An Imperial Possession

THE PENGUIN HISTORY OF BRITAIN

I: DAVID MATTINGLY *An Imperial Possession: Britain in the Roman Empire, 54 BC–AD 409**

II: ROBIN FLEMING *Anglo-Saxon Britain: 410–1066*

III: DAVID CARPENTER *The Struggle for Mastery: Britain 1066–1284**

IV: MIRI RUBIN *The Hollow Crown: A History of Britain in the Late Middle Ages**

V: SUSAN BRIGDEN *New Worlds, Lost Worlds: Britain 1485–1603**

VI: MARK KISHLANSKY *A Monarchy Transformed: Britain 1603–1714**

VII: LINDA COLLEY *A Wealth of Nations: Britain 1707–1815*

VIII: DAVID CANNADINE *At the Summit of the World: Britain 1800–1906*

IX: PETER CLARKE *Hope and Glory: Britain 1901–2000, 2nd edition**

* already published

DAVID MATTINGLY

An Imperial Possession

Britain in the Roman Empire,
54 BC–AD 409

ALLEN LANE
an imprint of
PENGUIN BOOKS

ALLEN LANE

Published by the Penguin Group
Penguin Books Ltd, 80 Strand, London WC2R ORL, England
Penguin Group (USA) Inc., 375 Hudson Street, New York, New York 10014, USA
Penguin Group (Canada), 90 Eglinton Avenue East, Suite 700, Toronto, Ontario, Canada M4P 2Y3
(a division of Pearson Penguin Canada Inc.)
Penguin Ireland, 25 St Stephen's Green, Dublin 2, Ireland (a division of Penguin Books Ltd)
Penguin Group (Australia), 250 Camberwell Road,
Camberwell, Victoria 3124, Australia (a division of Pearson Australia Group Pty Ltd)
Penguin Books India Pvt Ltd, 11 Community Centre,
Panchsheel Park, New Delhi – 110 017, India
Penguin Group (NZ), cnr Airborne and Rosedale Roads, Albany,
Auckland 1310, New Zealand (a division of Pearson New Zealand Ltd)
Penguin Books (South Africa) (Pty) Ltd, 24 Sturdee Avenue,
Rosebank, Johannesburg 2196, South Africa

Penguin Books Ltd, Registered Offices: 80 Strand, London WC2R ORL, England

www.penguin.com

First published 2006
1

Set in Linotype Sabon
Typeset by Rowland Phototypesetting Ltd, Bury St Edmunds, Suffolk
Printed in Great Britain by Clays Ltd, St Ives plc

A CIP catalogue record for this book is available from the British Library

ISBN-13: 978-0-713-99063-8
ISBN-10: 0-713-99063-5

For the Harolds

Contents

List of Figures and Tables   ix
Preface   xi

Part One
Introduction

1 The Spectre of Empire   3
2 Sources of Information and Rules of Evidence   21
3 'Nothing for us to Fear or Rejoice at.' Britain, Britons and the Roman Empire   47

Part Two
The Military Community

4 The Iron Fist: Conquest (43–83) and Aftermath   87
5 *Britannia Perdomita*: The Garrisoning of the Provinces   128
6 The Community of Soldiers   166
7 The Fashioning of the Military Identity   199
8 *De Excidio Britanniae*: Decline and Fall?   225

Part Three
The Civil Communities

9 *Forma Urbis*: The Development of Towns   255
10 Townspeople: Demography, Culture and Identity   292
11 The Urban Failure?   325

Part Four
The Rural Communities

12 The Villa and the Roundhouse 353

13 Provincial Landscapes 379

14 Free *Britannia*: Beyond the Frontiers 428

15 Rural Culture and Identity 453

Part Five
Comparative Perspectives and Concluding Thoughts

16 Different Economies, Discrepant Identities 491

17 'No Longer Subject to Roman Laws' 529

Bibliographical Essay 541

Index 581

Figures and Tables

Figure 1. Britain and the Roman empire in the mid-second
century.   22

Figure 2. Map of the British archipelago.   29

Figure 3. Peoples of Britain, including Ireland, in the Roman
period.   49

Figure 4. Southern Britain in the late Iron Age.   55

Figure 5. Changing garrison patterns in Britain under Roman
military occupation.   133

Figure 6. Military sites in southern Britain.   137

Figure 7. Military sites in northern Britain.   148

Figure 8. Hadrian's Wall and the Antonine Wall.   155

Figure 9. The province of *Britannia* and its sub-divisions. 229

Figure 10. The main towns and peoples of Britain.   262

Figure 11. The road network, major towns, small towns and
garrison settlements.   264

Figure 12. Rural settlement in southern Britain.   380

Figure 13. Rural settlement of Roman date in the East Midlands. 391

Figure 14. The villa landscape of the West Country.   396

Figure 15. Rural settlement and (inset) Roman material culture
in northern Britain.   430

Figure 16. Ireland in the late Iron Age/Roman period.   440

Figure 17. Comparative distributions of villas and
Romano-Celtic temples.   481

Table 1. Key dates in Roman history and of Britain in the
Roman world.   8

Table 2. Main campaigns and battles of the conquest phase. 97

Table 3. Wars and revolts, 84–211.   120

Table 4. Civil wars and secession, late first to late second century. 125
Table 5. Religious dedications from *Vindolanda*. 219
Table 6. Wars, civil wars and revolts in Britain, 235–409. 231
Table 7. The army of Britain in the *Notitia Dignitatum*. 239
Table 8. The *Antonine Itinerary* and the connectivity of towns in Roman Britain. 257
Table 9. The current state of archaeological knowledge of the principal Roman urban sites in Britain. 268
Table 10. Inscriptions recording public benefactions in British towns and small towns. 302
Table 11. Curse tablets from Britain. 312
Table 12. Urban defences in Roman Britain. 328
Table 13. The main phases of construction of urban defences. 330
Table 14. Religious identity in Britain defined by differences in practice. 521

Preface

The Pelican Histories of England were landmarks in the field and have
served their reading audience well through the second half of the twentieth century. As I sit typing the final words of my own book, I am very
conscious of the fact that Ian Richmond's *Roman Britain* was published
in 1955, exactly fifty years ago, and, with revisions, has remained in
print ever since. The story of Roman Britain has been written many
times; indeed, perhaps too often and rarely with the verve or insight of
Richmond. Consequently, and like other writers in this new series, I
have felt humbled and daunted by the task of writing an account for the
twenty-first century. Over recent decades Britain has become one of the
most heavily researched provinces of the Roman empire, but this in itself
makes the task of synthesis ever more difficult. Another challenge has
been to address the subject as a history of Britain, rather than of the
limited south-eastern part of the archipelago. Every telling of history is
a product of its age and while Richmond's account was from the twilight
zone of the modern colonial period, my perspective has been built up in
a much more sceptical post-colonial world, where 'empires' are no
longer assumed to have been benign civilizing powers. The realities of
Britain's status as an imperial possession are not all comfortable ones
for modern readers schooled on a vision of Roman imperialism as
essentially a civilizing force for good.

Writing this book has taken me far longer than Penguin or I anticipated (and here I must acknowledge the patience and persistence of my
editors David Cannadine and, most directly, Simon Winder). The delay
in part reflects the explosion of new publication in the last decade, and
in part my determination to bring a freshness of approach in comparison
with what has become a rather jaded format in some of the rival books
on Roman Britain. In short, I have tried to write a controversial book,

but one that will be accessible to a wide audience, a book that will make people think for themselves about issues, and that does not always have clear answers to difficult questions. In the process I have tried to dispense with a series of sacred cows – most notably the intellectually lazy recourse to the concept of Romanization (which ultimately means everything and nothing). In place of Romanization, I offer a framework of analysis based on three broad groups of provincial society (military, urban and rural communities) and the diverse identities that they gave rise to in responding to the challenges and opportunities of Roman rule.

The fact that this book is in a history series has determined something of its structure. The conventional narrative framework of Roman Britain is heavily weighted towards military matters, though I believe I offer a new interpretational slant on traditional approaches to these sources. My focus is on the broad features of military occupation and I have endeavoured not to get too bogged down in the minutiae of the dating of occupation phases at individual forts. I have also attempted to show how the community of soldiers intersected with the civilian communities, wherever possible introducing the names of real people into the account. At the same time, my exploration of the social and economic history integrates a wide range of archaeological evidence. A synthesis focused more single-mindedly on archaeological evidence would have produced a rather different sort of book and it was a deliberate choice to try to integrate discussion of conventional history with the sort of social issues that recent work in theoretical archaeology has highlighted. One of the problems we face in reconstructing the lives of ordinary people is the difficulty of interpreting their thoughts and actions from their use of material culture. I strongly believe that the massive accumulation of high-quality data, especially relating to finds assemblages, makes Britain a particularly suitable case-study for the investigation of discrepant identities in the Roman empire. This book can only offer a rough framework – it is my sincere hope that other researchers will help put flesh on these bones.

This is my personal vision of the history of Britain under Roman imperial rule and I hope to show that this was a rather different world from that encountered in many other books on the subject. At the same time, I am conscious that my viewpoint depends on the fact that I am standing on the shoulders of giants, whose achievements have made possible this re-evaluation. I hope that the book succeeds in bringing together the best of older and newer approaches to the subject. There is a necessary level of speculation here – though I would contend that key assumptions of more orthodox views equally lack substantiation in the preserved evidence and my text is suitably qualified at many points. Above all, I want to engage and excite readers both new to and expert in the subject, even if some may choose ultimately to disagree with aspects of my conclusions. The date range of my title defines the period within which I believe that it is reasonable to argue that part of Britain was considered an imperial possession, from the conclusion of Caesar's second campaign in 54 BC to the final revolt of the province in 409. This represents a lengthy interlude of foreign domination. As one reviewer of this book in draft succinctly put it, a key element of my view is that the 'Romano-British episode was nasty, brutish and long'.

My debts to others are myriad and I can only acknowledge a few here. The book is dedicated to the two Harold Mattinglys, who first illuminated the ancient world for me. Some of my earliest memories are of sitting on my grandfather's lap and hearing the myths of ancient Rome. My copy of his Penguin translation of the *Agricola* of Tacitus is among the most well-thumbed of all my books. My father has been a constant influence and I hope I have inherited some of his characteristic ability to ask really awkward questions about academic orthodoxies in ancient history. A third major influence was Barri Jones, my PhD supervisor at Manchester, who inspired me to commit to Roman archaeology. His early death in 1999 deprived me of a friend and adviser, and I have particularly regretted the loss of the opportunity to share drafts of this book with him. Tony Birley similarly nurtured my interests in Roman history and has remained a tremendous source of advice and support. Having provided extensive comments on early drafts of several chapters, he then made available to me (ahead of its publication) his indispensable *The Roman Government of Britain* and last, but far from least, undertook to read the entire typescript. As well as saving me from a truly embarrassing number of errors, he contributed much general wisdom and many insights on specific points to help me make this a far better book than it would otherwise have been. Numerous other academics and professional archaeologists have answered my questions, served as sounding boards for my wilder flights of fancy and sent me off-prints and texts of unpublished work. Particular thanks are due to Graeme Barker, Paul Bennett, Robin Birley, Roger Bland, David Breeze, Peter Carrington, Hilary Cool, John Creighton, Barry Cunliffe, Simon Esmonde Cleary,

S. S. Frere, Mike Fulford, Michael Given, Chris Gosden, Bill Hanson, Ian Haynes, Richard Hingley, Bruce Hitchner, Nick Hodgson, Rick Jones, John Manley, Martin Millett, David Potter, the late Tim Potter, Richard Reece, Tim Strickland, Roger Tomlin, Peter Wells, Steve Willis, Andrew Wilson, Roger Wilson and Greg Woolf. I must also express my gratitude to Suzanne Blackmore of Wyggeston and Queen Elizabeth I College, Leicester, who patiently answered questions about the current teaching of Roman Britain at A Level (as well as bringing the subject alive for my daughter Rebecca).

Since 1992, I have profited hugely from being part of the thriving Roman and Iron Age research cluster in the School of Archaeology and Ancient History at the University of Leicester. I am profoundly grateful to both short- and longer-term colleagues – Colin Adams, Graeme Barker, Richard Buckley, Neil Christie, Patrick Clay, Nick Cooper, Hella Eckardt, Andy Gardner, Mel Giles, Annie Grant, Colin Haselgrove, Simon James, Alan McWhirr, Rachel Pope, Jonathon Prag, Eberhard Sauer, Sarah Scott, Graham Shipley, Jeremy Taylor, John Vanderspoel, Marijke van der Veen, Jane Webster. I have also benefited from a terrific pool of Leicester postgraduate students with Roman interests (not all British focused), who have helped my understanding of the subject and particularly of new more theoretical approaches: Jennifer Baird, Andrew Birley, Alfonso Burgers, Fran Condron, John Coombs, Laura Cripps, Garrick Fincham, Colin Forcey, Gillian Hawkes, Anna Leone, Michelle Mann, Judy Meade, Phil Mills, Dominic Perring, Nick Ray, Judith Rosteff, Tom Rust, Irene Schrüfer-Kolb, Dan Stewart, Rob Witcher, Stephen Young. At another level, many of the more speculative ideas advanced here have been tried out on successive undergraduate classes, who have grappled with post-colonial thinking and the concept of identity with good humour and enthusiasm, coming up with some remarkable insights of their own.

In addition to Tony Birley, Paul Booth of Oxford Archaeology read the entire text with his habitual astuteness; many of his suggestions (plus information on new discoveries) are incorporated in my final version. Individual sections of the book were greatly improved by suggestions from the following additional readers: Neil Christie, Simon James, Richard Hingley, Colin Haselgrove, Bruce Hitchner, Mick Jones, Andrew Birley, Judith Rosteff. Joe Skinner produced the illustrations from my roughs, though Jeremy Taylor provided the raw data on which

Figure 13 is based. Simon Winder at Penguin was the ideal editor, gently persuading me to shed the excess baggage of an overweight first draft and providing perceptive and incredibly helpful guidance on how to sharpen the argument. Richard Duguid, Rebecca Lee and Chloe Campbell saw the book through production, with copy-editing input from Janet Tyrrell. Jenny Mattingly compiled the index.

It is customary to excuse those who read the draft work of responsibility for remaining errors. This is more than ever necessary here as in many ways this is an experimental, speculative and heretical book. In choosing not to follow every suggestion I have had from my readers, I have sought to retain the architectural structure of the book as I conceived it. In the end, this is my 'take' on the story and I unreservedly take responsibility for all remaining errors. This is a book about identity, communities and regions and in places there is a necessary level of detail to illustrate these themes. I hope that readers both familiar with and new to the subject will rise to the challenge this presents and will be encouraged to follow the bibliographical guidance for yet more detailed discussion of specific topics.

The book was completed during the 2004–5 academic year with the benefit of University of Leicester study leave and an AHRC Research Leave award. I am most appreciative of the support of my colleagues and especially of my Head of School, Marilyn Palmer. The observant reader may spot that a few paragraphs spread across several chapters are based on material published by me in rather different form (with fuller referencing) in the *Journal of Roman Archaeology*, and it is a pleasure to record my gratitude to its editor, John Humphrey.

I am grateful also to my wider family (parents, sisters and assorted in-laws) and friends who never lost interest in the project and did much to keep my attention focused on it through their questions. To Jenny, Rebecca, Susanna and Douglas I must extend special thanks. They have all lived this book with me and have helped me keep on track. Beyond the call of duty, they have read and commented on text, visited sites and discussed ideas. Above all, though, they created the time and space for me to write when I most needed to. Thanks to them, my great obsession has at last become *An Imperial Possession*.

University of Leicester
June 2005

NOTE ON DATES, PLACE-NAMES
AND MEASUREMENTS

All dates are to be read as years AD unless stated otherwise, when they are differentiated as 'BC'. Thus 43 for AD 43, but 55 BC. A few potentially ambiguous dates in the early first century AD have been so flagged. Ancient place-names are occasionally given in parentheses or used in Tables, but my normal practice has been to use modern place-names. The main exception to this rule is the key site of *Vindolanda* near Hadrian's Wall, where the modern location is actually best known by its Latin name. Names of Roman provinces are often used in preference to the geographically less precise designation by modern country. Whenever used, ancient toponyms, Latin technical terms and names of British peoples appear in italics. Where reference is made to modern British local government regions, I have followed the boundaries as displayed on the Ordnance Survey *Map of Roman Britain* (Southampton, rev. 4th edn, 1994), though in some areas these have been revised in subsequent local government reorganization. In addition to the figures illustrating this book, readers may find the Ordnance Survey *Map of Roman Britain* a useful resource for locating specific sites. Measurements are normally given in metric units, such as kilometres. Where a figure is stated in 'miles' this normally indicates 'Roman miles' of 1.48 km.

PART ONE

Introduction

I

The Spectre of Empire

This book tells the story of the occupation of Britain by the Romans. It is not the same sort of history that characterizes most other titles in this series, where narrative is built up around a multiplicity of written sources of evidence. True, the Roman period marks the crossing over from prehistoric to historic Britain, but the light shed by conventional historical documents is dim indeed. There are no large surviving Roman works specifically dealing with Britain; we come closest with the biography of Agricola, a first-century governor of the province, written by his son-in-law Tacitus. There are, of course, snippets of historical and geographical information to be gleaned from a wide range of other source material, but these are too often imprecise and of ambiguous interpretation. Inscriptions and archaeological evidence have been extensively employed in support of the written sources, though the essential weakness of the basic source material necessitates a great deal of interpolation to fill in the many gaps in the narrative. No matter how authoritative the voice, the writing of the history of Britain in the Roman empire has of necessity been in large part an impressionistic sketch.

My fundamental theme is the fate of Britain as an imperial possession during nearly four centuries of foreign domination. Good history is meant to be objective, not judgemental, but in studying so remote a period through so threadbare a set of sources, we face serious interpretative difficulties that oblige us to make choices about the shape of our accounts. Consciously or subconsciously most writers on Roman Britain have tended to form a view on whether or not the fact of Roman government was a positive thing. As a famous spoof history of Britain puts it, 'The first date in English History is 55 BC in which year Julius Caesar . . . landed . . . when the Romans were top nation on account of their classical education, etc. . . . The Roman Conquest was, however, a

3

Good Thing, since the Britons were only natives at that time.' This quote tells us nothing, of course, about ancient reality and everything about late nineteenth- and early twentieth-century attitudes.

Even today, more than half a century beyond the effective end of a British empire, mainstream views of the Roman empire are constrained by collective assumptions about the legitimacy of imperialism, with profound consequences for our reading and writing of that history. To take an Anglocentric view first, there is still a broad consensus in favour of the benefits of Roman rule outweighing the negative impacts it brought, and this is closely bound up with issues of national nostalgia for our own lost empire. As a result, we have a curious and ambiguous relationship with our Roman heritage, which is difficult to reconcile with the hard facts of Roman conquest and domination. In our national mythology, the Roman period is presented as one of development and opportunity far more than one of defeat, subjugation and exploitation. There is surprisingly little attention focused on the themes of resistance and underdevelopment.

In France, by way of contrast, Vercingetorix is a national hero and the site of Alesia celebrated as a memorial to Gallic resistance to foreign conquest. For all its English-language sales, the Asterix series is also a quintessentially French celebration of national resistance. The roots of this fascination with resistance may be traceable to the real-life events of the sequence of German invasions in 1870, 1914 and 1940. Despite a brief flirtation with the legend of Boudica (or Boadicea as they styled her), Victorian and Edwardian Britain sided pretty much wholeheartedly with the Roman invaders of Britain rather than with the subjugated natives. This was perhaps a natural response from servants of a great imperial state that at the height of its power in the late nineteenth century controlled one third of the territory and population of the world and that modelled itself in part on Roman structures. Britain's modern imperial role made most scholars sympathetic to the perspective and problems of the Roman state in its governance of empire and its civilizing mission in the frontier lands. The father of Romano-British archaeology in the early twentieth century, Francis Haverfield, summed up this attitude of underlying sympathy with modern colonialism:

The old theory of an age of despotism and decay has been overthrown, and the believer in human nature can now feel confident that, whatever their limitations, the men of the [Roman] Empire wrought for the betterment and happiness of the world.

This sort of nostalgic association with the colonizers and the ascribing of the best possible motives to them still underscore much writing on Roman Britain. The Romans brought towns, roads, stable government, the villa economy, art, culture, literacy, togas, baths and other elements of high culture. By the same token, the stereotypical native Britons in many popular accounts were at the time of conquest semi-naked, spiky-haired, tattooed and woad-painted barbarians, subsequently raised up by the experience of Rome to enjoy the benefits of civilization. This favourable vision of imperialism has for the most part been eagerly adopted in the popular image of Roman Britain. As an example, prominent Romans have been hailed up and down the country as the founders of many modern centres – a particularly notable case is Agricola, who occupies pride of place over the entrance to Manchester Town Hall among a throng of historical figures with Mancunian associations.

Rather different attitudes have developed, unsurprisingly, in northern and western Britain, where the history of rule from London in more recent centuries has led to the Roman period being equated as 'more of the same'. The tendency here is to present Rome as provoking resistance and non-conformity in terms that reflect the twentieth-century rise of Scottish and Welsh nationalism and Cornish regionalism. This has the potential to present as distorted a view of history as those who uncritically assert the natural justice of Roman rule.

Each generation of scholarship will tend to interpret the past in line with the perspectives and preoccupations of the moment. In attempting to write a new history for the globalized twenty-first century, I have been much influenced by recent dramatic changes of emphasis and interpretation. Studies of the pre-Roman Iron Age have been revolutionized by new theoretical approaches and Roman history is also starting to be affected by post-colonial perspectives. This book is very much concerned with the experience of people in Britain under Roman rule and as such it is far more social history than political history. It will explore the texture of life in Britain, making extensive use of archaeological material to supplement the meagre historical sources. This is a post-colonial history, in the sense that it questions aspects of the consensus model and attempts to widen debate about the nature and impact of Roman rule in Britain. There is inevitably much uncertainty and some speculation to fill the gaps, drawing on knowledge of the wider operation of the Roman imperial system and of other colonial regimes.

The Roman empire is often cited as the greatest that the world has ever known in terms of its extent, population, civilization and longevity (though one or more of these criteria might be disputed by the Chinese, the British or other modern imperial powers). It was certainly a yardstick against which the nineteenth-century imperial powers measured their achievements and from which they freely borrowed imagery, titles and style. Much of the early history of Rome concerned the progressive subjugation of the Italian peninsula in a more or less continuous sequence of wars. Anyone familiar with Livy's *History of Rome* will appreciate the remorseless nature of this process as year after year army levies were raised and sent off to fight, despite the expense and inconvenience that this imposed on a basically agrarian society. Compared to other ancient Italian peoples the Roman state was exceptionally aggressive and warlike. The unification of Italy, the Mediterranean and a large part of Temperate Europe under Roman rule was a lengthy process and achieved at huge human cost. For instance, more than 300 triumphs are recorded from the sequence of wars between 509 and 19 BC and a 'triumph' was only awarded for a victory in a battle that ended a declared war and killed at least 5,000 of the enemy. The total casualties must have far exceeded the minimum of 1,500,000 implicit in the figure. The human impact went much deeper than that, due to the practice of enslaving certain categories of prisoners taken in war. For example, in a five-year period of the Third Samnite War (297–293 BC), figures from Livy indicate that over 66,000 captives were enslaved from a variety of defeated enemies. The demographic impact of such relentless and ruthless warfare was probably profound, though in time the subjugated peoples were allowed to participate in the next round of expansion and in the foundation of colonies on captured lands. Latin colonies established from 334 to 263 BC are estimated to have required the seizure and re-allocation of over 7,000 square km of prime farming land to over 70,000 settlers.

The point here is that the Roman state could be a ruthless military power, inflicting major damage on its enemies. At the same time, she had mechanisms to reward peoples who submitted to her authority or who showed capacity to be reconciled to Roman rule after their subjugation. Specifically, the Roman model of provincial government involved a significant devolution of power to local authorities based around elite groups, whose wealth and status was often bolstered in the process. This 'beneficent' imperialism is an important aspect of the Roman case, but can be overstated if we want to assess the broader impacts on society as a whole.

Britain was a relatively late addition to the empire, by which time the nature of Roman expansionism had changed somewhat, due to the initiation of autocratic rule of emperors (*principes*) in place of the prior Republican system of government (Table 1 summarizes key dates and periods in Roman history and of Britain's incorporation in the empire). The emperors tended to be wary of allowing potential rivals unlimited opportunities to gain military glory, and future conquests were mostly carefully controlled. However, once selected as an imperial project, the invasion of 43 involved the use of exemplary force to impose as quickly as possible an understanding of Roman military superiority. That will have meant major British casualties and the taking of slaves. Nor was the conquest rapidly completed. Major campaigning continued until 83, almost two generations after Claudius launched his invasion. In between times the Boudican revolt of 60–61 had exacted a huge cost on both native Britons and on Rome. For the majority of Britons, it is clear that in the short term the Romans were very bad news and, even in the medium and long term, Britain in the Roman empire was a colonized and exploited territory. This was not a Golden Age, though the opportunities provided by the empire were golden for some individuals among the British elite and assorted immigrants into the province.

The Roman view of Britain can be partially explored, though we have to understand the nature of our surviving source evidence, discussed in detail in Chapter 2. A fundamental point is that the ruling metropolitan elite of the empire produced the bulk of our written evidence. It is unsurprising to find that they were enthusiastic supporters of Roman world domination. As a result, their writings must be presumptively suspected of bias and distortion in the presentation of historical 'facts' and in their interpretation. To a large extent the history that we construct from these sources is the history of the victors, and gives their gloss on events. The extent to which the values and attitudes of the leading Romans were shared in Italian society at large and across the many provinces of the empire is a moot point. It is clear, however, that the

Table 1. Key dates in Roman history and of Britain in the Roman world.

ROMAN WORLD	EVENTS IN BRITAIN	PERIOD
753 BC Traditional foundation of Rome	Early Iron Age in Britain	Rome ruled by kings
509 BC Traditional foundation of Roman Republic	Hillfort societies dominate Britain	Roman Republic
265–146 BC Period of Punic Wars with Carthage	Mid Iron Age in Britain	
120s BC Extension of Roman rule into southern Gaul	Late Iron Age in Britain First British coins	
50s BC Iulius Caesar's conquest of central and northern Gaul 54–51 BC Gallic revolt	55–54 BC Caesar's campaigns against Britain Client relations with British kings	
49–45 BC Civil war between Caesar and Republicans 44 BC Assassination of Caesar and renewed civil war	Client relations continue, bringing southern Britain and Rome into closer contact	Triumvirate (Antony, Octavian and Lepidus)
31 BC Battle of Actium (defeat of Antony and Cleopatra by Octavian)		Effective end of Republic with death of Antony in 30 BC
27 BC Octavian takes title Augustus (first *princeps*), rules until AD 14 AD 9 Loss of three legions on Rhine	Roman campaigns to Britain considered on several occasions	Start of Principate Julio-Claudian dynasty
14–37 Reign of Tiberius		
37–41 Reign of Gaius (Caligula) Plans invasion of Britain	AD 40–43, Cunobelin dies, flight of Verica to Rome	
41–54 Reign of Claudius	43 Claudius invades Britain	
54–68 Reign of Nero	60–61 Boudican revolt	
68–70 Civil war	Crisis with Brigantian kingdom	'Year of the Four Emperors'
69–79 Reign of Vespasian, followed by sons Titus (79–81) and Domitian (81–96)	83 Major victory of Agricola in Scotland 87 Withdrawal from northern Scotland	Flavian dynasty
96–98 Nerva, 98–117 Trajan	Main period of *Vindolanda* letters	Trajanic era
117–38 Hadrian	Hadrian's Wall built	Antonine dynasty
138–61 Antoninus Pius	Antonine Wall built	
161–80 Marcus Aurelius		

ROMAN WORLD	EVENTS IN BRITAIN	PERIOD
161–69 Lucius Verus		
180–92 Commodus	Warfare in Britain in 180s	
193–97 Civil wars	197 Clodius Albinus, gov. of Britain, defeated by Severus at Lyons	End of Antonine dynasty with assassination of Commodus
193–211 Septimius Severus, 211 Geta, 211–16 Caracalla 212 Roman citizenship extended to majority of population of empire	208–11 campaigns in Scotland Division into two provinces	Severan dynasty
235–84 Period of 'barbarian' incursions, civil wars and numerous emperors	260–74 Part of breakaway 'Gallic empire'	Third-Century Crisis
284–305 Diocletian, 286–305 Maximian, 293–306 Constantius, 293–311 Galerius	286–96 Britain ruled by Carausius and Allectus Post-296 division into four provinces	End of Principate Period of the Tetrarchy
306–37 Reign of Constantine 313 Edict of Milan, legitimizes Christianity 324 Foundation of Constantinople	Constantine proclaimed in Britain 306 British bishops attend council at Arles	The Dominate House of Constantine
337–63 Constantine II, Constans, Constantius II, Julian Brief resurgence of paganism under Julian (360–63)	350–53 Britain under rule of usurper Magnentius	
364–92 Valentinian I, Valens, Gratian, Valentinian II 378 Death of Valens at Adrianople	367–68 Barbarian Conspiracy in Britain	House of Valentinian
378–95 Reign of Theodosius I	383–88 Rule of Magnus Maximus	House of Theodosius
395–423 Reign of Honorius (in west)	Succession of British usurpers	
410 Sack of Rome by Goths	409 Secession of Britain	
476 End of western Roman empire	450s Growth of 'Saxon' power in south-east Britain	Germanic kingdoms in west Byzantine empire in east
1453 Fall of Constantinople	More than 1,000 years since end of Roman rule in Britain	End of eastern Roman (Byzantine) empire

Roman empire did not rest throughout its existence on a narrow Italian governing aristocracy. The Romans were a good deal more inclusive than many more recent empires, integrating the elite class of its subject peoples into the power structures of the state. Over time, many provincial aristocrats were incorporated into the ruling orders as senators and equestrians; indeed by the late second century there was a North African, Septimius Severus, on the imperial throne. There are grounds, then, for believing that to some extent the provincial elites around the empire adopted or incorporated elements of 'Roman' culture and social behaviour in the expectation of advancement in political, social or economic position.

The motivations behind power-sharing were potentially a good deal more complex than generally acknowledged and the rewards of empire (and the negative impacts also) were unevenly spread between the provinces. This is not to say that prominent Britons did not participate in the empire. Some probably enjoyed a level of influence and wealth that is hard to match in later imperial systems, where race and nationality have played a far more significant role in determining social position. Yet, Britons do not appear to have broken through in numbers to the very highest levels of Roman society. Because of the substantial military garrison, Britain as a whole probably endured more than its share of oppression. We do not have direct evidence for how British elite families felt about this, of course, but it is plausible that their commitment to the empire in general was in proportion to the rewards it offered them. To take this a stage further, we also need to consider what services Rome offered people below the level of the ruling elite.

What exactly was the view of Rome among the wider population of Britain? There are serious obstacles to our looking into the minds of people who were unenthusiastic about Rome. Unsurprisingly, the Romans were delighted to promote literary works of erstwhile enemies who embraced wholeheartedly the Roman way (Polybius the Greek and Josephus the Jew are famous examples). But there is a dearth of source material from any part of the empire on what Rome's opponents themselves thought. The reasons for this are not hard to find. The extant literature of the Roman world has been through a series of filters to determine what has survived, but the state itself could have a primary impact. For example, the library of Carthage was largely destroyed as a deliberate act after its capture by Rome, denying posterity an alternative view of the Punic Wars. In Britain with no pre-Roman tradition of literature, there is even less possibility of hearing the voice of dissent expressed unambiguously in the surviving literary sources. The best we can hope for is reference to events that attest to unrest, and we must always bear in mind that our knowledge of these events is mediated through the writing of people aligned with the Roman state and fundamentally unsympathetic to those who opposed it. The conventional historical sources at our disposal, then, are probably far from objective.

The problems raised by the potential bias in the Roman sources are particularly acute in relation to our understanding of late Iron Age Britain. Chapter 3 explores new theories and evidence for the nature of these societies and their relationship with the expanding Roman empire in the century leading up to the Claudian invasion.

The tendency in the past to equate the British and the Roman empires has led to a too ready and uncritical approbation of the Roman empire. It is fair to say that in some past series on the history of England / Britain, the Roman period has been presented as a prequel to the heyday of the British empire. The stress on Rome's civilizing mission, the universal benefits of her rule, and so on, has the effect of deflecting attention from the exploitative and repressive aspects of imperial rule. To some extent this contrasts with common perceptions of the Norman conquest, where the negative impacts have never been denied in quite the same way. The point is neatly illustrated in Tom Stoppard's play *Indian Ink* where an Indian is informed by an ex-Memsahib that: 'We were your Romans, you know. We might have been your Normans.' One of the underlying questions in this book is whether this supposed difference between 'nice' Roman and 'nasty' Norman conquerors of Britain is sustainable.

Nor has the British empire been immune from revisionist views. Fifty years of post-colonial studies have done much to dent its reputation. There is increasingly widespread scepticism of the extent to which it was ever run for 'the betterment and happiness of the world'. That is not to deny that there were many decent and humane individuals involved in the governance of the British empire who behaved honestly and with compassion to subject peoples, but the power dynamics of an empire are such that unscrupulous and less-principled individuals could have a disproportionate impact and were less likely to be disciplined for behaviour or bias that would have been unacceptable in Britain. The idea of the 'white man's burden' was largely a *post facto* attempt at self-justification and, when power was abused, how often was the excuse trotted out that the ends justified the means? Yet one of the interesting effects of post-colonial criticism of imperialism has been to reinforce such apologia. Many people do not like to have their preconceptions challenged in this way. In 1986 the performance of a new play by Robert Brenton called *The Romans in Britain* caused a furore because of the staged rape of a male Briton by a group of Roman soldiers. In part the outcry was to do with this being a graphic and shocking piece of sex and violence in a theatre, but for many people this was compounded by the fact that parallels were being drawn between Roman imperialism and the modern experience of Northern Ireland patrolled by British troops. The violence is the sort of plausible outrage that imperialism begets (and that we would prefer not to be reminded of).

There is an interesting consequence of the close alignment of many modern scholars with the Roman empire, in that these authors have missed a key ingredient of Britain's history under Rome. Far from being a close comparison with Britain's later experience of empire, the history of Roman rule provides a diametrically opposed perspective on imperialism and colonialism, with the boot very firmly on the other foot. In this book, considerably more emphasis than usual will be placed on the negative aspects of imperial rule and their impact on the subject peoples. Since there was no unified British identity as such, rather a mix of regional societies, the impacts also varied considerably across Britain. Britain's early experience of empire was thus far removed from its later one, as victim rather than perpetrator. This account may in a certain way shed new light on modern colonialism too, by emphasizing the experience of subject people, who were in their turn imperial possessions.

It is pointless, of course, to try to assess how the British regional peoples would have fared had the Roman conquest not occurred. The pre-Roman Iron Age societies were not necessarily any less exploitative of ordinary people, and, in taking a critical view of the impact of Roman imperialism, it does not necessarily follow that life would have been better without Rome. However, the longevity of Roman domination (about fifteen generations) meant that its impacts were profound, both positively and negatively. We must assess not just Rome's triumphs and achievements, but also the extent of her unpopularity and of resistance to her rule.

Empire can be defined as rule over very wide territories and many peoples without their consent. While ancient societies did not have as developed a sense of self-determination as modern states, the fact that subjugation was often fiercely contested militarily is symptomatic of the fundamentally non-consensual nature of imperialism. This book seeks to explore the nature of life under Roman domination from a variety of perspectives. It offers a critical and sceptical view of the nature of imperial systems. An empire is in general interested in its own mainten-ance, with regional development a secondary consideration, in itself underscored with self-interest. Wherever economic development did take place, there the state could extract more revenue. Where social institutions took root, there the state could govern more effectively and often more economically.

Recent work on the archaeology of colonialism has opened up entirely new perspectives on societies under imperial rule. Colonialism is essen-tially about the operation of power in situations that necessarily created or reinforced large inequalities within territories subject to exterior rule. Power is used to induce people to comply with imperial authority and to deliver up resources, but empires are inevitably also about the attempts by subjects to evade obligations, such as taxation. These power differences underscore the conventional history of action and response, but they also have correlates in the material world. This is where the archaeological record can help us to trace the impact of colonial rule on British societies under Roman rule. Roman imperialism has been defined as being focused on an inherent accommodation with local cultures (what is described as 'middle ground' colonialism). In this respect it has sometimes been contrasted with the approach of some more recent imperial projects that have had a much more violent and less respectful attitude towards pre-existing people on the land. The contrast is true to a point, but there is a danger that we may overlook the violent side of ancient empire in the process (see Chapters 4–5). At different times and places, and in separate relations with diverse social groups, it seems to me that the Roman empire could be both sorts of colonizing power. Similarly, looked at from the bottom up, there was probably a great deal of similarity between the lived experience of Rome's humbler sub-jects and those of more recent imperial regimes, especially as regards attempts to avoid taxation and other fiscal controls and legal restraints. These tendencies need to be considered alongside the social outlook of native elites who became most closely aligned with the geopolitical system.

Romanization is a key concept in many studies of Roman Britain and a further departure in this book will be my attempt to dispense with it after this brief introductory notice. Romanization was not a Roman concept, but it has a long pedigree in Roman studies, being traceable back to a tradition of study developed in the late nineteenth and early twentieth centuries that stressed the benign aspect of Roman rule and the cultural purpose of the Roman empire. Under this simple model the Romans brought the gifts of towns, villas, language, art and culture to grateful provincials and it was assumed that all of them perceived Roman culture as self-evidently superior to what they had before. Britons were thus depicted as enthusiastic participants in Roman lifestyle, with society undergoing progressive cultural evolution under Rome. Early excavation of Roman period sites in Britain focused on Roman forts, towns and villas, creating a research agenda that was predisposed to support these assumptions precisely because it focused on those elements of Romano-British society that were most closely aligned with a 'Roman' identity. Romanization has inevitably stressed the degree of *similarity* between Britain and the rest of the empire, while at the same time ignoring or downplaying the extent to which aspects of pre-existing British culture influenced developments.

The early enthusiasm for the approach in Britain and elsewhere in Europe was in part at least conditioned by the involvement of European scholars at the time in their own world of colonization and empire. A very close association between the scholarly view and the perspective of the imperial power was the predictable result. Some scholars talked of a Romanization policy on the part of Rome (somewhat akin to the equally specious insistence on the civilizing mission of white settlers in modern imperialism). Rather more surprising in my view has been the longevity of the Romanization paradigm into the post-colonial age, all the more so as Romanization suffers from other problems than simply being a hang-over from the period of modern imperialism. The model is unilateral, unidirectional and progressive, yet the archaeological evidence often stands in implicit contradiction of this. For instance, Romanization tends to reduce the question of cultural identity to a simple binary opposition: Roman and native. The fact that much of what we identify as 'Roman' culture in provinces like Britain in fact came from other provinces in northern and western Europe, rather than from Italy or even the Mediterranean region, should give us pause for thought. Moreover, attention has been drawn increasingly to the infinitely varied nature of the Roman cultural package found around the empire. Regionality and diversity should be just as important in our analysis as elements of homogeneity, but the Romanization paradigm is an obstacle to exploring these.

In reaction to the more traditional understanding of Romanization, attention has been directed to the role of provincial elites. In the older 'Romanization as policy' model the native recipients of Roman culture were denied an active role. However, according to the new thinking, people of the elite class were active agents, making significant choices about the adoption of Latin (as the language of official business), new styles of dress, architecture and literate behaviour, along with many other items of perceived 'Roman' material culture. People lower down the social hierarchy experienced a more diluted version of Romanization, a sort of 'trickle-down' effect, through emulation of their social betters. In effect, though, this 1990s model of Romanization is simply the flip side of the early twentieth-century one – both focus almost exclusively on the elite group in society, but in the former the indigenous elites were the active agents, in the latter they were passive recipients. The same tendencies have been recognized in studies of Roman Gaul, though again these effectively concentrate on a narrow social band at the top of society. It can be argued that these people were the most important in Roman provincial societies and that they are the most visible (though there is a whiff of self-fulfilling prophecy about this, since it is primarily these 'Romanized people' that the prevalent academic agenda has set out to trace).

A further problem with Romanization is that the motor of cultural change is assumed to have been 'emulation', without any unpacking of the baggage associated with that term. Emulation has been taken to mean a spontaneous and uncritical adoption of material culture or cultural traits. It is still sometimes assumed that everyone in Britain would have recognized the innate superiority of Roman civilization and have wanted to subscribe to the maximum extent possible in its material comforts (surely everyone would have preferred to live in a villa rather than a roundhouse?). Yet that question is one that the vast majority of the population would never have faced; some options were not widely available in ancient society – including easy means of changing wealth, rank and social position. The difficulties are most acute at the points in time, space and society where emulation ceases. Traditional explanations of why this occurs have focused on factors such as: latent persistence of earlier traditions; overt resistance; the view that Romanization was a veneer; and pre-Roman regional differences.

One of the main problems with regarding Romanization as primarily the result of the agency of local elites is that it diminishes the influence of the Roman state on the process. A key argument of this book is that identity is integrally bound up with power in society, and therefore the creation of provincial identities cannot have taken place in a vacuum, isolated from the power negotiations between the Roman empire and its subject peoples. What is often lacking is consideration of how these power dynamics operated, both top-down and bottom-up. Conventionally, Romano-British studies have tended to de-emphasize elements suggesting continuing traditions of the late Iron Age, such as the prevalence of the roundhouse in rural landscapes well into the Roman period. From many accounts and museum presentations you might easily assume these had been rapidly abandoned in favour of new building forms, notably Roman-style houses (villas). They were not. In later chapters we shall examine these sorts of issues in more depth and consider alternative approaches to culture change in Britain under Roman rule. While traditional approaches have tended to stress the degree of sameness of material culture in different provinces ('you've got baths, we've got baths . . .'), much greater attention needs to be paid to the often-substantial degree of regional variability that is present. Once we recognize that there was no single 'Roman' identity, the regional variation in the adoption and non-adoption of material culture is potentially far more informative about the character of a province such as Britain.

Binary oppositions have been widely employed in the literature on Roman Britain and these tend to set Roman and Briton apart in interesting (but cumulatively unhelpful) ways – Roman : Native British; Advanced : Primitive; Cultured : Uncultured; Forward-looking : Backward-looking; Literate : Illiterate; Desirable : Undesirable; Progressive : Conservative; Preferable : Rejectable; Complex : Simple. However, many aspects of human culture are not black or white but various shades of grey. This book will attempt to explore the intermediate points between extremes.

Globalization has become a much-trumpeted concept in the age of an unchallenged American superpower and there are certainly some similarities with Rome, even if in the Roman case 'global' has perforce to be defined more narrowly. There was undoubtedly cultural change in Britain and this was equally clearly related to Rome's 'global' dominance. A key characteristic of globalization is that geographical constraints recede and that people refashion their identities in awareness of this situation. Even before the Roman conquest, Britain was being drawn into a new cultural milieu centred on Rome. However, as with Romanization, globalization will prove no better a concept in seeking to understand Britain under Roman rule, if we use it to emphasize conformity rather than investigate diversity. If anything, globalization highlights the unintentional and random impacts of Roman culture on provincial societies.

A key argument is that there was no single stereotypical 'Life in Roman Britain', as some popular books lead one to believe by their emphasis on the adoption of towns, baths and villas. Rather, the (partial) occupation of Britain by Rome commanded varied responses at different times and, more significantly, from different people within Britain. The perspective of a Roman governor will undoubtedly have been distinct from that of a villa owner in the Cotswolds, a hill farmer in Yorkshire or a Syrian merchant operating in the province. Even in the late Iron Age, native British groups were displaying pronounced regional identities and these were exacerbated by imperial rule.

In seeking an explanatory model for this social variability, I have been drawn to the concept of 'discrepant experience' in post-colonial research on modern imperialism. We may understand this to mean the coexistence of very different perceptions of history, culture, and relationships between colonizer and colonized. These produce parallel but distinct histories, as in the rival French and Egyptian accounts of Napoleon's Egyptian campaigns. Since we lack native written transcripts of accommodation and resistance for Britain under Roman rule, my approach seeks to develop this idea by identifying 'discrepant identities' in the material culture. Most writing on Roman Britain has made certain assumptions and choices in ascribing value to Roman culture in Britain, with consequences for what has been studied and what has tended to be ignored in the archaeological record. This book explores a series of divergent perspectives of Roman imperialism in Britain.

The evidence of cultural change and social behaviour is reviewed in terms of three broad identity groups: the military community (Chapters 6–7), urban dwellers (Chapter 10) and rural societies (Chapter 15). These are fairly conventional divisions to make, but what distinguishes this book is the starting premise that these three broad communities did not share a single common culture, but that there were significant differences between them (and indeed further levels of divergence within each of these major communities). Just as the individual experiences of empire could vary widely, so too there were discrepant patterns of identity in response to Rome's occupation of Britain. In a sense, there are three parallel social histories within this book, relating to these broad groupings and the individuals they were made up from: the occupying army (Part 2), the towns (Part 3) and the rural settlements (Part 4, which considers both subjected territory and those parts of Britain that were not incorporated into the province).

Identity is thus the key analytical tool and I seek to demonstrate the existence of discrepant identities and of discrepant experiences of the Roman empire in Britain. But how was identity defined in the Roman period? Various factors can be suggested as bearing on individual and group identity in the Roman world: status; wealth; location; employment; religion; origin; proximity to the imperial government; legal status and rights; language and literacy; age and sex. Status incorporated various broad categories: slave, free, freed, dependent, independent, barbarian, Roman citizen, non-citizen, *humiliores*, *honestiores*, curial class, equestrian, senator, imperial household – including imperial slaves and freedmen. Wealth was not simply a measure of relative position above or below subsistence; how you made your money was also socially significant. A person's physical location in an urban, rural or military community (or in transit between them) was also contingent on behavioural norms. Possession of a craft skill, membership of a guild, or of the army were all significant identity markers. Religion could also be an important element, especially through membership of exclusive cults – Mithraism, mystery cults, Judaism, Christianity – but the nature of ritual practice was probably as significant to ancient worshippers as the name of the god addressed. Place of origin (whether geographical or ethnic) was frequently an important factor, though perhaps not as important as in the modern nationalist world. The over-riding demands of loyalty focused on the imperial state affected particularly those most closely linked to its power and governance structures. The nature of the judicial apparatus an individual lived under was also important – again it tended to define status groups. Language obviously served to define identity groups and differentiation between literate and illiterate was a key distinction in society. Age and gender are again universal attributes of identity, though with different weight attached in every society. In many cases, identity will have been a composite of several of the elements listed here. A crucial point is that identity was used not just to assert shared characteristics, but also to differentiate between groups in society. For example, part of the community of merchants living in London may have espoused a group identity that reflected their citizen status, foreign origins and their profession, while at the same time establishing distance between themselves and non-citizen foreigners and British-born traders.

Important infrastructural evolutions, such as urbanism (Chapter 9) and rural realignments (Chapter 12), are also central to an understanding of the impact of Rome. Another important approach of the book is the stress on regional differences, whether concerning the pattern of military garrisons (Chapter 5), or of provincial landscapes (Chapter 13) and extra-provincial territory (Chapter 14). In chronological terms, the long-term impacts of empire are assessed, focusing in particular on late Roman evidence of decline and change in society (Chapters 8, 11 and 17).

Chapter 16 reviews the evidence of the economic impacts of empire on the three communities and presents a final synthesis of the evidence of discrepant identities within and between each group. There are hints in the sources of a debate in Rome about the economic benefits that conquest of Britain would bring. In the early first century AD, the Roman geographer Strabo felt that the income gained by Roman taxation of pre-conquest trade would not be matched by more direct exploitation. Here he was probably picking up the 'official' line, at a time when the possibility of conquest was being played down. Archaeology is a prime tool in attempting to judge the validity of the statement and of the impact of Rome's political economy on the province.

What sets the history of Britain under Roman rule apart from other parts of the empire, or indeed, from other periods of British history? The province and later diocese of *Britannia* required the presence of a substantial garrison – at its peak more than one tenth of the available armed forces of the empire. As a result, this was an expensive province and one with a distinctly military character in comparison with many others. Furthermore, its insular position on the north-western fringe of the empire, its distance from Rome and the Mediterranean core of the empire, and its physical separation from the European landmass, combined to set it apart geographically. The Romans engaged in long-term military occupation and large-scale interference in life within and beyond the frontiers in the north and west of Britain. To be sure, this was a period of significant social and cultural changes, though these are susceptible to different readings. And for every winner under Roman rule, there were a hundred losers, with the gap between the richest and poorest in society widening as never before.

2

Sources of Information and
Rules of Evidence

The history of Britain in the Roman empire equates with proto-history in that our written sources are primarily external ones, that is, written outside Britain or by people who were of non-British origin. Comparatively little documentation survives that was produced in Britain itself and, as a result, the early history of the British archipelago can never be recovered in the level of detail of later epochs. The fact that this volume covers roughly 500 years, as opposed to the approximate century-spans of most other volumes in this series, is indicative of this difference. The explanation lies in the nature of surviving evidence and in particular in the quantity of documentary material available. Archaeology plays a disproportionately larger role in reconstructing a history of the Roman period in Britain and that makes for a very different sort of history. In this chapter, we shall explore the nature of the available sources of evidence and consider the sort of history that has been constructed from them.

The main problem lies in the depth rather than the breadth of the surviving literary sources. The earliest references to Britain are in Greek sources dating to the fourth century BC and there are relevant passages in Dark Age sources at the other end of Antiquity. Overall, around 100 ancient authors mentioned Britain in some context, but the vast majority of these were vague and fleeting allusions, peripheral to the main thrust of the documents they occurred in. The relative scarcity of literary sources and other written materials is primarily a product of their poor survival from classical antiquity. Extant literary works represent a tiny percentage of the total corpus of classical writers, and the selection of what is preserved owes much to chance and the whims of medieval copyists, though in general there is far less of early Greek writers than of Roman authors.

Figure 1. Britain and the Roman empire in the mid-second century, showing the position of the former at the northern extremity. Figures in parentheses indicate number of legions in each province

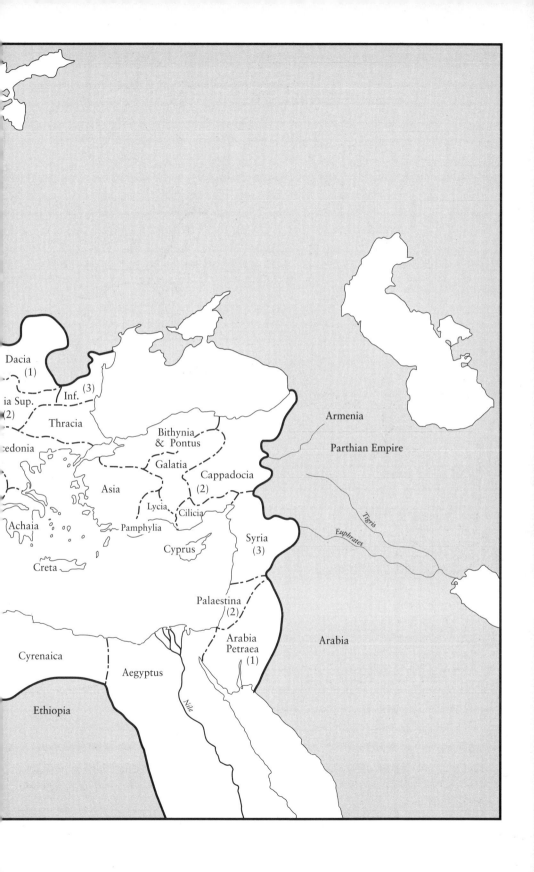

Similar limitations apply to the lesser documents of the past. Stone inscriptions are a vital source of regional information, but again survive in proportion to the local demand for building stone in later ages. The plethora of informal documents and transactions made on organic media (writing tablets, papyrus, parchment) are almost entirely lost to us, save in the most extraordinary conditions of preservation (anaerobic damp deposits or hyper-arid deserts).

A further problem confronting the historian of early Britain concerns its geographical location on the very north-western fringe of the Roman world (Fig. 1). The main island of *Britannia* projected north of the highest latitudes covered by the Continental provinces. Unincorporated peoples occupied the lands facing Britain to the east of the North Sea and all of Ireland on the west side. To the north, Rome never fully subdued a large part of highland Scotland, necessitating the development of complex land frontiers from the second century. The fact that *Barbaricum* surrounded it on three sides illustrates graphically that *Britannia* was an isolated island outpost of empire. This must have had significance throughout the Roman occupation, but in late Roman times it became increasingly critical. This set Britain somewhat apart from the rest of the empire – it was an end in itself, of course, but you did not pass through it en route for other provinces.

At a basic level, this isolation limits the profile of Britain in our ancient sources. It was not central to Roman politics or economic life and thus tended only to feature in an incidental way in the sources, when something significant happened there, or when someone of importance (or of future importance) went there. Although the Romans understood that the world was round, it was clear to them that the known inhabited parts did not fill the entire globe, but that a vast and fearsome Ocean bounded the landmass. A prime factor about Britain was its location in unknown *Oceanus*, as opposed to the known waters of the Mediterranean (*mare nostrum*). Despite the relative shortness of the Channel crossing, the dangers implicit in the ocean location were highlighted again and again, from the storms that wrecked or diverted parts of Caesar's invasion fleet, to the mutinous behaviour of the army assembled by Claudius at the prospect of the Channel crossing. The popular reaction in Rome to the Caesarian and Claudian invasions of Britain was evidently out of proportion to the actual military gains. Dio wrote of the award to Caesar of a twenty-day festival of thanksgiving, 'For seeing what was previously unknown had been revealed to sight and what had formerly been unheard of had become accessible, they regarded future expectations arising from these events as already realized.' Claudius made a point of fixing a naval crown on his palace in Rome 'as a sign that he had crossed, and as it were, conquered Ocean'. Even well into the fourth century, 'Ocean' maintained its hold on the imagination, with sources extolling the bravura victory of Constans over the 'raging waves of Ocean in winter time', following his crossing of the Channel well outside the normal sailing season. Another fourth-century source, Avienus, could still write of the 'abyss of Ocean, full of sea monsters'.

To some extent the Channel was more of a barrier to invasion fleets than to normal shipping and it is clear that there was considerable trade contact between Gaul and southern Britain by the first century BC, so some scepticism is needed with sources that present Britain as deeply mysterious and unknown at this time. The seasonality of maritime traffic was another factor that was of more concern to an imperial power than to individual traders. The island province was effectively cut off from the Continent for part of the year, outside the main shipping season that ran from March to October.

Britons as well as Romans held the Ocean in awe. Plutarch, for instance, mentioned the report of Demetrius on the remoter islands of the archipelago, 'some named after spirits and heroes . . . and held sacred and inviolate by the *Brettanoi*'. He witnessed a tremendous storm on one island, interpreted by the inhabitants as being due to the decease of a 'great one'. Other extraordinary portents of the northern latitudes, of course, included the length of the day and the coldness and harshness of the climate.

A further problem concerns how we read our source documents, given that they were primarily written from a distance by an alien elite, whose lives were closely bound to the maintenance of the Roman empire. We should not expect critical objectivity and, if we appraise the material carefully, we shall in fact find the converse. Such material requires very careful interpretation, though there is inevitably a tendency not to wish to cast aside the meagre crumbs of information that have survived for us. But we always need to be aware of where our sources got their information from (official documents or hearsay), of what biases may have consciously or unconsciously underscored the presentation of material, and finally of the fact that truth in history is elusive. More than one reading of events is possible, but most of what survives for us is history from the victor's perspective. That may suffice if we are simply seeking 'Roman Britain', but to understand 'Britain in the Roman empire' we need to give equal weight to other potential histories.

THE SOURCES

Historical works are naturally of prime importance, despite the dearth of surviving material. Although the writing of history was a well-established tradition by the time of the Roman conquest, many Roman writers were not critical researchers of their material. They would tend to repeat statements they found in their own sources, without considering the veracity or the continuing contemporary relevance of the information. The primary form of historical writing was the annalistic technique of cataloguing the wars and other chief events of the Roman state, best exemplified by Livy's monumental *History of Rome*, produced during the Principate of Augustus. For Roman imperial history, our two most important historical writers are Tacitus writing 98–*c.*120 and Cassius Dio *c.*220, though there are important gaps in the surviving manuscripts of their works. Cornelius Tacitus produced two key historical works, the *Annales* covering the period from Tiberius to Nero, and the *Histories* detailing the events of the civil war in 69 and of the Flavian period (though what survives goes only to autumn 70). He also wrote two further works with some historical content, a biography (*Agricola*) and the *Germania* – an ethnographic study of the Germans. Widely regarded as the most reliable Roman historian, nonetheless Tacitus had his prejudices and the rhetorical nature of this sort of historical writing must never be forgotten. He was above all a great moralist and it is clear, for instance, that he was almost obsessively negative about those he judged to have been 'bad' emperors. Tacitus is also infuriating as a source in that he rarely cited place-names and 'tribal' names in remote provinces, presumably omitted for the benefit of an aristocratic readership that did not want to be bothered with those sorts of barbarous details. This hampers attempts to make an exact reconstruction of the events he described. Equally frustratingly, some of the major lacunae in the surviving Tacitean manuscripts correspond to periods when Britain was most in the imperial spotlight, as at the time of the Claudian invasion. Dio is important because he filled some of the chronological gaps in Tacitus' account of the first century, though the second-century sections are poorly preserved. With the exception of the early third century covered by Dio and another Greek writer Herodian, few annalistic sources then survive until the last great historian of the Roman west, Ammianus Marcellinus, writing in the 380s. The earlier sections of his work, covering the second to mid-fourth centuries are entirely lost, but a detailed account of about twenty-five years of his own lifetime is preserved (353–78).

Biographical works, mainly focused on the lives of the emperors, represent an alternative historical tradition. The *Lives of the Caesars*, covering Iulius Caesar and the emperors from Augustus to Domitian, by Gaius Suetonius Tranquillus are justly the most famous and best reputed of this genre. Suetonius held administrative posts in the imperial household under Hadrian and certainly had access to important documentation to flesh out his biographical sketches. Later biographical accounts, notably the fullest one, the so-called *Historia Augusta* – which provides lives of emperors from Hadrian (accession 117) to Carinus (died 285), with a gap for the period 244–60 – are far less reliable. If Suetonius represents the 'broadsheet' tradition, then the *Historia Augusta* is the equivalent of the worst excesses of tabloid journalism. Much of the work is pure fiction, in particular the lives of 'junior emperors' and usurpers, and most of the lives of third-century figures. Yet for the emperors from Hadrian to Caracalla the author of the *Historia Augusta* summarized a good source, with lots of genuine information. For example, this is the only extant source that correctly credits Hadrian and Antoninus Pius with the initial construction of their respective walls.

The *Agricola*, written by Tacitus in 98, represents another type of biography. It is essentially a panegyric of his father-in-law, who was one of the most distinguished governors of Britain and who, Tacitus hinted, Domitian poisoned. Since much of Agricola's public reputation rested on his British service, Tacitus is unusually forthcoming about these events, though we need to keep in mind that he wrote the work to eulogize the man, not as a literal historical account. The meagre references to the (not inconsiderable) achievements of Agricola's predecessors as governor or to the actions of his successor show one side of this. You could also conclude from this account that the governor had pretty much a free hand, without reference to the ruling emperor – something we know to have been far from the truth.

The autobiographical account by Iulius Caesar of his campaigns in Gaul and Britain falls into a special category, somewhat akin to the much shorter, but equally self-promoting, *Res Gestae* composed by Augustus to trumpet his achievements for posterity. These two works, frustratingly evasive on many important issues, both contain important insights into affairs in Britain.

There are a number of important ancient works that can be classed as geography or ethnography, including works by Strabo, Mela, Pliny the Elder, Tacitus and Ptolemy. Modern commentators can easily criticize the geographical knowledge of the Romans because these works contain cardinal errors of measurement or placement – several Roman sources authoritatively place Ireland between Britain and Spain, while Ptolemy appears to have 'turned' the alignment of northern Scotland through ninety degrees. On the other hand, it is clear that Roman surveyors and map-makers, when they chose to, could work to an extraordinary degree of accuracy. Even at coarser scales of resolution, the Romans constructed maps of provincial territory based on systematic procedures and observations. Ptolemy noted the importance of daily observations by travellers going beyond the bounds of the empire to establish the geographical position of places visited. For instance, there are numerous references to measurements made of the length of the longest day of the year in remote locations, reflecting a desire to ascertain the latitude. Therefore, while geographical knowledge was far from infallible, it stands comparison with that of most pre-industrial societies. The archived information available to provincial governors and imperial officials on the ground may well have exceeded in quality that in the records and libraries of Rome or Alexandria.

A Greek historian of the first century BC, Diodorus Siculus, made a number of allusions to Britain, in part based on Caesar's account, but also quoting from earlier Greek writers whose works are now lost. For example, Poseidonius (135–50) who wrote about the Iron Age societies in Gaul, was an influential source for Caesar, Diodorus and Strabo. Drawing on the third-century BC Greek writer Eratosthenes (whose own works are now lost), Diodorus described a major triangular island called *Prettanike* set within an archipelago of many islands in the ocean. The nearest point to the continent was a promontory called *Cantium*

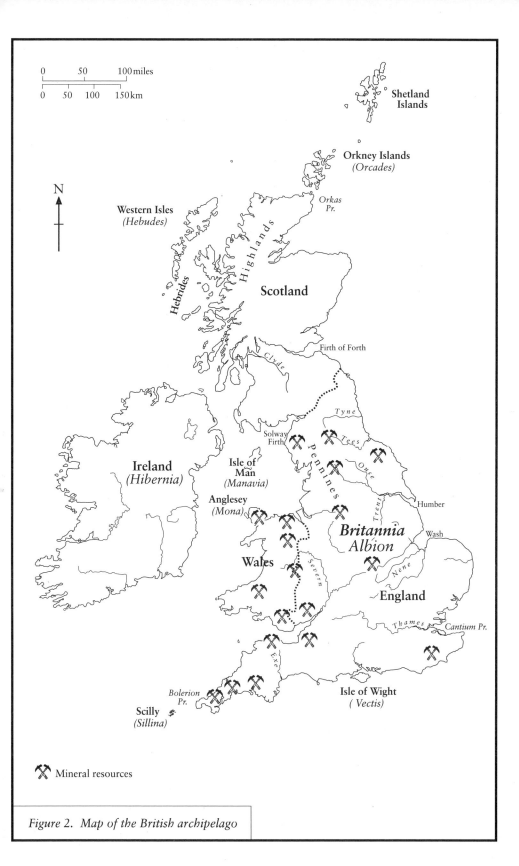

Figure 2. *Map of the British archipelago*

(see Fig. 2), with the other two points of the triangular shape being defined as *Bolerion* promontory (Land's End) – from which region tin was traded with Gaul – and the *Orkas* promontory (Caithness). He described the people as simple in their habits, old-fashioned in their ways, free of wealth and luxury and for the most part living at peace with each other, though he also mentioned reports of cannibalism and other barbarous traits. Two recurrent themes in the Greek writers were the existence of islands from which tin was traded (the *Cassiterides*) and the location of a mysterious island of *Thule* somewhere to the north beyond Britain. Neither of these locations was necessarily part of the British archipelago, though tin was traded from Cornwall in the latter centuries BC and Tacitus identified *Thule* with Shetland. The information on Britain in the early sources is thus very slight and vague, with the most reliable information in Diodorus derived from Caesar's campaigns.

Another Greek writer, Strabo, compiled an encyclopaedic geographical study, completed *c.*20. As well as summarizing the state of the dispute about the relative latitudes of Britain and *Thule* and other controversies, his account of Britain added significant details, reflecting the increasingly close contact between the island and Europe during the long reign of Augustus. For instance, he described how ships leaving Gaul on the evening ebb-tide could expect to reach landfall in Britain by the eighth hour of the following day and that there were four main cross-channel routes: from the mouths of the Rhine, Seine, Loire and Garonne – though the British landing points were not defined.

It is unfortunate in some respects that our more detailed geographical accounts, including the work of Pomponius Mela and Pliny the Elder, all date to the first century AD. Mela, writing just after the event, referred to the invasion of Britain as being about to reveal more clearly 'what Britain is like and what sort of people it produces'. Pliny the Elder, writing *c.*77, noted that over the course of thirty years Britain had been 'explored by Roman armies to the area not beyond the Caledonian forest', though his account did not mark much of an advance on his predecessors. He did at least provide a fuller list of 87 islands of the British archipelago, including mainland Britain, Ireland, 40 *Orcades* (Orkney), 7 *Acmodae* (Shetland), 30 *Hebudes* (Western Isles), with *Mona* (Anglesey), *Monapia* (Man), *Vectis* (Wight) and *Silumnus* (Scilly).

A very different sort of geographical study is that produced in the second quarter of the second century by Claudius Ptolemaeus (Ptolemy) of Alexandria. His *Geography* was a vast listing of place-names and geographical features from all round the Roman world, with latitude and longitude co-ordinates provided for many of them. Although no maps are preserved with the earliest manuscripts, maps can be produced from the data and provide us with a glimpse of one particular Roman view of the geography of the empire. Although of huge value for its listings of over 200 British place-names, 'tribal' ethnics, rivers and other geographical features, the *Geography* is far from infallible in its purported positions of things. The problem is particularly acute for fringe provinces such as Britain, since there are fewer alternative sources with which to correlate identifications. Particular difficulties with Ptolemy concern where he obtained his data from, as it is evident that his British section combined information from several different sources, not all contemporary with one another. Although he was probably writing in the 140s, many of his data seem to relate to the 70s–80s, while the distribution of the legions reflects the situation in the early second century. There is no reference to either Hadrian's Wall or the Antonine Wall and many of the sites in Scotland described as *poleis* (literally 'towns') and associated by Ptolemy with particular ethnic groupings are almost certainly references to Roman forts of the Flavian period, not native settlements. On the other hand, much of the information on southern Britain appears to be Claudio–Neronian in date, with some slight updating. One of Ptolemy's major sources was Marinus of Tyre, working around the mid-first century. Although Ptolemy goes to lengths to expose many errors made by Marinus, it is far from clear that Ptolemy had been successful in eradicating all similar lapses from his own account.

Yet, many modern writers have placed absolute trust in Ptolemy's ascriptions of specific locations to the territories of particular British peoples, even when these seem to defy logic. They could equally be the result of his having simply linked closely adjacent names written on a source map. We shall encounter these issues on numerous occasions later in this work.

The names for Britain vary in our sources. The earliest form of the name for the main island may have been *Albion*, and though this recurs throughout classical antiquity, the more common early form in Greek sources was *Prettanike*, later *Brettania* or *Britannia*. References to the 'Brettanic islands' normally meant Britain and Ireland, and Pliny the

Elder recorded that the entire archipelago was known as *Britanniae* (in later Roman times *Britanniae* also referred to the collectivity of the British provinces). Ireland had a more varied nomenclature over time: *insula sacra* (sacred isle), *Ierne, Iris, Ivernia* or *Hibernia, Iuvernia*. The name *Albion* has often been equated with the Latin word for 'white', suggesting a connection with southern Britain's white cliffs. However, it is more probable that the derivation is from a British stem meaning 'the land' or perhaps the 'mainland' within an archipelago such as the British isles. The name recurs in Irish writings as *Alba*, mostly defining Scotland, but sometimes the whole of Britain.

Another class of geographical sources comprises the itineraries and road maps of the Roman world (and documents derived from them). The Roman authorities maintained such listings of the places encountered along the main roads of the empire for very practical reasons. A public post system (*cursus publicus*) was set up to carry official travellers and messages, with changes of horses and accommodation facilities at regular intervals (*mutationes* and *mansiones*). The itineraries listed these sites and the distances between them along selected major routes, conveying the information either as a simple written list or in linear map form. The former is represented by the *Antonine Itinerary*, compiled in the early third century and listing 225 major roads across the empire including 15 routes and over 100 place-names for Britain. The sequential nature of the listing and the indication of both total and stage distances have been invaluable in identifying the modern locations of the bulk of these Roman names. Since some of the routes overlap and over half the routes start, finish or pass through London, it is possible to detect some of the errors that have been introduced into the document by medieval copyists in terms of variations in recorded spellings of place-names and mileages. The *Tabula Peutingeriana*, a thirteenth-century copy of a Roman road map of probable second-century origin, illustrates the second type of itinerary document. This remarkable map stretches out the topography of the empire on to a parchment roll *c.*7 m long, but only 34 cm high, with names of places and distances being marked along schematic road lines (somewhat in the manner of a modern motorway 'journey planner'). Symbols indicated the sort of amenities provided at sites along the way, allowing the traveller to distinguish between major towns and the minor intermediate locations. Unfortunately, because of damage to the western end of the roll, only a very small part of (southern)

Britain is preserved. What both these sources represent is the laying down of an infrastructure of imperial government in the provinces (see further Chapter 9).

Close correlation is possible between many of the sites listed by Ptolemy in southern Britain and the itineraries, though since the extant itineraries do not extend west of Exeter, into westernmost districts of Wales or much north of Hadrian's Wall, huge uncertainty remains about the placement of sites mentioned by Ptolemy in south-west, west and northern Britain. Another source derived from Roman itinerary data, known as the *Ravenna Cosmography*, suggests that other Roman maps did at one time exist for these remoter areas of Britain. Compiled by an anonymous monk *c*.700, the *Cosmography* is an error-strewn and disorganized listing of place-names from all over the empire. For Britain, the compiler listed *c*.300 names and appears to have been working from several maps, one at least of itinerary type, reading off names in a somewhat random manner within areas of the map, rather than in strict sequential order along roads. The plethora of copying errors – apparent in the garbled form of many well-established place-name forms – and the evident inclusion of some river names and other geographical features and ethnic names complicate the interpretation of the document still further. All place-names that are uncorroborated elsewhere are thus presumptively unreliable and their original forms uncertain. Despite increasingly ingenious emendations to the clearly corrupt forms of many place-names, the reality for the south-west and north of Britain is much the same as for Ptolemy: we know many place-names but very few can be fixed exactly.

The *Notitia Dignitatum* is another document that provides us with place-name data. This was an early fifth-century collection of administrative information for the entire empire, listing civil and military officials, military units and their bases. Preserved through an eleventh-century copy, it includes facsimiles of the original illustrations of official insignia. There are problems concerning its composition and purpose, since it appears to comprise documents datable variously to the late fourth and early fifth centuries and therefore is not a 'snapshot' view of late Roman administrative arrangements. There may well be lacunae in the surviving documentation, for instance in relation to military deployments in Wales.

Many of our geographical sources allude to the inhabitants of Britain, though generally in vague and stereotypical terms. There is, unfortu-nately, no work to compare with Tacitus' *Germania*, a classic study of the peoples beyond the Rhine and Danube. The epithets used to describe the people of Britain are revealing of the mind-set of Mediterranean writers encountering the Other: 'brutes', 'warlike', 'prone to fight for domination and booty', 'inhuman', 'savage', 'barbarians', 'fierce', 'fren-zied', 'raving', 'terrifying of aspect', 'tent-dwelling', 'living on milk and meat', 'pastoralists', 'cannibalistic', 'clothed in skins', 'naked', 'unshod', 'painted with woad', 'tattooed', 'swarthy', 'red haired', 'promiscuous', 'lawless', 'old fashioned', 'aboriginal', 'simple', 'modest and free of luxury', 'uncivilized', 'rich only in herds and lands'. These and similar terms are used about almost all of Rome's so-called 'barbarian' neigh-bours and should by no means be seen as representing the actual situ-ation on the ground. In fact, archaeological data very often reveal a rather different reality, but the Roman literary audience did not neces-sarily want truth, rather they sought confirmation of their own innate superiority and of the backwardness of others. The popular stereotype of Britons as half-naked savages who dwelt in non-agricultural land-scapes thus had an extraordinary longevity in the sources.

Caesar divided the peoples of Britain into two main groups: interior peoples who claimed to be autochthonous, and coastal peoples who he said were descended from Gallic (or Belgic) migrants. Near the coast, he observed, the population was large, living in numerous homesteads, cultivating cereals and raising cattle, using bronze and gold coins and iron currency bars. Their society had many similarities to peoples in northern Gaul, with the most civilized people being those of Kent. In the interior, agriculture was less common, with people living off milk and meat and dressed in skins. All the Britons used woad to paint their skin blue to render themselves more daunting in battle. Customarily they wore their hair long and were moustachioed. Groups of ten to twelve men shared wives, with children assigned to the paternity of the man who first slept with the woman. They used chariots in warfare, a very archaic tradition by Continental standards (where conventional cavalry had largely supplanted the chariot).

Strabo, clearly drawing on the Caesarian account but adding some additional details, gave a broadly similar picture. The Britons were evidently taller than the Celts of Gaul and not so blond. He mentioned having seen British boys in Rome standing half a foot taller than the tallest in the city. They were loosely built, bow-legged and lacking in grace. Their customs were like the Celts, but simpler and more barbaric, as in their use of chariots in warfare. They drank milk, but lacked the ability to make cheese, and were unskilled in horticulture and farming. Chieftains ruled over them and, though they lacked cities, they erected fortified enclosures in their forests, where they lived in temporary huts and penned their stock.

Tacitus left open the question of whether the first inhabitants of Britain were indigenous or immigrants, due to insufficient evidence, 'as one might suspect when barbarians are involved'. Nonetheless, he highlighted the variation in physical types, noting the red hair and large limbs of the people of *Caledonia* as being similar to the Germans, while the swarthy faces and curly hair of the *Silures* were reminiscent of Spaniards and the inhabitants of southern Britain were similar to the peoples of northern Gaul. Overall, he favoured the idea of migrations of people having contributed to this mixture of characteristics and he stressed the similarity of language to the Gauls. Unlike the Gauls, who had lost their edge under Roman rule, the Britons remained ferocious and expert in warfare, with their strength in infantry. All the same, Tacitus commented on their tendency to court danger and then panic when confronted by it. The nobles still drove chariots in warfare, though their retainers did the actual serious fighting. Although once ruled by kings, the peoples had become split into partisan factions under rival chieftains. This lack of cohesion and planned co-operation in opposition to Rome was very much to Rome's advantage.

Writing in the early third century, Dio described two large peoples of Scotland, the *Maeatae* and the *Caledonii*, into which earlier more numerous groups had merged. The *Maeatae* lived north of the Forth–Clyde isthmus, the *Caledonii* to the north of them. According to Dio, they inhabited wild and waterless mountains and desolate marshy plains, possessing neither towns nor farms, but living on their flocks, game and gathered fruits. They dwelt in tents and went unclothed and unshod, sharing their women and rearing children in common. They chose their boldest men as leaders because of their insatiable liking for plunder. In battle, they used chariots and small horses alongside infantry. They struck their shields with knobs on the hafts of their short spears to create a terrifying noise in battle. They were able to run fast, were steadfast in battle, and could endure privation and cold. They could live for days in marshes with only their heads above water and survive in forests on bark and roots. Herodian also referred to the ability of the peoples of northern Britain to endure living in marshes. He stressed their nakedness and unconcern about being covered in mud. In the absence of clothing, they adorned their necks and waists with iron and tattooed their bodies. They were extremely warlike and fought without armour, using small shields, spears and swords.

The sixth-century Byzantine historian Procopius provided a wholly mythologized vision of Britain:

In this island of *Brittia* the men of old built a long wall, cutting off a large part of it, and the air and the soil and everything else is different on the two sides of it. For to the east of the wall there is healthy air . . . and many men dwell there . . . and the crops flourish . . . But on the other side everything is the opposite of this . . . innumerable snakes and all kinds of wild beasts occupy the place as their own . . . and the natives say that if a man crosses the wall and goes to the other side he forthwith dies, unable to bear the pestilential nature of the air.

The use of language in all these sources was deliberate and served a variety of common *topoi* in classical literature on the barbarian 'Other', as, for instance, the emphasis on uncivilized ways of living. Taking agriculture and horticulture as the marks of an advanced society, the descent through pastoralism, to nomadism, to hunter-gathering communities, to utterly barbaric people living off roots and bark can be correlated with distance from the Roman empire. This was thus a schematic model of *Barbaricum*, not a representation of actual socio-economic states. The point is perfectly illustrated by Pomponius Mela: '[Britain] has peoples and kings of peoples, but they are all uncivilized and the further they are from the Continent the less they know of other kinds of wealth, being rich only in herds and lands.'

Another literary 'trick' was to use diminutives in describing the Britons and their institutions: *Brittunculi* or 'little Brits' is a dismissive term used on one of the *Vindolanda* tablets. Tacitus described Irish rulers as *reguli* or 'little kings', while Strabo similarly uses a term for 'petty monarch', rather than 'king', when describing the British rulers who appear to have had formal client status. The exceptions to this linguistic pattern are interesting: Cunobelinus was described as *rex Britannorum* or 'king of [more than one ethnic group of] the Britons', a title that has echoes in that of the man known either as Togidubnus or Cogidubnus in the post-conquest period, *rex magnus Britannorum* – 'great king of the Britons'.

Much in these descriptions was calculated to stress difference and distance between the Britons and an educated Roman audience, both in terms of their social habits and in the landscapes they occupied. Several of these accounts concluded by commenting unfavourably on the British climate – where the implicit comparison was with the Mediterranean. Strabo, for instance, noted the frequency of rain and of fog that combined to limit sunlight to only a few hours each day. Tacitus called the frequent rain and mists 'miserable'. The Scottish landscapes of Dio and Herodian were excessively marshy, with thick mists rising from them to give them a gloomy character. These sources created a hostile landscape and duly peopled it with alien people. The stereotypical images of British barbarians are contradicted in a number of important details by archaeological evidence (discussed in Chapters 3 and 14). The testimony of our sources is thus neither necessarily 'true' nor accurate in all details and they need to be carefully weighed with other evidence where possible.

Roman legal sources do not generally refer to Britain in particular, but have much to add about the administration of civil affairs and justice in the empire as a whole. A few rare finds of Roman legal documents from Britain, including part of a will from North Wales and documents relating to property sales and contracts, confirm that Roman law was applied to certain communities and in specific circumstances.

Christian sources specifically alluding to Britain are relatively rare, though the Church took over the Roman state's moralistic and stereotypical view of barbarians. Jerome in the fourth century stressed the cannibalistic and promiscuous behaviour of the *Attacotti*. The repetition of such tales does not make them any truer than the earlier stereotypes. On the other hand, after the western empire broke up, late Roman writers such as the diehard pagan Zosimus or the Christian Constantius provide our best evidence of events in Britain, while St Patrick's *Confessions* provides a link to Ireland. Similarly, Gildas in the sixth century and Bede in the early eighth century tried to make sense of the Dark Ages from a Christian perspective. At a certain point, however, the accounts shade across from the historical to the legendary. The problem is recognizing where that transition occurs.

If historical and geographical accounts of the remoter regions of the empire reflected the preconceptions, biases and stereotypes of ancient authors, this was even more the case for other works of literature, primarily poetry, but also including plays and novels. Literary tropes and conventions abound: the noble savage, the mythical status of Britain as a heavily forested land, and so on. Looking for words to evoke the wildest and remotest lands of the Atlantic west, poets freely incorporated the *Britanni* and the *Caledonii* into their verses. The historical significance of such poetic flourishes in Virgil, Horace, Lucan, Martial and Juvenal has been much debated, though the interest of the first three at least attests to the currency of discussion about Britain during the reign of Augustus.

The rise of literacy and of literate acts (both the writing/inscribing and the reading of those words) marks the Roman period out from both the late Iron Age and the Dark Ages that followed. Epigraphy is the collective term to describe the corpus of writing and inscriptions on a wide variety of media. Inscriptions on stone are perhaps the best-known class of epigraphy, serving a wide variety of purposes in Roman society. The Roman army was a major source of such inscriptions, erecting them to commemorate building projects, on altars and dedications to the gods and emperors, and as tombstones for deceased comrades and family members. Civil communities of the empire also adopted the epigraphic habit to varying degrees: to record private and public building schemes and dedications, to publicize laws and decisions, to celebrate the careers and achievements of notable people, to record votive and other religious acts, as well as to mark burials. In addition to engravings on stone, the Roman world made use of a very wide range of written communication, from inscriptions on copper-alloy sheets, to a variety of media for making everyday documents (writing tablets, papyri, parchment), to the marking of personal possessions, to inscribed votive offerings, to makers' marks or labels on pottery, metal ingots, brick and tile, lead pipes or leather, to information about transport or trade on pots and barrels, to graffiti on buildings or personal articles. Collectively these miscellaneous categories of writing are often referred to as *instrumentum domesticum* and they far outnumber the inscriptions on stone in number, though the vast majority of these texts are very short. Coins are another type of inscribed artefact that circulated widely within the Roman empire, carrying written messages on their faces. Pre-Roman encounters with Latin literacy were few but significant. The adoption of sophisticated coin legends by some of the southern peoples of Britain was already a development of the late Iron Age.

Most epigraphic materials present problems of preservation, legibility, reconstruction, translation and interpretation. The discovery of a further fragment or a minor change in transcription can substantially alter the accepted reading of a text. The style of writing involved in different forms of epigraphic document varied, and making sense of these requires knowledge of both ancient writing practice and conventions. For example, the cutting of stone inscriptions was a cumbersome and expensive process of communication, leading to the evolution of a complex set of shorthand abbreviations, somewhat akin to modern text messaging. There was also a range of other forms of epigraphic expression, often less well studied or less well preserved than the stone inscriptions. In assessing the epigraphic practices of Britain in relation to those of other regions of the empire, it is important to be aware of the differences as well as highlighting the similarities. We also need to understand very clearly how the differential preservation of the various classes of inscription influences our understanding of the extent and use of literacy in Britain.

The total volume of epigraphic evidence from Britain is comparatively small, though greatly augmented by a number of highly significant discoveries in recent decades. The first volume of the *Roman Inscriptions of Britain* (inscriptions on stone) contains only 2,400 entries, covering discoveries up to 1954, in comparison to more than 60,000 known from Roman Africa. New texts published each year in the journal of Romano-British studies, *Britannia*, normally amount to fewer than twenty, often very fragmentary. Of the total corpus now known, the vast majority originate from military sites and the epigraphy of the civil zone is comparatively poor. The stone inscriptions from Britain are supplemented in important ways by material from elsewhere in the empire relating to Britain. Typically, these inscriptions may provide details of careers of upper-class Romans who served in Britain, or provide additional details about military units or individuals known to have been in Britain. There are also important insights into regional contacts between Britain and the Continent.

Although Britain appears a relative backwater for stone epigraphy, it has produced some astonishing groups of more everyday documents. Such documents in longhand (cursive) script are far less commonly preserved, but, when found, present rather different challenges for modern experts. Finds of papyri in Egypt were for many years seen as unrepresentative of the Roman world at large and a peculiarity of that province. However, discoveries of caches of everyday documents written on perishable organic materials from other provinces continue to grow and it is now clear that the stone inscriptions represent the tip of an iceberg of documentation that sustained the Roman empire. Wooden writing tablets only survive in exceptional archaeological conditions, but have been recognized in permanently damp and anaerobic contexts in Britain (notably at *Vindolanda*, Carlisle, Caerleon, London). There were two main forms of writing tablet; the first fashioned from thin slivers of wood and written on in ink, the second comprising thicker wooden leaves with an inset hollow filled with wax and inscribed with a stylus. Although the wax has generally perished, scratches made by the stylus in the wooden backing are sometimes legible, though since these tablets were for repeated use they are often indecipherable palimpsests of successive documents.

The most extraordinary group of ink tablets has come from the fort at *Vindolanda* near Hadrian's Wall, though dating to the decades immediately before the wall's construction. The 'archive' represents the residue of military records of successive units that occupied the fort and of the households of their commanding officers. The types of document present illustrate the range of uses of written instructions and records within the army.

For the civil zone, there are few comparable documents of any length. The principal exception comprises the so-called *defixiones* or curse tablets, with notably large groups published from temples at Bath and Uley. These were generally engraved with a sharp implement in the soft surface of thin sheets of lead (or lead alloy) and the messages called on the gods to punish those who had wronged the dedicant. The majority of incidents concerned the theft of personal items by an unknown thief, with the most dreadful curses called down upon them 'whether man or woman, slave or free'.

This sort of documentation opens a remarkable window on to the world of Roman-period Britain, but we must bear in mind that it provides us with a highly localized and chronologically specific view. The rest is comparative darkness and therein is the nub of the problem of reconstructing the history of the people. We know that there was once a mass of relevant documentation produced by temporary residents, permanent immigrants and native Britons, but we have so little of it preserved that we are reduced to silence or analogy for the most part.

To what extent did native Britons adopt the 'epigraphic habit' and acquire the necessary skills to read and write? Literacy is a key sub-theme of my study of discrepant identities. The ability to read and write served both to unite and to divide the people of the province. For certain groups it was a key factor in defining their identity – as in the case of the Roman army. Being a user or reader could bolster the social distinction of select Britons, some of whom, according to Tacitus, were anxious to obtain a Latin education. These were people of property and wealth, but who also saw opportunities for social advancement under Rome. We shall look later at how different groups within Romano-British society deployed literate skills in varied ways as a means of defining their identity under Roman rule. Judged by the inscriptions on stone alone, the extent of literacy looks pretty low, though adding in other classes of data – such as graffiti on personal possessions, or the distribution of styli, writing tablets and seal boxes (used to secure writing tablets during transport or in storage) – gives an indication of rather more widespread usage. Nonetheless, there are grounds for suggesting that levels of literacy and uses of writing were specific to certain groups in society. At the top end, the major users of written communication of all types were the army and the provincial administration, followed by the local urban elite class and the largest rural estates. In the towns, writing underpinned administration, elite competition and status display, being variously used for census, land-holding and taxation records, personal correspondence, economic matters, legal process, religious activity, and so on. Rural literacy was far more exclusive at all times.

WHAT SORT OF PICTURE HAS BEEN CONSTRUCTED?

The nature of our written sources limits and directs the sort of historical research that is practicable today. From the literary sources, it is possible to construct at best only an outline history of the British provinces, one that is very unbalanced century by century because of the gaps in the surviving material. The first century is thus far better delineated than any subsequent century of Roman rule. The vagueness of many of the references to events in Britain has led to a natural tendency to extract the maximum from them, whether through clever textual emendations to improve the sense, through embroidering the story or through accepting information of dubious validity rather than discard any 'fact'. Overall, then, the broad narrative account of Roman Britain is relatively fixed in outline, but very threadbare in detail. New epigraphic discoveries modify this in only minor ways.

Much activity has focused on the identification of the place-names with physical ruins of Roman date. Clearly, the names of the British peoples, the Roman provinces, the major forts and towns, and so on, have much to contribute to our story. It is somehow reassuring to know the ancient names of rivers, coastal features and even some minor settlements, though the enthusiasm for correlating this sort of data can easily take us far into the realms of hypothesis. For instance, attempts to propose ever more ingenious identifications of places in Scotland risk much by not facing up to the frailty of our real knowledge. In fact, only a small handful of the places named by any of our sources from north of Hadrian's Wall can be located with precision. On the other hand, the Romans did not suffer this same problem, since having accurately located, named and archived the knowledge of features, peoples and places across the landscape, they evidently had the maps and documentary records to refer to when they chose to march their army north again. As in many imperial systems, knowledge equated to power and the geographical mastery of the colonized landscape was a prerequisite of domination.

An interesting aspect of the study of the place-names of Roman Britain concerns the origins of the toponyms. Despite the Latinized endings of names such as *Londinium* (London) or *Camulodunum* (Colchester), the roots of most place-names were British or 'Celtic'. Only about fifty of the *c.* 500 names listed in the standard compendium of Romano-British place-names were based wholly or partly on Latin words. The most common of these Latin elements were descriptive terms: *Portus Dubris* (the Port of *Dubris*, Dover), *Aquae Sulis* (The Hot Springs of Sulis, Bath), *Colonia Nervia Glevensium* (the colony of Nerva at *Glevum*, Gloucester). Other Latin elements include references to bridges (*Ad Pontem*), salt production (*Salinae*), or military needs (*Horrea Classis*, 'granary of the fleet'). However, purely British names far outnumbered these alien elements, even for newly established Roman forts. The names for coastal features indicate that much geographical information-gathering was mediated through British speakers, though the hybrid Latin/British names reveal the adjunct of Latin descriptors: *promontorium, insula* and so on. The Roman conquest of Britain thus did not involve the imposition of a new set of toponyms at the expense of local usage. British names for fortifications (*Dun-* and *-dunum*, *Dur-* and *-durum*) are frequently encountered as elements of names for Roman forts and towns, while *Venta*, the term for 'market', was used for three town names and in compound form at a further two sites.

Prosopography is the study of the careers of notable Romans, mainly from epigraphic evidence. It was a Roman upper-class custom to record and honour the careers of great men with inscriptions listing successive posts in the imperial service. Although relatively few such inscriptions are known from Britain, the epigraphic corpora from the core provinces of the empire reveal many details of Romans who served in Britain as governors, financial officials, legal experts, military commanders in the legions and auxiliary units.

Prosopographical and epigraphic studies also underlie our understanding of the governance of the Roman empire and of the sort of people who rose to the highest positions of power within it. In the absence of firm evidence from Britain for many aspects of Roman government, it is necessary to look at processes elsewhere in the empire to build our hypotheses. One must also admit the caveat that the Roman empire was not run according to an unvaried rule book and there are numerous examples of local variations in procedures and of the adoption of short-term, *ad hoc* solutions. When we employ analogy, therefore, we are constructing theories for further testing, not establishing fact.

What is missing? The answer to this question is a great deal. The Roman empire was essentially a literate empire, with many areas of life defined by written laws and subject to a minute level of documentation. Consider what we have lost at the upper end: provincial census data and the daily and archive records of military and urban/provincial administration. A few rare finds, such as writing tablets from *Vindolanda*, London and Carlisle, prove the existence of a mass of lost documentation. These missing data will inevitably render our models crude. We need only contrast the detail of the economic documents from *Vindolanda* with studies of the Roman economy based solely on the archaeological pattern of distribution of selected goods.

ARCHAEOLOGY

Whereas the body of literary documents is essentially static and epigraphic material accumulates only slowly, the already large volume of archaeological information is growing at a pace and covering a range of data that is unmatched for many other areas of the Roman empire. The publication of results inevitably lags behind the actual fieldwork and much work carried out by professional archaeologists as part of the planning process is 'published' only by archive reports (the so-called grey literature). Even limiting ourselves to the properly published material, the volume of available material is now overwhelming. Researching this book has brought home to me the increasing difficulties in producing a synthesis from such a mass of disparate data. Just like the written sources, however, archaeology comprises a wide range of different sorts of data and it is equally important to understand the rules of this evidence. Archaeological data comprise not only structural evidence of excavated sites laid down in successive strata, but also the artefacts (for example, coins, pottery, glass and small finds) and ecofacts (bones and seeds) preserved in that stratigraphic sequence. There are also non-invasive techniques for discovering or investigating sites, such as fieldwalking, aerial photography, earthwork and standing building survey, geophysical methods (resistivity, magnetometry and ground-penetrating radar). There is increasing exploitation of the underwater archaeology of wrecks. Study of inscriptions and artworks, such as mosaics or sculptured stone, are other specialist fields in their own right. There are corpora in progress of all inscriptions, sculpture and mosaics from Britain – all have been invaluable to me in working on this book – and the standards of reporting of finds assemblages in published reports are extremely high. The Roman army, urban archaeology, mortuary archaeology, Roman landscapes, Roman roads, Romano-Celtic religion, all attract their devotees. Finally and fundamentally, there is the archaeology of the late Iron Age and of sub-Roman Britain, often treated as separate intellectual areas with their own academic networks and agendas.

Britain is thus one of the most intensively researched Roman provinces from an archaeological perspective, and this offers huge potential, though the data are not without problems. In the first place, the intensive occupation and use of the British landscape over the last two millennia has degraded the physical survival of structures, through stone-robbing, over-building and agricultural activity. With the additional factor that buildings were often constructed in less durable materials in Britain than was the case in some of the core provinces of the empire, the structural remains are often less impressive and less easy to interpret. Secondly, our evidence favours what survives in the archaeological record, with a bias for inorganic over organic materials. We are more likely to find the remains of ceramic transport jars (amphoras) for wine than wooden barrels. The difficulty here concerns whether absence of amphoras means non-consumption of wine or whether the supply of wine is not visible to us archaeologically. On settlement sites, archaeology is largely a study of rubbish and ruins, with a strong presumption that ancient society was quite efficient at recycling materials of value. Metal artefacts, for instance, will tend to be much rarer than broken pottery in rubbish deposits, because they will have been selectively removed for repair or refashioning. Even the association between finds and findspots needs to be questioned. The assemblages that lie within the shell of a house are more likely to have arrived there after its abandonment as a dwelling than during its lifetime. The redeposition of earlier rubbish assemblages in later times is also a factor to consider. On multi-period sites, people often dismantled disused buildings down to foundation level to make way for later ones, adding to the archaeological difficulty of recovering detailed plans.

There are advantages of the archaeological data over the literary sources. We should note in particular that the archaeological evidence covers all sectors of society, not just the richest and most pro-Roman elements. If we are prepared to search for it, there is evidence to give us a bottom-up as well as a top-down view of society. At the same time, though, we must be careful in the assumptions we make about the value placed on and the use of items of material culture by different social groups. Can we be at all certain that a native Briton had the same conceptual imagination about, say, a red fineware bowl as someone on the governor's staff? This is a difficult question to answer, but the conventional approach has tended to assume that both placed a similar value on the 'Roman' identity of the bowl and that the former would have used it in emulation of the latter. Careful interrogation of the archaeological data should allow us to test such assumptions and to perceive more complex and varied identities being forged in Britain under Roman rule.

However, a prime weakness is that the conduct of archaeology is dependent on academic agendas and here we must reflect on the traditional focus of Romano-British studies on forts and frontier works, baths and urban buildings, rural villas, roads, the 'Roman' artworks and treasures (mosaics, wall-paintings, silver plate, coin hoards, and so on). For instance, comparison of numbers of excavations on different classes of Roman sites reveals that in 1921–25 military sites/major towns/villas comprised 75 per cent of the total. In 1991–95, these three types still comprised 68 per cent, although non-villa rural settlements had risen from 7 to 23 per cent of excavations. Given that the latter represent over 95 per cent of all Roman period sites, there is still a major imbalance in research effort. In pursuing this agenda over the last 100 years or so, archaeologists have consciously or unconsciously implanted a basic sympathy with Rome and its elite culture at the core of Romano-British studies. This is not a neutral position to adopt, though its consequences are rarely admitted. We can enrich the picture of Britain in the Roman empire through more excavations of low-status urban structures or rural sites.

3
'Nothing for us to Fear or Rejoice at.'
Britain, Britons and the Roman Empire

When Caesar invaded the south-east of England in 55–54 BC, amid much hype and spin at Rome, his political opponents held their breath and awaited word of this mysterious land. One of those opponents was the arch-Republican M. Tullius Cicero and, as news of rather mediocre results filtered back, you can sense his relief in letters to his friend Atticus and to his brother Quintus, who was in Britain with Caesar. He stressed the fact that, contrary to expectations, the campaigns had not yielded much gold and silver 'nor any prospect of booty except slaves' (adding snidely that such slaves were not expected to be accomplished in literature or music). His overall conclusion was 'that there is nothing there for us to fear or rejoice at'. Strabo, explaining why Augustus had subsequently chosen not to annex Britain, expressed the same sentiment:

For though the Romans could have held Britain, they have rejected the idea, seeing that there was nothing to fear from the Britons, since they are not powerful enough to cross over and attack us, nor was there much advantage to be gained if the Romans were to occupy it.

The campaigns of Caesar have often been written off by modern commentators as no more than a brief and inconsequential encounter. The real disruption was to come under Claudius a century later. Indeed, the Roman conquest of AD 43 is often presented as the end of the Iron Age in Britain, in much the same way that 1066 is held to mark the end of Anglo-Saxon England. This is wrong in several respects. Many of the islands of the British archipelago did not become part of the Roman empire in 43; some never did. There were also strong continuities in regions that were under Roman territorial control. Conversely, of course, neither does the year 43 mark the start of civilization and history in Britain. We must recognize that this is a date of convenience for

historians and archaeologists, a line in the sand, rather artificially segregating Iron Age archaeologists from Romanists. In reality, it marks just
one stage in a much longer process of integration of parts of Britain
with a wider European world. From the mid-first century BC there
was regular contact with the Roman world and this had profound
consequences for the late Iron Age societies in Britain. The impact of
this contact was unequal both across society and geographically, and
Iron Age studies increasingly highlight regional diversity and non-
conformity. When it came to the dramas of Roman invasions in 55–54
BC and AD 43, the reaction of the separate British peoples appears
to have varied. Parts of Britain were already embarked on a path of
convergence with Rome, long before the British peoples were fully aware
of Rome's existence. In archaeological terms, the key date may have
been the later second century BC, not 55 BC or AD 43.

Of our classical accounts, those of Caesar and Strabo are primarily
relevant to the peoples of southern Britain, while Tacitus, Cassius Dio
and Herodian provide more information on the northern peoples (Fig.
3). As outlined already, a fundamental problem is that they interweave
stereotypical attributes of barbarians and anachronisms with factual
information. Modern book illustrators have done much to promulgate
the view that all Britons went to war half-naked, without body armour
or helmets so as to display their spiky hair and massively tattooed bodies
daubed with blue dye. While we can accept that Roman forces did fight
some Britons adorned in this way, it is another thing to assume that it
was ubiquitous to British war-bands (although one can appreciate that
any blue-skinned warriors encountered would have made a lasting
impression). Mail shirts have been found in a number of late Iron Age
contexts and brooches and clothes pins are regular finds from Britain.
People certainly wore clothes and some at least went into battle suitably
armoured. The chariots that aroused the curiosity of our Roman sources
are also attested to by chariot burials in Yorkshire and Scotland and by
more widespread finds of horse brasses and chariot gear (as at Melsonby/
Stanwick and Llyn Cerrig Bach on Anglesey). However, chariot burials
in East Yorkshire seem to have ended prior to the Claudian invasion,
even if they may have lived on in folk memory much later. An outlying
example at Ferrybridge, dated to the mid Iron Age on artefactual
grounds, was surrounded by a ditch into which were deposited the bones
of at least 128 cattle. Radio-carbon dating has demonstrated that the

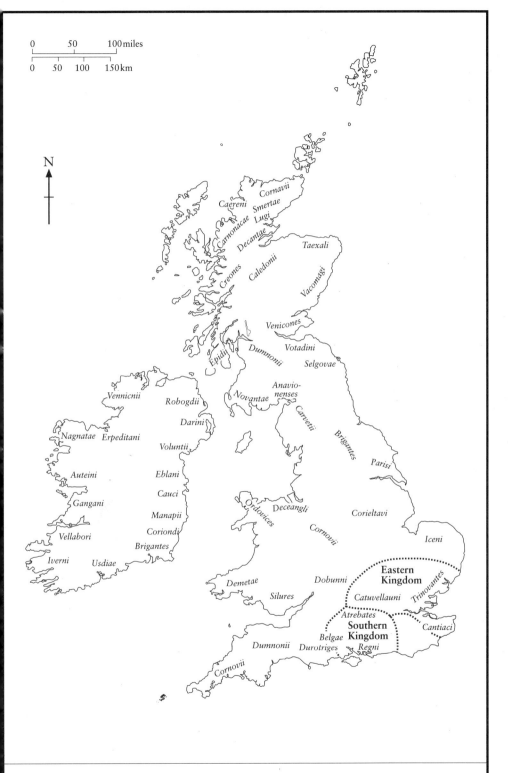

Figure 3. *Peoples of Britain, including Ireland, in the Roman period (information primarily based on Ptolemy)*

date of the feasting deposit was long after the initial burial, suggesting continuing recognition of the burial of a significant Iron Age leader well into the Roman period.

Comments in the sources on the lack of farming skills outside southeast Britain are plainly contradicted by the archaeological data. It suited the Roman mental model of progressive barbarism as one moved away from civilized lands, that one should successively encounter people who practised less advanced economies. When Caesar stated that the people living nearer the coast of Britain were agriculturalists, but those further into the interior were predominantly pastoralists, he appears in both cases to have been discussing the Home Counties, since his campaigns did not progress far north of the Thames. This is not an early allusion, as sometimes it has been taken to be, to a highland/lowland division of Britain. Moreover, it implies a pastoral/agricultural distinction north and south of the Thames that is not represented in the archaeological record. The sub-human characteristics later attributed to the most northerly Britons fall into this same category of exaggeration.

The Roman sources indicated a number of possible forms of leadership within British society – kings, petty chieftains, war leaders appointed by temporary alliances, spiritual leaders such as the druids, an elite 'class'. In Caesar's account, we learn that there were at least three separate kings in *Cantium* (Kent), but that the overall direction of the war was entrusted to Cassivellaunos, described as a paramount chieftain. There was wide variation in the precise form of authority and the ways in which it was transferred, whether by force of arms and personality or through inheritance. Britain was no more uniform in this respect than Gaul, where Caesar encountered a range of different forms of native authority. An important element of the Gallic scene was the support for leaders given by their clients and dependants in society. At least some of these Gallic chiefs appear to have maintained a regular force of followers (*comitatus*), normally a cavalry band who gave the leader 'distinction in peace and protection in war', to borrow a phrase from Tacitus, describing a similar Germanic tradition. The same trend may have been present in the British late Iron Age.

Another group of elite Britons were the *druides*, about whom much rubbish has been written. The druids were an important group of religious leaders within both Gallic and British society and received a particularly vitriolic write-up in classical literature. The politest comments described them as 'barbarian philosophers', but other references stress their involvement in human sacrifice, the secrecy of their practices, the dangerous prophecies they made about the impending end of the Roman empire, and so on. Their precise role in society is thus difficult to reconstruct with any certainty, but we can identify at least some of the reasons behind the Roman unease and distrust of them. They operated at a supra-'tribal' level within society and were thus a potential focus for concerted resistance to Rome. The Roman authorities thus deliberately targeted druids in both Gaul and Britain for violent eradication. According to Caesar, Britain was a major centre of the druidical order and attacks on the island of Anglesey were later to encounter druids and other religious 'fanatics' at the heart of resistance to Rome.

In sum, we need to reconsider the validity of the traditional view of late Iron Age society as consisting of a semi-naked warrior race, long-haired and hirsute, riding into battle in archaic chariots at the prompting of religious fanatics. This image comes through the accounts in our Roman sources, but is reinforced by our uncritical acceptance of such stereotypes. Understanding the Iron Age involves deconstructing the biases of ancient literary sources and modern preconceptions alike.

There is a continuing major debate about the ethnic identity of the pre-Roman populations of Britain, bound up with modern understanding of the term 'Celts'. The ultimate origins of native Britons also interested the Romans. In part the question is a linguistic one, in part cultural, in part determined by modern preconceptions. The Celts are commonly viewed as a pan-European Iron Age cultural group, some say civilization, with common language, physical characteristics, societal structures and material culture. Paradoxically, Celtic identity has become associated both with the modern centralizing politics of the European Union and with movements for self-determination on the 'Celtic fringes'. Modern notions of Celticity imply far greater uniformity of culture, practice and purpose across Europe than can be demonstrated by the archaeological evidence. The 'Atlantic Celts' of the British archipelago almost certainly had no ethnic sense of being part of a great Celtic civilization, even though they shared cultural affinities with Continental peoples. They need to be understood in their own terms as a distinct series of regional groupings. The practice in the rest of this book will be to avoid the term Celts in a British context for this reason, and to follow the Roman practice of referring to the inhabitants as Britons and their language as British. However, it is equally essential to qualify this by saying that at the time there was no sense among the various British peoples of their collective British identity and even the unity of the British language must be doubted.

The indigenous languages of Britain were certainly linked to a north European group known in modern times as Celtic and, while no doubt comprising numerous strong local dialects, these can be divided into two main groups. The larger of these groups is the Brithonic (Brittonic) Celtic, sometimes referred to as P-Celtic. It is attested in much of Britain with the exception of Ireland and parts of western Scotland, where Goidelic (or Q-Celtic) was the norm. P- and Q-Celtic differ most obviously in the replacement of a qu- sound in the latter by p- in the former. P-Celtic dialects evolved into the relict Welsh, Cornish and Breton languages and were similar to the dominant Continental branch of Celtic speakers. The Q-Celtic dialects underlie modern Irish, Scottish and Manx Gaelic, and were rare on the Continent, suggesting an earlier phase of language dispersal. However, with the exception of the Romano-British place-name evidence, a few personal names and the evidence of the later surviving languages of the Celtic fringes, there is little actual data to assess the linguistic pattern in Iron Age Britain and debate still rages among linguistic specialists. The possibility of survivals from an earlier non-Indo-European language within P-Celtic Pictish is a particular point of controversy.

In any event, it is evident that there were strong regional dialects throughout Britain – with some of the distinctions broad enough to be seen as separate languages by casual observers. As a general model, it is probably reasonable to infer that the peoples of mainland Britain spoke a range of P-Celtic dialects, with the closest linguistic similarities between adjacent groupings and divergence increasing with distance. The apparent dominance of Q-Celtic dialects in Ireland would have presented a more challenging linguistic barrier in that direction.

The material culture of the Iron Age peoples of Europe has long been recognized to reflect two broad artistic episodes, each with various sub-phases, known as the Hallstatt (c. 800–500 BC) and La Tène (c. 500–1 BC) cultures, after the type-sites where characteristic metalwork and art forms were first identified. The Hallstatt and La Tène cultures have provided the framework of Iron Age studies in much of northern Europe, and this remains a baseline also for British archaeologists. There is comparatively little material of the Hallstatt phase in Britain and Ireland, but material reminiscent of the La Tène culture is much more widely represented. La Tène artworks are characterized by fine curvilinear patterns and these styles became widely disseminated across Europe. In the simplest traditional models of Iron Age Britain, these were correlated with phases of migration into Britain during the first millennium BC, believed to have involved the importation of both language and material culture from Europe. Migrations of Belgic Gauls to Britain are referred to by several of our sources, including Caesar. However, the main transition points in southern Britain, from the early to mid Iron Age c.400/300 BC and from the mid to late Iron Age in the late second century BC, do not correlate neatly with social and material culture trends on the Continent. At these dates the British Iron Age communities differed from Continental ones in significant respects. Furthermore, north and west of a line extending from the Humber estuary to the Bristol Channel, the British Iron Age shows less distinct phases and is generally split between an early phase running on from the late Bronze Age to c.300 BC, and a later Iron Age beginning c.300 BC and culminating in the first centuries BC and AD.

The idea of Belgic migration models is thus less attractive to archaeologists nowadays, who prefer to stress the distinctive regional characteristics that distinguish the British Iron Age from Continental Europe. The truth may lie between the two extremes, with the linguistic evidence suggesting some small-scale movement of people, who perhaps succeeded in establishing themselves in leading positions within British groupings. The increased use of iron and new decorative forms on the Continent were imitated within these societies. This process may have occurred across a very broad time-frame, with many British groups adopting the new fashions without need of incomers imposing them. Indeed, the differences between the southern British Iron Age and Continental Europe in the late Iron Age are striking enough to suggest a strong undercurrent of continuity of British peoples and practices. For instance, the Continental La Tène culture was characterized by warrior inhumations, whereas male burials with weapons are extremely rare in Iron Age Britain, and, when encountered, clearly represent individuals of special status.

On the other hand, Diviciacus, a Gallic king of the *Suessiones* in north-eastern Gaul, evidently had lands and political interests in Britain around the time of Caesar. There is also evidence of Gallic refugees fleeing to Britain during and following Caesar's wars in Gaul and this may well be a reflection of a longer-term process, in which small bands of elite warriors and traders had crossed the Channel and integrated themselves into British groups. This is not to argue for a return to the Belgic 'invasion' hypothesis of old, but simply to acknowledge that perhaps not everything in the late Iron Age can be interpreted in terms of insular development.

THE BRITISH IRON AGE

A detailed synthesis of the British Iron Age is beyond the scope of this book. The focus here is on the key developments of the late pre-Roman Iron Age – broadly 100 BC and onwards (Fig. 4 shows some key sites). However, it is necessary to cast a glance back to the middle Iron Age, to set later innovations in their longer-term context.

The traditional 'heartland' of Iron Age archaeology has been the Wessex region of southern England. Many of the classic investigations were carried out here (Cranborne Chase, Little Woodbury, Maiden Castle, Danebury, Hengistbury Head). Early syntheses were understandably built up around this rich pool of data, but the applicability of the 'Wessex model' to other parts of southern Britain is increasingly questioned. Regional archaeologists are now starting to emphasize diversity and difference from the dominant Wessex paradigm. A key feature of the Iron Age was the hillfort, canonized in popular imagination by the impressive earthworks of sites such as Maiden Castle in Dorset, and this has been a major focus of study. Yet it has become increasingly clear that the hillfort was no longer so central to British societies of the late Iron Age.

The heyday of the hillfort was in the sixth–fifth centuries BC, when large tracts of landscape became organized around these fortified sites. There may have been a link between the rise of the hillforts and the emergence of a new style of elite group, initially producing a volatile situation with many short-lived hillforts, but gradually settling down and with some of the sites becoming more highly developed. Excavations at the classic Wessex hillfort of Danebury inform the model with high-quality data. Here the interior of the hillfort contained a comparatively

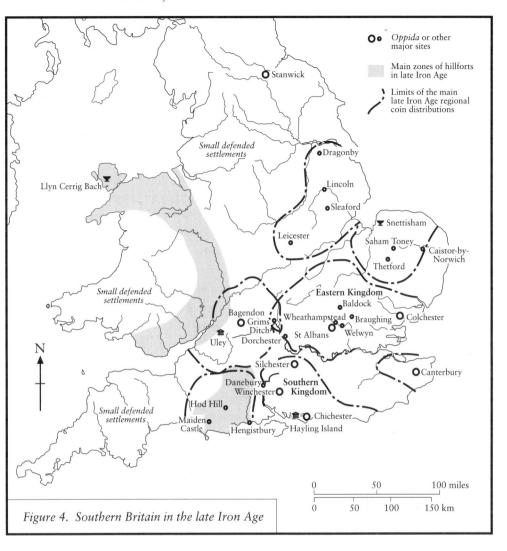

Figure 4. Southern Britain in the late Iron Age

small number of roundhouses around the periphery of the site, with the central area filled with numerous storage pits, some associated with ritual deposits. This may indicate both an important storage function, but also social devices employed to reinforce the authority of an incipient elite. By the fourth century, the pits were accompanied by small four-post or six-post rectangular structures, again interpreted as granaries, perhaps reflecting the successful manipulation of agrarian surplus by the elite. The religious function of the site appears to have become more overt in this later phase, with a series of 'shrines' near the centre. Animal bones from the pits indicate that stock-raising also played an important part in the 'economy' of the site. The power relations of Danebury have been modelled in terms of a warrior-aristocracy, dominating local areas from a strong-point, extracting and redistributing surpluses of crops and stock, but also placed in competition with neighbouring groups. Warfare and raiding may have been endemic in these societies.

Further major upheavals followed around the end of the second century BC, with the progressive abandonment of many hillforts in Wessex, though they remained important in a few areas of Britain, such as Dorset and the Welsh Marches. Defended or enclosed farmsteads became more common from this date, as part of a general development of rural settlement, and some of these sites had an elite character. New types of nucleated site also emerged or grew, including trading ports such as Hengistbury Head and low-lying foci, conventionally referred to as *oppida*.

Increasing trade contact with the Continent has been seen as a significant motif of this later phase, with elite power redefined in terms of access to and control of imported cultural symbols, such as wine and a range of paraphernalia associated with feasting and drinking. Localized chiefdoms were evidently replaced by larger territorial groupings, initially indicated by new regional pottery styles, later by distribution areas of Iron Age coinage groups. These appear to have been fluid identities and territories, rather than the fully fledged 'tribal' entities (*civitates*) enshrined later in Roman administrative structures. The abandonment of hillforts need not, of course, have marked an end of warfare and raiding, which rather were henceforth organized on a larger scale and over wider areas by kings in control of proto-states. The conquest of Gaul by the Romans in the 50s BC accelerated this process, by placing these incipient polities in direct contact with the globalizing force of an expanding empire. The importance of Rome as a focus of change, whether intended or not, has been enshrined in the application of core–periphery models, which anticipate greater impacts closest to and weakest impacts furthest from the core state in the 'tribal' periphery.

The prime critique of this model is that it is still very much focused on southern and south-eastern Britain. There is still a tendency to conceptualize Britain as a unified whole, rather than as a fractured and highly regional set of societies. On the other hand, the fact that one can find exceptional material in Scotland does not entirely invalidate the view that the proximity of Rome to south-east Britain became a significant factor. The key element of the core–periphery model, that territories closest to an expanding state tended to be more socially developed, still has the ring of truth about it, especially when we come to the events of the late Iron Age.

An important question arising from current debates is whether societies of the middle Iron Age were more egalitarian than those of the late Iron Age. This has some merits given the current lack of evidence for a single elite residence standing out among the other dwellings on sites such as Danebury. Some have gone so far as to argue that the mid Iron Age hillforts were great communal centres, not elite residences at all. If we accept that view, then the contrast with the highly stratified late Iron Age societies is all the more striking. Since the scale of socio-political organization in southern Britain moved up a level in the late Iron Age, then the emergence of a greater differentiation between the rulers and the rest is understandable. When the Roman empire erupted into northern Gaul in 57 BC, this introduced an alien world of status ideas and possibilities to Gallic and British societies, creating a new vocabulary of power.

Craft production and manufacturing also developed and expanded in the late Iron Age. The fast wheel was introduced to some pottery production, the lathe for working of wood and fine-grained stone. Regional pottery styles became increasingly standardized. Technological refinements can be demonstrated in metalworking and casting, glass production, salt-winning. The level of technical expertise involved in the more complex gold and copper-alloy work indicates the existence of specialist craftspeople in many communities. Gold and silver were rarely deposited until the late Iron Age, when metal artefacts in general became much commoner in society, and there is evidence for widespread trade/exchange of iron ingots (so-called currency bars) and salt. The rotary quern, though present from at least the fourth century, became increasingly widely distributed in the late Iron Age.

One of the most important advances in recent decades has been the improved knowledge of settlement and economy in the north and west of Britain. Far from being the heavily forested and wildly barbaric landscapes depicted by our ancient sources, it is clear that these were substantially cleared environments at an early date and that, by the late Iron Age, agriculture was well established in parts of the so-called highland zone. What were often dismissively referred to as 'huts' are now more correctly called roundhouses. These buildings, constructed in a wide variety of styles and materials, are the characteristic vernacular architecture of the Iron Age in most parts of Britain. They could reach genuinely large proportions – many are over 10 m in diameter – providing impressive internal spaces for social interaction and display.

In parallel with the increasing abandonment of hillforts, especially in the south-east and east of Britain, we can discern the rise in numbers and importance of a range of other settlement types. In many regions, the enclosed farmstead was a key type, elaborated in a series of regional variants. In some areas, unenclosed settlements were more numerous, whether individual farmsteads or nucleated clusters of roundhouses. The village-like appearance of some of these sites is reflected in the transition of a number of examples into 'small towns' during the Roman period. In the vicinity of Danebury, after occupation there was ended with the destruction of the main gate in a fire around 100 BC, a new local centre emerged at Bury Hill. The late Iron Age phase there was characterized by the high volume of horse bones, accompanied by a large amount of metal horse gear. 'Horse gear' here covers a range of decorative and functional elements of bridles, bits, chariot fittings, and so on. Bury Hill seems to have been short-lived and was followed as a local centre by another large enclosed site at Suddern Farm, where imported Roman wine amphoras appeared by the mid-first century BC, suggesting this was a high-status centre. Horse gear is also found on rural sites exhibiting elite characteristics (Gussage All Saints), and can perhaps be linked to significant growth in individual power within society.

Another important change is marked by the appearance in the first century BC of territorial *oppida*. Some occupied large plateau areas (as at Wheathampstead in Hertfordshire), but others occupied valley-slope or valley-bottom locations and enclosed vast areas within huge dyke systems. Activity within the *oppida* included domestic structures, coin production and varied crafts, though large areas within these dyke systems also appear to have been open ground. The *oppida* were undoubtedly among the most important political centres in 43 and were prime targets in the Roman conquest strategy. This group included *Camulodunon* (Colchester), *Verlamion* (St Albans) and *Calleva* (Silchester), along with Chichester, Bagendon near Cirencester and Stanwick in Yorkshire. The dykes could have provided effective control of centralized grazing lands for horses – already identified as an increasingly vital resource in the late Iron Age.

The first century BC and first century AD are often depicted as a period in which tribal identity, a sort of regional ethnicity, took root in Britain, to be given concrete form under administrative arrangements of the Roman empire. It has become conventional to describe the late Iron Age regional groupings by the 'tribal' labels attached to them by Ptolemy in the early second century. 'Tribe' is itself a contentious term, loaded with colonialist assumptions and potential anachronisms, and this book will generally speak of 'peoples'. From an archaeological perspective the evidence is somewhat contradictory and can just as easily be read as indicative of the rise of a series of regional kingdoms based on individual power. At one extreme, the late Iron Age in southern Britain was a story of dynastic rivalry (with Shakespeare's *Cymbeline* perhaps oddly prescient), while at the other, even in areas such as Ireland and Scotland, new forms of elite behaviour were changing the shape of society and emphasizing individual wealth, charisma and power. There are further clues to the nature of the southern British kingdoms because some of them started to issue coins.

The wealth of the British Iron Age is best symbolized by the exquisite craftwork and excessive showiness of the gold torcs (neck rings), of which a number of examples survived the pillaging Romans, with impressive hoards from Snettisham, Ipswich and Ulceby in eastern England. The largest group was found at Snettisham near the Wash in what appears to have been a ritual context, with a number of separate deposits of torcs and other valuables. Torcs took various forms from twisted or plaited rods of gold or electrum, to tubular forms, to plaited strands. The terminals at either end allowed the ring to be taken on and off, and were sometimes highly elaborate with cast decoration. Exquisitely fashioned and tremendously ostentatious as a piece of personal adornment, the torcs were also a useful means of storing wealth, with the heavier examples weighing more than the equivalent of 100 gold coins. The 'great torc' from Snettisham shows the stunning sophistication of British craftwork. The fact that torcs have been found across quite wide areas of Britain is highly significant. In addition to the three hoards already mentioned, there is a cluster of individual finds in Norfolk (Bawsey, Sedgeford, North Creake), and other isolated single finds at Netherurd (south of Edinburgh in Scotland), Needwood and Glascote in the West Midlands, Clevedon in Gloucestershire and Hengistbury Head on the Solent.

The finest items define our image of the craft expertise of the Britons (in the British Museum, the Snettisham torcs sit alongside the Battersea shield or the Waterloo helmet from the Thames). Horse and chariot gear was often highly decorative copper-alloy and enamel work. Various types of harness rings (terrets), bits, linch pins, loops and strap ends are known, with evidence that they were manufactured in matching sets. The expense of such fittings has to be set alongside the cost of the horses and the chariots, further emphasizing the wealth of individual Britons at this time. Caesar mentioned facing 4,000 charioteers, which, even allowing for hyperbole, suggests a very substantial number and lends support to the idea that chiefs may habitually have surrounded themselves with elite warrior bands (*comitatus*).

The funerary rites of the ancient Britons were as diverse as many other aspects of these societies. What is more perplexing is the fact that the vast majority of the dead appear to have been disposed of in some way that leaves no clear trace in the archaeological record. In place of formal cemeteries, in many parts of the country we encounter finds of disarticulated human body parts on settlement sites, suggesting that exposure of the corpse (excarnation) was routinely practised. The rituals that lay behind this are uncertain, but the defleshing of bones prior to disposal appears to have been a common tradition, differentiating the British Iron Age from Continental traditions. Even in areas where we have evidence of burial (inhumation) or burning of the corpse (cremation), it is clear from the relatively small numbers of burials known that not everyone in society can have been treated in the same way. Another consequence of the low level of formal burial in the British Iron Age is that a common depositional context for a wide range of artefacts is denied us, in contrast to the European Iron Age, where burial assemblages provide a mass of cultural material. The exclusivity of the British and the Continental practices can be overstated, as there is evidence of excarnation in northern Gaul and some burials in Britain parallel elements encountered in Gaul. However, the funerary rites of Britain appear to have been broadly differentiated from those of the Continent and to have shown great regional diversity.

A few rare warrior burials are known in Britain, in contrast to huge numbers on the Continent. A third-century BC example from Mill Hill near Deal in Kent comprised an inhumation with sword, shield and copper-alloy head-dress. At Brisley Farm (Kent), a double warrior burial has been found on the edge of a large roundhouse settlement. The warrior burials were inhumations within rectangular enclosures and contained the panoply of sword, shield and spear. Both burials date to the Augustan period and appear to have been the focus of later veneration.

The principal exceptions to the British tradition of excarnation (or scattered cremation?) are the so-called Arras culture barrow cemeteries in east Yorkshire and the Aylesford–Swarling culture burials of south-eastern England. The former comprise inhumations beneath small barrows, defined by rectangular ditched enclosures and sometimes grouped in large cemeteries (Wetwang Slack, Rudston). Some of the higher-status burials included two-wheeled carts or chariots and weapons, recalling Continental practices, though it is now mostly argued that a British group had adopted novel rites through a range of contacts with the Continent, rather than as a direct result of migration of a group from northern Gaul to east Yorkshire. It is apparent that this regional burial rite was disappearing by the later first century BC and most 'chariot' burials in Britain date to earlier centuries. The Aylesford–Swarling cremation burials are closely paralleled in northern Gaul and date from the later second century BC to the mid-first century AD. Most cemeteries were quite small, though a few larger ones are known (as at King Harry Lane, St Albans or Westhampnett, Sussex). Individual burials were generally relatively simply furnished, with the ashes contained in either a pot or a shallow pit and at most one or two other pots and perhaps a brooch or toilet implements included. A limited number of examples were richly furnished with imported goods, including Italian wine amphoras, copper-alloy vessels (many connected with the service of wine or food), brass-bound wooden buckets, and hearth furniture (so-called iron fire-dogs). The virtual absence of martial gear reflects a social peculiarity of the burial rite, rather than a characteristic of the society behind it. These burials are most densely concentrated to the north of the Thames, in the heartlands of the most powerful British kingdom of the pre-conquest period. The latest stages of the Aylesford-type burials took the rite to new levels of complexity, designed to highlight extraordinary individuals within society. These 'royal' burials at Stanway and Lexden (Colchester) and Folly Lane (St Albans) will be discussed in more detail below.

Ritual deposition of material goods played an important role in British society, even if more limited in funerary contexts than on the Continent. The major loci for ritual deposition were at religious sites based on sacred groves (*nemeton*) or watery locations. Deposition of valuable goods into rivers, lakes and bogs was a long-held tradition of prehistoric societies in northern Europe. Some of the most spectacular finds of Iron Age metalwork in Britain have come from such locations: the Battersea and Chertsey shields and the Waterloo helmet are the best known of many artefacts recovered from the Thames; the Llyn Cerrig Bach hoard of horse gear and other metalwork was deposited in a lake in Anglesey; a pony cap and two drinking horns came from a bog at Torrs in Dumfries and Galloway. 'Lindow Man', an Iron Age bog body from Cheshire, appears to represent another, darker aspect – human sacrifice. After eating a ritual meal, he was stunned by blows to his head, garrotted, had his throat cut and was 'drowned' in the bog. The dating evidence suggests a close correlation with the later first-century eruption of Roman armies into north-west Britain – to which the sacrifice may have been one response. Man-made wet places, including ditches, also appear commonly to have held special significance and were often marked by special deposits. Ritual deposition was not exclusive to the elite, as special structured deposits are also commonly identified in and around domestic structures on settlements at all social levels in both Iron Age (and Roman-period) society.

The development of sacred groves into more complex shrines marked with built structures can be traced at a number of locations (Uley, Hayling Island, Thetford), in each case accompanied by structured deposits of material. Similar temples also developed in Roman times at a number of major spring sites, such as Bath. Coins appear to have been regularly deposited in ritual contexts, both watery and of other type. Some sites seem never to have attained particularly complex structural form. An example in south-eastern Leicestershire consisted of a ditch separating two areas of ritual deposits – one of over 4,500 coins, the other of multiple deposits of animal bones, evidently the remains of ritual feasts. Although sharing some characteristics with Gaul, there are aspects of British ritual behaviour that gave it an insular character.

The late Iron Age peoples of Britain are generally believed to have been quite warlike, an impression reinforced by the evidence of impressive hillforts such as Maiden Castle and by the description of the Britons encountered by Caesar. The Britons were depicted as redoubtable warriors (though Roman sources tended to trumpet the prowess of defeated enemies). There are indications, however, that the style and scale of warfare differed in important respects from that of the armies of Rome. In Caesar's time, chariots were still used on the field of battle by the elite Britons but, although slightly unnerving, their impact appears to have been swiftly neutralized by the adoption of new tactics by the Romans. The key factor of chariot warfare seems to have been the ability to move rapidly about the battlefield; the noise and psychological impact of an advancing wave of chariots could induce panic in opposing forces, but were less successful against disciplined infantry formations. The use of cavalry was perhaps more significant and seems to have inflicted some defeats on Roman forces. The infantry appear to have been fairly lightly armed and armoured which, no matter how brave and skilful they were as swordsmen, will have placed them at a severe disadvantage in a pitched battle on ground of Rome's choosing.

One of the interesting aspects of the Roman invasions is the extent to which we can trace significant changes in the British approach to war. In seeking to resist Rome, the British peoples learned that numbers were all-important and that fighting pitched battles on Rome's terms was not generally to their advantage. A phenomenon recognized in later colonial situations is that an expanding state can act as a spur for social evolution among its neighbours – leading to organization in larger groupings and co-operation between groups. This is precisely what we see in Britain in the early first century AD, where the distribution pattern of coins produced by the peoples in the south-east indicates in broad terms the emergence of larger polities or socio-political groupings. This could, of course, have been linked to factors that were purely internal to those societies, but the adoption of minting and a range of Continental material goods by these groups suggest that the contact with the Roman empire was a significant influence. In this context it is surely significant that the peoples in the rest of Britain were markedly less changed in this period. In the north and west of Britain, Roman or Continental goods did penetrate, but there was simply not the intensity of interchange to elicit the profound societal transformations that we see in the zone of primary contact.

CAESAR'S BRITISH ADVENTURE

When Iulius Caesar led an expeditionary force to Britain in 55 BC, the resulting two campaigns trod a fine line between qualified success and outright disaster. Caesar needed both luck and skill to extricate himself and, on his return to Gaul in 54 BC, he found it on the brink of the revolt that was nearly to undo his astonishingly rapid conquest of 58–56 BC. Why had he embarked on such a risky and seemingly unnecessary war in Britain, when his Gallic conquests patently needed more careful supervision to ensure pacification? In his own account of his campaigns, Caesar gave several reasons for his British adventure, but it is not easy to disentangle which of these were of prime importance and which were *post facto* justifications. He cited the presence of British troops fighting alongside the Gauls, the threat posed by unsubdued British peoples to his Gallic conquests, and common links of culture between the British and Gallic peoples. Other reasons not made explicit by Caesar, emerge from a variety of sources. Cicero's remarks about the army's lack of success in locating silver sources in Britain strongly imply that Caesar had suggested that Britain had mineral resources worth tapping. The possibility of taking booty and slaves was an unwritten but significant factor in making decisions about committing troops, and Caesar presumably played up whatever intelligence reports he had to support the belief in substantial spoils being available for the taking.

However, part of the context of his decision lay in the extraordinary political situation of the day. The Republican system of government was under immense stress in the 50s BC because of the rival aspirations of the leading politicians and generals. The collective principles of Roman government were breaking down in the face of the huge possibilities of personal power that the empire presented. While in command of his province and enjoying the sort of run of success he had in Gaul, Caesar had enormous discretionary power in shaping events. Once his conquests were completed and his command ended, he would have to return to Rome and as a private citizen lose his immunity from prosecution. The course of events from 55 to 49 BC shows that Caesar was seriously concerned about surrendering his military command. In order to justify continuance of it, though, he also needed to demonstrate that the job was unfinished. He may also have reasoned that the more military glory he attained, the more triumphal celebrations his victories funded in Rome, the stronger his popular support there would grow.

With hindsight it is easy to point out shortcomings of the British adventure, notably in its planning. Although Caesar was a very experienced general, the British campaigns had an added amphibious dimension, which nearly proved his undoing. His first campaign took place late in the summer and with a limited force based around just two of his legions. When the first invasion fleet set out across the Channel, the cavalry got left behind because of contrary winds and delays in loading the horses. The landfall was in turn delayed while Caesar waited at anchor under the eyes of the gathering British forces for the cavalry to catch up, and then was obliged to force a beachhead without them, probably in the Deal area. The unsuitability of his ships for landing troops on an open beach caused further problems, and when his infantry finally did struggle ashore and break through concerted British resistance, the absence of the cavalry prevented him from inflicting maximum damage. Then a major storm prevented the second attempted crossing by the cavalry transport ships and severely damaged the fleet at Caesar's beachhead. Caesar's army was soon under effective siege, and two further victories were needed to extricate it. With his ships hastily repaired, Caesar departed for Gaul with little accomplished beyond the taking of a few hostages and not much new knowledge gained.

The second campaign was better planned and learned some lessons from the shortcomings of the first. Caesar had a much larger fleet constructed this time, the ships were modified to make them more suitable as landing craft, and he took five legions and 2,000 cavalry (a total force of c.30,000 troops). Yet, soon after a successful landing, his fleet was again damaged in a storm. A paramount wartime leader, Cassivellaunos, co-ordinated British resistance. He was a ruler north of the Thames and after Caesar forced a crossing of that river, the war broke down into a series of guerrilla actions. Some of the peoples north of the Thames now reached agreements with Caesar, among them the *Cenimagi* (perhaps the antecedents of the *Iceni* of Norfolk) and the *Trinovantes* of Essex, who had been assimilated into Cassivellaunos' kingdom after he had killed its previous ruler. Mandubracius, the son of the latter, had been brought with Caesar, having earlier fled as a refugee to Gaul, and he was now installed as ruler of the *Trinovantes*. With the help of his new allies, Caesar was able to locate the main base of Cassivellaunos (probably one of a number of extensive defended sites in Hertfordshire, such as Wheathampstead or Prae Wood, St Albans). Terms were reached with Cassivellaunos and other British chiefs, in which they gave hostages and pledged to pay an annual tribute and to respect the arrangements Caesar had made. He then withdrew to Gaul with his military reputation intact, if not much enhanced, to face the growing foment of revolt there under the leadership of Vercingetorix. But for that, it is conceivable that Caesar would have returned the following year to consolidate his successes and perhaps to start the process of territorial incorporation.

From a British perspective, Caesar's invasion will have had a very different resonance. Some peoples had sent envoys to Caesar in Gaul, offering to submit before his first campaign. It is clear that Caesar received at least one British prince as a refugee and he made additional diplomatic efforts to detach some groups from the anti-Roman alliance that would face the invasion fleet. A Gallic chief, Commios, was sent back with the British envoys specifically to foster pro-Roman sympathies (or at least neutrality).

Caesar did not receive the support in Britain he had been led to expect, a point demonstrated by the concerted resistance to the first landing and the fact that Commios was 'arrested' shortly after his arrival in Britain. The resistance involved a confederation of peoples in southern Britain, suggesting that the Roman invasion when it came was widely perceived as more threatening than existing differences between the diverse British peoples. At the start of the second season, British resistance was no less resolute, though the scale of the fleet caused them to withdraw from directly opposing the landing. Despite two major victories, Caesar struggled to impose his authority. Even after the capture of Cassivel-launos' stronghold, there was a further diversionary attack at his insti-gation on the fleet base by four kings in Kent, perhaps attempting to liberate British prisoners of war as much as to strike at Caesar's ships. Only after that was defeated did Cassivellaunos accept terms.

The campaigns had a tremendous impact on the popular imagination in Rome, representing not only a victory over new peoples, but also one over Ocean itself. The fact that Ocean had fought back and imperilled Caesar's forces simply served to raise the scale of the achievement. The Senate responded to popular clamour by granting an unparalleled public thanksgiving (*supplicatio*) of twenty days – and this after the first campaign in 55 BC. In reality, though, well-informed Romans could draw their own conclusions about the unfulfilled potential of Caesar's two campaigns. Cicero commented that practically the only booty was in the form of slaves, though these were in sufficient numbers for some of the 800 ships to be seriously overloaded on the return journey in 54 BC. The taking of hostages and the framework of treaties Caesar hurriedly set in place on the eve of his final departure from Britain have commonly been presented as a short-term settlement, with little continuing relevance once Caesar himself was distracted by weightier matters. On the other hand, the evidence of post-Caesarian Britain suggests that his campaigns did have a more decisive outcome, in bringing parts of southern Britain within the Roman orbit. His victories constituted the baseline for future political relations, in which Rome was established as the dominant military power in the region. For this reason, the title of this book takes 54 BC, rather than AD 43 as the starting point of the integration of Britain in the Roman empire.

Total British casualties in the two seasons of fighting may have run into tens of thousands of dead, wounded, enslaved or taken as hostages. The Romans lived off the land to a significant extent, seizing cattle and harvesting grain in the fields. The army will have seized material wealth as booty, whenever and wherever found. This represents a potentially major impact on the population of lowland Britain. In the aftermath of the second campaign, at least one pro-Roman ruler was installed. It is not uncommon for powerful states to nurture allies or clients beyond their borders and the Roman empire had a strong tradition of such relations with 'friendly kings'. The history of relations between southern Britain and Rome from 54 BC to AD 43 makes better sense when interpreted as interdependence rather than insular isolation.

BRITAIN BETWEEN THE (ROMAN) WARS

The diplomatic arrangements put in place by Caesar marked the start of a period of closer contact between the major southern British peoples and Roman Gaul. It is clear that diplomatic ties were maintained with selected British rulers, rather than with specific peoples. This is not to deny that distinct 'ethnic' British identities existed at this time, but simply to suggest that they were less significant in the actual definition of power, territory and allegiances at this point in time than the dynastic authority of a series of kings supported by client relationships with Rome. Clearly, this picture applies specifically to the south-east of England and should not be taken as a general model for other regions of Britain. The first of the two main clients, the eastern kingdom, had its heartlands to the north of the Thames (Buckinghamshire, Hertfordshire, Bedfordshire, Essex). This area has traditionally been identified as the territory of the *Catuvellauni* and *Trinovantes* peoples and it has often been assumed that the former conquered the latter to form a single kingdom. However, it is equally plausible that the Trinovantian king Mandubracius was able to extend his personal rule westwards. The southern kingdom extended between the Thames and the Solent (Berkshire, Surrey, Hampshire and west Sussex); its history can be related to the historical record of the 'flight' of the chief of the Gallic *Atrebates*, Commios (Commius in our Latin sources), to Britain around 50 BC. There is archaeological evidence for an increase in trade between Gaul and Britain post-Caesar and for this being progressively refocused away from the south-western harbours such as Mount Batten in Plymouth Sound or Hengistbury Head in Dorset towards the ports of these new kingdoms on the Solent, the Essex coast and Thames estuary.

From the late second century BC, in common with their neighbours in northern Gaul, the peoples of south-east Britain had started to use and then to mint coins. These were primarily high-denomination issues of gold and perhaps of particular utility in this type of society for making standard payments to reward a large war-host. The ultimate origin and inspiration of Celtic coins can be traced to a gold coin (*stater*) of Philip of Macedon (359–336 BC), portraying the head of Apollo on the obverse and a two-horse chariot on the reverse. The initial copies of this coin in the later fourth or early third century BC in Gaul were relatively faithful to the original, but through progressive recopying and deliberate abstraction the designs became both more varied and more bizarre, though the steps in the process can be plainly traced in the intermediate issues. Changes to the images were minor yet persistent issue by issue, though without abandoning the essential concept; hence their characterization as 'serial imagery'. The earliest coins in south-east Britain were second-century BC imports from northern Gaul, the so-called Gallo-Belgic series. The date of the appearance of these coins matches the period of major settlement dislocation and social change indicated by the decline of hillforts and signs of increasing social differentiation.

From about 80 BC onwards, British coin production was certainly well established in the south. This takes us down to the time of Caesar's campaigns, an event that marked a distinct transition point. The break with the past is reflected initially in the hoard evidence that shows that the post-Caesarian issues are rarely found in association with the earlier British serial image types. It would appear that there had been a systematic attempt to withdraw earlier coins and to remint to a new standard. By the 30s BC, innovative images were starting to appear alongside the traditional Apollo/horse serial imagery. Analysis of the gold content of the new-style coins shows that the evident reddish tinge to these coins represented a departure in metallurgical composition from the serial issues, which still maintained a yellowish hue. The former group was produced by the alloying of gold from a new source – refined gold – that perhaps originated within the Roman empire. The appearance of a legend on some of the British coins, naming Commios, marked another innovation. During the time of Augustus (30 BC–AD 14), a wider array of new coin imagery appeared in Britain, some derived from Roman prototypes, and now also including issues in silver and copper-alloy.

Before considering the coinage evidence further, it is necessary to reintroduce Commios to the narrative. He was initially a friend of Rome, being made king of the Gallic *Atrebates* after their conquest by Caesar in 57 BC, and playing a significant role in the negotiations with the British that followed up the military victories in both 55 and 54. Caesar rewarded his services with generous concessions – treating the *Atrebates* as an independent 'client' with suzerainty over some other north Gallic groups and giving them immunity from taxation. When the Gallic revolt broke out in 53 BC Commios was initially loyal to Caesar, but as the revolt reached its climax, he was drawn into the struggle and appears to have become one of the leaders of resistance. An attempt was made by a Roman commander Volusenus to assassinate him during a parlay and, although seriously wounded, Commios escaped. He continued to lead resistance and revolt against Rome, eventually succeeding in wounding Volusenus grievously in a fight. Hirtius, who completed the account of the Gallic Wars after Caesar's own death, noted that Commios offered hostages and terms to Mark Antony, then in command in northern Gaul, to 'live where he was bidden and do as he was told', provided he was not required to come into direct contact with any Roman. It was presumably at this point that he moved permanently to Britain, taking up residence south of the Thames. The implication of this account is that Commios was eventually reconciled to Rome as a client. Some unusual finds of treasure dating to this period – such as a fabulous hoard of gold jewellery found near Winchester – show that someone among the elite of the southern kingdom was receiving valuable goods from the Roman empire. The political legacy of Caesar's campaigns was thereafter based on a southern client ruler (initially Commios) and an eastern client king (Mandubracius).

Reconstructing the dynastic and political history of these two major kingdoms in post-Caesarian Britain is fraught with difficulty and will produce at best pseudo-history. The various reconstructions of lists of successive rulers of these regions differ in many details and the greater the precision of dates that is claimed, the more suspicious we should be. What is more accessible through the coin evidence is the ideological outlook of these rulers. Detailed analysis of the imagery and legends on this coinage has identified a consistent pattern of behaviour that is closely paralleled by the iconographical programmes developed at Rome itself to consolidate the personal rule of Augustus, the first emperor. The similarities are too close and too many to be coincidental and imply sustained and profound contact between the British rulers and the political world and culture of Rome.

The assassination of Caesar in 44 BC was a key turning-point in Roman society, plunging the Republic into a renewed period of civil war, from which Caesar's adopted heir Octavian was eventually to emerge victorious after the battle of Actium. In 27 BC Octavian took the new name Augustus and, in a series of political reforms, laid the foundations for autocratic rule (the Principate) within a framework that echoed the traditions of the Republic. The power of imagery in defining the *princeps* (emperor) was further experimented with for much of his long reign, over time establishing a series of very strong iconographic associations. This imagery was used to evoke a number of key ideas related to his power, prestige and ancestry. This new Roman visual language can also be traced in detail on the dynastic coinages of the eastern and southern kingdoms from the latter decades of the first century BC up to the conquest, and is paralleled by the coinage issued by other contemporary clients of Rome.

Commios was himself dead by the time the new imagery started to appear on British coins. The greatest innovation of his own coins was the inclusion of his name on one issue. In fact, it may well have been his death that directly brought about the change in imagery. His successor appears to have been Tincomarus, whose coinage (with Latin legends) stressed his dynastic link to Commios while also evoking Augustan legitimation imagery. It has sometimes been argued that Caesar's political arrangements with the British did not survive the prolonged period of civil wars and internal strife of the 40s BC. Augustus clearly had relations with individual British rulers and we know he received refugees from Britain, though these have often been considered very *ad hoc* arrangements. The coinage evidence suggests a different interpretation – that parts of Britain were effectively considered as integrated client states within the empire from 54 BC onwards.

The key to this surely lay in the Roman practice of demanding hostages (*obsides*) from defeated enemies. The absence of these British hostages from their homelands was sometimes prolonged and their exposure to Roman culture and martial society was clearly profound. Hostages from various client peoples are known to have established high-level contacts in Roman society, to have served as officers in the Roman army, and to have been first-hand witnesses of imperial politics at the centre of power. They returned as Latin speakers, sometimes with Roman citizen status, accompanied by noble companions who had been with them and shared their experience. Arminius, the German leader who masterminded the annihilation of Varus and three Roman legions in AD 9, had just such a history. Tincomarus and other major innovators in the Iron Age coinages in Britain were thus most likely princes who had spent a period of time in Rome or at any rate inside the empire.

Yet the dynamics of this contact situation were inherently unstable, as a political settlement based on individual power and agreements with Rome required renegotiation and renewal every time leadership changed, whether as a result of the incumbent's death or his overthrow. Client kingship was something that had to be agreed by Rome, so anyone seeking to establish their own rule, no matter what their support in Britain, would have to seek recognition from Rome. In succession matters, Rome may often have had a favoured candidate, though that does not mean she always got her way. We know of at least two British rulers who fled to Rome under Augustus and of others who did so on the eve of the Claudian invasion. The point is that such upheavals were most likely to have occurred at moments of succession to the two major client kingdoms that Rome recognized in Britain, rather than being a continuous problem.

Under Augustus, conquest of Britain was mooted several times, though the decision was ultimately against further military intervention on each occasion. There are indications that Augustus had started making active preparations for war in 34 and 27–26 BC and that he intended to lead a campaign in person. In 27–26 our sources refer to a proposed treaty with some Britons, so it is possible that the threat of imminent Roman invasion resulted in a new political settlement. It is conceivable that these events were linked to the deaths of Commios and his equivalent in the eastern kingdom. Augustus may also have considered action c.16 BC, when he was in Gaul, but in the event again decided on diplomatic solutions rather than direct intervention. Augustus increased diplomatic activity in Britain, recognizing certain rulers as clients and receiving refugees into the empire. Trade and exchange between Britain and northern Gaul reached new levels in this period, with material culture from within the empire increasingly being used as status symbols in British society.

Another threat of direct Roman action in Britain came under Gaius Caligula in 39–40. This seems to have coincided with the end of the long reign of the foremost ruler of the eastern kingdom, Cunobelin. According to Roman sources, just before Cunobelin's death one of his sons, Adminius, quarrelled with his father and was exiled and fled to the imperial court. Adminius seems to have persuaded Caligula that invasion of Britain would bring easy victory, and preparations were put in hand. By the summer of 40 an army and fleet had assembled at the

Channel and invasion seemed imminent. But the planned expedition ended in farce when Caligula evidently pushed the army close to mutiny. The troops were eventually ordered simply to collect seashells for the emperor's claimed triumph.

The late Iron Age coinages of the eastern and southern kingdoms reflect the close relationships of those parts of Britain with the empire. The imagery of Tincomarus (c.30–10 BC), for example, is entirely consistent with the idea that he might well have been in Rome during the 40s and 30s BC, returning to Britain just before Octavian's victory at Actium. The classical horseman of Tincomarus contrasts with the 'Celtic' horses of the serial coinage and this new style was echoed by a number of other British clients, sometimes with 'British' touches such as the horseman bearing a war trumpet (*carnyx*). Verica was another of the southern kings, again claiming to be a 'son' of Commios, and he is almost certainly identifiable with 'Berikos' who fled to Rome as a result of internal strife c.42. His coinage featured a wide array of images, much of it evoking key elements of the Augustan iconographic programme, and he expressed his position using the Latin term *rex*, in effect indicating the formal nature of his client status.

Overlapping with the latter stages of Verica's coinage is a series produced for Epaticcus, its distribution centred on the northern part of Verica's zone of influence. The iconography of the coins follows that of the eastern kingdom and Epaticcus announced his dynastic link with the ruling group of the eastern kingdom. Understandably, this has been seen as evidence that the eastern kingdom was aggressively expanding at the expense of its southern rival, leading to the expulsion of Verica by the early 40s. The few issues ascribed to Caratacus (a son of Cunobelin), who may have succeeded Epaticcus in this territory just ahead of the Roman invasion of 43, continued Roman-style themes.

The eastern kingdom was marginally slower to adopt the new styles, with the issues of Addedomarus (c.40–30 BC) and Dubnovellaunos (c.30–25 BC) generally continuing the serial tradition, but with the addition of the king's name on some issues. Tasciovanus, who became king c.25 BC and may have ruled down to c.10 BC, was the first ruler to experiment with the new image pool and his coinage features a variety of mythical or other beasts associated with Augustus. Other novelties included Roman-style portrait busts, seated figures and the naming of the mint site on some issues – *VER* for *Verlamion* – and the claim to be king, though the term used here was 'Celtic' *RIGON*. After the death of Tasciovanus there appear to have been a number of short-lived coinages issued by a series of shadowy individuals, prior to the emergence of Cunobelin as the undisputed ruler of the eastern kingdom *c.*AD 10.

The reign of Cunobelin marks the apogee of the late Iron Age kingdoms in Britain. His gold coinage is estimated to have exceeded more than 1 million struck pieces and dwarfs the output from all the other pre-Roman kingdoms. Cunobelin claimed on some coins to be 'son of' Tasciovanus, though the relationship may have been a filiation of convenience rather than of biology (as was perhaps the case also with Verica and Commios). The Roman practice of adopting successors offered a ready exemplar of how to promote such claims. Although the Roman sources were ultimately hostile to his memory, Cunobelin appears to have ruled for a lengthy period over a wide region with Roman support. Suetonius described Cunobelin as *rex Britannorum* (king of the Britons), which implies that he ruled over a large group of British peoples with imperial blessing. His client status is also indicated by the use of the *rex* legend on his coins.

Although occasional issues echo the earlier serial coinages, the proliferation and range of imagery on Cunobelin's coinage is astonishing and the pronounced classical style and quality of many of the late images suggests the presence of highly trained die-cutters or of Britons who had learned the craft inside the empire. By identifying with the iconographic programme of Augustus and the reinvention of Roman culture that took place in the Augustan age, the British dynasts proclaimed their allegiance to the emperor and constructed their own identity as powerful rulers. The coins reflect the close integration of these kingdoms within the Roman world. Indeed some of the late issues feature imperial portraits of Augustus, Tiberius or Gaius and the voluntary inclusion of such images must indicate an expression of allegiance. Yet, it would be equally wrong to portray Cunobelin as simply a Roman stooge. One of the interesting aspects of his coinage is the extent to which it combines allusions to Augustan art with more ambiguous symbols. His most characteristic obverse type with the ear of barley has often been interpreted as a reference to cereal production (evoking the grain exports noted by Strabo). However, it could equally be seen as a reference to British beer, as a counterpoint to the fashion for importing Roman wine to his court and to that of Verica (who had actually adopted the vine-leaf on some of his coins).

Client rulers, even in remote areas such as Britain, were controlled and manipulated in a variety of ways (providing levies for the Roman army, exaction of customs dues on trade with the empire), but interference in the succession process was probably the most significant and contentious area. It was clearly in Rome's interests when a client king died to have him replaced by one of the educated hostages from the pool held at Rome. The system did not always work smoothly, of course, and Rome could if necessary threaten annexation against client states keen to appoint a king other than the candidate favoured by Rome. There might be a lengthy interregnum while the issue of succession was sorted out. There are signs of this in the historical record in that Augustus considered campaigning in Britain, because 'the people would not come to terms with him'. A root cause of the Claudian invasion in 43 (and its antecedent threatened action under Gaius) was evidently the issue of what was to happen to the eastern kingdom on the death of Cunobelin. Finally, the Boudican revolt erupted when the Romans over-rode the wishes of the *Iceni* and decided to annex the territory after the death of its client king. These flashpoints in relations with client kingdoms were an occasional hazard, to be prepared for through diplomacy and the grooming of the *obsides*.

Sources related to the Roman invasion in 43 provide some detail on Cunobelin's sons: Caratacus, Togodumnus and unnamed other brothers who resisted Rome, Adminius who was earlier forced to flee to Gaius Caligula. Why had his family been thrown into conflict with Rome at this point? Cunobelin had a long and prosperous reign, and to judge from his coinage he was a long-term friend of Rome. But he chose a bad moment to decline and expire (he probably died between 40 and 43), creating a succession issue at a time when two new emperors (Caligula and Claudius) came to the throne in Rome in quick succession, each needing military glory to establish their popular reputation. Client kingdoms, whether loyal or not, were an attractive target in such circumstances.

Support for the view that the late Iron Age developments in south-east Britain represent the maintenance over a prolonged period of a client king structure by Rome can be sought in the archaeological evidence of settlements and burials. Unfortunately, comparatively small areas of the main *oppida* sites have been examined. At Colchester, there is evidence of intense craft production in the Sheepen area, while at Gosbecks, a few kilometres south, a potential royal enclosure has been identified in another area of intense settlement activity. Until excavations are carried out on this enclosure we can only guess at the physical structures of Cunobelin's court. Roman St Albans lies in the valley base, below a great series of dyke systems (the Devil's Dyke and Prae Wood). The focus of the late Iron Age site is harder to pin down here, though a major aristocratic enclosure was attached to the Devil's Dyke at Gorhambury. Buried beneath the forum of the later Roman town there is a major enclosure of at least two hectares in area, surrounded by a massive ditch. Much of the most intensive evidence for metalworking and coin production comes from the area immediately to the north and west of this. This may represent another 'royal' enclosure, though other possible explanations cannot be excluded. There is a series of other notable late Iron Age centres in the vicinity of St Albans, with varied evidence of industrial activity, settlement sites and cemetery features spread over large areas. Cow Roast/Ashridge to the west appears to have been a centre for iron-working, while Welwyn, Baldock and Braughing to the east all feature a mix of settlement complexes and rich burials. At Braughing, for instance, the complex covers an area in excess of 200 hectares and the richness of the material has been interpreted as evidence that this was a principal entrepôt of trade and distribution of imported goods within the region, though it seems to have passed its peak by c.AD 10. To the south of Welwyn a ritual site has been discovered at Essendon, where weaponry and hundreds of coins were deposited. The overall picture of late Iron Age settlements in Hertfordshire, Buckinghamshire and southern Bedfordshire is striking testimony to the wealth and high population density of the eastern kingdom.

The three principal centres of the southern kingdom were Chichester, Winchester and Silchester. A major sequence of dykes to the north of Chichester defines a huge area, within which the late Iron Age foci remain somewhat elusive, although at Selsey Bill finds of coins and gold work are suggestive. It is likely, though, that the main focus lay in the Chichester/Fishbourne area, where early first-century finewares and other finds highlight a high-status site and where post-conquest development also concentrated. Silchester is currently the best understood of the *oppida* sites, though somewhat atypical in being a very nucleated centre within a single main enclosure. Excavations have revealed traces of building and enclosure alignments, defined by roads running from three gates in the encircling ramparts. At both Silchester and Fishbourne it is increasingly suspected that some stratigraphically early rectilinear buildings were constructed in the pre-conquest period – again, something that is consistent with the idea that these were fully fledged client kingdoms. Imported goods found at Fishbourne, Colchester, St Albans and Silchester in particular have illustrated the special nature of these sites and of parallel finds from a number of unusual burials.

At Colchester, two main complexes of late Iron Age burials have been examined. The first at Lexden, near the Sheepen area of settlement, revealed a main burial beneath a tumulus of 30 metres diameter, surrounded by an oval ditch. A timber chamber appears to have been erected within a large central shaft below the mound and numerous artefacts were recovered from there, with many of them evidently having been deliberately broken before deposition. A small amount of cremated bone had also been deposited. The individual was someone of very high status and was associated with chain-mail and horse gear, but no weaponry. There were at least eighteen amphoras and numerous other pottery vessels, along with imported metal artefacts in copper alloy (boar, bull and cupid statuettes, along with a griffin attachment and other fittings from broken-up artefacts), silver (mounts, attachments and studs, a medallion featuring a portrait of Augustus in a coin of *c.*19–15 BC) and gold (fine filaments of ribbon). Other fragmentary finds included parts of the legs of a ceremonial chair (*sella curulis*) and stool. Overall the assemblage appears to date to 15–10 BC, perhaps coincident with the end of the reign of Tasciovanus. It was undoubtedly a burial fit for a client king and one that fully reflected the profound economic and political contacts between the eastern kingdom and Rome at this time. The chain-mail appears to be of Roman military type and, while this may have been a gift, we should not exclude the possibility that its owner had earlier served with an auxiliary unit in the Roman army. It parallels other finds of chain-mail from late Iron Age contexts (Baldock, Folly Lane) and parts of at least two cavalry parade helmets from south-east Leicestershire. Another elite burial ground was at Stanway, close to the Gosbecks site about three kilometres to the south of Lexden. This cemetery (whose use extended beyond the conquest) comprised five ditched enclosures, each containing central pits, in which various broken but unburnt artefacts and small quantities of cremated bone had been deposited. The locations were probably originally marked by low barrows, long since ploughed away. Satellite burials were found in some of the enclosures, including one of an individual dubbed the 'surgeon' because of the inclusion of a set of imported medical tools. That burial also contained the remains of a Roman board game with the pieces laid out for the start of play, numerous pottery vessels from Gaul, and wine amphoras.

Several burial grounds at St Albans have been excavated: King Harry Lane (on the west side), St Stephens (to the south) and Folly Lane (to the east). The burial rite at Folly Lane was highly distinctive. A two-hectare enclosure was constructed, defined by a large ditch, with its entrance facing south-west into the valley of the river Ver. Near the centre of this enclosure and probably closely contemporary with its construction, a large shaft was dug. The shaft walls were revetted with substantial timber linings and a free-standing square structure erected in the base of the shaft. This central timber structure was surrounded by a gravelled walkway, accessed by a ramp or ladder in one corner. From finds within the shaft, it appears that this structure was a mortuary enclosure in which a body was placed, possibly for some time, prior to its cremation. Deliberately broken material in the base and fill of the shaft shows that the body was accompanied by a wide array of possessions, including imported amphoras and finewares and metal vessels. The spoil from the shaft excavation had been raised into a mound, on top of which were signs of a cremation pyre. Immediately after the cremation and while the pyre was still hot, it appears that the mortuary chamber and shaft were deliberately slighted and infilled, with a token amount of the cremation material being deposited. A further deposit of the remains of the pyre was buried in a pit dug into the northern edge of the top of the shaft. Analysis of the burnt remains showed that the pyre had contained not only the bones/body of an individual, but also a wide variety of animal sacrifices (pig, cattle, horse, sheep/goat). Small quantities of molten metal or burnt material from a wide variety of artefacts attest to a rich panoply of pyre goods, including a chain-mail vest, horse and chariot gear, hobnail boots, silver and copper-alloy vessels, ivory furniture fittings, iron artefacts, fine pottery and amphoras similar to those in the shaft. A low turf mound was raised over the filled-in shaft and pit, while a post was raised on the adjacent pyre mound to mark the site of the actual cremation.

The date of the cremation appears to be c.55, to judge from the contents of shaft and pyre debris pit, though, given the interpretation of the mortuary structure, the individual could have died some time (perhaps years) previously. The nature of the rite and the possessions that accompanied the individual on to the pyre suggest that this was a British ruler or member of the dynastic house of the eastern kingdom. The mail shirt, horse and chariot gear suggest that we are dealing with a man. The ephemeral mortuary structures required considerable labour to construct and to demolish immediately after the funeral. While we cannot exclude the possibility that a leading Catuvellaunian chief had died before the Claudian invasion and lain in state for over a decade, before the cremation of his defleshed body and deliberately broken possessions, it is as likely that we are dealing with a British leader who had been invested by Rome with local authority in the aftermath of the conquest. The similarity of the funeral rite to that observed at Lexden and Stanway suggests that this was a member of the ruling family of the eastern kingdom. This also implies that some at least of the family of Cunobelin came to terms with Rome at an early stage and were treated sympathetically post-43. In the second century, a rectangular stone building was erected over the site of the pyre mound, with its entrance facing directly towards the turf mound over the shaft. This building has the form of a Romano-Celtic temple and represents the monumental counterpoint to a long sequence of ritual deposits in the vicinity of the original enclosure. This may be evidence for a form of ruler or ancestor worship, commemorating the site of the dead chieftain's funeral rites.

The burials from the other St Albans cemeteries are less exceptional, but even on a smaller scale they reveal a highly stratified society practising complex and mixed funerary rites. For instance, at King Harry Lane, a number of unusual cremations containing evidence of burnt pyre goods almost invariably occupy the centre of a series of rectangular enclosures (c.10–15 m sq). They appear normally to have been ringed by clusters of simpler cremations and several have inhumations around their margins or in the enclosure ditches. These cremations featured rich pyre goods, including metal and pottery vessels, animals, horse gear and furniture. To the extent that the native elite was employing Roman material culture, it was very much within a British cultural milieu and this practice continued into the early post-conquest period. Cremation was not simply limited to the eastern kingdom, but is also attested in the southern kingdom. The best-known example is the extensive site at

Westhampnett, near Chichester, where numerous cremations have been recorded, some in circular clusters, with associated pyre pits.

BEYOND THE CLIENT KINGDOMS

The peoples of Britain represent a microcosm of a broader pattern of changing identities in the late Iron Age world. In general there was a switch from communal expressions of status to individual and dynastic ones. The development of new forms of status behaviour reflected increased inter-regional contact, especially with Continental Europe. Although the effects were most profound in areas closer to mainland Europe, even in Ireland and south-eastern and eastern Scotland there are significant examples of La Tène-influenced metalwork. Atlantic Scotland and Ireland had the most distinctly insular cultural make-up, but the late Iron Age was still one of significant material changes. The process began before Rome reached the coasts of Gaul and Germany, but the presence of Rome from the 50s BC amplified the effects of contact with the European world.

The extraordinary developments in south-east Britain marked a departure from earlier Iron Age traditions. What of the rest of Britain in the period between Caesar and Claudius? Several other regions produced coins and show signs of settlement and social evolution that resemble in some respects the southern and eastern kingdoms. The coinage of Kent seems to fall within the same general model as that of the eastern and southern kingdoms, and for much of the period this region appears to have been attached to one or other of the main kingdoms, rather than being independent. In the other coin-producing areas – Norfolk, the East Midlands, the Severn/Cotswolds area and Dorset – the coins continued, with occasional exceptions, to follow the original serial imagery through to the end of the sequence. That suggests that these areas had rather different relations with Rome and that culturally they were more conservative.

Access to imported goods from the Roman world also appears to have been lower. It may be questioned to what extent these other groups maintained direct contact with Rome during this period. It is a reasonable supposition that the major kingdoms to the north and south of the Thames were encouraged to exercise their influence on other British rulers and groupings. The corollary of this, of course, was that it could lead to the expansion of the power and territorial scope of the major clients. Much that has been written of a Trinovantian/Catuvellaunian 'empire' goes far beyond the limits of the available evidence, but the expansion of the eastern kingdom is indicated by a number of factors. Perhaps most critically there is the testimony of Dio that part of the *Dobunni* (*Boduni* in the extant manuscript) was subject to the rule of Caratacus and Togodumnus 'although they were *Catuvellauni*'. The main heartlands of the *Dobunni* lay further west in the Cotswolds and Severn Valley, but *oppida* at Dorchester and Grim's Ditch and the linear Aves Ditch in eastern Oxfordshire can all plausibly be linked to the expansion of the eastern kingdom's power in this direction. The coin issues of Epaticcus in the northern sector of the southern kingdom in the years leading up to the Claudian invasion are another indication of the growing domination of the house of Cunobelin. However, that dominance may not have been achieved solely through warfare; the politics of dynastic marriages are as likely to have been used by the eastern kingdom (with Roman encouragement) to expand its area of control. Power was also potentially exercised by the extent to which the eastern kingdom controlled high-status imported and manufactured goods. Major clients could have influenced the behaviour of their neighbours through the distribution of status goods, and through new feasting practices and other social ceremonies to which outsiders might be invited.

The coinage generally identified with the *Iceni* of Norfolk featured the normal abstracted Apollo head/horse imagery, along with an Apollo/ wolf series and a boar/Celticized horse type. The legend *ECEN* on some issues could represent the 'tribal' name *Iceni*, though it would be a unique occurrence of an ethnic declaration on such coinage. The coin series of the *Iceni* evidently extended post-conquest down to *c*.60 and quite a lot of the inscribed issues could belong to a period from the late 30s onwards, when Rome may have started to seek out more developed relationships with the minor rulers in eastern and central England.

The coinage of the East Midlands was poorly known until comparatively recent times (fifty years ago it was uncertain whether the *Corieltavi* had struck coins at all), with new hoards adding substantial information. The coin series is now known to have been of long duration and some sophistication, and produced at several centres in Lincolnshire and

Leicestershire. The imagery rests on the standard serial types, heavily abstracted to the point where head of Apollo and horse are barely recognizable. Like the *Iceni*, there are silver issues featuring a boar/horse combination. The earliest inscribed (dynastic) issues appear to date to the late first century BC, with paired names often featured in the legends. It is likely that the series continued post-conquest for a time, though how many of the inscribed issues are as late as that is uncertain. The traditional tenor of the imagery of the coins would suggest that the *Corieltavi* were not formally a Roman client pre-conquest, though they were undoubtedly starting to adopt much of the late Iron Age social package that was evolving to the south of them. The east Leicestershire hoard contains a suggestive number of pre-Claudian *denarii*, along with over 4,000 Corieltavian coins. In the early post-conquest phase, leaders of the *Corieltavi* may have been formally accorded client status and continued for a few years to have issued coins.

The coinage attributed to the *Dobunni* of the West Midlands and lower Severn Valley was also very traditional in imagery. Legends were added to some issues from the late first century BC, but the meanings are uncertain. Dynastic names remain the most likely explanation, in emulation of the coins of the southern and eastern kingdoms. The Roman-style imagery of the southern and eastern kingdoms was eschewed, suggesting that the surrender of the '*Boduni*' to Rome in 43 marked the start of their formal status as Roman clients.

Finally, the people of Wiltshire, west Hampshire and Dorset (the *Durotriges* of Roman sources) produced a unique series of coins, though derived from the southern serial image pool. The final issues are among the most abstracted of the serial imagery. A few late examples bear the legend *CRAB*, though the vast majority of coins were anepigraphic. The coinage suggests again that the rulers of this British people were not formally clients before the Claudian invasion.

All of these secondary coin-producing peoples of southern Britain were direct neighbours of either the eastern or the southern kingdom and, coupled with other developments in material culture, it looks as if here too we see the development of hierarchical societies led by petty dynasts, in emulation of the most successful clients who had direct relationships with Rome.

Beyond the zone of the coin-producing peoples, things were different again. The *Brigantes* and *Parisi* of north-eastern Britain had some access to Roman and Gallic imports, but it is unlikely that either was formally part of the client network pre-conquest. By 47 at the latest, Rome had recognized Queen Cartimandua as a client, suggesting that the Brigantian confederation was normally under the control of a paramount chief at this date. The site of Stanwick is the best contender for a territorial *oppidum* in northern England. Devon and Cornwall, Wales and the Marches, north-west England and much of Scotland appear to have been characterized by social groupings organized at a rather different scale from the kingdoms of southern England. The typical settlement of the west and north was an enclosed homestead, accommodating at most an extended family group (on which see further, Chapter 13). In some regions there appears to have been a marked lack of differentiation or hierarchy between sites. Yet there are signs that these societies had the capacity to operate at higher levels of social complexity – as the evolution of Irish kingship indicates (see Chapter 14). These were more difficult regional societies to integrate into the Roman empire, but they were not predestined to failure/resistance.

Older theories of Belgic migrations have been replaced by an insistence on the insular evolution of British society, though most recently with some acknowledgement of closer links with the Continent and the assimilation of some Gallic groups into British society. The back-projection of knowledge of Roman political arrangements and the equation of Roman *civitates* with pre-conquest 'tribes' is clearly less secure than has generally been assumed. The alternative suggestion that some of our kingdoms of late Iron Age Britain were constituted around the prestige and status of individual leaders, rather than strictly speaking around ethnic identities, has much to recommend it. It allows us to understand the ready adoption of Commios (and perhaps some other Gallic refugees) into regional British societies, or the ability of Caratacus to transfer his 'paramount chief' status from Essex to mid-Wales. Paradoxically, it was through opposition to Rome and in what followed their defeat that the British peoples achieved a clearer set of 'ethnic' identities, as the Roman state made 'tribes' of subjected Britons.

Most recent studies of the Iron Age emphasize diversity and regionalization. Gone are the old certainties and generalizing models, almost banished are the 'Celts'. There still needs to be a recognition that Rome cannot be written entirely out of the picture. Although there were key changes underway at the transition from the mid to late Iron Age phases, there was a significant intensification and acceleration of such processes after Caesar, especially in the regions with the greatest contact with the Continent. By the time of the Claudian campaigns, a substantial part of southern Britain had already been adjunct client states for the best part of a century. Does this make the Claudian expedition a conquest, a reconquest, or a political rationalization of a territory already considered to be part of the empire?

The evidence for 'pro-Roman' attitudes can at best be described as opportunistic or pragmatic. Rome played an increasingly central role in the lives of the peoples of south-eastern Britain, but that does not mean that the British leaders were reconciled to eventual Roman take-over. People who might be conceived of as pro-Roman from their consumption of Roman goods (Italian wine, olive oil, metal tableware, medical tools, toilet utensils, board games) did so primarily as part of a new formulation of power and status within their own societies. This was not an uncritical adoption of Roman material culture and social practices, but rather the careful selection of certain prestigious elements of Roman culture to be used to accentuate social differentiation in Iron Age society and to construct new forms of elite identity. This will have worked not only within regional kingdoms, but also as a way of accentuating difference between emerging polities. The eastern and southern kingdoms, with their privileged access to imported goods, stand in contrast to their western and northern neighbours. This close contact with Rome did not necessarily predispose the British peoples as a whole to submit to military incorporation; rather it had the potential to make them more determined opponents of renewed invasion.

PART TWO

The Military Community

4

The Iron Fist

Conquest (43–83) and Aftermath

The Romans had developed a uniquely persistent approach to warfare in their conquest of first Italy and then the Mediterranean world. They lost occasional battles, sometimes catastrophically – as when Hannibal invaded Italy – but their refusal to accept terms of surrender and their commitment to raising new armies and fighting on meant that they were extremely difficult to defeat in drawn-out war. Some of Rome's greatest victories were the product of simple persistence in the face of the logic that said a war was lost. Their whole society became structured around the idea of war, and focused on the sacrifices, training and organization necessary to win.

However, it is not the case that the Romans always enjoyed huge technical or technological advantages over their opponents. Warfare in the ancient world was based around exchange of missiles (arrows, javelins, slingshot, ballista bolts, etc.) and hand-to-hand combat with a limited range of weaponry (sword, dagger, thrusting spear, club, etc.). Horses were often very important in ancient warfare, but the extent and significance of their role varied from region to region. Cavalry was an ideal force for medium-range hit-and-run raids, where small war-bands were involved. But really large-scale horse-borne armies were expensive to equip, maintain and to supply and were a comparatively rare phenomenon in the ancient world (the Parthians, Sarmatians and Huns were all peoples from the east). Cavalry was also much less effective against a disciplined infantry force that was able to stand its ground and hold its formation and many of the Mediterranean peoples had evolved infantry tactics and improved body armour to counter the in-built superiority of cavalry forces. At the same time this allowed them to put larger armies in the field. The Romans became masters of this sort of warfare, with heavily armoured infantrymen at the heart of their battle lines. By the time Rome came in contact with Britain, the scale of her recruitment base far outstripped the human resources of her opponents, and this was arguably her biggest asset in warfare. Although the elite troops of the Roman army were its heavy infantry (both of citizen and allied status), light-armed infantry and cavalry were also essential components and were recruited from those of Rome's previously defeated enemies who specialized in these areas. These auxiliary troops gave the army balance in battle, with the cavalry normally deployed on either side of the infantry line where they provided both defence for the flanks of the army and an offensive threat to the enemy forces, particularly when the latter were in retreat.

The Roman army differed in other important respects from that of many of its opponents. By the first century BC it had become a professional standing army, rather than a seasonally levied or irregular conscript force. There were set terms of pay and service, rules of military discipline, standardized equipment and training, a commonality of structure, and battle tactics which allowed units to be brought together to form a cohesive whole. Officers were regularly transferred from one unit to another and from one province to another. A particular characteristic was the careful approach to campaigning in enemy territory, with the army aiming to march ten to twenty miles each day and spend each night in a specially constructed defensible camp. Speed was not of the essence if, by methodical advance, the risk of ambush or surprise attack at night were lessened. These were significant advantages.

There is abundant evidence of Roman campaigning in Britain, most notably from Wales and north Britain where fighting was prolonged and repeated. This evidence takes the form of vestigial traces of the Roman temporary camps erected at the end of each day's march. Since an army on the march would construct a standard camp each day to suit its size, it is possible to recognize distinct series of camps, each presumably representing a different campaign or a different battle group. The evidence is most graphic in Scotland, where the Roman line of advance up Strathmore to the east of the Highlands is marked by successive sequences of camps. Although the dating of these camps is problematic and controversial, some are certainly attributable to the activity of Agricola's army and another, much larger series to the campaigns of Septimius Severus. The largest of these camps are over 40 ha (100 acres) in extent and could have accommodated a battle group of up to c. 50,000 men in tents.

The preferred option of the Romans was to engage in a full pitched battle on a site of their own choosing, with the light skirmishers (slingers and archers) engaging the enemy first, then the cavalry establishing superiority over the opposing cavalry (preferably driving them off the field) and the infantry closing with their opponents for savage hand-to-hand combat. If the cavalry were victorious, they could be relied upon to deliver further attacks to the flanks and rear of the opposing line. Superior body armour was provided for the rank-and-file Roman soldier, but was in more limited supply among his opponents in north-western Europe, and the Romans developed to a fine and bloody art the tactics of close-packed infantry warfare utilizing the murderous potential of the *gladius*, the legionary stabbing sword. The odds in a close-quarters battle were heavily in Rome's favour, even when faced by larger numbers. The fighting could continue for hours, until one of the combatants (usually the enemy) tried to disengage. As they fled the field, the Roman cavalry and light skirmishers would chase them down. In ancient warfare the highest casualties were often inflicted in the pursuit phase.

A key ingredient in the Roman approach to war was their ruthless attitude, which frequently extended to the use of exemplary force. Rebellious or recalcitrant peoples were slaughtered or enslaved without qualms, massive resources being poured into the crushing of even small groups of dissenters (as in the well-known siege of the Jewish fortress of Masada by the Dead Sea). Moreover, the Romans believed that they had divine sanction for 'empire without limits'. In these circumstances, it was easy for them to believe their strategic interests to be threatened by others, and, although Roman law forbade the state from declaring war other than in self-defence, the Romans built an empire on the principle of getting their retaliation in first. They were by turns aggressive and deceitful in their diplomatic dealings that backed up campaigning; breaches of treaties on the part of Rome far outnumber incidents of such behaviour on the part of her opponents. Although Rome could on occasion be generous to her defeated opponents, we should not underestimate the degree to which she was prepared to inflict massive social and financial penalties, through seizure of property and enslaving of people. After all, this was how campaigns and triumphal celebrations were funded.

This aggressive behaviour had a considerable impact on the course of her wars of conquest. Her enemies generally tired of the conflict before she did. Moreover, Rome showed considerable skill in the use of 'deterrence diplomacy', often achieving her aims simply by intimidation. The resources of the empire were not limitless and if every issue had to be resolved by armed intervention, then over time the force available to the empire would have been seriously diminished. It was in the interests of Rome to use the perception of her power (and of the latent force that lay behind it) to elicit compliance. It is also characteristic of imperial systems that the perception of huge power inequalities between the state and its opponents can create dynamic mechanisms for military and social control. Some degree of resistance is always to be anticipated and intimidation cannot work unless there is also a clear perception of what the alternative to compliance is. Part of the rationale for the exemplary use of force against subject peoples was to reinforce the message that Rome had the ability to compel those who did not readily accede to Roman demands.

The limitations on Rome's forces are clear in the history of military conquests in the first century. Expansionism had slowed considerably after the reign of Augustus, in part because the territorial control of the consolidated empire left few troops spare for further conquests. When additional conquests were considered, as in Britain in 43 or Dacia in the early second century, these required drawing substantial reserves of troops from other military provinces. As a result, the strategic considerations that determined the pace of the British conquest were not entirely local to Britain, but reflected changing priorities in the empire as a whole (sometimes also the whims of individual emperors). The overall slow progress of Roman conquest in Britain attests the fact that a consistently aggressive policy was not allowed to all its Roman governors. Troops were withdrawn on several occasions for participation in wars elsewhere, as *legio XIV Gemina* in *c*.67 and 70, and *II Adiutrix c*.86. The 'mystery disappearance' of *legio IX* in the early second century appears to have been due to its strategic transfer from the province rather than its loss in an unrecorded British catastrophe.

Roman victories required parallel diplomatic efforts to capitalize on the advantage gained. Some peoples were formally recognized as client kingdoms, as with the *Iceni* under Prasutagus, the *Brigantes* under Cartimandua and the kingdom of Togidubnus. From the Roman perspective such a policy of divide and rule produced clear short-term gains, but there was no expectation that such kingdoms would endure in the long term. The British perception may have been more optimistic, though the bungled annexation of the Icenian kingdom in 60 should have sent clear signals about Rome's intentions for other client kingdoms. As far as we know, none of the British client kingdoms after 43 was allowed to pass on from the first recognized client ruler to his or her descendants. In two of the three cases, the annexation required considerable military force. This was not war avoided so much as war postponed.

It is debatable, in fact, whether the use of deterrence was seen by the Romans as a mechanism for avoiding war, as opposed to one for waging war by other means. At least in the conquest phase, the diplomatic efforts seem to have been directed at isolating enemies from potential allies and releasing troops who might otherwise have been fighting on a second front. Roman deterrence was thus to a considerable degree a cynical use of power, manipulating and compelling subject peoples to make required responses.

The activities of the Roman army in the conquest phase will have had a profound impact on the peoples of Britain. Even in a professional army like the Roman one, the collateral damage to civilian communities was undoubtedly high. Some such activity was sanctioned by the army command to be deliberately provocative – burning villages and laying waste to crops and resources in the line of march were stock tactics for bringing the enemy to battle. Tacitus repeatedly used the word 'terror' to describe Agricola's campaigns in northern Britain. The behaviour of the Roman army was meant to intimidate people, to persuade them that resistance was futile. Strong resistance was met by extreme force, extending even to attempts to exterminate whole peoples. When frustrated in her attempts to deliver a conventional military defeat or to enforce peace on people who had resorted to guerrilla warfare, the Roman response was also to fight dirty.

Some modern writers have tended to minimize the impact of the Roman conquest, implying that its worst effects were quickly compensated by the transition to civil government and renewed local autonomy. This seems a naïve reading of the evidence available. The supposed benefits of Roman civilization were not widely distributed until several generations after 43 and the experience of military subjugation had a long-lasting impact on the province. A characteristic of colonialism in general is that the power of empires creates resistance and opposition. The story of resistance to imperialism, whether short-term as in post-Saddam Iraq, or long-term as in British India, needs to take account of the failure of imperial powers to obtain complete approbation and acceptance.

From the perspective of communities that resisted the invasion, the trauma involved was potentially very great indeed. Many men will have been killed in battle, others in 'mopping-up' operations afterwards. Women, children and elders will also have suffered from the damage that armies inflict both before and after battle (massacres, rape, random killings, burning and destruction of settlements, displacement as refugees, enslavement). In the aftermath of defeat and occupation of territory, a further series of impacts might be felt over a period of years: arrests and execution of suspected troublemakers, enslavement of elements of the population, forcible disarmament, seizure of property (especially portable wealth, crops and livestock), confiscation of lands.

Newly conquered people were regularly recruited into the Roman army for service on other frontiers. This had the joint effects of removing potential military opposition while pacification measures proceeded, furthering Rome's military aims elsewhere and introducing defeated people to direct participation in the empire. Two cavalry units (*alae*) and at least sixteen infantry/mixed units (*cohortes*) were raised in Britain from defeated peoples during the first century. The unit names reflect two designations of Britons (*Britanni* and *Brittones*), though it is uncertain whether the distinction has any clear geographical implication (say, southern and northern Britons). The majority of the regular auxiliary units appear to have been posted to the Danubian provinces (*Pannonia, Moesia, Dalmatia, Dacia*), for example the *cohors II Britannorum* at Regensburg. In addition, a number of irregular units (*numeri Brittonum*) are known on the German frontier from the second century. These British auxiliary units represent a series of initial levies totalling *c.*12,000 men, with supplementary recruitment requiring an average of between *c.*500 and 750 per year to make up numbers completing service or dying. By the reign of Hadrian, in line with developments elsewhere in the empire, it is probable that most recruitment of Britons was directed to established units already based in Britain, and the 'ethnic' units on the Danube lost their British character. The large size of the auxiliary garrison in Britain (*c.*30,000 troops) implies an annual top-up of *c.*1,200–1,500 men, or 12,000–15,000 men each decade. Although not on the scale of military recruitment enacted on the Gallic provinces (with *c.*100 units raised), in Spain (*c.*75), Syria/Palestine and Thrace (both more than 40), British recruitment was above the average for other provinces. Within Britain the impact of recruitment was probably unequally spread, with some peoples providing larger numbers.

The potential British casualties in the conquest period can only be very crudely estimated. Roman generals needed to have killed 5,000 of the enemy in a decisive battle to claim a Triumph, but under the Principate such honours were reserved for emperors. On the other hand, Tacitus specifies that there were 10,000 Caledonian dead at *Mons Graupius* (set against only 360 Roman fatalities) and some sources recorded 80,000 British dead in the decisive battle that settled the Boudican revolt. Tacitus was clearly sceptical about this last figure, but it may well represent total British deaths in the war and the Roman reprisals that followed. Taking account of the number of major and minor engagements in our sources and the nature of ancient warfare, somewhere between 100,000 and 250,000 Britons are likely to have perished in the conquest period 43–83. In the context of pre-industrial warfare and of a total population of Britain of *c.*2 million, these are very high figures – to which should be added a significant number of others who will have survived wounds, but whose lives were shortened as a result.

The military administration of conquered peoples placed wide powers in the hands of local military officers. Summary justice could be meted out, communities forcibly resettled, restrictions imposed on movement, trading and assembly. The presence of a military garrison created new power relationships in society, but these were very unequal ones – even common soldiers had considerable scope for exerting personal influence. This might take the form of casual brutality, extortion, theft, rape or imposing an unwanted sexual relationship. Under martial law, a soldier's word would normally count for more than that of a newly created subject. That is not to say that the army command took no action against soldiers who consistently abused their power; on the other hand it is probable that many enjoyed considerable latitude in their dealings with conquered peoples.

If those of the traditional elite who had survived defeat in battle were not sufficiently docile, others could replace them. Defeated communities were immediately liable to pay tribute or war indemnities, and to provide forced labour and animals for hauling goods. In theory, the surrender of a people to Rome involved the loss of control of all land to the state, and though much of this might in time be returned into various forms of private or local ownership, in the short term the uncertainty of the situation was clearly another powerful lever to exert pressure on people to conform to Rome's wishes. Conquered lands were normally surveyed and assessed by skilled military land measurers. Such surveys provided the state with detailed information on the nature, extent, quality and use of land. This formed the basis for more regularized tax assessments as and when a region was transferred into civil government. Roman campaigning and what followed on from it transformed much of southern Britain by the end of the first century.

THE RETURN OF THE ROMANS

Invasion was considered on several occasions after Caesar, under Augustus, under Caligula and under Claudius. Conquest had always been an option in dealing with British clients, particularly for an emperor needing an attention-grabbing military action. The desire to emulate one of Caesar's most celebrated achievements was greatest in those with the least military experience of their own. It is an interesting paradox that annexation when it came should focus on the British client kingdoms that had been most closely aligned with Rome in the period between the campaigns of Caesar and Claudius. Alliance with Rome carried dangers for these kingdoms because in the eyes of Rome they were already part of the 'empire without limits'. The accession of Caligula in 37 created the need for military glory to bolster his prestige. One result was the execution of the king of *Mauretania* and annexation of his kingdom, and this was followed quickly by preparations to invade Britain in 40. Regime change in client kingdoms offered the potential of quick victories, particularly if the elite order could be persuaded that their interests would be best served by compliance. What complicated matters in Britain was that Cunobelin had at least two grown-up sons, Caratacus and Togodumnus, who had a clear expectation of succeeding him in power. There is reason to believe, therefore, that the evident sharp deterioration in relations between the house of Cunobelin and Rome after 37 was a direct consequence of the realization in Britain that Rome intended to annex the kingdom on Cunobelin's death. Our sources imply that it was the British kings who became difficult and broke agreements, but it is at least as likely that it was the Roman change in policy that provoked the crisis in a hitherto close relationship. The flight of another son of Cunobelin, Adminius, to Rome was perhaps a consequence of Roman manoeuvring to get some in the ruling elite to collaborate. The same policy shift may also have destabilized the southern kingdom of Verica, since he was forcibly ousted just before the conquest of 43. It is unclear who replaced him, but his ousting could have been a consequence of his acceptance that he would be the last independent king. Adminius and Verica were used as pretexts for invasion in 40 and 43 respectively, but significantly neither appears to have been returned to power as a Roman client once the invasion was launched. Although in the event only the eastern kingdom was directly annexed in 43, with the southern kingdom being returned to the care of a new client ruler, one senses that realpolitik lay behind Rome's actions. Attempts to suggest that the Roman conquest was invited and encouraged by the *Atrebates* and other peoples threatened by the eastern kingdom's expansion seem to be far too accepting of a Roman perspective of these events.

The outline of the Claudian invasion is clear, though the detail is far less securely established. Under the command of Aulus Plautius, the army was assembled at the Channel, based around four legions, some 20,000 men, and a similar force of auxiliary units. The memory was still strong of Caesar's armies nearly being stranded by storms wrecking his fleet and there was difficulty in persuading the troops to embark. The troops' nervousness may also have reflected their unfamiliarity with amphibious landings and their perception of the difficulty of establishing a beachhead if strongly opposed. An imperial freedman had to shame them into taking to their ships.

There are two main versions of what happened next. We know that the fleet sailed from Boulogne in three groups, though it is unclear if these all landed together or at separate locations. The main landing is commonly assumed to have been at Richborough in Kent, though some scholars argue strongly that the initial target of the fleet was the Solent and a possibly warmer reception from pro-Roman elements of the southern kingdom. The issue is not currently resolvable, but the main objective of the first campaign was to cross the Thames and advance on Colchester. In either case, it is clear that the initial landing was unopposed, with the British forces perhaps misled, by news of the near-mutiny in Boulogne, into thinking that once again the invasion was postponed. But as the Roman army (or part of it) advanced from the base camp, it encountered a considerable British force at a river crossing. The Roman victory here was hard-fought over two days, with the future emperor Vespasian commanding *legio II Augusta* and playing a major role in the action. This allowed further advance to the Thames, where the British made their second major stand. Once again, the Romans were successful in the pitched battle and secured the river crossing. There was then a hiatus while Plautius awaited the arrival of the emperor Claudius before proceeding to the major objective of the campaign, the capital of the eastern kingdom at Colchester. Dio's account of the campaign implies that Plautius waited until he got to the Thames before sending word for Claudius to join him. In reality it is more probable that Claudius was on his way as soon as the successful landing was announced. Once Plautius had secured the crossing of the Thames and the line of advance on Colchester was open, he was obliged to wait for a brief period for the emperor to arrive. Claudius, plus a detachment of elephants which he brought with him, participated in the rapid siege and capture of Colchester. The large size of the site and its relatively unsophisticated defences militated against extended resistance here, but may also have facilitated the escape of large numbers of the British combatants.

In consequence, the capture of Colchester was far from the end of the war (Table 2). Claudius' visit to the front was evidently a whirlwind – and carefully orchestrated – tour. Dio says he was only in Britain for sixteen days, barely time for more than the advance on Colchester with his elephants, a series of battles (evidently with minimal Roman casualties), the capture of the *oppidum* and, in the immediate aftermath, receiving the surrender of some of the British leaders, though crucially not of Caratacus. An inscription from Rome on a commemorative arch mentions the surrender to Claudius of eleven (or more) British kings, presumably many of them yielding at this stage in the campaign. Some of these were recognized – though not necessarily immediately – as independent client rulers to allow Rome a freer hand in pursuing those who continued armed resistance. The Roman army roamed far and wide in lowland Britain in the years immediately following the invasion and even the nominal clients may have found their affairs placed under close control and supervision for a period. Caratacus, meanwhile, seems to have been adopted as war leader by a range of other British peoples in western Britain, but unfortunately our sources are silent on the sequence of events that took him from the fall of Colchester to Wales.

Table 2. Main campaigns and battles of the conquest phase.

DATE	PEOPLE	EVENTS	SOURCES
43	Eastern kingdom (*Catuvellauni, Trinovantes*) and allies. Southern kingdom (*Atrebates*)?	Invasion and targeted advance on capital at Colchester (*Camulodunon*). Defeats for British forces at two river crossings (including Thames) and before Colchester. Surrender of 11 British kings.	Dio 60, 19–23; Suetonius *Claudius* 17; CIL 5.920
43–47	*Durotriges, Dumnonii, Atrebates*	Activity of Vespasian with *legio II Augusta* – 30 battles, 20 hillforts, the Isle of Wight and 2 peoples subdued	Suetonius *Vespasian* 4
43–47	*Corieltavi, Dobunni*	Expansion of Roman power into East and West Midlands by other legions under overall control of Aulus Plautius	Dio 60, 21
47	*Iceni, Cornovii*?	First revolt by part of the client *Iceni* at forcible disarming of peoples between rivers Trent and Severn	Tacitus *Annals* 12.31
47–51	*Deceangli, Brigantes, Silures, Ordovices*	Campaigns of Ostorius Scapula versus Welsh peoples and minor rebellion among client *Brigantes*. Capture of Caratacus.	Tacitus *Annals* 12.31–6
52	*Silures*	Further attacks on Roman forts in Silurian territory	Tacitus *Annals* 12.38–9
53–54	*Silures, Brigantes*	Defeat for a legion in South Wales. Internal conflict among *Brigantes* threatens client queen Cartimandua – situation restored by two battles involving auxiliaries and a Roman legion	Tacitus *Annals* 12.40
57	*Silures*	Campaign of Quintus Veranius	Tacitus *Annals* 14.29
58–60	*Silures, Ordovices*	Major campaigns versus Welsh peoples culminating in attack on druidical centre on island of Anglesey	Tacitus *Annals* 14.29–30
60–61	*Iceni, Trinovantes*, others	Boudican revolt. Massive casualties on British and Roman sides. Extensive and bloody Roman reprisals	Tacitus *Annals* 14.31–9; Dio (Epitome) 62, 1–12

Table 2 – *contd.*

DATE	PEOPLE	EVENTS	SOURCES
69	*Brigantes*	Vettius Bolanus forced to rescue Brigantian client queen Cartimandua after revolt of her ex-consort Venutius	Tacitus *Histories* 3.45
71	*Brigantes*	Petillius Cerialis annexes Brigantian kingdom – numerous battles, some bloody	Tacitus *Agricola* 17
73–76	*Silures, Ordovices*	Final conquest of Welsh peoples by Iulius Frontinus	Tacitus *Agricola* 17
77–83	*Ordovices, Brigantes,* Caledonii	Campaigns of Agricola against a revolt of *Ordovices*, then northern British and peoples of Lowland and Highland Scotland. Advance up east side of Highland line culminates in battle of *Mons Graupius*	Tacitus *Agricola* 18, 20, 22–3, 25–7, 29–38

So far the Roman campaign had achieved its key objective, the conquest of the eastern kingdom. What happened after the departure of Claudius for his triumph in Rome is much less certain because of gaps in our sources. The invasion force was probably split up into a series of battle groups, to continue the work of subjugation in detail. *Legio XX* certainly remained at Colchester to take further the pacification and disarmament of the *Trinovantes*, singled out for special attention. The territory of the *Catuvellauni* centred on St Albans must also have been targeted in this phase. Over the next three years, two legions (*XIV Gemina* and *IX Hispana*) extended Roman control west, north and north-west, incorporating the territory of the *Dobunni* in the Cotswolds/ Severn estuary area and the *Corieltavi* in the East Midlands, and this had certainly been achieved by the start of the next governor's term in 47. Meanwhile, Vespasian was assigned the task of continued campaigning in the south-west with *legio II*. He is credited by Suetonius with fighting thirty engagements, receiving the submission of two warlike 'tribes' and more than twenty native centres and the Isle of Wight. One of the peoples involved was certainly the *Durotriges* of Dorset, the identity of the other more controversial. This was the iron fist in action, and graphic evidence of Roman siege warfare comes from Hod Hill, where a mass of ballista bolts fired into the densely settled interior attests the ferocity of the attack, and Maiden Castle, where a possible war cemetery of British dead has been found. Both these sieges of strongly defended hillforts attest the Roman commitment to the exemplary use of force in this phase of the conquest. There are similar hints of violent action ending occupation at a number of other hillforts in southern England and Wales that also may plausibly be assigned to the conquest phase (Bilbury Rings, Cadbury Castle, Spettisbury, Sutton Walls, Croft Ambrey, the Wrekin, Llanymynech).

The treatment of peoples defeated in this way was probably quite prejudicial in comparison with those who had acknowledged Roman suzerainty early on. Further measures may have been taken against these defeated communities, hinted at by the presence of a number of small Roman fortifications set up in a series of south-western hillforts. The implication here is of a far more repressive and intrusive operation of the army in enforcing the *pax romana*, again with the intention of making an example of those who resisted strongly. At the same time, Rome wooed individual members of the British elite in areas where suzerainty had been more readily acknowledged, convincing some at least that accommodation was better than resistance and that it offered possibilities for self-advancement.

The southern kingdom appears to have been large, corresponding geographically to three of the later Roman administrative *civitates*, the *Atrebates* based on Silchester, the *Regni* at Chichester and the *Belgae* on Winchester. These were probably all placed under the authority of the most important client king of the early post-conquest era, Togidubnus (the name is also rendered Cogidumnus or Cogidubnus, but the T- version is more in line with British nomenclature). There are many intriguing puzzles here. First, it is not clear in what circumstances the southern kingdom surrendered to Rome. Its re-installation as a client kingdom could be looked on as a sign of favour and as an indication that resistance had not been too long maintained. If the main landing was in Kent, it is possible that they submitted only after the fall of Colchester, and then perhaps as a result of Roman troops being specifically detached to their territory. This would logically have been *legio II* with Vespasian, and the kingdom would fit the bill as the second major people to submit to him. The presence of a campaign base below the villa at Fishbourne, a legionary base of some sort below the later town of Chichester and military finds at Silchester strongly suggest that the area was initially subject to military take-over, not immediately handed on to a suitable client ruler. Some of Vespasian's victories may well have been won here, before he tackled the tougher resistance in Durotrigian territory to the west. In any case, Tacitus' account appears to link the creation of the kingdom of Togidubnus with events in 47.

The second question concerns who Togidubnus was and why he was given this kingdom to rule. We do not know why the ousted king, Verica, was passed over. Perhaps he was already dead or too old or too hated by his people. It is probable that Togidubnus was a British prince who had been an exile or hostage at the imperial court, though a Gallic Celt is also a possibility. The similarity of name with the prince of the eastern kingdom, Togodumnus, would give pause for thought, were it not for the fact that Dio tells us that Togodumnus was killed in one of the early engagements with Rome. It is not inconceivable that Dio had simply got his facts wrong and there are parallels for Rome employing as a client ruler someone who originated in a neighbouring territory (Juba II of *Numidia* being given the kingdom of *Mauretania* is a good example). If Togidubnus was a renegade British leader, persuaded to change sides during the invasion, then this would have been a tremendous coup for the Romans, somewhat akin to the conversion of Josephus during the Jewish revolt from rebel leader to imperial panegyrist. Whatever his ethnic origins, the grant of the kingdom and of Roman citizenship to him may be taken as substantial rewards. He was far from being the only Briton seeking to find personal advantage in making his peace with Rome.

The scale of the initial Roman victory in the south-east left the British leaders with stark choices: fight to the death, flee westwards (as Caratacus chose to do), surrender and endure Roman rule, surrender and offer service to Rome. Other kingdoms whose rulers negotiated client status with Rome included the *Iceni* in Norfolk and the *Brigantes* in northern England. Elaborate post-conquest burials of native Britons at both Colchester and St Albans indicate that even in the Trinovantian and Catuvellaunian heartlands, some British aristocrats were allowed to maintain their wealth and status. While few Britons welcomed the invasion, the initial Roman victories constrained many to find an accommodation.

CONTINUED RESISTANCE AND REBELLIONS 47–69

Caratacus re-emerged in our sources as leader of the *Silures* and later the *Ordovices* in Wales in the late 40s. In the interim it is probable that he had continued his resistance as a war leader of other groups. However, this phase of activity is more than the story of one man's crusade against Roman domination. The sources for this period present the Romans as being on the defensive, responding to the provocation of native attacks and rebellious subjects. The reality was probably radically different, with the Roman army precipitating resistance by its own expansionist actions. The principal mineral resources of Britain lay in the highland zone in the west and north of the country and these appear to have been a key objective of the conquest from its early stages. If prominent leaders such as Caratacus were also seeking refuge in the mountainous western districts, that was all the excuse Rome needed for directing campaigns towards them.

When Aulus Plautius was replaced as governor by Ostorius Scapula in 47, the incoming commander found enemies invading the land of allies, perhaps Silurian raids into Dobunnic territory. Ostorius sent out his auxiliary troops to drive off the raiders and then took a series of further measures against the peoples who had already submitted. Tacitus suggests that the pacification of the previously conquered lands was incomplete and that Ostorius now disarmed even client kingdoms and extended direct territorial control into the regions bordering the Rivers Trent and Severn. It is possible that the lands of the *Dobunni* and the *Corieltavi* were now garrisoned (if not before), and their nominal independence as client peoples ended. But the forcible disarming was also extended to the *Iceni* in Norfolk, who had submitted to a Roman alliance without having been defeated in battle. The *Iceni* are said to have rebelled, though they may well have felt that they were simply resisting a Roman action that contravened their rights as clients. Tacitus says the Britons' chosen field of battle was a defended enclave, which illustrates the character of this so-called revolt. Far from being on the rampage, some part of the *Iceni* had refused to hand over arms, and retreated into a defended site. They only 'chose' the field of battle in the sense that that was where the Roman army found them. A direct attack by Roman auxiliary units on this stronghold broke the Icenian resistance. The *Iceni* were permitted to keep their client status, perhaps even the same ruler as before, and that too suggests that this was a spontaneous and relatively isolated act of resistance to Roman bullying, rather than a full-blown revolt.

Scapula next launched a series of campaigns against the hitherto unconquered Welsh peoples, starting with the *Deceangli* in the north. The latter avoided a pitched battle, but endured the full impact of a scorched-earth policy. The sources acknowledge that the approach was brutal, their territory being devastated, with seizure of substantial booty. There was a brief interlude caused by unrest amongst the *Brigantes*, and once again Roman units were sent into a nominally independent client kingdom to sort out trouble, with those who had taken up arms against Roman interests being killed. Then in 49 the offensive against the *Silures* in southern Wales was renewed, with the legion previously kept back at Colchester being moved up to occupy a forward position. Tacitus presented this as a defensive move against Silurian aggression, but the immediate sequel was the launching of offensive operations into Silurian territory. Caratacus eluded Roman attempts to force a decisive battle or to capture him, but was obliged to move northwards into the territory of the *Ordovices*, bringing them into the conflict. There Ostorius caught up with him and forced the British forces to give battle, though once again the field of battle 'chosen' by the Britons sounds more like an existing hillfort, hastily strengthened. A case has been made for locating this battle at the site of Llanymynech, a hillfort and copper-mining site, though once again conclusive evidence is lacking. The Roman victory here was only marred by the escape of Caratacus, though his wife, daughter and brothers were captured. Caratacus now fled north-eastwards into Brigantian territory. If he hoped to persuade the *Brigantes* to revoke their treaty, it was a miscalculation. Queen Cartimandua captured him by a ruse and handed him over to the Romans. To have done otherwise would have been equivalent to declaring war on the Romans herself, but the decision does not appear to have been popular within her own people, where a deepening chasm between pro- and anti-Roman elements was emerging. Luck favoured Caratacus in the end, however, as his proud and defiant demeanour won Claudius' clemency and he escaped execution in Rome.

Caratacus is a romantic figure in the story of resistance to Rome, not only for his military resourcefulness, but also for his consistent refusal to admit defeat. After each setback, he carried his resistance into a new area, rather than submit to Roman power (though this was a repudiation of his early life as a would-be Roman client). He is the opposite of the post-conquest client rulers, who at an early stage compromised and sought accommodation. Although Caratacus enjoyed numerous minor victories in his guerrilla war, every pitched battle he fought against the Romans ended in defeat and by degrees he was hounded across the country by an opponent of disproportionately greater military resources. This power inequality between Rome and the individual British leaders perhaps persuaded many others to negotiate for peace.

The war with the *Silures* was far from ended by the capture of Caratacus, though Rome may have made the mistake of believing it so. Once again our sources intimate that the *Silures* were the aggressors, but the action was for the most part fought out in Silurian territory, which the Roman army was evidently trying to pacify by force. There was a full-scale assault on a legionary detachment (vexillation) left in their territory to construct forts, leading to the deaths of the camp prefect and of eight centurions, together with the pick of their men. The loss of so many senior officers suggests a serious reverse. Soon after, a foraging party was attacked and the cavalry force sent to its aid was severely defeated. Further auxiliary units and legionaries were brought in to assist in this battle, but darkness fell before the Romans could inflict major damage to the enemy. No Roman casualty figures are given, but in total these two engagements probably accounted for well over 1,000 troops. For an army that took pride in avoiding casualties on this scale these were major setbacks. Tacitus speculated that either Rome had reduced the vigour of its operations believing the war to be over, or the Britons had been moved by some strange passion to avenge Caratacus. The more likely scenario is that Roman pacification measures in Silurian territory misjudged the preparedness of the *Silures* to lay down their arms. The construction of forts, the seizure of crops and animals by foraging parties, and the pillaging of Silurian settlements were provocative acts. After these two major actions, the *Silures* mainly reverted to hit-and-run tactics, though two Roman auxiliary units, incautiously engaging in pillage, were cut off by a larger-scale attack. Roman frustration with this obdurate resistance was such that they evidently declared their intent to exterminate the people or transport them – the extreme reaction of an imperial power to unremitting resistance. Presumably the words were matched on the ground by harsh deeds. This phase of the war was starting to look mishandled and, with no end in sight, Ostorius Scapula added to Rome's problems by dying in 52.

By the time the new governor, Aulus Didius Gallus, arrived, there was further trouble. The *Silures* had defeated another legionary force and there were renewed problems with the Brigantian client kingdom. The account of Tacitus is far from clear, but it appears that Silurian raiding parties had spread out beyond their own borders, though the advance of Didius with his army forced them to withdraw. The Brigantian situation suggests a reconsolidation of resistance to Rome. Cartimandua had divorced her husband, Venutius, and taken his shield-bearer as her new consort. This led to internal fighting, in which Rome clearly supported the queen. Venutius henceforth appears to have maintained a steadfastly anti-Roman attitude. Roman auxiliary cohorts and a legionary force fought two separate engagements against him, but they do not seem to have pursued his army beyond Cartimandua's boundaries. The destabilization of the Brigantian kingdom was to tie down Roman troops on her borders and demand periodic intervention for the next fifteen years.

The progress and cost of campaigning was almost certainly starting to be questioned in Rome. Tacitus is highly critical of certain governors of Britain for their lack of action, but we must remember that they were the appointees of the emperor, receiving detailed written instructions and being directly answerable to him. The relative inaction of Didius Gallus in the face of a series of unresolved military problems is better explained in terms of indecision in the imperial palace. The death of Claudius in 54 served only to lengthen this crisis in the central direction of the British conquest. Suetonius says that Nero considered abandoning the British conquest at some point in his reign, and the apparent suspension of campaigning during the first years of his reign is suggestive.

The appointment of Quintus Veranius as governor in 57 marked the relaunching of Rome's offensive against the *Silures*. Veranius was a man of proven military ability and, significantly, he had experience of mountain warfare. Although he died at the end of his first year of office, and Tacitus played down his achievements as a series of 'plundering raids', he would seem to have had a marked impact. The *Silures* disappeared from the pages of Tacitus at a stroke and the policy seems to have been continued against the *Ordovices* by his successor. Suetonius Paullinus, another military careerist with experience of mountain warfare, conquered Ordovician territory within two years and at the start of his third season of campaigning stood facing the island of Anglesey (*Mona*) across the Menai Straits. The island's population was swelled by a large number of refugees (or fugitives to use the Roman terminology). Tacitus gave the Roman view of the enemy lined up on the opposing shore: armed men, fanatical women bearing torches and druids invoking terrible curses. From a Roman perspective these were the remaining dregs of British resistance, further tainted by their barbaric religious practices such as human sacrifice. They could expect no quarter now they had nowhere else to run. In a well-planned amphibious assault, Suetonius Paullinus led his army across the Straits to 'cut down all they met'. There is little doubt that this was a massacre, followed up by the destruction of sacred groves.

Can we reconstruct a British perspective on these events? The period from 57 to 60 was a particularly traumatic one for the Welsh peoples. The Roman force comprised at least two legions and associated auxiliaries. There is every reason to believe that the style of warfare was deliberately brutal in an attempt to crush resistance once and for all. A stream of refugees will have been forced back ahead of the Roman advance. The severity of the Roman assault proved to be a costly miscalculation; for a policy conceived to intimidate and demoralize the Welsh peoples contributed to the outbreak of rebellion in the core areas of the province.

The druids are an enigmatic group in the historiography of the Roman world and may have had a significant part to play in British resistance. At the time of Caesar they were a powerful branch of the Gallic and British aristocracies, responsible for the oral transmission of religious lore and often wielding considerable political clout. By the first century Roman sources treat them as more of a curiosity than a serious source of power in society, but this seems incompatible with the increasingly severe measures we know that the Romans took against them in Gaul and Britain, culminating with attempts to exterminate them. The druids were a particular threat to Rome in that they were both the teachers and the practitioners of native religion and were the most likely focus for cultural resistance to Rome. In common with more recent empires, the Romans encountered strong revitalization movements after periods of apparent pacification. The druids were a focus for such resistance precisely because of their overlapping religious and political prestige. The pacification of the rest of Britain and the reinvention of British religion in a 'Roman' guise were thus bound up in important ways with the ruthless suppression of a group characterized by the Romans as religious fanatics. The Roman preparations for the assault on Anglesey will have been well-advertised; it is probable that in their hour of need the druids did their best to stir up trouble elsewhere in Britain. There were many other causes of the rebellion that now broke out in Icenian and Trinovantian territory, but the possibility of an undercurrent of profound religious reaction against Rome is hinted at by the accounts of the Boudican revolt.

We have two surviving accounts, from Tacitus and Cassius Dio, though they differ in points of detail. In identifying causes of the revolt, our Roman sources were influenced by the official need to find palatable explanations and convenient scapegoats. There is little doubt concerning the scale of the catastrophe that overwhelmed much of southern England. Tacitus described it as a disaster (*clades*) and even if the figures given for overall casualties were exaggerated, the bloodbath that was apparently enacted by both sides revealed a profound gulf between the Roman conquerors and their subjects.

The events can be quickly summarized. Prasutagus, the client king of the *Iceni*, had died and it had been decided to incorporate his territory into the province. This was mismanaged by the responsible financial official (procurator), Decianus Catus, and while Paullinus was engaged in his Anglesey campaign, the *Iceni* rose in revolt, led by Boudica, the widow of Prasutagus. The *Trinovantes* to their south, with many grievances of their own, joined them and the rebel forces went on the rampage. They defeated a legionary vexillation sent against them, overwhelmed the city of Colchester and its defenders, comprising colonists, an auxiliary unit and last-minute reinforcements of 200 men. They then marched on London. Paullinus had hastened back from Wales with a cavalry escort, but, being unable to organize an effective defence, he withdrew towards his forces marching overland from Wales and abandoned both London and St Albans to the rebels' onslaught. Shortly thereafter the under-strength Roman army met the British forces somewhere in the West Midlands, with complete victory going to the vastly outnumbered Romans. Paullinus then engaged in brutal punitive action against those implicated (the revolt having evidently spread beyond the two peoples originally involved), a process that was only terminated when he was replaced as governor in 61. Because of the number of incidents to be fitted into the narrative, it is generally agreed that the revolt actually broke out in 60, though the Tacitean account indicated 61.

Tacitus suggested a series of factors was responsible for the outbreak of the revolt and for its widespread impact. Prasutagus had made the emperor Nero co-heir to the kingdom with his two daughters, but Roman centurions and imperial slaves plundered the kingdom and his household. Several outrages were committed against the Icenian royal family and prominent nobles: Boudica was flogged, her daughters were raped, other members of the royal family were treated like slaves, and nobles lost their traditional lands. Tacitus implied that responsibility for this rested with minor officials abusing their power. Only at the end of this section of his account did he reveal the key information that these events had taken place in the context of the annexation of the kingdom and its incorporation into the province.

The *Trinovantes*, who had been under direct Roman rule since 43, were roused to revolt because of bitter hatred of the legionary veterans settled in the colony at Colchester. These veterans had evidently been abusing the British population of the area. Some people were evicted from their homes and lands, others treated as second-class citizens (perhaps some enslaved). The army turned a blind eye on these illegal acts and even encouraged them. The creation of a temple of the divine Claudius at the colony was also a major focus of discontent in that the Trinovantian elite was obliged to contribute to its elaboration and to annual ceremonies. Dio added important details about other fiscal embarrassments of the British elite. Claudius had apparently distributed substantial sums to British leaders in the early years after the invasion, presumably as a way of encouraging their collaboration in the creation of the Roman province. Decianus Catus had apparently been claiming that these had been loans not gifts and now must be repaid. Other prominent Romans had also loaned huge amounts of money to the British elite, the most notable being Nero's tutor and adviser Seneca, who had committed a multi-million sum and had suddenly called in the entire amount for settlement. Although Tacitus and Dio reduce the causes of the rebellion to a series of individual abuses, it is possible to see within this list of causes an indictment of the entire Roman system of colonization. The scale and ferocity of the Boudican revolt would suggest that this was not a settling of petty scores, but rather a grand confrontation that struck at the very heart of Roman governance in Britain.

The notion that people might rebel against the day-to-day reality of Roman occupation of their land deserves serious consideration. From a British perspective the sort of abuses mentioned by Tacitus may have been considered as neither unusual nor outside the normal experience of Roman rule at this stage in the life of a province. Conquest had doubtless been followed by a sequence of unpleasant measures. Routine brutality of soldiers towards civilians in this phase was to be expected and this rose in intensity depending on the degree of resistance shown. The status of communal and individual landholding was left ill-defined until territory passed into civil administration, and in many parts of lowland Britain this had not yet been achieved at the time of the revolt. Traditional religion was another target of repression. Overall, the complaints of the chief protagonists will have struck a chord with many others in southern Britain.

In contrast to the humiliating and humbling treatment of the British population at large was the marked latitude Rome allowed three groups closely aligned with the interests of the state. The first, of course, was the army. Troops became accustomed to the opportunities campaigning brought for seizing booty. Indeed, after the suppression of the revolt, when the brakes were put on further expansion for a time, the Roman legions in Britain appear to have become mutinous partly because of their lack of opportunity for plunder. There are plenty of hints in the sources that troops engaged in widespread raiding of enemy territory and exploited their power over disarmed civilians elsewhere to extort what they wanted. The foundation of the military colony at Colchester extended the possibilities for soldiers to profit from the British conquest beyond the term of their military careers. Although the colony was designed for retired legionaries, it appears that elements of the *Trinovantes* were also associated administratively with the city. These were the people who were being illegally forced out of their homes and off their lands by the colonists before the revolt. Tacitus stated that the serving soldiers encouraged the harassment in the expectation that they would be allowed similar licence themselves as further colonies came to be founded.

The second group comprised the heterogeneous non-combatant foreigners who had followed the army into Britain. They included slave-traders, merchants, artisans in various crafts and trades, money-lenders, agents for powerful individuals hoping to profit from a distance. A newly conquered territory, lacking a developed infrastructure and economy along Roman lines, offered great opportunities to people able to assist in the rapid creation of a facsimile province. The role of provincial Romans from outside Britain in the early history of the new province was thus profound. London, one of the main targets of the rebels, was apparently teeming with merchants and the same may be hypothesized of St Albans, lying as it did on one of the main routes to the north-west. There were few settlements worthy of the name 'town' in 60, but immigrant communities were probably important at all of them. A near-contemporary inscription from Chichester was erected on behalf of a guild of craftsmen on land donated by a man who was probably a foreigner.

The Gallic provinces across the Channel were an important contributor to this, not least because linguistic similarities made Gauls ideal interlocutors and intermediaries. After a century of Roman rule, large numbers of northern Gauls were in the vanguard of the active exploitation of the newly established neighbouring province. These people were targeted by the rebels in 60 not simply because they were perceived as pro-Roman or living in more wealthy communities, but because many of them had sought to profit from the conquest phase. We are not talking about individual acts of cupidity or wickedness, but a systemic effect of Roman colonialism. The same pattern was repeated in other provinces, where similar groups of 'Roman' traders and 'carpet-bagger' entrepreneurs occasionally got massacred. Yet despite the risks, the economic rewards of serving an expanding empire were a substantial inducement.

What of the third group, comprising those of the British elite who had acquiesced to Roman rule and been the recipients of Roman bribes, subsidies and loans? How compromised were they at this time? Some individuals had without a doubt adapted to the new order with pragmatism and profit. Togidubnus, the longest-lived of the client kings, is the classic example. The Romans used members of the existing elites to carry out much routine work of local government, allowing them to retain or enhance elements of personal prestige. This is demonstrated by rich burials of early post-conquest date at Colchester and St Albans, evidently made for British aristocrats following traditional customs. Client kingdoms, of course, provided larger opportunities for elite families to retain their wealth and power, but the line between ally and enemy of Rome could be a fine one. The families of Cunobelin and

Prasutagus provide good examples of the way in which those who had most closely co-operated with Rome could be rapidly transformed into victims by the system. Similarly, the Colchester temple of the imperial cult, designed as a religious focus for the province, depended on the investment of their personal fortunes by the chief families of the *Trinovantes*. Dio suggests that some of the leading British families had been lent money they did not want so that they could demonstrate that they were supporters of the provincial development by investing in a temple in a colonial city where they were effectively second-class citizens. The sudden rejection of seventeen years of compliance by a large body of the south-eastern elites was thus an extremely dangerous development from a Roman perspective as it exposed the fragility of the relationship that bound British subjects to Rome. The fact that Togidubnus seems to have remained loyal to Rome in this crisis and kept the peoples south of the Thames largely out of the revolt was probably critical to its suppression.

When the revolt broke out, Rome's forces were widely distributed in Britain. The *XIV* and *XX* legions were with Paullinus on Anglesey, and part of *legio XX* was evidently left there by Paullinus as the rest of the army marched towards London. *Legio IX* appears to have been split at this time into two battle groups and one of these, commanded by its legate Petillius Cerialis, had been severely defeated by the rebels, with *c.*2,000 legionary infantrymen slaughtered and only the cavalry escaping back to their base, probably Longthorpe near Peterborough. The other part of this legion was evidently based in Lincolnshire or Nottinghamshire, in an advanced position to keep watch over the *Brigantes*. The final legion was the *II Augusta*, with its main base at this time at Exeter, but with part of its forces again stationed elsewhere, perhaps at Kingsholm or at Alchester. Paullinus may have been marching south from Watling Street hoping to link up with this vexillation when the decisive battle took place. This is the most plausible explanation for the tragic story of Poenius Postumus, camp prefect of *legio II*. A camp prefect was a logical choice to be placed in command of a vexillation, but with the countryside in tumult and fearing attack, Poenius ignored an order to lead his troops out, and then fell on his sword when news of the Roman victory reached him. As a result, Paullinus had only about 10,000 men in total when the decisive battle took place.

They were greatly outnumbered by the rebel forces, though the high figure of 230,000 given by Dio must be exaggerated. On the other hand, it is apparent that this vast horde of people, which included many non-combatants, was neither well armed nor well trained. Earlier disarmament of conquered peoples must have had an impact on the availability of weapons, and in a fast-moving rebellion there was neither time to fabricate large numbers of arms, nor, evidently, was there the opportunity for rebel forces to pillage major stockpiles of Roman weaponry. While a core of Boudica's army will have been properly armed, therefore, many of the rebels will have had no body armour and will have been provided with makeshift weapons, such as agricultural tools. Through careful selection of the battlefield within a narrow valley, Paullinus equalized the odds further still. When deployed in a confined space, the rebels could not bring the full weight of their numbers to bear on the Roman line and the heavily armoured Romans slaughtered their opponents with no quarter given, even to women with the British baggage train. Roman battle losses were apparently 400 dead, against a probably inflated figure of 80,000 Britons.

Both our Roman sources record that the rebels had killed 70,000–80,000 Romans and provincials in their sack of three towns and numerous other settlements. Are these sorts of figures credible? The army losses must have been at least 7,000 men, to judge from the scale of reinforcements sent from the Continent. Colchester, London and St Albans were the major settlements attacked and loss of life was probably greatest at Colchester, because of the element of surprise. The rebels evidently took no prisoners and simply slaughtered all they encountered. Perhaps as many as 10,000 died at Colchester, but the population of London and St Albans had more warning of what was coming and many might have fled. Tacitus stated that Paullinus allowed some of the population to join his column when he pulled back from defending the town, but this was limited only to those who could keep up with the column (those with horses) and he appears to have excluded women. It is possible that the population of London had been relying on assurances of a military defence and were left inadequate time to organize their own safe evacuation, though some must have escaped by boat. St Albans, like Colchester, was something of an imposed town and may have had a strong presence of non-British people, alongside the native *Catuvellauni*. Fear of what they might encounter in open countryside may have constrained many of them from early flight. Their Catuvellaunian townsfolk may even have turned on them, once the governor's column had retreated up Watling Street. For various reasons, then, the casualties in the three towns may have been high, perhaps over 30,000. Total Roman and provincial dead could thus have approached 40,000.

The tales of British atrocities serve a clear purpose in the Roman story of the rebellion, in that they justify the extreme severity with which the Romans dealt with the revolt's aftermath. Their value as historical truth is harder to judge. But there is no doubt that the revolt was an explosion of anti-Roman hatred and the rebels had no desire to take captives for profit or for use in bargaining later. A key characteristic of the revolt was the slaughter of men, women and children who were perceived to be aligned with Rome. It is certainly possible that some were horribly sacrificed during post-battle celebrations in the sacred groves of British gods, particularly if the druids had been active in stirring up anti-Roman feeling. There is an uncanny parallelism in our sources between the near contemporaneous carnage of Romans slaughtering British priests, men, women and children in sacred groves on Anglesey and the followers of Boudica sacrificing 'Romans' after the fall of Colchester or London. Vengeance was a clear sub-text on both sides of this revolt and the ending of the war was not straightforward. Paullinus set about re-subjugating the implicated areas by 'fire and sword' and this extended not only to the most hostile peoples, but also even to those who had simply wavered in their loyalty. We may imagine that this meant ex-tremely repressive measures, including summary executions, widespread arrests and enslavements. Just how extreme the Roman action was is suggested by the fact that, although resistance became more fragmented and ultimately futile, many of the British refused to surrender for fear of Roman 'mercy'. Famine quickly became an additional problem (and may have contributed to the total reported casualty figures). Tacitus blamed the Britons for failing to plant the usual crops, but Roman seizures of supplies will have exacerbated the situation. North Wales and Anglesey appear to have been relinquished in favour of concentrating the army once again in the south-east and east.

The ferocity of Roman vengeance created a serious rift between the military governor and the new financial procurator, Iulius Classicianus. The latter finally took the highly unusual step of petitioning the emperor to remove Paullinus on the grounds that his behaviour was prevent-ing an end to hostilities, presumably with a significant impact on Classicianus' area of competence, raising revenues from the province.

Classicianus was from northern Gaul and thus a representative of the provincial elite who were beginning to profit from the empire. Although many of his Gallic compatriots had been victims of the revolt, his perspective was evidently that the empire could not be ruled by force alone, but must involve its subjects in a more productive dialogue. On the other hand, it is unlikely that his complaints to Nero, which were investigated by an imperial freedman Polyclitus, did more than speed the replacement of Paullinus. The new governor Petronius Turpilianus was accused of slothful inactivity by Tacitus, but seems to have brought the revolt to a close and started the process of stabilizing the province once again.

There is no doubt that the Boudican revolt had an enormous impact on the population, on urban and rural settlements, on the economic bases of trade and agriculture. Rome's prestige was also gravely damaged, both by the initial defeats and by the loss of control shown in victory. Both Petronius Turpilianus and his successor Trebellius Maximus were given little credit by Tacitus for the fact that the province was gradually restored to a semblance of order. What mattered more to Tacitus was that there was no forward progress towards the conquest of the rest of Britain during the 60s.

Further conquests in Britain were not ruled out, but simply deferred. Britain was deemed to need a period of stabilization and there were also other military situations demanding the emperor's attention. *Legio XIV*, arguably the most battle-hardened of the British legions, was withdrawn for service elsewhere in the late 60s, though the outbreak of civil war forced a change in plan.

CIVIL WAR AND THE
FLAVIAN ADVANCE

When Nero committed suicide in 68, believing he had lost control of the empire after a revolt broke out in Gaul and Spain, he left no obvious heir and the resulting civil war affected practically every province of the empire. The succession of rival contenders in 69, the 'Year of Four Emperors' – Galba, Otho, Vitellius and Vespasian – tested and exposed the fickle loyalty of governors and garrisons in the military provinces. Proximity was a key factor in deciding who gained the British legions' adherence. When Otho had supplanted Galba at Rome and prepared to meet Vitellius, the governor of Germany who was marching on Rome, he incorporated in his forces *legio XIV Gemina*, which had been awaiting transit to the East. Meanwhile the other British legions were persuaded to side with Vitellius, after a serious rift had opened up between Trebellius Maximus, the governor, and at least one of his legionary legates, Roscius Coelius. The British legions were in a near-mutinous state, encouraged by their commanders; this was attributed at the time to their frustration at the lack of campaigning opportunities and to their thus being denied some customary financial rewards. Trebellius had run an 'easy-going administration' and according to Tacitus 'never put the army to the test'; from a military perspective this may have meant greater encouragement of the British populace and a reining in of the soldiery's power and exploitative behaviour. The stand-off culminated in the humiliating flight of Trebellius from his province. The legionary legates were temporarily allowed to continue the government of the province by Vitellius, but had to send him reinforcements of 8,000 legionaries (about half their rosters). After Otho's defeat, Vitellius sent Vettius Bolanus as the new governor, along with the *XIV Gemina* (who were not entirely trusted by him after their earlier allegiance for Otho). When Vespasian entered the contest, he sought out *legio XIV* in particular and may have appealed to the other British legions on the basis of his earlier service in the province as commander of the *II Augusta*. As the final conflict between Vitellius and Vespasian drew near, the former demanded further reinforcement from the auxiliary units in Britain, but Vettius Bolanus resisted this on the grounds that he had military problems of his own. Nonetheless, the British legionary vexillations claimed earlier were in the centre of Vitellius' battle lines when the supporters of Vespasian defeated him in northern Italy in 69, and they presumably took heavy casualties.

Meanwhile in Britain, military indiscipline continued to be a problem, but Vettius Bolanus did not confront it directly. There was also renewed trouble in the north, where, once again, Venutius the ex-consort of Queen Cartimandua invaded her territory with outside help, sparking a revolt of at least part of the *Brigantes* confederation. Roman auxiliary troops were sent to Cartimandua's aid, but despite some minor victories were obliged to concede the kingdom to Venutius and take Cartimandua and her supporters back to Roman territory. The Brigantian client kingdom was now effectively at an end, with the territory left in the hands of an anti-Roman ruler, Venutius.

The succession of Vespasian seems to have been welcomed by the *II Augusta* and *XIV Gemina*, but more cautiously by the other two legions, *IX Hispana* and *XX Valeria Victrix*. Vespasian took steps to rectify this situation and Britain was to emerge as one of the key theatres of military action during his reign. Vettius Bolanus was allowed to remain in post until 71, when Petillius Cerialis was sent to Britain directly after crushing a revolt in the Rhineland, bringing with him a newly raised legion, the *II Adiutrix*, to replace *legio XIV* which had now left Britain for good. Cerialis was a close kinsman of Vespasian and also had British credentials, having commanded *legio IX* at the time of the Boudican revolt. Another Flavian adherent, Iulius Agricola, had been sent in 70 to take over command of *legio XX*. Cerialis was clearly instructed to resolve the Brigantian question in a more decisive fashion. Indeed the sequence of Flavian governors in the 70s all seem to have been selected on the basis of their military experience and loyalty to the Flavian emperors and were allowed great opportunities for waging offensive warfare. We know little in detail of the campaigning, but there were apparently many battles, some bloody, across a three-year period and with the *IX* and *XX* legions given ample opportunity to demonstrate their loyalty to the Flavian dynasty in the vanguard of the action.

The events leading to the Roman incorporation of the Brigantian kingdom are naturally blamed on anti-Roman forces, but there was no attempt subsequently to reinstall Cartimandua. A prime target was perhaps the major *oppidum* at Stanwick, which was destroyed at about this time, with a final phase of defensive modification uncompleted. It is probable that the confederation soon fragmented into its many constituent sub-groups and that campaigning targeted these one after the other. We do not know the fate of Venutius or his supporters, but the implications of the line of marching camps leading across the Stainmore Pass to Carlisle are that resistance was systematically pursued to the north-west, with the establishment of a fort at Carlisle raising the possibility that Cerialis extended Roman campaigning into Scotland. The Roman advance presumably also utilized the main south to north lines of advance on both sides of the Pennines. Although the best farming lands of the *Brigantes* were concentrated in the Vale of York and north Humberside, there was mineral wealth in the Pennine valleys. Tacitus does not appear to have liked Cerialis and damns him with faint praise, so it is impossible to reconstruct the detail of his conquests, but on the basis that the *Brigantes* were, according to the same writer, the most populous people of Britain, their defeat within three years was a considerable achievement.

Vespasian also gave a mandate for conquest to Sextus Iulius Frontinus who succeeded Cerialis in 73 or 74, this time directed at the unresolved problem of the Welsh peoples. Once again he was a man with active campaign experience (in the Rhineland) and the final conquest of southern and central/northern Wales shows that a massive concentration of Roman force was achieved. The subjugation of the *Silures* was evidently swift and their western neighbours, the *Demetae*, were also incorporated. By the end of his governorship, central and northern Wales was under direct military control. Here again, Tacitus' shorthand account denies us the detail, but the territories of both the *Deceangli* and *Ordovices* were involved. Agricola arrived to take over as governor in 77 to find that a cavalry unit stationed in Ordovician territory had been destroyed, but he seems to have completed the task of subjugating north-west Wales in a single short campaigning season, culminating with his invasion of the island of Anglesey. This was evidently unplanned and the lack of available troop transports suggests that Frontinus had not accomplished the task earlier. His troops swam or forded the Menai Straits regardless and retook the island held briefly in 60.

This campaign was a distraction from what was plainly Agricola's brief from Vespasian, the conquest of northern Britain. The scale and the speed of Roman advances in these years imposed their own constraints. For both the subjugation of the *Brigantes* and Wales, it is probable that Rome had achieved a significant concentration of her forces in Britain, with two legions and vexillations from the two others and the larger part of the auxiliary units (say 30,000–35,000 men in total). The problem was how to sustain this sort of campaign force for further expansion while at the same time securing pacification of the territory just subjugated. Although Cerialis brought significant legionary and auxiliary additions, there were no subsequent reinforcements of the provincial army in this phase, and indeed by the early 80s the opposite trend applied, as troops were withdrawn for wars in Germany and on the Danube. Two consequences followed from this. First, it is probable that the further Agricola and his army penetrated into Scotland, the smaller the actual force available to him will have been. The second point is that in order to maintain the largest number of active troops, the nature of the Roman subjugation of Wales and northern England may have been particularly brutal in seeking to neutralize opposition. When Tacitus put the famous words 'They make a desolation and they call it peace' into the mouth of the Caledonian chieftain Calgacus, he was using a literary device, not reporting actual speech. However, the sentiment may have been especially appropriate in the context of the Flavian advance. This was probably Roman imperialism at its fiercest and most remorseless.

The events of the campaigns of Agricola in northern Britain form the centrepiece of Tacitus' biography of his father-in-law. In his second season, there was consolidation of the conquest of northern England or southern Scotland. The third season saw a major push forward, right across Lowland Scotland as far as the Tay. The fourth season involved territorial consolidation, with a series of forts erected on the Forth–Clyde isthmus and on the approach roads from the south. The fifth season involved extending control in south-west Scotland, with a combined seaborne and land assault, ending with Agricola looking out across the sea towards Ireland and evidently recommending its invasion to the emperor. There was a change of policy in the sixth season, with the advance north of the Forth–Clyde line recommenced, with joint land and naval operations up the eastern flank of the Highland line. Agricola appears to have split his forces into several battle groups, but these may have been kept fairly closely grouped, since a night attack on the camp of *legio IX* was beaten off by the rest of the army coming to the rescue. In the seventh and final season, a further deliberate advance was made, leading to a decisive battle at *Mons Graupius*, somewhere near the northern limits of Britain. There is a clear line of marching camps, representing several phases of campaigns in Scotland, up Strathmore and into the Moray Firth area. Some of these with a distinctive form of gate (the so-called Stracathro type) are certainly Flavian, while others at 40 ha (100 acres) and larger conceivably fall outside the scale of camp required by Agricola. The largest Stracathro-type camp is of *c.*25 ha (60 acres) and this may have been adequate to accommodate his combined forces. There are also quite a few camps of *c.*12 ha (30 acres) known on the line of march and these may well represent the advance of Agricola with his army in two columns.

One element of the debate has been the precise dating of these events, with the current consensus favouring 77–83 for Agricola's governorship, rather than 78–84. The change may seem minor, but because both Vespasian and his son Titus died during this period, the question of who was deciding policy in Rome is actually critical. For a variety of reasons, the earlier dating works much better, with the policy changes and pauses in the advance reflecting the instructions of first Titus and then his brother Domitian. In this scheme, it was Titus who ordered a more cautious approach after the dramatic advance to the Tay, and Domitian who rejected Agricola's suggestion that Ireland was worth conquering and ordered him to advance again north of the Forth–Clyde line. Tacitus loathed Domitian and it is unsurprising that his role in determining policy in Britain was not acknowledged explicitly. The assignment of the felling-date of timber used in a major remodelling of the fort at Carlisle to the winter of 83–84 now offers strong additional support to the earlier dating of Agricola's governorship, as it is consistent with the start of changes in garrison deployment once the victory had been won.

A second point of contention is where exactly the battle of *Mons Graupius* took place, with the most recent assessments tending to favour a location close to or even beyond the Moray Firth. Somewhere near Inverness is highly probable given the decisions of two later High-land forces to stand and fight invading armies in that area (in 1201 and 1746). Once Inverness is reached, the Highland line is turned and defending forces are liable to fragment. At the battle of *Mons Graupius*, Agricola's army apparently faced a Caledonian force of 30,000, while he had 13,000 auxiliary troops and an unspecified number of legionaries (but probably no more than 10,000–12,000). Such was Roman confi-dence in the outcome of a pitched battle, that he put his auxiliary troops in the front line and held his legionaries in reserve. British casualties were put at 10,000, Roman losses a mere 360 men ('and few of note', crowed Tacitus). After the battle, Agricola dispatched his fleet round the far northern tip of Britain to confirm its circumnavigability and marched slowly back to his winter quarters, taking hostages on the way.

The account of these campaigns by Tacitus was, of course, un-ashamedly partisan. Agricola was depicted throughout as the model general, leading from the front in battle, being everywhere at once on the line of march, looking to the security of his troops and selecting the best camp sites, and so on. There is surprisingly little detail about his British opponents and much of what we are told of the British leader Calgacus looks like stereotypical invention. However, it is clear that Agricola did win for Domitian an impressive victory in the very far north of Britain and that this marked the culmination not only of the Flavian campaigning, but also of the entire process of conquest since 43. Tacitus claimed that Britain was at this moment conquered, but that this was almost at once let slip. Indeed it is clear from the archaeological evidence that the sequel to the battle, under Agricola's anonymous successor, was the creation of garrison points far into Scotland, but that this system was abandoned within three or four years.

THE AFTERMATH OF CONQUEST

When Tacitus announced that *Britannia* had been captured he was probably not exaggerating the significance of the moment. After *Mons Graupius*, the Romans had the opportunity to impose a military stranglehold on the Highlands, had events elsewhere not necessitated troop withdrawals and a strategic rethink of the military disposition in northern Britain. Failure to capitalize fully on the victory of Agricola was to necessitate the creation of a frontier and the exclusion of part of the island from direct Roman control. Because of the partial nature of the conquest, warfare between Rome and Free *Britannia* was a periodic occurrence thereafter (Table 3).

This must be considered very much a minimal listing of military unrest in Britain, given the lacunose state of Roman historical sources from the second century onwards. As an example of this, the problems in Hadrian's reign are normally confined by scholars to the period 117–20, followed by Hadrian's visit in 122 and the start of construction of Hadrian's Wall. A tombstone of a centurion from *Vindolanda* killed in battle (*interfectus in bello*) may well relate to this war, and fragments of a Roman monument found at Jarrow evidently mention the dispersal of the enemy, the recovery of the province and the subsequent erection of the mural barrier. There are also two inscriptions relating to unit commanders sent to Britain as part of a military campaign (*expeditio Britannica*) at some point in Hadrian's reign, one of whom led a force of 3,000 men drawn from the *VII Gemina*, *VIII Augusta* and *XXII*

Table 3. Wars and revolts, 84–211.

DATE	PEOPLE	EVENTS	SOURCES
117–19	Britanni (northern Britain?)	Source implies both rebellion within province and trouble with 'barbarian' neighbours. Establishment of Hadrian's Wall follows after his visit in 122	HA Hadrian 5, 11
128–30	Britanni	References to an expeditio Britannica and to serious losses incurred in Britain under Hadrian may suit a date in late 120s better than the attested unrest in 117	ILS 2726; 2735; Fronto, de Bello Parthico 2
139–42	Britanni (Lowland Scotland)	Advance from Hadrian's Wall into Lowland Scotland and Strathmore. Establishment of Antonine Wall	HA Antoninus Pius 5
138–61	Brigantes?	Doubtful reference to trouble with Brigantes and reduction of their territory	Pausanias, Description of Greece 7.43
163– mid-170s	Britanni	Threat of war necessitated dispatch of senior general and additional troops	HA Marcus Antoninus 8, 22
181–84	Peoples beyond wall	Major incursion across wall (but which one?) and serious defeat inflicted before Ulpius Marcellus won victories	Dio (Epitome) 72.8; RIC 437, 440, 451
197– 207	Maeatae and Caledonii	Disturbances affecting British frontier – large payouts to peoples in Scotland	Dio (Epitome) 75.5
208–11	Maeatae and Caledonii	Full revolt provides pretext for Severan campaigns into Scotland	Herodian 3.14–15; Dio (Epitome) 76.13, 15, 77.1

Primigenia legions. These men appear to have been replacements to make up losses in the British legions and this chimes with a reference in Fronto to serious casualties inflicted by the Britons in Hadrian's reign. However, a re-evaluation of the career paths of the two unit commanders has cast doubt on whether they could really have been in the province as early as 117. A date in the late 120s might suit better, suggesting a second period of unrest, and the posting to Britain of Hadrian's best general, Iulius Severus, c.130 may also fit with this – though he was swiftly withdrawn to deal with another serious revolt that had broken out in *Iudaea* in 132.

The limits of our understanding are also well illustrated by inscriptions recording military actions in the wall zone. Q. Calpurnius Concessinius, a cavalry prefect, erected an altar celebrating his slaughter of a war band of the *Corionototae*, an otherwise unknown native group – unless it represented an attempt to Latinize the British term *Cruithentuath*, later applied to the Picts. The text appears similar to a dedication at Carlisle (by a man presumed to be commander of the *ala Augusta*) that recorded a defeat inflicted on another British war band, or another altar from south of the Solway ford recording successful operations beyond the wall ('*ob res trans vallum prospere gestas*') under the command of a legate of *legio VI*. Further evidence of second-century campaigning is provided by the Roman siege works at Burnswark, which seem more consistent with an actual assault than with an exercise in artillery prac- tice. What is unclear is whether all these incidents were part of larger wars, or isolated moments of unrest. However, in each case, a context after the abandonment of the Antonine Wall seems probable, perhaps in relation to the attested warfare in the reign of Commodus.

The advance into Lowland Scotland early in the reign of Antoninus Pius seems to have been a premeditated expansionist move, involving the abandonment of the recently completed and costly wall of Hadrian and the subsequent erection of the Antonine Wall on the Forth–Clyde isthmus. Lollius Urbicus, the governor put in charge, was actively build- ing at Corbridge in 138–40, with operations evidently concluded in 142 and victory heralded by coin issues of early 143. Roman sources speak of Pius having 'conquered the Britons', but the location of the new frontier suggests that this was a relative success. Although military operations quite certainly extended north of the Forth–Clyde line, the victory was not so overwhelming as to allow a revisiting of Flavian plans for total conquest. The suspicion remains that this war was fought largely for opportunistic reasons, to give Antoninus Pius much-needed military prestige in the early years of his reign.

There have been long-running debates about the Antonine occupation of Scotland and the circumstances that led to withdrawal back to Had- rian's Wall by the 160s at the latest. A revolt in Brigantian territory has often been adduced, on slight evidence, for the mid-150s. The reference in Pausanias to the *Brigantes* being deprived of the Genounian territory could apply to another people called *Brigantii* in *Raetia* (with neighbours called the *Genauni*). There are coin issues from the mid-150s depicting a subdued *Britannia*, but the significance is unclear and if there had been trouble it could have been in Scotland just as well as northern England. More plausibly, the reasons for withdrawal were again bound up with Continental events, with a build-up of trouble on the Rhine frontier necessitating troop transfers from other provinces, including Britain, from the mid-150s. In any event, the final abandonment of the Antonine Wall appears to have been orderly and systematic.

There is a further reference to troubled conditions in Britain in the 160s, but the major military theatres in this period were in the East (161–66) and on the Danube frontier (167–80). The fact that Aurelius sent 5,500 Sarmatian cavalry, levied from one of the most dangerous trans-Danubian peoples, to Britain in the mid-170s could indicate a continuing military problem in the province, or it could simply reflect a need to place these potentially reluctant soldiers as far from their homes as possible. In any case, not all of these troops may have remained in Britain after basic training, as only one auxiliary unit of Sarmatians is specifically attested.

It is certain that there was a major military breakdown in Britain in the early 180s. According to Dio, the British war was the greatest of the early part of Commodus' reign, 'for the tribes in the island crossed the wall that separated them from the Roman army and did a great amount of damage, even cutting down a general together with his troops'. The 'wall' is often assumed to be Hadrian's Wall (and there is some contemporary damage at Haltonchesters, Rudchester and Corbridge), but it is clear that Roman outpost forts extended right up through Lowland Scotland at this date and that the Antonine Wall, though no longer garrisoned, could have functioned as a demarcation line in agreements with the *Caledonii* and *Maeatae*. The identity of the general who died is uncertain, but he was either the provincial governor or a legionary legate – indicating a very serious reverse. Commodus dealt with the crisis by 'sending Ulpius Marcellus against them'. Since Ulpius Marcellus was certainly governor of Britain in 178, he was either sent back to Britain *c.*184 after the death of his successor, or he was still there on his first tour of duty and served an extended term in avenging the death of one of his legionary legates. In either case, he was given a brief to launch major punitive action. Coins of 184–85 attest victories in Britain, from campaigning that probably extended well beyond Lowland Scotland.

Ulpius Marcellus was evidently a strong disciplinarian and his governorship seems to have heralded another period of unrest in the army in Britain, culminating in their support for the governor, Clodius Albinus, when he made a bid for the purple in the civil war of 193–97. The participation of troops from the garrison on the losing side in the civil war has conventionally been seen as the prelude to further native unrest in Britain. However, the evidence for a military crisis *c.*197 is now viewed as dubious, though there were some rumblings in the north. The first governor appointed by Septimius Severus, Virius Lupus, was evidently obliged to buy peace with the *Maeatae* for a large sum, and they were evidently in collusion with the *Caledonii* and in breach of treaty arrangements. By *c.*207 the situation had deteriorated further and the governor Alfenus Seneccio requested additional troops to deal with attacks. He got an imperial expedition instead, led by Septimius Severus himself and accompanied by both his sons, whom he was evidently anxious to remove from the dissolute lifestyle of the court at Rome.

The Severan campaigns of 208–11 represented the largest force sent against the peoples north of the Forth–Clyde isthmus. In addition to the British garrison, Severus also brought with him the Praetorian Guard and substantial contingents from the Continental armies. His younger son, Geta, was left in the civil province, with a brief to administer justice and to continue the government of the rest of the empire, aided by a council of the emperor's advisers. The elder son, Caracalla, accompanied Severus on the campaigns, returning each year to winter quarters at York. The huge expeditionary force is associated with some exceptionally large marching camps in Lowland Scotland and several groups north of the Forth–Clyde isthmus. The campaigns were presented in the sources as disappointing, with frequent skirmishes but no major pitched battles and considerable Roman losses to ambushes. The initial results may have been more substantial, with the negativity of our sources due to the subsequent disintegration of the Severan arrangements in northern Britain. Preparations for the first campaign had been elaborate and the army had advanced with deliberate slowness, advertising its power to shock and awe. British envoys had sued for peace even before the army reached Scotland, but had been rebuffed. Severus had a point to make and, though ill with gout and carried everywhere by litter, he intended to make it in person. The camps confirm a long slow advance up the east side of the Highland line to the Moray Firth at least. A victory was proclaimed, associated with the annexation of a large territory, probably focused on the lands of the *Maeatae* in Fife and Tayside. The construction of a legionary base at Carpow on the Tay may have been the centrepiece of the intended occupation of the territory of the *Maeatae*.

There was soon renewed trouble, when the *Maeatae* rebelled against their territorial incorporation. Severus responded with attempted extermination. In a second campaigning season, entrusted to Caracalla because of the emperor's increasing infirmity, the focus appears to have been more exclusively on the territory of the *Maeatae*, if a series of 25-hectare (63-acre) camps belong in this phase. The explicit instruction of Severus to his troops was to kill everyone, even the baby in its mother's womb. One result of this extreme 'war on terror' was that the *Caledonii* rejoined the war. In the winter of 210–11 Severus was preparing to take the field again himself, when he died on 4 February 211 at York. In the aftermath of the death of Severus, the bigger issue of the dynastic succession overshadowed the Scottish conquest. The sources move quickly from the death of Severus to the murder of Geta by Caracalla after their return to Rome and the seizure of sole power by the latter. It is quite obvious that Caracalla was anxious to return to Rome to secure his position there, but that does not mean that the British war was simply abandoned and with it the Severan plan for reoccupying part of Scotland. There had clearly been the intention for further campaigning in 211 and coins of that year indeed record a victory in Britain. The more likely scenario is that Caracalla entrusted a further campaign in 211 to one of his legates and initially at least continued with the plan to annex the territory of the *Maeatae* (and by implication Lowland Scotland as well). That would suggest that the campaigns in 210–11 had achieved a result of sorts.

The Roman army was not simply active against Britons; it was also involved in a number of civil wars and mutinous acts (Table 4). Acts of insubordination on the part of the soldiery are significant in that they show that the Roman army was not a machine, but a living, breathing and sometimes defective community. The invasion force in 43 initially refused to embark. On three occasions, resentment spilled over into violence against governors or other high officials. Trebellius Maximus was forced to leave the province in 69, and the future emperor Pertinax,

Table 4. Civil wars and secession, late first to late second century.

DATE	EMPEROR/PRETENDER	EVENTS	SOURCE
69–70	Vitellius	British legions mutinous towards governor Trebellius Maximus, but otherwise play only minor role in events	Tacitus, *Histories* 1.59–60
185–92	Commodus	Mutiny among British legions leads to downfall of praetorian prefect Perennis, but mutinous attitudes continue to death of Commodus	Dio (Epitome) 72.9; HA *Pertinax* 3.5–10
193–97	Clodius Albinus, Septimius Severus	Following assassination of Commodus (192) and Pertinax (193), Albinus (governor of Britain) challenges Septimius Severus. British legions involved in battle of Lyon in 197, where Albinus defeated.	Dio (Epitome) 73.15, 75.6–7; Herodian 2.15, 3.5; HA *Severus* 10.1–2

a disciplinarian governor in the 180s, was wounded in a mutinous attack by his troops. He had been sent to Britain specifically to restore discipline after the British army had sent a deputation of 1,500 men to Rome in 185 to complain about the actions of the praetorian prefect, Perennis. Commodus was persuaded by the British troops that Perennis was plotting against him and allowed Perennis and his immediate family to be purged. But he was also clearly concerned about the precedent set by the armed march on Rome of even a relatively small provincial force. Emperors had to listen carefully to the soldiery, but they also had to attempt to control them and the interests of the ruling (or would-be next) emperor did not always coincide with those of the provincial garrisons. Civil wars in 68–70 and 193–97 were simply the prelude to the period of endemic usurpers in the mid-third century.

The remoteness of Britain meant that the attitudes of British troops were not as influential in deciding the outcome of these power struggles as those of some other military provinces, and some such conflicts were settled before British troops were summoned. Nevertheless, it was in the nature of the Roman empire that troops were periodically pulled out of frontier provinces to contest the imperial throne. The British garrison will certainly have been seriously affected when Clodius Albinus lost to Septimius Severus at the battle of Lyon in 197 that decided the civil war. One corollary of these power struggles was the sub-division of provinces to limit the size of army available to individual commanders in the provinces. By 213 Britain was split into two provinces: *Britannia Superior* with its capital at London and two legions under the control of its consular governor, and *Britannia Inferior* with its capital at York and with the legionary legate of the *VI Victrix* now also praetorian governor.

Warfare was thus a significant part of Britain's history under Roman rule, and while it was not an ever-present factor in people's lives, it was a potential occurrence long after the initial conquest phase. The size of the provincial army could to some extent act as a deterrent against attack and reduce the impact of raiding by land or sea, but ultimately Britain was a military outpost of the empire.

The non-completion of the Roman conquest of Britain is a conundrum, especially as the creation of a frontier within northern Britain failed to provide full security. Surely Rome should have had the military strength to overcome the resistance of the northern Britons and in doing so to have opened the way for progressive reduction in the British garrison (as had happened in Spain, where the resistance of the mountain peoples had been similarly obdurate)? There are several possible explanations. Expansionist warfare in Britain was always an imperial 'project', requiring the direct input or thorough support of the emperor. The one moment when the complete occupation of insular Britain was within reach in the early 80s was undone because of military problems in other provinces. After the Flavian period, there were two main attempts to seek a larger territorial solution, under Antoninus Pius and the Severans, both relatively short-lived before the emperor's attention was taken elsewhere, leading to withdrawal to the line of Hadrian's Wall. The distances involved in the conquest and garrisoning of Scotland were also significant; it would have taken an army about forty days uninterrupted marching to reach Caithness from York. Successive campaigns revealed the difficulty of terrain, or local resistance and the relative lack of booty to be had from such wars. Imperial interest in this sort of conquest will have waned.

A second factor concerned resources and manpower on both sides of the frontier. It is clear that Scotland was more densely populated in the late Iron Age than once believed and would have required a large initial garrison. At key moments, Rome did not have the military manpower in Britain to spare for that and, in the long term, the army had a demanding role to play in internal security and administration of occupied Britain. Logistical inertia was another important factor in fixing the garrison pattern in northern Britain. The occupation of northern Scotland would have required maintenance of a string of garrisons along a single and vulnerable main road north of the Forth. Unlike in Wales and the Pennines, where networks of roads criss-crossing the mountainous landscape allowed garrison posts to be mutually self-supporting, Scotland was a dangerous blind alley. The generally low material wealth of the peoples of Scotland, the comparative lack of natural resources and doubts about the productive capacity of their lands to support both a substantial garrison and the local population were other disincentives to annexation.

5

Britannia Perdomita

The Garrisoning of the Provinces

The ultimate function of the army may have been to wage war, but its longer-term and continuing roles were to protect the emperor and to serve as an army of occupation in the provinces. Britain once conquered (*Britannia perdomita*) required garrisoning. Not all Roman experts like the term 'garrison', in that it seems to imply a primarily defensive aspect to military deployment. Here, it is used in a different sense to cover the way Rome utilized her army as an instrument of domination. Britain contains one of the largest bodies of evidence anywhere in the empire relating to the way Rome followed up conquest with military occupation.

The Roman empire imposed a mixture of imperial and self-rule institutions on its provinces. The balance between these elements of oppression and opportunity varied between provinces and even within them. There has been a tendency in Romano-British studies to view the benefits of occupation as outweighing the drawbacks. The reasons for this benign vision are bound up with the history of later empires – the British included – where the Roman army has been much admired for its organization and capability. At times there is a tendency to lose sight of the fact that this was an army of occupation and later a tool of state control – even locally recruited soldiers had a different sort of identity from other local groups.

The army played an important role in the administration of the province in all periods. This was especially profound in the first century before the establishment of widespread structures of civil governance in southern Britain. However, direct supervision of indigenous communities was much more protracted in northern and western Britain, where large regions never seem to have been released to the normal civil form of self-government based on towns. The attestation of forms of regional authority exercised by serving soldiers (*centurio regionarius* or *praepositus regionis*) is important evidence in this regard. Nor should we see any contradiction in this relationship between civil and military government. The provincial governor in the first and second centuries was both the pre-eminent military commander in Britain and the main civil administrator. Indeed, close examination of the mechanics of provincial government in the Roman empire illustrates the major contribution of military personnel. Governors brought few staff from Rome, and instead placed heavy reliance on troops seconded from the army. These troops were given titles (and in some cases higher pay) in relation to special duties on the governor's staff (*officium consularis*). Senior among these were the *cornicularii*, who appear to have had overall control of the running of the *officium*; *commentarii* involved with record-keeping; *beneficiarii* who fulfilled a wide range of functions, often running outposts (*stationes*) of the governor's office or specific operations; *speculatores* who were couriers and executioners; *frumentarii* who, over time, developed a specialized role as spies. In addition there were other classes of seconded soldiers serving as grooms (*stratores*), interpreters and bodyguards (*singulares*). The numbers are not exactly attested, but in a province like Britain, with a substantial military garrison, it has been estimated that the main body of the *officium* will have drawn c.300 higher-rank soldiers from the legions, plus perhaps a further 1,800 from the auxiliary units to serve in guard units and as grooms for the governor and his chief subordinates. The implications of this are that at any time there may have been over 2,000 soldiers operating in the civil zone of the province.

Troops thus continued to be a visible and active presence in southern Britain even when civil government was well established there. The governor had troops seconded to him in London and some would accompany him on his assize tours; the procurator almost certainly also had some troops assigned to him; Roman markets were often placed under supervision and small numbers of soldiers might be assigned to such duties; there were detachments of the Roman fleet in the Channel ports (with main bases at Boulogne and Dover) and customs dues were overseen there; messengers carrying military communications with the governor in London passed along the main roads using the public posting stations; larger bodies of troops on the move would frequently pass through the civil zone and be billeted on urban communities; army supply specialists were a constant presence and were able to requisition transport within set limits; army recruiters will have also been regularly seen; some extractive industry may have had troops in attendance; consignments of metals and specie will have been moved under military escort. The soldiers with the *officium* had specific responsibility for aspects of provincial record keeping, tax collection, census taking, land survey, and no doubt liaised closely with local civil authorities on these matters. In addition, the administration of areas of the province that retained a garrison was most probably carried out directly by military officers and their staff.

One of the reasons why the army was well suited to the needs of provincial government was that it was a largely literate organization that operated in a well-regulated manner. The dossier of documents from the Roman fort at *Vindolanda*, for instance, illustrates the complexity and scale of military bureaucracy. Written on wooden tablets, the vast proportion of the original documents of the Roman army administrators in Britain has perished. The nature and quantities of the documents from *Vindolanda* suggest that if, as seems entirely plausible, the pattern was replicated across all contemporary forts and government *stationes*, then the Roman bureaucracy in Britain was generating millions of documents each decade. There are clear indications that some at least of this material was well archived in retrievable files. Provincial government in *Britannia* was not characterized simply by *ad hoc* decisions and a laissez-faire attitude. The province was placed under a bureaucratic regime that was designed to administer and to exploit the province with reasonable efficiency by the standards of pre-industrial societies.

The precise size of the garrison in Britain at any particular time is unknown, but the combined evidence of inscriptions, the archaeological traces of numerous fortresses and forts and documents such as the *Notitia Dignitatum* indicate a large and sustained presence. There are also large gaps in our evidence, especially for the early conquest period, when epigraphic records are least helpful. Even the composition of the invasion army is uncertain, though it is generally assumed to have involved about 40,000 troops. The first-century army comprised troops of different types, in two main categories: legionaries (who were Roman citizens, at that time still mainly from Italy) and auxiliaries (cavalry and infantry) levied from non-citizen provincials. The initial legions were *II Augusta*, *XIV Gemina* (*Martia Victrix* after 61), and *XX* (*Valeria Victrix* after 61) redeployed from Lower Germany, and the *IX Hispana* from Pannonia in the Danube region. A chief centurion of the *VIII Augusta* decorated in Britain suggests that elements of that legion may also have participated. There will have been a roughly equal number of auxiliary troops, including units of Batavians (probably the '*Celtoi*', who swam across rivers on two occasions in the initial campaigns), but there are only a few certain identifications.

For long periods in the first century there were four legions of *c.*5,500 men and from the later first century until the fourth century the normal garrison was three legions (though the legions became much reduced in size in the later empire as new-style units emerged as the elite forces). In addition there was a large component of auxiliary units: *alae* (dedicated cavalry units), *cohortes equitatae* (mixed infantry and cavalry units) and *cohortes* (infantry). These units were normally *quingenaria*, of 480 men (600 for a mixed unit), or (more rarely) *milliaria*, comprising 800 men (1,040 for a mixed unit). The overall size of the garrison (on paper at least) may have grown from *c.*40,000 to 55,000 at its maximum in the mid-second century. This was an unusual concentration of forces.

Six legions are attested as having served at some point in Britain (*II Adiutrix* and *VI Victrix* in addition to the initial four), though vexillations of other units may have been sent for short-term missions. No fewer than twenty-one *alae* are known from Britain, including one of only a handful of *alae milliariae* in the empire, over seventy-five *cohortes* and at least twelve *numeri* and *cunei* (less regular auxiliary formations of the mid- to late second century and after). By way of comparison, units attested in *Africa/Numidia* (a far larger province) include two legions (one only briefly deployed there), four *alae*, thirteen *cohortes* and two *numeri*. Flexibility was a key element of Roman military dispositions and we now know that troops were moved around a great deal more than was once believed, especially in the first and early second centuries. A single unit might also be split between two or more forts, as well as providing troops for outpost duty in a range of intervening installations. Forts were normally built to accommodate the total manpower of a unit, but that does not mean that the full complement was necessarily in garrison for much of the time.

The origin of troops serving in Britain was overall very diverse, but was often influenced by Rome's tendency to recruit units from newly subjected people. Britain was a conveniently distant and isolated area to which to dispatch people whose pro-Roman sympathies were still in their formative stages. The tale of the *cohors Usiporum* is instructive. This unit was raised in 82 by a levy of the German people of the *Usipi*, and sent to Britain to join Agricola's army in the final push against the *Caledonii*. While undergoing drill instruction somewhere on the coast of north-west Britain, they rebelled, killing the centurion and other soldiers placed in charge of them, then seized three small warships. The pilots were killed or escaped, so the mutineers perilously sailed north alone, eventually circumnavigating the northern tip of Britain and sailing into the North Sea. There, after suffering great deprivations, they were shipwrecked on the Frisian coast and the survivors taken into slavery among the *Frisii*. This tale marks a signal failure of the Roman policy of incorporating defeated enemies into her army as swiftly as possible, and of then exploiting the manpower in fresh campaigns in other areas. But there were plenty of more successful examples – perhaps most notably the large number of units (re-)created in the Rhineland in the early 70s, following the suppression of the Batavian revolt by Cerialis. These 'new' units amalgamated elements of earlier auxiliary units disbanded as a result of their conduct during the revolt. Cerialis took a large number of these units from the Rhineland with him to Britain and put them to practical use immediately in the major wars that his governorship initiated. The four cohorts of Batavians and two of Tungrians were also at the heart of the action of Agricola's campaigns, and several are mentioned in the *Vindolanda* writing tablets at the end of the century.

THE CHANGING NATURE OF MILITARY DISPOSITIONS

Military deployments changed in character and focus over time (Fig. 5). There are gaps in the surviving evidence, but the sample of data available is broadly indicative. The types of forts occupied by the Roman army units were designed with regard to the category of troops. The legions were generally brigaded in large fortresses of *c.*20 ha (50 acres), while the auxiliary units were more commonly housed in forts of 1–2 ha (2.5–5 acres). Especially in the initial stages of the British conquest there is

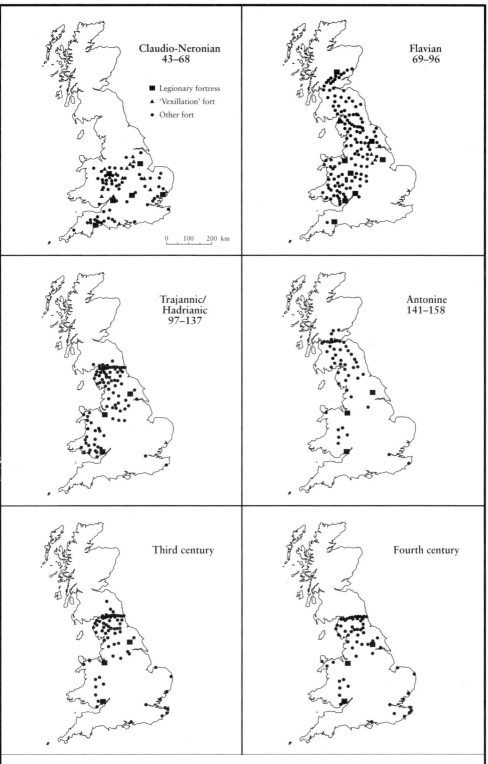

Figure 5. *Changing garrison patterns in Britain under Roman military occupation (not all forts in each phase were occupied contemporaneously)*

Within the figure (map legend and labels):

Claudio-Neronian
43–68

■ Legionary fortress
▲ 'Vexillation' fort
● Other fort

0   100   200 km

Flavian
69–96

Trajannic/
Hadrianic
97–137

Antonine
141–158

Third century

Fourth century

evidence for an intermediate size of site, often referred to as 'vexillation fortresses', of c.10 ha (25 acres) and in which it is thought battle-group detatchments of legionaries and auxiliaries may have been accommodated. There are over 250 known locations with fortresses or forts in Britain and many of these comprised sequences of rebuildings to different specifications at the same site. The cumulative total of forts constructed was thus probably in excess of 1,000, providing striking evidence of the scale of Roman military operations in Britain.

The Claudio-Neronian period (43–68) is notable for the relative paucity of forts in the south-east of Britain, the initial focus of the invasion. This pattern surely reflects a different approach to garrisoning in the early period. Initial troop deployments seem to have commonly involved mixed battle groups, comprising either both legionaries and auxiliaries, vexillations of legionaries alone or groupings of several auxiliary units brigaded in single fortresses of about half the size of normal legionary bases. Some of these larger bases served as winter quarters, others were advanced summer bases. This preference for keeping troops in battle groups of 2,000–3,000 men and their geographical distribution is a clear mark of intent that the Roman conquest was never intended to stop at the limits of the eastern kingdom. As Dio commented, after the completion of Claudius' campaign in 43, 'He disarmed the Britons and handed them over to Plautius, whom he authorized to subjugate the remaining areas.' The deployment was as much about the need to extend the conquest into additional areas as it was about securing the pacification of the territory of the eastern kingdom. The relative balance between fortresses and smaller forts was certainly very different in this phase. The locations of the forts and fortresses in the initial phase observe one of several requirements: proximity to the coast/navigable rivers or to roads (regional logistics); proximity to productive land (local supply); direct supervision of major late Iron Age settlements (tactical positioning); positions astride the major lines of advance (strategic deployment); proximity to limits of territories, so as to isolate peoples from each other and to facilitate simultaneous supervision of several groups (strategic deployment).

There was no attempt in this early stage to establish a blanket garrison pattern across the country and no linear frontier. Attempts in the modern literature to trace a frontier along the Fosse Way connecting Lincoln and Exeter are seriously flawed and there is no evidence to suggest that

Rome ever intended to limit her expansion in Britain at this point. Conversely, the mineral wealth of Wales and the Pennines provided a significant spur for expansion beyond the Trent and Severn and, while the sources imply that Roman territory was often subject to unprovoked attacks by the *Silures* for example, the physical deployment of Roman battle groups suggests rather that offensive pressure was applied by the massing of troops at the head of lines of advance. Where larger numbers of smaller forts start to appear in the pre-Flavian period – as in Devon, for instance – these were perhaps areas where pacification was prolonged and strongly contested.

Only from the Flavian period do we see a more general policy of spreading the garrison thinly in occupied territory, though there are continuing debates about the speed with which such networks of forts were constructed behind the advance of Roman troops. In Wales and the Pennines, new tactical deployments were devised to achieve the pacification and control of highland zones. In the aftermath of *Mons Graupius*, it is clear that Agricola's unknown successor initiated similar deployments in Scotland, but the scheme was abandoned within a few years. From the early second century there was an increasing concentration of troops in northern Britain, to be soon formalized as the Hadrian's Wall frontier. While garrisons were thinned out in other regions, by and large areas that had a military garrison at the start of the second century maintained some military presence thereafter. With the exception of a few years under Septimius Severus, when a return into northern Scotland appears to have been seriously considered, the basic shape of Roman troop deployments in northern and western Britain was much the same in the third century as in the second. The main difference after this time was a shift in emphasis towards coastal defence, not only along the Irish and North Sea coasts, but also on the Channel coast. The so-called Saxon Shore forts were established over a considerable period of the third and fourth centuries, but eventually represented a separate military command in Britain.

Some elements of the deployment were clearly linked to the exploitation of natural resources, as exemplified by the establishment of forts in mining areas (Charterhouse, Pumpsaint, Brompton, Brough-on-Noe, Whitley Castle) or at notable salt springs or salt mines (Droitwich, Middlewich, Northwich, Whitchurch). More detailed investigation of forts and associated settlements in other areas of natural resources could establish further cases. One interesting instance is the Roman road driven across Wheeldale Moor to the north of Malton in the Vale of Pickering. The rationale for this road and the two forts that sit at the northern and southern edges of the moor at Lease Rigg and Cawthorn has never been clear, but it is worth noting that the road connects the two major iron sources in the North York Moors in Eskdale and Rosedale (though to date no firm evidence of Roman exploitation has been found), and if extended north-east it would descend to Whitby, main source of British jet and one of the best natural harbours north of York. The Lake District is a similarly intriguing case of a substantial garrison being put into an area of relatively low population, but high mineral potential. More research at the fort sites there could determine whether mineral exploitation was a factor in the deployment.

Regional differences in garrison patterns perhaps reflect nuanced approaches on the part of Rome to her provincial subjects as well as varying levels of resistance. The location and longevity of garrisons within a particular region may also indicate both Rome's tactical approach and the relative success of pacification. The following section explores the regional character of military deployments, relating them where possible to British peoples mentioned in the sources. Dating at many sites is imprecise and this account will provide a broad outline, rather than attempt to reconstruct successive phases in minute detail.

South-east and south-west Britain

Out of the eastern kingdom Rome recognized two main peoples: the *Trinovantes* centred on Essex and parts of Suffolk and Cambridgeshire and the *Catuvellauni* of Buckinghamshire, Bedfordshire and Hertfordshire. The Roman conquest appears to have affected the two parts of the territory differently (Fig. 6).

In the Trinovantian area, one of the key early dispositions was the establishment of a legionary fortress at Colchester within the heart of the *oppidum*, with a possibly contemporary auxiliary fort nearby. The impact of the legionary force will have been highly significant – in numerical terms, a legion represented the equivalent of up to ten auxiliary units. In addition, there were several other forts, a vexillation fortress and a probable naval supply base in the region. This was not a blanket occupation of the territory, but rather focused on establishing control

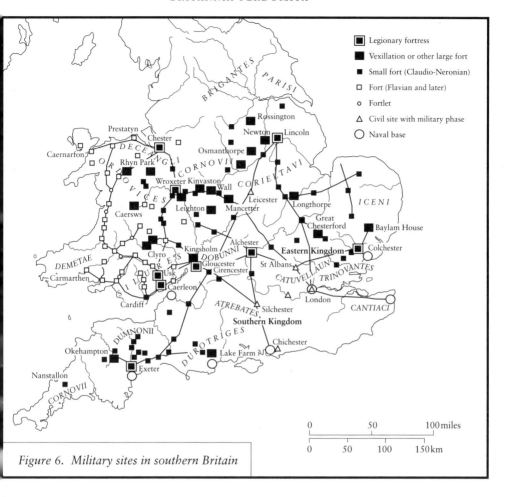

Figure 6. Military sites in southern Britain

at the key central site, supplemented by a few large bases around the periphery of the territory, where troops could influence affairs in neighbouring districts as well. The foundation of a colony in succession to the fortress at Colchester *c.*49 permanently removed territory from native British control, further indication of a relatively harsh approach to the *Trinovantes*.

The Catuvellaunian territory appears to have been much less supervised, especially now that a long-argued-for military fort at St Albans is being reinterpreted as a civil feature relating to the early town. The Folly Lane burial raises the possibility that Catuvellaunian territory may have been briefly organized as a client kingdom. However, there are military sites on roads leading north and west that appear to have lain close to the probable borders of Catuvellaunian lands. These include the fortress at Alchester in Oxfordshire (see below), and the presence of a vexillation fortress at Longthorpe near Peterborough is also suggestive. Again, we should see these not only as springboards for advance beyond the eastern kingdom, but as points from which the territory could be kept under surveillance and, when necessary, reached within a day or two by rapid march. Longthorpe is the probable location from where the unfortunate vexillation of *legio IX* marched against Boudica in 60. The scale of the rebellion they encountered resulted in their annihilation, but in less serious circumstances they would have provided a rapid and effective response to local unrest in the 'pacified' territories.

The site of London, controlling the lowest crossing point on the Thames and a river port, was a critical one in the conquest phase and a Roman military presence there from an early date seems certain. This fits with the artefactual evidence from London that conforms more closely with early military bases than with civil centres, though un-equivocal evidence of an early fort is lacking. The nature and scale of military activity thus remains imprecise.

The eastern kingdom's influence extended south of the Thames into Kent, technically the heartlands of the *Cantiaci*. Early Roman military activity is known at Richborough, which remained for much of the Roman period a major port of entry. Other early forts have been claimed, with less certainty. Dover was developed from the second century as the main base of the British fleet and a sequence of forts is known there. Otherwise, the main fortifications in Kent are all late Roman. However, the military control of the terminal points of the route through Kent from the Channel ports to London could have given early Roman Kent a profoundly military character.

The continuance of an Icenian client kingdom in Norfolk down to 60 kept Roman military posts at arm's length up to that point. But given the circumstances of the Boudican revolt, it is to be expected that Roman units were posted there in the aftermath. Although the Roman *civitas* centre of the *Iceni* was later established at Caistor-by-Norwich in eastern Norfolk, the most impressive archaeological evidence of the heartlands of the Iron Age polity lay in western Norfolk, focused on sites close to the Icknield Way, such as Thetford and Saham Toney. Several Roman forts have now been recognized in this area, including one at Saham

Toney (Woodcock Hall). The Romans built the Fen Causeway – a road across the Fens linking the vexillation fortress at Longthorpe with Peddars Way, the north–south Roman road established in western Norfolk. There was at least one fort in the Fens themselves at Grandford and perhaps others still to seek along the continuation of the Fen Causeway into northern Norfolk. A Roman military presence at Caistor-by-Norwich itself in the years following the Boudican revolt is plausible but unproven.

The initial fate of the lands of the southern kingdom in Sussex, Hampshire, Surrey and Berkshire is uncertain. There are military-style buildings below and adjacent to the Palace at Fishbourne, suggesting an early supply base. More significantly still, there appears to have been a military presence at Chichester close by. There are also numerous early Roman military finds from Silchester. One explanation is that the kingdom of Togidubnus was set up *c.*47, as a way of releasing troops initially deployed to that territory for expansionist campaigns elsewhere. Alternatively, some troops may have been provided in support of establishing Togidubnus as king. A third possibility is that Togidubnus modelled his own troops on Roman lines. What is apparent from the absence of later forts is that the kingdom was thereafter fairly successful in keeping Roman troops out of its borders and that the eventual incorporation of the kingdom into the province by the 80s was relatively smooth and did not require any long-term troop deployment.

The territory of the *Durotriges* in Dorset and Somerset was the scene of extensive Roman campaigning as a prime target of Vespasian. A vexillation fortress is known to have existed just north of Poole Harbour at Lake Farm and appears to have been occupied *c.*45–60. This implies a sizeable garrison in the territory for a generation post-conquest and there are additional traces of military occupation within a number of late Iron Age hillforts, as at Hod Hill, Maiden Castle, South Cadbury Castle, Ham Hill and Whaddan Hill. There were also more regular forts, for instance on the Fosse Way at Ilchester or at Charterhouse on Mendip. Inscribed lead ingots from the Mendip hills attest the involvement of *legio II* in mineral exploitation and indicate that production was under way by 49.

The picture of the military occupation of Dumnonian lands in Devon has been transformed over the last thirty years. The 1978 *Map of Roman Britain* featured only the legionary fortress at Exeter and two forts. The current total stands at a legionary fortress, a sequence of forts at North Tawton, and at least six other fort sites, as well as military occupation of an abandoned hillfort at Hembury. The bulk of these sites are located in eastern and northern Devon, indicating close supervision of the valleys of the Taw and Exe, and perhaps iron production on Exmoor. The earliest finds from Exeter suggest initial military occupation c. 50, though whether the site was immediately a full legionary fortress is unclear. Exeter certainly became the key military base of *legio II* in the south-west by 55 at the latest, and was in occupation until the mid-70s (though probably with a much reduced garrison by then). Forts at North Tawton and Okehampton were evidently situated on a route running west on the north side of Dartmoor. Another fort further west on this route at the crossing of the Tamar in the vicinity of Launceston remains a probability. The presence of two fortlets on the north coast and the route down the Taw valley strongly suggest a missing site at or close to Barnstaple, while numerous Roman finds from Plymouth harbour suggest a port and possibly fort site there. Overall, Devon appears to have been quite heavily garrisoned in the third quarter of the first century.

The people of Cornwall are normally treated as part of the *Dumnonii* because Ptolemy's *Geography* did not specify the existence of a separate group in this area. However, basic distinctions in the late Iron Age cultures of Devon and Cornwall strongly suggest that the people of the latter area had a well-developed and separate identity before the conquest. Since the name Cornwall appears to derive from an ancient form *Cornovia*, it is reasonable to surmise the existence of a people called the *Cornovii* here. A site called *Durocornovium* ('stronghold of the *Cornovii*') is also attested somewhere in the south-west in the *Ravenna Cosmography*. Only a single fort is at present known in Cornwall, at Nanstallon by Bodmin – evidently dating to the late 50s, but given its isolation (seventy kilometres from the nearest confirmed fort) it is probable that several others existed, perhaps corresponding with *Tamara*, *Uxellodunum* and *Voliba* in Ptolemy.

The take-over of the East Midlands is often considered to have been a relatively peaceful event. There are no explicit references to warfare with the major people of this region, the *Corieltavi*, or to their participation in revolts. Nonetheless, there are hints that incorporation was not entirely consensual. One explanation for a series of major hoards of Corieltavian coins from Yorkshire is that these were taken there by refugees from the Roman take-over of Corieltavian lands, presumed to extend between the east bank of the river Trent, the Humber and the Wash. The establishment of the Roman Great North Road, Ermine Street, drove an access route through the eastern part of this territory, with a sequence of forts along it. Along with the vexillation fortress at Longthorpe, these forts also facilitated the supervision of the Fens to the east and important iron deposits and farmland to the west. Lincoln lies at the point where the north road descended from the Jurassic ridge to cross the river Witham. An important Iron Age settlement existed at the crossing point by the Brayford Pool and an early Roman base probably lay just to the south of this (perhaps a vexillation fortress to match the one at Longthorpe). This early base was probably abandoned after the Boudican revolt and replaced with a legionary fortress on the north side of the river. This site remained a key military base until the late 70s, probably operating in concert with a series of vexillation bases on either side of the Trent (Newton on Trent, Osmanthorpe, Rossington). These latter sites appear related to intimidation of the *Brigantes* to the north or preparations for advance into their territory. Several smaller forts are also known on or close to the Trent. There were a further two possible forts near the Humber crossing. The overall impression is that the eastern lands of the *Corieltavi* came under concerted military supervision, centred on Lincoln, with territory for a *colonia* also being annexed in this area. A possible Roman military ditch beneath modern Leicester probably represents a small fortlet rather than something larger. There is a marked lack of other military sites in the Soar valley and the fact that the *civitas* capital was eventually located here may perhaps be seen as preferential treatment of the western sept of the *Corieltavi*.

Another key region that lay on a major line of Roman advance away from the south-east was the Cotswolds and related areas of Gloucestershire, Avon, Oxfordshire, Hereford and Worcester. This is normally equated with the people known as the *Dobunni* and, as with the *Corieltavi*, the general view has been that they were relatively favourably treated by Rome. The military deployment again modifies this view. The eastern limits of the territory of the *Dobunni* are uncertain, but are sometimes equated with the Cherwell in Oxfordshire.

The site of Alchester just north of Oxford has emerged in recent years as a key location in the early years of the conquest phase. It is now known that a major fortress underlies the later small town here and a timber post from the gate of its annexe has yielded a felling date of autumn 44 to spring 45. This is the earliest dendrochronological date from any Roman site in Britain and provides evidence of a base for a large battle group at the end of the second campaigning season. Alchester lay at the cross-roads of a Roman road leading east to west from Colchester via St Albans and on towards Cirencester and a south–north route linking Chichester, Winchester, Silchester, Dorchester, with potential continuations to the north and north-west towards Leicester and Wroxeter. There was also a second north–west route towards the Severn near Worcester. Alchester thus sat at the centre of a web of incipient communications and may have had a long life as a base in the conquest phase. In addition to the legionary base at Alchester, a fort at Dorchester-on-Thames secured the river crossing and controlled an *oppidum* there. A few kilometres south of the primary *oppidum* of the *Dobunni* at Bagendon a cavalry fort was established beneath the later town of Cirencester, again at an important road junction. This site was well situated to exercise close supervision of the primary native centre, but also served as a link between Alchester and a sequence of two major military bases at the Severn crossing at Gloucester. The legionary fortress at Gloucester was established only in the mid-60s, probably succeeding a mixed vexillation fortress at Kingsholm (tombstones of serving soldiers of the *cohors VI Thracum* and *legio XX* have been found nearby). The start date of the Kingsholm site could be the late 40s, with abandonment in the mid–late 60s. The implantation of a colony at Gloucester in the late first century will have detached territory from Dobunnic territory. The southern limits of the *Dobunni* are uncertain, though coin finds suggest that their influence extended as far as Bath (where an early military presence has been long suspected). Finds of military equipment also suggest a small naval base at Sea Mills with access to the Bristol Channel. All in all, there was a heavy garrison in Dobunnic lands from the 40s to at least the 70s.

The Marches and Wales

Tacitus focused on the *Silures*, *Ordovices* and *Deceangli* as the prime targets of Roman aggression in the 40s–50s, but huge bodies of troops were based in or passed through the lands of the *Cornovii* in Shropshire, the West Midlands, Staffordshire and Cheshire. Watling Street has for long been recognized as a key line of advance, with an impressive sequence of camps, legionary/vexillation fortresses and smaller forts along it between High Cross (the junction with the Fosse Way) and Wroxeter. There were vexillation fortresses at Mancetter, Kinvaston, Leighton and perhaps Wall, with a full legionary fortress established at Wroxeter *c.*58–77. In addition there were at least six smaller forts linked to this road. The vexillation fortress at Leighton and fortress at Wroxeter were built close to crossing points of the Severn and to a known late Iron Age hillfort, the Wrekin. Even if the main function of this deployment was to provide winter quarters for troops gathered for campaigning further west into Wales, the local impact caused by the presence of these troops on the people of the West Midlands must have been considerable.

Between the invasion corridors represented by Watling Street and Akeman Street/Ermin Street, an intermediate military route can now be recognized running north–west from Alchester. There are several possible fort sites along its line (for instance at Alcester and Droitwich) and on north–south routes connecting this route to Watling Street.

On the west side of the Severn, there were a number of bases in what may have still been Cornovian territory, including a major complex of forts and camps around Leintwardine. Brandon Camp near Leintwardine is another example of Roman re-use of an Iron Age fortification, with what appears to have been a supply base installed within an old hillfort. There is further evidence of Roman garrisoning of key sites in the Cheshire plain on land that may have been detached from Cornovian territory, notably at salt-producing sites and the legionary fortress at Chester in the 70s.

Some of these sites were founded early in the Claudian period and others continued to be occupied well into the Flavian period, or conceivably into the early years of the second century. This fifty-year military phase is longer than that for most of the civil zone and the level of garrisoning was also large. The *civitas* centre for the *Cornovii* was only fixed in the second century at Wroxeter.

In line with their internecine struggle with Rome in the mid-first century, the territory of the *Silures* in Glamorgan and Gwent was marked out for particularly thorough pacification and supervision. A broad distinction can be made between sites dating to the pre-Flavian period and those relating to the Flavian repacification of the territory. The earliest forts lay along a route running north-west from the Severn crossing at Gloucester towards the upper Wye valley, where a fortress at Clyro and a large fort at Clifford probably date to the pre-Boudican period. One advantage of this route was that it brought forces into closer proximity with the central Marches battle group, allowing mutual reinforcement. A more southerly access into the Wye valley passed via Weston-under-Penyard and Monmouth, reaching the river Usk at Usk itself, where a legionary fortress was established in the mid-50s. A number of other early forts are confirmed, including a coastal base at Cardiff, and some at least of this infrastructure seems to have survived the retrenchment following the Boudican disaster, contributing to the relative quiescence of the *Silures* in this period.

Following the Flavian completion of the conquest of Wales, very few of the earlier forts in south Wales were retained or reoccupied. The legion was moved to Caerleon, on the lower and tidally navigable Usk, with a small depot replacing the fortress at Usk. Only Abergavenny and Cardiff of the other pre-Flavian sites show any continuity. In southern Wales the deployment focused on a line of forts up the Usk valley, crossing the watershed between Brecon and Llandovery. The coastal road from Caerleon west to Carmarthen was marked by a few forts at key river crossings (Cardiff, Neath, Loughor) and there were additional lines of forts along transverse roads up the Neath Valley and up the east flank of the Taff valley. A further line of forts ran north-east of Llandovery into central Wales.

The Flavian deployment in Silurian 'territory' consisted of one legionary fortress and fifteen auxiliary forts, a daunting total, commensurate with a force of perhaps 13,000 men or about a quarter of the British garrison if all were held at full unit strength. The logic of the equation is that they cannot all have been occupied simultaneously or to full complement. The garrison was not much reduced in the early second century, though by the mid-second only the legionary fortress and a couple of forts remained (Brecon Gaer and Castell Collen). However, that lesser degree of supervision was to remain in place until late Roman times. Civil and rural development of the Silurian territory was late and abnormal, arguably as a result of the impact of military occupation and reductions in population and territory.

The *Demetae* of south-west Wales (Dyfed) appear to have remained out of range of Roman armies until the Flavian period and then seem to have been subdued comparatively speedily. By the mid-70s there were forts at Carmarthen (later to become the *civitas* centre), Llandeilo and several others in an arc near the putative north-eastern limits of the *Demetae*. This latter group of sites continued the road line running from Usk round to the western side of the main highland massif in Wales. The presence of a Roman road running west of Carmarthen towards Pembroke suggests the presence of a missing fort in the Milford Haven area. Overall, while it would be wrong to say that the *Demetae* were spared military occupation, this is a much lighter garrison in comparison with the neighbouring *Silures*, and none of these forts was still occupied by the mid-second century.

The north-eastern part of Wales (Clwyd) was not fully occupied until the Flavian period, although campaigning had been directed against the *Deceangli* as early as 47. It was once believed that the lack of Roman forts in this area denoted special treatment for this people. That picture is now changing with the recognition of at least three or four forts. The northern part of the territory contained significant lead deposits and if, as seems likely, the territory of the *Deceangli* was much smaller than some of the other Welsh peoples, this was a sizeable garrison, especially with the nearby legionary base at Chester from the 70s.

The *Ordovices* are normally assumed to have been a widespread group of clans active across a large area of north-western and central Wales (western Clwyd, Powys, Gwynedd, Anglesey). The island of Anglesey appears to have been the 'granary' of their territory, providing the largest area of good-quality farmland. Copper resources on Anglesey, at the Great Orme, in the Ceredigion hills of west Wales and in central Wales at Llanymynech may all have been under their control. There is no evidence of garrison posts being constructed until the pacification in the 70s under Frontinus and Agricola. However, pre-Flavian campaign bases are known in Cornovian territory around Wroxeter and at the advanced site at Rhyn Park near Llangollen. A case has been made for identifying a sequence of camps and campaign forts by the hillfort of Llanymynech as the scene of Caratacus' last-stand battle in 51.

The main principles of the Flavian deployment appear to have been to establish chains of forts along the main valley systems that bisected the mountains, and along the coastal plains on the fringes. On the northern coast Caernarfon fulfilled the double role of controlling the Menai Straits crossing to Anglesey and dominating the northern end of

Snowdonia. Other forts ringed Snowdonia and watched over the Lleyn peninsula. The upper Severn valley was also garrisoned, with forts at Caersws and Forden Gaer, and another at Brompton in relation to mining activity. Two legionary fortresses, a new one at Chester and an older base at Wroxeter, initially supported the auxiliary units. As in the territory of the *Silures*, garrison posts remained largely in commission down to *c.*120, but thereafter were radically reduced, until only a handful remained alongside the Chester legionary fortress by *c.*160: Caernarfon in the north, Caersws and Forden Gaer in the centre.

The overall picture of the garrisoning of Wales is an impressive example of how to control a mountainous landscape. Networks of roads, forts and fortlets connected the natural corridors. The end result was a regularly spaced pattern of garrison points, mainly in the valley bottoms or on the estuaries. The gap between adjacent forts was rarely more than 15–20 km, and in the event of trouble, assistance could often be sought from more than two directions. The main corridors of movement between mountain and coastal plain and between one upland zone and the next were controlled and the construction of roads increased the speed of communication. The Roman deployment was designed in part to control the spaces between the major British peoples, rather than simply occupying their heartlands. By segregating people and supervising contact between them, Rome applied the principle of divide and rule.

The policy can be considered reasonably effective, in that from 160 onwards a very significant reduction in the garrison was made, even if a few forts were maintained for centuries to come. On the other hand, not counting the pre-Flavian garrison posts, the intensive military occupation of much of Wales lasted for nearly fifty years.

Northern England

The *Brigantes* were described as the major people of northern Britain, extending from 'sea to sea' in an area perhaps equivalent to Yorkshire, Lancashire, Greater Manchester, County Durham and Cumbria. The heartlands lay in the Vale of York; for the rest of the area we should envisage a hegemonic confederacy of peoples. Initial Roman campaigns targeted the eastern lands, leading to the establishment of a major base at York. Roman control quickly extended to the lands of the *Parisi* in the Wolds to the east of the Vale of York and across the Pennines towards Carlisle, where the earliest fort was built with timber from trees felled between autumn 72 and spring 73. As in the conquest of southern and western Britain, there were a number of larger bases that seem to have been key gathering points for troops and supplies involved in the conquest of the north (Fig. 7). Sites of vexillation or legionary size include Chester, Lincoln, Newton on Trent, Rossington Bridge, Osmanthorpe, York, Malton and Corbridge, but in the course of the Flavian era these were replaced by a more dispersed pattern of deployment. Nottinghamshire, Derbyshire and south Yorkshire had been partially occupied in the pre-Flavian period, with forts at key river crossings and along the main lines of advance.

Several forts in the territory of the *Parisi* appear to have been established before the governorship of Agricola. The deployment encircled the Wolds with roads and forts, rather than directly penetrating them, hinting that the intention was to separate the *Parisi* from the *Brigantes*. Most of these sites were short-lived, though Malton remained a long-term military base in the Vale of Pickering into the fourth century. Other probably early Flavian forts include the line of forts flanking the southern edge of the Peak District from Derby towards Chester. The establishment of Chester and York as full legionary bases by the later 70s also required trans-Pennine links, notably the Manchester to York route.

The early deployment west of the Pennines appears to have skirted the edge of the Lake District and it may have been the late first and early second century before a network of forts was fully established at its heart. Additional trans-Pennine roads were also developed linking the garrisons along the Mersey to Solway route with those of the east side and ensuring a Roman presence in the main Pennine valleys and Dales. It must be stressed that this deployment was probably developed over decades rather than years and that the identification of many of these as 'Agricolan' is not secure.

North of York, several Flavian forts were developed along the line of what was to become Dere Street, notably at Catterick. Located at the crossing of the Swale just to the south of Scotch Corner, where routes fork towards Newcastle and Carlisle, Catterick became a long-term transit base for the northern frontier. The north-west road crossed the Pennines by the Stainmore Pass, descending the upper Eden Valley towards Carlisle. It was heavily garrisoned by the late Flavian period and remained a vital controlled route until late Roman times. Studded

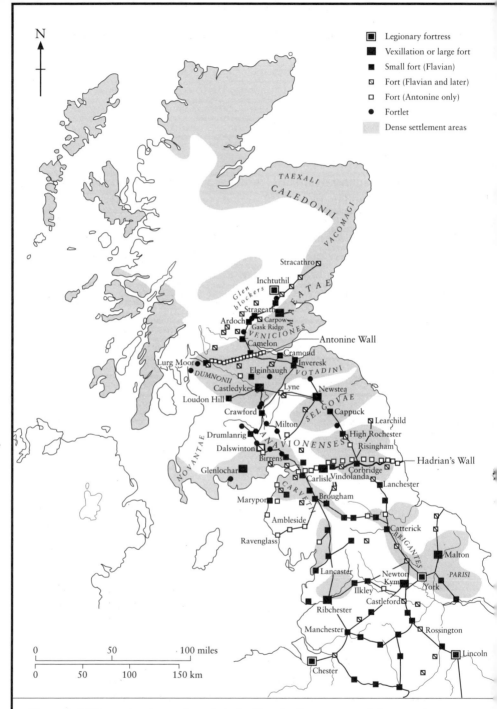

Figure 7. Military sites in northern Britain. Tone indicates areas of dense native settlements (cf. also Figure 15)

with forts along its length, Dere Street ran north from Catterick to Corbridge (where the vexillation fortress was soon replaced by a sequence of auxiliary forts). A branch road served second-century garrison points at the east end of Hadrian's Wall and the Hadrianic bridge on the Tyne at Newcastle. The construction of the Hadrianic frontier at the Tyne–Solway isthmus will be separately considered below.

A considerable portion of northern England remained under direct military supervision long after the *civitas* centre of the *Brigantes* was established at Aldborough. The scale of the garrison was also remarkably static between the late first and the third centuries: a legionary fortress and over fifty smaller forts spread across the region. The impact of such a large and prolonged garrison on the *Brigantes* must have been colossal. A corollary of this is that the territory under the direct administration of the civic authorities at Aldborough probably comprised only a comparatively small part of northern England, perhaps only a restricted area in the Vale of York. The long-term maintenance of the fort at Malton suggests similar loss of control by the *Parisi* of some prime lands in the Vale of Pickering. During the third century, at the latest, a third northern *civitas* was created for a group called the *Carvetii* ('Deer men') in part of the Eden Valley, though again the territory assigned may have been quite restricted in a region with a continuing military garrison. One result of the heavy military presence throughout the north was that the evolution of civic government and society was much less far-reaching than in southern Britain. The rest of the region was presumably maintained under direct military administration.

Scotland

It is particularly difficult to achieve precision about the location of British peoples in Scotland. Tacitus spoke only of the peoples of *Caledonia* in his account of the campaigns, though Ptolemy recorded numerous subgroups (Fig. 3). In both Lowland and north-eastern Scotland there were two main phases of Roman occupation, in the Flavian and Antonine periods. There are also signs of an intended, but short-lived, Severan re-occupation of Scotland in the early third century. A few outpost forts on the main routes north of Hadrian's Wall were maintained at other times during the operation of that frontier line. There were also large parts of Scotland, notably the Highlands and the Western and Northern

Isles, that were never formally garrisoned by Rome. What we encounter in Scotland thus differs from the rest of Britain, where garrisons were imposed and either eventually removed as pacification was judged complete, or else remained in place until late Roman times. Scotland saw three waves of Roman occupation with intervening and subsequent returns to 'free' status.

There has been much debate about the extent of fort construction under Agricola, as opposed to his unknown successor. On balance, it seems more probable that Flavian forts in Lowland Scotland between the Tyne–Solway and Forth–Clyde isthmuses date to his governorship of 77–83 and those north of the Forth–Clyde line to the consolidation of the conquest between 84 and 87, though exceptions may exist in both areas. The Flavian sites in Lowland Scotland were mainly established on two lines of communication: the first between Tyne and Forth from Corbridge to Camelon (with a major base at Newstead on the Tweed), the second from Carlisle to the Clyde Valley, passing via Annandale. There were also major forts at Glenlochar and Dalswinton in south-west Scotland in the Dee and Nith valleys. The overall impression is of a substantial garrison placed in control of the main roads north and exercising close supervision of the inhabitants of the Tweed Valley (the *Selgovae*), and of Nithsdale and Annandale (the *Anavionenses*). The scale of the military presence appears to have been lighter in the territory of the *Votadini*, more or less equivalent to Lothian. In addition to several known Flavian forts in the Clyde Valley, the probable territory of another people called *Dumnonii*, there are several candidates for forts established along the isthmus by Agricola. When the Romans abandoned the attempt to garrison northern Scotland, the initial stage of retrenchment (between *c.*87 and 105) seems to have also involved a strategic withdrawal to the southern Borders, with garrisons maintained in eastern Dumfries and in Selgovian territory in the Tweed Valley. The Hadrianic frontier represented another stage of contraction with some outposts left within striking distance of the heartlands of the *Selgovae* and of the *Anavionenses*, but with garrisons removed from their core territories.

North of the Forth–Clyde, it has long been noted that the Flavian forts fall into two groups: one set following the line of the Roman road north-east from Stirling (almost certainly the site of a lost fort) along Strathmore towards the Tay. Beyond the Tay, the road by-passed the legionary fortress at Inchtuthil and continued parallel to the Highland line at least as far as Stracathro, *c.* 50 km south of Aberdeen. The second group, the so-called 'glen-blocker' forts, lay west and north-west of this road, up into the eastern outlets from the Highland glens.

The glen-blocker forts were most probably built in the aftermath of *Mons Graupius*, their primary purpose being to separate Highland peoples from the relatively good farmland of the *Venicones*, based in Fife and lower Tayside, a point reinforced by a system of watchtowers developed along the Roman road on the Gask Ridge. Regardless of their date in the Flavian sequence, they seem to imply a high level of surveillance of movement both along and across the route. The heartlands of the *Venicones* have not yielded evidence of garrison posts, but it is also apparent that with a legionary fortress and about fifteen smaller forts along the north-western fringes of their putative territory, this people were under supervision. Indeed the prime evidence of Roman campaigns, represented by marching camps, shows that their territory was repeatedly targeted. The farmlands of Fife were presumably intended as a main source of supply for the northern garrison.

The 'glen-blockers' not only controlled egress from the Highland zone, but could also have served as bases for patrolling of the Highland glens. The system would have exerted a stronger grip on the Highlands had the line of forts been extended along the Moray Firth. There is still dispute about claimed forts in that area, but the northerly location of the legionary base would suggest that there was an original intention to deploy further units in the Grampian/Moray region. The better-quality farmland of parts of Moray will again have been of interest to Rome, but initially these lands were perhaps left in the hands of the local people (probably to be identified as *Taexali* and *Vacomagi*) under treaty terms. Had Roman occupation continued beyond 87, the garrison system would surely eventually have been extended into this region and possibly beyond to the far north and west. The withdrawal by Domitian of a legion and a substantial number of auxiliaries from the British garrison from the mid-80s made the intended deployment impracticable and even the existing one untenable. The initial retrenchment probably occurred rapidly from 87, involving a withdrawal south of the Forth–Clyde isthmus, but not yet as far as the Tyne–Solway.

The Antonine occupation of Scotland was at one time portrayed as comprising three phases and lasting (with brief interruptions) from *c.* 142

to the 180s. The last phase was generally dropped from the consensus model in the 1970s, with a two-phase history becoming canonical (c.142–55, 158–63). Only recently has this too been shown to be a seriously flawed theory, and the most probable scenario is that there was a single Antonine phase lasting from c.142 to 158. Abandonment of the Scottish forts and recommissioning of the Hadrianic frontier may have taken place progressively over several years. The changing interpretation is interesting for what it reveals about the frailty of the evidence.

Antonine dispositions resembled the Flavian ones, with many earlier forts recommissioned, though often to larger or smaller plans. Some additional forts were created, mostly replacing nearby Flavian sites. In Lowland Scotland the overall pattern was similar in both periods, being based primarily on the two main north–south routes. The Corbridge–Camelon line was re-established with a total of eight forts and two fortlets, while Carlisle–Old Kilbride at the western end of the Antonine Wall – incorporating two alternative routes up Annandale and Nithsdale – had eight forts and six fortlets. Newstead was once again a key site, marked out by a very large fort, with its own amphitheatre. There were a few additional forts on transverse roads linking the two main north–south lines. There were also outliers at Glenlochar and Loudoun Hill, again providing a measure of supervision of western districts. North of the Forth–Clyde isthmus, where the Antonine Wall now marked a major concentration of forces, there was an echo of the Flavian advanced garrison. Based on a line of forts along the road linking Camelon on the Forth with the Tay, the intention once again appears to have been to control and protect the farmlands of the *Venicones* in Fife.

The Severan occupation of Scotland was brief and inconclusive. Following the large-scale campaigns of Septimius Severus and Caracalla, there appears to have been an intention to re-establish control north of the Forth–Clyde isthmus. A vexillation fortress (11 ha/27.5 acres) was built on the Tay at Carpow and there is evidence from Cramond on the Forth of renewed activity in the Antonine fort there. Several late sources credit Severus with establishing a 32- or 132-mile wall across Britain, and while this seems most obviously to correlate with a major refurbishment of Hadrian's Wall, it is conceivable that Severus also considered recommissioning the Antonine Wall. Evidently built and possibly garrisoned for a year or two at most by detachments of the *II Augusta* and *VI Victrix* legions, the fortress at Carpow was well positioned to dominate Fife, probably the heartlands of the people named by Dio as *Maeatae*.

Rome may have treated some of the northern peoples of Britain with greater favour – one can point for instance to the smaller number of forts in the lands of the *Votadini* around Edinburgh or the *Venicones* of Fife. In practice, the garrisons of each occupied zone were comparatively heavy and the impact of the Roman presence is likely to have been high on all the peoples in Scotland. The Roman peace will have exacted its own cost: in animals, crops and tribute to the garrisons. When they withdrew, it is probable that the Romans continued to try to influence (or intimidate) from a distance.

General characteristics of the Flavian and later garrison pattern

Garrison posts constructed after 70 were generally smaller than earlier, at 1–2 ha (2.5–5 acres), and are normally presumed to represent accommodation for individual auxiliary units. However, a simple calculation of the number of Flavian forts raises a problem concerning the numbers of troops committed to the pacification of Wales, northern Britain and Scotland. In Wales alone, over forty auxiliary forts and three legionary fortresses were constructed in the period 70–96, implying a minimum garrison of over 35,000 troops if all forts were contemporary and fully manned. Given that this was a phase of major wars in north Britain, followed by the garrisoning of an additional territory even larger than Wales, we must question the logic of this. Yet, as we have noted, the early second-century deployment in Wales remained similar, with no more than a handful of forts entirely abandoned, but seven sites showing signs of being reduced in size, and a similar number where occupation is uncertain. The solution to the conundrum is that the Roman army deliberately created over-capacity in constructing forts and maintained many posts with detachments of the units they were notionally designed to hold. Other colonial armies have attempted similar 'smoke and mirrors' trickery to suggest the presence of a larger force than was actually the case. The *Vindolanda* tablets illustrate this flexible approach to garrisoning, with strength reports showing that significant numbers of troops were out-posted to other forts or absent on other duties. It is clear that the legionary fortresses at Caerleon and Chester had much reduced garrisons in residence for much of the second century, when the construction of the Hadrianic and Antonine frontiers and northern (and perhaps foreign) wars may account for the prolonged absence of substantial vexillations. It is thus highly unlikely that all forts were fully manned, with some units perhaps divided between more than one base or with token holding forces left in place, while the major part of the unit was elsewhere. Viewed from outside, the forts were of sufficient size to accommodate 500 or more men and any fort could be periodically reinforced if local circumstances warranted. The British perception will have been of numerous garrison posts and 'police' checks on the roads, but the actual numbers of Roman troops in a region at any time will have been harder to gauge accurately.

The Roman linear frontiers: Hadrian's Wall and the Antonine Wall

The construction of linear barriers was a distinctive feature of the Roman garrisoning of Britain, though it should be noted that the walls themselves did not mark the literal limits of Roman territory, which outpost forts indicate lay further north. The walls of Hadrian and Antoninus Pius respectively spanned the isthmuses of Tyne–Solway (*c.*120 km/80 Roman miles) and Forth–Clyde (*c.*60 km/40 Roman miles) (Fig. 8). Inevitably they have been the focus of much study and a relatively minute structural history can be written about them. Their construction was arguably one of the most significant phenomena in the second-century history of Roman Britain. The British walls represented something very new at the time in Roman strategy. Hitherto the army had generally eschewed the delineation and garrisoning of formal frontiers, relying instead on the establishment of numerous garrison points within an area and the construction of superior 'all-weather' roads connecting them. Although there are signs of an increasing importance being placed on a series of forts along a transverse road across the Tyne–Solway isthmus in the late first and early second century (the so-called 'Stanegate frontier'), this was not yet a physical demarcation line. The conceptual design and execution of the Hadrianic frontier works were radically different, echoing contemporary developments in Germany, where felling-dates for timber used in the first frontier palisades there demon-

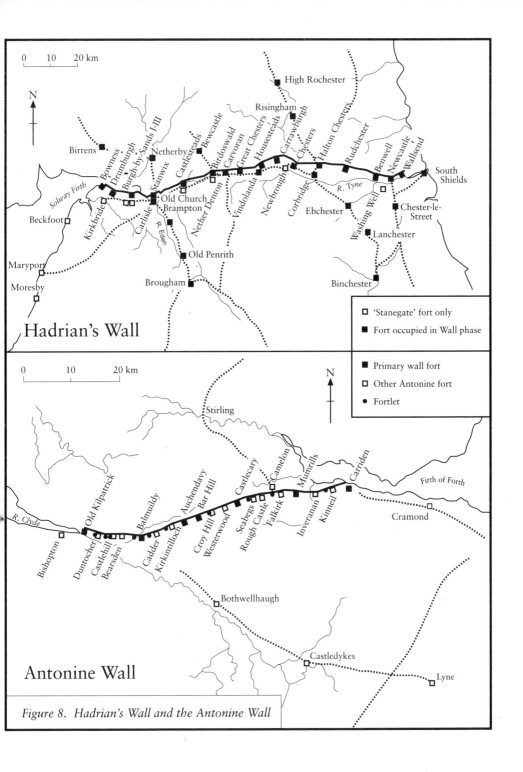

Figure 8. Hadrian's Wall and the Antonine Wall

strate the initiation of those works in the winter of 119–20. The intention was clearly to create a linear barrier for the control of movement through the frontier zone. The construction of the wall, initially under the supervision of a new governor A. Platorius Nepos, followed from a visit Hadrian made to Britain in 122 (though advance planning and logistical preparation may already have been under way). Given his known dabbling in architecture, it is almost certain that Hadrian had a say in its design. It may actually have been known as the *vallum Aelium* (the Wall of Aelius Hadrianus).

Hadrian's Wall comprised a complex series of installations, in part representing alterations to the original scheme – something that can be detected through the detailed archaeological evidence for the sequence of construction. All three of the British legions were involved, along with the British fleet (*classis Britannica*). Although inscriptions related to the primary construction do not attest auxiliary units, some were probably involved, working alongside the legions to whose command they were assigned, though perhaps directed to tasks that have left no documentary evidence, such as the digging of the ditch.

The principal element was a continuous wall curtain from the Tyne to the Solway, comprising a stone wall in the east and a turf wall in the western sector (most likely due to the change in geology making lime for mortar harder to come by). The initial plan appears to have been for a broad stone wall from Newcastle on Tyne to the river Irthing, with the turf wall running from the west bank of the Irthing to the Solway at Bowness. Variations in the width of foundation and wall structure allow the delineation of various phases of construction and some changes of plan. East of Newcastle, an additional sector of stone wall was soon extended along the north bank of the Tyne to Wallsend. West of the river Irthing, the turf wall was eventually replaced in stone (though the precise timing of this rebuilding is still debated). The wall would have stood to a height of *c.*6 m including its parapet, and it may have been whitewashed to make it a still more strikingly visual symbol of Rome's power. On the north side of the wall a large ditch (up to 9–10 m wide) was dug, except where the nature of the topography rendered its presence redundant, as on the cliffs of the central sector. In places, trap-pits have also been noted on the berm between wall and ditch, as near Wallsend. Along both the stone and turf sections, the original scheme envisaged a system of small fortlets at intervals of approximately 1 Roman mile

(1.48 km). Gates in the north and south walls of these 'milecastles' provided numerous potential points at which the barrier could be crossed, though some of the gateways in the central sector open on to a sheer cliff drop. Between each of the milecastles were two towers or 'turrets' at intervals of a third of a mile, with the north gate tower of the milecastles providing equivalent structures for observation and signalling.

Hadrian's initial intention appears to have been to utilize the forts along the Stanegate road as the source of troops for the milecastles and turrets, though he may have added additional forts to the existing series. However, at an early stage in construction, this decision was reversed and the main garrison points moved on to the line of the wall; traces of foundations of wall curtain and turrets have been found beneath some wall forts. An evidently near-contemporary decision was the construction of a further linear earthwork south of the wall curtain, the so-called Vallum (a misnomer, since *vallum* was actually the Roman term for the wall). This tripartite earthwork, comprising a central flat-bottomed ditch flanked by two mounds, deviates to avoid several forts, but is in turn over-ridden by one of the latest forts to be constructed in Hadrian's reign, Carrawburgh (130–38). There were controlled crossing points of the Vallum opposite each fort. The 'fort decision' thus had major implications for the construction programme and the functioning of the Hadrianic frontier, though not all the Stanegate forts were totally abandoned. Corbridge, *Vindolanda* and Carlisle all had later military phases. Finally there was an additional system of coastal defences down the Solway coast as far as Maryport, involving a series of forts, with intervening fortlets and turrets.

The total building requirements of the frontier in the period 122–38 were in the order of: 20 forts (including outposts), 100 milecastles/fortlets, 200 turrets and towers, 1 million m^3 of stone wall and 800,000 m^3 of turf wall, removal of over 5 million m^3 of material from the ditch and Vallum. This was one of the great engineering projects of the ancient world. It is estimated that a workforce of 15,000–20,000 men completed the bulk of this work in about ten years.

But what was the wall for? There was a war in Britain early in Hadrian's reign and the wall may be seen as partly at least a response to that. It is unlikely at this early date that the Romans saw it as a defensive platform behind which they would await attack; the preferred option was still to march into enemy territory at the first sign of trouble and to win victory in open battle at the expense of the enemy's lands, crops and resources. The fourth-century biography of Hadrian, probably following a Severan source, noted that Hadrian was the first to build a wall across Britain, suggesting that its function was 'to separate Romans and Barbarians', but that could be an anachronistic verdict on the failure of Rome's more expansionist aims in northern Britain. The defensive aspects of the wall are in places very impressive, as on the central crags, but elsewhere the wall does not always take the most topographically advantageous line. Nonetheless, the scale of the barrier and the addition of trap-pits in some sectors suggest that defence was a factor. Yet the presence of eighty gateways and undug causeways across the ditch introduced a large number of potential weak points if the primary function was to repel incursions. Indeed the gates imply a permeable demarcation line, where supervised crossing was not only allowed but also facilitated by the design specification.

The decision to move the forts on to the wall and to create a second barrier to the south is one of the most revealing aspects of the Hadrianic phase of use. Together the wall and Vallum formed a controlled cordon, with gates to both north and south, and native settlements between the two apparently abandoned at this stage (as at Milking Gap). The Vallum allowed army units to segregate themselves from civilians and to use the zone between the two barriers for grazing military pack animals and cavalry horses. Selected civilians who were counted as part of the military community may have been allowed to settle close to the forts between wall and Vallum. Other civilians could cross the barriers under escort or observation at specified crossing points, the installation of the Vallum serving to reduce the number of active gates on the wall. Regular movement across the frontier zone thus appears to have been anticipated, with Roman dispositions intended to control these in a labour-efficient way. Woe betide any native Britons who got caught in the vicinity of the wall without the requisite documentation permitting their presence. In sum, Hadrian's Wall was probably several things: a huge symbol of power that functioned as an effective deterrent to native aggression and facilitated customs control and frontier supervision. Most importantly, as originally designed, it did not entirely differentiate between Britons to north or south – both groups appear to have been considered as potential enemies, requiring intimidation and military supervision.

After Hadrian's death, his wall was soon abandoned and the frontier advanced to the Forth–Clyde isthmus. The milecastle gates were dismantled and the Vallum systematically slighted, though some forts may have been retained on a care-and-maintenance basis. The Antonine Wall resembles Hadrian's Wall in many ways – indeed part of the reason for the Antonine advance may have been not only to gain military glory, but also to emulate what was arguably one of Hadrian's most notable achievements. Once again we can detect changes to an initial plan for the monument, suggesting adaptation of a blueprint drawn up at a distance, once construction began on the ground.

The primary scheme seems to have been for a turf wall fronted by a large ditch from Carriden on the Forth to Old Kilpatrick on the Clyde, with six or seven major forts along its line at roughly 8- or 9-mile intervals and interspersed by a system of fortlets similar to the milecastles. It is still uncertain whether the wall included towers – if so, they were not constructed in stone. There were additional forts beyond the end of the wall on the Clyde and Forth and in advance of the east end of the wall, starting at Camelon. This scheme was soon modified, with some of the milefortlets being replaced by thirteen additional small forts, leaving a much closer spacing of forts, approximately every two Roman miles. Much of the evidence for a supposed second Antonine phase can in fact be interpreted as garrison changes at the original forts following the decision to add extra forts to the line. The effect was to make the gateways through the wall more strongly garrisoned. There was no attempt to replicate the Vallum here, though a military road was built linking the forts. As with Hadrian's Wall, epigraphic evidence shows the involvement of all three British legions in the construction work. Because of the lesser amount of stone used on the Antonine Wall and the shorter distance to be covered, the speed of construction was probably much quicker – perhaps as little as three to four years. Although the date of withdrawal from the Antonine Wall is still disputed, the general consensus is that around 158 the governor Iulius Verus instituted major refurbishment at forts on Hadrian's Wall and in the Pennines.

The recommissioning of Hadrian's Wall saw changes to the original scheme. The Vallum appears to have been left in largely derelict state and civilian settlements were now certainly allowed to approach close to the forts on the wall. A military road was constructed to the south of the wall to facilitate lateral movement in places where the Stanegate lay several kilometres to the south. In its modified form, the wall from Tyne to Solway was to remain a demarcation line down to the late fourth century.

INSIDE ROMAN FORTS

The archetypal Roman fort had a playing-card shape, defined by one or more ditches outside a wall or earthen rampart. The defences were not particularly impressive by the standards of other ages, and express a belligerent self-confidence in the army's ability to deal with opposition. There were normally four gates: in the centre of the short ends and a facing pair about two thirds of the way along the long sides. The main cross street (*via principalis*) ran between the two side gates, with the principal gate of the fort in the centre of the short side closest to the side gates. The interiors were divided into three broad zones: the *praetentura*, comprising the area between the main gate and main cross street between the two side gates (*via principalis*); the *latera praetorii* being a central range to the rear of the *via principalis*; the *retentura* or rear range extending to the rear gate and defences. The central range commonly comprised the headquarters building (the administrative hub of the fort) and the commanding officer's house along with other central facilities such as granaries or baths. The *praetentura* and *retentura* were generally given over to barracks and workshops. Legionary fortresses were much larger and more complex in overall layout, but normally followed similar lines.

Despite the basic similarities, fort layouts turn out to have been far more varied in points of detail. There was much experimentation and local flexibility, with forts tending to be built for specific units and to their specifications. When units were moved around and a new unit arrived at a garrison post this often involved substantial modification of the fort accommodation to match the incoming regiment's requirements. Cavalry and infantry utilized different styles of barrack blocks. Infantry were generally billeted with groups of eight men (*contubernia*), sharing a linked pair of rooms within a barrack block that typically contained ten pairs for the full complement of a Roman century of eighty men. The centurion in charge had larger accommodation in a suite of rooms at one end. Cavalry were organized in *turmae* of about thirty men, commanded by decurions. Excavations at Wallsend and South Shields have provided graphic evidence of their barracks, which again involved paired and interconnected rooms, but here with three horses stalled in one and the three troopers sharing the other. Cavalrymen often had slaves or servants as grooms and it is assumed that they must have been accommodated in the loft space over the stable room. In later chapters we shall consider the extent to which other non-combatants and civilians were part of fort life and how soldiers participated in garrison settlements that grew up outside forts.

Building the forts and fortresses was a huge undertaking for the army, especially the legions, in the early phases. Detailed calculations based on the legionary fortress at Inchtuthil allow estimates to be made of the materials required and the man-hours expended. For that single fortress of 22 ha (55 acres) and its associated support (in terms of gathering and transporting materials, providing security, and planned – but not completed – upgrades), a total of 16.5 million man-hours may have been required. That is the equivalent of 5,000 men working 413 eight-hour days or, making allowance for inefficiency, bad weather and so on, a legion spending the best part of two years engaged on little else. In reality the work was scheduled over a longer period of time and the fortress was still incomplete when abandoned in *c.*87, having been started in 83 or 84. Timber requirements can be estimated at *c.*22,750 tonnes, materials needed for masonry construction at 156,600 tonnes, roof tiles at 4,500 tonnes, nails at over 12 tonnes. When the fortress was prematurely abandoned, *c.*1 million iron nails (many bent on extraction) varying in length from 4 to 37 cm were buried in a pit. That much iron could not be left lying around for the locals to scavenge. At the same time that they were building Inchtuthil, the army in Scotland was also engaged in constructing at least twelve auxiliary forts north of the Forth. Individually they required about one tenth of the materials needed for the fortress, but cumulatively more than doubled the total material requirements and added an extra 7.6 million man-hours to the construction programme. These figures give some sense of both the huge resources in materials and manpower invested by Rome in the creation and maintenance of garrison posts, and some hint of local impact in terms of takeover of land, felling of timber, quarrying of gravel, sand and stone, cutting of turf and so on.

Potential figures for the economic impact of the garrison in Scotland, assuming a maximum force of about 25,000 troops, suggest require-ments of *c.*10,000 tonnes of wheat per year and *c.*8,000–9,000 tonnes of barley for cavalry horses and draught animals. Meat consumption by the garrison is conservatively estimated as approximately 2,000 cattle, 5,000 pigs and 5,000 sheep per year, and additional animals were required for sacrifices and for leather goods. The cavalry units required remounts, estimated at about 520 new horses each year. Some of this need was met by long-distance supply arrangements, but the army will also have regularly taken a large share of local surplus production, where that existed or could be stimulated.

One of the most important archaeological discoveries in British archaeology has been the recognition and retrieval of wooden writing tablets from anaerobic conditions of well-sealed early levels at the fort of *Vindolanda.* Written on with ink, these tablets are eloquent testimony to the day-to-day work and routine of the army units. They open a window on garrison life that is not reconstructable from the other data at our disposal. The *Vindolanda* documents can be divided into a number of distinctive types: strength reports and duty rosters, statements of accounts (some personal, some linked to military supply), contracts, military reports from outposts, requests for leave, personal letters. Many documents relate to the household of one of the commanding officers, Flavius Cerialis and his wife Sulpicia Lepidina.

One of the surprises of the *Vindolanda* material has been the picture it provides of the flexibility of military deployment at the fort. In Period 1 (*c.*85–92), it appears that the *Vindolanda* garrison was the cohors I *Tungrorum* and, when in Periods 2–3 (*c.*92–97, 97–105) the size of the fort was doubled to an area of *c.*2.8 ha (7 acres), this was to house the milliary *cohors VIIII Batavorum equitata*. In Period 4 (105–22) when the Batavians were withdrawn for service elsewhere, the fort was again remodelled for the return of the *cohors I Tungrorum*. However, it is possible that for some of the period 85–122, elements of more than one unit were in garrison alongside each other, as *cohors III Batavorum* is also mentioned in documents of Periods 2–3 and may have been present either in whole or in part at some point. More certainly, cavalry elements from the *cohors I Vardullorum* were in garrison alongside the Tungrians during Period 4, and towards the end of this period, when prepar-ations for work on Hadrian's Wall may have been under way, there were also legionaries present. This last piece of documentary evidence is valuable confirmation of something long suspected: that detachments of legionaries might on occasion have been brigaded with auxiliaries.

Units were regularly subdivided, as indicated by a strength report from Period 1 relating to *cohors I Tungrorum* under the command of Iulius Verecundus. This listed total strength at 752 men with 6 centurions, of which 296 men were present at *Vindolanda* (including 31 unfit for service) and 456 men absent. Absentees included a probable total of 337 and 2 centurions at *Coria* (Corbridge), 46 serving as *singulares* with the provincial staff, and smaller groups away at six other locations – including 6 men possibly in Gaul and another 11 doing something connected with military pay. This provides us with a radically new image of the Roman garrison pattern, much more flexible and varied than conventional models. Other documents highlight duty assignments within the fort, with very large numbers active in the workshops at the fort, others building a new bath-house, working at the hospital, tending kilns, working clay, involved with wagons and so on. The assignment of duties by craft specialization is important as it illustrates the extent to which the army could be very self-contained in terms of construction projects, manufacturing and transport.

A distinctive type of document was the *renuntia* or reports confirming 'all at their places who ought to be and equipment (inspected)'; these were probably daily notes prepared by the *optiones* and *curatores* (deputy centurions and cavalry NCOs) confirming that they had inspected the fort guards. These documents typify the routine activity of the garrison. That there were less regular inspections, with different remit, is confirmed by another tablet found at nearby Carlisle, relating to an internal audit of weapons in the *ala Sebosiana*. One of the decurions, Docilius, was deputed to make a list of the total number of troopers who were missing regulation lances (of two types) or swords. Another class of document at *Vindolanda* comprises short messages evidently to and from small groups of troops outposted from the main fort, but in its vicinity. These notes could request soldiers to return to *Vindolanda* or for supplies to be sent out to the outpost. There are twelve examples of letters written by soldiers to the prefect requesting permission to go on leave (*commeatus*), in some cases involving travel to Corbridge, where more developed recreational attractions no doubt existed.

Quite a lot of documents deal with aspects of military supply, though not all supplies were imported. Several tablets refer to the presence of a brewer called Atrectus (possibly a Gaul), either on the military payroll or a contracted civilian. The importance of beer as part of the military diet is emphasized by the appeal of an outposted decurion for more beer to be sent for his men. The unit also employed a range of specialists looking after livestock (both draught animals and those reared for consumption): tablets mention oxherds, a piggery and poultry yard. There were detailed records kept of food consumed within the fort, some specifically relating to the household of the unit commander, who quite literally counted his chickens.

The administration of justice over both soldiers and civilians is touched on in a number of documents. There are references to deserters, to individuals being beaten and others transported in chains (one to be deported 'out of the province'). Petitions to the commanding officer show that he had responsibility for dealing with petty crime on his patch – there are specific allusions to thefts and legal investigations under way. Soldiers owing money were liable to have their debts to men in other units brought to the attention of their commander.

The personal correspondence files of Flavius Cerialis include a number of letters to him as well as some of his drafts. Some dealt with military matters, others were social, including making arrangements about hunting nets. Correspondence with the provincial governor and with other units in the area was regularly maintained. One of the best ways to get on in the Roman world was to get yourself recommended for a job and there are allusions to such letters of recommendation, including both requests to Flavius Cerialis to use his influence on behalf of others and his own attempts to gain support for his career progression.

Soldiers made important relationships for themselves in the army, often referring to each other as 'brothers' (in arms). In several cases individuals chide old messmates for not having written in a while from their new postings. But the very fact that they maintained long-range correspondence at all is revealing about the military community and mutual support available within it. There are lots of allusions to goods being sent between soldiers (sometimes as gifts, sometimes with money promised in return).

Notably absent in the *Vindolanda* tablets are references to warfare or to perceived military threats. This was a garrison engaged primarily with administering its affairs and those of its district, building things, making things, trading and transporting goods that were consumed at the fort, earning and spending their wages, seeking justice or personal advancement. A fragmentary tablet referring dismissively to native Britons as *Brittunculi* ('little Brits'), who were unprotected by armour and did not throw javelins from horseback, was initially interpreted as an intelligence report, but is now viewed as more plausibly a comment on British native levies undergoing basic training for incorporation into the Roman army. This does not mean the period was without military action; indeed a tombstone from *Vindolanda* records the death of a centurion of the *cohors I Tungrorum* in battle. However, what is clear from the tablets is that the army was confident in its supremacy over the landscape and people of northern Britain and was proceeding methodically with the exploitation of both.

6

The Community of Soldiers

The Roman army in Britain, conventionally estimated to have numbered around 55,000 in the second century, constituted the most significant minority group within the province (less than 3 per cent of the total population). It had its own tight-knit communities and its own distinctive vision of what it meant to be Roman. Britain had the largest provincial garrison and one of the highest densities of military personnel in the empire, effectively 10–12 per cent of the army in 4 per cent of its territory.

The military garrison had a disproportionately large impact on the culture and economy of the province. But just how 'Roman' was the army? A key argument here is that the army had a strongly developed Roman identity, though a distinctive one when compared to other elements of the provincial population. The dependence of the army on the imperial treasury (known as the *fiscus* and *aerarium militare*) for pay, special handouts and retirement bonuses created special ties of allegiance to the emperor himself and contributed to the precise formulation of army culture. The Roman army was an institution that created its own sense of common identity for its polyglot soldiery, drawn from all corners of the empire (and even beyond its frontiers). One task of the military community was to transform levies from newly conquered people into servants of empire. Within the diversity of army culture there were structured elements, based on the use of Latin as the lingua franca, the Roman religious calendar (with a particular focus on the imperial cult), common standards of service, pay and conditions (unit structure, military discipline, the military oath, the hierarchy of ranks, literacy).

Military service and the social status and power that came with it affected the way soldiers interacted with civilians. Soldiers were comparatively well paid and well looked after by the state. Their involvement in provincial administration and the rights and privileges that were accorded them placed them above ordinary provincials in certain important ways. There was thus a distance between soldiers and civilians in the Roman world – demonstrable by examples in Roman literature of soldiers being more feared and despised than loved and respected by civilian communities.

The soldiery have in the past often been seen as great ambassadors of Roman culture, playing a leading role in its dissemination through the provinces. Recent studies have focused instead on the essentially self-serving use of material culture within the army, which to a large extent developed a separate version of Roman identity, distinguishing soldiers from civilians, rather than uniting them. To talk of the 'Roman army' as a monolithic institution is to obscure a significant degree of regional variation. The army in the eastern provinces differed quite radically from that of the west and we should perhaps think in terms of 'Roman armies'. On the other hand, some basic characteristics of the community of soldiers were widely disseminated, allowing troops regularly to be transferred between provinces and to be incorporated readily into the new situation. It is also clear that military identity was far from static and was continually refashioned, inevitably influenced by the cultural background of the soldiery.

What was the glue that gave the imperial army its cohesion, given that there were strong regional centrifugal tendencies present? One could cite the commonality of military dress, the ideological indoctrination of the soldiery based around the routine of camp life and training, the acceptance by the recruit of a package of new identity reference points (often including changes to personal names), the common language of camp Latin (*sermo militaris*), the foundation of the army's version of the religious calendar and style of religious practice. A military community recruited largely from the more warlike subject peoples quite naturally adopted the martial ethos that was at the heart of Roman culture. To join the Roman army, often under the duress of conscription, was nonetheless an opportunity to shift sides from defeated enemy to powerful winner. When Rome shipped the fighting strength of her enemies away from their homelands to represent Roman power in other provinces, there was a triple gain. The threat of revolt in the first area was diminished and the martial potential of subjected people turned to positive effect. Perhaps most important of all, the military community was reinforced by people whose experience of war, power and rewards would in due course turn them into supporters of the 'Roman' way of life that they experienced. For the most part, the community of soldiers was exclusive from civilians, other than those who lived alongside the garrisons. For that very reason many discharged soldiers chose not to move away from the military zone, but settled in civilian communities by forts and fortresses, where their identity and experience of army life could continue to be recognized.

The British garrison underwent many changes over the centuries of occupation, but only the legionaries were normally Roman citizens during the first two centuries. Average annual recruitment for three legions required about 600 individuals from a supporting population pool of c.50,000 citizens. In the first century, recruits were still sought outside the province and, even after the creation of three colonies for discharged legionaries and the growth of civil settlements outside the legionary bases where other veterans may have chosen to settle, it is doubtful if Britain could supply those numbers from eligible citizens before the extension of Roman citizenship under Caracalla.

In examining auxiliary recruitment patterns in a province such as Britain, we need to discriminate between newly raised units sent en bloc to the province and the origin of conscripts sent to long-established units. Overall, there appears to have been a strong preference for sending to Britain units originally raised through mass conscription in what we may term the 'Celtic' sphere – Germany (over 30), Gaul (25) or Spain (10), compared with a mere handful from the eastern provinces and Africa and comparatively low numbers from the Danubian provinces (fewer than 20). Where we know the previous posting of a unit, most instances involved transfer from one of the German provinces. In the initial invasion, it is logical that the auxiliary units attached to the legions brought from Germany would have accompanied them. This pattern was repeated later, when Petillius Cerialis brought to Britain a large number of units raised in the lower Rhineland in the aftermath of the Batavian revolt. Analysis of personal nomenclature suggests that both soldiers and officers of the Batavian and Tungrian units at *Vindolanda* were recruited from the same area of the lower Rhineland. Thus, for at least the first century of Roman rule, the cultural affinities of the bulk of the auxiliary troops were with northern Gaul and the Rhineland. Most of the initial batch of legionaries had also served there.

Over time the ethnic origin and the cultural outlook of units serving in Britain will have become diluted for a number of reasons. From the second century, Rome less commonly founded new 'ethnic' units through mass conscription, as opposed to reinforcing existing units with new conscripts and volunteers, often from the province in which the unit was based rather than its place of origin. Although in some provinces, voluntary enlistment became more common, the size of the army in Britain may have necessitated the maintenance of a degree of conscription among certain British peoples. The ethnic names of most units in Britain thus had less and less basis in reality (though the Batavians seem to have remained a major source of recruits in much the same way as the Gurkhas have retained a unique character in the modern British army). However, it is unlikely that all gaps in the ranks could have been filled purely by local recruitment; epigraphic information attests to the very mixed composition of units in Britain. Three mid-second-century altars from the fort at Birrens attest distinct groups serving in the *cohors II Tungrorum*, some from *Raetia* and others from two rural districts (*pagi*) in *Germania Inferior*, *Vellaus* and *Condustris*. Several inscriptions from Housesteads stress the dual identity of donors as soldiers of the *cuneus Frisiorum* and as Germans of the *cives Tuihanti*. There are several attested incidents of mass conscription and transportation to Britain of peoples from beyond the Rhine or Danube frontiers. In the later second century, for instance, 5,500 Sarmatian cavalry were transferred from the Danube region, following their defeat in the Marcomannic wars (though some at least of these may have been transferred out again later).

It is thus not the case that a British-raised defence force quickly replaced an initial foreign army of occupation. Although British recruits into the units serving in Britain will have increased steadily over time, it is important to recognize that there were still units levied overseas and that in most other units there was probably a distinctive diversity of ethnic backgrounds. Two features of the unit organization counteracted individual ethnic identities. In the first place, a soldier was placed within a strict hierarchy of power, and individual social identity was often expressed in inscriptions and sculpture in terms of rank. A second aspect was the existence of military 'clubs' (*collegia*) that provided additional social bonding for sub-groups of the soldiery and supported patronage networks within units.

CIVILIANS AND THE MILITARY COMMUNITY

The legions and auxiliary units comprised just one element of the military community. The cultural world of the soldiery was shared to some extent by select groups of civilians. It used to be believed that the literary and legal references to a Roman ban on marriages before the third century created a strict division between soldiers in their forts and civilians located just outside in settlements often referred to as *vici*. Detailed examination of finds from barracks at *Vindolanda* has revealed an interesting level of artefacts relating to women and children, suggesting their regular presence in the fort already in the late first century, and not just among the officer class. If women were living in barracks designed for the lower ranks of an auxiliary unit, this suggests that the demarcation between soldier and civilian was rather more fluid than the normal fort and *vicus* model allows. It is an illuminating paradox of the way the Roman army operated that it could ban serving soldiers from contracting marriage, but at the same time tolerate some unofficial 'wives' (not to mention slaves and other dependants) within the barracks at the fort. Considerations of space and safety may have had a part to play. A fort occupied by only part of its paper strength provided more potential for such arrangements. Similarly, in an early phase of a fort's existence, the security of camp followers in an external settlement may have seemed more precarious than when pacification was further advanced and a civil settlement better established. The *Vindolanda* evidence thus could relate to special conditions rather than normal practice, and more studies are needed. What it does reveal is that the relationship between soldiers and non-combatant civilians could be intimate, and these relationships may have blurred the identity of the two groups.

The civilians we are concerned with here were those who through choice or obligation lived alongside soldiers and whose lives were primarily devoted to servicing the military. They have sometimes been referred to as the 'frontier people', but since they were present wherever the army was, 'military community' is a more appropriate term. Civilian settlements have been recorded alongside many forts and though a few are epigraphically attested to have been designated as *vici*, it may be better to use a more neutrally descriptive term for these fort/*vicus* complexes. I shall refer to them below as 'garrison settlements', recognizing that there may have been a hierarchy of such sites and different degrees of military supervision or self-regulating autonomy. It follows that all the garrison settlements were a part of the military community and profoundly affected by its culture, economy and political outlook, in much the same way that modern garrison towns are often heavily dependent economically on the army and stand out from their surrounding districts in terms of the social values and material culture of their inhabitants.

The epigraphic and archaeological evidence of garrison settlements further illustrates the difficulties of separating soldier from civilian. We have already noted that slaves and women and children appear to have been present inside some forts. There were also military or official structures outside the fort defences at many sites, notably bath-houses and large complexes often described as *mansiones* (official rest-houses). Many forts had attached annexes, and sometimes these 'official' buildings were sited within the annexe alongside other buildings that look typical of the civil occupation. Some of the external buildings were also very well constructed, whether for dwellings or workshops, and it has been suggested that these could represent overflow accommodation or workspace for the garrison. An inscription from outside the fort of Malton, recording a gold workshop run by a slave, perhaps related to a civilian enterprise, but slave ownership was probably quite high throughout the military community. Certainty is impossible and few of these settlements have been excavated in any detail. However, the old belief in a rigid demarcation between soldiers inside and civilians outside seems much less acceptable on the evidence currently available.

How the garrison settlements were administered is controversial. Though used in a number of cases to describe civil settlements by forts, the term *vicus* in Roman sources is most fully defined in relation to small towns, as a small settlement below the level of a *civitas*, with streets but no walls, and administratively attached to a *res publica* or larger town. The term thus implies a dependent settlement. A key question is to what higher authority did the military *vicus* answer? It seems improbable that they answered to the nearest (often quite distant) *civitas*. The *Vindolanda* tablets have shown that the military had a complex and evolved bureaucracy, well suited to local administration, and there are clear references to military supervision of civilians. It is a reasonable assumption that the garrison settlements were initially established on state land (*ager publicus*) and therefore that anyone living and working within them would be liable to pay rent to the state through the unit in garrison. However, the inhabitants of some garrison settlements did act as a body, as inscriptions set up by the *vicani* at *Vindolanda*, Housesteads, Old Carlisle and Carriden indicate. The reference to '*vicus* people living at the fort of *Veluniate*' (*vikani consistentes castello Veluniate*) at Carriden reinforces the impression of nascent group identity, though a supposed reference to magistrates (*magistri*) of a *vicus* at Old Carlisle is now generally recognized to relate to the place-name, *vicani Mag(lonenses)* or *Mag(nenses)*. It is thus uncertain that all garrison settlements were normally designated as *vici*; the term could have been reserved for sites of a particular size, status or stage of development. Some of the larger garrison settlements, at Corbridge, Piercebridge and Catterick, were of substantial size, but may have remained under military supervision (for instance, of regional centurions), even at times when their garrison was removed.

Sites such as Wilderspool and Walton-le-Dale represent another type of garrison settlement. The former was located at the lowest fording point of the Mersey, coincident with the highest reach of sea-going ships. It is possible that an auxiliary fort existed on the north side of the ford, though the major settlement here was on the south side of the Mersey, just downstream of where the Romans built a bridge. The settlement was not only a major trans-shipment point for goods brought by sea for the north-western garrisons, but also evolved as a major manufacturing centre whose products were widely distributed across the military zone. It may have been established as a specialized military supply base, rather like Holt south of Chester. Walton-le-Dale occupied a similar position at the lowest crossing point on the Ribble and was also a heavily 'industrial' settlement. Sites like this, situated within the military zone, with a significant manufacturing and supply role in relation to the northern frontier garrison, probably came under military supervision as there are plenty of finds of military equipment to suggest the regular presence of soldiers. There were other centres of habitation in the Cheshire plain/Mersey basin that generally have a high manufacturing component, in some cases with an initial military garrison phase, but generally continuing to operate as small towns after the removal of garrisons (Whitchurch, Northwich, Middlewich). The recovery of an auxiliary discharge diploma at Middlewich provides a hint that the military character was not entirely lost as the forts were abandoned. Another site at Tarbock, near Liverpool, also produced tiles for *legio XX* at Chester in the second century. It is probable that the inhabitants of these centres, like those of the garrison settlements, saw themselves as part of the broader military community in Britain.

Who lived in the garrison settlements? Some civilians were directly bound to the soldiery as concubines, wives and families, or as slaves. On retirement, ex-soldiers may have chosen to live in close proximity to their former barracks in a garrison settlement. There were also groups of traders and craftspeople, who serviced specific needs of the army and who would not otherwise have been living in northern or western Britain. One problem with inscriptions from garrison settlements in Britain is that it is rarely certain in the case of men whether they were civilians or (ex-)soldiers and with women it is equally problematic to know if they were there as wives or in some other role. Where people came from, however, is often highly revealing, as in the case of Barathes, a native of Palmyra in the Syrian desert, who buried his British wife at South Shields.

The writing tablets from *Vindolanda* contain few references to the native British populace or to other civilians. Most of the recognizable civilians in the documents appear to be non-local traders and camp-followers. Revealingly, one of the few hints of brutality towards a civilian at *Vindolanda* concerned a foreign trader who had evidently been beaten with rods by a centurion. He wrote a letter of complaint about his treatment (either to the provincial governor or conceivably to the emperor Hadrian), which even in fragmentary form is evocative:

... he beat (?) me all the more ... goods ... or pour them down the drain (?). As befits an honest man (?) I implore your majesty not to allow me, an innocent man, to have been beaten with rods and, my lord, inasmuch as (?) I was unable to complain to the prefect because he was detained by ill-health I have complained in vain (?) to the *beneficiarius* and the rest (?) of the centurions of (?) his unit. I accordingly implore your mercifulness not to allow me, a man from overseas and an innocent one, about whose good faith you may inquire, to have been bloodied by rods as if I had committed some crime.

The very fact that this man wrote in Latin shows his close identification with the Roman military authorities. If he was not formally a part of the 'community of soldiers', he was by extension, since they were his reason for being present in northern Britain. There are other hints that many of the civilians servicing the needs of the *Vindolanda* garrison were likewise men from outside Britain. Personal nomenclature shows that some certainly had connections with northern Gaul and the Rhineland, where successive garrison units were raised.

The possibility of native Britons, especially women, being incorporated into these settlements over time has been much canvassed in the past. But even if soldiers eventually set up unofficial families alongside facilities servicing troops with drink, sex and a variety of trade goods, the character of these settlements in material terms stands far apart from that of native rural settlement in the military zone. Service in the army and close attendance upon the army were characterized by a distinctive set of cultural markers, reflecting a basic division in identity between these communities and native settlement in the frontier zone.

The main distinction in the frontier zone was thus not between provincials and non-provincials, but between the military community and Britons living either side of the frontier. The career inscription of Titus Haterius Nepos, who was governor of Egypt in 120, shows that he was responsible at an earlier stage for conducting a census of the *Brittones Anavionenses*, the people of Annandale in south-west Scotland. Letters at *Vindolanda* indicate that Haterius Nepos was in the neighbourhood, perhaps in command at Corbridge, and there are references in fragmentary tablets to a census and to the *Anavionenses*. All these instances suggest that the early relationship between the army and native northern Britons was one of exploitation. A prime purpose of carrying out a census of native lands was to determine tribute due and to provide a baseline for military conscription.

The design of Hadrian's Wall does not really suggest that its purpose was to 'separate Romans and barbarians', but rather that it was used to supervise 'barbarian' communities on both sides of the frontier. Did this view change over time? Development of a *civitas* of the *Carvetii* based on the agricultural land in the Eden Valley is a sign of limited development, but the economic and social evolution of large areas of northern Britain seems to have been stymied. Some have blamed the 'backwardness' of the frontier peoples for this, but an alternative possibility is that the military zone was deliberately maintained as a region to be exploited for the benefit of the garrison, with most land not released from direct military control to civil administration. In such circumstances, the separation between military communities and their native neighbours was great and was expressed most clearly through the overbearing Roman identity of the former.

The social consequences of Roman conquest merit further consideration. In many cases the British elites had their prestige severely weakened by defeat, by loss of control of lands, by depletion in their numbers, by loss of their portable wealth and right to bear arms, by transference of political and judicial power to the Roman state. Women were placed in a particularly vulnerable position, especially when they were enslaved or where they were left without their menfolk (through the death, enslavement or conscription of the latter). Large numbers of native women may have been forced through enslavement or necessity to work in brothels, or to enter into concubinage with soldiers. The Roman army imposed long service contracts on young men, refusing to allow them to contract legal marriages. Such a system can only have worked because the state unofficially sanctioned the presence of prostitutes and the taking of concubines around its military bases. Whether as concubines, prostitutes or legal wives, women were probably in short supply in garrison settlements. Tombstones suggest that soldiers were more likely to be commemorated by messmates in early service years and only by a 'wife' after ten or more years' service. The sexual needs of the younger soldiers were probably served by casual contacts (however organized) around military bases.

In the twentieth century, the Japanese empire provided prostitutes for its troops at a ratio of 1:40 and, although that figure is obviously meaningless for the Roman period, it may serve as illustration of the sort of impact involved. There is no epigraphic or archaeological evidence for military-run brothels in the Roman army, though it is possible that such services were organized as monopoly contracts, in much the same way that we find concessions for, *inter alia*, barbershops and shoe-makers at Roman mining sites. If the British garrison was *c.*55,000 at its peak, then, on a 1:40 ratio, 1,375 prostitutes might have been required at any one time. A very much larger number of women may have become involved in longer-term relationships with soldiers – primarily the concubines and unofficial wives of soldiers. If just one in four soldiers had entered into such a relationship by the time they had served in the army for ten years, the number of women affected at any one time could have exceeded 10,000. Some may have embarked on such liaisons willingly or opportunistically, but yet others only under coercion or out of necessity. This would potentially have had a long-term impact on society and one that extended far beyond the initial conquest phase. The power of the serving soldier, both economically and in terms of position in law, gave him advantages in wooing or buying local women. The strains on, and changes to, social structures may have been considerable.

MEMBERS OF THE COMMUNITY
OF SOLDIERS

The community of soldiers was a hierarchical society and the behaviour and perceived identity of members at different levels will have varied. At the apex of the military community were emperors, provincial governors, legionary legates and senatorial tribunes assigned to the British legions. These were men of the senatorial order, whose identity was normally defined in very different terms when in Rome. To serve in the army, with temporarily reduced opportunities for luxury and excess, was seen as character-building in line with the Roman military ethos. Sharing the discomforts of the ordinary men is a repeated *topos* of the good general in Roman literature. Military postings could be important stages on senatorial career paths, starting with a junior officer post (tribune in a legion) at around twenty to twenty-five years old. Command of a legion could follow the holding around thirty of a praetorship (junior magistracy) with the provincial governor of Britain selected from among the men who had held the senior magistracy at Rome (consulship), generally over age forty-two.

The remote location of Britain meant that visits by the commander-in-chief were rare indeed: only Claudius, Hadrian, Septimius Severus (with his sons Caracalla and Geta), Constantius I (and his son Constantine the Great) and Constans visited Britain when holding supreme power, though a number of pretenders were also proclaimed emperor while based in Britain (Clodius Albinus, Carausius, Allectus, Magnus Maximus, Marcus, Gratian and Constantine III) and several men who rose to the purple are known to have served in Britain (Vespasian, Titus, Pertinax, Gordian I and perhaps Theodosius I). Most of the emperors who visited did so for specifically military reasons and many of the pretenders were in positions of military command. The army thus conditioned the personal relationship of emperors with the British province.

Until the early third century, Britain was treated as a single province, governed by a man appointed by the emperor as *legatus Augusti pro praetore*. The British governorship was normally reserved for extremely high-ranking ex-consuls, with only *Syria* perhaps seen as more prestigious to the individual. The size of the army and the periodic opportunities to undertake military action there were what made the British posting so sought-after. When the province was subdivided, *Britannia Superior* with two legions remained an important consular appointment, whereas *Britannia Inferior*, with the York legion, was a praetorian command – that is, one awarded to senators who had held the office of *praetor*, but not yet the consulship. The provincial governors could expect to spend much of their time in relatively well-appointed quarters, though the relative lack of social equals, the constant presence of bodyguards and daily interaction with military administrative personnel will have meant that even in the civil part of the province, the governor had constant reminders of the military community. When active campaigning was authorized, the governor spent a substantial period living in a tent at the heart of his army and, even in peacetime, it is probable that regular inspections were carried out of the military zone, with accommodation provided in forts or garrison settlements. The correspondence of Flavius Cerialis at *Vindolanda* included a reference to an imminent meeting between himself and the governor.

The names of about thirty governors of Britain between 43 and 213 are preserved and the careers of several are known in considerable detail. The most famous, Gnaeus Iulius Agricola, is also one of the least typical, because of his length of governorship and his career path. The average term for a governor of Britain appears to have been about three years; Agricola got seven (and the opportunity to lead six major campaigning seasons). He also had an unusually long and close association with the province, having been a military tribune at the time of the Boudican revolt and a legionary commander in the early 70s (this triple service in the same province is unique among known senatorial careers). He was not from a well-known family, with both his grandfathers serving as equestrian procurators, though Caligula, in executing his father in 40, ended a promising senatorial career that had reached the praetorship.

Agricola's early career in imperial government was not particularly distinguished, but crucially he supported the Flavian cause at an early stage in the civil war that brought Vespasian to power. His modest family pedigree, his loyalty and his prior military experience there all recommended him for further service when Britain was made a key theatre of expansionist warfare in the 70s. It is equally apparent that Agricola's achievements in Britain gave Domitian good reason to sideline him after his return to Rome, as his success made him a potential rival.

Some other Flavian appointees held things in common with Agricola. Q. Petillius Cerialis was another early adherent to the Flavian cause, in his case perhaps through kinship with Vespasian, and he was rewarded with command against the Batavians and other rebels on the Lower Rhine frontier in 70, being sent from there to Britain as governor in 71. He too had earlier service as legionary legate in Britain. Sextus Iulius Frontinus, Agricola's immediate predecessor was a very distinguished senator, eventually holding the consulship three times (rare outside the imperial household). His early career is not known in detail, though he seems to have leapt to prominence by taking Vespasian's side in the civil war, and active service in Germany and Britain was his immediate reward. After his British victories, he held another military command in Lower Germany in the early 80s and the Proconsulship of *Asia* (western Turkey), a lucrative and prestigious posting. Subsequently he wisely concentrated on writing technical works, before re-emerging after the death of Domitian as a senior statesman under Nerva and Trajan, who both honoured him with further consulships. All three of these governors were special cases, selected for their known loyalty to the new dynasty and thus entrusted with prosecuting an expansionist war that was deemed important for the establishment of the Flavian dynasty.

There were many factors that could influence an emperor's choice of governor in Britain. When major military action was anticipated the choice would favour men with appropriate experience of generalship and this appears to have quite often been a factor in Britain. The most obvious examples in the early conquest period are Quintus Veranius (57–58) and Suetonius Paullinus (58–61). The former man's career had featured a five-year term as governor in Turkish *Lydia*, where he had acquired a reputation in mountain warfare. The latter was 'brought out of retirement' following the premature death of Veranius in office. He had served with distinction in mountainous terrain in Morocco and his

British victories, even if tainted by the Boudican revolt and its aftermath, guaranteed him a lasting reputation. As the senior ex-consul in 69 he played an influential role in support of Otho. Although the governorship of Britain generally marked the apogee of a general's career (especially if he had directed successful campaigns there), there are instances when governors were specifically selected for further commands after service in Britain. Sextus Iulius Severus was governor *c.*130, between service as governor in *Moesia Inferior* on the Danube and in *Iudaea* to deal with the Jewish revolt. He was described as the foremost of Hadrian's generals, and Cn. Iulius Verus, sent to Britain in 158, was probably his son and was again evidently selected with a special military mandate after service in Lower Germany.

Most of the early governors of Britain came from Italy or southern Gaul, but by the later second century an increasing number of senators came from further afield. Q. Lollius Urbicus was from the *ager Cirtensis* in Algeria and served with legions in Germany and Pannonia, before being given higher responsibility on campaigns in *Iudaea* and in Britain in 139–42. Another North African, Q. Antistius Adventus, a native of *Thibilis*, was governor of Britain in the 170s. He married the daughter of the legate of the *III Augusta* legion and the significant military component in his career perhaps reflects his father-in-law's initial patronage. He was at various times tribune of *legio I Minervia* at Bonn, legate of the *VI Ferrata* and *II Adiutrix* during the Parthian wars in the early 160s, governor of the military province of *Arabia*, a sectoral commander in the 'German expedition' of Marcus Aurelius and Lucius Verus in 168, and governor of Lower Germany and Britain. Another governor of this period, Sextus Calpurnius Agricola (163) may likewise have been an African and was apparently specifically chosen to go to Britain in a time of military difficulty.

The governors of the sub-divided British province after *c.*213 are for the most part more shadowy figures. Few careers of third-century governors are known in detail and many fail to specify their seniority or their specific province on surviving inscriptions. The most interesting case concerns Ti. Claudius Paulinus who served as legate of *legio II Augusta* in *Superior* a few years before returning to Britain as governor of *Inferior* around 220. In between he was governor of *Gallia Lugdunensis* and an extant inscription from France preserves the text of a letter of gratitude written by Paulinus in Britain to a man called Sennius

Sollemnis, recording material rewards and a job offer the governor had sent him. A statue of Paulinus was erected by the *civitas* of the *Silures* at Caerwent, demonstrating a relationship that continued after his period as legate at the nearby legionary base at Caerleon.

Legionary legates shared much in common with the provincial governors – indeed the legate of *legio VI* at York was also the governor of *Britannia Inferior*. It has been estimated that about 200 individuals were appointed to the British legions in the period 43–274, though the names of only about 40 are known. Of those, 14 were Italians, 4 were Spaniards (plus another 3 probables), 1 from North Africa (and 2 probables), 1 from Gaul, 4 from the eastern provinces, 1 perhaps from Dalmatia and others uncertain. Most had not previously commanded a legion, though in three cases the British command was given to men who had. A three-year tenure seems to have been the average. Both governorship and legionary commands were assigned directly by the emperor, and close friends will rarely have been selected to serve together. One role of the legates was to keep an eye on the political ambitions of the governor and the same operated in reverse.

Several hundred senatorial tribunes (*tribuni laticlavii*) served in the British legions in the period 43–274, though only three or four together at one time. The names of fewer than thirty are preserved. These positions, in the gift of the governor, normally extended for more than a single year and served to give young men of the senatorial class direct experience of the army and the military ethos. Titus, son of the future emperor Vespasian, held a tribunate in the early 60s, perhaps sent as part of post-Boudican reinforcement for *legio IX Hispana* commanded by his kinsman, Petillius Cerialis. About two thirds of the tribunes for whom we have more detailed career information went on to command legions, one third to govern military provinces. Britain was thus a good proving ground for senators who aspired to military careers.

The equestrian officers serving as the fifteen to twenty non-senatorial tribunes (*tribuni angusticlavii*) in the legions and in command of auxiliary units were numerically far more important. In the period from the Claudian invasion to the late third century, *c.*5,000 separate appointments to equestrian army posts in Britain will have been made, with some men holding more than one successive post in the province. Only about 300 names of individuals are known, mainly from inscriptions on stone within Britain. Before the system changed under the Tetrarchy at the end of the third century, equestrian posts in the army could be divided into a series of stages. The lowest stage (*prima militia*) comprised prefects of quingenary cohorts (more than thirty posts in Britain in the Hadrianic period), the *secunda militia* was for tribunes of the legions and milliary cohorts (about twenty posts), the *tertia militia* was for the commanders of cavalry *alae* (about twelve posts) and the *quarta militia* was with the single milliary cavalry unit in Britain, the *ala Petriana*. Although some of the highest posts were technically in the emperor's gift, the patronage wielded by the British governor was considerable, with over sixty posts in total. Nonetheless, wholesale changeover of officers was unlikely to occur with every new governor, as demonstrated by the case of Claudius Paulinus and his Gallic client, Sennius Sollemnis. The latter was honoured by an inscribed monument set up by the Council of the Three Gallic Provinces, which included the verbatim text of a letter to Sollemnis from the governor, apologizing that he did not have available a post as tribune and offering a supernumerary post on his staff and some extravagant gifts instead. Although some lengthy periods of service are attested in the early empire, the average length of appointment was perhaps around three years, with many post-holders serving under successive governors.

The study of the personal names and indications of origin of the equestrian officers shows that the majority were appointed from outside Britain and primarily from the western, Latin-speaking, half of the empire, though several individuals are known from Asia Minor. There are quite a few attestations of Africans, though this could in part indicate that they felt culturally far further from home than men from European provinces, leading them to indicate their *origo*, as seems the case with Cornelius Peregrinus of *Saldae* (Algeria). There are other groups of officers from Gaul/Germany, Italy, the Danubian region and the Balkans. There are relatively few cases where a British origin can be proposed; exceptionally, M. Statius Priscus, prefect of *cohors IV Lingonum* in the early second century, may have been born at Colchester. In the early empire, auxiliary commanders may have been selected in part to match the ethnic nature of the units. An unknown equestrian from *Ilipa* in southern Spain held his three *militiae* all in Britain, two with Spanish units, the other as tribune of *legio II*. Similarly, there are strong reasons for believing that Flavius Cerialis, prefect of the *cohors VIIII Batavorum*, came from the Batavian region of the Lower Rhine.

What were the motivations of the men who undertook service as unit commanders? Although the equestrian status indicates a prior property qualification of 400,000 *sestertii*, the salaried nature of army commands was important, as was the likelihood that there would have been opportunities to make additional financial gains from involvement in imperial government. The patronage system was one way in which an officer might benefit, but the opportunities to accept bribes and gifts must have been considerable. The *tres militiae* was also a set of steps towards still more lucrative imperial postings in the equestrian career path. A few years of relative discomfort on Hadrian's Wall might be followed by an assignment to a Mediterranean province, if one was lucky. Particularly for those newly enrolled in the equestrian order, it offered networking opportunities and a path of upward mobility. About ten officers who served in Britain were later enrolled in the Senate, and a further fifteen went on to higher procuratorial posts.

In the most astonishing case P. Helvius Pertinax ended up as emperor in 193. Pertinax started out as a schoolmaster, but switched to a military career, serving his *prima militia* in *Syria*, before gaining a legionary tribunate and commanding a cohort in Britain, followed by an *ala* in *Moesia*. He then advanced into the procuratorial branch of equestrian service with a junior post related to the *via Aemilia* and served as commander of the fleet on the Rhine, before being appointed procurator of *Dacia*. Further military service, in the emergency of a Germanic invasion of northern Italy, was followed by his adlection (enrolment) into the Senate and he soon had command of a legion in the Marcomannic war under Marcus Aurelius, where he is known to have won at least one major victory. He was subsequently governor of four military provinces, *Moesia Superior* and *Inferior*, *Dacia* and *Syria*, obtaining the consulship along the way. After a gap, he was recalled to public life in 185 with the task of governing Britain at a time when its army was evidently mutinous. On his return to Rome, he was prefect of the *alimenta* and then Proconsul of *Africa* and Prefect of Rome and consul for the second time. He was well placed and well qualified, despite his humble origins, to make a bid for the purple following the assassination of Commodus. This was an exceptional career, made possible by the humble origins of the man and the distrust sometimes shown by emperors for well-established aristocrats.

Also fairly exceptional was Q. Baienus Blassianus from Trieste who started his career as prefect of the *cohors II Asturum*, later commanded the British fleet (technically an imperial procuratorial appointment, not a military post in the gift of the governor) and ended up many years later as the Prefect of Egypt, one of the highest equestrian governorships. Another equestrian who made the transition from military commands to procuratorial positions had an unusually long connection with Britain. Maenius Agrippa from *Camerinum* in Italy first served as prefect of a cohort of Britons on the Danube, before being 'chosen by the deified Hadrian and sent on the British expedition' (as his career inscription informs us). He was tribune of the *cohors I Hispanorum* at Maryport for at least four years, before returning to the Danube to command a cavalry *ala*. Subsequently he returned to Britain as prefect of the British fleet and finally as imperial procurator of the province. Another man appointed to the tribunate of a British legion was Suetonius Tranquillus, the biographer of emperors, though he declined to take up the post.

The *Vindolanda* tablets reveal that Sulpicia Lepidina accompanied her husband Flavius Cerialis to his posting. Numerous documents from the building that was their home within the fort (the *praetorium*) relate to their personal correspondence and the management of the household. Among their regular correspondents were a number of other auxiliary commanders, including Aelius Brocchus and his wife Claudia Severa, based at a fort called *Briga* (perhaps Kirkbride to west of Carlisle) and probably also at *Coria* at another time. A letter sent by Claudia to Sulpicia inviting her to attend her birthday party is among the most interesting tablets. Other letters refer to further visits and to the loneliness of the women between-times. Claudia had her son with her, and small shoes and other finds at *Vindolanda* suggest that Sulpicia also had children. There were clearly a number of slaves, both male and female, in their households; some of them were clearly literate and drafted letters and documents. One of the most touching aspects of the correspondence between Claudia Severa and Sulpicia Lepidina is that the former added her personal greetings to the end of the letters drafted by an amanuensis.

Flavius Cerialis (or his father) appears to have been enfranchised by the Flavian emperors, and promotion to equestrian status may have been quite recent. What is striking from the documents is that he and his wife were well integrated into the behavioural world of the Roman elite. Several documents appear to be household inventories, one listing dishes, bowls, plates, and a variety of other vessels including egg-cups;

another containing a list of textile hangings, clothing (including tunics from Brocchus) and blankets. Although the *praetorium* of a fort was palatial in comparison to the amount of personal space allowed for the ordinary soldiers and junior officers, excavation of such structures show them to have been spartanly decorated. It is clear that aristocrats showed off their wealth and status by filling their houses with portable luxuries, that they could carry with them to the next posting – notably decorative textile hangings, drapes and carpets and impressive metal tableware. Another document mentions five curtains of different colours (red, green, purple and yellow) costing in total over 200 *denarii* – at a time when a legionary's annual salary was not much more. Pliny the Elder censured a first-century governor of Lower Germany for carrying 1,200 Roman pounds of silverware in his baggage, but less excessive and ostentatious displays were probably common in the elite military community.

A lengthy document spanning several years' activity appears to be a list of expenses in the *praetorium*, and includes a list of dining guests on specified dates, while other entries seem to give a detailed account of beer and chickens consumed. They suggest that the diet of the commander was not all that different in basic ingredients from the common soldiery, though the availability of meat and chickens and of wine and beer may have been more generous. In addition, though, there are documents that appear to deal with lists of more exotic (or simply less readily available) commodities, ordered up from a distance – including mustard, verdigris, resin, cumin, anise, grapes, nuts, potash and perhaps even opium.

Cerialis and Brocchus appear to have been keen hunters and there are references in the tablets to hunters, hunting nets and dogs. The sport could supplement the diet in the fort and the lists of foodstuffs include venison and roe deer (also present in the faunal assemblage). In a letter, Cerialis requested that Brocchus send him some new or repaired hunting nets, and from a list we learn that the Batavian cohort left behind (perhaps when it departed *Vindolanda c.*105) a number of different types of net. Hunting was a popular leisure activity of the Roman elite, in part because it was a restricted practice. Military commanders had more opportunities than others in Britain to indulge in large-scale hunting (and some may have been required to do so to furnish beasts for imperial shows). A famous inscription from Bollihope Common in Weardale was set up by the prefect of the *ala Sebosiana*, in celebration of the 'taking of a wild boar of remarkable fineness which many of his predecessors had been unable to bag'. Apart from the competitive element present here, indicative of peer emulation, this inscription is interesting for what it tells us about the relationship of the military to the landscape. The ability of the officer class to pay visits to each other accompanied by their spouses or to go off hunting in the vicinity of their forts indicates a general self-confidence about their place and power in the region. Such behaviour also sent a specific message to the native Britons about the dominance, the right to roam and the lack of fear felt by the Roman army.

Another important group within the community of soldiers comprised the 180 legionary centurions and the three camp prefects, men who were prospective additions to the equestrian order on retirement. They were evidently comparatively well paid, since some equestrians sought the steady employment of a legionary centurion in preference to the uncertain and potentially discontinuous postings as an auxiliary commander. There appears to have been no mandatory retirement age and centurions could continue in service for remarkable terms. Six of nineteen centurions known to have chalked up in excess of forty years' service included spells in Britain. T. Flavius Virilis was successively centurion in all three British legions, *II Augusta*, *XX Valeria* and *VI Victrix*, in an astonishing career of forty-five years. He had eventually left Britain to serve with the *III Augusta* in Africa and the *III Parthica* in Italy. His British wife Lollia Bodicca buried him in Algeria aged seventy. Legionary centurions were central figures in the community of soldiers since they had a foot in two social camps; some had risen from the ranks, while a few would go on to pursue equestrian careers after discharge. Cn. Pompeius Homullus is a high-flying example of the latter tendency with connections to Britain at two stages of his career. His early posts are uncertain, but he was a highly decorated first centurion (*primus pilus*) in two legions (*II Augusta* in Britain and *X Fretensis* in *Iudaea*) – implying a considerable previous track record. He served as tribune of three of Rome's urban units, before holding procuratorships in Britain and in Gaul and a final posting in Rome (*a rationibus*). Another extraordinary career is recorded in a long funerary inscription at Kasserine in Tunisia, covering two generations of centurions, both called Petronius Fortunatus. The older man served over fifty years in the army, being initially promoted to centurion following a vote among his fellow legionaries. He was centurion for forty-six years and served in thirteen legions including *VI Victrix* at York. His son was less fortunate and died young, while serving as centurion of the *II Augusta* at Caerleon. In contrast to these men, we should note that there are several examples of equestrians who took direct commissions as legionary centurions. One such was M. Iulius Quadratus from *Numidia*, who served in *Dacia* and *Africa*, before being transferred to the *II Augusta* in Britain, where he met his death 'on active service'.

Many of the known first-century centurions were from Italy; men like M. Favonius Facilis of *legio XX*, depicted in full-dress uniform on his tombstone from Colchester. There were some individuals from further afield, such as P. Anicius Maximus, camp prefect of the *II Augusta* in 43 who came from Antioch in *Pisidia*. Among the large number of centurions' names recorded on building stones from Hadrian's Wall, there are a few 'Greeks', perhaps mainly from the Danube region, along with several where an Italian origin is plausible, as well as others who have typically 'army' names, suggesting that they were descendants of provincial veterans. Although it is to be expected that the number of British-born centurions rose over time, the size of the legionary garrison in Britain and the fact that centurions showed much more mobility between provinces than did legions, would suggest that the centurionate was overall less affected by changes in recruitment and continued to be ethnically quite mixed. It has been suggested that a third-century tombstone from Chester of M. Aurelius Nepos, with a poorly executed image of the centurion and his wife, might represent a British-born man. Certainly the quality of the work compares unfavourably with the image of Favonius Facilis at Colchester.

Centurions were regularly assigned special duties, including commanding small legionary detachments (vexillations) or auxiliary units away from the main fortress. Sextus Flavius Quietus, when *primus pilus* of the *XX* legion, commanded an expeditionary force sent to Morocco in the 140s and after his return to Britain was appointed prefect of the British fleet. There are several references to 'regional administrators'. T. Floridius Natalis of the *VI Victrix* was *praepositus* in charge of a *numerus* based at Ribchester and its region. C. Severius Emeritus of the *II Augusta* was recorded as regional centurion (*centurio regionarius*) at Bath, where he restored a shrine 'wrecked by insolent people'. A letter from the *Vindolanda* archive mentions another *centurio regionarius* at

Carlisle and a fourth region is now attested, centred on the garrison settlement at Castleford (*regio Lagitiensis*). There must surely have been many more. Military officers serving as 'tribal prefects' (*praefecti genti*) are attested in other provinces, though not as yet in Britain.

Centurions evidently regularly owned slaves and sometimes the latter were named as heirs, becoming freedmen with the death of their masters. For example, Verecundus and Novicius, the freedmen of Favonius Facilis, erected his memorial. The longer a centurion lived the higher the likelihood that he might have a wife or have offspring to take on this role. Some of these wives may be strongly suspected as being British in origin; so Vibia Pacata wife of Flavius Verecundus who was stationed on the Antonine Wall, or Lollia Bodicca, whose name recalls Boudica.

Other legionary soldiers are not as well represented in the surviving epigraphic record as their officers. Their origins are not always clear, but the small sample of evidence suggests that at the time of the Claudian conquest the majority (81 per cent) were recruited in Italy, with the balance shifting by the end of the first century to present almost the reverse picture (*c.*20 per cent Italians). Most of the provincial recruitment was from veteran colonies in the western empire, notably *Hispania* and *Gallia*, but also *Germania*, *Raetia* and *Noricum*. Recruits from the eastern empire are also attested, but in small numbers. From the reign of Hadrian onwards there were evidently few Italian recruits in Britain and provincial recruits dominate the record. Some individuals had 'Celtic' names from which unusual Latin forms had been fabricated, and could have included men recruited in Britain. Examples include Condrausius from near Hadrian's Wall and Ecimius Bellicianus Vitalis from Chester. Iulius Vitalis who died at Bath described himself as a '*Belga*', indicating either a North Gaulish or a British origin. C. Pomponius Valens is another probable British recruit, as his origin is given as *Victricens[is]* on his tombstone found at London. The *colonia Victricensis* was another name for the veteran settlement at Colchester and that site will have been the first in Britain to supply qualified citizen recruits.

Several strands of evidence point to the presence of contingents of North African recruits in the army, notably the tombstone found at Birdoswald of C. Cossutius Saturninus from *Hippo Regius* (Algeria). A study of Roman pottery on the Antonine Wall and at the legionary works depot at Holt near Chester has identified African-style cookwares appearing (in one example from the pottery manufactory at Holt with a neo-Punic graffito), along with braziers and cooking stands of typical African form. It has been suggested that there may have been an influx of North African recruits into British legions and auxiliary units after the Mauretanian war in the 140s, to which British reinforcements, commanded by the *primus pilus* of *legio XX*, had been sent as part of the emergency response. Indeed the history of the army in Britain is punctuated by such episodic transfers of personnel out and in that could give a new cultural dimension to the garrison as a whole.

Whole legions were withdrawn in the mid-60s and in 70 (*legio XIV*), in the mid-80s (*II Adiutrix*) and in the early second century (*IX Hispana*), with replacements in 71 (*II Adiutrix*) and 122 (*VI Victrix*). We also know that there were major influxes of legionaries, to make up losses in the British regiments following the Boudican revolt and under Hadrian, and that British contingents were absent at various points in the first, second and third centuries, assisting in external wars. To some extent such movement of troops will have counteracted the tendency of increased local recruitment to create a predominantly British outlook among legionaries. Dedications to 'African, Italian and Gallic Mother-Goddesses' at York and to 'Italian, German, Gallic and British Mother-Goddesses' at Winchester (by a *beneficiarius*) suggest that the strong diversity among the legionaries continued into the third century.

It is increasingly recognized that the activity of the British legions extended well beyond their main fortress bases. Although there were only three main bases from the late first century, it is apparent that these were not continuously occupied to full capacity. The construction of the Hadrianic and Antonine frontiers may have been one factor behind this, but small legionary detachments have been detected at other sites, most notably Corbridge, Carpow and London. It is highly significant that such movement of legionaries continued after the division of the province, and the presence of detachments (and of *beneficiarii*) of the legions of *Britannia Superior* in the military zone of *Britannia Inferior* suggests a high level of military and administrative co-operation.

The contribution of legionaries to basic administrative tasks in Britain has been alluded to already. The role of the *beneficiarii consularis* and other staff of the governor's *officium* is largely invisible to us in the surviving sources. We can catch the occasional glimpse of where they were operating, but rarely do we get a clear sense of what they were engaged in. At some locations they seem to have had specific administrative bureaux (*stationes*), in other cases they may have been on *ad hoc* missions. What is clear is that they operated both in the military and civil zones of the province. *Beneficiarii consularis* are attested at *Vindolanda* (both in an inscription and in the tablets) and Housesteads, and at forts along the main roads north and south of Hadrian's Wall (Risingham, Greta Bridge, Lancaster, Lanchester, Binchester and Catterick). In the civil zone of the province, there are examples from the towns of Wroxeter and Winchester and the small town of Dorchester-on-Thames. Some *beneficiarii* were attached to legionary legates and tribunes; examples occur at Chester and London.

Auxiliary troops outnumbered the legionary contingent in Britain, probably by the 70s at latest, but there are only about eighty inscriptions attributable to auxiliary troops in Britain, the majority relating to the junior officers in these regiments (centurions and decurions). On the other hand there is a high probability that some of the inscriptions from garrison settlements that do not specify a regiment nonetheless related to soldiers. This is clear in some cases where images were included on the stone. M. Aurelius Victor's epitaph at Chesters only gave his name and age, but the image unambiguously depicts him as a cavalryman. Officers (even junior ones) had careers or career aspirations; their status within the hierarchy was normally specified by drawing attention to their rank with such-and-such unit. The same was not true of other ranks in quite the same way. Soldiers were more likely to give detail as they moved up the hierarchy (if they were on double-pay, a clerk, an NCO or a standard-bearer). Cavalry troopers, with higher pay and enhanced status, are by far the most commonly attested lower-rank troops. The act of erecting an inscription within a garrison settlement was a means of asserting membership of and position within the community of soldiers. The inclusion of the unit name may have been seen as optional and the extra cost of adding that information may in itself have been determinant. It is certainly clear that higher-paid soldiers, such as cavalry troopers, tended more frequently to identify their unit in funerary or religious texts.

The inscriptions set up by auxiliaries in Britain provide information about their nomenclature, origins, status and length of service. In theory at least, the auxiliaries were non-citizens and were signed on for 25–26-year terms. In practice, especially in the Claudian–Flavian period, many served longer, though citizenship might be awarded after twenty-five years. It is also clear that some soldiers were already citizens, especially true of junior cavalry officers, and this became increasingly common in the second century, when citizen sons of auxiliary soldiers were often recruited. There were also some block allocations of citizenship to units that had showed particular valour in battle. Longinus Sdapeze, son of Matygus, is typical of a group of Thracian cavalrymen. He served in the *ala I Thracum* and was buried at Colchester. Rufus Sita and Tiberius Claudius Tirintius served in *cohortes equitatae* of Thracians, dying at Gloucester and Wroxeter respectively. The first two of these men had assumed Latinized versions of their native names on joining the army, but they were not yet citizens. Tirintius had probably served more than twenty-five years and been granted citizenship. The three-part Roman name (*tria nomina*) of Sextus Valerius Genialis, also from the *ala Thracum*, shows that he was a citizen when he died at Cirencester, but he was of Frisian origin, rather than a Thracian. Yet others retained a more native appellation – such as the trooper of the *ala Indiana*, Dannicus, from Upper Germany, again buried at Cirencester.

The *Vindolanda* tablets have added substantially to knowledge of soldiers' names and lifestyle, though the mutual familiarity of personnel and the relative informality of many of the documents result in a lack of clarity of the precise status of many named individuals. Some letters contain greetings to or from 'messmates'. Of *c.*200 Batavian and Tungrian soldiers identified so far in the archive, most had a single name only and were not yet citizens. Quite a few of the names were clearly Germanic or Gallic and a few were Latinized versions of German or Gallic names, but the majority were straightforward Latin names – presumably in most cases selected for the men by their officers on their induction to the army. Several female names (Elpis, Verecunda, 'sister Thuttena', Crispa, Ingenua and Varranilla) were included in groups of people referred to as messmates (*contubernales*) and this fits with evidence already mentioned that some soldiers may have had 'wives' or concubines with them in the fort. The fact that such names are relatively uncommon suggests that the female component in the fort itself remained comparatively small at this date.

There was much amusement in the 1970s when one of the first *Vindolanda* letters to be deciphered turned out to refer to socks, sandals and underpants being sent to a soldier, but clothing turns up in many other documents now translated. Securing appropriate garments to withstand the northern winters was obviously a key concern of these men; it is also clear that much had to be brought in from a distance, even from Gaul. Money was another abiding obsession of the soldiery. Not only were they unusual in being salaried, they also had access to means of borrowing money, whether from each other or in advance of salary from the unit. Quite a few documents seem to comprise accounts of debts owing, with entries being scratched through once paid. The sums involved were mostly trifling (a few *denarii*), but several sums exceeded a year's pay and one exceptional debt of 2,000 *denarii* appears to have involved an officer. As well as clothing, soldiers were spending money on items of glassware, tableware, cooking pots, foodstuffs, salt, beer, firewood, boot nails, thread and shoe laces, metals, tallow or fat, blankets and towels, wooden sandals for the baths, and on repairs to possessions.

Units were responsible for providing the essentials, but soldiers engaged in lively trade for a wide variety of goods to improve the quality of their life, diet and wardrobe. A lengthy account of wheat distributions reveals the mixed nature of the military community at the fort. In addition to a number of individual soldiers of the auxiliary garrison, the document lists grain supplied to legionary soldiers and to a *beneficiarius*, as well as to 'oxherds in the wood', 'Lucco in charge of the pigs', a probable slave and someone referred to as 'father'. The overlap between what was technically military and civilians living alongside the unit may have been considerable.

Veterans formed a significant category of civilian members of the military community. Legionary soldiers received lands or cash payments on discharge after twenty-five years' service. At moments when there were large numbers of veterans to discharge (as after civil wars) and in general during the phase of continued expansion of the empire, emperors tended to settle groups of veterans in specially founded towns (*coloniae*) with associated land allotments. Such allocations involved confiscation of land from the indigenous peoples of the region. By the second century, it was more common for veterans to be directed either to an existing colony, where there was spare land, or simply given a discharge bounty and left to make their own arrangements. Some soldiers probably took the money and ran, returning either to their birthplace or to more convivial climates or to other provinces in which they had served and prospered. On the other hand, several factors may have favoured settlement of veterans in Britain, including the fact that many had acquired families in service and the likelihood that land was readily and comparatively cheaply available. For those choosing to settle in Britain, there were several choices. Many military service personnel undoubtedly will have been attracted by the concentration of ex-soldiers at the *coloniae* and the military character of such sites remained strong for generations. Colchester, Gloucester and Lincoln were the only three veteran *coloniae* in Britain and may have absorbed a significant number of discharged legionaries over time, not just when first established. On the other hand, the growth of substantial garrison settlements (*canabae*) alongside the major fortress sites at Caerleon, Chester and York offered another set of possible retirement locations and many legionaries may already have had families living there. The origins of recruits drawn from these settlements would have been characterized as '*castris*' (literally 'from the fortress'). A separate urban centre on the opposite bank of the Ouse eventually supplemented the garrison settlement at York and this new town was elevated to the rank of honorary *colonia* in the third century. Since the legion remained in place alongside the double urban centre, the military character of the place was very pronounced. Another regular destination for ex-legionaries within Britain will have been London, where many men may have spent time on the governor's business. Purchase of rural estates was another potential course of action.

Auxiliary soldiers received less materially on discharge, but many soldiers will have come out of service with accumulated savings and the sought-after award of Roman citizenship, recorded on bronze tablets issued to those men who required them. These 'discharge tablets' became rare by the late second century and were redundant after Caracalla extended citizenship. Presumably the decline in use reflects the fact that auxiliary units were increasingly recruiting individuals who already had Roman citizenship. Some diplomas of soldiers who had served in Britain have been found in other provinces, but, as with the legionaries, it is clear that many auxiliaries had acquired families in the garrison settlements by the time they reached the age for discharge and chose to settle in Britain. Some will have chosen to remain by their garrison post, perhaps using their savings to invest in a trade or business, others will have gravitated towards urban centres with a more military character or to areas with cheap land. Whether carrying the status of Roman citizens or not, the sons of veterans were prime candidates for voluntary recruitment.

Ten of eleven stone inscriptions recording auxiliary veterans relate to garrison settlements in northern Britain (Chesters, Old Carlisle, Old Penrith, Kirkby Thore, Ambleside, Greta Bridge, Malton, Templeborough), though in many cases the veteran appears to have moved away from the exact location where his unit was based. The remaining inscription is from the *colonia* at Lincoln. On the other hand, the evidence of discharge diplomas reveals a rather different picture. Of sixteen examples known in Britain, there are five from the military zone (*Vindolanda*, Chesters (two), Ravenglass, York), plus a further two from the Cheshire plain close to Chester (Malpas and Middlewich) and another from Stannington in south Yorkshire. Four additional examples come from towns (Colchester, London, Wroxeter and Caistor-by-Norwich) and four from rural locations (Walcot near Bath, Sydenham in Kent, Aldwincle in Northants and Great Dunham in Norfolk). The behaviour on retirement of auxiliaries thus splits into three groups: those who left Britain, those who continued to display very visibly their sense of belonging to the military community in Britain and those who blended more into the civil zone of the province. Some of the urban centres selected by the latter group were towns with a military profile, and Wroxeter was closer than most to the military zone. The man who retired there was from Trier in *Gallia Belgica*, not a Briton returning to his home town.

Civilians in the garrison settlements were numerically important. About 100 forts have produced evidence of associated external structures, and similar features may be suspected at other sites that have been poorly investigated. Not all the garrison settlements were the same, however, and it is important to recognize that some probably comprised little more than temporary shacks and tents flanking the approach road to a fort, while others developed over time into small towns of well-built houses. The legionary *canabae* were certainly large and relatively sophisticated settlements, reflecting the scale and economic power of the legions and the nodal positions they occupied in terms of communications and supply networks.

The inhabitants of the garrison settlements are difficult to separate off from the soldiery. As noted already, lower-rank soldiers included information on their unit much less frequently on inscriptions. For this reason, it is probable that many male funerary inscriptions erected outside forts, but lacking unit ascription, were nonetheless set up by soldiers or members of their immediate families. Clues to military status include possession of citizenship or references to wills and heirs (though these became less diagnostic features after Caracalla's citizenship edict). For the first and second centuries at least, such people, if not army personnel, were almost certainly incomers to the region. Many traders operating in the frontier regions will have seen themselves as intimately linked to the community of soldiers and it is interesting that their tombstones do not draw clearer distinctions between their employment and the soldiery. The case of the Palmyrene Barathes exemplifies this, and his status as a flag-bearer (military) or flag-seller (civilian) has been much debated on the basis of an ambiguous abbreviation on his tombstone. Given his age when he died (68), it is not inconceivable that he had been both.

There are quite a number of religious dedications from garrison settlements and dedications by identified military personnel seem to have provided the model for the texts whose dedicants are of ambiguous status. Tombstones are another important category, though divisible into a number of types: cases where a man was buried by his heir(s) or his wife, cases where a woman or child was buried by members of their family, cases where burial of an individual was paid for by a *collegium*. Examples of the third category include the burial of a slave at Halton Chesters by a *collegium conservorum*, implying the presence of considerable numbers of slaves at the fort. Military tombstones that do not mention widows or heirs are relatively common and were presumably paid for by military burial clubs. Some individuals who were buried by wives clearly died at an age when they would still have been active soldiers and their 'marriages' illegal if pre-dating the Severan reform of 197. On the other hand, discharge diplomas frequently mention 'spouses', though often to delimit their rights. Both indicate the existence of unofficial marriages. Overall, soldiers were more likely to be commemorated by their wives than the other way around. A survey of *c.*1,000 military tombstones across the empire identified 102 instances of wives commemorating husbands, against 55 cases of soldiers erecting memorials to their wives. The reasons for this pattern include the fact that many soldiers were probably much older than their wives, settling in to long-term relationships towards the end of their service. A couple buried together at Burrow-in-Lonsdale by their son provides a typical example: Aurelius Pusinnus was fifty-three and his wife thirty-seven.

The majority of tombstones of soldiers dying within the first fifteen years in service do not mention spouses and, where specified, the heirs were often fellow soldiers or perhaps freedmen of the deceased.

Commemoration of a person with a permanent funerary inscription (and sometimes a sculptural relief also) was widespread in Roman society, though in Britain it is very much more commonly attested in the military areas than elsewhere. As such it can be highlighted as a diagnostic element of the military identity. Soldiers engaged in displays of status and ostentatious commemoration aimed at their peers, at the upper end reflecting the career achievements of individuals within the service and at the lower end simply the financial wherewithal to leave such memorials behind them. The practice quite naturally extended, as resources allowed, to their families and households (including wives, children, brothers and sisters, freedpeople and slaves).

Despite the official line against recognizing soldiers' marriages before the end of the second century, it is nonetheless interesting that women played an important and visible role within the military community. The presence of commanding officers' wives has already been noted and legionary centurions at least had the right to marry while in service. Concubines of serving soldiers and wives of veterans had status through the position and earning power of their men. However, we should not take too rosy a view of the overall position of women in this society. Women were present in the garrison settlements for a number of reasons, but primarily in relation to the army. Since many of the younger soldiers did not take unofficial wives, it is certain that prostitutes were a valuable commodity in garrison settlements. How their business was organized is unclear, though the operation of brothels by entrepreneurs using slave women is a distinct possibility. Establishments serving drink to off-duty soldiers may well also have catered for sex in a room at the back. The importation of prostitutes from outside the immediate area could have reduced tensions with the local population. Wealthier and higher-ranking soldiers may have bought their own female slaves to serve them in a variety of needs, including as sexual partners. Marcus Cocceius Firmus, a legionary centurion in command at Auchendavy on the Antonine Wall, evidently had a female slave. Pompeius Optatus paid for a tombstone at Chester for three slave children from his household, and though his occupation is unclear it is highly probable that he was a serving soldier and that the reason for the memorial was that these were his own children with a female slave. The name of Aurelia Eubia, the wife of Aurelius Pusinnus, suggests that she might once have been his slave, since slaves were often given such Greek names. Barathes the Palmyrene erected a splendid memorial to his British wife Regina at South Shields, depicting her as a Roman matron. Yet she had started as his slave, being freed so he could marry her. The fact that she was a Catuvellaunian by birth and had been taken into slavery long after the conquest phase suggests that she may have been sold into slavery by her own family, in full knowledge that sexual exploitation would be part of her fate. Regina is a 'success' story in that she was freed and married by her owner, but there is an ominous, if unsurprising, gap in our evidence for the lowest tier of women serving the army.

Power differentials within provincial society were open to abuse in the obtaining of sexual favours. There were specific prohibitions on governors and military commanders contracting marriages with women from the province in which they were serving (though betrothals were permissible). This measure clearly aimed at protecting the interests of wealthy provincial families from having pressure exerted on them to contract marriages with senior members of the Roman administration. No such limitations were placed on the soldiery and their power in society will have made them a predatory threat to British women, though as the garrison settlements grew in size and demographic stability, the military community may have conducted its marriage market within better defined limits.

The names of some wives in northern Britain suggest that they were from well-established or status-sensitive military families. Aurelia Aia, who came from Salona and was daughter of Titus (presumably an ex-soldier), was married to Aurelius Marcus, a serving soldier at Carvoran in the third century. She is described as 'without any blemish'. Even where servile origins are suspected, as in the case of Aurelia Eubia, the commemoration stresses family norms. Her name even means 'respectable'. Gaius Valerius Iustus, a legionary at Chester, mourned his wife Cocceia Irene as 'most chaste and pure'. There are plenty of examples of growing daughters in garrison settlements, where it is clear that the family will have had strong concerns about reputation and marriageability. Aurelia Romana and Aurelia Sabina set up a memorial for their father at Greta Bridge, while Aurelia Quartilla (aged thirteen) and Iuliona (sixteen) are both attested at Risingham. There are also instances where it is clear that soldiers had taken responsibility for other relatives living in the garrison settlements: Dionysius Fortunatus buried his mother Aurelia Lupula at Risingham, Iulius Maximus did the same for his mother-in-law Campania Dubitata at Ribchester (along with his wife and six-year-old son). A German called Lurio at Chesters mourned his sister Ursa along with his wife and his son. Other examples show uncles commemorating nieces and nephews. Some of these relatives were acquired, but others had clearly followed the soldier to his posting.

There are, of course, also examples of women setting up memorials in their own right to relations. We have already noted that women were frequent dedicants of inscriptions to their husbands, but they also commemorated sisters and children. The implication here is that the act of commemoration was not simply dictated by the communal interest in soldiers and ex-soldiers, or in soldiers applying the principle to their families.

Personal nomenclature and to some extent religious preferences can help to identify ethnic minorities in the garrison communities. Again the distinctions between serving soldiers and civilian dependants are hard to discern. The issue is further complicated by the tendency for soldiers to take Latin names on enlistment and for nomenclature to be further affected by the gain of citizenship. Occasionally, we can do better. For example, more than sixty people of German extraction, some certainly women and children, can be identified in the Hadrian's Wall area, where a *cuneus* of *Frisii* and a *numerus Hnaudifridi* were based from the third century. One inscription from Housesteads recorded the deaths of [. . .]enionus, son of Venocarus, Gratus, son of Fersio, Romulus, son of Alimahus, Similis, son of Dailus, Mansuetius, son of Senicio, Pervinca, daughter of Quartio. The heir of the entire group identified himself as 'Delfinus, son of Rautio from Upper Germany'. The mix of Germanic and Latin 'army' names is very suggestive here. Units of Germans were an important component in the British garrison and some newly levied troops were still being sent to Britain in the later second and third centuries.

There is also a smattering of recognizably Gallic or British names, along with some Greek forms, from the frontier region. In addition to Barathes, there is another easterner, Salmanes, who buried his fifteen-year-old son, also called Salmanes, at Auchendavy on the Antonine Wall. The ethnic balance at any site will have varied considerably, but was probably quite mixed throughout the garrison settlements of northern and western Britain. What we are not dealing with are pristine settlements of local Britons, neatly attached to the forts and becoming 'Roman' as a result of close and prolonged contact. The garrison settlements may well have assimilated some native Britons, but those Britons will have taken their place within a social structure that was at all times a reflection of a broader military community with a distinctly cosmopolitan mix.

The fort of Brougham in Cumbria has yielded quite a large number of personal names, both on dedications to a local cult (Belatucadrus) and on tombstones. Comparatively few relate to the officer class and the site has often been held up as representative of the lower levels of 'frontier society'. One man identifies himself as a member of a cavalry unit, but the military associations of others, though likely, are unproven. Almost all the individuals are known by a single name only, which is a distinctive feature and supports the 'lower ranks' theory. Annius, Aurelia, Crescentius, Ianuarius, Iulianus, Lunaris, Pluma are straightforward Latin names that are highly suggestive of the military community, though some are rare or unparalleled. Annamoris, Audagus, Baculo, C[uno]vinda, Nittiunis, Ressona, Talio, Tittus, Vidaris and [. . .]orix may all be Latinized versions of British or north European nomenclature. Taking account of the difference in time, the overall characteristics of this group are not dissimilar to the soldiers' names in the *Vindolanda* tablets. This strongly supports the view that most people named in inscriptions from garrison settlements were serving officers or soldiers, retired soldiers, closely related to soldiers or veterans, or non-local traders who shared and emulated much of the cultural identity of the garrison. The identity of the Brougham community will be revisited at the end of the next chapter.

7

The Fashioning of the
Military Identity

The widespread origins, varied languages and differing social mores of the soldiery and the civilians in the garrison settlements created great cultural variability within the military community. This diversity reminds us that the Roman army was a human organization, built from the bottom up as the sum of its sometimes unruly parts. Yet, at the same time, there were significant common patterns of behaviour and social outlook that made the army an empire-wide and self-aware identity group of *commilitones* – 'fellow soldiers'. The culture of the military community was particularly strong in the garrisoned areas, but also permeated other areas of the province.

This chapter will look in more detail at what contributed to the military's distinctive overall identity and how this served both to reinforce its sense of oneness and to differentiate it from other groups in Britain. Just as important, though, was the fact that the notion of being Roman, and the social behaviours attached to it, differed markedly from that of civilians outside the military community. Far from being agents of '*Romanitas*', the army constructed its culture and identity to emphasize its power, its difference and its distance from ordinary civilians. The civilian groups that sought to emulate the military community were generally those linked closely to it, through marriage, agnate relations, or trade.

LANGUAGE AND LITERACY:
THE EPIGRAPHIC HABIT

The Latin language was an essential element of a Roman soldier's identity. Enrolment in the army often involved the taking of new names (or

Latinized name forms), swearing Latin oaths of loyalty and living under a regime shaped by Latin as the language of command and regulations. We have already noted the importance of written communication and written records in the day-to-day activities of the military community. The *Vindolanda* discoveries have revolutionized our view of the extent and scale of literate communication in the army outside Egypt. Wooden stylus tablets had long been known in the Roman world; their design, with a recessed wax-filled surface into which messages were incised, emphasizes the possible multiple reuse of each set. No one expected the northern provinces to produce evidence of huge quantities of a second type of tablet, written on in ink and designed for single use (or at most reuse of the back of a single-sided document). The nature of the documents clearly implies a very large annual output for a single garrison. Many letters found at *Vindolanda* were received from or addressed to other locations (Binchester, *Briga*, Carlisle, Catterick, Corbridge, London, *Ulucium*, York), and examples of ink tablets are now also known from Carlisle, London and Caerleon. The implications are that the large-scale use of such tablets was standard and wide-ranging in terms of the types of records and communications. The excavated context of the tablets suggests that many had been held in the prefect's records, but were disposed of when the fort garrison changed (a typical Northumberland rain storm seems to have extinguished a smouldering bonfire and preserved one of the main groups). The *Vindolanda* excavations have also yielded large numbers of stylus tablets, though transcription of the palimpsest scratches on their surfaces is rarely possible. Ink writing on the narrow edges of these stylus tablets has shown that they were also sometimes filed in boxes or on shelves (rather like CDs). This is clear evidence for the existence of a retrieval system in military record keeping. The production of leaf tablets must have been considerably easier and cheaper than the manufacture of wax stylus tablets and facilitated the mass communications of the Roman army. From what we now know, the army in Britain must have generated tens of millions of documents across the centuries of occupation.

Latin communication became ever more essential in polyglot and ethnically diverse units. Not all soldiers spoke Latin 'correctly', and some soldiers evidently remained illiterate. But literacy was an important element of getting promoted to higher ranks in the Roman army and the cachet attached to it cannot be overestimated, even if classical scholars may chuckle over the grammatical manglings of the 'camp Latin' that emerged. Soldiers who lacked good reading and writing skills were nonetheless obliged to operate in a system that depended on written communication and records. The use of written language was clearly at a far higher level than in other areas of provincial life. A striking aspect of the *Vindolanda* material is that the tablets were evidently produced by a large number of individual hands (several hundred have been recognized). There is no evidence that the fort's records were simply serviced by a small group of clerks and slaves. Although there is much variation in punctuation and abbreviation in the cursive script employed, it is also clear that soldiers were operating within a broadly common frame of conventions. There are, in addition, general similarities in form and content between the *Vindolanda* material and other army documents produced at the opposite end of the empire. Similarly, palaeo-graphical studies show that the handwriting is basically the same style of script as was used in Egypt (known as Old Roman Cursive), though with a great range of fluency in the hands, from elegant to ugly. It is a reasonable inference that a literate soldier newly transferred to Britain would have been able to recognize at a glance the general type and import of the documents used at *Vindolanda*.

There is plenty of evidence to suggest that some members of the garrison aspired to higher levels of literacy than others. Not surprisingly the unit commander's Latin stands out above much of the rest. This is indicated not simply by the quality of spelling and grammar applied, but also in the care of composition. Many of the letters in the Cerialis archive appear to be drafts of documents he sent and some of these show signs of crossings out as he worked at his constructions. There may well have been good models to hand for some standard types of documents, as similarities in phrasing of letters of recommendation known elsewhere suggest. There are a few clearly literary allusions, such as quotes from both the *Aeneid* and *Georgics* of Virgil, implying the presence of books in the households of at least two commanders in Periods 3–4. It is also fascinating to have documents written by women associated with the garrison, in the form of the addenda to the letters of Claudia Severa to Sulpicia Lepidina. Although her handwriting was rather stiff, it is probable that she had dictated the body of the letters to a scribe in fairly elegant Latin. However, many of the documents that were written by lower ranks contain vulgarized forms and spellings, and the literary competence can give some hints about the relative status of the writer when this is not otherwise clear from the document. Throughout the tablets one senses a strong feeling of comradeship, of shared values and loyalties. This is clearest in the repeated formulae that stress the shared experience of military life: 'brother and old messmate', 'lord and brother', 'little brother', 'my brother and my messmate'. Even the women shared this sense of close community, Claudia Severa referring to Sulpicia Lepidina as her 'sister, my dearest soul'. A final point to note is that some of the *Vindolanda* documents were probably written by or addressed to civilian traders operating alongside the army. The obvious example is the letter of complaint by the merchant who had been beaten. The use of literate communications in their dealings with the army distinguished them from the local population at this time and reinforced their sense of identity and common cause with the army.

Inscriptions on stone offer another window on the use of literacy in the military community. Taking Britain as a whole, the vast majority of all stone inscriptions recorded can be attributed to the military community. This is not simply a result of geology or preservation. The occurrence of inscribed material in town and country districts is simply less impressive. The 'epigraphic habit' was not just a matter of record of regimental building work or the preserve of the officer class. As already noted, religious dedications and tombstones were set up by and for individuals of different ranks, from humble privates to the unit commander. Commemoration of one's life and of the lives of one's relatives was evidently considered important within the military community. It is plausible from what we know of the military community that the behaviour of the commanders and officer class was emulated as far as practicable by lower ranks. The extension of the use of tombstones from soldiers to their families was a crucial ingredient in building the sense of group identity.

Even in the civilian parts of the province, where there is a general dearth of tombstones, those of soldiers and ex-soldiers predominate among known examples. At the very least this suggests a different priority given by the military community to epigraphic commemoration compared to the Romano-British population at large. In fact, the frequency with which inscriptions of any type from sites in the civil zone were erected by members of the military or imperial administration is striking.

At a more prosaic level, the personal possessions of soldiers were often name-tagged for ease of recognition – a scratched name on the underside of a red fineware (samian) cup would avoid disputes as to ownership. Such graffiti on samian vessels are more than two times more commonly reported from military sites than from civil ones (and the latter includes towns with a pronounced military character such as the *coloniae*). Similar patterns can be detected with other classes of marked personal possessions. On this basis alone it can be argued that literacy was much more widespread in the army than in other major groups in British society under Roman rule.

Pottery and small finds from *Vindolanda* allow us to perceive the true scale and extent of 'words on things'. Personal names were engraved post-firing on a wide variety of ceramic vessels (coarsewares, amphoras and finewares), and supplement moulded or stamped makers' marks on pottery and tile. Names are also found incised into bone and pottery counters/roundels, stamped on metal artefacts (including weapons and armour, a stylus pen, an iron knife blade) and cut into quern stones. Amphora fragments have yielded traces of painted inscriptions, indicating weights of vessels and contents and the names of merchants responsible for shipment. Other inscribed or stamped material includes stamped lead weights, lead seals, silver and jet rings, gemstones, copper-alloy spoons and other military metalware. Most spectacular, due to their rarity of preservation in normal archaeological conditions, are the organic artefacts with incised or branded marks and names, including large numbers of barrel staves or lids, other wooden artefacts and leather items and offcuts. An ornate horse chamfron from the Period 3 *praetorium*, intriguingly, was closely associated with another offcut marked VIILDIIDII SPONDII (here II stands for E) and Sponde is perhaps to be identified as the name of the horse of the governor's groom Veldedeius or Veldeius mentioned in the tablets. A fourth variant of this same man's name may be given on a tombstone found close to the wall, Vilidedius – a good illustration of the sometimes irregular orthography of Latinized versions of north European names.

The materials for stamping or marking artefacts have also been found. At *Vindolanda*, a branding iron C (retrograde) E is tempting to reconstruct as CE(RIALIS). Quite a number of potters' stamps are known from military sites, as well as at the major ceramic production centres in southern Britain. Dies in lead and baked clay have been found at the legionary fortresses at Caerleon and Chester and demonstrate that the Roman army even stamped its daily bread (by legionary century). The average Roman soldier thus lived in a world of words, used to convey information, to denote possession and to promote a literate identity.

CULTURAL AND SOCIAL TRAITS

The Roman army was hugely time-dependent. That is to say, its affairs were run on a singularly Roman concept of time, whether at the level of measuring the hours of the day to determine duty rosters or of denoting dates. Many of the *Vindolanda* documents are headed by calendar dates in the Roman system (for example, *vii kalendas Maias* for 25 April). We know from evidence elsewhere in the empire that the army used the religious calendar of Rome to give shape to ritual and ceremonial activity at the unit level. Several references at *Vindolanda* suggest that Britain was no exception. For instance, listings of more lavish foodstuffs for 24 June correspond to the festival of *Fors Fortuna* and there are other references to the *Saturnalia* and New Year's Day being marked by religious festivals. The careers of soldiers were also played out in the Roman time system, demanding long service terms of twenty-five years. It is notable that many military tombstones specify not only the age at death, but also the years of service completed.

The Roman soldiers were privileged in legal terms. Auxiliary troops for instance were the only non-citizens in the western provinces able to designate heirs under Roman law. Phrases on military tombstones identifying heirs and mentioning wills are clear pointers to the import-ance of this provision and to the fact that soldiers often had property or savings to pass on. Part of a Roman testamentary will found in a bog in northern Wales can almost certainly be attributed to a Roman soldier, following a legal form developed at the heart of the empire. There were also legal constraints on soldiers, such as restrictions on marriage and the recognition (or not) of the legitimacy of children. While the exclusion of children born to a serving soldier from receiving citizenship with him and his wife on his discharge was a serious issue, the fact that soldiers could leave legacies to unofficial wives and children mitigated this to some degree. Moreover, soldiers were adventitiously placed for making individual appeals or petitions to governors, and even to the emperor, for redress of legal difficulties. Juvenal implies that assaults on civilians by soldiers were not uncommon even in the city of Rome, but rarely led to convictions, because civilian complaints against serving soldiers were always heard by tribunals within the fort, not a civic court. He also asserted that property disputes involving soldiers were more expeditiously processed than civil ones. There is ample testimony in the ancient sources to military oppression of civilians, exploiting their power and privileges (for instance to requisition transport or obtain billets with civilians when on the move). Evidence from all corners of the empire demonstrates that soldiers persistently abused their position in relation to civilians. Occasionally, they met their match, though rarely through due legal process. A macabre burial from Canterbury contained two male bodies, bundled unceremoniously into a pit, with military belts and cavalry swords thrown in after. It looks like a double murder of off-duty soldiers, perhaps by civilians.

On the other hand, military discipline could be harsh. Centurions could be martinets, using their vine staffs to inflict corporal punishment. Military punishments included reprimands, fines, fatigue duties, transfers, loss of rank, and dishonourable discharge. However, soldiers, veterans and sons of veterans were immune from certain punishments, such as condemnation to the mines and hard labour, and would be spared torture. Not all the members of the military community had the same rights, but clearly the closer the individual was to the military, the better the position. Most importantly, garrison settlements predominantly contained people who experienced written Roman law and who had legal rights established by documents. This was another feature that distinguished them from the indigenous people of the military zone.

Military identity was also expressed through material culture. Publication of the corpus of Roman sculpture in Britain emphasizes the overwhelming predominance of military assemblages in some regions. The two largest collections by a wide margin relate to the western and eastern sectors of Hadrian's Wall, a total of 940 items that are almost entirely attributable to the military community. To give some idea of the relative paucity of non-military material, of 99 items catalogued for Wales (leaving aside a further 17 of uncertain attribution or provenance), 62 came from the legionary fortress at Caerleon and a further 16 from auxiliary forts or military supply depots, 15 from the *civitas* capital at Caerwent and 4 from the villa at Llantwit Major. Nearly 80 per cent of the material is thus from a context with clear associations with the military community.

The representational forms adopted by the military are interesting as a highly selective take on Roman provincial sculptural production. There was comparatively little accomplished work fully in the round and the most notable pieces come from the legionary fortresses. However, fragments of copper-alloy statues (including 'armoured figures', presumably emperors) at Caerleon and Caernarfon in Wales and at Carrawburgh and Carvoran on Hadrian's Wall hint at significant gaps in the extant corpus. These high-quality pieces will have been produced at specialized centres and shipped to the garrisons. They must have been quite common at Roman fort sites, but most will have been melted down eventually. Much more common are relief sculptures in the form of panels, on altars or on tombstones. A large amount of the anthropomorphic repertoire concerns representations of deities. Although some of these gods and goddesses combine Roman and British deities, the practice of anthropomorphic representation appears to be largely a Roman innovation in the north and west of Britain. There are comparatively few representations in these areas (mostly so-called 'Celtic' heads) that were perhaps produced by people outside the military community.

Military dress was an obvious and highly visible signal of a soldier's status and power. Three types of dress can be identified: standard issue armour and armaments for active duty; parade armour for ceremonial display; and casual dress for off-duty hours and perhaps for general wear around the fort. Within the army, distinctions in dress and finer accoutrements served to define grades and rank. Despite doubts that have been expressed about the extent to which legionary and auxiliary armour and armaments were mutually exclusive, for the first and second centuries at least soldiers would mostly have been able to ascertain the type of unit and the rank of fellow soldiers at a glance. From the third century, the appearance of all categories of garrison troops converged, while different styles were introduced for new mobile field army units. Military clothing styles were introduced to Britain at the conquest and differed in key respects from native British ones. That this situation continued for a long time well illustrates the essential separateness of the military community within Britain. From the viewpoint of a civilian, a soldier was easily recognized, even in off-duty dress, and was someone to be respected and feared, especially in a society where only the military regularly carried arms.

The distinctive plate armour known as *lorica segmentata* characterized the battle-dress of the Roman legionary in the mid-first century. The overlapping iron plates, mounted on leather straps, provided excellent protection in a pitched battle, but were too cumbersome and heavy for day-to-day wear. The auxiliary soldiers seem normally to have been equipped with chain-mail or scale-armour shirts, but again these will presumably have been worn only for certain duties, such as guard details or when on the march or detached duties away from the fort. Both legionaries and auxiliaries used substantial and showy metal helmets; shields were large and decorated with martial images and unit badges and symbols. Cavalry troopers generally had more elaborate helmets and decorated their horses with elaborate harness gear, connected by decorative copper-alloy fittings. The Roman soldier in full battle array was thus visibly well protected, but also carried images on his person emphasizing martial prowess and unit solidarity. The point is further illustrated by the numerous regimental standard-bearers, who topped off their helmets with distinctive animal skins. Arms and armour were issued to individual soldiers against deductions from pay. It was a major disciplinary offence for a soldier to lose his sword (no doubt because there was a clandestine trade in second-hand Roman swords to 'barbarians' beyond the frontiers). Equipment was recycled within units wherever possible, as illustrated by a Roman helmet from London with no less than four separate names stamped into its neck guard.

Parade armour was even more elaborate, especially for cavalry troopers. Several cavalry parade helmets are known from Britain (Ribchester, Newstead and numerous fragmentary examples). These helmets were sheathed with copper alloy moulded to represent hair, with a full face-mask hinged at the front. Silvering, tinning or gilding was applied in some cases to enhance the appearance still more dramatically. Cavalry mounts were also provided with embossed leather chamfrons and copper-alloy eye protectors. The god-like appearance of these riders in the cavalry practice manoeuvres (*hippika gymnasia*) was calculated ostentation. The location of parade grounds outside forts made the regular military displays a very public spectacle and the army did not miss the opportunity to reinforce its power and prestige through such theatricality.

Military tombstones are an important class of representation for several reasons: they introduced the concept of personal (if stylized) portrayals of individual people; they communicated ideas about military identity, power and superiority, and they imported certain norms of Roman funerary culture as used elsewhere. The practice of erecting stelae with busts, half- or full-length depictions of the deceased soldier appears to have been adopted in Italy in the Hellenistic period and spread from northern Italy to the Rhineland army in the early first century, whence it quite naturally passed to Britain. A number of fine examples date to the earliest years of the conquest period. The typical relief of a Roman infantryman depicted him in military dress, often in full armour. When shown unarmoured, soldiers are distinguishable by distinctive military belts, the wearing of side-arms, or a style of cloak associated with army personnel (the *paenula*). If a centurion, his swagger stick (vine staff) was prominently displayed (as Favonius Facilis at Colchester or Aurelius Nepos from Chester); if a standard-bearer, then his *signum* (as L. Duccius Rufinus from York); if a junior officer or clerical rank, then a small case for transporting writing tablets. Cavalrymen were generally portrayed mounted, mostly in the act of riding down a naked barbarian (Rufus Sita from Gloucester and Dannicus and Sextus Valerius from Cirencester are excellent illustrations of the type). The inclusion of the fallen enemy is a nice touch here, diverting attention from the unfortunate circumstances of the tombstone and instead emphasizing the power of the Roman soldier and the death of those who opposed him. Some cavalry tombstones combined two scenes, one of the deceased reclining on a banquet couch and a second of his horse being led by a groom. Over half the military tombstones known from Britain and the Rhineland are of cavalrymen, the remainder comprising roughly equal numbers of legionaries and auxiliary infantry.

Everyday clothing styles in the Roman provinces will of course have reflected the local climate and environment. Most garments in Britain were of wool and it would be strange indeed to find standard Mediterranean fashions of clothing. Soldiers wore belted tunics, with distinctive styles of cloaks in contrast to the loose-fitting and unbelted Gallic coat and wrap of many reliefs of male civilians. Military cloaks included the *sagum*, with a basic rectangular shape and secured at the right shoulder by a brooch, and the *paenula*, which hung down to a triangular point in front of the body and had a hood. Auxiliaries also introduced to regular use long-sleeved shirts and trousers. Leggings, neckerchiefs, underpants or loin-cloths, socks and hobnailed boots were other common features that served to make the average soldier better dressed and better shod than most civilians.

The tombstone erected for Flavia Augustina and her two infant children by C. Aeresius Saenus, veteran of *legio VI*, is a good example of a depiction of a military family group. Although the inscription records that both infants died (at different moments) at less than two years of age, they were shown as older children, effectively miniature adults. All four figures on the tombstone wore long tunics, thick cloaks and ankle-high shoes, the man and boy distinguished by the military style of their cloaks (the *paenula*). Both Flavia and her husband clasped scrolls (*volumina*) indicating their literacy. Other typical representations include banquet scenes, evoking not only funerary feasts but also the importance of dining in Roman society. Women were generally depicted in the guise of respectable Roman matrons, frequently seated, wearing their best clothes and jewellery, and occupied with 'suitable' tasks, like wool-working. The image of Regina from South Shields is a perfect example of this, though her servile background was admitted in the inscription. These various types of tombstones erected by the military community indicate through repeated motifs the attributes that exemplified the group identity.

The dress of women associated with the army may also have differed from everyday female costume in Britain. The Gallic coat, worn in longer style than for men, was the basic element, normally topped off with a cloak (a good example of this is the Murrell Hill 'lady' from Carlisle). Everyday wear of native British women in the first century was somewhat different, utilizing more brooches and combining long-sleeved bodice and overtunic and cloak. This suggests that army 'wives' may have pioneered new styles of fashion in the province. The decline in fibula use in the late second and third century suggests that female fashions in the civil zone may partially have shifted towards those of the military zone, though at present all the reliefs showing the 'typical' female dress of this period come from the military zone.

Another major class of sculpture concerns decorative details on building inscriptions, best illustrated by the extraordinary series of inscribed reliefs from the Antonine Wall recording the completion of specified lengths of the barrier. These 'Distance Slabs' are very diverse and many are relatively plain, but common elements include the depiction of the legionary emblems (Capricorn and Pegasus for *II Augusta*, wild boar for *XX Valeria Victrix*), winged victories, representations of Mars, imperial valour and perhaps *Britannia*, captive and dead barbarians (some ridden down by Roman cavalrymen), Roman standard-bearers and religious sacrifices. The largest and most complex of these is the Bridgeness slab, marking the eastern end of the wall. To the left of the inscribed text a Roman cavalryman rode over no less than four naked warriors (one headless, with arms bound). The right-hand scene depicted a formal Roman sacrifice of pig, sheep and bull (the *suovetaurilia* – generally a cleansing ritual). A high-ranking Roman, indicated by toga (probably the legate of the *II Augusta* whose flag was depicted at the rear), poured a libation at an altar, to the accompaniment of pipes as the animals were led for slaughter. The theme of bound and naked or semi-naked captives recurs on other stones and emphasizes the opposite destinies of Rome and her enemies.

Large-scale monuments and mausolea incorporating elements of mainstream Roman funerary iconography are also quite common at military sites, but extremely rare elsewhere in Britain. For instance, sphinxes and lions (often crouching over some prey) were often used as apotropaic guardians of the tomb, and pine-cone finials evoked immortality. These major tomb monuments advertised the status and cultural affinities of the leading members of the Roman community and the comparative lack of imitation at major urban centres is a striking illustration of different behaviours.

A dispassionate analysis of the vast bulk of the sculpture from the military zone, with the partial exception of the legionary bases, suggests a general shortage of professionally trained sculptors. Much of the carving looks like the work of people who were soldiers first and foremost and at best only part-time sculptors, or who were general masons rather than artists. Nonetheless, it is striking that even when the results were artistically naive or inept, the investment in the medium shows that its production was considered important for these communities. Some people have seen a growing British artistic influence in the sculptural naivety, and, for instance, view the large almond-shaped eyes and protuberant lips of many pieces as deliberate abstraction. Others would rather see it simply as bad art. The truth probably lies between the two extremes; as the military community became numerically more dependent on British recruits, British responses to anthropomorphic art will have influenced sculptural output. The key point to note is that the repertoire reflects a demotic military style of art. As we have seen, the messages were often relatively simple and unsubtle: emphasizing Roman power versus barbarian defeat and humiliation, personification of named deities, representation of members of the community of soldiers. These artworks were aspirational and representative of the military community, despite the lack of first-rate artists.

The availability of higher-calibre sculptors was somewhat better in London and at the legionary bases at York, Caerleon and perhaps even Chester (though the extant evidence is predominantly of rather clumsy sculptures). Marble pieces are known at York (notably a statuette of a nude male from the baths) and London (including the sculpture and reliefs from the Walbrook *mithraeum*, at least one of which was paid for by a soldier). There are also fine-quality limestone sculptures from York (a bust of Constantine) and London, and military influence is strongly suspected in the best pieces at Bath.

Short-term postings in army accommodation for governors, legates and commanders and the probability of moving on for legionary centurions were disincentives to investment in fixed or bulky artworks. The lack of mosaics, elaborate wall-paintings, and so on is thus to be expected. Only at the legionary garrison settlements do we encounter mosaics. The military community was predisposed instead to invest its money in metalware, jewellery and coloured textiles. Silver tableware was the service of choice for the senior commanders, but decorative copper-alloy vessels were within the range of higher-paid soldiers. Samian ware, some of it elaborately decorated with figured scenes, and functional metal vessels are fairly ubiquitous in military contexts. The decoration on metal and ceramic vessels as a rule picked up traditional Roman scenes: hunting, the classical pantheon of gods and myths, gladiatorial, martial and erotic scenes. Occasional metal objets d'art are found, such as a fine copper-alloy statuette of Commodus as Hercules from near Birdoswald – presumably the sort of thing a unit commander might carry with him. Glassware was also used at many forts and decorated examples are known. There appear to be basic differences in the consumption of glass at military sites compared to civilian sites and this may relate to different cultural choices as well as supply mechanisms. Decorated lamps are also much more commonly found at forts than in civil contexts and the choice of images frequently reflects traditional martial and religious values.

Elaborate brooches and belt fittings were often specific to, or are most commonly found at, military sites. Some belt and baldric fittings incorporated Latin inscriptions and military symbols, such as the eagle. Finger rings were commonly worn by the military, many with fine gemstones. It is striking that the *c.* 1,000 gemstones known from Britain deal exclusively with traditional Roman themes. Again there is a bias in the distribution towards military sites, though major towns also have generally produced large assemblages and they are relatively common at temples and villas in the south. Detailed analysis has suggested that there are specific types that were more prevalent at military sites: martial scenes (Mars, Minerva, Achilles, Ajax, Hercules, warships, standards, military equipment, eagles, regimental emblems), other gods and myth-ical heroes, fantastical beasts, allegorical scenes, personifications, emperors. Some striking examples of military 'type' have turned up on civil sites, hinting at the interaction of the military across Britain. As suggested by the Snettisham jeweller's hoard, manufacture of some intaglio gemstones was probably carried out within Britain, so the un-varied classical themes are significant. The investment was both for status display and for a specific social behaviour. These intaglio rings were designed for sealing letters, documents and packages, bringing us back once again to the emphasis on literacy.

A feature of many portable artworks is that they drew on a repertoire of generic Roman themes, both martial and religious. The religious reference points for instance were primarily with the classical pantheon and a few eastern cults imported to Britain. The intent of the minor art seems to have been to reinforce the strong connection between the soldiery and the Roman state, using imagery that was explicitly and unambiguously associated with the empire and its protecting gods.

Military supply and a degree of standard issues – of arms, armour, and so on – determined the pattern of consumption of a wide range of portable material culture in the army. Pottery supply was met in various ways, sometimes involving the creation of potteries close to military bases, perhaps run by civilians under contract to the army or occasion-ally by skilled soldiers. The alternative was to ship pottery long distances from southern Britain or even the Continent as part of the overall pattern of military supply. The distribution maps for a number of production centres in southern Britain are strongly suggestive of such contracts, with large concentrations of, for instance, Colchester mortaria or Black

Burnished cooking pots on Hadrian's Wall. That such patterns represented trade over several generations in some cases suggests that the purchasing power and contractual mentality of the army were key factors, rather than individual initiative of potters or specialist pottery traders. Some of the main centres supplying pottery to the army were also involved in the supply of other needed commodities, such as foodstuffs, salt, iron, and so forth. The types of vessels supplied to the army reflect the adoption within the army of a somewhat standardized version of food preparation, cookery and serving. The use of large mixing bowls (mortaria) for grinding and blending foods, of fairly ubiquitous deep cooking pots and of individual vessels for eating and drinking shaped the identity of soldiers of Rome just as much as the food that they ate. For many recruits, especially in the first century, enlistment involved adopting new culinary habits and a shift in diet.

We have already considered the way in which soldiers and those closely connected to them made extensive use of personal ornament, especially rings, brooches and other jewellery to highlight their membership of the military community. Certain types of fibulae have a distribution that is skewed towards military sites and can be considered as predominantly military types. The army was a substantial manufacturer of a wide range of artefacts, but it was also an important patron of craft activity and it should be no surprise to find skilled artisans working for the military market. Many Romano-British brooches featured Iron Age designs and technical metalworking skills, as with the so-called trumpet or dragonesque types. Fluid and curvilinear motifs were often inlaid with enamel, especially reds and blues. The popularity of these 'Celtic' styles is unsurprising in the context of a military community that was heavily recruited in north-western Europe.

The convergence of Roman and Gallic/British styles is particularly clear in a series of copper-alloy vessels (bowls and small pans – *trullae*) intricately inlaid with enamelwork. Since inscriptions on these name forts on the western half of Hadrian's Wall, it is pretty clear that the military community was the target market for these 'souvenir' products, and a centre of production in the north-west is to be expected (Carlisle?). The Rudge cup and the Amiens *patera* feature an abstract depiction of the wall and its crenellated forts, but the 2003 find from Ilam in Staffordshire is a much more hybrid piece, with a colourful curvilinear scroll of flamboyant 'Celtic' style running round the body of the vessel.

The inscription names four of the forts 'on the line of the wall of Aelius (Hadrianus)' (*rigore val(l)i Aeli*) and an individual, Draco – presumed to be the soldier for whom this was made. Related vessels have also been found at Brougham in the Eden valley (curvilinear design, but uninscribed), Beadlam in north Yorkshire (with only a fragment of inscription) and from Bath (with the wall design of the Rudge and Amiens type, but no inscription). The findspots of these vessels could be a useful guide to the activities of veterans after discharge.

Identity could be expressed by other social choices, such as how one illuminated one's dwelling after dark. The conventional Mediterranean lighting medium was the olive-oil lamp and there is evidence for both lamps and fuel being imported into early Roman Britain, with an over-whelming bias in distribution towards military sites and London. The level of lamp imports was not maintained in the second century, and the design of British open lamps and of candlesticks suggest that tallow fat and candles were the long-term choices as lighting fuel – suited to the nature of Britain's resources. However, the military community remained an important consumer of lighting equipment and by implication of a way of life that continued after dark under artificial illumination.

RELIGION

Modern views of religion in Roman Britain have tended to stress the importance of syncretism, that is, the mutual reconciliation of religious practice between two societies. It is assumed that this is what we should understand by the Roman concept of *interpretatio*: 'the interpretation of alien deities and of the rites associated with them', as Tacitus expressed it. What this meant in practice is normally assumed to be the name-pairing of a native British god with an appropriate Roman one, as in the case of Mars Cocidius, where it is assumed that the British deity Cocidius shared the martial attributes of Roman Mars, and that the name-pairing was adopted by both Romans and Britons. But the evidence for the practice of Roman religion in Britain is much more complex and less uniform than the model of consensual syncretism suggests. Three points will serve to highlight the problems. First, the military contribution to our knowledge of 'Romano-British religion' is very dominant and potentially distorting. Second, *interpretatio* should not be seen as benign integration, but rather as a colonial act of a ruling power, in which power asymmetries operated. Third, there was more to naming and worshipping patterns than *interpretatio*. In fact, 169 of 246 'Celtic' appellations in religious inscriptions from Britain refer to a British deity in isolation, 12 refer to both classical and non-classical without pairing them, and 65 only are instances of name-pairing (26 per cent).

The vast majority of all inscribed religious altars of traditional Roman type in Britain come from military sites. It is also striking that the military account for a much wider array of named divinities than are encountered in other parts of Britain, ranging from mainstream Roman deities, the imperial cult, eastern cults and other provincial divinities imported to Britain, to spirits of place and localized British ones. The temples in the military zone were either of typical classical form or of distinctive military type (such as the shrine of the standards in the headquarters' building of forts). Overall, what we can deduce is that the army operated in a traditional framework of practice, based on sacrifices in fulfilment of vows, cleansing rituals and calendar-based duties. The approach was formulaic and superstitious, seeking to win (or maintain) the support of the gods for unit and self. The state dictated that certain official cults be given a high profile in the religious calendar – notably Jupiter Optimus Maximus and the imperial cult. Many religious dedications made on behalf of the entire unit will have related to dates in the religious calendar or to cults that had special significance for a unit (or its commander). Large groups of dedications to Jupiter Optimus Maximus on behalf of units at the forts of Maryport (twenty-one) and Birdoswald (twenty-four) reflect an official practice of possibly annual dedication. Similarly, the assemblage of religious sculpture and inscriptions at Corbridge reveals a strong component of observation of the official religious calendar. There are a few more idiosyncratic inscriptions, such as the poem composed by M. Caecilius Donatianus at Carvoran in ten iambic *senarii* in honour of Virgo Caelestis. This sort of literary conceit was emulated by soldiers in other provinces, including two examples from the fort of Bu Njem in the Libyan desert.

Individual soldiers were acutely aware of local divine powers and the need to appease them – a tendency exemplified by the many dedications at Carrawburgh to the nymph Coventina, whose spring provided the garrison's drinking water. The varied origins of the soldiery in many units ensured a range and mixture of supplementary cults. The profound polytheistic tendencies of the Roman army are demonstrated in the case of the centurion M. Cocceius Firmus, who dedicated a series of four altars at Auchendavy to a total of eleven different divinities: Diana, Apollo, the genius of the land of Britain, Jupiter, Victorious Victory (linked to the health of the imperial family), Mars, Minerva, goddesses of the parade ground, Hercules, Epona and Victory. As with tombstones, it is much commoner to find higher ranks and officers dedicating religious altars with inscriptions, but other ranks also emulated this behaviour. Frumentius, a soldier of the *cohors II Tungrorum* at Birrens, got his money's worth by dedicating to 'all the gods and goddesses'. The cost could also be lessened by communal dedications erected on behalf of religious guilds (*collegia*) or other sub-divisions of the garrison. Among the altars where the status of dedicant is unspecified there were no doubt civilians as well as military personnel, though generally these will have been members of the military community, rather than indigenous people *per se*. Religious dedications by women show that the practice of inscribed communication was not exclusively the preserve of soldiers or of men.

The act of *interpretatio* was essentially about naming and in Roman colonialism naming and power went hand in hand. Victory in war heralded not only the defeat of her enemies, but also subjugation of their protective deities by the gods of Rome. Roman religious tolerance was that of the victor, and *interpretatio* was more of a monologue than a dialogue. Of the sixty-five instances of name-paired deities in Britain, thirty-six involved the Roman war god, Mars. It is no surprise to find the army at the forefront of such practices, and most of these dedications to Mars Cocidius, Mars Belatucadrus and the rest have been found in the vicinity of Hadrian's Wall. Indeed, studies of who was responsible for erecting paired-name dedications show that the majority were military personnel and most were officers or commanders. Where name-pairing occurred in lowland Britain there must have been special reasons why the individual chose to adopt it. Lower ranks in the army rarely bothered with explicit name-pairing and had no problem with simply using a British (or Gallic or Germanic) name on its own. The cult of the nymph Coventina at Carrawburgh has yielded fourteen inscriptions, of which two relate to unit commanders, one to an *optio* and one other to an officer of some sort. The other ten appear to be rank-and-file soldiers.

Even more striking are the more than fifty inscriptions of the Veteres (variously spelt Vitiri, Hveteri and so on), whose distribution focuses on the northern frontier and whose nature may be Germanic (as suggested by the Hv- spellings). Most dedicants were men, only two explicitly identified as soldiers; there were also three possible women dedicants. However, five of the dedicators had twin Latin names (*gentilicum* and *cognomen*) and another twelve had single Latin names, while thirteen names were British (or possibly Germanic). These people were in fact probably lower-rank soldiers and their families, rather than native Britons – a point reinforced if the cult had Germanic connections. The findspots of these inscriptions are almost without exception in the garrison settlements and as such are illustrative of a lower-echelon version of the pattern of religious practice at military sites. There are no equivalent altars and Roman-style shrines in native settlements away from the forts in the military zone.

There are a number of other cults whose worship in Britain appears to have been exclusive to the military community. Some seem to have been brought in with particular units, such as the Gallic Mars Camulus, and Mars Toutates and the horse goddess Epona or the German Mars Thincsus and Alaisiagae. Others were eastern cults with a particular appeal to the military, such as Mithraism. The hierarchical structure of this 'mystery cult', based on a series of levels of initiation, was well suited to the rank-conscious soldiery and also to the collective aspect of some religious practice (whether by unit or *collegium*). Virtually all the unambiguous evidence of Mithraic worship in Britain comes from military sites – even the Walbrook *mithraeum* in London seems to have had close associations with soldiers based there. A similar military distribution applies to numerous dedications to the Syrian god Jupiter Dolichenus.

The military community not only worshipped gods in standard ways, based on traditional Roman formulaic (and epigraphic) practices and using anthropomorphic forms, but it also built new types of structure within which to place altars and cult images. Antenociticus was a minor British deity only known at Benwell near Newcastle. The small shrine with apse built outside that fort thus symbolized an alien approach to religion. The extent to which the local native population translated their own worship of Antenociticus to this temple is uncertain and ultimately doubtful. In adopting native gods, soldiers imposed their own practices and requirements. The location of the vast majority of shrines close to forts and garrison settlements indicates that the convenience of the garrison was paramount, rather than the upgrading of an existing local sacred place. It must be doubted whether there was much religious integration of native and military communities, at least initially, and the epigraphic evidence essentially highlights the activity of the military community alone.

The most striking aspects of army religion are its promiscuous polytheism and its mixing of traditional religion with a wide range of other cults brought within a literate and anthropomorphic frame of reference. Garrison settlements and their forts were characterized by a proliferation of minor temples and shrines, dedicated to a very wide range of divinities and spirits, with acts of devotion often concretized by inscriptions or relief sculptures of the gods. The range of divinities and spirits evoked at *Vindolanda* (Table 5) and the mixed status of dedicants provides an excellent illustration from an extensively excavated site. Collective dedications focus on traditional army gods, such as Jupiter Optimus Maximus and Mars. Commanding officers were inevitably interested in appeasing the *genius praetorii* (the spirit of their own residence). Local cults also attracted the individual attention of Roman commanders, as in the case of Cocidius, but there appears to have been notably more interest in such local deities among the lower ranks. The dedication by the dwellers in the garrison settlement (the *vicani Vindolandesses*) is significant in that it espouses devotion to the imperial house and to the Roman smith god Volcanus. By contrast, the dedication on behalf of the *curia Textoverdorum* to a native goddess is one of the few pieces of evidence for religious practice by a native community in the area. It may have been erected under military supervision at *Vindolanda*, or possibly have come from an unlocated rural shrine. The former is perhaps more probable. The numerous dedications to the Veteres (and the variance in the spelling of the name) are also of interest. As noted already, the lack of specific allusion to unit among the dedicants does not preclude identification of many of them as soldiers of the lower ranks. Indeed the predominant association of dedications to the Veteres at military sites in northern Britain pretty much ensures that to have been the case. The cult would seem to have had particular appeal to ordinary soldiers.

Table 5. Religious dedications from *Vindolanda* (* indicates a text from Beltingham church, *c.*3 km south-east of *Vindolanda*).

DEDICATION TO	DEDICANT	*RIB* NUMBER OR REFERENCE
IOM (Jupiter Optimus Maximus), other immortal gods and the Genius of the *Praetorium*	Q. Petronius Urbicus, prefect *cohors IV Gallorum*	1686
IOM and Genius of the *Praetorium*	[. . .]	*Brit* 24: 366–7
IOM and the Genius and the guardian gods	Ve[. . .] Caecil[. . .] and *IV Gallorum*	1687
IOM	L. [. . .]gius Pudens, prefect and *cohors IV Gallorum*	1688
IOM	[lost]	1689–90
Mars Victor	Titus Caninius [prefect] and *cohors III Nerviorum*	1691
Fortune of the Roman People	C. Iulius Raeticus, centurion *legio VI Victrix*	1684
Genius of the *Praetorium*	Pituanius Secundus, prefect *cohors IV Gallorum*	1685
Mercury	–	1693
Neptune	[. . .]	1694
Silvanus	M. Aurelius Modestus, *beneficiarius consularis* and soldier of *legio II Augusta*	1696
Divine house and imperial *numen* and Volcanus	*Vicani Vindolandesses*	1700
Deae [. . .]	–	1701
Deo Ma[g]u[sa]no	–	*VindResRep* 2003, 59
Dea Sattada*	*Curia Textoverdorum*	1695
Cocidius	Decimus Caerellius Victor, prefect *cohors II Nerviorum*	1683
Deus Mogons and Genius loci	Lupulus	*Brit* 4: 329
Deus Maponus	–	*Brit* 2: 291
Matres and imperial *numen*	[. . .]ini	1692
Deae Matres	[. . .]	*Brit* 1: 309
Deo [V]ete[r]i	–	1697–8
Veteres	Senaculus	1699
Di Veteres	Longinus	*Brit* 4: 329
Di Veteres	Senilis	*Brit* 4: 329

Table 5 – *contd.*

DEDICATION TO	DEDICANT	*RIB* NUMBER OR REFERENCE
Deo Vetiri	[…]	*Brit* 6: 285
Deo Ve[…]	[…]	*Brit* 6: 285
Deo Hvitri	–	*Brit* 8: 432
Deo Hvutir[i]	[…]	*Brit* 24: 368
Ara Vitirum	–	*Brit* 10: 346
Deo V[…]	–	*Brit* 24: 369

DIET AND CONSUMPTION

The military diet was well regulated and distinct from that of many civilian groups within Britain. It used to be thought, on the basis of literary sources, that it was rather narrowly based on cereals and involved little meat consumption – a pattern probably more valid for campaign rations. Documents such as the *Vindolanda* tablets, in combination with archaeological evidence, have revealed a much more varied diet and a higher level of meat consumption than previously suspected. Supplies of cereals appear to have been a prime concern at *Vindolanda*, with regular accounts of wheat, barley and *bracis* (a cereal used in malting/brewing). Cereals were used for bread of different forms, semolina, porridge, pasta and gruel – key staples of the army diet. Barley may have been used both for brewing beer and as feed for horses and mules. From the tablets we can see that meat was also frequently on the menu at the fort, with a wide range of animals being consumed in different forms: pork, pork cutlet, bacon, ham, suckling pig, pig's trotter, pork crackling, pork fat, lard, goat, roe deer, venison, chickens, geese. Curiously there are no explicit references to beef or mutton and lamb, though bones of cattle and sheep are common at the site. In addition, there are references to fish, fish sauce, oysters, eggs, butter, beans, lentils, lovage, radishes, apples, plums, honey, olive oil, olives, pepper, spices, salt, wine and beer. However, many references seem to indicate soldiers purchasing meat specially, presumably to supplement the regular diet or for special occasions and sacrifices.

Animal bone assemblages from forts reveal a high proportion of cattle and pig bones relative to sheep/goat (ovicaprids). Legionary fortresses generally have higher occurrences of pig bones (c.20 per cent by number) than auxiliary forts, reflecting their higher status. Military sites as a group stand out in comparison to many rural settlements (where sheep/goat bones constitute in excess of 30–40 per cent of assemblages) and towns and villas (where proportions differ again). Almost half of military sites have over 70 per cent of cattle bones by count (indicative of a contribution of c.90 per cent of the weight of meat actually consumed). Some auxiliary forts have slightly lower cattle and pig counts relative to sheep/goat than was common for military sites in Gaul and Germany, but the difference is probably to be accounted for by the fact that the indigenous pre-conquest pattern in Britain was heavily sheep/goat dominated. The army in Britain had to draw its supplies in part from the existing base of production. Material from garrison settlements closely mirrors the fort assemblages and is distinct from small-town consumption patterns in the civil zone. Among wild species represented at forts, deer predominate, with hare also common. We have already noted evidence of organized hunting at *Vindolanda*.

Botanical remains are less regularly preserved in the archaeological record, but provide complementary evidence to literary evidence. Analysis of seeds in Roman sewage at Bearsden identified wheat, barley, bean, fig, dill, coriander, opium poppy, hazelnut, raspberry, wild strawberry, blackberry, bilberry and celery. Most cereals were probably levied in tax or bought from relatively local sources of supply, but there is evidence from Alchester, London, Caerleon and South Shields to show imports of grain from the Continent.

Amphoras for the transport of wine, olive oil, fish sauces and a range of other (mainly liquid) commodities are common finds at military sites. In addition, barrels were frequently used in the northern provinces, though rarely preserved as abundantly as at *Vindolanda*. They were perhaps most commonly used for moving salt-meat and beer. The regular and large-scale movement of such commodities further distinguishes the military community from contemporary civilian markets in the first and second centuries. The importation of olive oil from southern Spain and wine from Gaul, for example, can be linked to military contracts that operated beyond provincial boundaries. Although some civilian trade may have been affected by piggy-backing on the contracted exchange pattern, the overall distributions of amphora-borne commodities between civil centres and military sites differ. The military supply system was ultimately designed to provide the army with a varied and sustaining diet. Despite the fact that many of the soldiers serving in Britain originated in Temperate Europe, there was a Mediterranean aspect to it (the use of olive oil, fish sauces and wine). That said, it was not exclusive of regional preferences; it is clear that the Batavian cohort at *Vindolanda* consumed large quantities of beer, brewed on site.

DEVIATIONS FROM THE ARCHETYPAL MILITARY IDENTITY

In presenting the evidence for uniform and coherent elements of a military identity in Britain, this chapter has focused on the first centuries of Roman rule, but it must be emphasized that there was change over time and variability within the military identity. By the fourth century the predilection among soldiers for erecting monumental inscriptions appears to have ended and the military community as a result becomes less visible for us. Even at earlier dates, though, discrepant behaviour is to be expected given the widespread origins and background of the soldiery on the one hand, and, on the other, the likelihood of a steady growth in recruitment of British-born individuals in the second and third centuries. It bears repetition that the common assumption that local recruitment rapidly replaced external levies from other provinces, as is clear in second-century *Africa* for instance, may overstate the speed and thoroughness of the transition in Britain. For one thing the British garrison size was extremely large (perhaps four times that of *Africa*) and the number of colonies and legionary *canabae* relatively small (about one sixth of the number in *Africa*). The epigraphic evidence for both legionaries and auxiliaries in Britain gives very few hints at local recruitment and rather more attestations of overseas origins.

Other identity markers can be discerned here and there, whether stressing ethnic origins, adherence to an imported Germanic cult or distinctive dietary or culinary habits. However, notwithstanding hierarchical differences and diversity in its ranks and units, the Roman army did generate a profound sense of community and shared the cultural identity of the soldiery with certain closely associated groups of civilians.

Quite a high proportion of the people who initially made up the population of the garrison settlements were probably ex-soldiers, foreigners or outsiders to the local areas where garrisons were set up.

Assuming the native British element in such settlements rose over time, the impression one has is that in the process they were assimilated into the military community and took on its strongly developed identity. There is negligible evidence for this army culture being exported out from the garrison communities to the wider rural communities of north and west Britain. Some at least of the womenfolk of the military community were native Britons, as Regina the Catuvellaunian at South Shields, an anonymous Cornovian woman at Ilkley and Verecunda Rufilia, the Dobunnian wife of Excingus, who was probably in the garrison at Templeborough. None of these women was from the locality of the fort where she was buried.

At one level, diversity within the cultural evidence of the garrison settlements may simply indicate differences in status between soldiers and dependent civilians, officers and other ranks, or legionaries, cavalrymen and auxiliary infantry. But ethnic and unit identity may also have been significant factors on occasion. Even when the recruitment base of auxiliary units bore no relation to the implied ethnicity of the unit name, the regimental history and traditions of individual units remained important. Successive units at a single fort site may thus leave rather different material traces.

In the third century we can still find units with a strongly ethnic character in Britain. The presence of German troops at Housesteads is revealed not just by the inscriptions of the *numerus Hnaudifridi* and *cuneus Frisiorum*, by the Germanic divinities extolled (Thincsus, Alaisiagae – Beda and Fimmilena – Baudihillia and Friagabis) and by expressions of specific German identity, but also by the presence of Frisian pottery at the site. Fundamentally, though, the German garrisons at Housesteads represent a variant on the military identity, not a dramatic departure from it. The possible identification through ceramic traditions of African contingents in legions (*VI* and *XX*) and auxiliary units in the mid-second century has been mentioned already. While it is clear that in some respects these soldiers blended quite well into the military community during their service lives, it is also probable that such people retained a lasting sense of difference in their domestic lives.

A startling instance of this is provided by the published excavation of a Roman military cemetery in the upper Eden valley at Brougham. This cemetery was established *c.*200 and was in use for about a century before being abandoned. A total of about 200 cremation burials has been excavated, with evidence of the ash variously deposited in urns, in the grave, with only a small part of the pyre debris included, or, in a few cases, no human remains at all. The date of the cemetery makes the predominance of cremation over inhumation a little unusual, but not unparalleled for the army. Fragments of twenty-five inscribed tombstones are known from the site, along with four additional fragments of sculptural tombstones. Although the presence of soldiers is not explicitly stated in the texts, some of the pyre debris included fragments of weapons and other finds of distinctive military type and some fragments of relief tombstones look military. Three individuals were allegedly aged seventy or more years, and several burials were of wives or children. The people commemorated had either 'Celtic' (10), Latin (3) or German (2) names. Previously the nomenclature had been taken to indicate that the bulk of the 'Celtic' names were probably local Britons. However, analysis of the burial rite and the grave goods suggests a much more Continental aspect to the cemetery as a whole. There are several iron bucket pendants of a type that is hitherto unparalleled in Britain and seems to relate to the trans-Danubian region of central Europe. A number of the cremations appear to have included whole horses with the deceased – again without parallel in Britain, but with possible Continental and Germanic parallels. There are other finds that have specific links to the Germanic and trans-Danubian regions, including groups of unusual glass beads. The 'Celtic' names could evidently be appropriate to such people. Taken together, the burial rite and finds strongly suggest a group with strong ethnic connections with the trans-Danubian or Germanic regions, while the grave markers stress adherence to commemorative norms of the military community. If there were native Britons from the region among the inhabitants at this garrison community in the third century they are rather hard to spot in material terms. The women and children associated with the soldiers here shared many of their cultural peculiarities. All in all, this seems a perfect example of the potential complexities of the military community, both in terms of what was held in common with other soldiers and how much unusual cultural baggage could also be present at a single garrison post. The Brougham cemetery also presages a key development of the later empire, the Germanization of the Roman army.

8

De Excidio Britanniae

Decline and Fall?

The late Roman history of Britain is dominated by perceptions of decline. This is exemplified by the post-Roman view of British writers such as Gildas, probably writing in the early sixth century:

The Romans therefore informed our homeland that they could not go on thus plagued at frequent intervals for expeditions that required so much effort, nor could the marks of Roman power, that great and glorious army, be worn out by land and sea on account of unwarlike and roving bandits. Rather they urged the Britons to stand on their own two feet, to get accustomed to bearing arms . . .

(*De Excidio Britanniae* [*On the Destruction of Britain*])

The theme of decadence and destruction is present in late Roman writings too and this view of the calamitous abandonment of Britain by the Romans as the western empire descended into chaos has been hugely influential in shaping modern thinking about late Roman and sub-Roman Britain. At root this was seen as a product of the declining efficiency of the Roman army and the progressive stripping away of the best troops for action elsewhere, leaving the British provinces both vulnerable and increasingly expensive to maintain. Yet there is a danger here of moving from history to literary trope based on the theme of decline. We need to examine the evidence for change in the late Roman period, to try to understand its causes and effects, and to appreciate evidence of stability alongside signs of difficulties. A basic understanding of the political changes that the empire underwent between the early third and early fifth centuries is necessary to set this debate in context.

There was a partial breakdown of the Principate in the middle of the third century, as a result of disastrous foreign and civil wars, endemic usurpation and assassination at the political centre. The effects of the 'Third-Century Crisis', as it is generally known, were profound, even though the empire stabilized itself. There were over twenty recognized emperors and numerous co-regents and usurpers between 235 and 284, few of them dying peacefully in their beds. Precariously ruling emperors and usurpers alike gathered troops to fight off 'barbarian' and Persian attacks and to stamp out rivals. Vexillations from the British legions, for instance, are known in *Germania* and *Pannonia* in the period 255–60. It is probable that many other units and detachments were called away for protracted service on the Continent and some may not have returned.

In the twenty-one-year period from 235 to 255 alone there were ten legitimate emperors, but just as recovery was getting under way with the joint rule of Valerian in the east and his son Gallienus in the west, another low point was reached in 260. Valerian was defeated and captured by the Persian King Shapur I (later dying in captivity) and there were incursions across the European river frontiers, with an army of *Iuthungi* penetrating down into Italy. Following a dispute about booty recovered from this retreating war-band, Marcus Postumus, the general in command of the Lower Rhine army, declared himself emperor in opposition to Gallienus. Rather than attacking Gallienus, Postumus effectively created a replica imperial administration and court within a part of the western empire. The Gallic empire, as it is known, involved the provinces of Gaul, Germany, *Raetia*, Britain and Spain in what was effectively a secessionist state run on Roman lines. It endured for fourteen years and brought a degree of stability to the north-western provinces. After the assassination of Postumus in 269, there was a succession of shorter-lived Gallic emperors – there are only two surviving coins (one from Oxfordshire) to mark the extremely brief reign of Domitianus – before Aurelian reunited the breakaway state with the empire in 274.

The impact of the raids of *Franci*, *Iuthungi*, *Alammani* and others across the Rhine and Danube was out of proportion to their actual numbers or the physical damage they inflicted. Above all, they instilled a sense of fear and a crisis of confidence in the Roman army that had not existed before. There was a consequent shift in the balance of power across Rome's European frontiers and heightened levels of warfare. In response to the real or imagined 'barbarian' threat, the imperial capital was shifted northwards to Milan. By the end of the century, there were additional imperial capitals, each in close proximity to one or more of the major field armies.

The level of political instability in the mid-third century led to many

ad hoc changes in provincial government. Unsurprisingly, imperial para-
noia about potential rivals reached new heights and, increasingly, provincial governors and military commanders came to be appointed from
the equestrian order. This heralded the further rise of the professional
soldier in Roman society, and many emperors of the third century (and
later) came from relatively humble origins, with a background in military
service not in the traditional aristocratic pursuits of the senatorial order.
Most of the third-century emperors originated in the Balkan region,
rather than the core Mediterranean provinces that had supplied the bulk
of earlier ones.

There were major reforms of the empire's administrative and military
structure under a series of strong emperors at the end of the third and
in the early fourth century. Diocletian, who came to power in 284,
devised over several years a new system of power-sharing in a bid to end
the shambles that imperial succession had become. He first appointed a
fellow Augustus, Maximian, and divided the empire into eastern and
western halves, though he was always the senior partner in the joint
rulership. Subsequently, both men appointed a junior Caesar – effectively an heir apparent. The Tetrarchy, as this new system is known,
provided a generation of stability before it broke down with the intervention of the army supporting a rival claimant to the western empire.
The new emperor was Constantine the Great and his proclamation
occurred in Britain in 306.

The Tetrarchs and Constantine brought in a series of major reforms,
the latter building on the work of the former. We should view these as
being aimed fundamentally at restoring the stability of the Roman state,
not at creating an entirely new version of 'Rome'. In particular, many
provinces were further sub-divided, creating more than double the
number of provincial commands, but now grouped under a series of
twelve regional *dioceses*, controlled by senior civil administrators called
vicars (*vicarii*). Groups of dioceses were assigned to a series of regional
praetorian prefects. The Diocese of Britain (Fig. 9), established by 312
and comprising the four provinces of *Maxima Caesariensis, Flavia
Caesariensis, Britannia Prima* and *Britannia Secunda,* was placed under
the overall authority of the praetorian prefecture for the Gallic region.
One of the main effects of the new political structure was to increase
the links between Britain and the near Continent, where the praetorian
prefect (and at times a western emperor) had a main base at Trier.

The provincial governors (*consulares* or *praesides*) now rarely had command of any troops, these being devolved to separate military commanders (*duces* and *comites*). These generals were placed under the authority of new senior commanders for cavalry and infantry (the *magister equitum* and *magister peditum*). The events of the third century had created a distinction between the frontier troops and new-style mobile units who accompanied emperors (the *comitatus*). This too was crystallized by the early fourth century into a basic distinction, in terms of pay, conditions and role, between field army units (*comitatenses*) and frontier troops (*limitanei* and *ripenses*). More will be said below about these changes in military organization.

The basic structure of the early fourth century appears to have endured through to the end of provincial life in Britain. The locations of the British provinces and their capitals are imprecisely known, though it is fairly certain that *Maxima Caesariensis* was in south-east England, with London as its capital (Fig. 9). *Britannia Prima* appears to have been focused on western England, with either Cirencester or Gloucester as capital. The East Midlands probably comprised the heart of *Flavia Caesariensis* with Lincoln as capital, in which case *Britannia Secunda* was northern Britain with its centre at York (or vice versa). By the later fourth century there may have been a fifth British province, though even its identity is disputed. It apparently already existed when it was recovered from enemies in 368 by Count Theodosius and renamed *Valentia*. It may simply have been a rebranding of *Maxima Caesariensis* or another of the existing four. These issues are not resolvable at present and provide a perfect example of the limitations of our knowledge of late Roman Britain.

Another major development of the fourth century was the progressive rise of Christianity. Subject to severe persecution under the Tetrarchs, it was recognized by Galerius and Constantine as a legitimate religion in 311/313; late in his life, Constantine was the first emperor to convert. Despite a number of pagan 'revivals' during the fourth century, the Christianization of the empire was complete by the 390s when Theodosius I outlawed all pagan worship.

A third trend that gained momentum during the fourth century was the increasing 'Germanization' of the western empire, as a result of the resettlement of Germanic groups inside the frontiers and their increasing numerical predominance in the imperial armies. Although they adopted

Figure 9. The Province of Britannia and its subdivisions

something of the ethos of the military community, their weight of numbers and cultural difference led to profound changes in Roman society at large and in military identity in particular. When Theodosius I died in 395, the repercussions of these changes came to the fore. Although his son Honorius was nominally emperor in the western provinces from 395 to 423, real power was effectively held by a succession of military chief ministers, of whom Flavius Stilicho is the best known. Of Vandal descent, Stilicho was the *de facto* ruler of the west and clearly made increasing use of barbarian federates in the Roman armies he commanded. Germanic groups were incorporated either as *laeti*, who were permitted to settle in a region, with the requirement that they provided troops for regular units, or they were simply recruited en bloc as federate allies as need arose. The flow of Germans into the empire was also a means of relieving pressure on the frontier regions, as migration of the Huns from the east forced others westwards and southwards. Coupled with the impact of external attacks and civil war, the effects of such Germanic groups on provincial society in Continental Europe were dramatic. Britain was to some degree insulated from the worst of this, but the island was not immune from the forces of change.

The record of warfare (and events in Britain in general) is even more fragmentary for the third and fourth centuries than for the second (Table 6). As in earlier periods, there appear to have been relatively rare major threats to the British provinces, though with episodic evidence of raiding and low-intensity infiltrations by seaborne raiders. Some of the more serious military situations may have resulted from secession or civil war, as in the campaign of the western Caesar, Constantius Chlorus, to retake Britain in 296.

The story of Carausius and Allectus illustrates an important theme in the history of late Roman Britain – its reputation as a breeding ground for usurpers to imperial power. Carausius was a Menapian from Belgium who had distinguished himself in Maximian's first war in Gaul. As a result, and because he had experience as a sailor, he was given a special command in 286 to put together a fleet to clear the seas of German pirates who were raiding the Channel coasts. He appears to have been very successful in this, but there were suggestions that booty recovered was being siphoned off by him, rather than returned in proper measure to provincial communities or the treasury. When he learnt that Maximian had ordered his execution he 'usurped the imperial power and

Table 6. Wars, civil wars and revolts in Britain, 235–409.

DATE	EMPEROR (PRETENDER)	EVENTS	SOURCE
235–280s		Third-Century Crisis in Roman empire – frequent civil wars	
260–74	(Postumus and successors)	Britain part of breakaway 'Gallic empire' during mid-third century	*RIB* 2260
276–82	Probus (unknown)	Probus defeats further attempts at secession of Gaul and Britain	HA *Probus* 18.5; Zosimus 1.66.2
286	Maximian	Carausius appointed to command of defence against seaborne raiders (*Franci* and *Saxones*, *Picti* and *Scotti*)	Aurelius Victor 39; Eutropius 9.21; Panegyric on Constantius Caesar 11–12
286–96	Maximian, Constantius (Carausius and Allectus)	Britain and northern Gaul seceded from empire under Carausius. Boulogne recaptured in 293 and Britain retaken by Constantius after amphibious landing in 296	Aurelius Caesar, *de Caes* 39.20–21; Panegyric on Constantius Caesar 11–20
305–06	Constantius I	Constantius campaigns in northern Britain against *Caledonii* and *Picti*	Aurelius Victor 40; Eutropius 10.1–2
306–12	Constantine (Maxentius)	Constantine declared emperor in Britain on death of father Constantius (306); takes British levies in final campaign for dominance in western Empire versus Maxentius (312). Britain sub-divided into 4 provinces at some point before 314	Zosimus 2.15.1
312–14	Constantine I	Constantine possibly campaigned against unknown enemy in Britain	Eusebius, *de Vita Constantini* 1.8, 25
342–43	Constans	Winter visit to Britain by Constans – linked by Ammianus to some issue with scouts (*areani*) of northern frontier	Julius Firmicus Maternus, *de errore profanarum religionum* 28.6; Ammianus 28.3.8
350–53	Constans (Magnentius)	Revolt of Magnentius in Gaul, with British support. Major reprisals in Britain	Ammianus 14.5

Table 6 – *contd.*

DATE	EMPEROR (PRETENDER)	EVENTS	SOURCE
360	Julian	Raids of *Picti, Scotti, Saxones* and *Attacotti* on Britain	Ammianus 20.1, 26.4
367–68	Valentinian	Barbarian conspiracy – Count of Saxon Shore killed and *Dux Britanniarum* 'ambushed'. Situation restored by land/naval campaigns of Count Theodosius in north and south Britain	Ammianus 27.8, 28.3
382/383?	Gratian	Magnus Maximus defeats *Picti* and *Scotti*	Chronicle of 452
383–88	Gratian (Magnus Maximus)	Revolt against Gratian led by British commander; initial success but defeated in Italy	Gildas, *De Excidio Britanniae* 14–15; Zosimus 4.35–7; Orosius 7.35
396–98	Honorius	Stilicho (or a subordinate) campaigns in Britain against *Picti* and *Scotti*	Claudian Stilicho 2.247–55; Eutropius 1.391–3
406–07	Honorius (Marcus, Gratian, Constantine III)	Sequence of three British usurpers deplete troops in Britain to defend Continental territories	Orosius 7.40; Zosimus 6.2
408–09	Honorius	Britain under serious attack by *Saxones* but devoid of effective troops, looks to own defence	Zosimus 6.5.2–3

seized Britain'. It is clear that for some time Carausius also controlled parts of northern Gaul and its Channel ports, and coin legends referring to no less than nine legions indicate that he had vexillations from the armies of Britain, Germany, *Moesia* and Italy under his control. His army may not have been big enough to make a bid for glory, but it was adequate to defend a substantial territory.

Initial attempts to dislodge him were unsuccessful, not least because he had control of the sea, though by 290 it looks as though much of the Continental territory had been reclaimed by Maximian, even if an initial attempt to cross to Britain had ended in failure. Carausius sought accommodation with the ruling emperors, issuing coins with himself,

Diocletian and Maximian under the legend *Carausius et fratres sui* ('Carausius and his brother (emperors)'). It is apparent that some sort of temporary truce existed between them, due to other pressing military problems. But in 293, Maximian dispatched his newly appointed Caesar, Constantius, first against Boulogne, Carausius' remaining outpost in Gaul, and then against Britain itself. The siege of Boulogne was achieved by blocking the mouth of the river Liane with wooden piling, denying access to the harbour. By the time Boulogne fell, Carausius was dead, assassinated by Allectus (perhaps his praetorian prefect), who assumed his position and became the chief target for the invasion of southern Britain that followed in 296, after lengthy preparations. The Roman fleet, commanded by Asclepiodotus, managed to evade the rebel fleet in the Solent and the forces of Allectus were swiftly routed and Allectus killed in a decisive battle. By accident or design, part of the fleet arrived in London just in time to prevent its sack at the hands of the remnants of the rebel army.

Our Roman sources are unreliable witnesses to the rise and fall of Carausius – several of them take the form of lengthy panegyrics in honour of Constantius and Maximian. As is generally the case when history is told by the victor, it is to the detriment of the loser. From this perspective, Carausius and Allectus were little more than 'pirates', their army a 'deluded band of piratical rebels'. The archaeology and the coinage of this period suggest that there was something more to Carausius' rule. He clearly aspired to be accepted as an equal by the ruling Augusti and ruled as if an emperor. The length of time it took for his territory to be reunited with the western empire reveals his military strength. There are clear parallels with Clodius Albinus or the Gallic emperors, who were left in control of similar territories until Septimius Severus and Aurelian were ready to move against them. Some scholars have hypothesized a major attack across Hadrian's Wall in 296 as a result of the withdrawal of garrisons to fight for Allectus in the south, though the evidence of an attack is circumstantial and unconvincing. There are signs of Tetrarchic rebuilding at wall forts following the reintegration of Britain, though this was required by dilapidation of buildings, not their destruction in hostile action.

In 305 Constantius returned with an army to campaign against the northern British people, now known as the *Picti*. As with Septimius Severus before him, there are hints that he penetrated far to the north, though without achieving resounding success against elusive enemies. He carried his emulation of Severus a stage further when he died at York in July 306. His son Constantine was proclaimed Augustus by the troops, launching a protracted and climactic struggle for supremacy between a bewildering cast of Augusti, Caesars and usurpers. The presence of Constantine in Britain was no accident. In 305, Diocletian and Maximian had both announced their retirement as Augusti and the promotion of their Caesars, Constantius and Galerius. But when the identity of the new Caesars was announced in May 305, both Maximian's son Maxentius and Constantine were passed over in favour of close associates of Galerius. Constantine was at this time with Galerius at *Nicomedia* and managed only with extreme difficulty to get approval of his father's request for him to join him on the British expedition.

When Galerius accepted the *fait accompli* of Constantine's proclamation by agreeing a compromise that saw the latter take the lesser title of Caesar below Galerius' appointee of Severus as western Augustus, Maximian's son Maxentius launched his own revolt. Chaos ensued – interspersed by odd years of accommodation between the competing factions in the Tetrarchy. The complex details of Constantine's rise to supreme power and the ending of the Tetrarchic experiment in power-sharing need not concern us. By 312 he was the acknowledged power in the west (a position consolidated by Licinius' victory over Maximinus in the eastern empire in 313). In 317 Constantine became the dominant Augustus of these surviving two, and the process of the reunification of the empire under his sole rule was completed in 324. Although Constantine had started his imperial rule in Britain and had spent his initial period as Caesar based at Trier, after 313 his interests moved increasingly eastwards to the Balkans and beyond. The creation of his new capital at Constantinople after 324 had far-reaching effects. *Britannia* did not entirely drop out of the picture, as there are hints of an expedition or expeditions in the period 307–14 and Constantine accepted the title *Britannicus Maximus* between 315 and 318, suggesting a victory there, though whether against a usurper or against the *Picti* or other external enemies is unknown.

One of the sons of Constantine, the emperor Constans, evidently made a mid-winter visit to Britain in 342–43, though the precise circumstances are uncertain. A brief allusion in Ammianus Marcellinus appears to link this in some way with the *areani*, frontier scouts based on or north of Hadrian's Wall. Given the timing of the expedition, a crisis with a possible usurper in the south is perhaps just as probable.

In 350 Constans was assassinated and one of his field army commanders in Gaul, Magnentius, proclaimed as ruler in his place. After the defeat of Magnentius in 353 by the eastern emperor Constantius II, severe reprisals were exacted against those in Britain who had supported the usurper. A Spanish imperial agent Paulus was sent to arrest some members of the army, but soon extended his inquisition to civilians. There was evidently 'widespread slaughter and ruin' as a result of fabricated charges and the affair culminated with the despairing *vicarius* attempting to kill Paulus, before committing suicide. Such were the hazards of Britain's position as a military province, from which troops and financial resources might be drawn off to support usurpers against legitimate emperors.

The military situation appears to have been worsening in the early 360s, with references to seaborne raiding by a variety of external groups. This culminated in a serious military crisis, the so-called Barbarian Conspiracy of 367. We have an unusually full account of this incident in Ammianus, undoubtedly due to the fact that the general sent to relieve the situation was Count Theodosius, father of Theodosius I, who was emperor at the time Ammianus was writing. This should alert us to the possibility that the significance of this attack may have been greatly exaggerated by Ammianus. There was evidently a rising pattern of coastal raiding at this time by bands of *Saxones* from the North Sea coast of Holland, *Picti* from Scotland, *Attacotti* and *Scotti* from Ireland. In 360, we know that Julian had had to send a senior general Lupicinus to Britain in winter-time – always a sign of crisis – in connection with attacks by *Picti* and *Scotti*. What made the attack in 367 out of the ordinary is that these various and geographically far-flung enemies appear to have co-ordinated their actions in a carefully planned assault on the province. Roman scouts (*areani*) from the northern garrison were implicated in betraying the province, perhaps by passing information on the relative weakness of Roman military dispositions in one direction and inaccurate intelligence in the other. Quite how the different groups in Ireland, Scotland and the North Sea coast drew up and communicated their plan is unclear, but their initial successes were striking – slaying one of the pair of senior Roman generals and ambushing (and presumably killing) the other. The first man was Nectaridus, described as 'Count of the coastal district' and thus probably Count of the Saxon Shore, while the second general, Fullofaudes, was styled duke, thus presumably *dux Britanniarum*. The attacking forces were evidently widely scattered through the province, well south of Hadrian's Wall, and their devastation included pillage, arson and murder.

The western emperor Valentinian I happened to be in northern Gaul in the summer of 367 and marched towards the Channel ports, sending on in advance his *comes domesticorum*, Severus. This man was soon recalled and replaced by Iovinus, the *magister equitum*. The former may have got no further than Boulogne, but the latter was evidently not close by when Valentinian fell dangerously ill at Amiens – an event that necessitated the return to Gaul of a general as senior as Iovinus. A third-choice general, Theodosius, was thus sent to Britain late in the campaigning season of 367, probably with the rank of *comes rei militaris*, though we are not explicitly told this. Theodosius crossed from Boulogne to Richborough with only four units of the field army and immediately encountered marauding bands in the vicinity of London. Having recovered some booty from these raiders, he entered London and apparently over-wintered there. He used the winter months to increase the forces at his disposal by calling back to the colours soldiers who had gone AWOL during the crisis. This shows the precariousness of his position, having crossed with only *c.*2,000 men. The enemy were evidently still at large and further military action followed in 368 by land and sea, in which Theodosius was supported by the appointment of a new *dux*, Dulcitius. Eventually Theodosius restored peaceful conditions and disbanded the treacherous *areani*. Ammianus claimed that an entire province had been recovered from enemy hands and renamed *Valentia*. In addition to the barbarian forces, Theodosius dealt with an insurrectionist plot fomented by a certain Valentinus, who had been exiled to Britain.

Although the impact of the Barbarian Conspiracy should not be downplayed, it is significant that the threat was met with a tiny expeditionary force and those elements of the provincial army that had survived the initial barbarian onslaught (probably quite a high proportion if they stayed within their forts). Theodosius is praised by Ammianus for the thoroughness of his reforms of the British administration and military dispositions. Some of the rhetoric has echoes of the *topos* of the 'good general' encountered many times in Roman history and was particularly appropriate for Ammianus' purpose in addressing his account to Theodosius I. We are told that he 'restored cities and forts of the garrison . . . he protected the frontiers with sentries'. The problem is that archaeologists have seized on this and virtually any building work of later fourth century date tends to be assigned to the aftermath of the Barbarian Conspiracy. Theodosius himself may not have been present to oversee much of whatever rebuilding and strengthening was required, since he seems to have returned to the court of Valentinian by late 368. Much of the reconstruction work in the province must have post-dated the victory completed in 368, perhaps under the unknown military and civil successors to Theodosius.

Yet another usurper was proclaimed in Britain in 383. Magnus Maximus went on to defeat and kill the western emperor Gratian, before falling to the eastern emperor Theodosius at Aquileia in 388. His earlier career is uncertain, in part because he was adopted as a potent figure in early Welsh literature and became as mystical a figure as Arthur, in part because of the usual antipathy for failed usurpers in Roman sources. Maximus probably had a lengthy military career. He had evidently served under Count Theodosius in 367, so may have been sent to Britain specifically because of his prior knowledge of the military situation there. His position in Britain in 383 is not known, and one of our sources says that his revolt was partly the result of peevishness with Theodosius I (possibly his kinsman) for not having given him 'honorific office'. However, since he had command of military forces, and won a victory over *Picti* and *Scotti*, he must have had the rank of either *comes* or *dux*. The former title would imply command of *comitatenses* units and the success of his coup in winning over the army on the Rhine would suggest that he had initial support from some field army units with him in Britain. Similarly, the statement in our sources that he withdrew troops from Britain to support his bid for power makes best sense in the context of high-grade troops, rather than, for instance, the *limitanei* units of the northern frontier. This brings up another frequently evoked theme in the history of late Roman Britain, namely the repeated stripping of the British garrison by usurpers. There is no doubt that men such as Clodius Albinus, Constantine I, Magnentius, Magnus Maximus and Constantine III will have taken the best-quality troops from Britain to support their causes in key campaigns on the Continent. But the quality of parts of the British garrison had changed by the end of the third century. Far from denuding Britain of all troops, these usurpers may well have deemed that many frontier units were better left where they were as they were unlikely to be much help in the sort of warfare that would be required in Gaul or Italy.

The last active Roman campaigns in Britain that we have a record of were due to the intervention of Flavius Stilicho. The panegyric poet, Claudian, alluded to victories c.398–99 over *Saxones*, *Picti* and *Scotti*, but the ambiguity over whether Stilicho himself went to Britain to direct these operations perhaps favours the view that the action was carried out by a subordinate. It is often suggested that this was the point at which Rome established the office of *comes Britanniarum*, with command of a small group of field army units evidently specially levied for service there (but later recalled to the Gallic prefecture). Any remaining field army units in Britain in 407 were undoubtedly taken to Gaul along with the usurper Constantine III when he launched the bid for power that brought about the end of the British Diocese.

CHANGES TO MILITARY STRUCTURE IN THE LATE EMPIRE

The army of Britain in the fourth century was dramatically changed from the army of the second century, notwithstanding the fact that many of the unit names remained the same and that some of the old garrison posts were still in occupation. Our most important document concerning the late Roman army is the *Notitia Dignitatum*, the administrative listing of government officials and army units (along with their headquarters). The British section of the *Notitia* was probably compiled in the 390s, though final revisions of other sections of the document continued to c.428, by which time the British information was long redundant. The list reflects the changes in military structure that had occurred since the third century (Table 7). One section records the garrisons on the line of Hadrian's Wall (*per lineam valli*) and in north-west Britain under the authority of the *dux Britanniarum*, and features almost exclusively old-style *cohortes* and *alae*. These units were probably much smaller in size than their second-century antecedents. Figures as low as 50–100 men have been proposed (or about 10 per cent of their former strength),

Table 7. The army of Britain in the *Notitia Dignitatum*.

TYPE OF UNIT (AND APPROX. SIZE IN MEN)	*COMES* SAXON SHORE	*DUX BRITANNIARUM*		*COMES BRITAN- NIARUM*	TOTAL
		HINTERLAND	WALL AND NW		
Old-style units					
legio (<500)	1	1			2
cohors (<300)	1		16		17
ala (<300)			5		5
New-style units					
cuneus			1		1
numerus	4	10	1		15
equites	2	3			5
milites	1				1
Comitatenses					
numerus (1,000)				3	3
equites (500)				6	6
Total	9	14	23	9	55

though the most recent studies suggest that in the early fourth century at least the average auxiliary unit may have still contained *c.*200–300 men. By contrast, the hinterland forts in north-east Britain (also assigned to the *dux*) included *legio VI* at York, ten *numeri* and three units of *equites*. The size of these units is likewise uncertain, but the legion probably numbered no more than 500 men by this date and other units at most 200–300 men. The separate command of the 'Saxon Shore', under a *comes*, included *legio II Augusta*, one other old-style cohort, with the bulk of troops in new-style *numeri*, *equites* and *milites* units. All of these units were technically frontier troops (classed as *limitanei* or *ripenses*). There are further entries to a small force of field army troops under the command of the *comes Britanniarum*. The overall size of the army in the fourth century, assuming the *Notitia Dignitatum* to provide a typical picture, was a small core of perhaps 5,000–6,000 *comitatenses* and perhaps no more than 12,500 *limitanei*. In other words, the total strength of the army was only about a third of that in the second century.

But there are indications that the *Notitia* lists are incomplete. There is, for instance, no mention of forts in Wales (though several continued to be occupied into the late fourth century) and there are quite a number of forts in northern Britain that do not feature in the *Notitia* where late occupation is attested. As in the earlier period, part of the discrepancy may be due to units being split between more than one garrison post, with only one recognized as their primary base. Nor is there an explicit mention of any naval force, though it is difficult to see how coastal defence could have functioned without one.

The debate about the extent to which there were field army units present in Britain as a regular part of the garrison is more difficult to assess. Some commentators suggest that the *Notitia* listing of *comitatenses* based there was a late departure, implemented by Stilicho. The lack of reference to a *comes Britanniarum* in the events of 367 is often held to be crucial evidence for the earlier absence of field army troops. The presence of field army units would have required a higher-ranking officer to command them. Both Gratianus, father of the emperors Valentinian I and Valens, and Theodosius apparently served in this way as *comes rei militaris* in Britain on emergency missions. Gratianus was sent at some point in the late 340s, Theodosius in 367 and, in between, a *magister equitum*, Lupicinus, commanded another expeditionary force in 360. There were good reasons why the western emperors should attempt to limit the number of top-grade troops assigned to Britain, given its reputation as a spawning ground for usurpers. But the Diocese also faced military problems in the later fourth century and continued to produce usurpers through the actions of its soldiers down to the early fifth century. It is hard to see how a man like Magnus Maximus could have succeeded in winning over the Rhine army if he had only *limitanei* units under his command. Thus, despite the claim in one of our sources that Maximus felt his position unequal to his dignity, it is likely that he was a *comes* in command of a small contingent of *comitatenses*. If field army units were not permanently based in Britain in the later fourth century, it is at least a strong possibility that the known list of *comites rei militaris* is incomplete and that field army troops were temporarily deployed in Britain on additional occasions before the permanent creation of the post of *comes Britanniae* or *Britanniarum c.*398.

Irish federates (*Attacotti*) possibly settled in south-west Wales in the second half of the fourth century and there are several references to Germanic groups in Britain, hinting at the presence of *laeti* or federate forces. After defeating Vandals and Burgundians in 277, Probus evidently sent the survivors to Britain, 'where they settled and became useful to the emperor when someone rebelled'. This sounds like a continuation of the earlier policy of sending newly defeated enemies to Britain for safe induction into the Roman army. Carausius also made extensive use of 'barbarian' elements in his army, and the eventual defeat of his successor Allectus in 296 was portrayed as largely a victory over Franks. When Constantine was proclaimed emperor by the army in Britain in 306, one of the leading instigators behind the move was the German king Crocus, commanding a unit of *Alamanni*. In 372, Valentinian dispatched another Alamannic king to Britain, with the rank of tribune over 'a large and powerful contingent of *Alamanni*'. This last sounds like a command of a regular unit, rather than *foederati*, in which case the unit may have been recruited from *laeti* already in Britain. There should be a presumption that both regular units of Germans and federates were viewed as a mobile resource by emperors and pretenders. They are therefore unlikely to have been a permanent fixture, but were undoubtedly from time to time a significant factor in the army in Britain. The field army units, any *ripenses* units and federate troops were those most likely to accompany a usurper to the Continent, as under Magnus Maximus and Constantine III.

Study of Roman fortifications in Britain provides further illustration of the changing nature of the military community. Hadrian's Wall continued to be garrisoned down to the end of Roman Britain and the lack of explicit evidence for wholesale violent destruction would suggest that it was relatively effective as deterrent and defence against land-based attacks from the north. The major threat in the late Roman period came from the sea, with *Picti* by-passing the Wall, *Attacotti* and *Scotti* probing across the Irish Sea, and the *Saxones* in the southern area of the North Sea and Channel coasts. There was a British fleet in the Channel in the early imperial period, with a main base in a *c.*12-ha fortress at Boulogne. The last epigraphic testimony of the *classis Britannica* dates to the mid-third century, and the fleet was probably formally disbanded and its personnel and ships subsumed into new arrangements for coastal defence that developed in the later third century. A separate reference in the *Notitia* to a *classis Anderetianorum* attached to the *magister peditum per Gallias* at Paris might represent a late transfer away from Britain of a naval contingent originally attached to the fort of Pevensey (*Anderita*).

The most striking indications of the changing threat are the sequence of fortifications built in south-eastern Britain from the early third century onwards, eventually unified as the command of the *comes litoris Saxonici per Britanniam* in the *Notitia*. The name 'Saxon Shore' has provoked rival theories that this was either the shore exposed to the Saxons or that Saxon mercenaries were in fact employed to garrison the defences by the early fifth century. The balance of probability is that the Saxons gave their name to the coastlands that they were attacking. The British evidence needs to be taken in parallel with the picture of similar defences along the Channel coast of Belgium and France; it is certain that at times these were placed under a unified command, at others that there were separate but related military authorities. The earliest British sites were at Dover, Brancaster and Reculver, where forts of relatively conventional playing-card shape were established in the early second, late second and early third century respectively. There was further development of the system in the third quarter of the third century, with additional forts at Burgh Castle, Walton Castle, Bradwell, Richborough, Dover, Lympne and Portchester. These late third-century forts had a very different form, comprising rectangular or trapezoidal ditched enclosures, with thick, tall walls and externally projecting towers. There was generally only a single gate, as opposed to the four of the traditional Roman fort. Pevensey was exceptional in being oval in shape, though otherwise of the same architectural style.

The character of the later forts is overtly defensive, though the interiors have not yielded evidence of closely packed buildings. The lack of the regular barrack lines of earlier periods could in part be due to poor preservation at some sites; some baths and possible headquarters buildings built in more durable materials are known. It is perhaps significant that these forts were of similar size to earlier auxiliary forts. If they were designed to house fewer than 100 men they could have been made more easily defensible by reducing the length of the enceinte, though even with small groups of soldiers present, their high walls will have made them relatively secure against investment by raiders. On the other hand, as in other periods, there is no reason to believe that they were permanently garrisoned by hundreds of men. Out-posting of some troops into other military installations and nearby towns would be one factor, the smaller size of late Roman units another. They could also have accommodated civilians, especially members of the military community, and finds of female artefacts from Portchester suggest as much. The naval function of these bases is also clear from the fact that they do not in general link in with the Roman road network, but are sited by harbours or beach anchorages. The locations require the presence of sailors and patrol boats at some or all of these forts. A reference in the late Roman military writer Vegetius may relate to forty-oared scout ships operating in British waters, with sails, rigging and crew in camouflage green.

The forts under the command of the Count of the Saxon Shore evidently spread across more than one of the British provinces. Indeed, they make most sense when considered with the Continental forts and defended towns of the Channel coast. There are about twenty relevant sites spread along the coast from west Brittany to Belgium, and the *Notitia* attests at least two relevant military commands: the *dux tractus Armoricani et Nervicani* in the west and the *dux Belgicae secundae* in the region from the Pas de Calais to the Rhine mouth. Both these sections in the *Notitia* make explicit reference to the first-named site as being located 'on the Saxon shore'. Boulogne appears to have been an important site in late Roman times as earlier, with a fortified town laid out over the demolished barracks of the *classis Britannica* in the late third century. However, the fleet (*classis Sambricae*) and two *limitanei* units listed in the *Notitia* were based at other harbours along the Belgic coast. The *dux tractus Armoricani et Nervicani* had a wide territorial brief, crossing the boundaries of five Gallic provinces, with nine military units under his authority (none explicitly naval).

The list of the Count of the Saxon Shore gives a particular focus on southern Britain, but archaeological evidence shows that other parts of Britain also saw strengthening of coastal defences. In south Wales a new fort was constructed *c.*260 at Cardiff, following the model of the later Saxon Shore forts. Similar, but smaller scale, were a fort with external towers at Lancaster and a fortlet at Caer Gybi by Holyhead. Up the west coast of Britain, forts continued to be occupied on the navigable reaches of other rivers or anchorages (Caernarfon, Chester, Ribchester, Ravenglass, Maryport), and some old forts may have been reoccupied (Loughor, Neath, Caerhun), supplemented by fortified towns (Gloucester, Carmarthen, Caerwent, Carlisle) and watchtowers (near Caernarfon and Holyhead).

The east coast was also fortified north of the Wash, with a probably military presence at Brough-on-Humber, backed up by the legionary fortress at York. The fort of South Shields controlled the mouth of the Tyne. In between, a system of substantial signal stations was constructed in the second half of the fourth century between the Humber and Tees (Filey, Scarborough, Ravenscar, Goldborough, Huntcliff, and possibly Sunderland). Conventionally ascribed to the revitalization of fortifications post-368, the surviving signal stations form a coherent series, with a substantial masonry tower within an outer enclosure with projecting towers. They are paralleled by a similar enclosure on Alderney in the Channel Islands. What is missing in the Yorkshire series is a Roman harbour for the towers to signal to. The best harbour on this stretch of coast is at Whitby, where a dense cluster of Roman finds has been recorded, though no coherent structural evidence has yet emerged beneath the medieval and modern harbour town.

The British legions were reduced in size and importance through the third century. The process appears to have begun early at Caerleon, where the main baths were abandoned *c.*230, and vexillations of the legion are known on the Continent in the 250s. Inscriptions show that Caerleon was still the headquarters of *legio II Augusta* in the mid-third century. The latest inscription dates to the 270s and there are signs of major demolition of administrative buildings in the 290s – linked by some to the exigencies of the years of Carausius' breakaway 'empire'. There are ample parallels in the third century for substantial out-posting of legionaries on a long-term basis to small forts, so the seeming abandonment of large parts of the fortress need not necessarily signal the legion's final departure from the site. By the time of the *Notitia* the only relic of the legion was recorded at Richborough, but the exact moment of final departure from Caerleon is uncertain. There was some continuing occupation within the northern part of the fortress to at least the mid-fourth century and coins of later fourth-century emperors are rare, but present. One of Caerleon's main extra-mural areas at Great Bulmore was abandoned from *c.*290 and it is possible that its inhabitants subsequently took up residence inside the fortress, alongside any remaining troops. The evidence from Chester is similar, with evidence of demolition of barracks around 300, with little evidence of occupation inside the defences, though the baths and headquarters buildings were evidently still in use for a while into the fourth century. At any rate, *legio XX*, last heard of in the reign of Carausius, did not survive into the *Notitia* lists. Only the *VI Victrix* appears to have remained at its old base at York, though again the archaeological evidence to support this is elusive. The south-western defences, fronting on to the Ouse, were remodelled with projecting towers in the early fourth century, but internal evidence is more ambiguous. As at Chester and Caerleon, the active size of the unit was probably reduced over a period in the late third century and this was formalized in the fourth.

In addition to the coastal fort at Cardiff, late military activity in Wales is attested by major refurbishment or remodelling of forts at Forden Gaer (late fourth century), Caernarfon (in use throughout the century), and by minor phases at a number of other sites. There thus appears to have been a small garrison of sorts in Wales down to close to the end of Roman Britain, though the apparent absence of Welsh sites in the *Notitia* lists has tended to drive the assumption at many sites that any activity by that date was civilian. There is a danger of circularity here and the absence in the lists of specific posts, such as a Severn estuary command, does not rule out the possibility that this was a significant one for parts of the fourth century.

For northern Britain, we are on surer ground with the literary and archaeological evidence. An interesting aspect of the *Notitia* list is that most of the regiments recorded along Hadrian's Wall were present at the same fort in the third century, whereas units at coastal sites and along the trunk roads of northern Britain show much greater variance from earlier garrison patterns. Thus, while there does not seem to have been major reorganization of the garrison of the wall, there was a more dynamic restructuring elsewhere. On the other hand, a Tetrarchic inscription from Birdoswald and plenty of archaeological evidence from other wall sites demonstrate a significant phase of renewal of the northern garrisons around 300.

The changing nature of military posts is reflected even more clearly by auxiliary forts, where traditional barrack blocks (comprising long, narrow rectangular ranges designed to hold at full capacity a century of eighty men) were often replaced with shorter rows of semi-detached 'chalet' buildings, butted up against each other. Various interpretations have been offered, such as the possibility that these served as married quarters for individual soldiers and their families or as accommodation suites for smaller groups of soldiers. Recent studies have demonstrated, however, that the so-called 'chalets' are rather less irregular than originally thought and that they originated well within the third century at *Vindolanda* and Wallsend. The use of a common spine wall and the regular placement of hearths within them suggest that these were still highly regulated spaces. Moreover, some appear to be a variant on the standard cavalry barracks of the second century, but with the number of paired-room suites (one for horses, one for men) reduced from nine or ten to five. These cavalry examples cannot have been for individual soldiers and their families, because the stables are suited to three or more horses. These semi-detached barracks thus appear to have been a standard type of late military construction and their design implies smaller numbers of soldiers present in the average auxiliary fort, with the reduction in the order of *c.*50 per cent. In the latest phase at South Shields (constructed *c.*286–312) there were apparently ten blocks, each with five *contubernia* units. There is some evidence that the late imperial army favoured six-man sub-divisions, rather than the eight-man *contubernia* of earlier times, and on this basis the fort had a potential garrison of 300 men. In reality, of course, the full contingent may not have been present all the time and roster numbers may have been progressively reduced from the mid-third century to the end of the fourth century.

The available evidence suggests that most auxiliary units were about half their second-century size from about the mid-third century onwards, though forts were still constructed on approximately the same size footprint. This suggests a more generous allocation of space, or increased numbers of non-combatants being accommodated alongside the troops. Coupled with the steep decline in legionary troops (demoted to the same status as the other *limitanei* by the end of the third century), this represents a major reduction in the overall provincial garrison.

The garrison settlements outside many forts show a corresponding decline in activity in the fourth century, but if soldiers continued in garrison it seems inconceivable that some of the civilian members of the military community did not also remain. There may have been an increasing presence of civilians inside the forts, especially if rosters dropped below the notional unit size suggested by the built accommodation. The situation may have varied from fort to fort, and even within forts, as circumstances dictated. Artefactual evidence from one of these 'chalet' barrack blocks at Housesteads indicates the presence of women only in the larger officer's quarters, but the South Shields excavations have located an increased incidence of infant burials in the fourth century, in contrast to isolated examples later. There were also signs at that site of increasingly irregular remodelling of interior spaces after 370, perhaps hinting at less regimented arrangements.

The reduction in the size of the provincial garrison has traditionally been presented as a cause of Roman Britain's decline. Yet, in another way, the changes of the later third and fourth centuries could be read as indicating a more cost-efficient approach to the British provinces. If substantial reductions had occurred by the mid-third century, effectively halving the garrison, and the province was not 'lost' for another 160 years, that might say something about the relative economy of the later Roman arrangements compared to the overkill of the second-century army. The construction of towers and outposts implies a continuation of the wide-ranging activities of the garrison, though it was now even more thinly spread. And while it is true that there were some military crises in this period, were these any worse than those that had arisen from time to time under a larger permanent garrison? Britain remained comparatively heavily garrisoned to the end, but it was also a relatively peaceful region by the standards of the western empire. Practical experience had shown that the Roman military community could still fulfil its role at less cost to the state and to the provincials.

CHANGES TO THE MILITARY COMMUNITY AND MILITARY IDENTITY

There were significant changes to the material practices and identity projections of the military community. There are, for instance, very few inscriptions erected by soldiers in the fourth century. The reduced use of the epigraphic habit is paralleled elsewhere and in part at least reflects broader changes afoot. But, given that the literate statement was such a key part of the military identity in the earlier period, it was a striking departure. Several factors were perhaps at play. Finds from Syria and North Africa of military archives comparable to the *Vindolanda* tablets and dating to the mid-third century, show that the army still operated in a highly literate manner, and papyri from Egypt demonstrate that such practices continued well into the fourth century. However, the longer-term changes in the imperial army, with the rise of German troops in the field army units and the effective downgrading of the *limitanei*, had implications for recruitment and promotion in both types of unit, perhaps with less emphasis than before on literacy. One of the few certain later fourth-century military texts from Britain, dedicating a signal station on the Yorkshire coast, is barely intelligible as Latin.

Similarly, changes at the commanding officer level promoted different types of people to the top of the military community, replacing the Mediterranean-dominated equestrian class with career soldiers from the German, Danubian and Balkan regions. The fact that even commanding officers of military units in Britain no longer routinely recorded their building works or made dedications or erected tombstones to family members underlines changing attitudes to the epigraphic habit. No surprise then that lower ranks abandoned it. Pay and conditions in the British *auxilia* and units were progressively eroded, so the material wherewithal to engage in epigraphic commemoration was also reduced. Finally, the increasing prominence of Christians during the fourth century impacted on traditional pagan styles of worship in the army as elsewhere. All these factors diminished the tendency of the British military community to express its literacy through the epigraphic habit in the fourth century. There was a corresponding decline in the use of sculptural stonework, though harder to pin down by date.

This does not mean that the military identity or the sense of a community of soldiers was lost. It was now expressed in new ways, perhaps with an increasing emphasis on personal appearance. Arms and armour evolved in the third century, partly through the necessity of being found wanting against enemies from Free Germany and from the East. Traditional Roman infantry warfare was increasingly only effective against other people who fought in the same way, and in the third century that mostly meant other Romans in the numerous civil wars. The 'barbarians' were now well armed and had evolved improved tactics, notably of cavalry warfare. To the extent that Romans continued to win battles, it was often due to the large-scale incorporation of Germans into the army. The plate armour (*lorica segmentata*) disappeared, to be replaced by chain-mail or scale armour, and the rectangular legionary shields were supplanted by oval ones for all classes of troops. One consequence of this was a blurring of distinctions between legionaries and auxiliaries. The evolution of the field army placed a new emphasis on cavalry and mobile infantry, equipped with a range of missiles as well as swords.

Within units, the relative uniformity of dress in terms of garments and colours will have reinforced the sense of group identity. Germanic groups incorporated in the imperial armies often maintained their own traditions of dress and battle gear, but used dress accessories to integrate with the broader military community. As in earlier times, soldiers advertised their status by means of distinctive belts, on which they openly displayed their arms, accompanied by military styles of cloaks and brooches. The crossbow brooch type is particularly characteristic of the Roman army and high officials in the late empire. It was worn as a cloak fastener on the right shoulder, with the head pointing downwards. Belt fittings can be divided into characteristic types of third- and fourth-century date, and show a tendency over time towards wider styles of belt (5–10 cm) and still more elaborate ornamentation. Some types of decorative metalwork, including chip-carved buckle plates and fittings, were strongly adopted by the army and, consequently, by Germanic groups. The uniformity of this material was enhanced by its production in state-run arms workshops (*fabricae*), for instance those serving the army and officialdom on the Rhine and Danube frontiers and in northern Gaul. Finds from Britain are all from the south-east, suggesting that they may have been linked to government officials, to members of field army units or to German federates. The inclusion of belt fittings and sometimes weapons in late Roman graves in the north-western provinces – at a time when grave goods were less and less common due to the influence of Christianity – is another indication of the military community pursuing its own cultural agenda.

The rising recruitment of Roman armies from their Germanic neighbours (and sometime opponents) is often attributed to difficulties with maintaining enlistment numbers within the provinces. From the reign of Diocletian conscription was stepped up again and hereditary service introduced for sons of soldiers. Evidently voluntary enlistment had been in decline – no doubt depressed by the spate of invasions and civil wars. In some regions and some sectors of society, service in the army was unpopular, particularly among provincials who had had bad experiences of the haughty exclusiveness of soldiers. By the fourth century, part of military recruitment targeted landowners, requiring them to supply soldiers in proportion to the size of their estates. The selection of the required 'volunteers' was inevitably resented. An alternative was to recruit large numbers from the Germanic groups settled along the frontiers and increasingly within the empire. These peoples, often with martial traditions, had inbuilt advantages over recruits drawn from farming communities and may have been more enthusiastic about the opportunities that army service offered. Britain was affected by the changes in recruitment, even if the units of *limitanei* still drew extensively on the local garrison settlements. The shift in the military hierarchy towards men of Germanic or Balkan origin is evident in the careers of senior officers linked to Britain in the fourth century (Gratian, Nectaridus, Fullofaudes, Stilicho), though Count Theodosius and Magnus Maximus were Spaniards, and a short-lived usurper in 406, Gratianus, was probably of British origin. The influential role played by the Alamannic unit commander Crocus in the proclamation of Constantine illustrates the importance of Germans in the command structure, as does the Alamannic tribune Fraomarius. By contrast, several of the known civil governors (*vicarii* and *praesides*) were of Gallic origin (Flavius Sanctus, Flavius Jovinus, Victorinus).

Pay in the fourth-century army was increasingly in kind rather than hard cash, while service terms remained long (twenty to twenty-four years). More important than the meagre salary was the chance of donatives (often paid in bullion rather than coin). Higher ranks qualified for higher ration allocations – an important consideration for those taking on family responsibilities. Sons of soldiers also were issued with rations (at least down to 372), emphasizing the necessarily close spatial links between military units and garrison settlements. There is little firm evidence about rates of pay, but it is clear that field army units received more than the *limitanei* and *ripenses*, and thus had more resources and more motivation to show off their status in material terms. Promotion within the field army would open up the gap still further.

What we need to think of increasingly, therefore, is the emergence of different military identities, related to the type of unit. In general terms we might expect that the more Germanic-style of military culture would correlate with the presence of comitatensian troops or German federates, rather than the *limitanei*, though the latter were not immune to some elements of the new fashions, such as crossbow brooches. However, finds of the standard late Roman military belt fittings are rare on fort sites in northern Britain and in the Saxon Shore command (admittedly the dearth of cemetery excavations at these sites may contribute to this picture). Most late 'military' metalwork finds have tended to come from southern towns, such as London, Dorchester or Winchester, suggesting that field army units may have been billeted there. The alternative explanation is that civil government officials also utilized these new symbols of power and authority and had taken over part of the duties previously fulfilled by military personnel on secondment to the provincial administration.

The evidence from the forts of northern Britain suggests that the soldiers retained a coherent pattern of discipline until late in the fourth century, and by implication a distinctly separate identity from the wider world of civilians outside their garrison settlements. The receipt of rations and other goods in kind, the privileges attendant on military service, such as exemption from poll tax, and bonuses on honourable discharge, still set the community of soldiers apart. The long-term stability of garrison postings at Hadrian's Wall forts through the third and fourth centuries no doubt gave many of them an increasingly local recruitment base and identity. The slow decline of these units towards the status of a militia makes it unlikely that they were normally called on to take part in the wars of usurpers across the Channel. Perhaps what we see here is a weakening of the sense of being *commilitones* in a global army, to a stronger regimental one in which sons followed fathers as a hereditary duty.

In Rudyard Kipling's celebrated poem, *The Roman Centurion Speaks*, we encounter a Roman officer unwillingly packing up to leave Hadrian's Wall after forty years' service, as the curtain comes down on the end of empire in the far north. The cultural identity of his invented soldier, of course, had more to do with contemporary ideas about the mission of officials of the British empire. The reality in early fifth-century Britain was that the military community had polarized into three main groups: the troops on the northern frontier, other units of *limitanei* or *ripenses* in the hinterland of the wall and southern England, and the field army units (when present at all). The first of these groups was probably recruited predominantly from the garrison settlements of northern Britain and its sense of corporate identity was significantly diminished in the face of regimental tradition, local attachments and diminished motivation. The second and third groups were more mobile and received recruits drawn from a wider area and backgrounds. The field army units were the most upwardly mobile group of soldiers, who had the greatest incentives to use material culture to project their sense of power and self-importance.

The roles fulfilled by the different sorts of troops in Britain had also deviated one from the other, with the northern garrisons still rather focused on general security and supervision of peoples on both sides of the frontier. The coastal defences reflected a new role in combating seaborne raiders and placing troops in new military situations. The field army units were the most flexible and also potentially the most burdensome on the civil population in terms of their billeting and provisioning. Their deployment was flexible, with units moving between Britain and the Continent as situations developed.

Finally, it is worth emphasizing that reduction in the overall size of the British garrison by the fourth century may have had positive impacts on the economy of the province as a whole, by reducing both the upfront and hidden costs of supporting the military community. Far from the picture we started with – a province in anarchic decline – for long periods in the fourth century, Britain may have been relatively quiescent militarily in comparison to the near Continent. As we shall see, some areas of British society reached new levels of development and wealth at a time of relative peace. Although generally dismissed in historical accounts as an army that fell well short of its early imperial apogee, the late Roman soldiery in Britain remained comparatively efficient and a lot cheaper to maintain. At the same time, they continued to be a sharply defined group, to a large extent separated off from the rest of society.

PART THREE

The Civil Communities

9

Forma Urbis

The Development of Towns

Towns have for long been viewed as the corollary of forts in the Roman colonial system: central to the success of Roman administration and symbolic of a supposedly rational accommodation with the imperial power. Once pacified by the army, a region would be handed over to civil administration based on towns. So runs the conventional wisdom, though, as we shall see, there are complications, not least the fact that the majority of the subject people lived in the countryside. Two issues must be raised right away, because they go to the heart of what made Britain different from many other provinces. The Mediterranean heartlands of the empire were generally regions where urbanism was well established at the time of incorporation and the administrative structures of towns were fundamental to the governance and taxation of provinces. Roman provincial government thus was built on the principle of adapting, where possible, existing structures of urban administration to serve the imperial project. But what happened when the empire extended to regions with no towns or with only embryonic urban structures? Provincial territory was generally acquired in a series of relatively rapid advances with many of the annexed territories being clear of large garrison forces within a century at most, allowing the civil governance model to thrive. What were the consequences, then, when the empire ceased to grow and military occupation of some provinces became a much more long-term affair?

The administration of the empire in the first century relied on provincial governors, many appointed directly by the emperor, though some through the Senate. Governors of provinces with significant bodies of troops like Britain were almost invariably the emperor's men. Their military responsibilities have already been reviewed. Civil administration was another major role, especially as this related to matters of justice, public order, communications and transport and the supervision of urban communities. Financial responsibilities in imperial provinces like Britain were delegated in part to specialist bureaux headed by equestrian procurators. They must have liaised very closely with the governor and may have shared access to certain archives relating to census data and so on. The governor's prime civic responsibility was thus to administer justice and maintain order, so that the procurator and his staff could maximize the financial return of the province for the emperor. The governor was also the conduit by which petitions from provincial communities and individuals passed to the emperor. Although there was not a single location formally designated as the provincial capital, there was generally a *de facto* centre where the provincial governor, the procurator and the bulk of their staff were based. This tended to be a major town, often at a hub in the road and communications network. Governors did not spend all their time there, of course, and in addition to campaigning with or inspecting the army, we know that they made annual assize court tours of the civil province. Crimes of a certain severity were automatically referred to the assize courts held before the legate in a limited number of the major towns. The governor and his retinue will have passed through and stayed in other centres en route. Over the course of a typical three-year appointment as governor, a legate would have visited most of the major urban centres in the province. The same sort of factors will have made the procurator's finance-related job peripatetic as well.

The development of towns in Britain was closely linked to the road network that facilitated not only military control, but also civil administration. The *Antonine Itinerary*, which lists fifteen routes within Britain, illustrates the importance of official peregrinations (Table 8). The itineraries often do not follow the shortest distance between places, but seem to take circuitous routes to take in the legionary fortresses and all the major towns in Britain (assuming that the site named as *Praetorium* can be equated with Brough-on-Humber). Three routes (*II–IV*) deal with the minor variants in journey for officials arriving at or departing from different Channel ports. London was the hub for seven routes and an eighth passed through it. Other major hubs of the communications network were York and Silchester (both named in four routes). Where routes started at a site other than London, they frequently began at a port, or a site accessible by boat, suggesting that officials might travel

Table 8. The *Antonine Itinerary* and the connectivity of towns in Roman Britain. Names in bold are major towns; [ship] indicates the possibility of an official arriving/departing from a terminal point by sea.

ITIN.	START [CONNECTS WITH]	FINISH [CONNECTS WITH]	MAJOR TOWNS ON ROUTE	OVERLAPS WITH [CONNECTS WITH]
It. I	*Bremenium* (High Rochester) [limit of Roman territory north of wall]	***Praetorium*** (Brough-on-Humber?) [ship]	Corbridge?, Aldborough, York, Brough?	It. II, V
It. II	*Bratobulgium* (Birrens) [limit of Roman territory north of wall]	*Rutupiae* (Richborough) [ship]	Carlisle, Aldborough, York, Chester, Wroxeter, St Albans, London, Canterbury	It. I, III, IV, V
It. III	***Londinium*** (London) [It. II, IV, V, VI, VII, VIII, IX]	*Dubris* (Dover) [ship]	London, Canterbury	It. II, IV
It. IV	***Londinium*** (London) [It. II, III, V, VI, VII, VIII, IX]	*Lemanis* (Lympne)	London, Canterbury	It. II, III
It. V	***Londinium*** (London) [It. II, III, IV, VI, VII, VIII, IX]	***Luguvalium*** (Carlisle) [ship]	London, Colchester, Caistor-by-Norwich, Lincoln, York, Aldborough, Carlisle	It. I, II, IX
It. VI	***Londinium*** (London) [It. II, III, IV, V, VII, VIII, IX]	***Lindum*** (Lincoln) [It. V]	London, St Albans, Leicester, Lincoln	It. II, VIII
It. VII	***Regno*** (Chichester) [ship]	***Londinium*** (London) [It. II, III, IV, V, VI, VIII, IX]	Chichester, Winchester, Silchester, London	It. XV
It. VIII	*Eboracum* (York) [It. I, II, V, ship]	***Londinium*** (London) [It. II, III, IV, V, VI, VII, IX]	York, Lincoln, Leicester, St Albans, London	
It. IX	***Venta Icenorum*** (Caistor-by-Norwich) [ship?]	***Londinium*** (London) [It. II, III IV, V, VI, VII, VIII]	Caistor-by-Norwich, Colchester, London	It. V
It. X	*Glannoventa* (Ravenglass) [ship]	*Mediolanum* (Whitchurch) [It. II]	None	It. II
It. XI	*Segontium* (Caernarfon) [ship]	*Deva* (Chester) [It. II]	Chester?	

Table 8 – *contd.*

ITIN.	START [CONNECTS WITH]	FINISH [CONNECTS WITH]	MAJOR TOWNS ON ROUTE	OVERLAPS WITH [CONNECTS WITH]
It. XII	*Moridunum* (Carmarthen) [ship]	*Viriconium* (Wroxeter)	Carmarthen, Caerleon?, Wroxeter	It. XIII [It. XIV]
It. XIII	*Isca* (Caerleon) [It. XII, XIV, ship]	*Calleva* (Silchester) [It. VII, XIV, XV]	Caerleon?, Gloucester, Cirencester, Silchester	It. XII, XIV
It. XIV	*Isca* (Caerleon) [It. XII, XIII, ship]	*Calleva* (Silchester) [It. VII, XIII, XV]	Caerleon?, Bath?, Silchester	It. XIII
It. XV	*Calleva* (Silchester) [It. VII, XIII, XIV]	*Isca Dumnoniorum* (Exeter) [ship]	Silchester, Winchester, Dorchester, Exeter	It. VII

out by sea to some locations and then have followed a peregrination back towards London.

Iter II covered the journey from beyond the west end of Hadrian's Wall to the Channel in a series of zig-zags, first going over the Pennines to Catterick and York, then recrossing the Pennines to Chester, then back south-east along Watling Street passing Wroxeter, St Albans and London. *Iter I* also has the look of a military route, descending from the eastern outpost fort of Hadrian's Wall to York and, probably, terminating at the military base and potential *civitas* centre at Brough-on-Humber. *Iter V* runs from London to Caistor-by-Norwich via Colchester (this part of the route repeated in reverse as *Iter IX*), then to Lincoln, York, Aldborough and Carlisle. Routes *VI* and *VIII* partly overlapped, both running north-west from London up Watling Street, before turning north-east up Fosse Way (taking in St Albans, Leicester and Lincoln), with *Iter VIII* continuing on to York. *Iter VII* connected Chichester to London by a very circuitous route via Winchester and Silchester (linking the three centres of the client kingdom of Togidubnus). Two routes in the north-west appear exclusively military, the first connecting Chester to Caernarfon (*Iter XI*), the second running south from the fort at Ravenglass to Whitchurch just south of Chester (*X*). *Iter XII* ran from Carmarthen to Wroxeter, via the legionary fortress at Caerleon. Caerleon was the origin point for two routes to Silchester (*XIII–XIV*), the first via Gloucester and

Cirencester (though the latter is omitted from the extant list by a copyist's error), the second passing by Caerwent and crossing the Severn estuary to take in Bath en route. The final route (XV) went from Silchester to the south-western town of Exeter, via Winchester and Dorchester.

Inclusion of a route in the official itineraries of the province should indicate that it fell within the purview of the *cursus publicus*, and will have been provided with official posting stations (*praetoria* – also referred to as *mansiones* and *mutationes*) for official travellers to change horses at and when necessary obtain overnight accommodation. Larger supply centres also provided vehicles for the movement of heavier goods and may have had warehousing for storage of goods. The *mansiones* appear to have been located 20–35 Roman miles apart, with intermediate *mutationes*, where horses could be changed. There has been much debate about the type of facilities to be expected at these sites, though in reality there was no single blueprint. Large courtyard houses, often associated with separate bath-houses, have been noted both at garrison settlements (Melandra, Newstead, Caernarfon) and in large (Caerwent, St Albans, Silchester) and small towns (Chelmsford, Godmanchester, Wall). They have typically been identified as *mansiones*, though this should not preclude other interpretations of some of these buildings or of other types of structure actually having served as *mansiones*. Where no facility existed, the official traveller had powers to demand accommodation and animals from civilians, within prescribed (but often abused) limits. It is clear that these facilities were set up to deal with different classes of official travel-ler, from officers and officials, to couriers and soldiers. Soldiers detached from their units for administrative duties (*beneficiarii* and similar appointments) may have helped run these establishments, though when-ever possible costs and the provision of animals were devolved on local municipalities. It is a reasonable assumption that the *c*.110 locations named in the *Antonine Itinerary* for Britain either had developed facili-ties or were obliged to provide appropriate services to official travellers. There were probably others on a number of other important sections of roads not included in the *Itinerary*, but marking the most direct line between places – notably the main north road from London.

Roman administrative and military needs underwrote the process of development of communications within Britain. Towns were another important element of the innovative infrastructure that evolved in Britain in response to the colonial project.

THE FUNCTION OF ROMAN TOWNS

In an idealized vision of Roman provincial administration towns were semi-autonomous units of local government, assigned specific territory and often given fiscal and judicial responsibility for larger areas of the countryside. Some towns were founded for the settlement of legionary veterans, others for indigenous groups whose identity as separate peoples (*civitates*) was recognized by Rome, yet others formalized the status of settlements of more mixed origin, including trading centres. We have noted that some of the garrison settlements could also have had a designated urban status conferred on them. All of these oversaw the local administration of justice, the collection of taxes and other specific obligations to the state, served as authorized markets and regulated their own local affairs. Towns were accorded different statuses and only the higher levels were obliged to take on a specifically Roman urban constitution. In practice, especially in areas lacking a strong alternative model, urban governance tended to imitate Roman forms. Although there is surprisingly little surviving evidence of local government offices from Britain, what we have suggests acceptance of a Roman model of town councils, paired magistrates and perhaps junior financial officers. Most of the surviving evidence comes from the periphery of the urbanized part of the province, such as the magistrate (aedile) of the *Parisi* known at Brough-on-Humber, the councillor of the *Carvetii* with quaestorian rank (and presumably financial responsibilities) at Old Penrith or the dedication set up by the council (*ordo*) of the *civitas Silurum* at Caerwent. These few instances strongly support the view that the administrative structures of the major British towns were conventional ones.

The legal status of towns needs to be understood as hierarchically related to privileges enjoyed by their citizens. There were three main categories of major towns: *coloniae*, *municipia* and so-called *civitas* centres. The *colonia* was a chartered town of Roman citizens, with a constitution modelled on Rome's own. Many *coloniae* were founded on conquered territory for the settlement of discharged veterans. In Britain, three veteran colonies are known at Colchester, Gloucester and Lincoln. Their presence is often presented as being in some way helpful to the continuing pacification process, but as they always involved the annexation of territory from defeated peoples we should not neglect the punitive implications of their establishment in specific locations. Although citizens of a *colonia* were also Roman citizens, it is clear that some colonies had attached groups of the indigenous community (*incolae*) who were not citizens and thus had very much second-class status within the town. This appears to have been the case at Colchester and was a contributory factor in the outbreak of the Boudican revolt. Once a province was established, other urban communities might petition for honorary promotion to *colonia* status, as appears to have been the case for York and almost certainly London.

A *municipium* was also a chartered town and ex-magistrates normally had the right to acquire Roman citizenship. Both *coloniae* and *municipia* were obliged to adopt Roman law, which would have had major implications for their populations and for their territories. The population will have been quite mixed in such towns and not all inhabitants will have been formally citizens of the town; foreigners were a significant minority. St Albans is commonly cited as the only *municipium* known in Britain, though York was described as a *municipium* when Severus died there in 211, before its further promotion to *colonia* status before 237.

The *civitas* centre is generally understood to have been the designated chief town of a distinct people. In the Mediterranean world, these were often geographical more than ethnic distinctions and centred on long-established urban centres, some of them historically city-states. In north-western Europe, the *civitates* were identified by Rome from the plethora of 'tribal' and regional groupings encountered. Although of lower status than the chartered towns, they fulfilled similar functions of local government and were allowed to apply local customary law or local constitutions where such things existed. Across the empire, there was a general pattern over time for the more successful of such *civitas* towns to be promoted to either *municipium* or *colonia* status. It is believed that sixteen British *civitates* were formally constituted around towns, including St Albans (promoted to a *municipium*) and a third-century creation at Carlisle. A further three sites have been suggested as other late additions to the list of *civitas* centres – Corbridge, Water Newton, Ilchester – though evidence is far from certain in each case.

There were thus twenty to twenty-four major towns in Roman Britain, including four or five *coloniae* (the status of London is uncertain, but it probably achieved this rank) and at least one *municipium* (Fig. 10). The remaining fifteen major sites lack evidence that they ever received higher

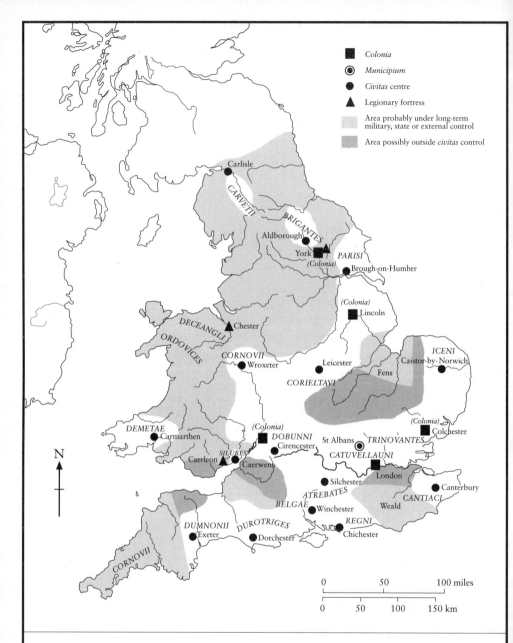

Legend:

- ■ Colonia
- ◉ Municipium
- ● Civitas centre
- ▲ Legionary fortress
- Area probably under long-term military, state or external control
- Area possibly outside *civitas* control

Places and peoples:

Carlisle · *CARVETII* · *BRIGANTES* · Aldborough · York *(Colonia)* · *PARISI* · Brough-on-Humber · *(Colonia)* Lincoln · *DECEANGLI* · Chester · *ORDOVICES* · *CORNOVII* · Wroxeter · Leicester · *ICENI* · Caistor-by-Norwich · Fens · *CORIELTAVI* · *DEMETAE* · Carmarthen · *(Colonia)* *DOBUNNI* · Cirencester · St Albans · *TRINOVANTES* · *(Colonia)* Colchester · *SILURES* · Caerleon · Caerwent · *CATUVELLAUNI* · London · Silchester · Canterbury · *ATREBATES* · *BELGAE* · Winchester · Weald · *CANTIACI* · *DUMNONII* · *DUROTRIGES* · Exeter · Dorchester · *REGNI* · Chichester · *CORNOVII*

N

Scale: 0 — 50 — 100 miles / 0 — 50 — 100 — 150 km

Figure 10. The main towns and peoples of Britain. Shading indicates hypothetical areas of the province that were probably detached from the control of the native civitates and other towns

status than as native *civitas* centres (though there is a probability of promotion to *municipia* in some cases, notably Cirencester, York and London). The number and density of *civitates* is substantially below the number recognized by Rome in Africa, Gaul or Spain and there was a much lower level of further promotion to *municipium* or *colonia* status.

Below these three categories of towns there were other large nucleated settlements that we might also recognize as urban. Small towns, as they are known, are a large and diverse grouping and will be separately treated at the end of this chapter. Some at least, though, were administratively subordinate to the major towns and will have had close relations with them. There were over 100 minor urbanized settlements and villages of varying complexity, though there is no scholarly consensus as to where to draw the line between town and non-town (Fig. 11). The principal physical distinctions between the major towns and minor towns consist in the presence or absence of regular road grids and forum/ basilica complexes. However, some of these so-called small towns were provided with defensive circuits similar to those of the major sites and there is a degree of overlap between the two groups in terms of size. The enclosed area of the major towns varied from 128 ha/316 acres (London) to *c.*6 ha/15 acres (Carmarthen), while for small towns the range is 18 ha/45 acres (Water Newton) to *c.*1 ha/2.5 acres (Cave's Inn).

There are fundamental limitations to our knowledge of the Roman towns of Britain, not least as a result of the subsequent success of many of the locations selected as urban centres. About two thirds of the major towns of the province lie beneath modern urban conurbations and most of the rest beneath villages or close to later towns that have quarried them for building materials. The most extensively investigated town is the greenfield site of Silchester, but new excavations are casting doubt both on the accuracy of the picture derived from excavations carried out more than 100 years ago and the site's typicality. At St Albans, where there have been successive waves of investigation during the twentieth century, each phase of work has shown up the inadequacies of previous interpretative models and changed the picture substantially. Towns are large sites – typically about 40 ha (100 acres) in Britain – and generalizing for the whole from a small sample examined will always be fraught with difficulty. The problems are even worse in the deeply stratified deposits below modern cities, where the choice of where to dig is mostly determined by modern developers, not research questions.

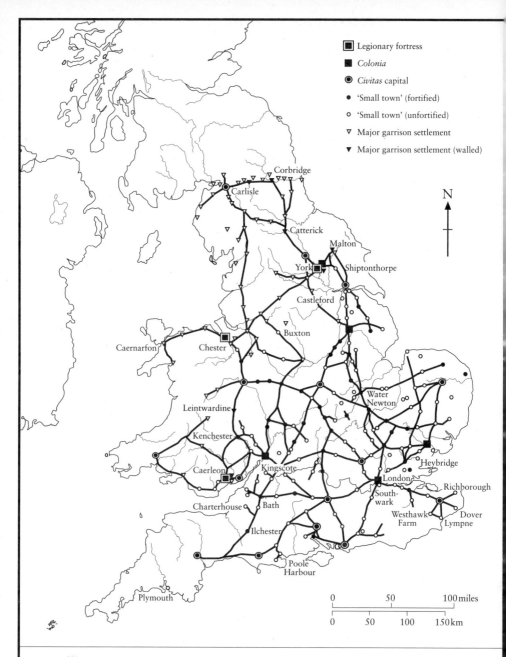

Legend:
- ■ (with border) Legionary fortress
- ■ *Colonia*
- ◉ *Civitas* capital
- ● 'Small town' (fortified)
- ○ 'Small town' (unfortified)
- ▽ Major garrison settlement
- ▼ Major garrison settlement (walled)

N

Corbridge
Carlisle
Catterick
Malton
York Shiptonthorpe
Castleford
Buxton
Caernarfon Chester
Water Newton
Leintwardine
Kenchester
Heybridge
Caerleon Kingscote
London
Charterhouse Bath Southwark Richborough
Ilchester Westhawk Farm Dover Lympne
Poole Harbour
Plymouth

0		50		100 miles

0	50	100	150 km

Figure 11. The road network, major towns, small towns and garrison settlements

Further work at any British town has the capacity to alter our understanding substantially.

The information presented above from the *Antonine Itinerary* represents the developed form of the provincial infrastructure and we need to be careful not to assume that this was a well-elaborated plan from the start, rather than (as seems much more probable) that it was the culmination of a lengthy process of decision-making and negotiation. London was the key site in the developed administrative network, but it is evident that it did not assume this position until some years after the invasion of 43. The earliest evidence of a settlement at London appears to be no earlier than *c.*50, though Tacitus described the site as 'famous for its wealth of traders and commerce' in 60. There is no evidence that the provincial administration had moved there before that date, although the burial of the procurator Classicianus at London in the mid-60s suggests that he at least had based his operations on the site and many people have argued that the entire civil administration was moved there from Colchester in the post-Boudican period. On the other hand, it is not clear that there was much 'civil' administration to be done at so early a date. The organization of provincial administration with a main centre at London was thus more a development of the Flavian period, with a first timber amphitheatre dated to *c.*70. By the late first century, a fort was established at Cripplegate for the soldiers detached from their normal units for service as bodyguards for the legate.

The early road network of the province, in so far as it can be differentiated from the later one, reflects the existence of several rival foci to London in southern Britain, including the fortress/*colonia* at Colchester and the fortress at Alchester. The latter site is interesting as the presence of the fortress gave to the subsequent small town here a regularity of plan that is uncommon outside the major towns. It is conceivable that the site was at some point considered for urban development as a *civitas* centre (perhaps for an eastern group of the *Dobunni*), but that for some reason it failed to take off. Rome certainly had the ability to conjure 'tribal' identities out of the air when it suited, as when the client kingdom of Togidubnus was annexed in the later first century and no fewer than three *civitates* created from its population (the *Belgae*, *Atrebates* and *Regni*). That Alchester did not become established as a major town is surely indicated by its absence from the *Antonine Itinerary*. The relative failure of what had initially been a nodal site on the early Roman communications web is in part at least attributable to the rise of London as the key centre of the road network. There may well be other examples of failed potential *civitas* centres, particularly from the early Flavian period.

Another point that has rarely been discussed is how autonomous the client kingdom of Togidubnus was from Roman interference. It is quite probable that he was not installed as client for some years after the invasion. The passage in Tacitus that mentions him associates the arrangement with the governorship of Ostorius Scapula (47–52):

Not only were the nearest parts of Britain gradually organized into a province, but a colony of veterans also was founded. Certain domains were presented to King [T]ogidubnus, who maintained his unswerving loyalty right down to our times.

This suggests that the release of substantial territories to the control of Togidubnus may not have occurred before *c.*50. The evidence of substantial military structures at Chichester and nearby Fishbourne could fit in with this, though the slow handover of the 'Atrebatic' area is at odds with the view that this area accepted Roman rule peacefully, if not joyfully. Even in areas where large garrisons cannot now be traced, military supervision for the first few years after the invasion seems a real possibility.

ORIGINS AND EARLY DEVELOPMENT

Two issues have been highlighted by recent debate on urban origins in Roman Britain. First, many sites have yielded evidence for a substantial late Iron Age presence, in some cases taking the form of proto-urban *oppida*. Second, there is a very high incidence of early Roman military features underneath the planned layouts that were developed by the late first or second century. Commentators vary in the interpretational weight they place on one or the other factor in discussing urban origins. The current consensus view emphasizes the role of native communities in urban development, rather than making it dependent on military supervision and encouragement. While this nativist perspective is much in sympathy with the work of late Iron Age specialists, some Romanists see this revisionist view as demanding a little too much passivity on

the part of the imperial power. The debate is essentially about structure (Roman administrative requirements) and agency (native British
responses).

The ancient reality may well have been a good deal subtler than most
scholars acknowledge. On the one hand, the towns in Britain involved
an act of creation by the imperial government in choosing between the
different legal categories with their assigned status levels and specific
functions in the decentralized local government structures (Table 9).
The socio-political profile of the first-generation townsfolk will have
affected the degree to which the state adopted an interventionist or a
laissez-faire attitude: the Roman state would have had different expectations in dealing on the one hand with military colonists from a Roman
urban background and on the other with the indigenous peoples of
northern Britain. The speed and circumstances of surrender or acknowledgement of Rome's suzerainty by the British peoples may also have
affected the urban status initially accorded to them. The more trouble-
some or intractable a native grouping, the more closely supervised they
may have been. It is clear that, following the Roman invasion of Britain
in 43, the military presence at a few native centres was comparatively
brief and that urban development was under way by the 50s, while other
sites remained military bases much longer.

Client rulers played a major role in the early development at several
sites. Thus Iron Age *oppida* at (or close by) Silchester, Winchester and
Chichester are normally identified with the southern kingdom assigned to
Togidubnus and all show signs of early development as towns. Togidubnus had probably spent time at Rome and may be presumed to have
had experience of the expected urban model. But were these really towns
of fully Roman type? The idea that these were in some sense showcase
'Roman' towns under Togidubnus rests largely on several inscriptions
from Chichester. A possibly pre-Flavian dedicatory inscription from a
temple to Neptune, Minerva and for the welfare of the imperial house
was erected on behalf of king Togidubnus and the guild of craftworkers
(*collegium fabrorum*) in the town on land donated by a man called [. . .]ens
son of Pudentinus. A second, and certainly Neronian, dedication slab
evidently came from another monumental building in this central area
within the town. Both these dedications were on Purbeck 'marble' and
attest construction of masonry buildings in the third quarter of the first
century. On the other hand, the street grid at Chichester does not seem

Table 9. The current state of archaeological knowledge of the principal Roman urban sites in Britain (most of the so-called small towns are omitted).

ANCIENT NAME	MODERN NAME	STATUS	DEF. AREA (HA)	LPRIA ORIGINS	ROMAN FORT	PUBLIC BUILDINGS
Camulodunum, Colonia Victricensis	Colchester	colonia (V)	47	(O)	LF	T, Th, C
Lindum	Lincoln	colonia (V)/4C p.c.	40	(*)	LF	F, T, B, A
Glevum, Colonia Nervia Glevensium	Gloucester	colonia (V)	19		LF	F, T, B, A
Eburacum	York	colonia (H)/3C p.c.	40		(LF)	F, T, B, A
Londinium, Augusta	London	?colonia (H)/p.c.	128		F & (F)	F, T, B, Am, A
Verulamium	St Albans	municipium	79	O	F?	F, T, B, Th, M, A
Isaurium Brigantum	Aldborough	civitas	22	(*)	F?	B
Petuaria Parisiorum	Brough-on-Humber	vicus/?civitas	6		F	Th
Venta Silurum	Caerwent	civitas	18		F?	F, T, B, Am, A
Venta Icenorum	Caistor-by-Norwich	civitas	14		F?	F, T, B, Am, A
Durnovernum Cantiacorum	Canterbury	civitas	52	O	F?	F, T, Th, B, A
Luguvalium Carvetiorum	Carlisle	civitas	28		F	T
Moridunum Demetarum	Carmarthen	civitas	6		F	B, A
Noviomagus Reginorum	Chichester	civitas	39	(O)	F	F, T, B, Am
Corinium Dobunnorum	Cirencester	civitas/4C p.c.	88	(O)	F	F, T, B, Th, Am, M
Durnovaria Durotrigum	Dorchester	civitas	33	(H)		F, Am, A
Isca Dumnoniorum	Exeter	civitas	36		LF	F, B
Ratae Corieltauvorum	Leicester	civitas	48	*	F	F, T, B, A, M

ANCIENT NAME	MODERN NAME	STATUS	DEF. AREA (HA)	LPRIA ORIGINS	ROMAN FORT	PUBLIC BUILDINGS
Calleva Atrebatum	Silchester	civitas	42	O	F?	F, T, B, Am, A
Venta Belgarum	Winchester	civitas	55	O	F?	F, T
Viroconium Cornoviorum	Wroxeter	civitas	77	(H)	LF	F, T, B, A, M
Lindinis	Ilchester	?civitas	10	(O)	F	
Coria	Corbridge	?civitas	15?		F	T, B, A
Durobrivae	Water Newton	vicus/?civitas	18		F	T

Key to Abbreviations
Status: V = veteran; H = honorary; p.c. = provincial capital (includes third-/ fourth-century divisions)
LPRIA (Late Pre-Roman Iron Age) origins: O, (O) = *oppida* on site/nearby; (H) = hillfort nearby; *, (*) = other settlement on site/nearby
Roman fort: LF, (LF) = legionary fortress precedes town/contemporary with; F, F?, (F) = fort precedes/probable fort precedes/fort in contemporary occupation with town
Public buildings: F = forum/basilica complex; T = temple(s), B = baths; Th = theatre; Am = amphitheatre; C = circus; A = aqueduct; M = market

to have been laid down until the 70s at the earliest and there is prior evidence of some sort of Roman military phase at the site. It is possible that the early buildings were part of a temple complex at a site that still lacked key characteristics of a town, even if it was a centre of the court of Togidubnus.

At Silchester it is clear that the late Iron Age *oppidum* established *c*.50 BC had already by the conquest taken on a somewhat regular internal arrangement based on the junction of several main roads at its centre. The alignments derived from these roads run at a diagonal to the subsequently imposed Roman street grid. Silchester is often celebrated as the classic example of a planned town in Roman Britain, though close inspection of the overall plan reveals anomalies. Quite a few stone buildings were misaligned to the grid and several streets are also oddly oriented. This relates to the very long-term influence of the layout of the earliest settlement, even after the superposition of the rectangular road grid in the mid- to later first century. Excavations in insula IX in the north-western part of the town have revealed not only numerous buildings taking one of these alignments, but that some of them were rebuilt again and again to the same off-axis pattern down to the third century. Beneath the Flavian forum, traces of another massive timber building arranged round a courtyard have been noted. This dated to the Claudian period and is interpreted as a proto-forum in the published report, though the function is in fact unclear. It relates to the period of the client kingdom and represents the earliest appearance of the north–south, east–west alignment of the later Roman town. There were other significant pre-Flavian buildings, including a bath building, and a number of stamped imperial tiles of Neronian date are known, though none in a structural context. Nonetheless, it is clear that Silchester boasted a building or buildings with tile roofing by the 60s. The amphitheatre dates to the 60–70s, exceptionally early for a civil site. The revised road grid was probably Flavian and the timber forum complex appears to date to c.85. The forum is actually slightly out of alignment with the north–south aligned street grid, suggesting that the Flavian forum/basilica complex was established first. The main road from the forum leads east towards a large *temenos* containing two Romano-Celtic temples. This sanctuary was evidently important, as the main approach road from London later deviated around it to enter the town.

Who was responsible for the developments at Silchester? We have a rather hybrid sort of 'town', incorporating Roman-style monuments and functional buildings at an early date, but lacking key administrative elements and overall coherence of planning before the Flavian period. It all suggests the experimentation of a client king with knowledge of Roman society, but administering his territory under different rules from those that would apply later. There is quite a lot of Roman military metalwork from the early levels at the site, but what this represents is uncertain.

St Albans likewise lay alongside an *oppidum* site (with a prominent enclosure underlying the later forum). There is no conclusive evidence for a military occupation here and by c.50 impressive timber buildings existed on a number of street frontages. The Folly Lane burial dated to around 55 adds a new dimension to the discussion. It is a distinct possibility that for the first few years after the Roman conquest this site was also placed under client rule of a trusted British chieftain. The early development here seems to have excluded military intervention in construction projects, but may have involved craftsmen from Gaul.

Some unusually aligned streets within the town appear to link with the Folly Lane enclosure, where a Romano-Celtic temple was erected over the burial site. Here again, then, there is a curious mixture of Roman and non-Roman influences in the initial development of the site.

Another site where urban development is believed to have started early is Canterbury, though the actual evidence for the first phases is pretty thin. There was certainly a late Iron Age settlement by the crossing of the river Stour, but its character does not appear to have been much changed in the first decades after the conquest. The road grid is slightly irregular, suggesting several phases of development, perhaps not originating until the late first century and focused on the area around a trapezoidal religious enclosure at the centre of the site, with at least two Romano-Celtic temples within. There is little evidence for major development in the town before c.80–100 and the partial road grid seems to take its orientation from the Dover road, rather than, as one might expect, from the Richborough road. The latter road appears to aim directly, though obliquely, towards the temple enclosure at the heart of the site. The current picture is hard to square with the conventional view of Roman urban development and the early activity here looks more like the continuation of an Iron Age settlement focused on a religious site, with the first evidence for the formalized *civitas* centre not before the later first century.

A completely different model must be advanced for Colchester. There the Romans constructed both a legionary fortress and a fort within the vast area defined by the earthworks of the great *oppidum* of the eastern kingdom, and it is clear that the *Trinovantes* were initially placed under full military supervision. The creation of a true urban focus began c.49 when the legion was moved forward in support of the military advance to the west and a veteran colony established. The colony reused some of the buildings of the legionary fortress, but, fatally, demolished the defences on the east side to allow the construction of a huge temple of Claudius and other public spaces. This community also included native Britons (*incolae*), who were obliged to participate in and contribute financially to the development of the town. The apparent lack of enthusiasm on the part of the *Trinovantes* for this enforced and regimented urbanization had its sequel in the Boudican revolt when they rebelled with the *Iceni* and sacked the town. When the town was re-established, the *Trinovantes* were penalized (uniquely among the major south-eastern peoples of Britain) by being denied their own separate *civitas* capital. The redeveloped *colonia* was unusually well provided with public amenities by the end of the first century, including the only known British example of a circus for chariot racing.

Two other veteran colonies were founded towards the end of the first century at Lincoln and Gloucester, and like Colchester they made use of the site of abandoned legionary fortresses. While Colchester had a strategic function to play in the pacification and urbanization of the core of the early province, the later two sites were designed to enhance the potential for urban growth towards the fringes of the expanded province. At Colchester it is clear that, although much capital was invested in a grand temple complex, some at least of the original settlers were living in converted barrack blocks left over from the fortress phase. A similar spartan and utilitarian style of domestic architecture characterized early Gloucester, and some reuse of military buildings is attested there too. At Lincoln the construction of the stone forum was not undertaken for some years after the foundation of the site in the late first century, with the town making do with either a paved open area or a timber structure. There are, then, aspects of the Roman colonies that do not conform to the view that these were intended to be prestige towns advertising an urban policy of the Roman state. Rather this looks like veteran settlement on the cheap. On the other hand, heavy investment in temples and in imperial imagery was a priority at these sites. The only attested fragments of bronze equestrian statues from Britain, presumably depicting emperors, came from the colonies of Lincoln and Gloucester, and a further fragment from the Icenian native settlement at Ashill near Thetford was perhaps plundered in the Boudican sack of Colchester.

The development of a number of the native *civitas* towns bears similarities to the processes just observed. Exeter and Wroxeter were both founded on the sites of abandoned legionary fortresses, with the road layout being based on that of the fortress. It is hard to escape the conclusion that these towns were established by state dictate on land that Rome had previously confiscated from the local *civitates*. At Exeter a pre-existing military bath building was demolished to make way for the new forum complex (perhaps initially in timber and only in stone from the second century). A somewhat similar phenomenon occurred at Wroxeter, where the traces of an unfinished bath (though not precisely dated) lie beneath the town's second-century stone forum. In these cases,

Rome deliberately demolished serviceable or adaptable structures of the military phase and offered little more than a level site and some advice on planning to the local *civitas*.

Of the remaining major towns, some military activity is proven (Cirencester, Carmarthen, Brough-on-Humber, Carlisle, York) or suspected (Canterbury, Leicester, Caerwent, Caistor-by-Norwich, Dorchester, Aldborough). It is difficult to reconcile this pattern for major towns with an insistence on the primary importance of pre-Roman political geography in determining town designations (though that obviously was a *part* of the equation at Canterbury and Leicester). Rome's exercise of the considerable powers endowed by the conquest or surrender of the British was a significant factor in redrawing the settlement map, overlapping with her need to impose a new communications network. But the process was neither random nor without reference to the socio-political structures found in existence. We should not underestimate the extent to which the political structures of the late Iron Age could have been speedily and usefully adapted to serve the administrative needs and urban preferences of the Roman state. It is a false picture of Roman imperialism to imply that Rome had no policy of urbanization towards conquered peoples. The recent discovery of an Augustan town beyond the Rhine at Waldgirmes suggests that military engagement may have been considerable in the earliest phases of some incipient urban centres. Urban development was an active bilateral relationship in which the balance of coercive power (when needed) lay with Rome. While it would be naive to continue to espouse the view that urbanism was unilaterally imposed on the 'backward' Britons by the imperial power, it seems equally short-sighted to ignore the potential for state intervention in the affairs of the early *civitates*. The distinction between military and civil administration was neither clear nor comfortable for much of the first century and, especially after the Boudican revolt, Rome had every reason to be suspicious of the subjugated Britons.

London stands out from most of the early towns in that, at first sight, its development may not have been politically motivated. Many scholars now argue that the town began as a commercial centre, perhaps following initial military prospection of a safe Thames anchorage and crossing point. Some early military activity is suspected here; if in connection with the main phase of early urban development 50–55, it was perhaps as a supply base. The fact that the Thames seems to have formed the boundary between various late Iron Age groups made the site ideal in other respects as a port of trade outside the control of any one group, though there is no evidence of any equivalent Iron Age site. Tacitus stressed the presence of numerous merchants at London at the time of the Boudican revolt and it is possible that the settlement had special status as a result of the presence of Roman citizens, perhaps as a *conventus civium Romanorum*. Such communities are well attested elsewhere in the western empire and not infrequently coalesced into chartered Roman towns.

Equally, though, we should not ignore the potential role and needs of the state in the early development at London. Situated at the natural hub of the shipping and road communications networks, London was to develop as both a logistical and operational base for the provincial armies. Tacitus does not enlighten us as to whether London or Colchester was the effective provincial capital in 60 (giving a rather ambiguous indication of London's status). Archaeological evidence, however, for the pre-Boudican town demonstrates that it developed on both the north and south banks of the Thames crossing. The northern settlement was focused on the river frontage, the river crossing and two roughly parallel east–west streets. Southwark consisted of a *c.*12 ha (30 acre) settlement on two tidal islands on the southern side of the crossing and in the earliest phases perhaps represented a more secure location for officials to have been based at. A concentration of finds of Roman military equipment and of Claudian coinage in Southwark is certainly suggestive of the regular presence of soldiers, although no fort has been located, unless a military-style ditch at the southern end of the northern isle provides a pointer. Demolition debris at points close to the river frontage derived from masonry buildings of pre-Boudican and pre-Flavian date, virtually unparalleled at this time. It is possible that the procurator may have been based here and there was certainly a good deal of imported goods passing through the site. Further substantial and expensively decorated buildings in Southwark date to the second and third centuries, in one case associated with an inscription that appears to list a legionary detachment responsible for construction of something. Soldiers are sometimes attested constructing buildings in civil contexts, but most commonly these were buildings for their own use or of official function. Southwark thus probably had some sort of official building complex at its heart.

The principal growth of London was on the north bank, where the late defences enclosed 128 ha (316 acres). This is about 50 per cent larger than the next largest towns in the province and two to three times the average size. London was also unusual in that it generally acquired public buildings earlier and on a grander scale than other Romano-British towns. The construction of a hugely enlarged forum and basilica complex in the early second century is suggestive of the site having acquired higher urban status, perhaps as an honorary colony, if, as seems possible, the site was already a *municipium* from the creation of its first forum and basilica in the Flavian period. In the pre-Flavian period, occupation was concentrated on the area directly north of the crossing point, with a substantial linear spread along the road extending west beyond the Walbrook stream. There is no conclusive evidence for an early military fort, though possible military ditches have been located in the Aldgate area. What stands out in the early levels is the volume and range of imported goods, of manufacturing activity and of storage of goods. The entrepôt function of the early settlement seems clear.

By the later first century, there was increasing evidence of Roman officials being based in London, at least for part of the year. Stamped roof tiles and writing tablets marked by the office of the British procurator indicate his presence, and there is unequivocal evidence of an imperial slave in London *c*.100. The construction of the Cripplegate fort correlates with references in the *Vindolanda* tablets to soldiers being detached for service there. There is also evidence in the tablets of a groom of the governor's staff being at London and this complements numerous epigraphic and sculptural attestations to other soldiers seconded to the governor's *officium*. The *Vindolanda* evidence has also highlighted the need for administrative archives – no matter how peripatetic governors or procurators were, their offices needed a home base.

An additional administrative office was created in the Flavian period, that of legal expert or *iuridicus*. The *iuridicus* was effectively an assistant governor, and the early holders (C. Salvius Liberalis and L. Iavolenus Priscus) were evidently men of senior senatorial rank who had already commanded legions and were on course for the consulship. Later holders were less senior and only irregularly appointed (probably when governors were on extended campaign). Indeed, the prolonged absences of Agricola campaigning in northern Britain have been seen as a key factor behind the reinforcement of the civil administration in the 70–80s, but it is apparent that this was a period in which there were dramatic extensions to the civil province, through annexation of the kingdom of Togidubnus and the delineation of additional British *civitates*. All of these officials and bureaux required facilities and even if archaeologists have been too hasty to label any substantial complex in London as a 'governor's palace', there was undoubtedly a concentration of high-ranking individuals to accommodate. The administration will have been a highly visible element within the town from the late first century onwards. London always remained the senior posting when the province was subdivided later and was the probable base of the civil governor (*vicarius*) of the British Diocese in the fourth century.

Only rarely was urban genesis the result of Rome's response to the economic enterprise of traders operating alongside and in the wake of the military deployment in the new province. For the *civitas* centres and *coloniae*, Rome selected communications nodes, commonly coincident with, or close by, Iron Age centres or Roman forts from which the native people had been supervised in the initial stages of pacification and integration. The garrison settlement to town transition can best be understood as the result of the native population being required to take up residence at a new site in response to the decisions of the Roman administration. We should also note that the transitional phase from military rule to civil government via a self-regulating town could be quite a drawn-out process. The last troops in the *civitas* territory may not have been removed until some years after the lifting of military administration; conversely, it is unlikely that street grids will have been laid out before the release of territory from military control.

The origins and subsequent development of Romano-British towns have conventionally been set into a series of phases. Claudio-Neronian initiatives included Colchester, London, Canterbury, St Albans, Chichester, Silchester, Winchester. Flavian expansion saw additional sites at Caistor-by-Norwich, Cirencester, Dorchester, Exeter, Leicester, Wroxeter, Lincoln, Gloucester, with Hadrianic stimulation responsible for a further clutch of towns at Caerwent, Carmarthen, Brough-on-Humber, Aldborough. The geographic correlates of this are a series of waves of urbanism moving out from a focus in the south-east, to encompass the Midlands, the Marches and the south-west, before finally breaking on the shore of south Wales and northern Britain under Hadrian. The model implies too regimented a pattern, rather than seeing urban development as a continuous process. There is also a temptation to assume too readily that the final pattern of urbanism was already decided at an early stage and that there were no false starts. An alternative approach is to think more in terms of a series of varied individual negotiations between Rome and the peoples of Britain. If the broad chronological divisions have any real relevance, it is in terms of an initial phase (43–70) where there were few 'urban' sites, and these mostly of hybrid form. With the exception of Colchester, the others may have been under unusual authority – client kings (Chichester, Silchester, Winchester), perhaps tribal prefects (St Albans, Canterbury) or Roman citizens or officials (London). The Flavian period saw a move towards establishing more conventional urban government with this stage marked by the appearance of fora, road grids and so on. Some sites progressed comparatively little in the next generation and it was not till the second century that the provision of a wider range of urban facilities was fulfilled, with an increased use of masonry construction for public buildings.

The key urban sites of the early period at Colchester, St Albans and London all originated at about the same time (49–50), but as the result of three very different negotiations, respectively with veteran colonists and the Trinovantian *incolae*, with a possible client ruler of the *Catuvellauni* and with traders. Chichester, Silchester and Winchester are often treated as a package, but they may have had very different histories. None of these sites had progressed very far in pre-Flavian times towards being typical Roman towns (though the traces of early phases in other provinces, such as Gaul, have also proved remarkably elusive). Nonetheless, the assignment of a large territory to a client who was evidently pro-Roman represents successful and sustained negotiation on the part of at least one British leader.

The picture of dramatic Flavian expansion and urban development owes much to excavations at St Albans, where the stone forum dedication of the late 70s appears to provide graphic illustration of a much-quoted passage from Tacitus:

Agricola had to deal with people living in isolation and ignorance and therefore prone to fight; and his object was to accustom them to a life of peace and quiet by the provision of amenities. He therefore gave private encouragement and official assistance to the building of temples, public squares and good houses. He praised the energetic and scolded the slack; and competition for honour proved as effective as compulsion.

However, the urban history of St Albans has been through at least three major revisions since early excavations there in the 1930s. An early military phase now seems highly doubtful and the influence of the Catuvellaunian population much more significant. Overall, the pre-Flavian development of St Albans looks rather curious as a Roman town; rather it seems to be a new sort of British settlement, involving some novel buildings, such as the range of shops and workshops destroyed in the Boudican revolt. With that exception, there was comparatively little in the way of 'Roman' structures for Boudica to destroy. Equally, recovery of the site afterwards was slow, with little reconstruction datable before the mid-70s. When the site was redeveloped, however, it seems to have been on rather different lines, with a regular street grid provided, along with forum/basilica complex – perhaps to mark the refoundation of the site as a *municipium*? The new discoveries make it far less plausible that the site was already a *municipium* at the time of the Boudican revolt and Tacitus' allusion to this status must be an anachronism. The central enclosure was suppressed in the Flavian revival and the area of the gridded settlement, defined by a bank and ditch, now covered c.48 ha (117 acres). By the end of the first century, the town had a running water supply, public baths, a market hall, although the first theatre was not established until c.140.

The extent to which the Flavian era was a boom period for other early towns is now increasingly called into question with the redating of stone structures at a number of sites and/or the recognition of timber predecessors (as with the Flavian forum at Silchester). In many cases, initial steps taken in the Flavian period (such as laying out the road grid) seem not to have been capitalized on until a generation later. The Trajanic/Hadrianic era is now emerging as a particularly significant phase at many sites. At Wroxeter, for example, the completion of the stone forum and basilica in 130 marked a revival of building activity at a site that seems to have struggled initially to get started. Indeed it is increasingly clear that the pace of development was very slow after the foundation of many other sites. There are indications of important projects such as forum/basilica and baths not being completed until the middle years of the second century in many cases.

Thus, apart from the veteran colony at Colchester, early urban development was generally of hybrid form, reflecting short-term arrangements for managing territory to the rear of the advancing army. Only in the Flavian period can we see clear evidence of a decision to move the *civitates* of south-east Britain towards normalized self-rule based on Roman-style towns, starting at sites such as Chichester, Silchester and Winchester when they were incorporated into the province proper. The rebranding of St Albans (and perhaps London) as a *municipium* appears to date to the early 70s, broadly contemporary with the first road grids at Canterbury, Caistor-by-Norwich and possibly other sites. The exact dating of this cannot be pinned down precisely and it may have happened in phases, with a significantly advanced timetable once Agricola's northern conquest was completed. Additional *coloniae* at Lincoln and Gloucester mark a stage in the late Flavian (Domitianic) extension of civil rule and it is logical to think that the neighbouring *civitas* centres of Leicester and Cirencester were created at the same time. The street grid at Leicester appears to date to *c*.100 and the evidence from Cirencester also points to a late first-century date. It is of course possible that sites that received gridded layouts in the late first century had earlier civilian activity pre-dating the formal assignment of *civitas* status. Indeed at Leicester traces of Iron Age roundhouses of the conquest phase later gave way to rectilinear buildings on a variety of alignments, with at least one major stone building close to the forum, but at an angle to the later street grid. If Leicester and Cirencester were only effectively towns from *c*.100 (and the same might apply to other 'Flavian' *civitates*, such as Dorchester, Exeter and Wroxeter), questions remain concerning how we should characterize evidence of activity pre-dating the imposition of road grids and fora.

What were the physical attributes of a town in Roman Britain? The question is important because for some experts it bears on the status of the settlement. Did a British town have to have certain categories of building in order to be considered fully urbanized? There were typical features of towns in the western Roman world that we might look for: planned/gridded layouts; forum/basilica complexes; classical-style temples; other Roman-style buildings; theatres, amphitheatres and circuses for chariot racing; baths; aqueducts and sewers indicative of improved water supply; arches/gates and walls; orderly extra-mural cemeteries and so on. An obvious problem is that there were numerous exceptions and departures from this sort of list. Moreover, the process by which urban communities acquired amenities was often lengthy.

The Roman government was loath to donate urban facilities at its own expense, so the extent and speed of provision of amenities reflected investment of local resources. Overall, the major towns in Britain probably eventually came to possess a majority of these characteristics precisely because these were part of the identity package of Roman urbanism. However, a retarded pace to urban development is typical of Romano-British towns in general. In part it must reflect the non-availability of capital (whether due to shortage of assets or to social preference) within the British *civitates* to pay for the endowment of the full suite of Roman-style amenities. There are many deficiencies in the archaeological evidence, but, as Table 9 reveals, few Romano-British towns have yet produced evidence for more than a bare minimum of public buildings and epigraphic evidence for public donations of all types is minimal compared to more normative provinces.

The question of who would have paid for public buildings in Britain is crucial to an understanding of this phenomenon. There is little reason to believe that significant assistance was provided by the military (outside the *coloniae* or perhaps London). This is supported by analysis of decorated architectural stonework from Britain, which shows clear discrepancies between military sites and the urban centres. The latter have more. in common with the architectural styles of towns in northern Gaul, suggesting that masons were drawn in from there initially, rather than from the army. Links between ornamental stonework in different towns suggest that they were the products of a relatively mobile workforce.

The provincial capital may have benefited from some state funds or the private largesse of imperial officials (one thinks particularly here of the truly massive second-century forum/basilica at London – though that project took many years to complete). But it must be doubted that state funds were at all widely used in this sort of way, particularly among the *civitas* centres. A marble-clad monumental archway erected at Richborough in the late first century – probably in commemoration of the completion of the British conquest under Domitian – is so unusual that it must have been an imperial project. Richborough was not a *civitas* centre, of course, but the main port of entry into Britain and thus a logical choice of location for such a public monument. Most towns would have had to rely on the generosity of their leading families and on their ability to generate income in other ways. However, since the majority of the Romano-British towns were below the rank of *municipium*, they would have been able to gain little income from set payments by public office holders (and in any case the paucity of elite housing at most British towns suggests small councils). In principle, participation in the Roman empire and its governance opened pathways of opportunity for provincial elites to consolidate their power in society. The conventional maps of Britain show very large territories assigned to the British *civitas* centres, with the implied potential for their elites to dominate if not monopolize the exploitation of these. The record speaks otherwise and a key argument of this book is that the territories assigned to the British towns were much smaller than generally believed.

Forum/basilica complexes were the living heart of Roman towns and provided colossal prestige buildings and open space for assembly, public business, justice and administration. With the possible exception of the *coloniae*, fora in Britain were distinctive in that they generally lacked *capitolia* (or indeed other integral classical temples). The arrangement of the basilical hall alongside the colonnaded forum piazza bears some resemblance to the plan of military headquarters buildings, but it is now widely acknowledged that the similarity need not imply direct transmission from military to civil architecture, still less that soldiers were behind the construction of the first British fora. At Silchester, and possibly also at Lincoln and Exeter, there are traces of a timber predecessor to the stone forum, while at London, the massive stone forum (166 × 167 m) and basilica (167 × 52.5 m) of the second century can be shown to have been constructed around a far smaller first-century predecessor that was left standing until a late stage in the process. The building programme for the second forum/basilica in London appears to have been protracted, with several serious setbacks to the work caused by fire or subsidence. Started in *c.*90–100, the basilica was evidently not completed until *c.*130. Improved knowledge of fora at other British towns (Caerwent, Caistor and Leicester) has served to emphasize the degree of variance that existed between them in size and arrangement.

The religious architecture of Romano-British towns is most notable for the shortage of classical-style temples, that of the imperial cult at Colchester being by far the most impressive example, though there were evidently classical precincts or temples at Lincoln, Gloucester, London, St Albans and Bath. The canonical Roman temple sat on a high podium approached by steps and comprised a rectangular structure with a colonnaded porch, pitched roof and triangular pediment. These temples were often set in paved courts, with altars in front of the steps to give ritual reinforcement of the frontality of their design. The main chamber of the temple (*cella*) housed the statue and cult items, but public ceremonies took place in the open air. The architecture thus reflects the nature of religious practice, not simply fashion. Although other examples of pedimental temples no doubt existed, it is clear that the predominant form for temples, even urban ones, followed a different model in Britain. This was the Romano-Celtic type with a square, polygonal or circular *cella* and a concentric ambulatory. Architecturally the type combines elements of classical tradition (stone walls, columns, etc.) with a distinctive concentric plan. It is very unlike traditional Roman temples of Mediterranean form, but typical of civil communities in northern Gaul. The distribution of these temples in Britain covers major and minor towns, and rural sanctuaries; there are very few examples known from garrison settlements, or from rural locations in far western and northern Britain. In British towns they can occur in isolation or in groups of two or more within an enclosure (as at St Albans, Silchester, Canterbury, Caistor-by-Norwich).

No Roman circus for chariot racing had been identified in Britain until the discovery in 2004 of suggestive remains 400 m outside the walls of Colchester. The arena appears to have been 350 m long by 70 m wide, with seating constructed upon two earthen embankments supported by buttressed walls. Amphitheatres for staged hunts of wild animals, combat sports and gladiatorial displays are attested in comparatively few Romano-British towns. The same applies to theatres, especially when one considers that *c.*100 theatres are known in Gaul. Further discoveries are to be anticipated, much as in recent decades we have seen the identification of a theatre at Colchester in the insula adjacent to the Temple of Claudius, or of the first-century amphitheatre at London. An amphitheatre at Colchester, a theatre at London and theatres and amphitheatres at Lincoln and Gloucester are among the most probable 'missing' amenities. On the other hand, some towns may have possessed only one or the other amenity, using it for a range of entertainments; St Albans provides a classic example of a hybrid structure combining features of both theatre and amphitheatre, a type well represented also in northern Gaul. Only Cirencester has at present yielded evidence of both a theatre and an amphitheatre. The detailed structural sequences of these major entertainment facilities can be assessed for a number of sites (amphitheatres: Silchester, Cirencester, Dorchester; theatres: St Albans, Gosbecks/Colchester, Canterbury). In most cases, the urban theatres were sited in close proximity to significant temple precincts (Canterbury, Colchester, St Albans), providing confirmation of the pattern observed at a number of rural or 'small-town' religious sanctuaries where theatres or amphitheatres are known (Gosbecks, Frilford). Only in the centre of Colchester is the theatre associated with a classical temple, all the others being of Romano-Celtic type. The function of these buildings in religious festivals as well as for more conventional Roman-style 'entertainments' seems clear, and the spatial relationship between sacred precincts and theatres in particular may give useful clues as to the whereabouts of theatres in those towns that so far lack evidence. If there were additional circus arenas in Britain, these were most probably located outside the other *coloniae* and London. Even if restricted to a minority of the British towns, the presentation of gladiatorial fights, animal hunts and chariot races were archetypal urban entertainments in the Roman world and strongly associated with the urban identity as a result.

Baths were reasonably commonplace structures, although more military than urban examples have been excavated in Britain. An important distinction to be drawn is that between small bath-houses, designed for either private use or for small numbers of paying customers, and the larger public baths that represent the investment of much larger resources to service a significant number of people at any one time. Many towns, including numerous small towns, have produced evidence for baths of the former type; the larger public facilities are more clearly a feature of the major towns. The construction of public baths at many sites seems to have been a lengthy process, with a mid-second-century date now favoured for the completion of a number of the best-known examples (Leicester, Wroxeter). The provincial capital London, Silchester and the small town of Bath were unusual in having large stone bath-suites by the 70s–80s, but all these sites can be argued to have been exceptional. St Albans has three known sets of baths, an early but small facility of the first century, a larger suite of probable second-century date and a sizeable extra-mural establishment close to the Folly Lane temple.

The erection of public baths generally demanded the construction of an aqueduct to carry the water supply and provision of sewers to dispose of the waste. It was this requirement of additional infrastructure that made baths such an encumbrance on communal resources. There is scope for much more work on the scale of provision of all three elements of hydraulic engineering at Romano-British towns. The speed with which these amenities were available in a given town and their durability over time may well be a very good index of the relative success or otherwise of urbanism.

Excavations in London, Gloucester and York have focused attention on harbour facilities, with the uncovering of sections of quay and of adjacent commercial warehouses. The massive scale and the constructional detail of the series of well-preserved timber quays and wharves from London in particular provide a record of unique importance in Roman archaeology and serve to emphasize the significance of Roman harbours in the tidal rivers of north-western Europe. Even towns at the navigable limits of river systems developed some facilities, as at Lincoln.

Up to the 1970s, the late Roman stone houses that were excavated in the nineteenth and early twentieth centuries at Silchester and Caerwent dominated discussions of domestic housing in Britain. That has changed dramatically since the publication of landmark excavations at St Albans. Subsequently the boom in rescue excavations in London and many other historic towns has revealed a wealth of evidence for long sequences of domestic buildings constructed in a range of materials (timber, half-timber, dried clay bricks, wattle and daub, cob, stone, etc.). Of particular note has been the work on Roman timber buildings, whether traced through patterns of post-holes and sleeper beam trenches or, in optimum cases, through the discovery of preserved timber in waterlogged conditions. It is now evident that timber construction was very sophisticated in Britain, that the expertise was in part pre-Roman and that, despite the fire risk, timber (or part-timber) construction was the norm in British towns into the second century. Both external and internal decoration of timber buildings could be lavish. An increase in stone construction from the second century marks a distinct departure from the normal vernacular tradition of both pre- and post-Roman times.

One of the most important conclusions to emerge is that the early towns consisted largely of relatively utilitarian buildings, often with narrow road frontages, but running back for some depth. Some of these structures, particularly the open-fronted strip buildings, can be associated with commercial or craft activities; they were most densely concentrated on the major streets leading from the gates to the centre. Others represent the earliest domestic housing, of simple form and cheap construction. Some strip buildings reveal an increasing complexity over time, with a workshop opening off the frontage and living rooms behind. Examples from London of timber-framed or clay-walled buildings with painted wall plaster and tessellated or mosaic floors show the potential for even simple building types to be given interior make-overs. Property divisions were frequently observed over long periods and through several phases of rebuilding.

Before *c.*150, there was a notable absence of more elaborate, elite residences, such as can be identified in the plans of the late Roman phases at Caerwent and Silchester. The second half of the second century was a crucial phase for the development of more prestigious forms of urban residence. The typical initial form of these buildings, with some rooms decorated with mosaics and wall-paintings, resembles most closely the winged corridor villa, already established in rural areas by this date. The construction of similar buildings in the town may indicate the fuller participation of the rural elite in urban life. By the third and fourth centuries, the most luxurious house plans reveal an adaptation of the winged layout into a three-sided or courtyard plan. Important questions remain to be answered, however, not least the extent to which study of domestic and commercial zones of the town can supply valid criteria for assessing the long-term pattern of urban growth and decline.

A fundamental feature of the Roman town was the rectilinear character of most buildings within it. Taken together with the adoption of masonry construction or stone footings this may be a useful indicator of the evolutionary progress of towns and small towns. From an early date, the typical structures lining the streets of towns in Britain were rectangular, in contrast to the countryside where the roundhouse remained the commonest vernacular form in many regions. However, examples of roundhouses have now been discovered in early phases of Roman London (Gresham Street), and further discoveries at other major urban sites are to be anticipated. Current evidence suggests that they were more common at 'small towns' (Alcester, Godmanchester, Baldock, Ashton, Heybridge, Westhawk Farm), though sometimes confined to the first two centuries or to the periphery (Alchester, Towcester). This may prove to be a useful diagnostic to the emergence of a distinctive urban identity at major towns that set them apart from lesser centres, where architecture remained more mixed.

DIFFERENT URBANISMS: THE 'SMALL TOWNS'

The 'small towns' do not form a single neat class nor is it at all easy to categorize them, as there is considerable overlap between classificatory groups (Fig. 11). At one extreme, some of the small towns appear to have shared characteristics with the major towns, allowing the potential for promotion into the latter group. The status of potential towns has implications for the identity of inhabitants at these settlements. Some large nucleated sites remained closely associated with Roman forts throughout their existence and are better considered as garrison settlements (as Catterick). There were also sites with a primarily economic function, including mining settlements or pottery production sites, or with a central religious focus. Yet other sites appear on close examination to have been rural villages. The people of the small towns thus represent all three of the main identity groups proposed for Britain and the cultural traits presented may have been quite varied.

The legal status of most sites is uncertain, though we know from epigraphic evidence that a few at least were designated at some point as *vici*. It is clear that these sites could not simply come into existence, grow in size and take on specific functions without reference to the imperial government along the way. Crucially, the acquisition of defences and of marketing functions were scrupulously controlled and limited by the state; the more significant of the small towns, therefore, must have had some recognized status within the overall hierarchy of urban sites. The British *civitates*, each with their single administrative centre, were comparatively widely separated from each other, giving Britain a low overall density of major towns. The administrative structure was to a greater or lesser extent based on the confederation of septs or sub-groups, leading to the subdivision of the *territoria* assigned to each *civitas* into districts or *pagi*. An example is given on a writing tablet from London, referring to a wood located in 'the *pagus Dibussu[.]* in the *civitas* of the *Cantiaci*'. Some small towns may have been assigned minor administrative functions in response to the geographical isolation of particular *pagi* from the *civitas* capital. The distinct twin clusters of rural settlement in Kent around Canterbury (the *civitas* centre) and Rochester (a possible *vicus* serving as administrative centre for a *pagus*) provide a suggestive example.

The origins of the small towns are still debated. As dissatisfaction has grown with traditional models emphasizing military origins, attention has come to focus on the significant numbers of sites revealing activity in the late Iron Age, or on the sort of locational factors that might favour one site over another for growth. However, neither the pre-Roman geography nor the superimposition of a new communications and administrative structure on the country seem to have been significantly more deterministic of small-town growth than the supposed congruence with military forts. The interplay of these three factors can probably account for the origins of the vast majority of the minor urban sites in Britain. That should be no surprise in the colonial situation of the frontier regions of the Roman empire, especially when the concept of nucleated centres was already well established in late pre-Roman developments. The further development of towns, large and small, can best be understood in terms of their differences in morphology, their varied status, functions and identity.

The morphology of small towns is quite distinct from the major towns. While the latter had regular street grids, forum/basilica complexes and a range of other distinctive public buildings, as a rule these were not to be found in the minor towns. Where more grandiose structures existed, these were commonly associated with some special function (commonly religious), such as the temple and baths complex at Bath or the temple and amphitheatre at Frilford. The vast majority of the structures excavated at small-town sites are of humble domestic or artisanal function, including circular Iron Age houses alongside rectilinear types. The most typical form is the strip building, set narrow end on along the street frontages and often of considerable size (examples of *c.*10 × 20 m size are attested). Strip buildings often reveal traces of manufacturing processes and are normally assumed to be the combined houses and workshops of artisans. Wealthy houses are generally uncommon, rarely more than one or two at any one site, making the exceptions such as Bath or Ilchester (both with numerous mosaics) stand out. Some building types seem to be most closely paralleled by rural structures, such as the winged corridor villa or aisled barns, illustrating the thin interpretative divide between small town and rural village. Other special facilities, such as small bath-houses and large courtyard buildings, are normally explained by reference to official functions, such as *mansiones* used by official travellers, though the similarity of these buildings with the market buildings (*macella*) at the major towns should be noted. Romano-Celtic temples were among the most commonplace and significant structures within small towns, in a minority of cases associated with extraordinary facilities such as theatres (Gosbecks) or amphitheatres (Frilford).

There was considerable diversity of morphological evolution among small towns, and five broad categories have been proposed. Sites often developed at the junction of two or more main roads with limited development of subsidiary lanes behind or between the through routes (Brampton, Braintree). An alternative was a linear development of settlement along the frontages of a single road, with minimal evolution of settlement behind the road frontages (Wall, Hibaldstow). Some sites acquired an irregular street system around a cross-road or linear settlement (Water Newton, Kenchester, Richborough). A few irregular street systems were not dependent on the pattern of through route(s), though in some cases possibly influenced by underlying Roman forts or other structures (Irchester, Kirmington). Finally, a few sites had some planned element of a street network (Alchester, Ilchester, Catterick, Corbridge).

Broadly speaking it was the developed roadside settlements and the semi-planned settlements that constituted the most plausible 'potential towns' among the British small towns, while the other categories in general appear to have been smaller, less evolved or more rural in orientation. This impression is reinforced by close examination of the location of specific types of building at individual sites. There is great variance in the density of buildings along the main frontages and the presence and size of associated plots of land and yards behind them. Ribbon developments of strip buildings were commonly complemented by demarcated allotments attached to the rear of the structures (as at Ashton, Baldock, Hibaldstow, Tiddington). Even sites with somewhat more complex plans of irregular streets have proven to be largely rural in orientation, as at Heybridge in Essex or Westhawk Farm near Ashford, Kent. The large numbers of roundhouses add to the impression that these sites were more villages than towns. At the other end of the spectrum, the emergence of a 'public' or cultural focus at the centre of some settlements distinguishes them from the majority of small towns. Sites such as Water Newton, Corbridge, Godmanchester and Ilchester show evidence for significant remodelling of the heart of the site and the construction of major stone buildings.

Small towns are also attested on the Continent, especially in Gaul, which had *c.*60 major towns and hundreds of secondary agglomerations. The extent to which the differences between small towns were due to variance in function or activity needs to receive greater attention. Official involvement at these sites could be due to a number of factors, from army supply and recruitment, to market supervision, to overseeing local taxation, to management of imperial estates or enterprises, to the smooth running of the provincial communications. Reference has already been made to *mansiones*, though there is less certainty as to what to expect to find in structural terms at the lesser wayside stations (*mutationes*). In the early empire the establishment of a road station favoured localized economic development around the official buildings; in time, some of these settlements may have succeeded in gaining permission to hold markets or to build defences. Some of the minor defended sites along the main roads of the province may even have had defences constructed by the state to protect some very specific functions within the late Roman communications and supply system.

Some small towns lay adjacent to substantial villas (as at Great Casterton, Ancaster, Kingscote, Gatcombe) and it is possible that their origins and growth were bound up in the economic relations of large estates (private or imperial). The acquisition of periodic market rights by private estates was highly sought after in the Roman world, with many such requests turned down. However, it is highly unlikely that privately owned 'small towns' would have been granted leave to construct defences before the late empire, and this may help to eliminate some possible candidates.

The prime example of a small town centred on a religious sanctuary is Bath (*Aquae Sulis*). The heart of the walled town is occupied by a classical temple and associated bath complex constructed around the sacred hot spring. The construction of a canalized reservoir at the springhead and the erection of the monumental stone temple and bath complex occurred at an early date, 65–75, when few of the major towns possessed any buildings of comparable scale and grandeur. Military or official links with the development of spa sites in Gaul and Germany provide parallels. The subsequent growth of a substantial small town around what must have been one of the premier British cult sites seems entirely appropriate. Although on a less grandiose scale than Bath, a number of other small towns had a significant religious focus (Buxton, Frilford, Harlow, Nettleton, Springhead and Wycomb) and several of these sites also reveal pre-Roman origins. One important aspect of such temples is that in rural districts of the Roman world it is by no means uncommon to find marketing activities associated with sanctuaries. Once again such rights were closely regulated by the state and were by no means straightforward to obtain. But a religious site could advance a persuasive case to the imperial government concerning the need for fairs to coincide with regular festivals. It is as well to bear in mind, then, the potential economic importance of major religious sites as venues for periodic fairs and markets.

The productive industry, market role and overall economic situation of the small towns became stronger than some major urban centres in the late Roman period. Water Newton, with its impressively developed urban core and extensive industrial suburbs, is the classic example, but many other sites yield evidence for a range of craft activity being carried out there. In a few cases this seems to have been on a significant enough scale to suggest a degree of industrial specialization. This is most clearly seen at sites such as the lead-mining town of Charterhouse and at Droitwich with its brine springs for salt production. Mining and large-scale salt production were special categories of industrial activity, normally treated as state monopolies. At these two sites at least we may reasonably raise the possibility of state control of the extractive procedure (whether by a junior procurator on the spot or through supervision of contractors). In most other cases of industrial specialization at small towns, market forces were a chief stimulus to craft production. At certain periods and places, those market forces may have been heavily influenced by the requirements of army supply, as in the Cheshire plain where a group of sites were engaged in multiple craft production involving salt, pottery, tile, glass, iron, bronze, lead, leather and textiles. Some centres of the Romano-British pottery 'industries' were located in the suburbs of small towns (Brampton, Brockley Hill, Mancetter, Water Newton), though the most important late Roman producers were rural based. It would be hazardous in the extreme to attempt to evaluate the degree of economic dependence (or otherwise) of these various sites on such production, but it is possible to distinguish between sites that were more orientated to this type of activity and those whose activities were primarily related to farming. Overall, it is clear that a large number of supposed 'small towns' belong more properly with the rural community.

Studies of larger nucleated settlements in northern and western Britain suggest radically different political conditions in comparison to the rapidly demilitarized southern regions, in part perhaps due to the slow relaxation or continuation of military administration. The more limited progress towards urbanization here may perhaps be attributed to two factors. First, it has been argued that the late Iron Age societies of northern Britain were less centralized and less hierarchical and therefore potentially more resistant to (or less enthusiastic about) urbanization. Second is the simple fact that the presence of a very large military garrison in the northern territory imposed constraints on the form of civil administration. Some parts of this territory evidently passed from military jurisdiction to civil government (Aldborough, York, Brough-on-Humber, Carlisle), but other areas remained effectively under military supervision throughout the Roman occupation. Civil development at sites such as Catterick, Castleford and Piercebridge thus had more in common with the military community than the urban communities of southern Britain. On the other hand, the garrison settlements of the north and west fulfilled many of the functions of the towns and small towns of the south, though in terms of material and cultural identity they conformed to the norms of the military community, rather than the urban culture.

10

Townspeople

Demography, Culture and Identity

The hesitant beginnings of urbanism in Britain led on to a less than golden second century heyday, followed by early decline. Nonetheless, the towns represent dramatic change from pre-Roman social and architectural norms. They were centres in which new ideas about status and identity were played out, leading to the creation of distinctive communities. These communities differed in crucial respects from the military one and also from those of the countryside. They also show some disparities, as well as similarities, with Roman urban communities in other provinces.

The urban community was much more diverse and less tightly structured than the military community and as a result there were several different urban identities at play. In part these relate to different sorts of towns, with the *coloniae* and the provincial capital(s) distinguished from other centres, but in part they also relate to other individual identity markers, such as origin, profession and status. Interactions with the military (especially at towns that developed from garrison settlements) and with rural settlements were other important variables and the essential interconnectedness of the three communities must always be remembered.

The military community (including other members of the official bureaucracy) maintained a visible profile in the towns of the province, whether fulfilling functions of government, passing through on furlough or settling there on retirement. Despite the notional autonomy of towns as self-governing communities, they were subject to Roman regulation, interference and supervision in many areas. These soldiers and officials of state used specific identity traits to distinguish themselves from the provincial townsfolk.

Roman urban government was plutocratic and the towns of Roman

Britain, as elsewhere, were ruled by oligarchies (councils drawn from the richest people in the community). In general, the governing (curial) class is disproportionately more visible in the surviving epigraphic and archaeological record than people of lower status. Archaeological evidence (in the form of elite housing at the best excavated sites) suggests that the British curial class was not particularly large and a low average of 30 councillors (*curiales*) per town is suggested here, giving a total for our twenty-four major towns of 720 individuals (representing a 'class' of perhaps five times this size including their families – say 3,600 (0.18 per cent of an estimated total population of *c*.2,000,000). When we come to look for signs of identity groups, they should be one of the most prominent, not only because they fulfilled roles that demanded certain types of behaviour, but because they used Roman material culture and identity markers as a means of enhancing their own prestige within British society. Similar patterns of behaviour can be traced in many other provinces, where Rome specifically targeted the elite in society – once pacification was ensured – to share in power and the opportunities that an expanding empire presented. The problem for the British however was that they were 'Johnny-come-latelys' into an empire that had practically stopped expanding and they lay at its very outermost edge.

In any new province there were other groups seeking to gain financial advantage from the evolving situation. Where the army went, merchants, skilled craftsmen and speculators followed to take advantage of the necessity of rebuilding the subjected societies once peace was declared. One of the causes of the Boudican revolt was the financial embarrassment of a section of the British elite, who had been lent very large sums so that they could fund some of the 'reconstruction' work. Deprived of much of their land and independence, the Trinovantian aristocracy was obliged to contribute to the construction of the Claudian temple at Colchester. The scale of the indebtedness is indicated by Dio's comment that Nero's tutor and adviser Seneca personally had 40 million *sestertii* bound up in loans in Britain (a multi-million fortune in any age). His decision to call in these loans 'all at once and in a heavy-handed manner' was evidently one cause of the revolt. The implication of this incident is that Romans from the highest level of society downwards were involved in the economic exploitation of Britain and the Britons. The corollary of loaning money to the British elite was to ensure that there were suitable things for them to spend money on, and the flood of traders and craftspeople into London, for instance, is a clear indication of the commercial opportunities. This is not to say that there were no British craftsmen possessing the necessary skills in some areas, but in a new age of competitive conspicuous consumption, immigrants dramatically swelled their numbers. Foreigners remained an important minority in Britain long after the conquest and as we shall see they often asserted their identity through difference rather than by trying to blend in. Foreign merchants and craftsmen already possessing Latin had inbuilt advantages in dealing with the Roman army and administration; native Britons wishing to compete had to learn to operate in new ways.

Another distinctive group comprised slaves and male and female freed slaves. While the institution of slavery is now socially abhorrent, it was a commonplace of ancient society that wealthy people had slaves, much as upper- and middle-class households had live-in servants in early twentieth-century Britain. Slaves had clearly been a feature of Iron Age societies also, to judge from examples of slave chains, so we should not contrast a wicked slave-using Roman society with a fabulously pure and egalitarian precursor. On the other hand, Roman Britain was a 'slave-using society', but not a fully 'slave society' in the sense that the latter term can be applied to Roman Italy (where 10–25 per cent of the population was of servile status) or the southern states of pre-civil war America. Slavery operated in Britain in two ways. Slaves were undoubtedly exported from Britain as part of the process of conquest and even at later times individuals were enslaved (or possibly sold into slavery by impoverished families). Many of these British slaves may have ended up being sold elsewhere, rather than within Britain. Slaves from various sources were also sold or brought into Britain and sold there. However, their availability and cost probably kept the proportion of enslaved to freeborn very low.

We can be reasonably sure that there was a provincial slave market, to judge from two documents discovered in London relating to sale and purchase of slaves. The first of these seems to contain the instruction 'turn that girl into cash', while the second is both more detailed and intriguing. It records the purchase of a slave by Vegetus, himself slave assistant to an imperial slave Montanus. The object of the purchase was a girl from western Gaul, who went by the name of Fortunata, though the legal formula does not preclude other possibilities ('or whatever name she is known by') and elsewhere she is referred to simply as the 'girl in question'. It may seem paradoxical that a slave should own another slave, but this was possible due to the ability of skilled slaves in responsible positions to accumulate savings (a *peculium*), which might ultimately also be used to buy their own freedom. In this case we have no less than two levels of slaves owning other slaves. The sum of 600 *denarii* (2,400 *sestertii*) was quite a considerable one (about two years' salary for a contemporary legionary soldier), but for imperial slaves involved in managing imperial property in Britain the opportunities to accumulate funds must have been considerable. Freedmen and slaves of the imperial household were a very important sub-group of the provincial administration, with a particularly strong role in financial management. An imperial freedman often served as the immediate deputy of the equestrian provincial procurator and other freedmen and slaves of the *familia Caesaris* undertook many junior fiscal duties.

Rural slaves and those committed to hard labour in mines and quarries had a particularly wretched time, but certain categories of domestic slaves and those involved in business operations could fare better, especially if literate, skilled and energetic and prepared to put up with the sexual demands of their owners. Although a great stigma attached to being a slave, and freed slaves were debarred from certain public offices, an interesting phenomenon of the Roman empire is the extent to which some slaves and freed slaves developed a strong sense of identity and unashamedly advertised their status in inscriptions and adopted patterns of behaviour that consciously aped aristocratic society.

Common townsfolk are much less easy to distinguish clearly, but must at all times have constituted the majority of urban dwellers. They were the craftspeople and shopkeepers who occupied the majority of the simpler domestic units in towns. Decorative improvement to some of these 'strip houses' suggests a specific form of group identity linked to their urban location. While they were to our eyes less Roman than the urban elite or the military community, they were at least distinct from many rural dwellers. Although rarely attested in the stone epigraphy, people from this stratum of society appear to be well represented in the minor religious ephemera and in graffiti on personal possessions.

THE EPIGRAPHIC HABIT

The use of the Latin language was a key diagnostic of identity, but, even in the towns, British will have been the everyday language of communication for the majority of inhabitants. Latin, and to a lesser extent Greek, were languages of business, officialdom and status display. Tacitus may have exaggerated slightly when he said that the British elite was desperate to get their sons educated in Latin, but it was an undoubted truth in post-conquest Britain that knowledge of Latin was a key to advancement in Roman society. The urban evidence reveals different aspects of identity being reinforced through writing at several levels in society. Combining the evidence of stone inscriptions and *instrumentum domesticum* (and excluding the small towns and garrison settlements), the strongest epigraphic signatures among the towns are in descending order York, London, Colchester, Cirencester, Silchester, Lincoln, Wroxeter and Gloucester. The importance of the *coloniae* and provincial capitals in this group is clear.

Similar preferential patterning in urban inscriptions is also detectable in Gaul, though there the overwhelming majority of Latin inscriptions were concentrated at towns and small towns along the two main overland routes from the Mediterranean to the Roman army bases on the Rhine; parts of Britanny and Western Gaul were virtually anepigraphic. An important point here is that the decision to adopt or not adopt Latin as a means of communication was bound up with the mechanics of the empire, it was not simply a matter of individual free will. Certain locations, certain sites will have registered far greater levels of literacy as a result of simple geopolitics.

Where people originated from has provided a strong element of identity formation in many societies. Funerary and career inscriptions make it clear that this was the case in certain sectors of Roman society. The most common group in Britain to state their origins were soldiers and officials, such as C. Pomponius Valens, a *beneficiarius* buried at London who recorded his *origo* as *Victricensis* ('from Colchester'). Unsurprisingly, many civilians who followed the practice were among those living in garrison settlements and presumably were influenced by the prevailing military tendency to state an *origo* or a 'tribal' ethnic. Examples include native women married into the garrison settlements, Regina of the *Catu-*

allana natio at South Shields, Ved[. . .] *civis Cornovia* at Ilkley and
Verecunda Rufilia *cives Dobunna* at Templeborough. When we turn to
the epigraphic testimony from the towns (and excluding obvious soldiers
or officials) there are comparatively few such declarations and the overwhelming majority relate to foreigners. Most of the examples occur at
sites where the military community and officialdom had a high profile
and may have given a lead (London, Colchester, Lincoln, Bath). Rare
British examples include a citizen of *Cantium* attested at Colchester,
and, more unexpectedly, Lossio Veda, a Caledonian, also at Colchester.
It could be argued of course that most Britons did not feel it necessary
to state their origin when they were consecrating an altar or getting
buried in their hometown. On the other hand the infrequency with
which Britons are attested outside their home communities in Britain or
elsewhere in the empire cannot be a true reflection on the extent of their
mobility. Most of the instances where we can trace a Briton abroad can
be related to the army, as Novantico from Leicester, who served on the
Danube under Trajan, or M. Ulpius Quintus from Gloucester, attested
as a secret policeman in Rome. Making a public statement about origin
appears to have been much more frequent among the inhabitants of the
coloniae and the military community and by extension with those
Britons or other outsiders who interacted with these communities. An
alternative view is that sense of place was less strongly felt by Britons,
or that their sense of belonging to a Roman town was less important
than other aspects of their identity.

In the Roman world many individuals also used inscriptions to
publicize their profession and rank at whatever level of society. Upper-
class Romans in Italy disdained manual work and tradesmen, but a profession was often something that defined one aspect of identity and
provincial inscriptions frequently mention it. Examples from Britain are
again dominated by the military, but include merchants and craftspeople.

Over twenty merchants who operated in Britain are known by name
– a tiny proportion of the actual numbers. Two sanctuaries to the
goddess Nehalennia on the North Sea coast near the mouth of the Rhine
(Domburg and Colijinsplaat) have produced over 150 dedications made
by sailors and merchants, and several identify individuals as being
traders with Britain. Other evidence in Britain supports the origin of
many of these merchants in northern Gaul or the Rhineland. Originating
from Bourges in France, a trader (*moritix*) M. Verecundius Diogenes

settled at York. Two other cases of merchants with strong connections with the *colonia* at York are known. At Bordeaux, M. Aurelius Lunaris dedicated an altar, made of Yorkshire gritstone, to celebrate his successful arrival and advertised his status as a *sevir* at both York and Lincoln. L. Viducius Placidus, a citizen of Rouen, donated a shrine at York in the early third century. This group shows the behaviour of merchants working closely with the military community and its urban ancillaries in the *coloniae*. London provides another example of a *moritix*, Tiberinius Celerianus, a native of the *Bellovaci* (north of Paris) – who also claims to be a 'Londoner' in the dedication. The term *moritix* appears to derive from a Celtic word for seafarer and thus has specific connotations of transmarine trade at the Belgic/British fringes of empire. There is a third example in a text from Cologne on behalf of C. Aurelius Verus, a freedman *negotiator Britannicianus moritex*. The choice of the word in preference (or in addition) to the more normal words for merchants and shippers (*negotiator, nauta, mercator, navicularius*) suggests that it evoked some special sense of identity, perhaps relating to a guild.

Three inscriptions from a small temple at Silchester attest dedications by individuals on behalf of a guild of 'foreigners dwelling at Silchester' (*collegium peregrinorum consistentium Callevae*). These resident aliens were perhaps traders of some sort and the use of the term *consistentium* recalls the '*vicani consistentes castello Veluniate*' from the fort of Carriden in Scotland. The implication in both cases is that the dedicants were asserting their difference from those born in the place and that this was important to their sense of identity. The ability of the traders referred to at York, Lincoln, London and Silchester to have a visible civic role or profile in towns where they were not citizens is surely significant in this context. Freedmen and traders with money could serve as officials of the imperial cult (*seviri Augustales*) in *coloniae* or have membership of guilds elsewhere. The first-century dedication by the *collegium fabrorum* at Chichester may likewise have been largely a guild of foreign craftworkers brought in to carry out the building projects of Togidubnus. The man who donated the land and was perhaps leader of the project was [Pu]dens, son of Pudentinus. The mention of a *collegium* suggests the presence of foreign artisans. The significance of the donation of land at the very heart of the urban area by an individual whose father's name was already 'Roman' suggests a non-British landholder at this early date.

Several texts refer to religious roles, most notably an inscription attesting the existence of a priest (*sacerdos*) of Sulis at Bath. There is also a dedication from the same site of a soothsayer (*haruspex*) and another seems to relate to a *collegium* involved in the running or upkeep of the temple there. An anonymous treasurer who set up a dedication to the Matres at Chichester may also have been associated with a *collegium* and a dedicant at Caerwent obtained freedom from liturgical liability to a religious *collegium* as a result of his gift. The provincial council in Britain was another body organized to promote the imperial cult and a slave of the council has been identified in a text at London.

Priscus son of Toutius was a stonemason from the Chartres region employed on projects at Bath. Sulinus son of Brucetus, also from Bath and possibly a native in that his name evokes the deity Sulis, called himself a sculptor. Cintusmus a coppersmith who recorded his fulfilment of a vow on a copper-alloy plate at Colchester is another example of the urban artisan adopting the epigraphic habit. Many craftsmen marked their goods for commercial reasons and the migration of some potters from the Continent to Britain and within the new province can be tracked from the evidence of stamps.

A striking aspect of the British inscriptions communicating details of profession, status or career pattern is the paucity of texts set up by the curial class, with the majority of the available evidence coming from the *coloniae* (though even there they are rare). Colchester has produced two possible equestrians, Lincoln a decurion and *curator*, a decurion of Gloucester died at Bath and some specially produced municipal tiles from Gloucester appear to name magistrates, while York has evidence of three decurions and an equestrian (an ex-prefect of *legio VI*). For the *civitas* centres the evidence is meagre indeed: a *senator in civitate Carvetiorum quaestorius* from Old Penrith (itself a garrison settlement) and an aedile of the *vicus Petuariensis* (Brough-on-Humber, itself a site that may well have had a continuing military influence). The curial status of some other individuals is implied by their funerary monuments, nomenclature or other distinguishing features. Crucially, they chose not to communicate this status explicitly.

Prior to its extension to the bulk of the empire's subjects under Caracalla in 212, possession of Roman citizenship was another point of distinction. At Dorchester, a reconstructed inscription commemorates [. . .] Carinus *civi [R]om(ano)* on behalf of his wife Romana and his children Rufinus, Carina and Avita. Full citizenship is often deducible from the donor's possession of *tria nomina*. We have evidence of several members of the local elite at Chichester possessing Roman citizenship at an early date – most notably Tiberius Claudius Togidubnus. An engraved signet ring from the Chichester locality belonged to Tiberius Claudius Catuarus, probably another member of this ruling family. Lucullus son of Amminius erected another inscription from the site. The father's name here recalls the son of Cunobelin who fled to Rome in *c.*39. His name is given as Adminius in the Roman sources, but appears as Amminus on the Celtic coinage ascribed to him. It is an interesting, though unprovable, possibility that his son may have returned to the court of Togidubnus.

Slaves and freed slaves, as we have already noted, were another group in society that sometimes advertised their status (which was also in a sense their profession) in epigraphic form. A clear example is the statue erected in the *colonia* at York by an imperial freedman. Another imperial freedman, Aquilinus, evidently paid for the restoration of a ruined temple or shrine to Jupiter at London, in association with three other named individuals who were probably imperial slaves. At Colchester, Imilcho (an African name), freedman of a non-Roman citizen with the Celtic-sounding name Aesurilinus, erected a marble votive slab. Another freedman, Vettius Benignus dedicated an altar to Diana in fulfilment of a vow. All these freedmen were imitating the epigraphic habit of upper-class Romans in making public donations of buildings or statues or conventional religious dedications. Freedmen were sometimes commemorated by their former owners, but were often attested as heirs (some may have been freed only on the death of their owners). A tombstone in Purbeck marble from London memorialized a legionary centurion and his two brothers on behalf of unnamed freedmen. Calpurnia Trifosa is an example of a freedwoman, who buried her husband and former owner, C. Calpurnius Receptus, priest of Sulis at Bath. Slaves were more often commemorated than active dedicators in their own right. Another urban slave, a fourteen-year-old youth, is attested on a tombstone from Gloucester. But Anencletus who set up a tombstone to his wife Claudia Martina was apparently a slave of the provincial council in Britain. The combination of means and literate ambition is clear.

Soldiers were also an important group of slave-owners, particularly in the officer ranks and cavalry troopers. There are several dedications to the goddess Sulis at Bath, invoking her help in guaranteeing the health and welfare of serving soldiers, erected by their freedmen, who may have been sent specifically to the shrine. An unmarried soldier might make his freedman his heir as was probably the case of a veteran of *legio XIV* at Lincoln.

Entertainers will have been another distinctive and probably itinerant group, though little evidence for individuals survives. Attempts to identify a female gladiator (*gladiatrix*) from ambiguous funerary remains at London have not generally been accepted. However, there is a simple graffito from Leicester, probably of amatory intent, linking Verecunda an 'actress' (perhaps a euphemism for prostitute) and 'Lucius the gladiator'.

The types of inscriptions erected in towns are revealing of underlying social attitudes, though the small sample available limits the analysis. Sacred structures (shrines, temples, altars, statues, religious precincts) predominate over public complexes or entertainment buildings. Individual dedications of buildings and other benefactions outnumber those made on behalf of corporate bodies such as *collegia* or *curia*. However, the majority of the recorded benefactions were relatively small in scale, though precise sums are not mentioned. Where the social standing of the dedicator is indicated, most relate to distinct user groups, the provincial governors, the military, freedmen, civil magistrates, corporate bodies such as *collegia*, Roman citizens. Only about 16 per cent (of seventy-nine known dedicants) cannot be assigned to one of these categories, in some cases simply because the inscriptions are incomplete.

The inauguration of new public buildings was inevitably a less common experience – perhaps a once-a-generation event in many British towns, requiring prolonged fundraising. Even the *coloniae* initially lacked potential donors of really major wealth, being founded from groups of discharged legionaries with relatively standardized retirement packages and savings to draw on. As noted already, there are only two certain references to equestrians from British towns, both from *coloniae* and dating to well after the initial phase of urbanization. No person born in Britain is known to have achieved senatorial status. The reality of urban development in Britain was that the provision of the major public buildings in British towns relied on public subscription, rather than spectacular one-off individual donations.

The pattern of public benefaction in Britain is not dissimilar to that

Table 10. Inscriptions recording public benefactions in British towns and small towns (excluding northern garrison settlements beyond York).

LOCATION	STRUCTURE	DONOR(S)	REFERENCE
London	Temple of Isis (restored)	M. Martiannius Pulcher, provincial governor	*Britannia* 7 (1976) no. 2
London	Temple of Jupiter(?) (restored)	Aquilinus, imperial freedman, and three others who may have been imperial slaves	*Britannia* 7 (1976) no. 1
London	Shrine to Matres (restored)	District of town (*vicus*)	*RIB* 2
Lincoln	Temple rebuilt	Imperial freedman	*Britannia* 10 (1979)
Lincoln	Architrave of public building	District of town (*vicus HRAPO Mercuresium*)	*RIB* 270
Lincoln (Nettleham)	Arch at suburban temple to Mars Rigonemetes	Q. Neratius Proxsimus (Roman citizen)	*JRS* 52 (1962) no. 8
York	Temple of Serapis (*serapaeum*)	Claudius Hieronymianus, legate of *legio VI*	*RIB* 658
York	Arch and shrine erected	L. Viducius Placidus, citizen of Rouen, on land given by order of town council	*Britannia* 8 (1977) no. 18
York	Shrine (restored)	[. . .]sius (name/status unclear)	*RIB* 656
St Albans	Forum/basilica complex	*Civitas Catuvellaunorum* or *municipium Verulamium*	*JRS* 46 (1956) no. 3
Cirencester	Jupiter column and statue (restored)	Lucius Septimius, provincial governor	*RIB* 103
Chichester	Temple of Neptune and Minerva erected	Guild of craftsmen (*collegium fabrorum*) using land presented by [Pu]dens son of Pudentinus	*RIB* 91
Wroxeter	Forum/basilica complex	*Civitas Cornoviorum*	*RIB* 288
Brough-on-Humber	Stage building (*proscaenium*)	M. Ulpius Ianuarius (Roman citizen and aedile of the *vicus Petuariensis*)	*RIB* 707
Winchester	Shrine of Matres (restored)	Antonius Lucretianus, *beneficiarius consularis*	*RIB* 88
Dorchester (Oxon)	Altar and screens erected to IOM and numen Augusti	M. Varius Severus, *beneficiarius consularis*	*RIB* 235
Dover	Shrine of Matres erected	Cordius Candidus, *strator consularis*	*Britannia* 8 (1977) no. 4

LOCATION	STRUCTURE	DONOR(S)	REFERENCE
Bath	Façade of Seasons restored and repainted	Claudius Ligur[...] (Roman citizen with southern Gallic cognomen), C. Protacius (Roman citizen with north Italian cognomen) and a *collegium*	*RIB* 141
Bath	Sacred space (*locus religiosus*) restored	C. Severius Emeritus, *centurio regionarius*	*RIB* 152

of the other north-western provinces in numerical terms, though there are some peculiarities. The participation of the military was far higher in Britain and in Germany than in the Gallic provinces. In common with *Gallia Belgica* and the lower Rhineland, there are few dedications on behalf of urban magistrates from Britain and more collaborative activity by *collegia* and other corporate bodies, suggesting a lower level of individual benefaction (what is known as euergetism) in these regions. On the other hand there was clearly a range of activity in British towns that required funds to be raised, including the various public buildings, the sacred complexes and the festivals and events associated with all these venues. The balance of the epigraphic evidence suggests that the British urban elite were less competitive with one another both in donating and in recording their benefactions. Many of the religious dedications may be seen more as an aspect of ritual practice than of competitive display, but if we limit our view to the few indubitable cases where the construction (or repair) of a structure was at issue the pattern is fairly stark (Table 10). These nineteen inscriptions identify twenty-six dedicants as follows: two provincial governors, a legionary legate, three members of the governor's *officium* (two *beneficiarii* and a *strator consularis*), two imperial freedmen and three probable imperial slaves, a regional centurion, two towns or *civitates*, a town council, two subdivisions of towns (*vici*), two guilds (*collegia*) and just seven individuals. The last group comprises a Roman citizen who was also a foreign merchant, four other Roman citizens whose names suggest origins in Italy or southern Gaul and thus perhaps either ex-legionaries or sons of ex-legionaries. That leaves an incomplete name in one of the York dedications, where one might suspect an ex-soldier or Roman citizen donor, and Pudens son of Pudentinus at Chichester in a first-century context when few British notables had Latinized their nomenclature in such a way. The likelihood is that that man too was a foreigner. Public dedication of buildings in Britain thus seems to have followed one of two main courses: corporate action by towns or *collegia*, or individual donations by officials, soldiers, foreign merchants and entrepreneurs. That is not to exclude the possibility of individual dedication among the British elite, just to observe that it was far from the norm.

There are few stone inscriptions from Gloucester but the other colonies at Colchester, Lincoln and York along with London provide a useful sample of patterns of dedication at the upper tier of British towns. Most of the material relates to very modest acts of religious devotion, such as the dedication of altars or metal plaques in acknowledgement of the fulfilment of vows. London has yielded the widest variety of dedications, as well as statuary from the *mithraeum*, the so-called 'Screen of the Gods' and fragments of a monumental entrance to a temple in the south-west of the town, and structural elements of several temples. Dedicants range from imperial officials such as the governor M. Martiannius Pulcher and the imperial freedman Aquilinus who respectively restored temples of Isis and of Jupiter, to the provincial council of Britain, to one of the districts of the town, as well as individuals such as the Gallic trader Tiberinius Celerianus. Another imperial freedman restored a temple in the forum at Lincoln. York has produced one of the most interesting texts, recording the donation by another Gallic trader and *sevir*, L. Viducius Placidus, of an arch and shrine to (probably) Jupiter and the *genius loci* on a site provided by decree of the town council. Another important inscription records the erection of a *serapaeum* (temple of Serapis) by the legionary legate of the *VI Victrix*, Claudius Hieronymianus – an important reminder of the peculiar character of York, where three major sites lay in close proximity to one another – the legionary fortress, the garrison settlement (*canabae*) and the *colonia*. Most of the minor dedications at York were altars or simple plaques, but a few were accompanied by relief carvings of the gods, one being erected to Fortuna for the welfare of P. Maesius Auspicatus and his son by their freedman. None of the *civitas* centres has produced much epigraphic evidence of dedications and it is surely significant that in several cases the only such text found records donations by outsiders.

The use of commemorative funerary inscriptions is another characteristically Roman practice that seems to have been little adopted among the urban dwellers in Britain. About 130 tombstones have been published from southern Britain. This figure excludes all examples from long-term military bases, like Caerleon and Chester, and serving soldiers from York. Of the 130, about 60 were possibly civilians, 40 related to military personnel or imperial officials and the rest are uncertain or fragmentary. For comparison, securely military tombstones from Caerleon, Chester and York number over 100. Furthermore, over 70 of the 130 tombstones come from the five *coloniae*, the urban centres most closely linked to the military community. Although some of the clearly military stones from the civil zone were erected in the conquest phase when troops were based at Colchester, Gloucester, Lincoln and so on, some are evidently later in date or relate to retired veterans. It is also probable that some of the ostensibly 'civilian' tombstones in fact related to people with connections to the military or officialdom.

The exceptions, as always, are interesting. A merchant (*moritix*), M. Verecundius Diogenes, paid for inscribed stone sarcophagi for his Sardinian wife and himself at York, where he was a *sevir* of the colony and thus possibly a freedman. Although he was from Bourges, he had evidently made his home in York, to judge from the fact that he pre-ordered his own sarcophagus there. Foreigners were an important sub-group among those using tombstones (with about ten identifying themselves as such); Tulia Fortunata the wife of Verecundius was a Sardinian. Volusia Faustina was unusual in being described on her tombstone at Lincoln as being of local origin (*civis Lindensis*), though the implication is that she was the daughter of an established veteran family with Roman-citizen status, not that she was British. Another feature of the extant civil tombstones is the preponderance of people with Roman-style nomenclature, whether certainly Roman citizens or bearing Latinized versions of Gallic or British names. The Tammonii family at Silchester had Latinized a British name and was probably part of the curial class there. Nemmonius Verecundus from Cirencester possessed another possibly 'British/Gallic' name. There is a sprinkling of others, including Mantinia Maerica, Candida Barita, Iulia Brica and Iulia Velva, all from York. These are possible candidates for British wives of members of the military community and are thus somewhat exceptional. Almost a third of the *civitas* centres in Britain have never yielded a civilian tombstone, a pattern that cannot be wholly explained by reference to post-Roman stone robbing or shortage of suitable stone in the first place. The gaps in the distribution map of tombstones and the general paucity of certainly British families adopting the practice are highly revealing of social attitudes.

The evidence strongly indicates that only a very select group or groups in urban society in Britain chose to commemorate their family members with permanent stone inscriptions. It is of course possible that a larger number of graves were marked in a cheaper manner with painted wooden signs, but the surviving record even in areas with abundant stone resources is not encouraging of the view that the epigraphic habit was widely adopted for funerary use by the civil community in Britain. Those who did were predominantly people with links to the military community (whether serving soldiers or retired veterans) or officialdom, or foreigners and traders, or local elites who used the act of commemoration as a means of differentiating themselves from the rest of society.

As already noted, Roman religious practice was often based on literate actions and was highly formulaic, even contractual, in the way it represented human interaction with divine powers. Much activity concerned petitioning the gods for assistance or the fulfilment of vows and promises made as part of such petitions. In the military community we have seen that this communication with the gods was often given solidity in the form of inscribed altars, slabs or plaques. To some extent this sort of religious behaviour can also be traced in the urban centres of the province, but the extent to which it was the dominant form of religious discourse is debatable.

Religious practice in late Iron Age Britain was rather different, though permanent structures were starting to be built at some sacred groves and spaces. Some early shrines were sited at highly visible points in the landscape, typically on hills, and separated from the main settlements. Ritual activity included sacrifice of animals and feasting, as well as the deposition of personal items, typically martial equipment, personal ornaments and coins. These last aspects of British religious practice were readily translatable into the Roman ritual of sacrifice and ritual deposition, though the sort of personal items deposited often changed. Another very strong feature of British religion was the deposition of material in watery contexts like rivers and bogs.

The Romano-Celtic temple was the predominant type of urban religious architecture. The form was perhaps better adapted to the north

European climate than the normal Mediterranean types. Temples generally stood within a sacred enclosure (*temenos*) and quite often seem to have been constructed in groups of two or more together. Some of the earliest datable examples in Britain were constructed in towns, rather than in isolated rural locations, suggesting an important link between religion and an emergent urban identity. The temple form is very unlike the types generally encountered on the northern frontier and emphasizes the closer links between the urban population and northern Gaul and the non-military parts of the Rhineland, where it was also common. An obvious question is to what extent the different form enshrined discrepant religious practice between military and civilian communities. To answer that we must consider the associated epigraphic and artefactual data.

Engraved altars were far less common in the civilian community than among the military community and some at least of the urban examples can in fact be attributed to soldiers, veterans and other members of the imperial bureaucracy. Two examples from London have already been mentioned and there were altars set up by *beneficiarii consularis* at Winchester and Dorchester (Oxon), numerous examples of altars relating to military personnel at Bath and another at Caerwent and a dedication by an imperial freedman at York. Civilian dedications of altars include Similis of the *Cantiaci* at Colchester, a Roman-citizen *curator* at Lincoln, three altars by Roman citizens at York, one by Lucullus at Chichester, an altar to Silvanus by Sabidius Maximus and two to the Suleviae by Sulinus son of Brucetius and by Primus at Cirencester. From Bath there are altars dedicated by freedmen, by a Roman citizen and others by Peregrinus from Trier and Sulinus son of Maturus. This is a small haul from such a large number of sites and once again Roman citizens, freedmen and foreigners dominate the list. Sulinus son of Brucetius was a sculptor, but we lack specific details of the status of the other four potentially British dedicants. What this highlights is the possibility of significant differences in religious practice between the urban communities and the military ones already discussed.

Rather more common than altars in southern Britain are plaques recording religious dedications and the fulfilment of vows. These were sometimes committed to stone, and there are several instances of marble (or Purbeck 'marble') being used – as in the dedication to the emperor's *numen* and Mars Camulus from London by a Gallic trader, or the series of texts set up by the *peregrini* at Silchester, or the Togidubnus text at

Chichester. Dedications on metal plaques also appear to have been common, either in the shape of ansate panels or leaf- or feather-shaped, or occasionally of more intricate design. Many were in copper alloy, sometimes gilded, occasionally in silver or in gold/gold leaf. A further form of votive dedication took the form of individual copper-alloy letters. Fixing holes for small nails in both the plaques and the letters shows that they were designed for attachment to walls or specially designated structures within the temple compounds. These plaques and letters occur not only at urban temples, but also at rural shrines and they appear to be particularly characteristic of religious practice in southern Britain, though a few votive plaques are known at military sites in the north.

Some at least of these dedications used conventional Roman formulae to record the fulfilment of vows, but there are also anepigraphic examples of leaves/feathers and the votive letters suggest semi-literate communication alongside the fully literate. Many of the personal ornaments and coins found at shrines may have been deposited without an accompanying 'written' document. For some worshippers the communication with the gods was internalized rather than externalized. It is certain that not all the transactions with the gods will have involved blood sacrifice; the pouring of libations, using ritual flagons and shallow dishes (*paterae*) was a popular and cheaper alternative. It would be wrong to imply that the choice was purely an economic one. The evidence of material investment in domestic housing would suggest that there were townspeople who could have afforded larger and more ostentatious sacrifices on the lines of those of the military, but there may have been a preference for smaller-scale sacrifice favouring animals such as sheep or fowl or for libation-type offerings.

Another point of major divergence with the military community relates to the specific cults observed. It is true that there are abundant images of classical gods in southern Britain, in the form of relief sculptures, statuettes, gemstones and mosaics. However, there is a surprising dearth of religious inscriptions from the towns of Roman Britain. Some identify the deity portrayed by the conventional Roman name, as in the early dedication to Neptune and Minerva at Chichester. Jupiter, Mars, Mercury, Diana and Silvanus are attested at one or more towns, along with inscriptions to the genius of the place. There are also a number of instances of *interpretatio Romana*, such as Silvanus Callirius, Mercury

Andescocivoucos or Mars Medocius at Colchester, Mars Rigonometes near Lincoln or Hercules Saegon at Silchester. The ambiguities of religious identity are sometimes alluded to directly, as in the statue erected to 'Mars Lenus also known as Ocelus Vellaunos'. Both Mars Lenus and Mars Ocelus are paralleled within Britain and Vellaunos is paired with Mercury in Gaul. The identities of the dedicants who employed the practice of religious name-pairing are not always clear, but of two texts to Mars Lenus and Mars Ocelus at Caerwent, one was by a soldier, the other a full Roman citizen. Similarly, two out of three dedications to Sulis Minerva at Bath were on behalf of Roman citizens, one a serving legionary centurion. The exception was the possibly British sculptor Sulinus. From Colchester, there are several unusual dedicants to paired gods, including the Caledonian Lossio Veda and Similis of the *Cantiaci*. Although neither expresses a specific military connection, it is possible that both these men were veterans and thus influenced by army practices. A third dedicant was a freedman. The overall impression is that people who evoked paired divinities were either soldiers, ex-soldiers, high-status individuals or groups that emulated elite practice, as was often the way with freedmen. The two identifiable craftsmen to make explicit pairings (a sculptor and a coppersmith) were both potentially professionally involved in making representations of the gods and might be expected to have had heightened awareness of such hybrid identity.

There are also instances where a classically portrayed god or goddess is named by a British name only, as with the Suleviae, a sub-branch of the popular mother goddess cult of northern Europe, attested at Cirencester, Colchester and Bath. There are several other dedications to mother goddesses (Matres) from southern Britain. Other examples of divinities of British or north-western origin include Nemetona and Sulis at Bath. In the latter example, the goddess is sometimes referred to in the conflated form Sulis Minerva, often as Sulis alone, but never as Minerva alone, although the cult statue was a fine free-standing copper-alloy representation of the classical Roman goddess.

Eastern cults, such as that of Mithras, appear to have been far less commonly represented in southern Britain than among the military. The exceptions are predominantly found at the cosmopolitan and military-influenced centres of London and York. The *mithraeum* at London, the only certain urban example, contained several individual dedications linked to ex-military men or provincial officials. Membership of the

Mithraic cult was itself selective and exclusive and appears to have been particularly favoured by the military and merchants.

There is of course evidence relating to the imperial cult from a number of towns, most notably Colchester and London. The former was evidently the centre of cult activity with its grandiose classical temple to the deified Claudius, and there are extant dedications to the imperial *numen* and to imperial victory. London has also yielded a dedication to the imperial *numen* set up by the provincial council, whose main role was the propagation of the imperial cult in the province. The relative paucity of other dedications (Bath, Lincoln, Caerwent, Brough-on-Humber) stands in marked contrast to numerous examples in the military zone. It also increases the suspicion that some at least of the dedicants were from the military community.

Religious practices were thus profoundly changed by the Roman conquest, in the context of a drastically unequal power relationship. The Roman elimination of the druidical priestly order is the most obvious example of that. What emerged subsequently was a mixture of Roman word- and iconographic-power in the naming and depiction of the gods, set against adaptive strategies by Britons in reshaping practice in ways that allowed them a different religious identity from the army and other aliens. The different emphases in cults followed and in naming patterns, in temple architecture and in ritual practices, surely attest the emergence of hybrid types of religious experience. There was no one form of Romano-British religion and the same sanctuary could accommodate different sorts of ritual acts – as certainly seems to have been the case at Bath.

A distinct peculiarity of religion in Roman Britain was the widespread use of so-called curse tablets (*defixiones*). At one level this appears to be a distinctly 'Roman' practice, generally using the Latin cursive script to record binding spells in relatively standardized and quasi-legal terms on thin sheets of lead, which were often folded or rolled before deposition. The curses typically sought revenge on someone who had wronged the dedicant; in the vast majority of the 300-plus recorded British examples the complaint concerned theft of belongings. Similar material has been recorded in other provinces, though in fact the overwhelming emphasis in Britain on issues relating to theft is quite unlike the pattern elsewhere, where curses relating to litigation, to competition, to commercial enterprises and to erotic or amatory adventures are also common. Curse tablets occur at a wide range of British sites, both urban and rural, but – with a single exception – not on military sites. Given the extent of excavation in the military zone, this seems unlikely to be due to sampling bias. Of the urban sites, by far the largest group is from Bath (about 130), followed by London (eight, including one from Southwark), Caistor-by-Norwich, with possible examples or related magical texts from Silchester and Wroxeter, and other small towns including Wanborough, Kelvedon, Chesterton-on-Fosse, Leintwardine, Braughing and Higham Ferrers. Further discoveries are to be expected.

A typical example of a curse from Bath concerns the theft of a copper-alloy vessel:

The person who has lifted my bronze vessel is utterly accursed. I give (him) to the temple of Sulis, whether man or woman, whether slave or free, whether boy or girl, and let him who has done this spill his own blood into the vessel itself.

This text was written from right to left, with part of the injunction to the god repeated on the back. The careful language used to ensure that the retribution should cover all eventualities is typical of curse tablets. Various expedients were adopted to keep the transaction with the goddess secret and to secure the awful power of the curse. Examples of mirror writing, as well as right to left ordering, are known; one or two incomprehensible texts are suspected of being written in British dialect using Latin cursive. As well as rolling or folding, curses were sometimes pierced with nails. At Bath they seem to have been routinely thrown into the sacred spring, though at other sites disposal into pits or incorporation into other votive deposits may have been followed.

The large number of tablets from Bath may distort the picture somewhat, since a number of them could relate to thefts from careless visitors to the bathing complex attached to the temple, where clothing may have been left unattended. However, several of the thefts of metal vessels seem to represent domestic burglaries, as is explicit in one Bath tablet and implicit in the long list of personal goods lost in the Caistor-by-Norwich example (Table 11). The fact that several individuals named suspects in their pleas to the gods would again suggest a domestic context, rather than random pickpockets in a public place. Most of the items lost were relatively minor and the people making the dedications were a mixture of ordinary types with a single Latin or 'Celtic' name. Only at London do we have explicit reference to Roman citizens – and there they were

Table 11. Curse tablets from Britain.

PLACE/GOD	SUBJECT OF CURSE	REFERENCE
Bath/?	Theft of person or thing called Vilbia, by one of named list of suspects	*Tab Sul* 4
Bath/?	Theft of a rug	*Tab Sul* 6
Bath/?	List of names	*Tab Sul* 9
Bath/?	Theft of bracelet	*Tab Sul* 15
Bath/?	Names thief . . .	*Tab Sul* 16
Bath/?	List of names on pewter plate	*Tab Sul* 30
Bath/?	Theft of ploughshare from Civilis	*Tab Sul* 31
Bath/?	List of names 'may their life be weakened'	*Tab Sul* 37
Bath/?	Stolen property to be given (to Sulis?)	*Tab Sul* 38
Bath/?	Response to false accusations	*Tab Sul* 40
Bath/?	Theft of horse blanket?	*Tab Sul* 49
Bath/?	List of 11 names; lists of names	*Tab Sul* 51; 95; 96
Bath/?	Theft of cape from Lovernisca	*Tab Sul* 61
Bath/?	Deomiorix curses burglar who has stolen from his house	*Tab Sul* 99
Bath/Mars	Something to be given, unless . . .	*Tab Sul* 33
Bath/Mars	Theft of silver ring	*Tab Sul* 97
Bath/Mercury	List of names with curse applying also to their families	*Tab Sul* 53
Bath/Sulis	Theft of 6 silver coins	*Tab Sul* 8
Bath/Sulis	Thefts of hooded cloak from Docilianus; cloak; headgear?; cloak; hooded cloak	*Tab Sul* 10; 43, 55, 64, 65
Bath/Sulis	Theft of bronze vessel	*Tab Sul* 44
Bath/Sulis	Theft of two silver coins from Arminia by Verecundinus	*Tab Sul* 54
Bath/Sulis	Theft of cloak, tunic and horse blanket	*Tab Sul* 62
Bath/Sulis	Theft of bathing tunic of Cantissena	*Tab Sul* 63
Bath/Sulis	Theft of an iron pan from Exsuperius	*Tab Sul* 66
Bath/Sulis	Sanction against perjury sworn at spring of Sulis	*Tab Sul* 94
Bath/Sulis Minerva	Theft of cloak and bathing tunic from Solinus	*Tab Sul* 32
Bath/Sulis Minerva	Theft of 5 *denarii* from Docca	*Tab Sul* 34
Bath/Sulis Minerva	Vengeance on those who have wronged dedicant	*Tab Sul* 35

PLACE/GOD	SUBJECT OF CURSE	REFERENCE
Bath/Sulis Minerva	Curse?	*Tab Sul* 45
Bath/Sulis Minerva	Theft of pan from Oconea	*Tab Sul* 60
Bath/Sulis?	Theft of pair of gloves from Docimedis	*Tab Sul* 5
Bath/Sulis?	Theft of various items (not preserved) or phraseology suggesting theft	*Tab Sul* 36, 38, 41, 47, 52, 57, 100, 102
Bath/Sulis?	Theft of 6 silver coins from Annianus, with list of named suspects	*Tab Sul* 98
Brandon/Neptune	Theft of iron pan	*Britannia* 25, no. 1
Braughing/?	Indecipherable text	*Britannia* 18, no. 8
Brean Down/?	Theft of *caricula* (wheelbarrow?)	*Britannia* 17, no. 6
Caistor-by-Norwich/Neptune	Curse relating to theft of wreath, bracelets, cup, mirror, head-dress, leggings, 10 pewter vessels, cloak?, 15 *denarii*	*Britannia* 13, no. 9
Chesterton/?	Theft of garment	*RIB* 1, 243
Clothall	Curse on Tacita	*RIB* 1, 221
Eccles villa/gods	Reference to property stolen by Butu?	*Britannia* 17, no. 2
Farley Heath/?	Mention of sum of 4,000 *denarii*	*Britannia* 35, no. 2
Hamble estuary/Neptune	Theft of gold *solidus* and 6 silver *argentioli*	*Britannia* 38, no. 1.
Kelvedon/Mercury	Thief to be made to pay	*JRS* 48, no. 3
Leintwardine/?	List of names	*JRS* 59, nos 31a/b
London/?	Curse against T. Egnatius Tyranus and P. Cicereius Felix	*RIB* 1, 6
London/?	Curse against Tretia Maria	*RIB* 1, 7
London/?	Names Plautius Nobilianus, Aurelius Saturninus and Domitia Attiola and 'any who were absent'	*Britannia* 34, no. 1
London/Diana	Theft of head-gear and band	*Britannia* 34, no. 2
London/Metunus (Neptune)	Vengeance requested against listed individuals	*Britannia* 18, no. 1
Lydney/Nodens	Theft of ring	*RIB* 1, 306
Marlborough Downs/Mars	Theft of something?	*Britannia* 30, no. 3
Old Harlow/Mercury	Curse in affair of heart?	*Britannia* 4, no. 3
Pagan's Hill/?	Theft of 3,000 *denarii* from a house	*Britannia* 15, no. 7
Ratcliffe-on-Soar/?	Theft of mule (?), 2 bags and other items from the house	*Britannia* 24, no. 2
Ratcliffe-on-Soar/?	Theft of gaiters, an axe, knife, pair of gloves	*Britannia* 35, no. 3

Table 11 – *contd.*

PLACE/GOD	SUBJECT OF CURSE	REFERENCE
Uley/Mercury	Theft of draught animal from Cenacus by Vitalinus and Natalinus	*Britannia* 10, no. 2 (*Uley* 1)
Uley/Mercury	Saturnina curses thief of linen cloth	*Britannia* 10, no. 3 (*Uley* 2)
Uley/Mercury	Theft of a gold ring, iron fetters from a house	*Britannia* 10, no. 4 (*Uley* 3)
Uley/Mercury	Biccus gives to god what stolen from him	*Uley* 4
Uley/Mercury	Theft of bridle	*Britannia* 20, no. 2 (*Uley* 5)
Uley/Mercury	Curse against 3 individuals who have harmed farm animal	*Britannia* 20, no. 3 (*Uley* 43)
Uley/Mercury	Theft of 2 wheels, 4 cows and many small belongings from house of Honoratus	*Britannia* 23, no. 5 (*Uley* 72)
Uley/Mercury	Theft of linen, cloak and 2 silver coins	*Uley* 52
Uley/Mercury	Theft of cloak	*Britannia* 26, no. 1 (*Uley* 55)
Uley/Mercury	Curse on those behaving badly towards dedicant	*Britannia* 26, no. 2 (*Uley* 76)
Uley/Mercury	Theft of gloves	*Britannia* 27, no. 1 (*Uley* 80)
Uley/Mercury	Theft (?) of piece of silver plate and four rings	*Britannia* 29, no. 1 (*Uley* 50)
Wanborough/?	Curse relating to theft?	*Britannia* 3, no. 1
Weeting with Broomhill/?	Theft of item	*Britannia* 25, no. 2

the object of the cursing. It seems plausible, therefore, that the curses reflect a general and repeated phenomenon in southern Britain in the face of minor thefts. In the absence of adequate policing or redress for humble people, they solicited the aid of the gods to visit terrible vengeance on malefactors using literate skills to make their petitions.

The Bath tablets reveal a great variety in the handwriting, with only two out of 130 demonstrably produced by the same hand; though, since the material preserved in the spring appears to be a random sample of about 300 years of deposits, this does not exclude the possibility that there were professional scribes operating at the shrine. However, many of the texts were very poor copies from specimen texts and look like

DIY curses on pre-prepared blanks. A number of completely blank lead sheets and some pseudo-inscriptions, which are essentially illiterate texts, suggest that cursing was not limited to the fully literate. The lead blanks and scribal assistance (if such there was) were evidently cheaply available if people felt it worth doing for the sake of relatively minor losses.

The fixation of the British on the vengeful protection of the gods against acts of theft requires further comment. Most of the appeals at Bath were to the British deity Sulis (only a few distinguishing her as Sulis Minerva), though a few curses address Mars or Mercury. From other sites we have Metunus (perhaps for Neptune), Neptune and Mercury. The formulaic nature and language of the tablets is characteristically Roman, as is the written and contractual nature of the exchange with the god. But, in fact, the pattern of near-exclusive use of 'theft curses' is unparalleled in other parts of the empire, and this strongly suggests that this was a British peculiarity, with literate lower-order Britons latching on to a form of petition that made them feel more powerful in the face of judicial indifference. The curse tablets can be read as a transcript about the workings of Roman imperialism – with divine help being recruited to help subjects address some of its shortcomings. One reason for the lack of interest in this religious practice in the army was that soldiers enjoyed better protection in and above the law.

The ritual deposition of metal goods in watery contexts was a distinct trait of Iron Age society and is well attested in pre-Roman Britain. The practice continued in Roman times, especially in rural contexts, but also in some towns. One of the reasons for the popularity of the Bath spring may have been that it spoke to this pre-Roman tradition for at least some of the worshippers. The Walbrook stream, cutting north–south across Roman London, may provide another example. It has been noted that there is a concentration of religious structures and dedications along its banks. The Walbrook stream was gradually infilled during the Roman period and an exceptionally rich haul of artefacts has been recovered from its bed, though this has sometimes been interpreted as deliberately dumped rubbish to consolidate the land for construction. However, the presence of some substantial deposits of metal artefacts has raised the possibility that some at least of the material may represent ritual deposition in the stream during the Roman period. Consideration of finds securely provenanced to the stream bed reveals broad similarities with the material used to revet the banks, leading recent accounts to downplay the ritual significance. Yet the proportion of copper-alloy and iron artefacts was higher than in most archaeological rubbish deposits and the superb preservation of the ironwork in particular shows that many artefacts were in perfect condition (undamaged and unbroken) when deposited. That some at least of the metal artefacts were ritually deposited remains a possibility, especially when taken with the many human skulls found in the northern part of the valley. If the deposits are typical of rubbish disposal in Roman London, then it attests a remarkably throw-away society here, by the standards of the ancient world, where normally a higher degree of recycling of metals in particular might be expected.

Literate people are attracted to literate objects as a means of demonstrating their facility with the written word. Makers' marks and information painted, incised or branded on to goods are commonly encountered in urban assemblages. Urban dwellers with some education often chose to mark their personal possessions, as a protection against the casual thefts discussed in the previous section. A survey of inscriptions on portable artefacts reveals that, though common in towns, they occurred at levels below the very high ones encountered at military sites. That may suggest that the threshold level of literacy was lower in the towns and that as a result it featured less generally in defining identity. There seems little doubt that those who could read and write utilized and flaunted the fact, relative to their means. Silver, copper-alloy and pewter vessels and eating utensils such as spoons were often decorated with writing – makers' stamps, owners' names and encouraging slogans ('good luck to the user'), or simply the weight – and thus value – of the metal. Items might be prepared for votive deposition by the addition of the god's name, as in a group of pewter and copper-alloy vessels from the spring at Bath. Most major finds of Roman plate and cutlery have been made in rural hoards, but the presence of individual pieces from urban sites (Colchester, London, Lincoln, Silchester, Caistor-by-Norwich, Canterbury, Bath) indicates that use of metal tableware will have been an important diagnostic of social standing and wealth there.

Certain types of literate artefacts appear to have a predominant distribution at urban centres. Glass mould-blown cups depicting chariot racing, accompanied by inscriptions hailing the victor and bidding the defeated charioteers farewell are known from London, Colchester,

Gloucester, St Albans, Canterbury, Caistor-by-Norwich and Carlisle. Similar vessels featuring both gladiators and charioteers are known from London, and cups with only gladiatorial scenes from London, Colchester, Gloucestershire, Wroxeter, Dorchester and Leicester. The prestige value of these items and their extreme rarity outside urban contexts suggest targeted purchases in places where these sorts of entertainments were put on. Engraved glass vessels have a wider circulation, including military sites and villas, but add additional towns (York, Exeter, Caerwent, Cirencester, Silchester).

Not all personal artefacts lent themselves to bearing inscriptions. They were rare on brooches, but finger rings were more commonly used by both civilians and soldiers to convey written messages, whether retrograde for use in personal seals or clearly readable on the ring, The information conveyed varied from declarations of love, wishes of luck or long life, personal names (or *tria nomina* initials indicating people of Roman citizen status), imperial loyalty statements, to statements of religious affinity. About half the inscribed rings came from town sites, with the majority of the rest from military sites and relatively small numbers from temples and rural sites. The same broad pattern is true of inscribed gemstones.

Inscribed bone roundels, normally identified as gaming pieces or counting pieces, are another category of artefact with a strong representation at major urban sites, accounting for 48 per cent of the material, with a further 9 per cent relating to sites of dual urban/military status such as Corbridge, and only 38 per cent military, and less than 5 per cent rural. Inscribed pottery roundels are concentrated at Colchester. Inscribed weights show a more predominantly military bias, and many of the urban sites where they have been recorded had a military phase. There are some notable concentrations at specialized small towns such as the mining settlement of Charterhouse. Lead labels and sealings were most commonly associated with the Roman military, so the recovery of over thirty examples in urban contexts is of interest. The seals attest movement of imperial goods, of those of the provincial authorities, of consignments for specific legions and auxiliary units, and, in a far smaller number of examples, urban authorities and private individuals. A seal of the town of Gloucester found at Cirencester is thus far a unique attestation of a civil seal, though an enigmatic example from Leicestershire conceivably related to the *civitas Corieltavorum*. Military or official

seals have been found at London (numerous examples), Leicester, Cirencester, Silchester and York among the major towns, with seals of more
ambiguous content also recorded at Silchester and Aldborough. What
these categories of artefacts show is that towns, like military sites, were
a focus for literate and numerate trade activity, in some cases involving
the adoption of new counting and weighing standards and in part at
least overlapping with issues of military or official supply.

MATERIAL MATTERS

The representation of people in sculpture was in many ways a fundamental element of Roman society and was one of the best ways, other than
through coinage, for emperors to portray their appearance to their
subjects (as indicated by fragments of imperial sculptures from London,
York, Lincoln, Gloucester, Cirencester). A peculiarity of British (and to
some extent northern Gallic) urban society was the lack of honorific
statues – with the exception of imperial statues – erected to prominent
individuals. Both statues and inscribed bases to individual citizens are
notably rare. The early third-century dedication from Caerwent in
honour of Tiberius Claudius Paulinus, ex-legate of *legio II Augusta* and
soon to take up position as governor of *Britannia Inferior*, illustrates
the importance of this form of civic action, but also reinforces the point
that this sort of thing was fairly exceptional in Britain.

Two female heads from Bath appear to be attempts at portraits,
though one at least of these is of very indifferent execution. A crude
human head from a house at Caerwent is more probably a representation
of a deity in a domestic shrine than a portrait of the owner. The absence
of non-religious statuary and the dearth of inscribed tombstones at most
towns is striking. There are limited examples of representations of the
deceased on civilian tombstones and most of the surviving examples
appear to relate to the extended military community at sites such as
London, Lincoln, York, Chester, Carlisle and Corbridge. A tombstone
from Lincoln erected by Aurelius Senecio, a decurion in the town, for
his wife Volusia Faustina is an example from the curial class in a *colonia*.
The tombstone of Philus from Cirencester depicts a standing figure
wearing a hooded cape to keep out the weather. He was an immigrant
from Besançon in Gaul. The general rule would appear to be that

members of the military community buried at urban sites were sometimes depicted on their tombstones; well-to-do 'resident aliens' and the
most aspirant members of the curial class, such as Roman citizens in the
coloniae, occasionally followed the same practice. The avoidance of
self-representation of townspeople at large was not connected with lack
of trained sculptors, as the amount of religious statuary and relief sculpture in particular demonstrates. Finance may have played a part, but, as
with civic inscriptions, one suspects an element of social choice here.
For many Britons, leaving written memorials of their lives and works
and representations of the person did not appeal and they constructed
their Roman identity without these aspects. By contrast, a small minority
of urban dwellers consciously used such strategies to enhance their
difference within the community and to stress their close identification
with Rome.

A corollary of the shortage of explicit depictions of civilians is that it
is difficult to judge the impact of Roman dress and hairstyles in Britain.
One recent account of 'Life in Roman Britain' states on near-consecutive
pages that men will rapidly have adopted Roman-style dress post-
conquest and then admits it is difficult to find actual depictions of the
toga. There are just two, both from the military zone, presumably
relating to high-status Roman administrators like the governor. It was,
of course, illegal for non-Roman citizens to wear the garment, and,
outside the army and the *coloniae*, numbers of full citizens were almost
certainly low until the third century. Other possible depictions include
statues of a Roman *genius* rather than real people. The available evidence
suggests that the standard form of civilian dress in Britain, as in other
north-western provinces, was the Gallic coat, a wide-fitting tunic, over
which a hooded cloak was commonly worn. Women wore a longer
version of the Gallic coat, along with underskirts and cloaks. The textiles
were typically diamond twills and probably dyed a variety of colours.
Most of the iconographic evidence from Britain is late second to third
century, but there is supporting evidence for significant change over time
in British clothing fashions. Earlier dress styles for both men and women
in Britain appear to have made more extensive use of brooches to fasten
garments and these are abundant finds in late Iron Age and first- and
second-century contexts, but much rarer by the late second and third
centuries, reflecting the adoption of the Gallic coat by that date. It is
thought that women's dress in the early Roman period was similar

to that of women in northern Gaul and the Rhineland, consisting of long-sleeved bodice and a *peplos*-like overtunic, fastened with several brooches. Male attire is less well documented in the early Roman period, but the number of brooches suggests that both men and women wore them and expressed something of their identity through local variation in fibula type. It has been observed that the evolved Roman dress of the north-western provinces obscured such regional differences, evoking instead a generic civilian identity.

The citizens of the *civitas* centres were not without classical pretensions, but in general they constructed their Roman identity in different ways from the military community. There is quite a lot of evidence for investment in lavish interior decoration in the form of wall-paintings and mosaics. We noted earlier that mosaics are virtually unknown at garrison settlements, with the exception of the legionary bases. Military wall-painting tended to consist of plain or simple bands and blocks of colour (*contra* the impression given by recent reconstructions of Roman buildings at South Shields and Wallsend). However, in the towns both mosaics and intricate wall-paintings are far commoner. Of the major centres, only Caistor-by-Norwich, Carmarthen and Carlisle have not yielded any mosaics or tessellated pavements, and over thirty have been recorded at London, Colchester, Gloucester, Silchester, Cirencester, Dorchester, Caerwent, with more than ten examples at York, Lincoln, St Albans and Leicester. Although these were primarily a feature of the largest town houses, they were not exclusively so, as recent excavations in London have demonstrated. Some typical strip buildings, with workshops or shops in the end nearest the street, showed development over time in the domestic quarters to the rear in the form of tessellated floors and painted wall plaster. The earliest urban mosaics are late first century in date from London, though there is little evidence for polychrome figural pavements before the mid-second century. There are notable groups of late second-century mosaics from St Albans, Cirencester, Leicester and Aldborough. Although there are comparatively few mosaics of indubitably third-century date, there was then something of a boom in the first half of the fourth century.

Where the wall-paintings and mosaics were figurative, they drew on classical mythology and conventional Roman themes for inspiration. Second-century examples in mosaic include a wrestling match between two cupids from Colchester and a splendid lion seizing a deer and a

Neptune from St Albans. Even in the fourth century pagan themes remained strong, as in the great Orpheus pavements of the West Country. The mixture was highly eclectic and surely represents the distinctive interests of the patrons in British towns and villas.

Mosaic inscriptions are fairly rare, but fragments with letters are known at London, Colchester and Aldborough. Painted inscriptions or scratched graffiti have been recorded on wall plaster at London, York, St Albans, Silchester, Cirencester, Wroxeter, Leicester, Caerwent, Dorchester ('Paternus wrote (this)'), and Exeter. The graffiti are generally secondary additions, sometimes implying change in use or downgrading of a high-status room. The twenty-four examples from Blue Boar Lane in Leicester include obscene allusions in Latin ('and who, catamite [. . .] you?'). They demonstrate the existence of a literate substrate in urban society who expressed themselves by putting their names and jocular insults on the walls of an opulent second-century house, at a time when it was semi-ruinous and converted in part for manufacturing activity.

Early excavations of Romano-British towns tended to give the impression that these were pleasant garden cities, with little manufacturing. One of the major discoveries of recent decades of urban archaeology is that many towns were more densely built up than was previously appreciated and that craft activity was both varied and prevalent. The street frontages of the earliest settlement at London were rapidly filled with long narrow workshops. One of the earliest substantial buildings at St Albans comprised workshops and shops. We have also noted the early establishment of a craftsmen's guild at Chichester. These settlements were thus active centres of production of various branches of metalwork, enamelling, pottery, glass, bone-working, carpentry, leather-working, shoemaking, clothing and textile production, mosaic and decorative arts, and so on. They were also prime points of consumption of new styles of artefacts that defined different versions of Roman identity. British craftspeople will soon have been absorbed by these settlements and trained in making new types of artefacts. Production spread also to the smaller settlements that were established along the Roman roads and in relation to natural resources. Indeed, by the later Roman period, the small towns were increasingly important in the provincial economy.

To some extent all urban inhabitants consumed material culture in a way that defined their identity as town-dwellers and as subjects of the

Roman empire. The political and economic roles of urban settlements made them focal points for the production, distribution and marketing of goods. These patterns of supply overlapped with, but also differed from, military logistical arrangements. Within the range of available goods in towns, different groups could select what suited their wealth and aspirations.

Against a background of rural conservatism in diet, towns stand out as centres of significant change in Roman Britain. The consumption of meat was generally dominated by an increased reliance on cattle and pig and lower levels of sheep/goat than on rural sites. The 'typical' town profile is close to the normative military one and urban meat supply appears to have followed similar specialized processing and distributive models. Separate zones for slaughtering, horn processing and tanning can be identified at some sites, distinct from secondary butchery waste and implying a measure of regulatory control. Taking account of the relative meat value of the three main groups of animals attested, it is estimated that at Silchester cattle may have contributed 68 per cent, ovicaprids 4 per cent and pigs 28 per cent of meat. The British preference for beef thus has a long history and urban consumption was higher than on the Continent. Other innovations of Roman diet included the widespread distribution of fish and shellfish to urban centres, the rise in the exploitation of domestic poultry and the increased use of techniques for preserving meat through smoking or salting. The last aspect extended the consumption of meat across the year and emphasizes an important duality of meat-eating in Roman society as both an occasional (religious) and everyday (commonplace) occurrence. The evidence from temple sites in southern Britain suggests a greater prevalence of ovicaprids and poultry as sacrificial victims (smaller and cheaper, but also sometimes appropriate to the cult, as at Uley) and a general absence of fish, shellfish and game. Assemblages with larger proportions of cattle and pig bones and with these additional species represented thus probably reflect 'secular' patterns of consumption. The age profile can also be revealing and large numbers of very young animals may also be indicative of sacrificial deposits.

Imports from the Continent of typical Roman liquid commodities such as olive oil, wine and fish sauces can be identified from the distinctive ceramic containers used to transport them. These amphoras are not as common as one might expect at British urban sites and reveal a divergence between urban and military communities. While there is enough evidence to show that all three were consumed in the towns, the level of occurrence is very low in comparison to Mediterranean sites. For example, a total of 1,700 amphora sherds was recorded in an assemblage of over 55,000 sherds of Roman pottery from one excavation in Leicester. Over 80 per cent of these were fragments of the large Spanish olive oil amphora (Dressel 20), which is the most commonly attested amphora in Britain. Numbers of wine and fish-sauce amphoras were generally low. Mediterranean urban assemblages can often comprise 50 per cent or more amphora sherds. The range of products and sources of supply were also much more varied in the imperial heartlands. It is clear that the level of occurrence at most British towns (London may be a partial exception) do not indicate long-sustained bulk imports. Once again, the exceptions to a general pattern of non-adoption of oil and wine highlight the behaviour of a minority of citizens who regularly consumed these. By and large, though, Britain remained a 'butter and beer' culture. Indeed, we can identify evidence in the ceramic assemblages for the dissemination of new styles of drinking equipment, notably large indented beakers for beer drinking.

There is a common assumption in the literature that the Roman period must have brought improvements in health and nutrition to the population of Britain. The palaeopathological data provide some cautious support for this optimistic view. Although there was a rise in tooth decay, perhaps linked to more fermentable carbohydrate in the diet (oral hygiene will have been generally poor), a small minority of skeletons reveal evidence of malnutrition or dietary deficiency (less than 7 per cent). Stature increased slightly for men, though dropped marginally for women. More detailed studies are needed of large urban cemeteries to assess the extent of regional divergence from this picture.

Cemeteries also reveal unusual demographic patterns in urban society. Women and children tend to be dramatically under-represented in the later Roman inhumation cemeteries in Britain (Cirencester, Winchester, London, Poundbury/Dorchester). Although infant burials are occasionally encountered within the urban area, it remains probable that children were disposed of in separate cemetery areas or by another means that leaves little trace archaeologically. A male to female imbalance is harder to explain, though in the earliest phases of urbanization at centres like London there appear to have been comparatively fewer women, judging by the predominance of male personal ornaments over female ones. This is perhaps indicative of the immigration of traders and craftsmen. However, even in late Roman cemeteries the under-representation of women remains and is difficult to explain satisfactorily. It is conceivable that towns continued to have imbalanced populations in later centuries or that the pattern recurred as a result of social change. It is to the late Roman changes in towns that we shall now turn.

I I

The Urban Failure?

The theme of the decline and failure of towns is central to debate about the fourth century in Roman Britain. One traditional view presents the history of towns as progressive and unilinear until the collapse of Roman authority in the early fifth century. Despite the fifth-century crisis, people have sought to demonstrate threads of continuity between Roman urbanism and the re-emergence of the town in the later Anglo-Saxon period. However, the accumulation of archaeological data threw this into doubt long ago, leading to suggestions that the Roman town, as traditionally understood, had effectively failed by the end of the third century. Life in towns, it has been argued, went on into the fourth century, but on a different basis, perhaps more related to individual power than civil authority. One recent study has attempted to chart decline systematically, using a wide range of parameters. The conclusion is strongly in favour of early decline, but dates the change to the second half of the fourth century. A more median line between the two extremes of vitality or decline has also had advocates, admitting quantitative and qualitative change in urban life, but maintaining the view that it was still vigorous until well into the fourth century.

The extent of the changes in urban society is clearest in the archaeological record. There are virtually no fourth-century inscriptions from British towns, no sculptural artworks, no tombstones. These are trends that were already present in the earlier centuries, but far less pronounced then. Pagan monuments in towns were particularly vulnerable to the changing religious politics of the empire, which moved from the persecution of Christians to the persecution of pagans within the course of the fourth century. Unsurprisingly, pagan cults became less flamboyant and less conspicuous in the urban centres as the fourth century progressed, but there is not the evidence one might expect to show

Christianity dominating the townscapes and providing a new focus for civic munificence, as it did in some other provinces. On the other hand, large stone town houses continued to be built well into the fourth century, there was a flourishing of mosaic art focused on a number of towns, and the province has yielded a number of late Roman silver plate hoards, signifying unexpected levels of personal wealth for the topmost tier in society. While some people might point to the early collapse of Rome's imperial project in Britain, others can write of the fourth century as a 'golden age'. The evidence, at first sight contradictory, can perhaps be best understood as the emergence of new forms of identity in response to combined political, economic and social changes. Regional differences between towns in the east and west of England now also increased.

TOWN DEFENCES

Defensive circuits and gates were important classes of monument in Romano-British towns. The diversion of funds into the construction of stone walls in the third century was both cause and symptom of more widespread change in late Roman towns. However, the creation of walls and embankments around urban settlements began far earlier in Britain than elsewhere, being datable to the first century in a number of cases, with numerous second-century examples, and the majority of urban sites, including many small towns, had defences by the end of the third century (Table 12). This is a very unusual pattern within the empire as a whole and it can reasonably be asserted that it reflects a particular insular dimension of urban identity.

Study of the defences of Romano-British towns has concentrated both on the accumulation of structural detail and on setting those data in a chronological and interpretational framework. Britain was unusual among the provinces of the western empire both in terms of the large number of towns that received defences before the end of the second century and the type of defensive circuits that were built. However, the older view that there was a virtual moratorium on the construction of urban defences elsewhere from the reign of Augustus to the mid-third century is no longer credible. Comparison with frontier regions of Africa, for instance, would suggest that defences may have been somewhat more common from the second century in areas with a perceived level of insecurity. On the other hand, in Gaul and Germany the provision of town walls before the third century was very clearly linked to urban status, with half the attested examples being *coloniae* and only eight examples (33 per cent) being *civitas* centres and with only two examples at small towns. The British examples dated before 200 are more broadly spread across the urban hierarchy and include London, the *coloniae* and virtually all the *civitas* centres and eighteen small towns. The British penchant for walls backed by earthworks also stands in marked contrast to the Continent, where free-standing walls are more common. This appears to have been an insular tradition, as does the provision of defences at so many small towns. There are other significant differences, notably that British defensive circuits generally encompassed a larger area of the core of the settlement than did the later Continental examples and did not make extensive use of *spolia* from earlier buildings (Lincoln's lower town walls and London's riverside walls being exceptions here). These partly reflect the long timescale of urban defences in Britain.

The archaeological evidence is conventionally placed within a framework that emphasizes five main phases of development (Table 13). There has been much debate concerning the coherence of these phases of construction and of the possible historical contexts to which they relate. On one side are those who believe that the erection of defences was so closely controlled by the state that the grouping of dated examples must reflect the rapid implementation of an imperial policy at a given moment in time. For the second-century earthworks, for instance, it has been argued that all must be of late second-century date on the basis of applying the latest dating for one example to the group as a whole. That context has traditionally been sought in the events of the civil war of 193–97, when Clodius Albinus is presumed to have prepared the towns of Britain for unrest as he made plans to take the major part of the garrison to contest the imperial throne. Some commentators now favour a date in the 180s, though yet others have objected to the idea that there was a single constructional context (whether proactive or reactive to a crisis). They propose that development could have taken place at different towns across much of the second century. There are inherent difficulties of dating defensive circuits in terms of the latest artefacts sealed beneath them. The underlying assumption made by those who see the construction of the earthworks as contemporaneous is that only some major security threat could have persuaded the Roman emperor to grant

Table 12. Urban defences in Roman Britain (featuring the major towns and the largest small towns only).

ANCIENT NAME	MODERN NAME	STATUS	AREA (HA)	1ST C	2ND C	3RD C	4TH C
Camulodunum	Colchester	*colonia*	47	E	S+E		
Lindum	Lincoln (upper city)	*colonia /* 4p.c.	17	ME*	S/E	++	++
	Lincoln (lower city)		23		ES	T	++
Glevum	Gloucester	*colonia*	19	ME*	S/E		BT
Eburacum	York	*colonia /* 3p.c.	40			S?	
Londinium	London	*?colonia /* p.c.	128		S		BT++
Verulamium	St Albans	*municipium*	79	E	E	ES	BT
Isaurium Brigantum	Aldborough	*civitas*	22		E	S/E	BT
Petuaria Parisiorum	Brough-on-Humber	*vicus/?civitas*	6		E	S/E	BT
Venta Silurum	Caerwent	*civitas*	18		E		S/E, BT
Venta Icenorum	Caistor-by-Norwich	*civitas*	14		E?	ES	BT
Durnovernum Cantiacorum	Canterbury	*civitas*	52			ES	BT
Luguvalium Carvetiorum	Carlisle	*civitas*	28			S?	?
Moridunum Demetarum	Carmarthen	*civitas*	6		E	S?/E	
Noviomagus Reginorum	Chichester	*civitas*	39		E	S/E	BT
Corinium Dobunnorum	Cirencester	*civitas* /4p.c.	88		E	S/E	BT
Durnovaria Durotrigum	Dorchester	*civitas*	33		E	S?/E	
Isca Dumnoniorum	Exeter	*civitas*	36	ME	S?/E	S?/E	
Ratae Corieltavorum	Leicester	*civitas*	48			ES	
Calleva Atrebatum	Silchester	*civitas*	42	E	E	S/E	
Venta Belgarum	Winchester	*civitas*	55	E	E	S/E	BT?

ANCIENT NAME	MODERN NAME	STATUS	AREA (HA)	1ST C	2ND C	3RD C	4TH C
Viroconium Cornoviorum	Wroxeter	*civitas*	77		E	S?/E	S?/E
Durobrivae	Water Newton	*vicus/?civitas*	18			ES?	BT
–	Great Chesterford	?	15				S
Coria	Corbridge	*?civitas*	?15				
Lactodurum	Towcester	?	10–11		E	S	
–	Alchester	?	10.5		ES?	ES?	
Durovigitum	Godmanchester	?	8/11		E	ES	BT
Lindinis	Ilchester	*?civitas*	10		E		S?
Durobrivae	Rochester	*?vicus*	9.4		E	S/E	
Aquae Sulis	Bath	spa	9.3		E	S?/E	
Magnis	Kenchester	*?vicus*	8.4		E		S? BT
–	Great Casterton	?	7		E	S/E	BT
–	Irchester	?	8		E	S?/E	
Caesaromagus	Chelmsford	?	7		E		
Cataractonium	Catterick	?	5–6				S
Cunetio	Mildenhall	?	6/8		E?	E?	S, BT
–	Dorchester (Oxon)	?	5.5		E	S/E	+
–	Brampton	?	6		E?	E?	

Key to abbreviations
E = earthwork defence
ME = military earthwork defence reused
S = stone wall
ES = contemporary earth rampart and stone wall
S/E = wall cut into front of earlier rampart
T = towers added
BT = bastion towers added
p.c. = provincial capital
+ or ++ = evidence for other additions or significant modifications

Question marks indicate that the date of a feature is uncertain.
The * on early phases at Lincoln and Gloucester indicate that these circuits date to the very end of the first or early second century.

permission for such an unprecedented scheme. On the other hand, it could be argued that the impetus came from the towns and not from the state. It is possible that a general petition by the British towns for leave to construct defences was granted around the mid-second century in recognition of special conditions in this frontier province. Not all the towns would necessarily have been able to take advantage of such a privilege immediately, but civic pride as much as fear could have motivated them to imitate those towns that were able to set the trend.

Table 13. The main phases of construction of urban defences.

PHASE	MAIN CHARACTERISTICS
1	Earth and timber defences were allowed at only a few sites during the first century (e.g. St Albans, Silchester, Winchester).
2	The *coloniae* received walls in the later first century or early years of the second century, reflecting their prestige status, their quasi-military function and a desire to avoid a repeat of the Boudican sack of Colchester (Colchester, Gloucester, Lincoln).
3	Many towns gained earthwork defences during the second half of the second century (but, NB, London was endowed with a stone wall *c.*200).
4	During the third century, stone walls were added to the front of many earlier earthworks (or, in a few cases, erected contemporaneously with new earthwork circuits).
5	Bastion towers were added to the front of many wall circuits in the second half of the fourth century (and in London a riverside wall was constructed to supplement the land walls). Other evidence of strengthening or refurbishment of circuits. Broader ditches added outside walls.

The issue remains unresolved, but it is clear that by the end of the second century it was normal for the major British towns, and a good number of the small towns also, to have defences. Most scholars are agreed that the addition of masonry walls to the front of the earthwork (or as free-standing walls) need not be related to a single historical context in the third century, with some town walls being dated as early as the Severan age and others as late as 280. Similarly, although it has been the fashion to attribute the addition of bastion towers and strengthening of defences at a number of sites to the events following the intervention of Count Theodosius in Britain after the crisis years of 367–68, that too has been challenged (with some examples now dated to the mid-fourth century or earlier). The lesson to be learned is that, in the absence of unequivocal historical references or epigraphic evidence, there will be problems of fit between dating frameworks for defensive circuits based on the *terminus post quem* principle and the application of unitary historical explanations. Table 12 summarizes the current state of knowledge about the urban defences of the major towns and the largest of the small towns. The overlap in size and the similarities in phases of development for certain of the lesser sites are striking.

What were defences for? Answers have tended to concentrate on their military value in times of crisis. The Boudican revolt had seen the destruction of three towns lacking defences and this failure may have encouraged the more permissive attitude to their provision at a comparatively early date at other British towns. The literary sources suggest that the prime military threat in late Roman times came from small groups of seaborne raiders. Even in the absence of any significant numbers of soldiers stationed at a walled town, the existence of defences significantly elevated the risks for the attackers and may have prompted them to seek softer targets. But walled circuits provided more than simply emergency cover for the civil population. The threats of banditry were reduced and towns and their associated markets were easier places to police if gates could be shut at night.

Walls and gates could also have been symbols of civic status, competition and pride. At several towns it is clear that gates were designed as especially grandiose elements, with masonry structures being constructed in association with earthworks at St Albans and Cirencester, for instance, and the Balkerne Gate at Colchester incorporated an earlier monumental archway. Appearance more than defensive capacity was clearly a significant concern, and earthworks and walled circuits delineated the urban sphere and emphasized status.

The very large circuits at many sites, far exceeding the densely built-up core of towns such as St Albans, Wroxeter and London, would also suggest that defensive issues were secondary. Even the addition of projecting towers on the exterior of the walls in the fourth century may have been less defensive in intent that at first appears. At St Albans, such towers were only added to the stretch of wall on the south-east side visible on the approach from London. Any enemy considering an attack on the town would quickly work out that the rest of the circuit was far weaker, but the addition of a few towers provided a grand façade to greet, for instance, the governor visiting from London.

In summary, defensive circuits fronted by wide ditches presented a significant obstacle to small raiding parties, reinforced the sense of community of the main towns, facilitated policing and projected ideas about status. It is unlikely that the state put much of its own resources into the provision of urban defences, so towns would have had to find the means to fund them, to the detriment of other aspects of the civic building programme. Other provinces might have more magnificent public buildings, but the British towns may have felt compensated by their walls. The emergence of new forms of identity within towns may have also favoured the construction of boundaries, as a psychological reinforcement of the degrees of difference between urban and military communities, between townsfolk and countryfolk. Many towns possessed extensive suburbs outside their walls, of course, and the extent to which these were rendered non-urban as a result merits further investigation – for instance, there are suggestive differences in coin-loss patterns (based on comparisons of coins found in urban and suburban contexts). Defences around a core part of the urban centre were symbolic of *urbanitas*, a particular sort of lifestyle. For a farmer bringing produce to market or for a soldier moving along the provincial roads, the entrance to a town was marked by a physical transition from one identity realm to another.

The shape of the enclosed area may give us further clues to the underlying mentality behind their construction. Although almost all major British urban centres had regular rectilinear road grids, the defensive circuits often took on a polygonal form. The chief exceptions were the veteran *coloniae* where a rectangular form was favoured, even in extensions beyond the original line of legionary fortress defences that provided their initial basis. However, many of the *civitas* centres showed a preference for a different layout, based on multi-sided shapes or ovals. The third-century wall at Silchester bore an uncanny resemblance in shape and area to the long-buried late Iron Age inner earthwork. While emulating the higher-echelon towns in possessing defences, the adoption of a style of layout that evoked late Iron Age *oppida* reveals a less straightforwardly 'Roman' urban identity at play. The fact that many of the early urban circuits were earthworks, rather than masonry walls, further emphasizes possible links with memories of a British proto-urban past.

The fifty or so walled small towns are more of an enigma, since such sites were less likely to have had the resources to pay for their circuits; indeed many small towns never received walls and the majority of those that did appear to be late in date. In a number of cases, particularly with the smallest defended enclaves attached to roadside settlements, we may suspect the state to have taken action to protect some important function of the site (for example, a series along Watling Street may have been part of the public post system or have served as tax-collection points or grain depots for military supply). Some walled small towns could have marked the crossover points along the major highways between individual provinces within the late Roman Diocese of Britain. At the larger settlements, the potential towns and walled garrison settlements, the construction of defences may only have proved feasible for the community if the building programme was spread across a number of years.

CHANGE AND REORIENTATION

There were a number of reasons why towns shrank in size or diminished in vitality. In addition to broader economic trends, we should remember the role of natural disasters. In the Mediterranean, earthquakes were a major hazard, especially during a period of heightened seismic activity in the 360s. By contrast, in the timber-and-thatch towns of the north-western provinces, fire was the greatest danger and, to judge from the archaeological evidence, it had a significant impact. The Boudican destruction of Colchester, London and St Albans set back the urban programme in Britain by a generation. Both St Albans and London also suffered major fire damage in the mid-second century, due in part to the large numbers of buildings that were of timber construction alongside the stone public buildings. At St Albans, this can be dated to 155–60 and affected about a third of the built-up area. In parts of the core area, rebuilding was a slow process and some plots were still empty 50–100 years later. There appears to have been a reduced level of economic activity after the fire, with fewer workshops than in the early Antonine phase. There are hints of a further major fire in the town in the late third or early fourth century, though the effects of this are less clearly mapped. London seems to have been even more prone to fire damage, with extensive destruction attributed to major conflagrations in the late

Flavian, Hadrianic and Antonine periods and more localized incidents of third- and fourth-century date. The Hadrianic fire (*c.* 120–25) appears to have been the most extensive, although the forum and basilica complex was spared. Rebuilding on many sites was relatively quick, but less dense and with less evidence for commercial and manufacturing activity, suggesting that by the mid-second century the town was economically past its prime.

Other factors that could have affected the vitality of later Roman towns include the impact of plague and other contagions. There is historical evidence of plague reaching the western empire in the 160s and demographic models for the later empire continue to attribute a significant impact to cyclical outbreaks thereafter. However, there is no certainty that it ever reached Britain – for once, Britain's isolation and dead-end status may have worked to its advantage – and if it did the effects were probably focused on major ports, such as London. In any event, towns in antiquity were unhealthy enough places without the incidence of plague. Especially when densely built up and populous, they were net consumers of people – that is, they could not sustain their population levels by natural reproduction, but had to attract additional migrants from the surrounding countryside or further afield. An important question to pose, therefore, is whether this balance was maintained in the fourth century and later, or whether a reduction in economic migration into towns reduced their long-term sustainability.

Some caution is required in interpreting decline in commercial and manufacturing activity at major towns. One obvious issue is whether the diminution in activity there was compensated for by growth elsewhere, most notably in the small towns, which have been interpreted as becoming more important economically in the late Roman period.

The late Roman civil administration of Britain is shadowy indeed and it is only because of the chance survival of the bureaucratic listings in the *Notitia Dignitatum* that we can sketch the outline. The *Notitia* provides us with the names of five provinces within the British Diocese (*Maxima Caesariensis, Flavia Caesariensis, Britannia Prima, Britannia Secunda* and *Valentia*). The first four of these names also appear in the earlier *Verona List*, dating to *c.*312–14. It may well be that *Maxima Caesariensis*, which had a governor of consular rank, was centred on London, but we lack independent proof of that. There is an inscription from Cirencester that refers poetically to a *rector* or ruler of *Prima*

Britannia, L. Septimius [...], that is commonly accepted as evidence that *Britannia Prima* had its capital there. Maps of Roman Britain routinely shuffle the positions of the remaining two provinces, *Britannia Secunda* and *Flavia Caesariensis*, with proposed capitals being York and Lincoln. The truth is we do not know even these basic facts. The *Notitia* does supply the additional information that London was the base of the finance minister and keeper of the Privy Purse for the Diocese. There was an active mint in London at some points in the fourth century, reflecting its role as a regional treasury. It is thus probable that the *Vicarius* of Britain was also based there. A final piece of information in the *Notitia* concerns the location of a state weaving works (*gynaeceum*) at a town called *Venta*, though with no further clue as to which of the three British sites with this name was meant. What we can establish from these various snippets is that towns remained important elements of the late Roman provincial administration of Britain.

Excluding milestones, there are few unequivocally fourth-century stone inscriptions from Britain that shed light on the late towns. The Cirencester text of the *praeses* L. Septimius marked the re-dedication of a Jupiter column, and perhaps dates to the early fourth century (though some favour the brief pagan revival in the early 360s under Julian). About 150 Jupiter columns are known, mainly in north Gaul and Germany, and the monument clearly conflated Roman and northern European pagan practices. The Cirencester monument is the only certain example in Britain, and the fact that its dedicator was the governor raises questions about its wider relevance to British urban religious practice.

A series of building stones from Hadrian's Wall attests the involvement in renovation work of contingents from the *civitates* of the *Durotriges*, *Dumnonii* and *Catuvellauni*, but the assignment of these texts to reconstruction post-368 is entirely hypothetical and they could be earlier in date. They do at least suggest that the *civitates* were still meaningful political units in late Roman times. Assuming that they are of third- or fourth-century date, they represent trans-provincial movement of labour corvées.

Given that the imperial bureaucracy was larger in the fourth century than in the first or second, the lack of civic epigraphic testimony is telling. The senior officials of the Roman state were not exhibiting the epigraphic habit in the same way as before and though similar trends can be observed in other provinces, the picture from Britain is particularly stark. In part the change reflects broader shifts in Roman society, which was increasingly dominated by people of humble origin from the European military provinces. The old-money aristocracies of the Mediterranean provinces were increasingly sidelined. The values of the new ruling order were somewhat different and thus their identity package was quite distinct. The decline in public inscriptions and honorific statues brought the western empire more into line with northern European trends. However, this was not an illiterate bureaucracy, as documents such as the *Notitia* or the imperial rescripts gathered in the Theodosian and Justinianic Law Codes demonstrate. It was the public display of literate skills that was now more muted and other aspects, notably dress, ornamentation and social ceremony, were given greater prominence. The tendency for civil officials to imitate the dress fashions of the late Roman army was another manifestation of the change in the ruling order and it is probable that some members of the provincial elite may likewise have adopted Germanic fashions of brooches and belt fittings.

Our image of a typical Roman town is focused on the impressive public buildings that lay at its core and that had involved a great deal of conspicuous investment in the second century in particular. The fact that at many towns we find these buildings falling into disrepair or ruin, or having a radically changed function, by the fourth century is thus often hailed as signalling the decline of town life more broadly. The evidence is clear in a number of specific cases, but the situation was not uniform in all towns. The forum/basilica complex was central to public administration in the early empire, so major changes in these buildings ought to be significant. Modern excavations at Silchester have demonstrated that the basilica was given over to metalworking by the end of the third century, though of a relatively well-ordered kind and not simply some sort of squatter activity. The basilica at Caerwent was largely demolished by the mid-fourth century, after which time metalworking hearths and furnaces were erected within the nave and aisle spaces. At Wroxeter, the forum and basilica were fire-damaged around 300 and not rebuilt, while at Leicester the basilica and the adjacent market both appear to have been damaged beyond repair by a fourth-century fire. The Gloucester forum ranges were demolished and replaced with a cobbled surface. London, as perhaps the foremost centre of late Roman administration, is even more striking. Its huge forum/basilica complex had been systematically demolished around 300. Exeter's forum/basilica appears to have been renovated in the mid-fourth century at least, though it too was demolished at some point in the late fourth century to be succeeded by open ground and metalworking activity, then by a cemetery. That at Caistor-by-Norwich was rebuilt on a reduced scale in the late third century (though after lying derelict for perhaps fifty years following a major fire).

What is the significance of the loss or change in use of the prime civic spaces of the earlier townscapes? First, it is clear from the time that it took some towns to construct these amenities in the first place that local administration did not depend on their possession. The functions of civic administration and the local judiciary could be fulfilled without a forum/basilica complex. The extension of Roman citizenship in 212 brought larger numbers of people under Roman law, as opposed to local customary law, and will have increased the importance of the assize courts. One reason for the multiplication of governorships may have been to provide additional magistrates in a more standardized legal system. Local courts at the *civitas* centres may have been rendered less significant or obsolete in consequence. The loss of the basilica at London is harder to explain, but the second-century building may have been too large and expensive to maintain. London's court (which must still have existed) may have relocated into a smaller building elsewhere within the town. In all these cases, though, we need to recognize that what followed on was not disorganized squatter occupation, but a regulated reuse of public space, whether for systematic metalworking, as open space, or as a quarry for building materials.

Other categories of civic buildings reveal similar patterns of changed use or abandonment in the fourth century. The theatre at St Albans appears to have been very dilapidated by the late third century and, despite signs of a final refurbishment around 300, within a short while the orchestra area was being used as a municipal rubbish tip. The close association between theatres and temples (and by implication with pagan festivals) could account for the progressive loss of this sort of facility during the increasingly Christian-dominated fourth century. The same pattern seems in general to hold for amphitheatres, as at London (also redundant *c.*300), reflecting changing attitudes to public bloodletting as sport. Again, the loss of such public amenities must be offset against the systematic use of the buildings as rubbish dumps, for instance, implying a continuing administrative authority.

Of fifteen major public bath buildings, nine were still operational *c.*300, but none a century later. Large bath buildings were very expensive to maintain and run and the progressive loss of such facilities in towns may initially at least reflect a more selfish investment by the elite in smaller-scale bath-suites in their town houses and on their villa estates, rather than an outright rejection of Roman-style bathing. The meticulous excavation of the baths basilica site at Wroxeter has revealed evidence of continued orderly use of the structure long after its original function ceased in the early fourth century. Even when the roof was removed, the floor was carefully repaved with reused stone roof tiles, perhaps as an open market space. Regulation of public space by an urban authority appears to have continued here well into the fifth century, before the site was finally taken over by what looks like an individual remodelling of the area around a timber hall.

The late Roman/late antique town was thus very different from the high imperial town, with less need of public building complexes, reduced investment by the elite in the maintenance of amenities such as major baths and in entertainment buildings that were often linked to pagan festivals, such as theatres, or to practices that were abhorrent to Christians, such as amphitheatre games. Nonetheless, the early onset and the extent of change within the British towns are striking.

Analysis of the occupation pattern in 1,400 domestic structures in Romano-British towns suggests a sharp decline by the later fourth century. There are of course various factors that could contribute to this apparent collapse of occupation in towns, not least the vulnerability of the latest archaeological phases to subsequent disturbance or truncation. The virtual cessation of manufacturing and marketing networks by the early fifth century also limits severely our ability to date later activity at these sites, but the pottery supply and coin lists should be stronger for the later fourth century than they are. Compilation of data on the fills of rubbish pits and wells from Roman London, for instance, has revealed a dramatic fall in the volume of material after 150; the late Roman period, although showing partial recovery from a nadir in the period 150–250, is notably low in comparison to the early second-century town. This is relatively typical of towns in eastern England, some in the west seeming to have fared better, as at Cirencester.

In terms both of the aggregate figures for occupancy of domestic buildings in general and of the detailed structural evidence of housing at specific sites, the data indicate that occupation levels in Romano-British towns remained quite high into the early fourth century, but showed significant reduction after 350. On the other hand, large and well-appointed town houses were far more a feature of the late Roman town in Britain than they had been of the early phases of urbanization. These were rare before c.150 and the maximum levels of occupancy occurred between 200 and 350, with an overall peak c.300. The essence of this analysis is that the numbers of elite houses occupied plummeted after 350 in line with the overall pattern for domestic structures, so that only about one tenth the number remained in 400 as had existed in 300. Architecturally, the elite urban house followed Roman fashions in design and decoration. Some of these were winged corridor houses similar to the classic rural villas typical of the northern provinces, but others were courtyard houses of more Mediterranean aspect. Interior decoration commonly comprised mosaics and painted wall-plaster, generally closely following Mediterranean models. The aisled-hall house, frequently encountered in rural villas and perhaps more evocative of British traditions, is relatively rare among the urban elite residences. In broad terms, then, the trend in elite urban housing reflects the consolidation over time of an increasingly 'Roman' private identity that is at variance with the evidence for the loss of significance of civic buildings and public display. At least down to the mid-fourth century, most towns had the personnel to fulfil the required functions of urban-based local government.

Some caution is needed about the generality of the late Roman reduction in the density of urban activity. The long-held view of Silchester as a garden town, with low-density stone housing, stands corrected by recent excavations in insula IX that have shown a previously unrecognized density of timber buildings along the road frontages, between the known stone buildings. Many of these commercial properties continued in occupation down to the end of the fourth century. The relative lack of later disturbance to the latest Roman levels and the comparatively large open-area excavations have been important factors in achieving this new vision. At present the site is exceptional in the way it appears to buck the trend of economic decline.

Individual buildings evidently remained in occupation until a very late date, but the extent to which these were exceptional survivals is controversial. The key evidence comes from excavation of insula

XXVII.2 at St Albans. Here, it is argued, a substantial courtyard mansion was constructed in the last quarter of the fourth century, with over twenty rooms, many with tessellated or mosaic floors and one room with underfloor heating. Subsequent modification and rebuildings on the same site appear to demonstrate the vitality of St Albans well into the fifth century. However, the structure is thus far unique for both St Albans and Britain at this date. It cannot serve as the basis of a general model of urban vitality and continuity into the fifth century. Indeed a recent reconsideration of the evidence has suggested that the initial construction of the house could be considerably earlier than the original excavator suggested and more in line with the normal pattern of late town houses.

The existence of rural types of building within the late towns is well established and some clearly retained their farming function in relation to cultivated land close at hand, as in a complex on the fringe of Cirencester. Coupled with the apparent decline in commercial and manufacturing activity at major towns, this has prompted some to question whether the balance of activity at towns was shifting away from traditional 'urban' lifeways towards rural ones.

Another major point of debate about the state of the late Roman towns of Britain concerns the interpretation of deep deposits of dark earth that have been recorded at a number of sites overlying the rubble marking Roman abandonment horizons – examples include London (and Southwark), St Albans, Canterbury, Lincoln, Gloucester and Winchester. No surfaces or structures have been identified within the dark earth layers, but they do contain Roman artefacts. One traditional interpretation of these soil layers is that they represent localized areas of the townscape that became devoid of buildings in the fourth or early fifth century and were given over to cultivation. The discussion about the nature of the dark earth is still unresolved, with some experts claiming the soil to be certainly imported and dumped to enable cultivation, others that the build-up of organic-rich layers could be the result of new patterns of rubbish disposal within abandoned areas of the town, yet others that it may represent the biological transformation of *in situ* occupation levels through the action of a particular type of worm, in combination with an increased use of simple mud walls for urban houses. The first two interpretations support the general view of overall decline in urban function and population levels, the last alternative implies that late Roman occupation was a good deal more dynamic than indicated by the remains of stone-walled houses. All the interpretations attest something other than passive decay within largely abandoned sites. If building plots had been abandoned, they were put to new use, whether as allotments or for rubbish disposal.

Public buildings may have been a dispensable luxury, but there were other civic services that were perhaps less so. Maintenance of streets, water supply and cemeteries provides complementary evidence of the relative vitality of Romano-British towns. Much has been made of the apparent functioning of a piped water system at St Albans well into the fifth century, implying the continued maintenance of an aqueduct. Overall, the evidence from towns in Britain suggests that rainwater collection, wells and springs may have been more important sources of potable water than expensive long-range transport of water by aqueducts. London and Southwark have yielded close to 100 wells and the extensively excavated sites of Silchester and Caerwent 76 and 16 wells respectively. Some of these were undoubtedly still functioning in the fourth century. However, the detailed evidence from London shows a decline in the overall number of active wells and the migration of elite housing across the townscape from areas previously provided by wells or public piped water supply to the area of the lower Walbrook, where an active springline still functioned. The implication is that with an increasingly less reliable public system of supply, the wealthier inhabitants chose to relocate their houses to areas where they could most easily tap groundwater supplies.

Once again, the most significant change may have occurred in the later fourth century. One reason for the final failure of public bath complexes could have been problems with maintaining an aqueduct-fed water supply. There are indications of blocked sewers at York and a number of other sites. Maintenance of roads (especially resurfacing) was comparatively rare in the later fourth century and at Gloucester one road near the forum was not only abandoned but was being actively quarried by the 390s.

Another clear indicator of the state of urban services concerns rubbish disposal. Urban societies produce a lot of waste, both organic and inorganic, and need to evolve strategies to dispose of this or suffer the consequences of unhygienic conditions, smell, rodents, and so on. Extraction or burial of rubbish from the core of an urban site would be the expected response of an orderly society. Removal to external dumps by communities required transport animals and vehicles, labour to collect and carry it and land outside the town on which to dispose of it. There is evidence that some Roman towns elsewhere in the empire made such provision, but in general it is probable that burial was the more common response. Some major developments in British towns offered unprecedented opportunities to dispose of accumulating rubbish – as the mass of material deposited behind the timber riverfront wharves or the partial infilling of the Walbrook valley in London both demonstrate.

Repeated references in the modern literature to unburied rubbish and increased urban squalor would seem to herald significantly declining standards. On the other hand the evidence is not entirely straightforward. The final Roman phases in British towns stand out as a period of ruins and rubbish because of what followed them, whereas earlier periods of activity were often capped by further development. Much rubbish in Roman towns was incorporated into each successive act of construction – thus material from a building destroyed in a fire in the mid-second century might be incorporated in the foundations of the next building on the site. But what if, as seems clear in a number of instances, the site had stood derelict for fifty years before redevelopment? A vacant lot might serve as an open rubbish heap for a considerable period, before the next builder on the site faced up to the problem of where to put the accumulated material. Early Roman towns may thus occasionally have been rather squalid environments.

Nonetheless, a reduction in building activity and progressive abandonment of buildings in the later fourth century clearly increased the amount of unburied rubbish. It is human nature not to wish to carry rubbish further than necessary and in the case of night soil the nearest street was evidently far enough. Bearing in mind that the use of animals for transport of goods and people will have introduced a good deal of ordure on to the average urban street, the tolerance of human waste being added to the mix is perhaps a little less surprising. More bulky items could be disposed of in a variety of ways, but recourse to 'fly-tipping' rather than digging a big pit in the back yard is a typically selfish human response. We can trace this sort of activity in empty houses and building lots (St Albans), accessible sections of urban defensive ditches (London) and so on. Private dumping in town ditches must have been officially discouraged, but if no civic rubbish collection was practised, how could the urban authorities regulate the accumulation of rubbish within the town? One possibility is that they could attempt to direct rubbish disposal towards selected locations, such as public buildings that no longer served their original function. The late fourth-century infilling of the orchestra of the theatre at St Albans with domestic rubbish may have been a pragmatic use of the space and, rather than suggesting increasingly anarchic conditions, it may represent a continuation of urban authority. If the urban population shrank considerably in the later fourth century, then the scale of the problem of rubbish disposal was also correspondingly reduced in comparison to earlier urban phases. In sum, there is no doubt that, in common with most pre-industrial societies, the late Roman town was dirty and smelly, but whether this was actually worse than the conditions in earlier centuries is far from certain.

Cemeteries are potentially an excellent measure of the vitality of urban life. Until quite recently there were few well-published, large-scale excavations of Romano-British cemeteries, making generalization hazardous. This picture is rapidly changing and one area of archaeology where we can now detect a pronounced expansion of data in the fourth century concerns cemetery data.

Late Roman funerary practices were diverse, in part aligned with trends in other north-western provinces, in part providing dim echoes of traditional insular preoccupations. As in much of the western empire, cremation was gradually replaced by inhumation in the late second to third centuries as the predominant rite. Though a number of cemeteries have yielded late third- and fourth-century cremations, these are rare at major urban sites and more representative of the military, minor settlements and rural communities. Many British towns have produced evidence for the emergence in the fourth century of large, managed inhumation cemeteries outside their walls, in areas distinct from earlier cremation grounds. It is equally clear that these cemeteries did not continue far into the fifth century, but, as with other key elements of urban life, fundamental practices and behaviours ceased.

Poundbury by Dorchester, Lankhills by Winchester and Bath Gate by Cirencester all continued in use as organized burial grounds to the late fourth or early fifth century at the latest. The Newarke Street cemetery at Leicester appears to be predominantly a later fourth-century development and, like Poundbury, features Christian burial traditions. A number of small towns have also been shown to have had extensive fourth-century inhumation cemeteries (Ilchester, Dorchester-on-Thames), but some sites have revealed a pattern of individual burials (or small groups) close to the edges of defined 'backlands' plots, standing behind individual buildings on the road frontage (as noted at Shepton Mallet, Ilchester, Alcester). Similar features have even been noted in suburban contexts outside some of the major towns, as at Leicester. There was clearly a strong distinction between traditions of interment in a public cemetery outside the settlement and in private 'familial' plots in close proximity to domestic structures. The latter tradition may well be a more rural practice and its appearance at towns in the later fourth century is another indication that at some sites there may have been a blurring of old distinctions.

While the cemeteries of Roman London were largely engulfed by the rapid nineteenth-century expansion of the city, the existence of substantial burial grounds has been demonstrated on the west, north and east sides of the walled Roman town and across the river on the southern flank of the Southwark suburb. In recent decades, a sample comprising c.300 cremations and 1,000 inhumations has been excavated from several of the main cemetery areas. In general, cemetery areas moved outwards from the town, as expansion occurred from the first century onwards. In consequence, some early burials have been found within the area that was later walled; conversely, at the unwalled South-wark settlement, late Roman contraction of the occupied area saw late burials cut through earlier buildings. Some inhumations were in wooden coffins, while in many cases only the presence of a shroud can be surmised. There are a few rare examples of lead-lined coffins (some with elaborately decorated lids) and some lead and timber coffins featured chalk packed around the body (a practice similar to gypsum burials recorded at York and suggested as a Christian preference). A small number of stone sarcophagi have been recorded and sometimes these contained lead inserts, as in the case of a rich female burial from Spitalfields.

In extensively excavated inhumation cemeteries, the majority of sexed skeletons were adult males. The most extensively excavated area of London's eastern cemetery had a male:female ratio of 1.7:1, only 25 per cent of skeletons were of children/adolescents, and these figures are typical. Given the probable level of infant mortality in the Roman world (perhaps 50 per cent died before age ten), children should proportionally outnumber adults in cemeteries. The explanation of these apparent demographic imbalances could relate to social practice (an adult male was more often granted the expense of an individual burial), or alternatively in different strategies of, and separate areas designated for, disposal for women and children, or it could reflect some genuine peculiarity of late Roman urban society, with a preponderance of males due either to greater rates of migration of men from countryside to town or to the impact of female infanticide. Rural cemeteries and the Poundbury data show a far closer balance in men to women in the population at large, so the answer is more likely to relate to social practices of disposal of the dead at some urban centres. The women and children who made it into these cemeteries may have been disproportionately representative of selected elements of society.

Perceptions about status and identity have been one of the chief motors for funerary ritual and practice. Status can be reflected in several different ways: through the funeral process itself, the treatment of the body, the location of burial, the provision of material goods for the deceased, the construction of the grave and surface marking of the spot. In many societies, expensive ceremonies and rituals mark death and burial as a means of both paying respect to the deceased and reflecting the social status (real or projected) of the family and heirs. While the bulk of the urban population does not seem to have embraced epigraphic commemoration, and high-status masonry above-ground structures are uncommon, the comparative rarity of intercutting of graves suggests that the location of graves was generally visible (wooden markers or low mounds?) and remembered for some time. High-status burials at towns represent a small minority of the interments and seem to confirm that even in late Roman times the urban elite remained a restricted group in society. They may also have used both urban cemeteries and rural burial grounds associated with villas.

Whereas cremation burials of the early empire were frequently accompanied by grave goods, either placed on the pyre with the body, or directly in the grave with all or part of the pyre debris, the late Roman burial rite marked a distinct change in fashion. Such items occur in only a minority of inhumation burials and Christian influence seems to have exacerbated a trend that was already present in pagan cemeteries. Where there were inclusions in late Roman burials these are almost invariably of great interest. Patterns of deposition suggest some distinct regional peculiarities, though with broad similarities in status-marked burials at both urban and rural sites. Shoes appear to have been a frequent inclusion (most easily identified when of the hob-nailed variety) and more often accompanied males in Essex, but with a more equal male to female distribution of shoes/boots in burials in Dorset and Somerset. The growing body of evidence reveals huge complexity and diversity. A key distinction to be made concerns whether the personal artefacts were worn by the body interred, or whether these items were simply placed alongside a shroud-wrapped corpse. If we see a clothed body adorned with personal ornament and accompanied by grave offerings, such as pots or glass vessels, as essentially non-Christian, it is apparent that some parts of the country demonstrated continuing pagan identities more strongly than others. The West Country from Dorset through Somerset, Avon and Gloucestershire stands out, for instance, as a region of strong pagan tradition. The similarity between burial rites in town and country suggests that the primary identity markers being displayed were ones of religious and social status. To the extent that 'urban' and 'rural' identities were expressed in funerary ritual, it was the location and internal organization of the cemetery that conveyed the clearest sense of difference.

One of the most interesting groups of material in burials concerns new styles of belts, indicative of official status and on the Continent generally closely associated with the field army and officials. These sometimes occur in association with the crossbow brooch, another high-status item. The later fourth-century cemetery at Lankhills, Winchester, has yielded a clearly defined group of these unusually furnished burials (also including a female equivalent with bracelets and other jewellery). Links can be drawn with a pair of male and female graves at Dyke Hills, Dorchester-on-Thames. The closest parallels for these graves in terms of rituals and personal adornments are from the Rhine frontier region and the possibility that they mark the presence of Germans has been much canvassed, though with no agreement as to whether these people were elements of the field army, irregular levies from an allied people (*foederati*), other imperial officials (not necessarily Germans) or simply members of the provincial elite adopting the trappings of the powerful. The likelihood is that this group was expressing a strongly held sense of identity that differentiated them from their fellows in the late Roman towns and they may well have been German. An involvement in late Roman government is also highly probable. Further examples of these distinctive late Roman belts, brooches and accoutrements come from other towns in southern Britain, including London, Water Newton and St Albans.

Some of the late Romano-British burial rites conform to Continental practices, but others suggest more insular traditions. A peculiarity of many British cemeteries in the civil zone is the inclusion of individuals or groups of decapitated people. These burials are not attested at military settlements, or at Colchester and Lincoln. Exceptional examples have been noted at London, Gloucester and a number of other major towns (Chichester, Winchester, Dorchester, Cirencester, Leicester, York), but the type is more common at small towns and rural sites.

Another key issue with late Roman cemeteries is how to distinguish between pagan and Christian burials, especially in the early phases of Christianity, when practice was hybrid, showed continued adherence to some earlier pagan traditions, and when burial grounds were less segregated on religious lines. A number of factors have been identified as potentially indicative of Christian practice: west–east orientation, supine posture, lack of or few grave goods, clustering around special enclosures/mausolea, and plaster or gypsum packing around selected special burials. When found in combination there does seem a higher likelihood in the interpretation. One of the most convincing cases of a Christian cemetery is at Poundbury (Dorchester), which provides the largest single sample of excavated burials. The burial ground is made up of a series of linked enclosures that may have been in broadly contemporary use, and analysis suggests that some areas of the cemetery were possibly pagan, alongside a core area with strong Christian associations. This latter area was characterized by west–east aligned burials, with comparatively few grave goods, but with other indications of higher-status burials being present (lead coffins, plaster burials and a few mausolea with painted decoration).

Burials inside the town limits were proscribed by Roman law and, with the exception of infant burials which are not uncommon beneath buildings and the odd apparent murder pit, British towns seem to have followed this pattern until near the end of their life. Exceptions appear in the fifth century, in the form of a multiple grave from Canterbury, or burials within the fora at Exeter and Lincoln (the last example associated with the early church beneath St Paul in the Bail).

The fourth century was marked by cataclysmic changes in religious practice across the empire – commencing with a wave of savage persecutions of Christians and ending with the situation reversed and paganism proscribed. A key step was the outlawing in 341 of pagan temples within urban limits, though the archaeological evidence does not support quite so abrupt a cessation of pagan activity within towns. On the other hand, one of London's main classical temple precincts was replaced by a complex interpreted as a palace of the usurper Allectus (dated by dendrochronology to 293–94), and the temple at the small town of Godmanchester was demolished in the late third century. However, some pagan structures endured well into the fourth century, as at Bath and the London *mithraeum* (though the latter was perhaps rededicated at some point in the fourth century to Bacchus). Coin dedications at Bath had diminished considerably by the mid-fourth century and ceased by *c.*390. In fact an overall survey of the dated examples of Romano-Celtic temples (both urban and rural) reveals that numbers peaked in the early fourth century, in much the same way as did town houses, mosaics, villas and so on. Late fourth-century repressive measures taken against pagan cults emphasize the fact that in some areas paganism remained strong.

More surprising perhaps is the relative lack of evidence of urban churches in Britain, although across the Roman world churches in the urban core are relatively rarely documented until the late fourth century. A large basilica partially excavated near the Tower may conceivably represent the late fourth-century cathedral of London, though a secular use of the building cannot be excluded. A small timber church was inserted into the centre of the forum piazza at Lincoln, beneath the later church of St Paul in the Bail, and may date to the late Roman period. Given that there were at least three British bishoprics at the time of the Council of Arles in 314 (London, York and Lincoln), there ought to have been churches at these centres dating to the first half of the fourth century. Other possible Christian churches remain poorly published (Icklingham), controversial (Silchester) or unexcavated (Wroxeter).

British bishops do not seem to have proliferated in the same numbers as those from other provinces (or they did not attend later councils en masse) and this suggests that the impact of Christianity within the towns was a qualified success. The three bishops and a priest who attended the Council at Arles in 314 presumably represented the four provincial capitals. Three British bishops at a Church Council at Rimini in 360 had only been able to attend through the support of state funds for their travel expenses, because of a lack of private support. This might suggest an impoverished and small British Church, but there are suggestions of greater wealth and vitality. For example, there is some evidence of the activity of bishops beyond the three or four main towns and of the accumulation of wealth within the Church. A lost silver dish of probable British manufacture from Risley Park in Derbyshire refers to its presentation to a church by Bishop Exuperius. Fragments of lead pans used in salt production from Cheshire mention both a Bishop Viventius and another clergyman. The involvement of the Church in manufacturing activity is paralleled in other regions. The location of the see of Viventius is uncertain, though the recognition of a probable church at Wroxeter suggests one possibility. Lead tanks with Christian symbols have been found at several sites in eastern England and may have served as baptismal fonts.

A major hoard of late fourth-century Christian silverware found at the small town of *Durobrivae* (Water Newton) included four inscribed silver vessels out of a total of nine recovered, an inscribed gold roundel and nine inscribed silver votive plaques out of seventeen examples in the hoard. The inscriptions on two of the vessels indicate that they had been specifically presented to a church as offerings, one by Innocentia and Viventia, the other by Publianus. The dedication of the latter refers explicitly to 'prostrating myself, Lord, I honour your sacred sanctuary'. The plaques are similar in design to the leaf-shaped votives of pagan tradition employed at shrines in southern Britain in earlier times. One of the votive plaques bears, in addition to a large chi-rho, the inscription *Iamcilla* or *Amcilla votum quod promisit conplevit*, perhaps best rendered 'The female servant of the lord (*ancilla*) has fulfilled the vow which she promised.' This is simply a Christian expression of a long-established form of worship as we have seen in earlier chapters.

The urban story of Britain in the Roman empire is one of retarded development and premature contraction. The explanation of the changing nature of towns is in part an economic one, but it is in part also socially contingent. It is a paradox that the towns provide some of the most striking evidence of physical change under Roman rule, often on a monumental scale. Yet, although urban centres played a crucial role in shaping political and economic development, and in determining the material culture, social outlook and identities of a significant group of the population, Roman urbanism did not endure. This can only partly be blamed on what followed after. The roots of the urban culture propagated by Rome were too shallow and the social bedding in which it was planted not fertile enough. The evidence presented here suggests that not only were the late Roman towns very different in appearance and outlook from their early Roman precursors, but that they experienced profound change and decline in the period after 350. Well before the notional 'end' of Britain as Roman territory c.409, it will have been increasingly clear that town life as people knew it was not sustainable, and by 450 at the latest it had gone completely. What endured beyond that point within the old urban centres was a different sort of life and was based on new political or social structures. The early Germanic rulers of eastern Britain did not need towns.

PART FOUR

The Rural Communities

12

The Villa and the Roundhouse

A fundamental principle of Roman provincial government was the differential treatment of defeated or submitted enemies, and a specific context of differentiation was land. The settlement of the land after conquest was often a protracted process, in which the army, specialist surveyors known as the *agrimensores* (literally 'land measurers') and the various branches of imperial government (provincial governors, juridical legates and procurators) all played their part. Although Britain was one of the last provinces to be added to the empire, the treatment of land there can be assumed to have followed in broad terms the established practice of centuries of Roman expansionism. The following quote from one of the *agrimensores*, Siculus Flaccus, summarizes the process.

Certain peoples, with pertinacity, have waged war against the Romans, others having once experienced Roman military valour, have kept the peace, others who had encountered Rome's good faith and justice, declared their submission to the Romans and frequently took up arms against their enemies. This is why each people has received a legal settlement according to merit: it would not have been just if those who had so frequently broken the peace and had committed perjury and taken the initiative in making war, were seen to be offered the same guarantees as loyal peoples.

As a starting point, the lands of defeated or submitted peoples (*dediticii*) were considered the property of the people of Rome (imperial property was in some ways a sub-set of this broad category), to be disposed of as she chose. Some lands were habitually seized and re-assigned in specified allotments to Roman colonists (typically time-expired legionary veterans). A proportion of conquered territory commonly remained as state lands (*ager publicus* and later frequently in the form of imperial estates), which would be leased out and yield revenue. Lands were also reassigned to subject peoples in proportion to their perceived merit (*ager assignati*), often after a suitable interval of military control and uncertainty. Lands were attached to a *civitas* or other major town in two ways, directly and indirectly. Direct allocations often included a grant of land to a town, which could be rented out to provide a source of income to support the local administration conducted there. The administrative and financial territory of a town also covered lands indirectly assigned to its control. These generally included substantial areas in private ownership or lease-hold, whether created by Rome through personal gift, direct sales or long-term leases. All of the lands that were not state owned or allocated to colonists appear to have carried a *vectigal* or tribute payment; again, the level of this may have been scaled to reflect the relative favour in which particular groups were held. Direct land sales within the broad territory previously controlled by a particular group could open up ownership to outsiders, whether retired soldiers, Romans from outside Britain (notably from Gaul, but extending up through society to include senators) or incomers from other regions of Britain. External proprietors might sub-let to native Britons or supplant them.

Looked at from another perspective, in extreme cases native Britons might find their lands definitively alienated (after an initial period where they had been permitted to remain on their traditional farms in return for paying tribute) or that they had been converted into tenants of a private estate of an absentee landlord. On the other hand, preferential treatment for certain favoured Britons is to be expected. As Siculus Flaccus noted: 'among the defeated not all saw their lands seized. In practice, the dignity of certain individuals, the gratitude or friendship of Rome impelled the victor to concede to them their own traditional lands.'

The initial conquest of Britain thus brought about major changes in land proprietorship and, to a lesser extent, land occupancy. The establishment of colonies involved assignation of land, the army carved out legionary territories, the Roman state designated large tracts as *ager publicus* or imperial property (especially in areas with natural resources). It is apparent that even after a first land deduction, an indigenous community might find a second block of territory taken away for a growing colony in the vicinity – there are hints of just such problems at Colchester before the Boudican revolt.

Many rural districts were placed under the supervision of urban centres, whether *coloniae*, *municipia* or *civitas* centres. The regional juridical power of the magistrates of the *coloniae* was the greatest, followed by those of *municipia*. The *civitas* centres may have had far less extensive regional responsibilities and, while it is certainly possible that they may have supervised some of the small towns (*vici*) and rural districts (*pagi*) in their vicinity, this should not be considered a foregone conclusion. Although we cannot reconstruct the fine detail from the surviving evidence, we should imagine a mosaic pattern of landholding across Britain, with the state in one form or another controlling a large amount of territory and a mixture of other block holdings assigned to communities (urban, native peoples, sub-tribal groups) or to individuals or to religious interests. The individual legal settlement between Rome and urban communities will have differed markedly in terms of the amount of land assigned to the town, sold or given to private individuals in its vicinity and the extent to which the local community was expected to supervise financial and administrative affairs across a wider area.

The conquest of Britain and its long-term occupation was no act of altruism; the exploitation of its land and resources was fundamental to the success of the province. While it has been fashionable in recent years to emphasize the participation of the British elite in this and to minimize the potential role of colonists, it is important not to forget that military and other settlers potentially played an important role in many parts of the country – perhaps disproportionate to their numbers. In addition to the legionary veteran colonies at Colchester, Lincoln and Gloucester, settlement of discharged soldiers was probably widespread. For instance, twelve auxiliary veterans are epigraphically attested in southern Britain (two in Norfolk, one in Northamptonshire, one at Lincoln, one in Essex, three in Cheshire/Shropshire, one in London and one just south of the Thames in Kent, two in Gloucestershire). Since the visibility of such veterans is affected by a number of factors, this must represent a minuscule proportion of the total of military personnel who settled back into civil life within the province. The native British contribution to the rural landscapes of the province cannot be denied, of course, but it needs emphasizing that these were equally imperial landscapes, constructed by and for a colonial society in which native Britons participated alongside others, subject to legal and financial limitations. Parallels of a sort exist in the settlement of *Dacia* (modern Romania) after the bloody annexation at the beginning of the second century. Roman sources have for long been interpreted as implying that *Dacia* was repopulated with large numbers of settlers following the 'extermination' or enslavement of much of the local population. However, archaeological research suggests a more mixed population in the countryside, incomers and indigenous peoples living alongside each other.

Britain under Roman rule comprised a series of predominantly rural societies whose history was largely unwritten and in consequence has been poorly integrated into conventional accounts of the province. A common stereotype of the Roman countryside is that it was structured around elite estates with distinctive Roman-style farms (*villae*) at their centre. The presence in the countryside of substantial numbers of sites of less characteristically Roman type has rarely been given proper recognition.

At all times, the rural population of Britain under Rome will have far outnumbered its urban population (the latter probably never much more than 200,000) or its military community – perhaps in the order of 200,000, including associated civilians. An estimated rural population of *c.*1.6 million (80 per cent of the total) seems entirely plausible, given current knowledge of rural settlement. However we wish to play these figures, in common with other provinces Britain was essentially a rural society. If Roman-period population was in fact higher than 2 million, the bulk of the extra numbers will have been in the countryside.

Aerial photography has had a far more dramatic impact in British archaeology than is the case for the Mediterranean countries, but its value is all the greater when combined with field survey. The total number of late Iron Age and Romano-British sites in England alone is now over 100,000. Although the quality of the data is variable, the sheer quantity of information and its geographical coverage creates dramatic new possibilities for analysing settlement at local and provincial levels. It is on this foundation that future studies of the rural geography of Roman Britain will be built.

A fundamental problem to address is the extent to which the academic agenda has prioritized some parts of the landscape and certain settlement types over others. This is best illustrated by reference to the Ordnance Survey *Map of Roman Britain*. The main categories of site included have remained fairly consistent since the early editions (though nomenclature has changed slightly, the underlying criteria for selection have remained solidly Romano-centric): major towns (*coloniae*, *civitas* capitals), defended small towns (scttlement, defended), a selection of other nucleated undefended settlements (essentially those along the major roads of the province), spa towns, villas, other substantial rural buildings, temples, legionary fortresses, forts, fortlets, signal stations, supply bases, temporary camps, frontier works, roads, milestones, lighthouses, aqueducts, artificial watercourses, mineral extraction sites, salt-making sites, pottery/tile-production sites, Roman barrows or mausolea, major hoards. Strict site-selection criteria have been applied, but with the specific aim of illustrating the major 'Roman' categories of site. What we see are primarily the features of government and domination, and of elite society.

What is not mapped is important: a large number of substantial villages/hamlets (especially those away from the main road network), cemeteries, distinctive regional settlement types – such as fortified major settlements in the north and west of Britain (for instance, the rounds of Cornwall, nucleated defended sites in Wales, brochs and duns in Scotland). This creates a fundamental problem in attempts to map Roman-period Britain. In areas where Roman site 'types' are uncommon (notably, but not exclusively, Cornwall, Wales and northern Britain), the maps appear empty apart from Roman military installations standing guard over large capital letters denoting 'tribal' names. In reality, these were areas where different rules of government operated and indigenous settlement followed a variety of trajectories. Even the largest native sites are excluded as settlement sites on the Ordnance Survey map, though, to take one notable example, the hillfort of Traprain Law in Scotland is marked (but not named) as the location of a major hoard. Clearly it is impractical to plot on a small-scale map every roundhouse and indigenous site, but even in the use of categories of nucleated settlement, the selection seems to be in favour of the most 'Roman' examples. The desire to avoid clutter on a small-scale map is understandable, but what is omitted from such maps is the settlement evidence relating to the vast majority of the population, especially in the north and west, where hardly any non-military sites are actually shown. These academic priorities produce a map of 'Roman Britian', rather than of 'Britain in the Roman empire', and it is important to remind ourselves that these are not the same thing at all.

The net result of this sort of mapping is to suggest greater homogeneity than was the case and to leave difference under-explored. My alternative vision stresses the heterogeneity of rural settlement and seeks to bring out more detail of the regional variability in settlement morphology and to give greater consideration to the less 'Roman' sections of the landscape than is conventionally done. In this diversity lies an important clue to the evolving cultural identity of different groups.

Accounts of Roman rural development tend to generalize, looking for common denominators like villas, road networks and small towns. On the other hand, varied archaeologies have been left by different geographical and social groupings, reflecting divergent regional histories and distinct rural identities. When we examine the regional landscapes as they were remodelled under Roman rule, we can distinguish a number of key features that characterize Britain as a province under imperial rule: the concentrations of military sites, the network of roads and the associated posting stations along them, the financial and security controls at the major harbours and markets, the towns and aqueducts, changes in religious sites and practice. The variability that we see in rural settlement change is also indicative of changing identities under the influence of the imperial regime. These developments in rural settlement must also reflect broad changes in the nature of landholding and ownership. Regional differences in settlement history under Roman rule may also correlate to some extent with variance in the negotiation of power between defeated British groups and the empire.

Maps often portray late Iron Age Britain as carved up into a series of contiguous 'tribal' territories, corresponding exactly with the *civitates* recognized by Rome. The sizes of these implied *territoria* are vast – most being equivalent to at least two modern counties. This conventional picture of massive *civitas* units is more problematic than generally admitted; the truth is that we do not know much at all about the extent of the landholdings of either the late Iron Age or Roman-period peoples of Britain. For instance, the widely assumed correspondence between Iron Age coin 'territories' and Roman *civitates* does not stand close scrutiny. To some extent the post-conquest *civitates* were simply a matter of administrative convenience and we cannot assume exact territorial or social correlation with pre-existent Iron Age groups. Although I shall associate named peoples with particular geographical regions, these are by no means certain ascriptions, and a key argument is that the territories directly allotted to them by Rome were smaller than commonly assumed.

On the other hand, it was certainly the case that Rome found it convenient to delegate a good deal of local administrative responsibility to the towns of the empire. This meant that rural districts (*pagi*) some way from a defined *civitas* and its assigned core territory might be placed under the administrative supervision of the *civitas*. But the extent to which large areas of the countryside may have been differently administered by army or financial officials also merits consideration. Figure 10 (p. 262) offers a hypothetical vision of how this sort of mosaic pattern might have operated, though there is no more hard evidence for this reconstruction than for the more conventional view of enormous *civitas*-based administrative districts.

When considering the rural landscapes around towns, we need to distinguish between the territory directly controlled by the urban centre and the broader hinterland and hierarchy of settlements that it interacted with. It is also pertinent to consider the different forms of landholding that were practised in Roman provinces. In other parts of the empire, urban territories were generally smaller than those commonly envisaged for Britain, with very large areas of the surrounding landscape given over to private estates, imperial or state lands, religious land, regions under the control of the army, and so on. Our image of the geopolitical map of Britain needs revising accordingly.

A fundamental tool of imperial government was accurate measurement of the extent and quality of landholdings and the Romans were skilled in this area. Iulius Frontinus, governor in the mid-70s, wrote that there were three basic types of land in the provinces: that which was divided and assigned (centuriated), that which was surveyed only in outline (delimited) and that which was not defined by any measurement (*ager arcifinus*). The last of these was clearly a general term also for all the land declared *ager publicus* but left undelimited.

In some conquered territories, notably those of the western Mediterranean conquered in the latter centuries BC (Italy, southern Gaul, Africa, Spain, the Balkans), massive schemes of orthogonal land survey were superimposed across huge areas. These rectilinear systems – commonly known as centuriation because of their basis on squares (*centuriae*) of *c.*706 m side – have often left distinctive traces in the modern landscapes. The prevalent angles of field boundaries and the incorporation of regular perpendicular grids of roads (*limites*) within the field systems are the tell-tale markers of ancient centuriation. The lack of certain evidence for centuriation in Britain has often been commented on, though by the time that Rome invaded Britain, such major schemes of landscape transformation were becoming rare in newly conquered territories. On the other hand, *Ammaedara*, a Flavian colony founded on the site of a decommissioned legionary fortress in North Africa, was linked to a formal gridded land survey of its *territorium*. It is thus probable that centuriation schemes once existed around the three first-century *coloniae* in Britain, in relation to the allocation of standard land grants to veteran soldiers. It is much less certain that centuriation was employed on a wider scale, for instance, with regard to lands re-assigned to native *civitates*.

However, the absence of evidence of widespread centuriation of the British landscape does not equate with a lack of rigour on the part of Rome in delimiting and quantifying existing landholding arrangements within the province. The writings of the *agrimensores* show that their work continued throughout the Roman period and that in addition to formal centuriation they were frequently employed to carry out more basic surveys of conquered land, measuring area and assessing quality as a basis for taxation and provincial records. Pre-existing field systems were often assessed and adopted as the basis for provincial records. The establishment of the provincial census was undoubtedly a major task of the fledgling Roman bureaucracy in Britain, leading to the codification and registration of British landholding patterns in an unprecedented level of detail.

Centuriated land and delimited land normally had elaborate maps (*formae*) made to illustrate the overall shape of the scheme and the detail of individual allotments as a form of guarantee to those allocated the land. Although no *formae* were made of the *agri arcifini*, it is clear that surveyors were also active in these landscapes. In place of the minutely detailed surveys conducted in centuriated landscapes, the main purpose in *agri arcifini* was to define in broad terms the extent of lands and the appropriate level of tribute to be levied on the local community. In all types of land, territorial limits of neighbouring blocks were physically established and marked by boundary markers (*termini*), which could take the form of stone or timber pillars, or upturned amphoras, or of marks on standing trees or natural features such as hills, slopes, water courses, watersheds, or built/dug features such as walls, ditches, roads and so on, in part following the custom of the region. Siculus Flaccus specifically mentions the role of *magistri* of the rural *pagi* to extract from the farmers the necessary labour for the establishment and maintenance of the country roads, which connected settlements, but also helped define property boundaries.

A major change under Roman rule was thus that land was quantified, surveyed, subject to title and ownership rights as never before. The Roman penchant for written documentation is sadly not matched by survivals, but the discovery of a writing tablet recording the sale of a small wood in Kent, bordered by other land units in private ownership, is a signal exemplar of just how much documentation has been lost. The purpose of this documentation and land survey was not bureaucracy for bureaucracy's sake; it was the key to Roman exploitation of Britain. Taxation and tribute assessments depended on written records, based on major land surveys and the formal census. All British lands will have been subject to taxation or tribute (*ager stipendiarius*) and this might have been either cash-based or (more likely in the first century) in kind. Tribute conditions often also involved the provision of a given number of military recruits for the Roman army, and the fulfilment of labour or pack-animal liturgies (for instance in relation to mines and quarries, the road and transport system). Such terms were generally defined at the communal rather than the individual level.

The apparent lack of evidence for centuriation in Britain is less surprising today than it was a few decades ago, when the extent of pre-Roman land clearance was believed to be far smaller. It is now clear that there had been considerable expansion of Iron Age farming, indicated by the development of field systems in many parts of Britain. So-called 'Celtic fields' survive in many upland areas such as Wessex or northern England, but aerial photography has revealed traces of similar systems across extensive parts of lowland Britain. Exploration of the landscapes of Nottinghamshire and southern Yorkshire has been particularly important in this regard, revealing the existence of hitherto unsuspected semi-regular ('brickwork') field systems of late Iron Age date extending across a vast area once thought to have been still forested in Roman times.

In the initial post-conquest phase, the situation will have been relatively straightforward, with lands by and large claimed for the Roman state, with the exception of such territory as was parcelled off to client rulers, whose loyalty was recognized in an immediate and exemplary way, although these lands were no doubt expected to be tributary contributors in much the same way as the annexed provincial territory. The emperors will have begun establishing their own land portfolios almost immediately, and these will have grown progressively through confiscations and inheritance. Many British groups were, of course, initially allowed to remain in effective occupation of their traditional lands, subject to such restrictions as the army might impose and to the obligation to make tribute payments. As a condition of good behaviour and depending on the forward movement of the Roman army, the long-term status of these lands would ultimately be addressed as part of the process of transferring groups from military to civil administration. Evidence from other provinces shows that such arrangements were normally negotiated with individual *civitas* groups; radically different outcomes for neighbouring peoples resulted from Rome's judgement of their relative loyalty, merit and progress.

The landscapes of Britain were thus transformed under Rome in major ways. The driving through of major roads, the physical demarcation of lands of different uses and for different stake-holders, new types of site and some introduced plants (such as orchard crops) and an expanded architectural lexicon – all these contributed to dynamic change. But much also echoed late Iron Age practice in Britain and to a lesser extent in northern Gaul. The landscapes of Britain under Rome were characterized by types of isolated and nucleated settlements, enclosures, fields, tracks and paddocks. These contrast with the extreme regularity of centuriated field systems elsewhere or the strict application of Mediterranean models of settlement. Britain was in this sense, as in so many others, a peripheral possession of the empire, with distinctive traditions.

Some areas of Britain stand out from their surrounding districts in terms of their archaeology, and this can occasionally be linked to the existence of natural resources that were of importance to Rome. Rome had a number of options with regard to the exploitation of such resources: direct extraction; indirect extraction through contracts issued to individuals or companies; indirect extraction by tapping into pre-existing activity through tribute assessed in kind; re-assigning the lands to native communities for them to develop the economic value of the resource; maintaining the lands on which the resources lay as state/imperial property but deferring full exploitation. Comparative studies from other provinces, in the absence of explicit evidence from Britain, would suggest that Rome carefully evaluated the resources available from conquered territory and that deposits of minerals, decorative stone and salt were quite routinely taken into and maintained under state control. Where not exploited directly, there was some preference for issuing contracts to private contractors with the appropriate experience to exploit the resource, rather than placing the onus on local initiative and capital. Where the resource was difficult to exploit efficiently on a large scale, as in the case of coastal salt-working, it is probable that Rome obtained a share of production in lieu of rent or taxation due from local communities. In my vision of a mosaic of different land types, these resources were jealously guarded by the state and were not generally returned to the full control of British *civitates*.

PRE-ROMAN AND ROMAN LANDSCAPES

Our picture of the pre-Roman, Roman and post-Roman landscapes is increasingly detailed. Pollen evidence, derived from cores taken from lakes and peat bogs, provides dated sequences of landscape change. Macroscopic analysis of plant remains (typically carbonized seeds) illustrates the range of both cultivated plants and weed species. Rare survivals of structural timbers and charcoal residues can indicate species present and whether woodland management was practised. Analysis of animal bones likewise provides species lists, and some measure of their relative abundance, but also vital additional data relating to comparative size, physical characteristics and age at death (often indicative of whether the animal was raised primarily for meat or for secondary products such as dairy or wool). Finally, the material culture of farming leaves many traces: ploughshares, scythes, rotary grain mills, wool combs are easily recognizable for what they are. Built farmyard structures can be equally diagnostic whether they be byres, granaries or corn-drying ovens.

From a consideration of the environmental data, it is now clear that land clearance and farming were much more advanced in prehistoric Britain than archaeologists once believed. These new data reveal the large scale and broad range of Iron Age farming and its relative sophistication. Iron Age landscapes were once believed to have been characterized by small areas of human settlement and farming, separated by tracts of dense woodland and marshes, providing a convenient explanation of gaps in the settlement data. Improved environmental knowledge and increased information on rural settlement patterns have demonstrated this image to be false. The major phase of woodland clearance, according to the pollen record, was in the late Bronze Age, over 3,000 years ago. This process continued in many parts of Britain throughout the Iron Age and the instances of Roman date where tree/shrub pollen counts first fall below 50 per cent of recorded pollen are by far outnumbered by those of the late Iron Age.

Regional differences in vegetation history can increasingly be traced. The south-east of Britain saw progressive woodland clearance throughout much of the Iron Age, building on substantial clearance of Bronze Age date. There is ample evidence for agricultural activity, extending to substantial grain storage facilities at many sites, extensive field systems, and so on. East Anglia saw continuing woodland clearance in the Fens and some appearance of cereals before a major phase of marine incursion reduced human activity there. A pollen core from Breckland in Norfolk hints at a more heavily wooded landscape that was giving way to heathland in the late Iron Age. South-west England has produced a varied record, with the Somerset Levels for instance remaining more heavily wooded for longer into the Iron Age. The great moorland massifs of the far south-west such as Dartmoor, Bodmin Moor and Exmoor had all been substantially cleared of tree cover in the Bronze Age, and there are indications that the late Iron Age landscape was a comparatively open one, with numerous settlements practising both stock-raising and agriculture. Pollen samples from the Midlands generally reflect substantial woodland reduction through the Iron Age, though some locally important stands evidently remained. Both north-west and north-east England have produced evidence of major woodland clearances of later Bronze and early to mid Iron Age date. A large group of pollen cores from the area of Hadrian's Wall suggests that the landscape clearance accelerated in the late Iron Age. There are botanical data that also demonstrate a considerable extension of agriculture at that date, especially in the north-east at sites such as Thorpe Thewles. Both Scotland and Wales show evidence of substantial woodland clearance in the Bronze Age, with an accelerated or revived rate of clearance in the late Iron Age and/or Roman period. Cereal pollen appears in many samples from all the upland areas of Britain.

The Iron Age saw dramatic advances in and expansion of agriculture and stock-raising across Britain. Cereal cultivation, once believed to have been very much a speciality of southern Britain, in fact was well established in the north and west by the latter centuries BC. People had divided up large areas of the landscape with field systems and other boundary features, centred on numerous settlements, typically of round-houses. Emmer wheat (*Triticum dicoccum*), the traditional grain of Neolithic and Bronze Age Britain, was progressively less important in comparison to spelt wheat (*Triticum spelta*) and, to a lesser extent, bread wheat (*Triticum aestivum*). Hulled six-row barley (*Hordeum vulgare*) was the most widespread of the less high-quality grains. Both oats (*Avena*) and rye (*Secale cereale*) were also cultivated in pre-Roman times. The expansion of the range of grains indicates the spread of agriculture beyond the dry and light soils favoured by earlier farmers, with spelt and barley in particular being suited to a wide range of conditions. Experiments at a reconstructed Iron Age farm at Butser Hill, Hampshire, have shown that many of these grain types could have produced high yields, opening the prospect of an era of surplus pro-duction. Weed assemblages also illustrate the extension of agriculture to wetter or heavier soils and this is backed up by widespread evidence of cereal pollen in upland locations of northern and western Britain. Other field crops included peas (*Pisum sativum*), beans (*Vicia faba* var. *minor*) and flax (*Linum usitatissimum*). Livestock included cattle, sheep and pigs as the three predominant species, though with some significant regional variations in their relative importance (cattle were less common on downland areas with poor water sources, sheep were rarer in wetland environments). Other common domestic animals included horses, dogs and domestic fowl, the last a late Iron Age introduction.

The cumulative picture of the Iron Age landscapes is one of mixed woodland and open land by the late Iron Age. Areas of denser forest were comparatively rare and in a few areas woodland had been reduced to a very low threshold. There is some evidence from waterlogged sites to suggest that woodland management took place in the form of coppicing. Perhaps the greatest change in the rural landscapes of Britain involved the extension of farming on to more varied soils, indicating a whole range of agricultural improvements. Far from being a country of primeval forest and limited agricultural development, it is now clear that farming was evolving rapidly and dynamically in many regions of

Britain during the mid to late Iron Age. Yet the Roman period *was* one of significant change, and just as our evaluation of pre-Roman conditions has had to be revised, so our expectations of the rural history of Britain under Rome also require review.

The natural and agrarian landscapes of Roman Britain were in many respects similar to those of Iron Age Britain in ecological and environmental terms. While this was not a phase of revolutionary and wholesale change in farming, key distinctions appear to be an upward shift in the scale of rural production and greater diversification. For instance, there were important new plant varieties introduced during this period: the grape vine and orchard crops such as apples, medlars, cherries and plums; many garden plants such as asparagus, beet, cabbage, carrot, celery. The look of the countryside itself changed; travellers could have been under no illusion about the nature of the imperial landscapes they were crossing. Far evolved beyond the traditional routes of the Iron Age, the presence of a substantial network of engineered roads, with bridges at many river crossings, presented a new framework for movement. The roads connected forts, towns, markets and religious centres – all of which were to a greater or lesser extent marked out as different from what had gone before. Approaching towns, our travellers would pass cemetery areas, industrial suburbs and, occasionally, aqueducts that again represented dramatic and visible change to the landscape. Even in more conservative rural districts, change would be visible in the form of occasional more Roman-style buildings and probably an enhanced tendency to demarcate property boundaries.

Notions about progressive change inhibit analysis of the Roman-period landscape history. It is sometimes assumed that there was uni-linear economic growth and raised standards of living under Roman rule and that this was a self-evident goal that everyone will have aspired to. Put another way, there has been a tendency to see every rural site as a potential villa, that required only improvement of farming practices, new markets and the slow accumulation of capital resources by an eager peasantry to be achieved. There are several objections to this. As already noted, we can now demonstrate that agriculture was highly evolved in late Iron Age times in many parts of Britain. In parts of northern Britain, compared to precocious Iron Age expansion, the level of Roman-period exploitation appears to have been at best static or perhaps even curtailed. Studies of farming technology and analysis of the range and yield of cultivated plants and animals have shown that the degree of change between Iron Age and early Roman farming was relatively slight, with more significant waves of innovation occurring in the latter centuries BC and in the later Roman period. Why was this so?

A clear trend in many areas of Britain was the innate conservatism of vernacular architecture. If 'Roman Britain' was the land of the villa, then 'Britain in the Roman empire' was characterized overall by the roundhouse. Although increasingly supplanted in some regions by rect-angular house forms, it was equally enduring in others. One explanation, of course, is that the issue of whether to embrace new styles of rural building was more pertinent to the upper echelon of late Iron Age society than to the bulk of the populace. A more fundamental objection is that even among the British elite groups we should not assume an unerring desire to adopt Roman architecture, manners and graces. Had the Roman model been so overwhelmingly potent, it is indeed strange to note the slow uptake of villa architecture in many parts of the country. Even elite settlements show a considerable conservatism of approach through the early centuries of Roman rule, despite the construction of some early villas that could have served as models.

Current syntheses suffer from an over-emphasis on upper-echelon sites such as villas. They make general assumptions about the progressive impact of Roman conquest, and the improving effect on the economy of native Britons. They use the dichotomy of a villa-dominated civil zone and a landscape of roundhouses in the military zone. The selection of site plans and reconstruction drawings in many books demonstrates the way that subconscious assumptions lead us to filter out native features. Roundhouses are normally omitted from views of villas, though there is increasing evidence that the two structural types existed side-by-side. There is no denying the importance of villas in our assessment of rural change, nor of the socio-economic significance of the people who were able to fund specialized construction work of this sort. But it is both more problematic and more interesting to look beyond these villas at what else the countryside has to tell us about regional histories and trajectories.

The garrison history has already made clear the existence of long-term regional differences. At the most general level, we can conceive a tripartite division of British landscapes between areas under various forms of civil governance, areas under military administration and extra-provincial areas. Within each of these broad categories, we can hypothesize further levels of difference.

We can only guess at total numbers of rural settlements, and indeed at the overall population of Britain in the Roman period. Estimates of the maximum population have varied wildly over the years, from 400,000 to 500,000 suggested in the earlier twentieth-century accounts, to a 1980s range of 4 to 6 million. Many commentators feel the truth may lie between these two extremes, and a very conservative estimate of 2 million for the mid-second century is adopted here. One of the key factors in the rise in estimates of population has been awareness of a much greater density of Romano-British rural settlement as a result of aerial photography and field survey. A classic study of the making of the English landscape in the 1950s was dismissive of the impact of the Romans – based on the c.100 towns and small towns and 2,500 rural sites of all types then known, the conclusion was that much of Britain was still engulfed by forest or was uncultivated wasteland.

There has been an explosion of new data revealing a density in many parts of the country approaching one site per sq km. This has significant implications for considerations of the potential cultivated area and population, although not all sites were occupied contemporaneously, nor can we assume that we are close to recovering the total ancient site universe. In fact, discoveries continue at a high rate, representing a 40 to 100-fold increase in knowledge of ancient settlements in the second half of the twentieth century.

On the other hand, the total number of known villa sites has grown much more slowly than other categories of rural site, largely because this class of site has a more distinct archaeological signature, with the result that a larger percentage of these elite residences are already known (for example, in the 1950s, villas accounted for c.20 per cent of rural sites, today they represent c.2 per cent). The ancient reality was probably even starker, since the numbers of unidentified lesser rural sites will far outweigh the numbers of 'lost' villas. The archetypal rural site in Britain was thus not a villa and the villas were likely outnumbered 25:1 or more by other forms of settlement, most with a distinctively Iron Age pedigree in Britain, others of hybrid forms reflecting the impact of new ideas concerning construction and the use of space.

It is sometimes assumed that the villas represent economic development in Britain and that the less-developed (that is non-villa) landscapes of the north and west are indicative of poor socio-economic evolution. That view is probably too simplistic and we also need to look at other possible explanations. Another way of categorizing territory might be as landscapes of opportunity and landscapes of resistance, with many gradations in between the extremes. This has the advantage over the traditional model in that it introduces another element beyond economic potential to the equation and does not assume that all Britons wanted to live as rich Romans did, or that Rome wished all parts of Britain to see the same sort of development. We have already noted the process of negotiation between the Roman governing power and the indigenous inhabitants about the question of land allocation. This was an unequal negotiation between victor and subject people and did not follow a uniform pattern.

The 'most successful' regions thus did not equate neatly with the best agricultural areas and in certain cases we can speculate on the reasons why. Similarly, the relative poverty and underdevelopment of the west and north can only partly be explained by reference to land quality or social make-up of the people. Some areas of Britain were viewed by the Roman state as more suitable or deserving of opportunity and advantage and some were viewed as more resistant and undeserving. The possibility that practical considerations also played their part in determining the nature of land settlement cannot be excluded. For instance, the exigencies of military supply could have affected Rome's arrangements in the west and north to the long-term disadvantage of the local population. The attitude of the native Britons is another important factor, especially in so far as they felt that the empire presented them with opportunities. Alternatively, the extent to which they found themselves disadvantaged by the resources granted them may have promoted resistance, however subtle or passive.

THE VILLA IN BRITAIN

The villa is one of the best-established categories of rural settlement in Roman provincial studies, although in reality the definition applied varies wildly between different areas and from one scholar to the next. The ancient sources defined the villa as a rural house, but it is clear that they were thinking in terms of a house owned by someone of social standing, not peasant hovels, and they discriminated between the more luxurious type (*villa urbana*) and productive farms (*villa rustica*), though in reality the two elements were commonly represented at a single site. In the Mediterranean provinces, however, archaeologists have tended to reserve the term 'villa' for the major sites with signs of luxurious living or large-scale productive facilities. Lesser structures, even if stone-built and with tile roofs, are generally described as farms or farmsteads. For Britain, a different approach has mostly been taken: a basic definition of a villa is 'a rural building of Roman aspect' (key diagnostic features are the use of stone or brick/tile, rectilinear plan, tessellated pavements or mosaics, bath facilities). One problem is that classification focuses on the 'house' element, whereas in most cases there were ancillary structures present, though these have frequently been less well-explored archaeologically. This sort of catch-all description also faces the objection that it must cover wide variation. Compare, for instance, huge country houses such as Woodchester, covering *c*.14,000 sq m and comprising over fifty separate rooms and corridors, with smaller buildings such as the 200 sq m, five-roomed building with timber porch at Lockleys. In recent years there has been increasing scepticism of the utility of so broad a definition of the 'villa', though it is not easy to see where to draw the boundary between the two extremes just described. On the other hand, it will be apparent that the choice of a more Roman style of building over a more traditional form was in itself a significant one and that the discrimination has some validity. The Lockleys site, for instance, despite its early appearance as a simple row house, went on later to develop further architectural characteristics that favour its eventual classification as a villa.

Just how many villas were there? The minimal position is represented by the Ordnance Survey map, listing only 278 villas and 285 other substantial buildings, for a total of 563. A published gazetteer lists *c*.2,500 possible sites and represents a maximal position, since some of these are questionably villas. For the sake of my argument here, let us say there were 2,000, representing only about 2 per cent of the 100,000 rural sites of late Iron Age and Roman date now known in England. Palatial villas were exceptional – perhaps only twenty to thirty across all Britain – with the vast majority of other villas being small, medium or large farms, some decorated with tessellated pavements or mosaics and representing widespread displays of modest wealth. Many of these sites were late developments of the third or fourth centuries.

A series of distinctive types of villa has been identified on architectural grounds. This includes (from simplest to most complex): rectangular houses; corridor houses (rectangular houses fronted by a corridor or portico); winged corridor houses (same as previous but with the addition of projecting rooms or ranges at the end of the corridor façade); aisled houses (perhaps a development from late Iron Age prototypes); villas with courtyards (buildings arranged around at least three sides of an enclosed yard); elaborate villas of large scale and architectural elaboration (often with courtyards). As noted already, there is huge variation in scale and pretension between these different structures and it is important to consider other factors than simply the architectural type. Room counts, calculated floor area, the richness of interior decor, presence of bath-suites (and scale of these facilities), can all give an impression of the relative grandeur. As a rule of thumb, we might consider as 'small villas' sites with fewer than ten separate rooms, as 'medium villas' those sites with ten to twenty-nine separate rooms and as 'large villas' those with over thirty rooms.

The distribution of villas closely echoes the area of developed urban centres, predominantly in the south and east and with comparatively few in the north and west. However, this often-remarked north–west/south–east separation disguises a great deal of additional variation in the density, typology and dating of villa settlement within Britain. There were comparatively few early Roman villas, and the majority of villas, and virtually all the grandiose houses, were of relatively late construction, especially in the fourth century. This has important implications, rarely fully considered, for our understanding of the impact of Rome on the countryside in the initial centuries after the conquest.

Villas do not occur everywhere or in equal numbers in the civilian zone of Britain and this has often been interpreted as reflecting degrees of economic or social success. It could also indicate differing patterns of land tenure. The general absence of villas in the Fenland, on Salisbury Plain and in parts of the Weald has sometimes been seen as evidence that these areas were maintained as imperial estates. However, there are no good reasons for thinking that imperial estates would have been devoid of villas, since such properties were often contracted out to private individuals to run for profit. In North Africa, for instance, large imperial estates at the heart of the agricultural zone were studded with farms, villages and villas. Nevertheless, the absence of villas in parts of the British landscape may indicate different forms of land-holding, with less emphasis on private ownership of 'estates' and perhaps more on communal access to resources and land. The more probable candidates for imperial estates may in fact be found in areas of higher villa development, where rural culture and identity also stand in contrast to the average development. However, villas were not the exclusive preserve of any one group in society and different possibilities of ownership and occupation should be considered. They could relate to any or all of: representatives of the Roman emperors and the state, absentee landowners, the army, members of the British *civitates*, settler groups (notably discharged soldiers with capital to invest), private individuals (both British and from overseas), religious or entrepreneurial bodies.

What do villas signify? The question is not easy to answer, especially in view of the heterogeneity of sites in Britain. Some villas evoke comparison with the 'stately homes' of more recent British aristocracy. This is especially true of the large, multi-roomed sites, with lavish use of mosaics, painted wall-plaster, imported marble, statuary and so on. There is an interesting historiographical link here, in that the first villa excavations in the eighteenth and nineteenth centuries often took place on the estates of landowners who were keen to establish a connection with Roman antecedents.

There is ample evidence from other parts of the empire to show that there was a strong tradition of elite construction of luxurious rural houses, often contained within productive farm complexes. The elites in the Mediterranean provinces were strongly linked in to the practice of government and display at urban centres, so they generally maintained households in both town and country, moving between the two areas, and making use of bailiffs and tenants to conduct the economic exploitation of their lands. It is uncertain whether the British elite behaved exactly as those in Italy or Africa; the presumption should perhaps be that there was a degree of difference. There is some evidence to suggest that by the fourth century elite wealth was being spent more lavishly on rural building projects than in the towns, though it also remains to be proved that those responsible for the most extravagant villas were also members of the urban governing class, as opposed to imperial officials or wealthy immigrants or largely absentee owners from other provinces. The eighteenth-century British aristocracy was more country-based, though many maintained houses in London or major resorts, such as Bath, and we should be cautious about assuming too close a degree of similarity between them and the owners of major villas. There is no doubt, however, that the large villas as a group were elite residences of considerable scale – in the most impressive examples comparable with almost any others north of the Alps.

Another idea is that villas were elements of Roman-style estates, where landownership and tenancy were controlled by formal deeds and legal documents of types that were indisputably Roman. To this extent the villa was symbolic of economic relationships as well as social ones. But the long time-lag in the widespread adoption of villas (and the uneven spread even in south-east Britain) suggests that the construction of a villa was an optional extra and not a necessary condition of a Roman-style estate. Many farms that lacked villa-type buildings will nonetheless have been fully documented landholdings in the Roman manner. On the other hand, in the north and west of Britain, the relative absence of villas suggests the possibility that most of the land there was accorded different status in law.

Villas have most commonly been viewed as Roman-style farms. That is to say, farms that took on an architectural form that echoed urban standards of construction in sharp contrast to the norms of both the late Iron Age and of the Romano-British countryside in general. The choice of rectangular building plans, often using mortared-stone walls or foot-ings and making use in some cases of heavy roofing materials, such as tiles or slates, will have contrasted with predominantly curvilinear building types, such as the roundhouse, and a general preference for timber, wattle and daub, and thatch. Even a small 'villa', little more than a three-roomed cottage, could still represent an architectural statement about identity and aspirations.

The development of villas mirrors the slow evolution of towns in Britain. There were few villas in the first century and some at least of these appear to have been exceptional commissions, perhaps to indulge imperial officials, prominent immigrants or uniquely important native Britons. Some of the earliest villa development took place in the south-east, essentially in the area within which the coinage of the eastern and southern kingdoms had previously circulated. The best-known example is the palatial villa at Fishbourne, just outside Chichester, generally identified as a residence built for Togidubnus. This building is outstanding for first-century Britain in terms of its scale, its architecture, its use of marble and mosaics.

There are a few other well-appointed medium villas of early date and again these may have represented special construction projects. A good example is The Ditches villa, established within an Iron Age enclosure closely adjacent to the *oppidum* at Bagendon. The rarity of early stone villas of any degree of elaboration is shown by the fact that fewer than ten villas with second-century mosaics are known for the whole of England. More commonly, early villa development is represented by small rectangular timber structures replacing Iron Age roundhouses at a number of sites.

There was undoubtedly a major phase of development in the third and fourth centuries, representing a gradual growth in numbers rather than a sudden revolution. Many sites reveal a long sequence of gradual accretion of signs of wealth and luxury (additional rooms, baths, hypo-causts). Numerous long-established rural centres only developed stone-built 'villa' buildings in the late third or early fourth century. In the fourth century, a number of structures were built or expanded on an exceptional scale and lavishness of ornamentation (Bignor, Chedworth, Turkdean, Woodchester are the obvious examples). It needs to be stressed that these were exceptions not the norm.

The reasons why there was enhanced villa development in the fourth century have been much debated, with explanations often focusing on an assumed in-migration of wealthy Gallic families, fleeing barbarian invasion in northern France and buying up British estates. The increased fragmentation of the Roman imperial bureaucracy in Britain following the Diocletianic reforms has also been highlighted as a possible expla-nation of some of the most exceptional villas. Others have argued that the fourth century marks the apogee of Roman economic development in Britain, with some local families achieving previously unheralded levels of wealth. There are objections to each of these theories, though the truth may encompass all of them.

There has sometimes been a tendency to describe Roman rural develop-ment as a natural, unilinear and ever-upward trend. However, the process of villa construction was retarded in many regions and numerous villas did not survive in use through to the end of the provinces' existence; in-deed many had already failed by the mid-fourth century. Moreover, the level of investment in construction and maintenance was sometimes beyond the pocket of the owners. For instance, some bath-houses at villas appear never to have been completed and heated up, illustrating what an expensive and lengthy business the construction of such facilities was.

NON-VILLA SETTLEMENT IN THE COUNTRYSIDE

Traditional British roundhouses have often been dismissively referred to as 'circular huts', subconsciously emphasizing their difference from elite villa houses. Some excavations have revealed a transition from roundhouse to villa on the same rural site and this sequence has been identified as a key element of the 'Roman' countryside. However, there has been an increasing recognition that the roundhouse was a much more enduring feature of the Romano-British landscape and that the social understanding of this building form was variable and complex like the 'villa'. Even at villa sites, circular buildings were constructed through much of the Roman occupation. Moreover, roundhouses should not automatically be viewed as low-status or poor dwellings. Although these were commonly constructed of non-durable materials (timber, daub, thatch), the dimensions of the larger roundhouses are impressive, with internal diameters commonly in excess of 5 m and examples as large as 16 m recorded. These were substantial constructions and provided extensive internal spaces, which shaped many social rituals and inter-actions in traditional British societies. The larger and more elaborate roundhouses were thus impressive markers of a sophisticated society.

Parallels from other colonial societies alert us to the potential com-plexities. The memoirs of Nelson Mandela contain an illuminating description of his guardian's farm in the Transkei. Jongintaba was a local chieftain recognized by the British colonial authorities, and his home consisted of two whitewashed rectangular buildings of European style, complete with tin roofs, and a cluster of 'rondavels' (superior roundhouses). The European-style buildings were a visible symbol of his colonial powers and responsibilities, and Nelson had seen nothing like them in an African village before he arrived there following his father's death. Social behaviour and use of space at Jongintaba's 'villa' was complicated and transitional between two traditions. The rectangular buildings were used for receiving and entertaining people, but the chief's extended family continued to sleep and carry out many other daily activities in the six traditional roundhouses to the rear. This is not to imply that villas in Britain should be read in this way, but it raises interesting questions about social choices that are taken in colonial societies. Can one assume, as some commentators have in the past, that Britons if they had the choice would automatically have adopted the comforts of the villa over the roundhouse? The comparatively slow and uneven take-up of villa building may suggest otherwise for at least some part of the British elite. The other main possibility to consider here is that the economic and social encouragement offered by Rome was highly focused on a small group of the British elite class.

Roundhouses were thus present even on villa sites, but were actually far more ubiquitous generally within the rural landscapes, though each region tended to have its own distinctive character. There were also Iron Age traditions of rectilinear building, so the increasingly common appearance of rectangular structures from the first century could be due either to trends already present in Iron Age society or to Roman influence. Until the florescence of villa building in the third to fourth centuries, much of Britain remained dominated by native forms of rural settlement, with a thin veneer of new types of buildings and structural forms. The persistence of pre-Roman building forms for domestic use was even more common and consistent in the north and west of Britain.

However, it would be wrong to imply that building forms were unchanging. The construction of stone buildings marked a major departure in many parts of the countryside, even if not all examples were rectangular in form. There are examples of substantial stone-footed round buildings of late second- to fourth-century date and some at least were evidently for domestic use. Other possible functions of circular structures include shrines or industrial or agricultural buildings. A major change during the Roman period was the widespread addition of rectangular buildings to the traditional curvilinear forms. Many of the new structures utilized timber and daub just like the roundhouses, but some adopted more complex carpentry techniques (indicated by sleeper trenches or footings for sill beams rather than earth-fast posts) and some buildings incorporated tile or slate roofs. The latter are significant markers of change as the technology and tolerances of supporting a heavy solid roof are very different from those for a thatch construction.

One of the most popular forms of rectangular building in Roman Britain was the aisled hall. Sometimes described as 'aisled barns', these appear to have been multifunctional structures, with excavated examples serving both as domestic accommodation and a range of agricultural functions. Some aisled halls can be dated to the first century and it is possible that the form was already present in south-east Britain in the pre-conquest phase. At any rate the aisled hall can be seen as a peculiarity of Britain, there being no strong correlation with the vernacular architecture of the nearest provinces in Gaul and Germany. There appears to have been a major expansion in numbers of aisled buildings from the second century onwards.

The older view of aisled buildings was that they represented accommodation for bailiffs and workers and/or served as ancillary farm buildings on villa estates, but increasing numbers are now known where the aisled house, often with its main walls constructed on stone footings, was clearly the main dwelling on an estate, with mosaics and bath units incorporated into a subdivided aisled plan. The collapsed gable end of an example at Meonstoke provides a graphic illustration of the architectural refinement and impressive vertical elevation of these structures. The aisled hall became a standard architectural feature in many parts of the civil zone and it is to some extent a hybrid form, common to both villa and non-villa sites. It combined the large internal space of the roundhouse, with the same flexibility of use, but it could also reflect adoption of new structural forms and an increased scale of architectural display. Some scholars have speculated on the suitability of such large communal spaces for a society still based on extended clan groups. The precise details of these social relations are generally elusive, given the quality of archaeological evidence (though an attempt has been made to define functional and gender divisions within an aisled villa at North Wanborough). It is increasingly clear that the social architecture of many rural sites in Britain differed significantly from Continental parallels. Even in the adoption of Roman outward forms of architecture and display, British societies followed their own local rhythms.

Many late Iron Age rural settlements were erected within enclosures, to be characterized as 'compounds'. A typical compound site might have two to three roundhouses in contemporary occupation, suggesting that the social unit present was an extended family or clan. Although there are examples of isolated homesteads, these compound sites indicate that British society commonly revolved around such extended units. Attempts have been made to identify the same tendency at some villa sites, where within an enclosed 'compound' the domestic accommodation appears to be duplicated (among the clearest examples are villas such as Halstock, Rockbourne, Gayton Thorpe, with two houses of relatively equal size and status). Such 'unit villas' as they are known may indeed be evidence of a British tradition translated into Roman architectural terms, but the arguments have sometimes been pushed too far in this direction, with almost every villa plan being re-evaluated for its possible divisions between extended family groups. An intriguing example is a double villa at Bradford-on-Avon, where despite near identical ground-plans the two buildings seem to have had very different functions. If we see unit villas everywhere, we are in danger of replacing one over-generalizing model with another. Nonetheless, the archaeological evidence suggests that they were a potentially important feature of indigenous rural society.

Another area of great interest is the nucleated rural settlement – essentially, villages or hamlets. This group in part overlaps with the class of sites often described as small towns, especially when they occur alongside major roads (though the broad class of secondary agglomerations are often not tied into the main road network). There is an increasing recognition of the existence of villages alongside villas, and some of these were no doubt integrally linked to one another. On the other hand, some villages evidently had pre-villa origins and other examples are situated some distance away from villas. They represent another pre-Roman social tendency in parts of Britain for people to live in larger social groupings and the fact that we should find some element of continuity of such settlements under Rome should not surprise us.

13

Provincial Landscapes

This chapter seeks to develop some of the themes outlined above on a region-by-region basis (Figs 12–15). There is a danger of oversimplification in presenting succinct regional summaries, especially as some areas could by themselves provide the material for book-length treatments. However, the aim here is simply to demonstrate regional diversity of rural landscapes and development. This non-conformity of landscapes and settlement patterns across the province illustrates the unequal and unique sequence of negotiations between Rome and the subject British peoples.

SOUTH-EASTERN BRITAIN

The eastern counties

The *Trinovantes* of Essex had lands confiscated to provide the *territorium* for the *colonia* at Colchester and no doubt also taken into imperial ownership. It appears that the *Trinovantes* were formally attached to the *colonia*, rather than being allowed to develop a separate *civitas* centre. Rural settlement thus relates to native Britons, veteran settlers (and their descendants) and other incomers who were able to purchase estates. Because of the history of conquest, revolt and colonial settlement, the contribution of the British elite to high-status settlements was lower here than in many parts of southern Britain.

The evidence for elite rural settlement is meagre, with only about thirty-five villas or probable villas known, few of large scale. At Rivenhall, a villa with a nearby nucleated settlement could well have formed the core of a large private estate. Chignall St James was another winged

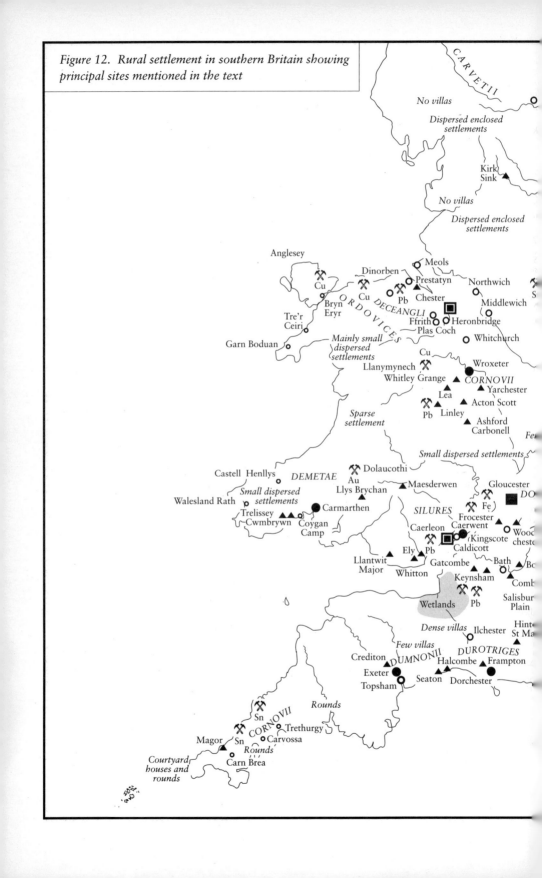

Figure 12. Rural settlement in southern Britain showing principal sites mentioned in the text

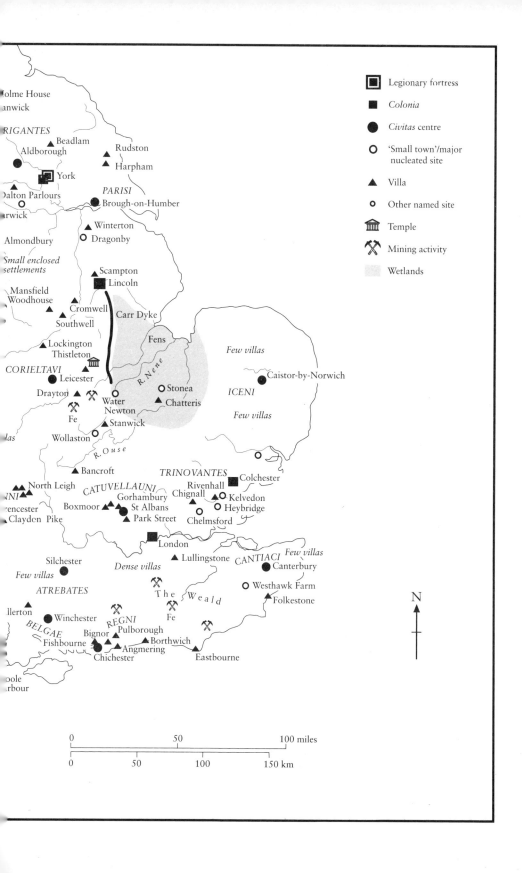

Holme House
anwick

RIGANTES

Beadlam
Aldborough
Rudston

Harpham

York

PARISI

Dalton Parlours
arwick

Brough-on-Humber

Winterton

Almondbury
Dragonby

*Small enclosed
settlements*

Scampton

Mansfield
Woodhouse
Lincoln

Cromwell
Carr Dyke

Southwell

Fens

Lockington
Thistleton

Few villas

CORIELTAVI

Leicester
Caistor-by-Norwich

Drayton

Stonea

ICENI

Fe
Water
Newton
Chatteris

Few villas

Wollaston
Stanwick

las

R. Ouse

Bancroft

TRINOVANTES
Colchester

North Leigh
Rivenhall

NI
CATUVELLAUNI
Chignall
Kelvedon

encester
Gorhambury
Boxmoor
St Albans
Heybridge

Clayden Pike
Park Street
Chelmsford

London

Silchester
Lullingstone
CANTIACI
Few villas

Few villas
Dense villas
Canterbury

ATREBATES

Westhawk Farm

llerton
The Weald
Folkestone

Winchester
Fe

BELGAE
REGNI
Bignor
Pulborough

Fishbourne
Borthwich

Angmering

Chichester
Eastbourne

*oole
rbour*

N

0   50   100 miles

0   50   100   150 km

corridor villa of some pretension. Some of the known villas appear to have comparatively early origins in the late first or second century, several succeeding late Iron Age settlement at the same locations.

The Essex area contains a high density of 'local centres' or villages and they more or less match the villa sites for numbers. These nucleated settlements can be interpreted in a variety of ways. Some may have been related to villa estates (as at Rivenhall), while others may have had administrative responsibility for rural districts. However, the vast bulk of settlement sites in Essex and southern Suffolk comprised a mixture of isolated farmsteads or nucleated complexes of such structures, generally of roundhouse type.

The western districts of the kingdom of Cunobelin fared somewhat differently. The environs of the *civitas* capital of the *Catuvellauni* at St Albans contain one of the highest densities of villa settlement. However, the pattern is not uniform across the landscape and some of the diversity perhaps relates to the parcelling up of the Chiltern Hills into a number of different forms of landholding. For instance, the area east of the city has revealed few villas, while that to the west has many, despite minimal ecological differences. The total number of villas recorded is about 130 known sites and about 100 probables. In parts of the Chilterns these villas are very evenly spread across the landscape, with sites every 2–3 km. A small but significant group show early origins, and a number of sites were built on late Iron Age settlements, with a plausible case for continuity rather than confiscation being made at some sites (Park Street and Gorhambury). But the probability seems high that some villas related to immigrants, rather than Britons.

The most extensively excavated site is Gorhambury, situated less than a kilometre from St Albans and originating early in the first century as a prominent enclosure. Through several phases of activity, an inner compound contained the most impressive buildings, while an outer one generally held more utilitarian buildings. The earliest structures were all of timber, from roundhouses to a possible pre-conquest aisled hall. The first stone buildings were built *c.*100, with a simple rectangular main residence and a small bath-house, though roundhouses continued to be built in the outer enclosure. Around the turn of the second/third century there was extensive enlargement of the main house into a winged corridor villa, now incorporating its own bath-house. After a period of semi-abandonment or contraction of the site in the mid-third century, renovations were made to the villa structures in both enclosures in the later third century, before the site entered a prolonged decline in the fourth century leading to the end of its effective life by about 350.

First-century bath-suites have been identified at Park Street, Gadebridge and Boxmoor, and are generally interpreted as the adoption of Roman architectural styles by some of the surviving indigenous aristocracy in the post-conquest period. But we cannot exclude the possibility of the take-over of some lands by immigrants, especially post-Boudica, nor does the presence of a few villas indicate that the *Catuvellauni* en bloc embraced the new styles. The cluster of early villas is just that, and represents a small minority in the countryside at large.

In the outlying parts of the zone traditionally ascribed to the *Catuvellauni*, the pattern of villas is heavily biased towards the river valleys of the Nene and the Ouse in the north and the Thames Valley in the west. Most sites were of relatively simple form of small to medium size. The major phase of development was the late second to early third centuries, with limited infilling thereafter and strong indications of a general decline by the mid-fourth century. The Nene Valley had significant clusters of villas between the small towns of Irchester and Water Newton. The increase in knowledge of non-villa settlements here is noteworthy, with over 500 sites known today, compared with only 36 sites in 1931. Some nucleated settlements and villages originated in the late Iron Age, but others appear to have been associated with villas, as at Fotheringhay, where the village was strung out along a linear trackway with a villa at its south-eastern end. Stanwick is another example, where extensive excavation around a villa revealed a contemporary village of numerous roundhouses.

The most common settlement type was the isolated farmstead, generally comprising single enclosures, sometimes with associated field systems. Some sites consisted of more complex sets of enclosures and several buildings, as at Wakerley in the Welland Valley, where a sequence of late Iron Age roundhouses and enclosures was augmented in Roman times by rectangular timber buildings, including a late second-century aisled building. A D-shaped compound at Odell was established in the early first century; here habitation continued to be in roundhouses until the fourth century when a rectangular timber house was erected.

Combined survey and excavation in the area of Wollaston in the Nene Valley has produced evidence of dramatic change in the landscape in the form of a Roman-period vineyard. Although introduced to Britain in Roman times, the grape vine never commanded the importance that it came to have in Northern Gaul and the Rhineland.

The heartlands of the *Iceni* in Norfolk, the Fenland and Suffolk were another territory blighted by the Boudican revolt. Roman reprisals were protracted and the *Iceni* will have borne the brunt of this. The amount of territory left in their direct control will have been only a fraction of the lands controlled by the Icenian elite at the height of their power. This conclusion is supported by the extremely small size of the *civitas* capital at Caistor-by-Norwich – the implication of the attenuated urban amenities being a meagre territory and a weak and small local elite.

The pre-60 heartlands of the Iceni were in western Norfolk, around sites such as Thetford and Saham Toney, so the move of the *civitas* centre to eastern Norfolk may in itself be indicative of punitive action against the western territory. The creation of imperial estates on Icenian lands is certain, given that the *Iceni* had tried to circumvent full annexation by offering half the kingdom of Prasutagus to Nero. After the revolt, Nero will have demanded at least as much territory to pass to his *patrimonium*. Other lands confiscated from dead or defeated Icenian nobles may have been put up for sale to private individuals, and the location known as *Villa Faustini* c.40 km along the road south of Caistor-by-Norwich is suggestive of a major private estate of this kind.

There are very few certain villas in Norfolk and the most prominent sites are large nucleated centres, mostly located on or adjacent to Roman roads and engaged in a range of activities including pottery production, salt-making and metalworking. Four sites appear to have had a strong religious focus (Thetford, Hockwold, Walsingham and Wicklewood).

The Fenland around the Wash was an important wetland area. Settlement and salt-making were already well established on fen islands in the late Iron Age, and the Roman activity represents intensification rather than colonization of a virgin landscape. There are hints in the coin record that the *Corieltavi* had privileged access to the Lincolnshire Fens and the *Iceni* to the central and eastern Fens in the late Iron Age. The traditional view is that following the Boudican revolt all of this area was developed as an imperial estate. The role of the state in managing the expansion of settlement in some way is supported by the development of an extraordinary settlement focused on a great stone tower at Stonea Grange, a stone aisled building at Chatteris, also in the central fen area, and an atypically large villa complex at Castor by Water Newton on the fen edge. Several major dyke systems along the western edge of the Fens appear to be ancient in origin, most notably the Carr Dyke. Once interpreted as a navigation canal, this is now seen as first and foremost part of a major drainage system. Stonea Grange was clearly an important and highly unusual site, with large masonry buildings constructed in the second century as part of a planned urban settlement, though it never seems to have fully established itself and was radically scaled down after 200. By contrast, most fen settlements were very conservative in layout, types of building (roundhouses and simple rectangular structures), construction materials used and material culture present.

Although Roman imperial power played an important role in shaping the Fenland landscape, the active contribution of indigenous social groupings should not be overlooked. The indigenous inhabitants made status displays that differed in important respects from those of communities on the fen edge. Rather than view the lack of villa development and eventual abandonment of settlements like Stonea as a sign of innate failure of the populace to rise to the 'opportunities' offered to them by the state, this can be read as a transcript of resistant adaptation and rejection of Roman norms. Although villas are absent, changes in building type and in the occurrence of 'elite' material culture markers hint at specific local patterns of adaptation to Roman rule. For instance, among the settlements on the silt fens, where drainage was dramatically improved in Roman times, we can identify two distinct groupings of sites with elite cultural markers – in the northern Fens this mainly takes the form of changed architectural elements (such as the construction of tiled roofs), while to the south, it is the presence of portable wealth that distinguishes a number of sites amidst the generally poor background material culture. Below the level of the potential control sites, such as Stonea, Chatteris and Grandford in the central Fens, settlement on the silt fens and on the islands within the peat fen was concentrated as a series of clusters, each of which was linked to the fen edge by a main trackway or canal.

An attractive alternative to the 'imperial estate' model is that some part of the region was retained as *ager publicus*, with native Britons allowed occupancy in return for rents and taxes levied in terms of products that the state required. Apart from salt, wetlands may have been important sources of other commodities required in quantity by the state, including animal products (meat, hides). The meat that was raised in the Fenland could have been exported in salted form in barrels to the frontier zones.

Close by to the west, the fen-edge landscape was very different, with the successful development of the small town of Water Newton and a villa-dominated landscape, revealing the construction of distinctive rural identities, suited to population groups with different relationships with the Roman state.

The south-eastern counties

The *civitas* of the *Cantiaci* was centred on Canterbury, though studies of the canton have tended to assume that the territory covered the whole of Kent and perhaps eastern Sussex. This seems unlikely for a number of reasons. The main Roman ports of entry into Britain lay on the Kentish coast, and the land between the provincial capital at London and these ports was prime real estate for investment by incomers to Britain – whether speculators from Italy and Gaul or imperial agents. There were also natural resources to consider. In Kent, for instance, there is a dense pattern of villa development north of the Weald, but a virtual absence of such structures within the zone of Wealden iron production. This suggests that the territory of the *Cantiaci* as defined by Rome focused on northern Kent, with the southern zone organized in some different way. In the northern area, most villas lay some distance to the west of Canterbury, clustered in the main river valleys (Darent, Medway) or the creeks of the Thames estuary. A minimalist reading of the evidence would limit the *civitas* of the *Cantiaci* to north-eastern Kent only, with the iron- and timber-rich Weald under some form of imperial control and the north-western sector leased or sold to private land-holders. It is also possible that some land in Kent was assigned to the town of London or run as imperial estates (as in the case of Ickham villa between Canterbury and Richborough).

The largest and richest villas in the area thus may not have been connected with the Cantiacian elite. This seems certain of the palatial villa constructed in the second century close to Folkestone, which utilized stamped tiles produced by the *classis Britannica*, though the identity of the person for whom it was constructed remains uncertain. The most extensive and earliest villa in the Medway Valley at Eccles is another candidate for outside influence and capital investment. The first stone building here dates to *c.*65, with several rooms possessing tessellated floors and a separate bath-house also of early date. A further major villa at Darenth extended over 1.5 ha and comprised at least six main building complexes, including a winged corridor main range, with two near-symmetrical annexes and two large aisled buildings. The lifespan of this villa ran from *c.*100 to the end of the fourth century. The most famous Kentish villa is that at Lullingstone, though the main house was quite modest in scale, even if well appointed, in some of its phases. It was first constructed around the end of the first century and underwent a complex series of expansions and modifications, before a final phase starting *c.*385 under Christian owners.

There are numerous smaller villas of simpler morphology – primarily winged corridor houses and aisled buildings – and several examples of large villages or small towns (Charlton, Westhawk Farm). However, the largest category of rural site comprised roundhouses within simple ditched enclosures. Only in the late Roman period did larger numbers of the houses within these sites take on a more rectilinear form, but by then many rural sites in east Kent were contracting or being prematurely abandoned.

The primary focus of late Iron Age and Roman settlement in Sussex comprised the light soils of the South Downs and the Chichester coastal plain. To the north, the heavy clays of the Weald, with iron and timber resources, again constituted a separate region, whose exploitation followed a different trajectory. The *civitas* of the *Regni* with its capital at Chichester represented a Roman rationalization of one part of the large client kingdom ruled by Togidubnus. There are a number of exceptionally early elaborate villas in the region (Fishbourne, Angmering, East-bourne, Pulborough and Southwick) and a crucial question is whether these early villas pre-dated the incorporation of the client kingdom into the province, or whether they were a consequence of that upheaval – perhaps as a palliative to the leading indigenous families. At any rate, it is clear from the unusual architecture and materials utilized – including Mediterranean-style plans, mosaics, marble floors and other marble components – that these were special commissions dependent on skills and materials that were provided from external sources. At Fishbourne itself, a sequence of development has been recognized, starting with the so-called 'proto-palace', subsequently greatly enlarged in the later first century into one of the best-known, but least typical, villa plans in Britain. The occurrence of identical flue tiles at Angmering, Eastbourne and Fishbourne links these sites as a group. Pulborough and Southwick share other architectural similarities and peculiarities with Fishbourne. The dramatically enlarged palace at Fishbourne has been variously interpreted as a retirement home for Togidubnus or for his direct family, or as a suitable base for Roman administrators sent to oversee the transition of the kingdom to provincial territory. Fishbourne would certainly have appealed to aristocratic Roman tastes in its late first-century form, but the family of Togidubnus had also been exposed to the high life at Rome.

Although the region saw considerable villa development in later centuries, this was generally much more modest in scale and in many cases seems to represent gradual transformation of indigenous settlements into Roman-style houses. Several examples are known of villas where the main building took the form of an aisled hall, a pattern also common in Hampshire. At some sites there was a sequence of rectangular timber buildings, before the appearance of the first stone house in the third century or later.

A feature of many of the Sussex and Kent villas was the decline and abandonment of sites near the coast during the fourth century. This has been variously ascribed to the impact of Saxon raids or of the military garrisons of the Saxon Shore forts. At any rate, both regions are notable for the relative lack of wealthy villas in the fourth century, with Bignor being a singular exception in Sussex. This villa was situated beyond the north slope of the South Downs, close to Stane Street linking Chichester and London, and seems to have originated as a rectangular timber structure by the late second century at latest. It was upgraded to a simple stone row house in the early third, and further embellished with a corridor and simple projecting corner rooms. The transformation of this modest villa into one of the largest and most elaborate villas in southern Britain in the fourth century is unexpected and highly atypical of this region. The final form of the villa focused on three extensive ranges of luxurious apartments around a large inner court, with additional structures constructed around a large secondary yard. The entire complex covers an area of 1.5 ha and comprises at least seventy rooms, many with mosaic or tessellated pavements. While Bignor stands comparison with some of the select group of larger villas of the West Country, it is unique for south-east England at present.

Most of the Sussex villas cluster along the coastal plain, some at the heads of creeks and inlets, or in the fertile south-facing valleys of the South Downs, or on the Greensand formation that lies just to the north of the South Downs. Large numbers of non-villa settlements are also attested in these same preferential areas of the landscape. On the Down-land, many settlements appear to have evolved directly from late Iron Age antecedents, with a gradual shift towards rectilinear structural forms in preference to the earlier roundhouses. Many of the sites represent isolated farmsteads, but there were some larger settlements. An example at Park Brow consisted of five small rectangular houses, one with a tile roof, window glass and red-painted plaster on its wattle-and-daub walls.

The central southern counties

Much of the territory of the northern *Atrebates* has vanished under the dormitory belt of London's western commuters. The plans of the excavated villas show considerable variation, with relatively few of winged corridor type. Only two sites have been suggested as early villas – Ashstead and Walton Heath. The distribution of Roman sites shows a concentration along the springlines at the edge of the Downs and along the Greensand and Gault beds, but a few villas are also known on claylands. In a generally sparse settlement distribution, there were slight concentrations of sites close to Stane Street within 10 km of the small town of Ewell and in the area of the Alice Holt pottery production in the Farnham area. The hinterland of the *civitas* centre at Silchester has demonstrated strong continuities with late Iron Age dispersed settle-ments, but few villas of any note.

The *civitas* of the *Belgae* appears to have been artificially created by Rome, with its capital at Winchester. The core territory of the *Belgae* was evidently in Hampshire and southern Wiltshire, representing the south-western portion of the southern kingdom. The settlement of Hampshire has many similarities with that of West Sussex, although lacking evidence for early sumptuous villas. Most villas were compara-tively modest in scale, with many exhibiting signs of evolution on pre-existing native sites. Land divisions and field systems of demonstrably pre-Roman date were commonly maintained in active use through cen-turies of Roman rule. The gradual embellishment of the British farms with the trappings of the villa estate has been traced in some detail at a series of villas (Grateley South, Houghton Down, Fullerton, Werwell). One interesting feature is the prevalence of the aisled hall at many of these sites, sometimes as an ancillary building, but occasionally developed as the main residence and aggrandized with baths, mosaics and underfloor heating.

A particular feature of the distribution map of Roman-period settlement in this region is the absence of villas from the geographically extensive area of Salisbury Plain, although eleven villages of Iron Age and Roman date are known there. Some of the villages were on a considerable scale, such as the most famous example at Chisenbury Warren – a 6-ha site containing about eighty buildings flanking a curving lane and linking to extensive field systems covering at least 80 ha. There has been much debate about the reasons for the absence of villas here, with many commentators favouring the idea that this was an imperial estate. That the land was held in some different form of arrangement from villa estates can be readily admitted, though whether imperially or state-owned, or assigned as communal lands to a British sub-grouping, cannot be determined. Similar settlements have been recorded elsewhere on the Downland of Hampshire, around Chalton, for example, where a detailed survey of *c*.20 sq km revealed no fewer than three villages, fourteen 'farmsteads' and four masonry buildings, set within a dense pattern of regular fields.

The East Midlands

The heavy clay soils of the East Midlands were for long thought to have been thinly populated, as were its flood-susceptible valleys and fenlands. More recent research has shown a high density of Roman-period settlement, the majority comprising dispersed farmsteads and settlements of roundhouses (Fig. 13). This map is an excellent example of the high densities of non-villa settlement now attested in many regions. The foundation of a legionary fortress and then a veteran *colonia* at Lincoln perhaps indicates punitive action against some elements of the *Corieltavi*, and effectively created a new focus of power in the eastern part of the region. The extent of Corieltavian land and authority was thus probably limited under Rome to the western sector, focused on the *civitas* centre at Leicester. The predominance of heavy clay soils around Leicester could indicate that the *civitas* was established

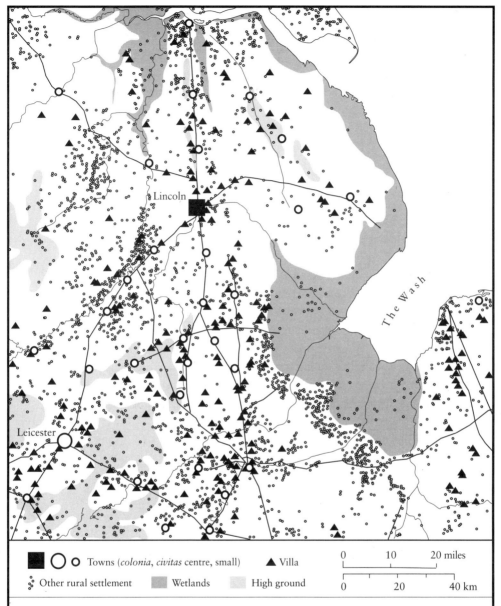

Leicester

Lincoln

The Wash

Figure 13. Rural settlement of Roman date in the East Midlands. Note the relative paucity of villas and the dense areas of non-villa settlement, as in the Fens

on less favourable land in the western sector of the Iron Age territory. A further complication was the presence of significant iron ore deposits in southern districts, and these were evidently exploited on a large scale in the Roman period. Some degree of imperial control or financial interest is perhaps to be expected, especially in the initial stages.

About 100 villas are known in the northern East Midlands, but few were medium to large villas (Southwell, Scampton, Winterton, Thistleton and Mansfield Woodhouse) and none was of really palatial scale. An interesting aspect of these larger villas is that they are mostly outside the probable territory of the *Corieltavi* – several are beyond the Trent or up near the Humber. Winterton is one of the most fully excavated, at its greatest extent comprising a U-shaped arrangement of buildings focused on a main villa range flanked by perpendicular aisled buildings. These early third-century structures had succeeded a series of stone-footed circular buildings and a simple rectangular timber building of second-century date. The prominence of the circular elements in the early architecture of the site and of the aisled halls stresses the continuity with British vernacular traditions here, though the evidence of a series of extensive rectilinear boundary ditches around the villa suggests the systematic demarcation of a landed estate. At a number of other villas in the region the main buildings lay within a double-ditched rectangular enclosure (Cromwell, Lockington), perhaps again an indication that these sites sought to differentiate themselves visibly from the more typical sub-rectangular or curvilinear enclosures employed at the majority of rural settlements.

Most of the villas cluster on the river gravels or on the lighter soils of the limestone ridge north and south of Lincoln and on the west side of the Lincolnshire Wolds. A few villas are known north and west of the Trent Valley, outliers from the main distribution. The example at Mansfield Woodhouse was a late second-century development on a site with evidence of first-century roundhouses and early second-century timber structures. Mosaics were comparatively rare in villas in the East Midlands, though tessellated pavements were somewhat less so, and bathing facilities were more often provided within other buildings rather than as free-standing structures. Many 'villas' were essentially developed aisled houses, often with tessellated pavements and heated rooms inserted into one end (Epperstone, Great Casterton, Drayton).

Non-villa sites are increasingly well known, especially through aerial survey, though the sample of excavated examples remains small. The most common rural site of the late Iron Age and Roman period was a small enclosed settlement of less than 0.5 ha, typically comprising one or more roundhouses within a ditch and bank. The enclosures were generally either D-shaped (Colsterworth and Enderby) or vaguely recti-linear (as at Wakerley, Willington). These sites were commonly isolated from one another, though sometimes associated with evidence of linear boundaries, field systems or trackways. Nucleated settlements were also common, generally comprising groups of physically linked enclosures that are in some respects similar to the isolated farmsteads. These settle-ment forms were present in the late Iron Age and continued to predomi-nate in rural districts for much of the Roman period. At Dragonby, however, there are indications that the roundhouses of the late Iron Age gave way to large rectangular buildings, many of the aisled hall type, with metalled roads and wells constructed in what was a well-ordered settlement.

In comparison with some other areas of Roman Britain, the evolution of villas was slow before the end of the second century, and they were always few in number. The evolution of traditional native settlements of roundhouses or of aisled halls into villas can be traced at a number of sites.

Aerial photographic evidence from Lincolnshire shows that the Roman-period landscapes varied considerably. North of Lincoln on the limestone ridge and on the Wolds, the pattern was dominated by dis-persed settlements, with few field systems linking between sites. South of Lincoln and in the Fens, on the other hand, there were larger settlements, frequently linked to one another by trackways and field systems.

The West Midlands

Oxfordshire was a possibly liminal zone between Iron Age polities, and settlement was dominated by a series of large low-lying *oppida* at Dorchester-on-Thames, Abingdon, Cassington and Salmonsbury, as well as Grim's Ditch on the Cotswold edge. The Cotswolds had a high density of villa sites, clustered mainly within its valleys or close to the Roman road from Alchester to Cirencester. There was one exceptional courtyard villa at North Leigh, with over fifty rooms. This palatial complex was ornately furnished with mosaics and other high-status markers. The site seems to have developed over a simple early villa dated to *c.*100, only reaching its apogee in the fourth century. North Leigh was the most successful of a group of precocious villas producing late first-century material that all lay within the area defined by Grim's Ditch at the southern edge of the Cotswolds (others being Shakenoak, Ditchley, Bury Close, Callow Hill and Stonesfield). These sites would seem to indicate some special arrangement with a favoured group, arguably British given the location.

Ditchley villa comprised a winged corridor house, set at the centre rear of a rectangular walled and ditched enclosure. In front of the main house was a centrally placed well, with to one side a circular stone-footed building (originally interpreted as a threshing floor, but now paralleled by stone-footed roundhouses at other villas such as Shakenoak and Islip). At the front of the enclosure were two further rectangular stone buildings, one a granary. This villa and another at Islip have a strong planned aspect to their layout, and the combination of rectilinear and round buildings appears to be part of the original scheme. At Shakenoak, the winged corridor villa of the mid-third century was later partially abandoned, with an aisled hall subsequently developed as the main residence and a stone-footed circular building constructed. In terms of architectural evolution, this site seems to demonstrate a strong reversion to British preferences for aisled buildings and the circular form.

One of the problems with examining non-villa settlements in Oxfordshire is that many of them are poorly preserved archaeologically because of the regional building techniques employed. In the late Iron Age period, roundhouse construction methods shifted from earth-fast posts to mass construction techniques, such as solid cob (earth) walling, and these features have proved hard to detect archaeologically. Late Iron Age and Roman period settlements most often comprised small enclosures (less then 1 ha) containing one or more roundhouses (Watkins Farm, Northmoor, Gravelly Guy). There were comparatively few village-like sites, though they did exist (Bowling Green Farm, Stanford in the Vale, Cote).

Large expanses of the Thames Valley landscape have been traced in detail through aerial photography and reveal clusters of small fields and paddocks around Roman-period settlements, often with trackways connecting sites or leading away from the infield systems to access more remote pasture lands. At several sites, there were large open spaces at the meeting point of tracks, somewhat akin to village greens (Gravelly Guy), and again an association with stock management may be suspected. The general picture of the Thames Valley is of comparatively few villas, but interconnected clusters of other sites within irregular networks of fields and trackways. An area of very regular rectangular fields in the immediate vicinity of the town at Alchester and the gridded layout of that small town represent a much more rigorously planned and locally superimposed landscape.

It is clear from both the broader settlement data and specific excavated sites in the Thames Valley that there were significant discontinuities in site morphology and occupation patterns, especially in the early post-conquest phase and again around 130. Many new foundations occurred in the mid- to late second century, probably including a large percentage of the known villas, creating a new settlement pattern. There are only a few rare examples of earlier villas or proto-villas, as at Barton Court Farm. At Claydon Pike, a late Iron Age phase characterized by curvilinear enclosures was succeeded by a rectilinear layout of enclosures, corrals and tracks, with two aisled buildings in one enclosure and a possible shrine in another. Army connections are hinted at by finds of military equipment and fittings and a military graffito (though other explanations are possible, such as a discharged soldier settling down to farm). Late Roman activity comprised a small row-house villa within irregular enclosures unrelated to the early Roman boundaries. Whatever the original significance of the site, it illustrates well the dynamic nature of rural settlement and the real potential for the landscape to be transformed in successive phases.

Roman settlement in Warwickshire featured very few villas (fewer than fifteen, mostly south of the Avon) and none of any great wealth. The vast majority of settlements were sub-rectangular enclosures, mainly for individual farmsteads, but occasionally forming larger complexes (as at Wasperton). Overall, the area was one of only modest change across the Roman period.

The western Cotswolds, commonly identified as the heartlands of the *Dobunni*, have produced some of the most impressive evidence for a transformation of the countryside and for the growth of elaborate and large-scale villas (Fig. 14). The late Iron Age coinage assumed to relate to the *Dobunni* was quite extensively distributed across Gloucestershire, northern Somerset, southern Warwickshire and west Oxfordshire,

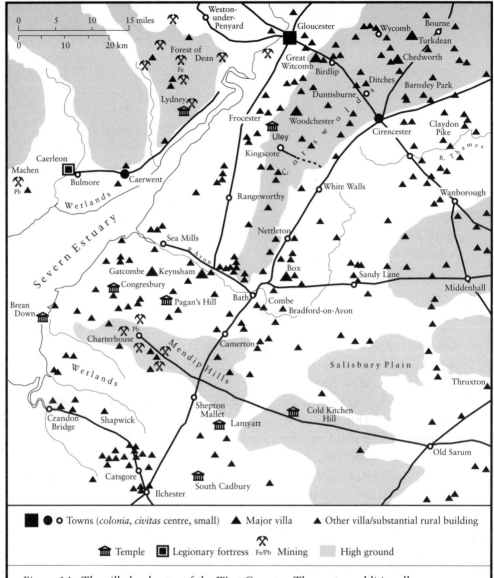

Figure 14. *The villa landscape of the West Country. There were additionally many non-villa sites across this landscape, producing one of the highest overall densities of settlement*

suggesting a broad zone of influence. The late Iron Age regional *oppidum* lay within extensive dyke systems at Bagendon and the establishment of the *civitas* capital at Cirencester involved a move of only a few kilometres southwards. Instead of hailing the *Dobunni* as one of the great success stories of Roman Britain, it is worth reflecting on other possible interpretations of the settlement evidence. The foundation of a veteran colony at Gloucester, for instance, indicates significant erosion of Dobunnic territory.

The majority of the approximately fifty villas known in Gloucestershire lie in the rolling hill country of the Cotswolds, though a few are found in the corridor of land between the hills and the river Severn (as at Frocester Court). These villas include some very large and elaborate examples, such as the palatial complex at Woodchester, and the somewhat comparable sites at Spoonley Wood, Great Witcombe, Turkdean and Chedworth. Chronologically, villa development in Gloucestershire was notably retarded until the later second century and the main phase of development on most sites cannot be put before the late third century. Some sites appear to have been new creations of the fourth century, the period when most villas reached their apogee. An interesting exception is the small villa at North Cerney, discovered within an Iron Age fortified enclosure known as The Ditches, immediately north-west of the Bagendon *oppidum*. This modest winged corridor house appears to have originated in the mid-first century and, in the reverse of the regional trend, was abandoned by the late third century. It is certainly tempting to see this early Roman-style residence as having been supplied to order for a local notable – perhaps even the same family that had controlled the prestige enclosure in which it sat? Although it was one of the earliest villas in Britain, this was no Fishbourne in scale and lavishness.

The villa at Woodchester contained at least sixty-four rooms arranged around two or possibly three courts spread over *c.*2 ha. Finds from the site underline its uniqueness: marble statuary and paving, mosaics, and architectural elements including columns, bases and capitals. The main reception room contained the largest mosaic pavement known in England, over 15 × 15 m, and containing *c.*1.5 million tesserae; overall, mosaic floors covered almost 1,000 sq m within the complex. There are few clues as to the ownership of this extraordinary complex, but it is possible that it was at the heart of a very large estate, and perhaps linked to other large settlements of West Hill Uley (5 km west) and Kingscote

(8 km south). Uley was a notable religious centre, unusual for the literate dedications of its users. The settlement at Kingscote comprised over seventy rectangular buildings (many stone-walled) spread over a 30-ha area.

The other villas that stand out as exceptionally wealthy are all located within 18 km of Cirencester, and appear to have reached their greatest extent in the fourth century. Chedworth has produced evidence of an early second-century origin and seems to have developed in a piecemeal fashion, until the elements were drawn together in the late third or fourth century, to emulate the appearance of a double courtyard villa. Despite suggestions that it was perhaps a religious centre, the complex fits best with the exceptional group of large-scale villas – as indicated by its over forty separate rooms, including two bath-suites and at least fifteen mosaics. Turkdean villa, only discovered in 1996, was another double courtyard complex (140 × 80 m), with further detached ranges. It also has an apparent start date in the second century, with major expansion in the fourth. The probable selection of Cirencester as the capital of one of the four late Roman provinces of Britain might account for some of these late high-status villas, but there may equally have been economic factors at play. The ornamentation of these villas was supported by a regional school of mosaicists at Cirencester, whose products found their way into at least thirty rural sites (a high percentage of the known villas in comparison with other regions).

Frocester Court is the most extensively excavated villa west of the Cotswolds. Here a simple row house within ditched enclosures was given an increasingly elaborate winged corridor façade, by the fourth century fronting on to a walled courtyard garden, though the main house never boasted more than about twenty rooms. The winged corridor plan and the general size (25–30 m frontage) are repeated at many other modest Gloucestershire villas (for example Farmington, Barnsley Park).

Large numbers of enclosed settlements, with traditional building forms such as roundhouses, are also now known in the Cotswolds. Stone-footed circular buildings have also been noted at upper-echelon rural sites (Barnsley Park, Bourton-on-the-Water); variously interpreted as byres and shrines, it is as likely that these were dwellings.

The Avon Valley, with the notable hot spring at Bath, and the Mendip hills with their lead/silver deposits, may have been linked to the Dobunnic territory in pre-Roman times. Although Ptolemy assigned

Bath to the *civitas* of the *Belgae*, this can be questioned on various grounds. On the other hand, prior association with the *Dobunni* is no safe indicator of how the area may have been handled administratively by Rome. The Avon Valley contains a distinctive cluster of villas, with foundation dates generally in the later third century. Of this group, Box is a large courtyard villa of over forty rooms. Another large site at Gatcombe also appears to have a late Roman floruit, though there were evidently earlier structures beneath the stone buildings. Fragmentary traces of a probable villa have been located (in a railway cutting), but the most remarkable feature of the site is the large number of ancillary rectangular buildings, including two aisled halls, contained within a *c*.6-ha enclosure wall. Quite a range of manufacturing activity was noted in relation to some of these buildings.

A further major courtyard villa was Keynsham. Although only partially excavated, this site was of grand scale and architecturally elaborate, with hexagonal rooms at either end of the main range. An inscription possibly relating to an imperial tenant was found at a neighbouring site. In contrast to the Cirencester area, there is a marked absence of second-century villa construction, or of clear indigenous antecedents at many sites. The inscription of an imperial freedman from a villa site at Combe Down just outside Bath indicates the existence there of an imperial estate. The mineral resources of the Mendip hills were initially exploited under direct military control and later contracted to private companies, presumably under procuratorial supervision. A dedicatory inscription from Bath by a *centurio regionarius* implies that direct military supervision in this region may have extended into the second century. The substantial changes in rural society from the later third century, notably the dramatic increase in villa construction, could indicate a new pattern due to land sales or leases.

The south-western counties

The *Durotriges* of Dorset and Somerset put up stern resistance to the Roman advance in the 40s and it is no surprise to note that villa development in this area was also retarded, in much the same way as the evolution of the *civitas* centre at Dorchester. It has been suggested that Ilchester became an independent *civitas* in its own right in the late Roman period, and that town is certainly highly unusual among small towns for the degree of planned layout and the number of mosaics found there. A series of well-dated villas has revealed origins no earlier than the late third century (Fifehead Neville, Hinton St Mary, Halstock, Dewlish), up to ten generations post-conquest. The only clear exception to this is the villa at Rockbourne, close to the Hampshire border in the eastern part of the area, where mid-second-century structures have been traced. In the northern part of the putative *civitas* territory, around Ilchester in Somerset, there are signs of slightly earlier beginnings of villa construction, but still within the third century (Bratton Seymour, Thornford, Westland, Ilchester Mead). There are also a number of villas in this area of exclusively late third- or fourth-century date (High Ham, Spaxton, Lufton).

On the Somerset wetlands, there was a general absence of villas, with the exception of a site at Wemberham, which might have been an estate centre. The comparative lack of wealth accretion among the native communities who worked this landscape (as in the Fens) fits with a high degree of state exploitation, the lack of cultural evolution with a degree of passive resistance on their part. Poole Harbour in Dorset was another area where salt production was practised and this locality stands out for a number of other commodities that were extracted or produced there and widely distributed within the province. Purbeck marble and Kimmeridge shale were important decorative stones in Roman Britain and both were being exploited on a significant scale within a very few years of the conquest. Black Burnished pottery produced near Poole Harbour enjoyed an extraordinarily wide provincial distribution, indicative of the unusual economic relationships of the area.

Even in the most 'developed' areas of the British provincial landscape, then, success was relative and conditional on a range of factors, including local volition and wealth, alongside imperial prerogatives and outside investment. There were also regions of profound conservatism, where traditional architectural styles and landscape forms co-existed with novel features long into the Roman period. The chronology of development varied markedly from one region to the next and some areas reveal more than one phase of profound change. There is evidence of both precocious development and premature decline – the latter especially true of parts of eastern England.

WESTERN AND NORTHERN BRITAIN

Eastern Devon

Exeter was the centre of the most south-westerly *civitas* of normal type, though, as already noted, it is less certain that Dumnonian territory included Cornwall. The evidence for rural settlement in Devon reveals apparently divergent development of the Exe valley and eastern Devon from the rest of the county. The only paved Roman roads in the south-west peninsula are found in Devon, notably the southern section of the Fosse Way, which connected Exeter with Ilchester, Cirencester and the Midlands, and a west to east route towards Dorchester. There is a trace of a route leading west from Exeter, though it is uncertain how far it extended.

The territory of the *Dumnonii* contained very few villas, even if others lie undiscovered beneath the extensive permanent pastures of the modern landscape. An example of a winged corridor villa with six or seven rooms lies south-east of Crediton, set within a rectangular enclosure. At Holcombe, a villa developed on the site of an indigenous farm with late Iron Age origins. Late first-century rectangular timber buildings were replaced by two aisled halls, one with stone footings, by the end of the second century. The eventual form of the villa in the early fourth century represents a series of extensions to a stone-footed aisled hall into an elongated rectangular range of about fifteen rooms and 50-m frontage, linked by sections of corridor or veranda. An unusual feature is a great octagonal structure, perhaps a bath, added to the south-west end of the range in *c.*300 (comparable with similar late features at Keynsham and Lufton in Avon and Somerset). Other villas are known near the Dorset/Somerset border, in the Exe Valley, and along the coast at Otterton Point and at Honeyditches near Seaton. The Honeyditches site is unusual in that it comprises simple rectangular stone buildings in association with a third-century bath-house, along with two long, timber barrack-like structures. Since a stamped tile of the *legio II Augusta* has been found, a connection with the military cannot be excluded. The complex was built over a native double enclosure farmstead of roundhouse type and was occupied from the second to the fourth century.

Relatively few nucleated sites of Romano-British types are known at present along the Roman road network, though Pomeroy Wood between Exeter and Honiton shows the potential for unsuspected sites to be added. The Pomeroy Wood settlement extended for at least 700 m east–west along the Roman road. In its second- and third-century phases it consisted predominantly of a series of timber roundhouses and four-post granaries, some within demarcated compounds. There are indications of a change in the character of the settlement in the later third century when the roundhouses were abandoned. West of Exeter, there is evidence of some sort of enclosed settlement succeeding the Roman fort at Bury Barton, a site that may correspond with *Nemeto Statio*. Another small centre existed at Topsham, again developing on what appears to have been a military site.

Non-villa settlements are largely known through aerial photography. They are morphologically of late Iron Age and Romano-British date – an interpretation supported at the limited number to have been investigated (as at Hayes Farm). These ditched enclosures are mostly quite small (less than 1 ha) and in both rectilinear and curvilinear form. There seems to be a greater concentration of rectangular enclosures in south Devon than elsewhere. An excavated example of the rectangular enclosure type is Stoke Gabriel, associated with an oval stone-footed house and with occupation evidence spanning the first to the fourth century. Although the internal buildings within these rural sites are often not well preserved, a range of structural types is represented, from round and oval houses to small villas.

Cornwall and western Devon

What then became of the rest of the south-west peninsula? Western Devon and Cornwall is in many ways a land apart from much of the rest of southern Britain. Distance is a factor – Land's End to London is as far as London to the Scottish border. The landscapes of Devon and Cornwall are dominated by areas of moorland, the most notable being the granite masses of Dartmoor and Bodmin and the sandstone uplands of Exmoor. Another geological feature, the Culm measures, is responsible for heavy clay soils covering a large part of northern and western Devon and north-east Cornwall. The many tidal river systems that cut into the landmass contributed to the difficulties of overland communication. The most significant of the river systems flowing to the south are the Tamar and its various tributaries leading into Plymouth Sound, and the Fal and other tributaries of the Carrick Roads. The Taw and Torridge, Allen and Camel are the major northern streams. Before the construction of modern road bridges near the mouths of some of these rivers, the main communication route through this territory ran down the central watershed, along the line still followed by the A30 road. The potential for communication by water was somewhat better, with major natural anchorages in Plymouth Sound, the Fal estuary and elsewhere.

Modern interpretation identifies the people of Cornwall as a sub-group of the *Dumnonii*, on the basis of a correlation of Ptolemy's double toponym *Dumnonium sive Ocrinum Promontorium* (promontory of the *Dumnonii*, or *Ocrinum* promontory) with the Lizard peninsula. The absence of any name in Ptolemy for the equally prominent headland south of Dartmoor could indicate that what were two separate toponyms in his sources had been erroneously conflated by him. If *Ocrinum* was the Lizard, then *Dumnonium Promontorium* could have been related to the Salcombe peninsula of southern Devon, marking the approach from the west to Dumnonian territory focused on the Exe valley. This fits far better with discernible cultural differences between Devon and Cornwall in terms of their late Iron Age ceramic styles, with distinct Cornish cordoned wares not generally found east of Plymouth, and with a separate tradition of south-western decorated ware in east Devon. The different ceramic tradition of Cornwall continued into the Roman period with the production of so-called Gabbroic wares utilizing distinctive clays from the Lizard peninsula.

Cornwall has often been written off in books on Roman Britain as lacking the human or other resources to develop the normal infrastructure of the civil province. Yet the area was not without natural resources and advantages. Its mineral reserves, notably tin, but also copper, lead and even gold, have at various points in history attracted speculators and supported substantial mining communities. These rich mineral resources were an obvious element for the state to set aside for its own exploitation. The sea was also another potentially important resource, not only for fish and other marine products, but also for the possibility of trade with Continental Europe. The late prehistoric harbour at Mount Batten on Plymouth Sound is a key site, perhaps identifiable with the tidal island called *Ictis*, the chief entrepôt of early trade. There were prolonged connections especially with the Armorican people of Brittany. In the

Roman period, the sea routes round the Cornish peninsula were important for maritime traffic up the west coast of Britain, though some overland transport to harbours in the Bristol Channel was also undertaken to obviate the long and dangerous sea passage round Land's End.

Nor was this region an empty wasteland in the late Iron Age. Dispersed defended settlements called rounds, with bank and ditch systems enclosing small clusters of large oval dwellings and roundhouses, are particularly common in Cornwall and west Devon. It is estimated that their average density is between one per 2.2 to one per 4.5 sq km, with about 1,500 sites now known, most less than 2 ha in area. Many of the excavated examples originated in the late Iron Age and continued through the Roman period, though some were constructed entirely within the Roman period. Most show limited development over time, either architecturally or in terms of material culture. As a group they suggest a society that was less hierarchically organized than those of south-east Britain, and perhaps predominantly structured around family units of roughly equal status.

'Cliff castles' were another settlement category; essentially small hillforts located on defensible coastal promontories, rarely larger than 2 ha. There are only seven hillforts in Devon and Cornwall in excess of 6 ha, one at least of which probably played a significant role in the settlement dynamics of the late Iron Age and Roman period. Carn Brea was expanded from an original Neolithic defensive core, with Iron Age walls creating a series of distinct enclosures within the overall 15-ha area. The potential significance of the site as a centre of power in the late Iron Age is illustrated by a hoard of at least seventeen Gallic gold coins of c.50 BC. Its function and role can only be guessed at, but its location near Camborne in one of the main mining districts is suggestive.

Rounds were generally located on lands with some arable potential and there is a notable concentration in the Penwith peninsula and Lizard area, where extensive field systems are known. A mixed economy, with agriculture an important component, is also indicated by finds of querns and sickles. The most completely excavated round is Trethurgy near St Austell. The interior of the enclosure (0.2 ha) was quite densely packed with buildings in an arc around a central cobbled area. In total nine main phases of occupation were identified, dating between the mid-second and the sixth century. The predominant dwelling form here and at many other round sites comprised large thick-walled single-roomed oval structures. Several at Trethurgy revealed traces of hearths in the floor and two buildings had preserved traces of screened off areas at one end of the oval room. The larger houses had a floor area of 80–140 sq m and the construction of these houses, with complex roof structures designed to eliminate central supports and to maximize interior floorspace, was a major undertaking for these small communities – probably numbering somewhere between 20 and 50 souls at a site like Trethurgy. Although the material culture of these sites was relatively poor (at Trethurgy the vast majority of the pottery assemblage consisted of local Gabbroic wares), occasional finds of coins, samian pottery, amphorae, Black Burnished ware and Roman glass vessels demonstrate some involvement with markets. These contacts appear underdeveloped economically and comparatively irregular. On the other hand, evidence of iron-smithing and recovery here of a tin ingot suggest that the exploitation of metal resources played a role in the local economy.

So-called courtyard houses were an important class of (generally) unenclosed site. These were stone-built ovoid complexes, comprising paved courtyards surrounded by small irregular rooms let into the massively thick walls. Sites typically comprised small hamlets of the courtyard houses, as the classic examples of Chysauster and Carn Euny. At both these sites, there is also evidence of another distinctive type of structure, souterrains or underground chambers. These have a limited distribution in the extreme south-west of Cornwall, though there are many parallels in Britanny to the south, and in Ireland and Scotland. Goldherring and Porthmeor are examples of courtyard houses built within rounds, showing some overlap between these categories.

What typifies all these types of settlement is their intermediate size between individual homesteads and large nucleated centres, suggesting a marked lack of hierarchy and social differentiation. The vast majority of these sites were either for extended family units or small clans. The plethora of sites of relatively small size cumulatively supported quite a large dispersed population. If we take the lowest population estimate of twenty people for a round and assume a maximum figure of 1,500 contemporaneously occupied rounds in Cornwall, this would suggest a peak regional population of c.30,000. Overall, the Cornish peninsula is notable for the relative poverty of its rural sites in material terms, the lack of integration into the provincial cultural and economic mainstream, and the relatively unchanging nature of these sites across several centuries.

There are gaps in the archaeological record concerning how the Roman state controlled Cornwall and west Devon. Given the mineral wealth around the granite formations of Penwith, Kerrier and Blackmore, and between Bodmin, St Austell and Penzance, it is highly unlikely that all official interest ceased with the withdrawal of first-century garrisons. It is equally problematic that no Roman harbour settlement has ever been confirmed on the tidal Fal estuary, and Roman activity on Plymouth Sound remains poorly delineated, though these are two of the best natural harbours in Britain. Over sixty separate coin finds, including at least eight hoards, have been made at different points within Plymouth, mainly on the central (northern) and the eastern promontories covering an extensive area overlooking the Sound. The coins span the first to fourth centuries in date. Other unusual finds include a bronze statuette and a small bust, while building materials including Roman tile have been found in Sutton Pool on the north shore facing the Mount Batten peninsula. Roman material has also been found at locations extending up the banks of both the Tamar and Tavy rivers. Cumulatively, this is impressive evidence that Plymouth overlies an extensive area of Roman settlement around the Sound. It seems clear that Roman settlement had expanded far beyond the Iron Age entrepôt on the Mount Batten promontory on the east side of the Sound. The position of these harbour facilities on the north and east side of the Sound suggests a connection with possible Roman-period mining on the flanks of Dartmoor.

No such convincing case can yet be made for the identification of a major harbour on the Fal estuary in Cornwall, though one or more sites might be expected there close to the other main mining district in the south-west. The creeks of the Fal estuary have all been navigable until relatively recent times and the anchorages could be some distance upstream. East of Truro, a large sub-rectangular enclosed site of 2.3 ha at Carvossa has produced an unusual assemblage of pre-Flavian fine-wares, glass and bronze fibulae and this is one of a cluster of unusually large sites close to the navigable limit of the Fal. The assemblage from the evidently indigenous settlement at Carvossa is reminiscent of Roman military sites of this period and may suggest the presence of a 'missing' fort or port nearby.

The only two known 'villas' in Cornwall are located close together, at Magor and Rosewarne, within the mining district east of St Ives Bay.

Magor has been shown by excavation to have a long history, being established as a 'villa'-type building by the mid-second century, within what appears to be an earlier enclosure of late Iron Age type. Rosewarne is known only from the discovery of fragments of tessellated pavement, implying the existence of a substantial masonry building, though this could as easily have been a bath-house on a mining settlement as a villa. The significance of these sites is unclear – they were certainly not part of a more widespread pattern of villa estates – and an association with mining or metallurgical activity seems most probable. We can only speculate as to whether these were residences of Roman officials in charge of a mining district or of private contractors or lessees or native Britons operating the Cornish mineral fields. The architectural features of these sites should remind us that this was still very much a colonial landscape, a point reinforced by five third-century Roman 'milestones' from Cornwall (perhaps in fact boundary stones for imperial mining regions?).

If this western territory had been under the control of the *civitas* of the *Dumnonii*, it seems extraordinary that the differences between Cornwall and the Exe Valley should be so marked, and that the opportunities for the development of mineral extraction and trade so comprehensively missed. The lack of widespread change and development in settlement and relative poverty of the material culture of the indigenous sites in Cornwall are in fact relatively typical of the military zones of Britain. The most plausible reading of the archaeological evidence is that the territory of the *civitas* of the *Dumnonii* was limited by Rome to eastern Devon, centred on the Exe Valley, with much of the rest of the south-west peninsula held in some other status – perhaps as *ager publicus* or imperial property. Indeed, evidence of large-scale Roman iron-mining and smelting on Exmoor, close to the location of early forts, could indicate the additional separation of northern Devon from the effective control of the *Dumnonii*. The people of Cornwall were probably known as the *Cornovii*, though they were apparently not allowed to develop as a fully independent *civitas*.

The Scilly Isles form the most south-westerly outpost of the British Isles and represent an extreme version of what has been observed on the mainland. An added complication is that the Scilly Isles have been increasingly slipping beneath the Atlantic and what was in Roman times a much larger main island (ancient *Sulina* or *Sillina*), now comprises many separate islands. The archipelago and associated shoals is a notoriously dangerous place for sailors, though there was clearly periodic contact with the mainland. The isolation of the islands did not put them beyond the reach of Rome, as is shown by ancient references to Rome sending political or religious troublemakers into exile there.

The Marches

The Welsh Marches appear very different from the lower Severn valley. There are fewer than ten villas in the Shropshire plain and none of these is of any great size or complexity. Rural settlement has been partly elucidated through aerial-photographic survey of the upper Severn valley and the Wroxeter Hinterlands survey, centred on the cantonal capital of the *Cornovii*. However, the late Iron Age and Roman settlement remains difficult to trace in detail because of a regional tendency towards aceramic material culture that seems to have remained pronounced on rural sites of Roman date. This paucity of rural ceramics stands in contrast to the relative abundance of such material at Wroxeter itself. Even villa sites defy normal expectations, as at Whitley Grange near Wroxeter, which produced fewer than seventy sherds of pottery from several seasons of excavation. A few nucleated centres have yielded larger quantities of material goods, such as Meole Brace (*c.*6 km west of Wroxeter), though the fact that the amphoras and storage jars attested here were not also distributed to the minor rural settlements undermines the general interpretation of these sites as local markets within the *territorium*.

The typical settlements of the territory were dispersed enclosed farmsteads, though there is a greater prevalence of rectangular enclosures near Wroxeter and of curvilinear ones further away. Both types seem to have Iron Age origins and to have continued into the Roman period. At Sharpstones Hill an irregular rectangular enclosure contained a central roundhouse, later replaced with a rectangular timber building of simple form. At a few sites only can one suggest a sequence from pre-Roman enclosure to villa. Most notably this appears to be the case at Ashford Carbonell, where a major sub-rectangular enclosure of presumed Iron Age or early Romano-British date underlay a walled compound, enclosing a small winged corridor house and an aisled hall.

Engleton and Ashford Carbonell villas were both modest winged corridor structures, while Lea Cross possibly, and Acton Scott certainly, conformed to the aisled hall type, with a bath-house eventually being inserted into one end of the structure. Rural mosaics are known at Whitley Grange, Lea Cross and Yarchester. Several of the stone buildings in the region may not be conventional villas at all, as seems to have been the case with the site of Linley, a possible control site for a mining operation, attested by a discovery of lead pigs here and the physical traces of linear trenches on the hill above.

At Duncote Farm, close to Wroxeter itself, a sequence of reorganizations of landscape was noted, with irregular Iron Age field systems replaced by a regular pattern of rectangular fields in the early second century. The boundary ditches were subsequently infilled, before being overlain by a major rectilinear enclosure of industrial usage in the late Roman period. The evidence suggests a series of upheavals in the establishment of rural property boundaries, with the first major change corresponding to the foundation of the city. This sort of drastic impact on property boundaries appears to have been most intensive in close vicinity to the city.

A complicating factor in this area was prolonged contact with the military and other state authorities. The mining resources of the Welsh borderland were valuable and were not necessarily assigned to the benefit of the urban community. Contractors under licence may eventually have worked the lead mines at Linley and the copper mines at Llanymynech; there is no evidence to link their control directly to the *Cornovii*. Similarly the nucleated settlements of the Cheshire plain – sites such as Northwich, Middlewich and Whitchurch – had a pronounced industrial focus and were probably separate in some degree from the core territory of the *civitas* (whether as part of the *prata legionis* based on Chester or as minor garrison settlements).

Wales

The landscapes of Wales, like those of Cornwall, were more challenging than those of south-east England, though not without potential for the development of mixed farming and other forms of economic exploitation. Mountain massifs dominate the centre of Wales, but these contained their own bounty in the form of a range of mineral deposits. Lowlands are located around the coastal fringes of the massif to south, west and north and down the land border of the Marches. There are good cultivable soils in the coastal plains of South and West Wales from

Pembroke to the Wye and to a lesser extent along the North Wales coast. The island of Anglesey has in many historical phases been an important arable farming resource for North Wales. Running out from the mountains are many rivers, dissecting the narrow coastal plains and creating obstacles to easy movement around the skirt of the uplands.

In south-west Wales, there was a preference for small defended sites, many with multiple enclosures. Simple enclosed sites, similar to the Cornish rounds, are known in Wales as raths. Of nearly 600 'hillforts' recorded in Wales, 230 enclose less that 0.4 ha and the territory of the *Demetae* appears to have contained the majority of these. One of the best-known examples is Walesland Rath, an oval enclosure, with single ditch and rampart, pierced by two entrances. The interior was initially densely packed with structures, including at least six timber roundhouses and numerous four-poster granaries. The large grain-storage capacity at Walesland Rath demonstrates the evolved mixed farming regime of this area in the late Iron Age. The site was abandoned following the conquest, with reoccupation only in the third century, when a stone-footed rect-angular building and Roman pottery occur alongside roundhouses. The Roman occupation here appears markedly less impressive than the later Iron Age phases.

Several other sites in Dyfed show a pattern of transition from enclosed settlement to Roman-style farm, beginning as enclosed sites in the Iron Age tradition and developing rectilinear stone buildings, generally described as villas. The two clearest examples are Cwmbrywn and Trelis-sey near Carmarthen, where the buildings were of mortared-stone con-struction. Although of simple row type, the former site incorporated a small bath, the latter a hypocaust. Cwmbrywn also boasted the most westerly 'corn-dryer' of Romano-British type yet known. Occupation ran from the mid-second to the fourth century. In terms of complexity and ornament these are near the bottom of the range of 'villa' sites in Britain and there are few other candidates in the region. Llys Brychan near the upper end of the Tywi valley is a distinct and exceptional outlier. Evidently of third-century and later date, this site is only partially known, but was stone-built with painted plaster, tessellated floors, hypo-caust heating in at least two chambers and a tile roof (later replaced with heavy slate). Some atypical explanation must account for its unique inland location.

As well as small hillforts and ring-works, there were promontory forts and numerous enclosed settlements. Open settlements were present, but in the minority. Of the more complex defended enclosures (ring-forts), the neighbouring sites of Woodside and Dan y Coed and Pen y Coed provide good examples of a type that is reminiscent of the Iron Age 'banjo-enclosures' of Wessex, with a probable function related to stock control. The richest phases of these sites were in the late Iron Age and the defences at Dan y Coed were evidently slighted and the site possibly abandoned for a period during the conquest phase. Nonetheless there was later first-century occupation here and a transition from timber roundhouses to rectangular buildings of simple type. Both sites seem to have suffered further decline in the second century.

Coygan Camp is an example of an excavated promontory site. This settlement started in the middle Iron Age, but continued to be occupied into the Roman period (though with a first-century hiatus). Palaeoeconomic data show that it was a specialized pastoral settlement. The range and number of artefacts present was atypical of many sites of this type and late Roman activity included third-century counterfeiting of coinage.

Smaller and simpler enclosed sites were the predominant settlement type, varying from oval and circular to sub-rectangular in shape. Internal buildings were typically roundhouses, with the largest enclosures containing several buildings. Castell Henllys was a thriving late Iron Age roundhouse settlement, but was abandoned around the time of the conquest, and a smaller undefended farmstead established just outside its defences.

The combined evidence suggests some volatility, despite the apparent similarity of settlement types before and after the conquest. Many excavated sites show periods of discontinuity, before being reoccupied at a later date. The mid- to late first century marked one cut-off point, sometimes accompanied with evidence for deliberate slighting of defensive features or settlement relocation to less defensible or open positions. There was another phase of settlement instability and abandonment evident at some sites in the second century. Current interpretations of the settlement data have not taken full account of the potential impact of Irish migration into this part of Wales in the fourth century and later.

The small size of Roman Carmarthen and the relative poverty of even the largest of the rural centres are strong indicators of a restricted territory. The mountainous fringe to the north and north-east of Carmarthen has been recognized as archaeologically distinct from the rest of Dyfed, with sparser settlements outside the river valleys of the Tywi and Teifi. The Roman military dispositions sought to control the middle and upper reaches of these valley systems and to exploit the mineral resources of the mountains. It is thus quite probable that this land was excluded from the territory assigned to the *Demetae*. The extensive civil settlement by the gold mine at Dolaucothi outlasted the removal of the military garrison there in the early second century and occupation appears to have continued into the fourth century. Either a procurator or a contractor leasing the mining site and its supporting infrastructure from the state perhaps supervised this site.

The *Silures* of Glamorgan/Gwent are known to have provided stiff resistance to the Roman advance. The first-century governor Scapula was so incensed by their repeated attacks that he is said to have ordered their annihilation. That this was not carried out to the letter is clear from the foundation of a *civitas* of the *Silures*, with its centre at Caerwent, one of the smallest of the Romano-British urban centres and somewhat in the shadow of a legionary base at nearby Caerleon. The development of its territory exemplifies the treatment of a native people allowed to pass under civil administration on much less advantageous terms than most other urbanized Romano-British communities.

The region includes the Gower Peninsula, the Vale of Glamorgan and the low-lying parts of Monmouthshire, arguably the largest contiguous area of better-quality land in Wales, subdivided by the Neath, Taff, Usk and Wye rivers. The depiction of the *Silures* by the Roman sources as wild men from the hills is interesting, since the archaeological evidence strongly points to their heartlands lying in a zone of permanent settlements and a mixed-farming economy. The Roman settlement pattern was influenced by the long-term presence of elements of *legio II Augusta* at Caerleon, the *civitas* centre at Caerwent and several small towns and garrison settlements, such as Abergavenny, Usk, Bulmore, Monmouth, Cardiff and Cowbridge. Within their local areas, these sites may have had some impact on rural settlement and economy. The settlement hierarchy was similar to Dyfed (though evidently with more upper-level sites): hillforts and promontory forts, simple enclosed settlements of oval and rectangular form and generally of less than 0.5 ha area. Some of these enclosures developed as farms or villas of Roman type.

There are signs of social and economic development that came close to the 'normal' pattern for civil territory. In particular, there was clearer and more distinctive development of Roman-style buildings at rural sites. Ten certain and five probable 'villas' are now known, mostly located within a few kilometres of the coast. Whitton is a good example of a defended enclosure that showed continued activity into the Roman period, over time evolving into a villa. Early first-century roundhouses were superseded, starting in the second century, by several phases of rectangular stone buildings, some utilizing tile or Pennant sandstone slate roofs. One of the buildings incorporated a simple hypocaust, another had a veranda and may have been two-storeyed. This is one of a number of sites showing this sort of sequence from native rectangular enclosure to villa in Glamorgan (others include Llandough and probably Llantwit Major). The villa at Ely near Cardiff was a substantial L-shaped complex incorporating bath-suite, a portico with dwarf columns, mosaic and tessellated pavements and tile roof. Occupation apparently ran from the late second to the early fourth century. Biglis (Moulton) and Dan y Graig are known from geophysical survey to have been corridor houses. The largest and most sophisticated villa in Glamorgan was that at Llantwit Major (Cae'r Mead). This complex grew in size and complexity from an initial stone phase in the later second century. In its fourth-century heyday, it comprised suites of buildings arranged around two courtyards, covering almost 1 ha in area; impressive features included a dining-room, mosaic, baths and a large aisled hall. It stands out from other villas of South Wales, with the possible exception of the imperfectly known site of Maesderwen near the headwaters of the Usk, beyond the Brecon Beacons. Only the bath-house of that site is known, but the number and quality of its mosaics indicate that it too represents something extraordinary at the regional level.

These two unusually opulent sites, for which there may have been some exceptional explanation, should not distract us from the reality of the rest. The typical villas in Glamorgan and Gwent were generally of small to medium size and of modest pretensions, though several were equipped with small bath-houses and mosaics or tessellated floors. The overall distribution of these 'villas' was generally well away from the cantonal capital at Caerwent. There were only three villas close to the town and the vast majority lay beyond Cardiff in South Glamorgan. Croes Carn Einion is an isolated example close to Caerleon, and Oystermouth a western outlier on the Gower.

Some of the rectangular enclosures of late Iron Age type demonstrate another trajectory of development from the villas. Mynydd Bychan was an Iron Age settlement with timber roundhouses, which were subsequently rebuilt in stone, reflecting a simple updating of a traditional building form. There are numerous other examples of roundhouse settlements defined by banked enclosures continuing in occupation into the late Roman period, such as Caldicot or Thornwell Farm.

A further major change attributable to the Roman period was the reclamation of a large area of coastal wetlands along the Gwent Levels. Recent survey has confirmed the Roman date of improved wetlands and of extensive field systems. An inscription at Goldcliffe recorded the construction by a legionary detachment of '33 Roman feet' of something (from the location surely connected to this coastal drainage work) – the clearest indication of military involvement in such schemes. The associated settlement sites were generally of timber, though evidently with good access to Roman material culture. It is uncertain at present whether the settlers on these reclaimed pastures were locals or incomers. The main phase of the reclamation appears to date to the second–third centuries, with little material post-dating the mid-fourth century.

A further ingredient in the settlement pattern was the presence of the legionary base, with its attendant garrison settlement (*canabae*) and additional nucleated settlements that were created or grew up around other forts or along the roads connecting sites. One important and unusual site is Bulmore, a linear settlement situated about 2.5 km east of the Caerleon fortress. This 'suburb' consisted largely of stone strip buildings set at right angles to the road and the earliest to be built were provided with legionary roof tiles, implying official encouragement for its creation. It has been suggested that Bulmore may have been established as a settlement for veterans. The legion will have had a large territory (*prata*) carved out of Silurian lands and the settlement of veterans in the vicinity will have required access to additional land. It is possible that the lands controlled by the army and veterans extended up the Usk valley as far as Usk itself, down to the sea at Goldcliffe, east to Bulmore and west to Roman lead/silver-mining sites and associated settlements at Draethen and Risca. That would amount to over 200 sq km of prime farmland and other resources confiscated from the *Silures*. It also raises questions about Silurian access to the farmland of south Glamorgan, since the legionary *prata* may have imposed a geographical separation between these lands and the *civitas* centre at Caerwent. From this perspective, was south Glamorgan in fact re-attributed to the *Silures* by Rome, or did villa development there reflect the activity of veterans or other members of the military community? The territory assigned to the *Silures* could well have been limited to parts of Gwent alone.

The *Deceangli* or *Decangi* are believed to have occupied the area from the Dee to the Conwy in Clywd, with the upper Dee valley marking the effective southern limits. At the heart of this area, there were substantial lead/silver reserves in the Clwydian range. The eastern limits of the pre-conquest people may originally have extended into the northern Cheshire plain and the Wirral, where there was an important Iron Age and early Roman maritime entrepôt at Meols. Their territory was garrisoned initially and the legionary fortress at Chester was established either on Deceanglian or Cornovian land. No *civitas* centre is known and the region appears to have remained under military supervision.

Assessment of the settlement history of this region is complicated by poor site visibility and the aceramic character of much rural settlement. The emerging picture though is of lowland enclosed settlements within and on the flanks of the valleys of the Dee and Clwyd and along the coastal strip. These were mostly small univallate sites; finds of Roman material remain rare. The 2.5-ha hillfort of Dinorben was slighted in the first century, but was reoccupied in the third century, when it may have served primarily as a temple or religious centre.

The garrison settlement at Chester was the closest thing to a major urban centre, with an additional suburban settlement to the south of Chester at Heronbridge – somewhat reminiscent of Bulmore by Caerleon. A pottery and tile production centre at Holt was also clearly under military control and suggests that the military territory extended at least 12 km in this direction. A settlement of over 10 ha at Plas Coch near Wrexham, with stone buildings, wells and 'corn-dryers', may also be in some way related to the legionary territory and its supply needs. Other significant sites in terms of size and Roman-style buildings were garrison settlements (as at Prestatyn, Ruthin, and possibly Rhuddlan) and probable industrial settlements associated with mining, such as those at Prestatyn, Flint and Ffrith. The Deceanglian communities may well have been integrated into the mining and metallurgy activity as a labour pool, as also seems to have happened in north-western Spain. The settlement at Flint (later first century until the mid-third) included a stone-built administrative building complex, developed from a timber predecessor, as well as baths and stone and timber strip buildings. Tiles of *legio XX* show the official nature of the site, and the main building is interpreted as the headquarters of a Roman mining official. Prestatyn has also yielded tiles of *legio XX*, a bath-house and workshops within the limited area of the settlement excavated. Ffrith has produced finds of legionary tiles, a bath-house and other timber and stone buildings. Prestatyn and Ffrith show a main phase of activity in the later first and second centuries, with more limited activity thereafter. These three sites that ring the Clwydian mountains from which the lead was extracted offer as comprehensive an example as one might wish of the Roman mode of exploitation of a conquered territory possessing potentially lucrative mineral reserves. Lead pigs from the area were stamped '*Deceangl*' in the first century, acknowledging just whose lead and silver the Romans were taking. The impact of Roman occupation on the *Deceangli* thus appears to be largely negative, with their lands mostly annexed to military or imperial control.

The people of north-west Wales were the *Ordovices*, if we are to accept at face value the comment by Tacitus that Agricola launched his attack on Anglesey following a rebellion by that people. On the other hand, earlier references to them in the campaigns of the 40s imply that they occupied territory nearer to the Marches and to the *Silures* of South Wales. It is commonly accepted therefore that they controlled lands between Anglesey and the upper Severn Valley. The area of northern Snowdonia has received particular archaeological study because of the extraordinary preservation there of numerous upland sites. The majority of these are situated at 150–250 m altitude along the north-western edge of the ridge of uplands that runs roughly parallel to the Menai Straits. These relict landscapes offer a remarkable window on to a style of life and settlement that shows little sign of Roman influence. It is equally clear from proper assessment of the more low-lying areas of Anglesey and Arfon that the *Ordovices* were not simply pastoral hill-dwellers but that they also possessed many enclosed settlements on the available arable lands.

The upland settlement includes a number of large hillforts, such as Garn Boduan, Conwy Mountain and Tre'r Ceiri, of which the last was certainly in use at the time of the conquest and for some centuries thereafter. Other common types of settlement in the upland area include variations on the theme of dispersed homesteads in oval, rectilinear and polygonal enclosures. There were also unenclosed settlements of roundhouses, some set in small-scale field systems. The standard form of dwelling in the Iron Age was represented by circular stone footings and this tradition persisted strongly into the Roman period, though some rectilinear forms did appear alongside. Recent research has also demonstrated that there were timber- and clay-walled roundhouses, some in unenclosed settlements, alongside the stone-footed structures.

The low-lying sites of Anglesey and Arfon had a somewhat different morphology, with one important group comprising rectangular enclosures with earth ramparts. Ten such sites are now known on Anglesey, and an excavated example at Bryn Eryr shows occupation of timber roundhouses from the mid-first millennium BC to the late Roman period. Other examples have yielded evidence of some rectangular buildings, as at Rhuddgaer and Caer Leb. The impression derived from the artefact-poor, upland settlements of a very fragmented and isolated society requires revision as more work is done on the sites situated on the better farmland. Both Bryn Eryr and Bush Farm, Gwynedd, have revealed lowland roundhouse settlements with access to a wide range of Roman pottery and material goods. For instance, the 600 Roman sherds recovered from Bryn Eryr represent at least 100 separate vessels, and over 400 sherds from Bush Farm a minimum of 76 vessels. Similarly, the site of Din Lligwy on Anglesey was a polygonal enclosure, containing a mix of roundhouses and rectangular stone buildings in good-quality masonry, and had an exceptional range of Roman pottery and coins in comparison to the upland sites. Its location close to the Roman copper mines on Parys Mountain may account for its privileged access to Roman material. Conductors or lessees evidently ran the Roman copper-mining at Parys Mountain on behalf of the state, to judge from the evidence of stamped ingots. The associated settlements and administrative centre for this activity are still to seek.

Snowdonia remains a somewhat under-populated part of the archaeological map, but the *Ordovices* appear to have had interests well to the south-east. A dense cluster of sites in the upper Severn region and around the major hillforts of Old Oswestry and Llanymynech should pertain to them. The latter site is one of the largest in Britain, enclosing 57 ha, with a major copper source at its centre. A substantial Roman mining operation was installed here, though little is known of its operation or its associated settlement sites.

The *Ordovices* developed no towns or villas and, as with the *Deceangli*, the evidence for wealth accumulation in their territory is limited to one or two exceptional native settlements. In the later second century, three of the five known auxiliary forts still occupied in Wales were in this region (Caernarfon, Caersws and Forden Gaer). This suggests that the mineral wealth of the mountains and the arable wealth of Anglesey were siphoned off in a variety of ways, to the benefit of Rome and the relative impoverishment of the indigenous people.

Northern England

The *Brigantes* are commonly (and misleadingly) depicted as occupying a vast area of northern Britain, extending up both sides of the Pennines from northern Cheshire and South Yorkshire to just beyond the Tyne–Solway isthmus. This is largely because Tacitus described them as the most numerous people of Britain and Ptolemy specifically stated that they extended from sea to sea. Given the physical dimensions of this territory and the diversity and separation of the constituent blocks of land that make it up, the reality was undoubtedly more complex. At a basic level there are major differences east and west of the Pennines, which form an upland watershed between discrete river systems running to the North Sea and the Irish Sea. There are also significant changes in settlement morphology and material culture as one moves south to north up either side of the Pennines. If the *Brigantes* really exercised authority 'sea-to-sea', this was most probably the result of confederation and hegemonic controls of other northern peoples. A number of other apparent ethnic names are known from literary and epigraphic sources: *Parisi* of northern Humberside, *Gabrantovices* of the North Yorkshire coast, *Setantii* of northern Lancashire, *Carvetii* in the Eden Valley, *Tectoverdi* perhaps in the Tyne Valley.

Settlement in both Iron Age and Roman times seems to have followed similar geographic trends, being denser in the valley systems and low-lying areas, and in general sparse in the Pennine uplands, the Lake District and the North York moors. The most important pre-Roman centres were on the east side of the Pennines, and this was certainly where the Romans later located the *civitas* lands of the *Brigantes*. There were numerous hillfort sites within the territory as most widely defined; though with many fewer to the west of the Pennines – where the main examples are, from south to north, Mam Tor, Ingleborough and Carrock Fell, with Burnswark in Annandale a possible northern outlier.

East of the Pennines, Almondbury in Carrickdale, Barwick in Elmet and the *oppidum* of Stanwick have all had their advocates as the chief centre of Brigantian power. At any rate, their heartlands appear to have lain in the Vale of York and the lower valleys of the Dales, within the triangular area defined by a line linking Almondbury, Barwick and York as the base, and with Stanwick as the northern apex. The large site at Stanwick, with elaborate systems of earthworks, is reminiscent of the southern *oppida*, with a potential inner compound at the Tofts, which may have served as a royal residence to judge by elite imports from the Roman world of pre-Flavian date. There was little activity here from the Flavian period onwards, indicating the abandonment of this site as a centre of the people.

The Romans created a new centre of the *Brigantes* at Aldborough (*Isurium*), on the river Ure, north-west of York close to where the Dales debouch into the relatively broad and fertile valley of the Ouse. It is doubtful that the Romans continued to consider all the other peoples of northern Britain as *Brigantes*. A separate *civitas* may have been created for the *Parisi* in east Yorkshire, though their main centre was apparently treated initially as a *vicus*. Both the Vale of York and the north Humber area have produced evidence of villa-type buildings, though they are still few in number (around thirty probable sites). Almost all fall within the main low-lying corridors of good arable or mixed farmland, with a few in the broad valley systems on the edge of Wolds or moorland areas. This 'villa landscape' is restricted to the eastern side of the Pennines; there are no viable candidates to the west, even in the Eden Valley, where the *civitas* of the *Carvetii* was organized by the third century. The most westerly outlier is at Kirk Sink in the heart of the Pennines near Skipton, a key location in the Aire gap that marks one of the easiest trans-Pennine routes. This site was developed on a native enclosed settlement, with roundhouses replaced in the second century by a small rectangular building with tessellated pavements, a bath and hypocausts. The uniqueness of its position makes explanation difficult, but whatever it represents, it is atypical of the regional pattern. The regions west of the Pennines also differ from those to the east in terms of material culture, stock-raising practices and economy – adding further weight to the argument that the pre-Roman confederation was at best somewhat artificial and that, under Rome, Brigantian territory was much more narrowly defined. A significant number of the major garrison settlements of northern Britain were also concentrated in the area east of the Pennines, as at Adel, Doncaster, Castleford, Newton Kyme, Malton, Piercebridge and, most notably, Catterick. These sites put further constraints on the territory assigned to the control of the Brigantes.

Half of the eastern group of villas are located within the area normally associated with the *Parisi*. These villas fall in two main groups on either side of the Wolds, the first close to the possible *civitas* centre at Brough-on-Humber, the other in the Vale of Pickering. Some of the villas close to Brough and Malton were ornamented with mosaic pavements (Brantingham, Beadlam, Harpham and Rudston) and tessellated pavements have been noted at several others. Several of these villas are known to have developed on the site of earlier indigenous enclosed settlements (for example, Rudston).

To the north of Aldborough, there is a thin distribution of villas and other Roman-style buildings close to Dere Street. There is also a small group of villas around York, including at least one example, at Dalton Parlours, where the villa was superimposed in the second century on an earlier Iron Age site comprising a series of curvilinear enclosures, though a gap in occupation is probable here. Although small baths and mosaics were a feature of some of these sites, they were generally on a small to medium scale. We cannot assume that native Britons were responsible for the majority of the northern villas, not least because of the rival urban centre at York and the long-continued military occupation at Malton and York, undoubtedly generating associated veteran settlement. The legion, the *canabae* and the later *colonia* at York must all have had access to rural territory in the Lower Ouse region. Settlers or wealthy residents in the civil centres at York could certainly have aspired to own villas. Thus, although some of the villas no doubt belonged to the urbanized elite of the *Brigantes* and *Parisi*, they were by no means the only candidates as villa builders.

There are a few outlying villas known beyond Catterick, notably Holme House by Piercebridge fort and perhaps Old Durham (where only a bath-house is known). Holme House was developed as a villa in the second century, rather earlier than most of the north-eastern villas. To a basic row house was added a small bath-suite and a heated dining-room. The interpretation of these sites is uncertain, and in the past the close proximity to military sites has received most attention. However, there are now additional sites known at Chapel House Farm and Quarry Farm, suggesting that the farming potential of the Tees Valley may have been a factor.

North of the Tees, rural settlement was characterized by dispersed rural settlements, many comprising simple roundhouses within rectangular enclosures of 0.2 ha or less in internal area. In lower-lying locations these tend to comprise ditch and embankment, in the rockier upland areas a simple wall or mound of piled rubble sometimes sufficed. In the late Iron Age, there are indications that this was a region of innovative and expanding agriculture, with new forms of cereals, additional land being cleared and agriculture extending into upland locations. Botanical evidence shows the cultivation of a range of cereals at different sites from at least the mid-first millennium BC, along with possible evidence for movement of grain between producing and consuming sites.

Among the best-studied settlements are those of upland Northumberland, due to their superior preservation. At one end of the scale there are quite large enclosed sites, such as Greaves Ash, with more than thirty roundhouses spread across its interior and a series of subsidiary enclosures just beyond. More common are oval or sub-rectangular enclosures with one to four roundhouses, such as Knock Hill or Kennell Hall Knowe. Many of these sites show continuity from the late Iron Age to the Romano-British period, with little evidence of morphological change post-conquest and a relatively poor exposure to Roman material culture.

South of the river Aire, in the angle between the Pennines and the Trent, there is evidence of very extensive late Iron Age field systems and many associated sites, but few villas or Roman-style buildings. The main exception at present is a small cluster of sites south of Doncaster. In general, the field systems, some of considerable regularity, and simple enclosed settlement types (such as Dunston's Clump) appear to have continued well into Roman times. The character of this area in settlement terms appears to have been distinct from that of the Vale of York or the Trent Valley in the post-conquest period.

To the west of the Pennines, small enclosed settlements again predominated, but the morphology of the enclosures was more commonly curvilinear in contrast to the rectilinear settlements east of the Pennines. The settlement pattern of the Mersey valley and northern Cheshire is poorly known because of the combination of modern conurbations, much permanent pasture and the fact that Iron Age society here was virtually aceramic. The Ribble valley has produced some settlement evidence, but higher densities of sites have been noted in the Lune Valley and the Eden Valley systems further north. With the addition of the Solway coastal plain, these are the areas that stand out as being more populous. Settlement within the Lakeland massif was widespread but generally of low density. Near the Solway, enclosed settlements appear to have had slightly later origins than in other parts of northern England, and excavated examples of these sites, especially rarer rectilinear enclosures, appear to have been constructed within the Roman period. The major settlement sites of the north-west were all garrison settlements associated with long-term forts, as at Manchester, Ribchester, Lancaster, Ambleside, Brougham, Carlisle. Only in the third century was a *civitas* centre created for the *Carvetii*, with the civic territory perhaps quite restricted in size within the Eden Valley and lacking any villas.

Roman military occupation was long maintained in northern Britain, with large areas apparently remaining under permanent military administration. The relative under-development of Aldborough, Brough-on-Humber and Carlisle and their attached territories strongly implies continued intervention or influence of the military community. The local civilian input to the larger garrison communities at Corbridge, Catterick, Piercebridge, and so on, may well have grown over time, but the extent to which native Britons became leaders there is very uncertain. Outside the limited areas of urban and villa development in the north, settlements were generally relatively impoverished in terms of material culture and lacking architectural signs of elite status. For many people in northern Britain, the *res publica* to which they were answerable was the state, represented by its governors, financial officials and military commanders and regional administrators.

Scotland

The late Iron Age (200 BC–AD 78) brought in major change in social and economic organization among the peoples of Scotland (Figs 7 and 15, pp. 148 and 430). In most areas, social organization was characterized by dispersed small settlements, suggesting a high degree of social fragmentation into family groups or clans. There are signs, however, of collective action and centralized power – evident in the creation of some boundary features and progressive deforestation. Moreover, after a period of comparative isolation from southern Britain and the Continent, there was a degree of reconvergence of art and material culture between the regions.

The principal peoples of Lowland Scotland, as reported by Ptolemy, were the *Votadini*, *Selgovae*, *Novantae* and *Dumnonii*. In addition, the *Anavionenses* of Annandale were another significant group encountered by Rome. There is nothing in Ptolemy's account to indicate whether the peoples he mentioned were centralized kingdoms, tribes, petty chiefdoms or loose and temporary alliances of normally warring clans.

Settlements in southern Scotland were characterized by variations on the roundhouse, with many stone-built structures as well as timber ones. These sites had more in common with those of the heavily garrisoned areas of northern England than with those of northern Scotland. They show limited development of elite architecture or material culture over time, whereas those further north and west reveal indications of greater social differentiation, including distinctive types of elite residence, the brochs and duns (discussed in fuller detail in the next chapter). On both sides of Hadrian's Wall, there appears to have been a broad zone of rural settlement that remained relatively homogeneous and under-developed throughout the Roman period.

The *Votadini* have traditionally been seen as a widespread people covering the eastern region from Hadrian's Wall to Lothian on the Forth estuary, though some revision is necessary. This is a zone of numerous hillforts and large defended sites, though many of these appear on current evidence to have been established far earlier in the Iron Age and some were already out of use by the first century. At Broxmouth (East Lothian), a hillfort had been abandoned and an unenclosed settlement built over its defences by the time of the Roman invasions. Another site at Dryburn Bridge started off as a settlement of roundhouses surrounded by an oval palisade, but was later an open site of ring-ditch houses. By the time of the Roman conquest settlement was also more widely distributed in smaller farmsteads.

There are reasons to suggest that the core territory of the *Votadini* was broadly coincident with Lothian and centred on one or more major sites, within an area of dense settlement. The hillfort of Traprain Law

(16 ha) dominated the arable farmland of the coastal plain east of Edinburgh and appears to have been a significant site throughout the Roman period. The similar volcanic crag at Edinburgh has also yielded evidence below the Castle of high-status occupation in the Roman period and this site was to emerge as the capital of the sub-Roman kingdom of the *Goddodin* (clearly the successors of the *Votadini*).

The pre-Roman settlement pattern of this fertile agricultural area shows a densely settled landscape, with evidence for division of parts of the landscape by pit alignments (as in the Esk Valley). The density of enclosed settlements in parts of East Lothian is particularly striking (around Traprain Law more than one site every sq km) and implies a large population. Some of the traditional Iron Age settlements lay within oval or circular enclosures, but a distinctive cluster of rectilinear enclosures, again in the area of Traprain Law, seems to be Roman in date and probably represents a morphological innovation of the Roman period (paralleled by similar sites close to Hadrian's Wall in Northumberland and Cumbria). The lack of a dense network of garrison points in East Lothian and the maintenance of activity at Traprain Law have generally been interpreted, surely with some justification, as indicating a relatively favoured status accorded to the *Votadini*.

The location of the territory of the *Selgovae* is bound up with the issue of the southern limits of the *Votadini*, though there is a general agreement that it must have included part of the central Borders region and their capital has commonly been identified with the 16-ha hillfort of Eildon Hill North in the upper Tweed Valley. The problem here is that, on Ptolemy's authority, Votadinian territory is generally believed to have extended down the east coast of the Borders region, across the Lower Tweed Valley and through the eastern Cheviots towards the Tyne Valley. Accordingly, modern maps frequently place the *Selgovae* in an area running south-west of the upper Tweed, close to the main route between Carlisle and the Clyde. As neat as that may look on a two-dimensional map it does not make good sense of the archaeology. If the possibility is admitted of gross error in Ptolemy's attribution of sites in the south-east Borders region to the Votadinian area, then, more convincingly, the lands of the *Selgovae* can be argued to have extended east down the Tweed Valley to the sea. The presence of Roman marching camps and forts in the lower Tweed Valley also makes better sense if these were the lands of 'hostile' *Selgovae* rather than supposedly 'friendly' *Votadini*.

The evidence of Roman-period native activity on Eildon Hill North is comparatively poor, and there are indications that the hillfort defences may have been slighted before the Roman arrival. However, the Tweed Valley was a significant locus for ancient farming and settlement, while much of the central Borders region is rough hill country. The presence of a major Roman base at Newstead would suggest that this was a significant location for Roman control. Ptolemy placed *Trimontium* within the territory of the *Selgovae* and this is the strongest clue we have to the location of this people in the Tweed Valley and its tributaries. Survey work around the Roman fort at Newstead has examined native settlements. These were mostly enclosed roundhouses, some of timber construction, others with stone footings. Enclosures of both oval and sub-rectangular form are known, but dating evidence is slight at present.

There are many small late Iron Age/Roman stone settlements in the Cheviots, generally circular stone roundhouses within oval or sub-rectangular enclosures; in some cases these were terraced into the hillslope and are characterized as 'scooped settlements'. The economy of these upland sites was primarily based on stock-raising, but traces of cultivation (cord rig) and clearance cairns suggest that agriculture was also a factor. The dense groupings of such sites near the headwaters of the southern tributaries of the Tweed should probably be attributed to the *Selgovae*, though similar upland sites near the headwaters of the North Tyne, Redesdale and the river Coquet could relate to a distinct group.

The *Novantae* are generally agreed to be a people of south-west Scotland, centred in the Wigtown/Mull of Galloway area (the Roman 'promontory of the *Novantae*'). It is unclear how far their lands extended east through Dumfries and Galloway. Both are areas of fairly dense settlement, but of somewhat different character, with more duns and crannogs (timber lake dwellings) found in the western cluster and more multi-vallate defended settlements and hillforts in the eastern area, centred on Annandale. Roman garrisoning appears to have focused much more on the latter area, evidently the territory of the *Anavionenses*, known from the *Vindolanda* tablets, but not mentioned at all by Ptolemy. Here native settlements were generally within circular enclosures, often multi-vallate, including a number of hillforts. There were few associated field systems.

North of the *Novantae* and *Anavionenses* and west of the *Votadini* and *Selgovae* were the *Dumnonii*, fairly certainly the people of Clydesdale. The spread of greater Glasgow obscures a substantial part of their core territory. A number of duns are known, particularly in Ayrshire to the west of the Clyde Valley, though brochs are very rare. There are also a few souterrains, suggesting the possibility of more extensive unenclosed settlement within the valley itself.

Overall, the military occupation of the Scottish Lowlands was relatively brief in length: ten to twenty-five years under the Flavians, Hadrianic outpost forts limited to the main roads north of the wall, about twenty-five years of Antonine occupation and limited outposts thereafter, apart from the few years of the planned Severan reoccupation. The impact on settlement and society in the region is strikingly slight at first glance. Settlement types appear to have been predominantly the same as those of the late Iron Age, with little evidence of Roman impact on the overall settlement dynamics.

Compared to northern England and Wales, few forts in Scotland have revealed evidence for substantial development of garrison settlements. At present these are limited to some of the Antonine Wall forts, and the major Lowland forts on the Forth and in the Borders region – Cramond, Inveresk, Newstead, Easter Happrew and Castledykes. The garrison settlements disappeared with the removal of their garrison, suggesting that these sites had little to do with local people and were primarily service communities of the army of occupation.

Finds of Roman material culture have been made at over 200 indigenous settlements in Scotland, but while these are quite widespread, they are by no means evenly distributed (see Fig. 7 above and Fig. 15 below). There are several discrete clusters of finds and to some extent they conform to the suggestions made above about core native territories in Lowland Scotland. For instance, there is a large group in the eastern Borders region, with a focus in the Tweed Valley and northern Cheviots (coincident with the proposed heartlands of the *Selgovae*), another in Lothian (the *Votadini*), another in the coastal area of Dumfries and Galloway (*Novantae and Anavionenses*) and another in Ayrshire and the Clyde Valley (*Dumnonii*). On the other hand, there is a large blank area in the western Borders and northern Dumfries and Galloway, suggesting some degree of separation between the heartlands of the main peoples.

*

There was thus huge variation in the rural histories of different parts of Britain under Roman rule. While villa development was clearly an important factor in the south-east (Fig. 17, p. 481 below), it was geographically varied and chronologically unsynchronized. It is suggested here that significant areas of the landscape, especially those with unusual natural resources or pertaining to peoples who strongly resisted Roman rule initially, were separated off from the lands assigned to the administrative control of the British *civitates*. In the west and north, the situation was even starker, and the socio-economic stagnation of the Roman period both contrasts with late Iron Age developments and highlights the stifling control of Rome and her garrison. Britain's ultimate status as an imperial possession is most clearly delineated in these varied landscapes.

14

Free *Britannia*

Beyond the Frontiers

Written sources, spanning the period of Roman rule in Britain, demonstrate that practical knowledge of and direct and indirect contacts with unincorporated parts of Britain were considerable. The surrender of a king of the Orkneys to Claudius in 43 has often been regarded as unreliable testimony of a fourth-century writer, Eutropius, but some finds of unusually early Roman material on the Orkneys suggest that we should not rule it out entirely. The ancient sources presented these outlying societies as primitive, degenerate and unchanging, whereas the archaeological evidence often hints at different relationships and impacts of the contact situation between the imperial power and its neighbours.

There are also smaller islands around Britain, the largest being *Ierne* (Ireland) . . . concerning this island I have nothing certain to report, except that the people living there are more savage than the Britons, being cannibals as well as gluttons. Further, they consider it honourable to eat their dead fathers and to openly have intercourse, not only with unrelated women, but with their mothers and sisters as well.

This quote from Strabo's *Geography* reflects not so much the ignorance of the classical world about its remote north-western fringes, as the prejudices and stereotypes that Mediterranean peoples employed to characterize 'barbarian' neighbours. Strabo was writing in the reign of Augustus, when official policy was to eschew direct involvement in the British archipelago. The accusations of cannibalism and polygamy, evidently based on no reliable testimony, were standard Roman accusations in relation to barbarian peoples, here elaborated to incorporate the most extreme imaginings of degenerate behaviour – paternal cannibalism and incest. In this chapter, we shall look at the relationship between the expanding empire and her northern and western neighbours. The Roman period can ultimately be seen as one of major change in the north and west and the social transformations in the societies confronting Rome had major repercussions for the future history of Britain.

NORTHERN AND WESTERN SCOTLAND

Despite repeated references in the Roman sources to the 'Caledonian forest', implying a relatively uncleared and unfarmed landscape, the picture now emerging is that Scotland was substantially deforested by the end of the Iron Age. The surviving stands of forest perhaps inevitably caught the attention of the Romans, mindful of the earlier slaughter of three legions in the German Teutoberg forest, but Rome's failure to conquer and hold the northernmost region of Britain cannot be simply ascribed to the difficulty of the terrain. Since this was also an area of considerable late Iron Age economic and social development, neither can it be attributed to the primitive state of the societies of the far north.

A division can be made between three groups of peoples of Scotland north of the Forth–Clyde isthmus: those east of the Highland line up to the Moray Firth, those in the northernmost tip of Scotland and on the Orkneys and those inhabiting the Atlantic shores and islands to the west (Figs 7 and 15). The peoples to the east of the Highland massif, following Ptolemy, were the *Venicones*, *Vacomagi* and *Taexali* based on the mixed-farming lands of Fife, Perthshire, Angus and Moray (Tayside and Grampian). Archaeological evidence attests to dense settlement in the Roman period all along the corridor between the Highland line and the North Sea coast, corresponding to the territories of these peoples, and items of Roman material culture are not uncommon in this region. The far north of Scotland (the Highland districts of Caithness and Sutherland) was home to the *Cornavii*, *Smertae*, *Lugi*, *Decantae* and *Caledonii*, though the precise location of these groups is inevitably much debated. The peoples of the western Atlantic coast mentioned by Ptolemy were the *Epidii* in Kintyre and the *Creones*, *Carnonacae* and *Caereni* probably in Argyll and Easter Ross. All these names appear to be British Celtic in origin and the forms suggest that we are dealing with P-Celtic speaking

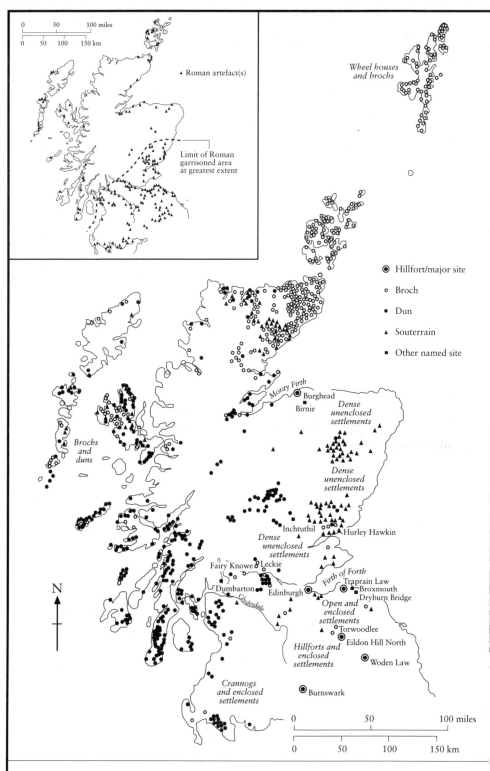

Figure 15. *Rural settlement in Scotland showing principal regional patterns and sites referred to in the text and (inset) Roman material culture in northern Britain*

groups. However, the name of the *Epidii*, though at first sight indicating a P-Celtic group, relates to an area of very strong Gaelic (Q-Celtic) linguistic evidence. Although once believed to be the result of a late antique invasion of the region by the *Dal Riata* of northern Antrim, it is equally plausible that this part of the Highlands, separated by the mountainous 'Spine of Britain' from the populous lands of eastern Scotland, was much more closely linked culturally and ethnically with Ireland over a prolonged period.

The usual problems of pinning down Ptolemy's peoples geographically are made even more difficult by the fact that few can be related to named sites or geographical features, though the *Epidium* promontory is identifiable as the Mull of Kintyre. A large group of names (*Epidii, Creones, Carnonacae, Caereni, Caledonii, Cornavii, Lugi, Smertae, Decantae*) have no associated sites listed, suggesting that direct Roman contact with these peoples had been limited. As a starting point, we can assume that these were in areas where no Roman forts were established in the late first century and that the names were collected during the rapid circumnavigation of northernmost Britain in 83.

The relative status of all these names should not be considered equal – some may have been the ethnics of relatively small communities based on clans, others more regional peoples. The archaeology of Atlantic Scotland differs profoundly from that of Lowland and eastern Scotland and appears to reflect very localized groupings. By contrast, Tacitus emphasized a great confederation of Caledonian peoples under a war leader, Calgacus (the name meant 'swordsman'). After their final defeat in 83, Agricola sent his fleet on to circumnavigate the northern tip of Britain, presumably making brief contact with some of the peoples mentioned in Ptolemy's list, while he marched his army back south, passing through the lands of further new, but unnamed, groups (perhaps within the Highland line itself). The names that were selected from the information obtained from local informants, and the precise forms recorded, probably had as much to do with the interpreters accompanying the army or the fleet as with reality. Most do not recur outside Ptolemy's list (see Fig. 3).

It is a moot point whether all the peoples reported by the sources existed before the coming of Rome, or whether some at least coalesced in response to the Roman threat. The danger presented by Rome certainly seems to have sparked higher levels of confederation between regional groups and, in place of the earlier multiplicity of ethnic names, the late Roman sources refer to broader regional groupings: by the early third century, *Caledonii* and *Maeatae*, and, from the fourth century, *Picti*. This parallels evidence from Germany, where the long-term presence of the frontier led to the emergence of larger and larger 'tribal' confederations in response to or in opposition to Rome. By the sub-Roman period, some of these entities in Scotland appear to have become minor kingdoms (*Gododdin*, the *Picti*, Strathclyde, *Dal Riata/Dalriada/Scotti*).

The threefold division of the northern peoples receives some support in the archaeological record of settlement evidence and material culture, though the differences were more profound between the peoples of eastern Scotland and those of the north and west, who shared many characteristics. The main areas in which hillforts are found were the Lowlands and the zone east of the Highland line. Smaller defensible sites characterize the settlements of the Atlantic zone, known as brochs in the northern area and duns in the west. These hint at basic differences in the scale of communal organization, with larger units in the south and east and a more fragmented clan structure to the west and north. Although some of the larger hillforts in the Lowlands were abandoned before the Roman period, later occupation of this type of site is attested and other classes of substantial settlements are also known, both enclosed and unenclosed. The settlement evidence suggests that the Romans burst in on a relatively stable set of societies, who had been increasingly turning to settled farming, and reanimated their warlike tendencies.

To the north of the Forth–Clyde isthmus, the major zone of Roman military control in successive phases of occupation was the low-lying valley systems and low hills on the eastern flank of the Highlands (broadly Fife and Tayside). This area is notable for the numbers of unenclosed settlements, comprising clusters of roundhouses, many with the subterranean passages and chambers called souterrains. The interpretation of souterrains has varied from refuges, to storehouses, to ritual structures, without any consensus emerging. A combination of all three is possible, though their utility for defending people and property would only be effective against small-scale raiders who feared to spend more than minimal time plundering a settlement once the local hue and cry was taken up.

Aerial photography in recent decades has greatly expanded the numbers of known sites between the Forth and the Moray Firth. Earlier hillforts seem in general to have been abandoned before the Roman invasions, rather than as a consequence. Here the pattern is broadly similar to that in the Lowlands. As in other areas east of the Highlands, relatively few brochs and duns are known, though some settlements were enclosed. There are a few rectilinear enclosures similar to those in Lothian, but in the absence of excavation their date and interpretation is still uncertain. Although there are no late Iron Age field systems north of the Forth to match the complexity of those found in Lowland Scotland, the density of sites and the finds of rotary querns and souterrains at many sites indicate a farmed landscape, rather than 'cowboy' country. The impression is that the peoples of this area, the *Venicones* and the *Vacomagi*, were comparatively stable and peaceful in the period leading up to the Roman invasions, with an expanded (and growing) farming economy, including cereal cultivation.

The settlement archaeology of the peoples of Atlantic Scotland, the west and northern coasts and islands, stands out as somewhat different. The Highland zone is rich in lake settlements (crannogs) built out on stilt-platforms from the shores of the lochs. These range in date from the first millennium BC to the first millennium AD. The investment of labour in constructing such sites suggests that they had prestige value within society as well as functional utility as defensible settlements. Environmental evidence shows that they were involved in a mixed farming economy.

Duns and brochs were the other upper-echelon settlement types in the west and north, with the term 'dun' being a catch-all for substantial stone-built houses, often fortified or within enclosures, that fall outside the definition of the classic broch. They are particularly common in Argyll, and the islands of Mull, Skye and the Hebrides. There is an outlying cluster in the central Grampians to east and west of Loch Rannoch.

Brochs were tall tower houses, generally built up as two concentric stone walls, with chambers, galleries or stairways within their width (which can be over 5 m at the base). There are traces of timber floors within some of the towers and indications that the main residential part may have lain at first floor and higher levels, with the ground floor perhaps used for corralling stock, and so on. Some brochs lay at the centre of village-like clusters of cellular houses of irregular form and some sites were enclosed within earthworks or ditches (Gurness on Orkney is a good example). The full evolution of broch architecture appears to date to the latter centuries BC and first century AD (as Howe on Orkney). By the early centuries AD there were many brochs, particularly in coastal locations on the mainland and on many of the islands. For instance, Orkney had at least twenty broch villages. On Shetland and the Western Isles broch villages are unattested, though settlements based on another type of elite residence, the wheel-house, are quite common. The wheel-house was a semi-subterranean roundhouse of distinctive type – often dug into coastal sand dunes. It generally comprised a long, covered entrance passageway and a main circular chamber up to 10 m in diameter, with the roof being in part supported on a ring of narrow stone piers, arranged spoke-like around the central hearth. The distributions of brochs and wheel-houses are more or less exclusive of one another, though the significance of this difference in architectural fashion is not clear.

Brochs, duns and wheel-houses represent the top end of a tradition for stone roundhouse construction, in the case of brochs extending vertically into substantial tower houses (the tallest extant example at Mousa on Shetland is over 13 m high). The significance of these sites is, of course, much debated, but there can be little doubt that these were expensive structures, reflecting huge prestige on those that could muster the available labour. The villages of poorer houses clustered around the brochs lend support to the idea that these were centres of local authority and power within a fragmented clan-based society. They represent social hierarchy in the societies least in contact with Rome, and rare examples of brochs and duns in both eastern and Lowland Scotland suggest that they too enshrined traditional values within northern British society. The brochs and duns in the east and south do not appear to date earlier than the first century and to some extent may reflect a reaction to the Roman invasions of those areas, not because they offered better defence against the Roman army (they did not), but because they symbolized high status and a particular sort of defiance.

The Roman garrison pattern did not impose blanket control of the fertile territories to the east of the Highland line, but segregated them from the Highlands, isolating the lowland territories of these peoples from their western highland neighbours. Some commentators have suggested that these farming communities were in some measure placed under Roman protection against 'Celtic cowboys'. However, the reality is that the inhabitants of eastern Scotland were numerous and were themselves a prime military objective for Rome. The archaeological evidence is unequivocal here. Fife and Tayside are liberally covered with marching camps of Agricolan, Severan and probably other dates as well, recalling the slow and systematic progress of an army that our Roman sources tell us despoiled the land as it went, in an attempt to bring the enemy to battle. No doubt the population retreated as far and as fast as they were able before the Roman advance, but there seems little reason to doubt that the *Venicones* and the *Vacomagi* counted among the main 'enemies' beyond the Forth–Clyde isthmus in terms of manpower and wealth. In a similar way, the Severan campaigns appear to have paid particular attention to this region, suggesting that the people then known as the *Maeatae* were the successors of the *Venicones* and *Vacomagi* on the same fertile lands.

Ptolemy placed the *Caledonii* along the line of the Great Glen from Loch Linnie to Inverness, but later sources clearly referred to a group with wider geographical range. Ptolemy's limited geographical reference could relate to the short-lived Roman settlement post-83, when the Caledonian peoples may have been broken down into a series of manageable groups east of the Highland line and the broader name deliberately applied to fragmented Highland groups. The experiment was not a success and by the late second century the sources speak of *Caledonii* and *Maeatae* as the two major groups in opposition to Rome. If the latter were the combined populations of Fife and Tayside, then the former were probably the peoples of Moray (successors of the *Taexali*) and the Grampian Highland regions. The peoples of the Atlantic coast and western Highlands may have occasionally sent assistance to their eastern and northern neighbours, but they were in general more insulated from the Roman world.

By the early fourth century, Roman sources speak of the '*Picti* and other Caledonian peoples' and the latest accounts speak almost exclusively of the *Picti* as their chief opponents in northern Britain. The name *Picti* in Latin means simply 'painted ones' and could indicate that the Romans, when confronted with a higher level of confederation in the north, simply employed a blanket descriptive term, perhaps reflecting a regional penchant for war-paint or facial tattoos. However, the name

Picti and the territorial designation Pictland (*Pictavia*) had a long after-life in post-Roman Scotland and it is more probable that the term was a transliteration of a native word or personal name. Studies of the Picts have often dwelt on supposed mysteries and problems relating to this kingdom, but in reality we know considerably more about this people than about most of the other early historic British groupings. They can be seen as the people of north-east Scotland, comprising the zone north of the Forth–Clyde isthmus and extending to the far north. To the west, their culture penetrated into the Highland line, but was limited on the Atlantic coast. Their heartlands can be identified by place-name, artistic and artefactual evidence with Moray, Tayside and Fife. In other words the Picts appear to represent the increasing union of *Caledonii* and *Maeatae*, though at what point we can speak of a Pictish kingdom is uncertain. There are hints in the material evidence that we might sub-divide the Picts into northern and southern groupings, corresponding to the earlier division between *Maeatae* and *Caledonii*, separated by the Mounth, the eastward spur of the Highland line that extends to the coast near Aberdeen.

The Pictish language has elicited much discussion, especially around the possibility that it might be a relict pre-Celtic tongue, though most commentators would now accept that it was probably a distinct dialect of the P-Celtic grouping. Recent research on the Picts has suggested that, far from being unusual and unique, they fit well within our picture of the northern British neighbours of Rome, and their evolution in many respects mirrors that of other groups. Although the general areas of Pictish influence are clear, the main centres of Pictish power are archaeologically somewhat elusive, though the major promontory fort that once existed at Burghead on the Moray coast was almost certainly one of them. A number of other forts were newly developed in this period, as at Dumbarton Rock, or imposed upon prehistoric fortifica-tions, as at Craig Phadraig, or on long-abandoned Roman military sites, as at Inchtuthil. Pictish centres known in the early medieval documentary sources do not coincide in all cases with archaeological evidence, but a cluster of sites is indicated around the Tay (including Scone and Dun-keld). The overall impression from the evidence is that in the late Roman period there was a renewal of construction of fortified centres in eastern Scotland, associated in many cases with self-confident stone relief-carvings in a distinctive British style. Although treated by Roman sources as a barbarian nuisance, the sub-Roman sources and archaeological evidence attest the emergence of a sophisticated Pictish kingdom.

Other peoples linked to the *Picti* in late Roman accounts of raids on the Roman provinces of Britain were the *Attacotti* (perhaps from southern Ireland) and the *Scotti*. The exact origins and location of the *Scotti* at this time are disputed, but they appear to correspond with the *Dal Riata* of Argyle and Antrim. Whether these Gaelic speakers were originally from Ireland and migrated to the Kintyre peninsula in late antiquity or the early medieval period, or whether they represented the close alliance of Gaelic speakers on both sides of the Irish Sea over a prolonged period is uncertain. However, what seems clear from the fragmentary historical record is that an area of western Scotland that had initially been marginal in terms of interaction with Rome, became very much more important in late Roman times. It was also distinguished from Lowland Scotland and Pictland by linguistic and cultural differences. We shall return to the *Scotti* later in this chapter, but the significance of seaborne raiding in late Roman times must be stressed and the very isolation of such people may have helped protect them from easy retaliation on the part of Rome.

The distribution of finds of Roman material culture provides additional insights into the regional groupings in northern Scotland. North of the Forth–Clyde isthmus the most notable clusters of finds are in the Stirling region and Fife (*Venicones*) and in Tayside (*Vacomagi*), with a thinner spread in Grampian and along the Moray Firth (*Taexali*). Beyond that in the north and west the distribution is sparse and essentially coastal, with minor clustering in Caithness and Orkney and in Argyll. There is comparatively little material from the Western Isles. Access to and use of these imported goods varied markedly between areas, with 40 per cent of excavated Lowland sites having Roman material, but only 25 per cent of those in 'free Albion' to the north and west. Those parts of Scotland that were at some point taken within the province had a different relationship with Roman material goods from areas that were always outside direct Roman control, and in these latter areas finds are often of unique artefacts, rather than of mixed groups. While the major part of the material has been recovered as site finds on settlements, some important groups have come from burials and hoards. Perhaps unsurprisingly, almost all the hoards have been found in Lowland and eastern Scotland, reflecting the impact of Roman campaigns.

In general, burials with Roman grave goods are rare, and are concentrated in eastern Scotland.

There is very little pre-Flavian material, suggesting limited contacts between Scotland and southern Britain before Agricola's campaigns. The majority of finds date to the Flavian and Antonine periods, showing that most Roman imports arrived in the region during the phases of military occupation of the Lowlands. Many artefacts are found in chronologically later levels at native sites, suggesting some degree of curation of prestige goods. Silver *denarii* of post-Antonine date are fairly common, providing evidence of Roman payment of subsidies to the northern peoples to keep the peace – an expensive policy also well attested on other frontiers. A roundhouse settlement at Birnie near Elgin on the Moray Firth has yielded two coin hoards, both certainly Severan in date and comprising over 600 *denarii* in total. The coins were evidently in leather bags, placed in pots and buried around a substantial roundhouse within the settlement. At this date a legionary soldier would receive around 600 *denarii* per year, so this was a substantial sum. Other material of third- and fourth-century date occurs at a smaller number of elite sites and appears to have been less widely distributed in society.

Many of the finds of Roman material concern just a single artefact at a site, but some settlements evidently had access to larger numbers of Roman goods in a range of types and materials. Regional differences are also clear in the assemblage composition. In the eastern Borders, we can identify significant differences between the richer elite sites, including brochs such as Torwoodlee and hillfort centres such as Traprain Law (most notable for its silver treasure, but with much other Roman material besides), Eildon Hill North, Camphouse and Edinburgh Castle, and from one of the rectilinear enclosures at Lilliesleaf. This appears to be strong supporting evidence for the existence of some hierarchy in this region, with important centres getting privileged access to Roman goods and using them to demonstrate their social prestige. In the western part of the Borders region, extending into Dumfries and Galloway and Ayrshire, there is less evidence for elite sites, with just two sites standing out from the rest, Whithorn and Buittle. In general the quantities of Roman goods at individual sites in this region were smaller and more evenly distributed.

North of the Forth–Clyde isthmus, the percentage of sites with only one Roman find rises, but there are again a number of elite sites with notably larger and more varied assemblages, including the brochs of Hurly Hawkin, Fairy Knowe (where 30 per cent of the artefacts were Roman imports) and Leckie. The hierarchy becomes less pronounced moving into Grampian, where many sites have Roman finds, but few of any great value. A series of ritual deposits in Covesea Cave and the Pictish site at Burghead stand out as the only notable exceptions at present. In the far north and the Atlantic west, the Roman finds comprise only a tiny percentage of the overall assemblages and there are no sites that have anything approaching the richness of the Lowland imports. Orkney and Caithness are the areas that show the greatest range of finds, but always in small quantities.

With the exception of the coins, most of the artefacts found on native sites can be divided into two categories – those connected with eating and drinking and those used for personal adornment. It is interesting that samian ware was more common than coarse wares, as this is the inverse of the normal picture on Romano-British sites and forts within the province, suggesting that this had enhanced status value beyond the frontier. Roman weapons and metal artefacts are occasional finds, but it is probable that what survives is a tiny fraction of the amount originally present and thoroughly recycled by the northern British.

IRELAND

'Fort discovery proves the Romans invaded Ireland', proclaimed the newspaper headline in the *Sunday Times* on 21 January 1996, setting off a modern political furore. The claim was based on an unexpected concentration of finds of Roman material goods at Drumanagh, a coastal promontory fort near Dublin (Fig. 16). The *c.*16-ha site is defended by multi-vallate earthworks along its landward side and overlooks a bay, which could have served as an anchorage. The site is a large and important one, and, although the scale of both the defended promontory and the nature of the defences are unusual, it has an essentially native Irish, not Roman military character. Although the metal-detector finds that provoked the speculation about a Roman invasion have not been published, they apparently do not include Roman military artefacts, while pottery, coins and other Roman goods could have reached Ireland by a variety of alternative mechanisms. But if not evidence of a Roman

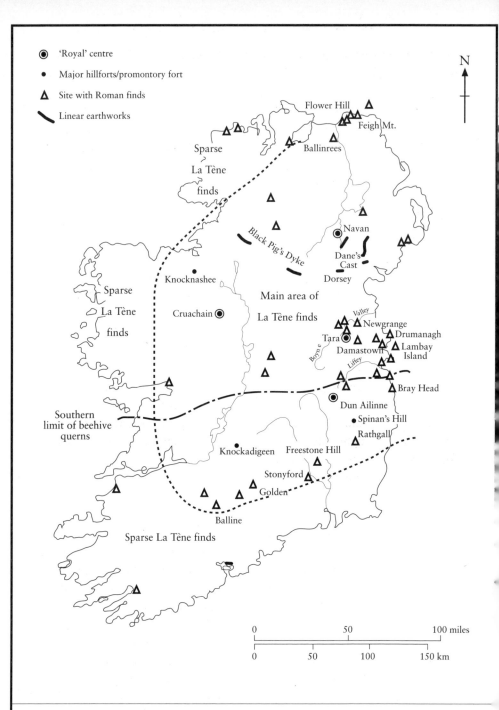

Figure 16. Ireland in the late Iron Age/Roman period, showing pricipal sites mentioned in text and findspots of Roman material. The dashed lines show the southern limit of beehive querns and the southern and western limits of the main area of La Tène material culture

military presence (and the newspaper headlines were clearly well off the mark), what does Drumanagh have to tell us about the relationship between Ireland and the Roman empire?

The main evidence in favour of Roman military intervention in Ireland focuses on the events of the late first century. When Agricola lined up his army along the western Scottish shore at the end of his fifth campaign in 81, he was evidently shaping a recommendation to the emperor Titus that he be allowed to lead an army in that direction, claiming that Ireland could be easily conquered by a single legion and some auxiliaries. But, unbeknown to Agricola, Titus was already dead and his brother Domitian would authorize a renewal of northern campaigning beyond the Forth–Clyde isthmus instead. A near-contemporary poetic allusion in Juvenal's second satire to the 'advancement of arms beyond the shores of *Iuverna* [Ireland] and the recently captured Orkneys and the mighty Britons with their short nights' has suggested to some that Agricola's wish for a Roman military expedition to be sent to Ireland was granted, perhaps under the command of his unknown successor. However, there remains no archaeological evidence for the activity of the Roman army anywhere in Ireland. It is perhaps more probable, if the source has any basis in fact at all, that the force of arms involved some form of support for an Irish chieftain who had a client relationship with Rome. Just such an individual sought refuge and support from Agricola, having been forced to flee his home area. Early Irish history is full of accounts of exiled chiefs returning to claim back their lands, as in the example of Tuathal Techtmar, who has sometimes been identified – totally speculatively – with Agricola's refugee chieftain.

What is very clear both from Tacitus and from Ptolemy is that Roman geographical knowledge of Ireland and the Irish Sea was dramatically increased in the late first century by the conquest of first Wales and then northern Britain, opening up naval supply lines around the west British coast. As resistance on the mainland was crushed, it is also plausible that a trickle of refugees will have crossed the Irish Sea. This may well account for some unusual discoveries along the eastern seaboard, as at Lambay island, just off the mainland close to Drumanagh. Here, a series of inhumation burials included a warrior burial with a long sword, shield and other ornaments. Other finds from the site included a mirror, two decorative sheet-metal artefacts, brooches of first-century types, a bangle and a beaded torc, all in copper alloy. There was also a jet bangle.

The parallels for beaded torcs are almost all from northern Britain (broadly in the lands of the *Brigantes*) and the jet artefact also points to this region. The lack of Irish artefacts and the uniqueness of the assemblage in an Irish context strongly suggest that this was a community of refugees from mainland Britain, perhaps part of the faction that had most strongly opposed the Roman advance. The island location, close to the major promontory fort and harbour at Drumanagh also hints at a group cautiously seeking to establish a foothold in a new political setting and lacking either confidence or numbers to occupy a position on the mainland.

The relative proximity of Ireland to the British mainland meant that there was always the likelihood of contact between the two, despite the stormy reputation of the Irish Sea and the supposedly unfriendly and warlike disposition of her people, emphasized by writers such as Solinus. The shortest sea crossing is about 22 km from Fair Head in north-west Antrim to the Mull of Kintyre, but Belfast Lough to the Mull of Galloway is only *c.*40 km and Drumanagh to Anglesey *c.*90 km. The Roman conquest of the western seaboard of *Britannia* and the increased use of the waterway to supply the army in the north must have had consequences, whether intended or not, for east–west shipping also.

Ptolemy's geographical account of the Roman empire opens with his account of the *Prettanic* Isles – Ireland (*Ivernia*) and Britain (*Albion*) – and it is interesting that he devotes almost half as much space to unconquered Ireland as to conquered *Albion*. This reveals much about Roman interest in Ireland at this time and the extent to which both its coastline and its internal political structures were the subject of close investigation. Altogether there is a heavy emphasis in Ptolemy's listing towards coastal features such as might be reported by merchants and other mariners: no fewer than six coastal peninsulas or promontories, fifteen rivers, thirteen islands, three coastal settlements and sixteen peoples whose lands touched on the various coasts. On the other hand, the co-ordinate locations of a group of seven 'towns' (*poleis*) are specifically stated to be 'inland' centres. The list is not without interpretational difficulties, but the consensus of opinion places the main peoples as follows (Fig. 3, p. 49). Starting in the north-east and moving south, the *Robogdii* (in Derry and Antrim), *Darini* (Antrim) and *Voluntii* (Armagh and County Down) were the main groupings of the modern province of Northern Ireland. The *Eblani* occupied modern County Dublin with a principal coastal site at *Eblana* (perhaps Drumanagh?), with the *Cauci* along the Liffey valley to the south and west. The south-eastern sector from Wicklow to Wexford was the territory of the *Manapii*, *Coriondi* and *Brigantes*. The latter group probably extended along the southern Waterford coast. The peoples of Cork and Kerry were the *Usdiae* and the *Iverni*, with the *Vellabori* in the Limerick area on the west coast. Running up the west coast, Ptolemy listed the *Gangani* (County Clare?), *Auteini* (Galway), *Nagnatae* (Mayo, Sligo), *Erpeditani* (Leitrim, Fermanagh?), and *Vennicnii* (Donegal).

The ethnic names given here are probably several steps away from the forms that were actually pronounced in Ireland. These written forms are more akin to P-Celtic speakers than Q-Celtic speakers, though all other evidence points to the bulk of the population of Ireland being in the latter language group. This has caused unnecessary consternation, since Ptolemy's list ultimately drew on sailors' reports and it is probable that the most accessible witnesses to Irish Sea trade at this date were Brittonic speakers operating from the mainland. The three coastal settlements are all named after a local people: *Eblana* and *Manapia* on the east coast and *Nagnata* on the west. The reporting of the inland centres is also indicative of external witnesses, two sites are known simply as *Regia* or 'royal seat', a third is simply called *Dunon* (meaning 'fortification') and *Ivernis* is evidently a chief place of the *Iverni*. The remaining forms (*Rhaiba*, *Laberos*, *Macolicon*) may be Irish toponyms. Two of the inland sites *Ivernis* and *Rhaiba* had been visited on midsummer's day by someone with the knowledge of reckoning its length in hours). The over-riding impression of Ptolemy's evidence is that it reflects the observation of Brittonic-speaking traders/intermediaries, rather than of native-born Irish and that it must provide only a partial and snapshot view of a more complex reality.

The early medieval literary classic, the *Ulster Cycle*, presents an additional complication in Irish studies. This work is a window into the late Iron Age world of Ulster and a source of unparalleled potential for reconstructing elements of its history. However, there are clear difficulties in using evidence that takes a highly mythologizing approach to issues of foundation and the role of heroes, such as Cúchulainn. Other problems concern potential anachronisms embedded in the tales. For instance, detailed analysis of the texts has shown that the references to dress, weaponry and material culture are based on early medieval realities, and do not correspond to the archaeological evidence of late Iron Age societies. Yet it would be perverse to discount entirely the Irish perspective that the *Ulster Cycle* represents. After all, is it any less fantastic than the perspective of some of our classical sources? It is generally agreed that the events that they present related to the first century BC or first century AD, preserved as a folk-tradition. Treated cautiously, the early Irish tales and annals can contribute to our understanding of the self-perception of Rome's neighbours.

The society revealed by the *Ulster Cycle* was fragmented into a number of distinct kingdoms or tribes (*tuath*), often at war with or raiding each other. There were kings and queens, heroes and villains, pagan gods and druids. There is archaeological support for the regional fragmentation from Ulster, where we can identify differences in material culture for instance between Antrim and Armagh (ring-headed pins in the former, fibulae in the latter). The Bann valley in the north also stands out from southern Ulster (Fermanagh, Monaghan, Armagh and Cavan). *Emain Macha*, the great royal centre of the *Ulster Cycle*, is generally identified with the chief site of this area at Navan. The rule of kings (*ri*) is a strong theme in the early Irish sources and is confirmed by Tacitus, referring to the exiled Irish prince (*regulus*). The recurrent theme of exiled kings and leaders suggests that rule was not hereditary, but dependent on prowess and prestige. Another repeated theme in the *Cycle* was competition and conflict between five regions (*Ulaidh* (Ulster) in the north, *Cruchain* (Connaght) in the west, *Laighin* or *Galian* (Leinster) in the south-east, *Mumha* (Munster) in the south-west and *Mide* (Meath) in the centre). An obvious question is how the kingdoms of Ulster, Connaght and the rest mapped on to the picture derived from Ptolemy. It has been argued plausibly that the *Ulaid* (Ulstermen) evolved from the group referred to by Ptolemy as the *Voluntii*, but overall there appears to be a lack of correlation between the Irish folk memory of their history and the Roman colonial vision enshrined in Ptolemy's lists. The precise relationship between the kingdom of Ulster and the late antique *Dal Riata* of north-eastern Ireland and Kintyre/Argyll in Scotland has also been much debated. The *Dal Riata* were Gaelic speaking and probably corresponded to the *Scotti* or *Scoti* of late Roman sources who were on several occasions in league with the *Picti* against Rome. The idea of a mass migration in the late Roman period of *Scotti* from Ireland to Argyll is now much less canvassed than it was. It is clear that the people of the western Highlands and islands were much more closely allied over a long period to the Gaelic-speaking Irish than the Brittonic-speaking inhabitants of the rest of Scotland, and that the emergence of the *Scotti* was a much more long-term process.

The inland centres named by Ptolemy cannot be correlated exactly with the royal centres of the Irish sources, though *Emain Macha* might well be the northern site described simply as *Regia*. There is archaeological evidence for a series of inland centres that should equate with the major assembly and inauguration sites of the *Cycle* and with Ptolemy's list. Although several of these sites have enclosing earthworks, the placement of ditches inside embankments at Navan, Tara and Dun Ailinne suggests that these were not defensive in nature, but defined large ritual complexes.

Navan Fort (5 km west of Armagh) is a circular enclosure of *c.*5 ha area, its interior dominated by a ring-work with a diameter of 50 m and a mound 40 m in diameter. The structural detail and phasing is debated, but the ring-work contained a large (16.3 m diameter) roundhouse and overlay an earlier massive circular building of over 20 m in diameter. The mound contained an extraordinary circular structure, 37 m in diameter, with outer vertical plank walls, the central space divided by a series of concentric rings of posts arranged around a massive central post. The accepted reconstruction of the building shows it as a roofed structure of *c.*12 m in height – in appearance a giant version of the roundhouse. There was no hearth within the structure, such as might be expected if it had been used for regular assemblies or feasting. The felling date for the timbers used in this building was 95–94 BC. Shortly after construction, the building was infilled with stones to a depth of 2.8 m and finally covered over with turf, to give a total height to the mound of over 5 m. Quite what it represents is hard to determine, but ritual use is most plausible and the scale certainly demonstrates the ability to muster considerable numbers of people. One of the most intriguing finds from the site was the skull of a North African Barbary ape dating to the latter centuries BC, and again demonstrating the importance of this royal site. It implies either direct contact with Mediterranean people or with people who had such contact themselves.

Tara is the largest and most complex of the other so-called royal sites. The earliest sources describe it as capital of *Brega* (Meath) and later it was the acknowledged centre of the High Kingship of Ireland. There are about forty separate structures spread over almost a kilometre along a ridge. The main enclosure (5.9 ha), defined by a bank and internal ditch, is oval and contains a series of other monuments, including a late Neolithic passage grave (on which a monolith known as the 'stone of destiny' was at one time erected) and two conjoined enclosures, defined by twin embankments on either side of a ditch. About 100 m to the south of the main enclosure was a smaller enclosure with bank and internal ditch, while immediately to its north was a triple-banked enclosure or ring-fort. Beyond this was a rectangular bank-delimited enclosure (c.180 × 30 m). Further enclosures or mounds lie slightly to the north-west on sloping ground and there were evidently additional prehistoric burial mounds scattered here and there over the hilltop. The majority of the structures at Tara are unexcavated, with the exception of the ring-fort, which has produced material of early Roman date, and the interpretation of many elements remains uncertain. However, it is clear that we are dealing with a very long-lived site of ceremonial importance.

Cruachin was the principal royal seat of Connacht west of the Shannon and is identified with a site near Tulsk (Roscommon). This is another complex ceremonial site, with almost fifty monuments of varied type and date. A large mound (88 m in diameter), known locally as Rathcrogan, appears to have been the focal point for a group of other enclosures and ring-barrows. There were also some linear earthworks arranged in pairs, perhaps to form ceremonial avenues, the longest over 600 m in length. Only limited excavation work has yet taken place, but the identification of the site with the Iron Age kingly centre seems secure (though some of the monuments may be earlier or later in date).

Dun Ailinne (Kildare) is a large single oval enclosure (13 ha) on a prominent hilltop, with once again the ditch inside the surrounding bank. It has been identified with the *Aillinn* of the early written sources and the early royal centre of Leinster. Near the centre, excavation has revealed three successive circular Iron Age structures, defined by concentric rings of palisades (respectively 22 m, 28.5 m, 37 m in diameter). Within the largest and latest of these palisade rings stood a circle of large free-standing timber posts (25 m diameter), with a small round building at its centre. There are indications also of possible ritual feasting in the vicinity. Finds span the latter centuries BC and early centuries AD, and include Roman brooch types and other finds.

These so-called 'royal' sites stand out from the background archaeology of the late Iron Age in Ireland, though the four examples described above were not the only sites with huge ritual structures. The excavated examples all featured non-defensive enclosures (ditches inside banks), and massive, complex structures that are generally not associated with occupation debris and hearths. These features strike a chord with the literary tradition of royal sites for great assemblies and fairs (*óenarchs*) and for the performance of complex pagan ceremonies linked to the kingship, such as inauguration. As yet, however, there is little evidence for dense habitation at the royal centres. From a different perspective, these Irish royal centres, with their vast ritual complexes, raise interesting questions about conventional interpretations of the proto-urban functions of mainland British *oppida*.

Although most of the excavated hillforts of Ireland have not yielded evidence of late Iron Age occupation (and many may have originated in the late Bronze Age and been abandoned well before the latter centuries BC), it is certainly possible that some of these large enclosed sites might prove to be additional royal centres – especially where they appear to have incorporated earlier barrows or other ritual features in a manner reminiscent of Tara. Most hillforts were comparatively small-scale – typically a few hectares in area, with only a limited number exceeding 10 ha. There are some larger examples (Knocknashee, Sligo, at 22 ha and Knockadigeen, Tipperary, at 16 ha), but the massive enclosure of 132 ha at Spinan's Hill, Wicklow, is so far unprecedented. It is also possible that some of the coastal promontory sites and inland hillforts were occupied in the late Iron Age, though they were not numerically significant by that date. The concentration of hillforts is in any case variable across Ireland, with rather fewer known in the north than the south. The promontory hillfort at Drumanagh was certainly occupied in the first–second centuries and a number of other sites have yielded traces of activity in Roman times (as at Freestone Hill, Kilkenny).

A key settlement type in Irish archaeology is the ring-work or rath – essentially a defended homestead. These sites are generally smaller than one hectare and are mostly circular in form with round or rectangular houses inside. Raths are extremely common throughout Ireland (more than 10,000 are known in Ulster alone) and although the vast majority are unexcavated and some examples have been shown to date to late antiquity and early medieval times, others can certainly be attributed to the late Iron Age and have yielded Roman finds (Carrag Aille, Limerick).

Closely paralleling the landscapes of Wales, Cornwall and parts of Scotland, where similar site types abound, the defended farmstead was the archetypal form of lesser settlement. Another feature that links the rural archeology of Ireland with western and northern Britain, is the souterrain, often found in association with raths.

The articulation between the fragmented demography of small clan-based rath settlements and the kingdoms of the Irish histories was clearly facilitated by the already discussed royal assembly sites, built around a 'calendar' of meetings, ceremonies and fairs. Lesser kings might owe allegiance to greater ones and pull regions even closer.

The economy of Ireland in Roman times has received comparatively little attention to date, in part because of poor preservation of animal bones on many sites. The average size of livestock was small by modern standards, though a larger volume of data is needed to assess whether there was any improvement in husbandry to match that attested in mainland Britain under Roman rule. One of the few positive things classical writers had to say about Ireland concerned the quality of its pasture lands (though Mela tempered this by the observation that they were so lush that, unless restrained, cattle 'would burst from feeding too long').

The history and archaeology of Ireland in Roman times at first appears to have had little to do with the Roman empire or with mainland Britain. The late Iron Age kingdoms, developing a distinctive regional style of the La Tène culture, and with elaborate rituals of kingly power, appear very inward-looking. The southern borders of Ulster when its centre was at Navan appear to have been defended by massive linear earthworks (such as Black Pig's Dyke, the Dorsey, Dane's Cast). All of this suggests a preoccupation with other Irish peoples and a turning of the collective back on the Roman world. But that may well be too simplistic a view and overstates the continuities of life implicit in the *Ulster Cycle*. This is where the discoveries at Drumanagh take on their true resonance, because here we encounter a different sort of site, a coastal entrepôt perhaps, that opened a doorway between the Roman province and its Irish neighbours.

Finds of Roman material culture have been made in many parts of Ireland, though unsurprisingly perhaps the greatest concentrations of findspots are in the eastern half of the country. A particular cluster in the Boyne Valley and down the coast from there to the Liffey can now be seen to focus around Drumanagh and surely illustrates the extent to which this site served as a portal for Roman goods, however exchanged or brought into Irish society. Typical copper ingots from the Roman mines in Wales are known at Drumanagh and just inland at Damastown, suggesting trade in more substantial things than mere baubles. The function of Roman material culture within Irish society is interesting. Partial excavation of the area in front of the massive Neolithic chambered tomb at Newgrange in the Boyne Valley has yielded a large group of Roman artefacts, evidently a series of small-scale deposits (twenty-five coins run from Domitian to Arcadius). Several of the gold coins had been worn as pendants or amulets. The finds included a number of gold items and illustrate ritual deposition around an earlier monument, which continued to be imbued with religious significance. The Hill of Tara has also produced quite a wide range of Roman imports, including samian ware, glass and various copper-alloy artefacts. Other Irish 'royal' sites with Roman finds include Dun Ailinne and Roman coins and other artefacts have been recorded at the hillforts on Freestone Hill (Kilkenny) and Rathgall (Wicklow).

Another cluster of early Roman finds exists in north Antrim, including two large hoards located on the coast at Feigh Mountain (500 coins) and Flower Hill (300 coins). Aside from coins, copper-alloy fibulae of 'Romano-British' types are quite widely attested, both as stray finds and on settlement sites. Diagnostic Roman pottery, such as samian or Arretine ware, is also represented in site finds, though often in much later contexts than its production, suggesting curation of such exotics within Irish society.

One very unusual find is an engraved oculist's stamp on a piece of fine-grained slate, possibly associated with a burial near Golden in Tipperary. Whether this was the last resting place of an enterprising specialist trader from the Roman empire, treating the eye-sore Irish, is unknowable, but it is not unthinkable. A cremation burial from a rath near Stonyford (Kilkenny), with the ashes contained in a Roman glass cinerary urn, capped with a bronze mirror and accompanied by another glass flask, is so unusual as to suggest the strong possibility that this person was not native to Ireland. In similar vein, an inhumation cemetery was located in the nineteenth century at Bray Head (Wicklow), with the extended skeletons associated with second-century coins. Both inhumation and the inclusion of coins were not native Irish customs.

Somewhat similar inhumations, but lacking coins, are attested also at Betaghstown (Meath) and Knowth in the Boyne Valley. At Newgrange a cut-down terminal from a traditional Irish gold torc was ritually deposited alongside one of the standing stones ringing the great Neolithic passage grave. The item was inscribed in Latin capitals: SCBONS·MB and though the precise meaning is uncertain, the import is clear – this belonged at some stage to someone who knew Latin letters. However, before we leap to the conclusion that all of these cultural anomalies represent foreigners coming to or settling in Ireland, we should reflect on the possibility that Irish people may have served on ships involved in the Irish Sea trade or been recruited to serve as auxiliaries in the Roman army. They could have brought new customs, artefacts and ideas back with them from overseas.

In chronological terms there is something of a gap in the distribution of Roman goods in the third century, but the fourth and early fifth centuries are much better represented, with two major hoards conforming to the literary reports of Irish raiders. The Ballinrees hoard, near the north coast in Londonderry, comprised 1,506 coins and 15 silver ingots (including two examples of ox-hide shape with stamps) and hack silver weighing over 5 kg. The plate consisted of cut-down fragments of bowls, platters, dishes and spoons. The latest coins suggest a date in the early fifth century. The two stamped ingots read CVR MISSI and EX OF PATRICI, indicating an official controlled source within mainland Britain. The hoard at Balline in Limerick near the west coast consisted of two intact hide-shaped silver ingots similar to those from Ballinrees and parts of two others, along with three fragments of silver plate, a beaded rim of a bowl, a corner of a tray and a hunting scene from a platter. There were no coins associated. Three of the ingots were stamped: EX OFFIC ISATIS, EX [chi-rho symbol] OFC VILIS and EX O NON. The complete ingots from the two hoards have similar weights of 314–18 g (close to a Roman pound of 325 g). Parallels for two of the ingots have been found at sites in Kent, though that need not indicate the location of a supposed Irish raid, since the silver was probably part of official distributions of ingots manufactured close to one of the silver/lead mining areas in western Britain. While the hack silver is suggestive of a raid against the civil zone of Britain, it is also possible that the silver ingots could have been used to pay Irishmen recruited into the late Roman army. Perhaps the most important historical conclusion to be drawn from this is that they could represent either activity on the part of native Irish. The peoples of Ireland were interacting with the Roman empire in new or enhanced ways in the late empire.

The material culture of the Irish Iron Age only marginally intersects with the main currents of the European Hallstatt tradition. Although there are some fine examples of high-status La Tène metalwork, both imported and of local production, in the north and centre, the south-west is virtually devoid of La Tène influence. Archaeology thus hints at a profound divergence between the north and south of Ireland in the latter centuries BC, with the north closer to the pattern of development on mainland Britain. Torcs, fine copper-alloy work and horse-gear highlight the emergence of a powerful elite in the latter centuries BC, notably in Ulster. The point is even more forcibly demonstrated by the distribution of rotary beehive querns, another late Iron Age innovation. These are limited almost exclusively to the north and centre of the country.

The evidence certainly supports the view that on the eve of Roman contact some areas of Ireland were cultural backwaters. Interestingly enough the most dynamic La Tène culture seems to equate well with the territory of the Ulster kings as represented in the *Cycle* and of their arch enemies in the kingdom of Connaght to the west. The evolution of extraordinary ritual centres of kingship within a landscape of primarily dispersed settlement is striking and stands in contrast to the late Iron Age of, say, Scotland, Wales or Cornwall. The impact of Rome on this situation is difficult to assess fully and requires more fieldwork at key sites. But there is some evidence to suggest a shift of political and social power southwards, as attested by the more extensive Roman finds in the Boyne Valley and the hinterland of County Dublin. Clearly the site of Drumanagh is a prime location requiring further work in this regard. Among the prime exports from Ireland may have been slaves, the product of existing inter-regional raiding.

The Balline treasure and a number of other finds of Roman goods in the south-west in the late Roman period hint at a change in the regional fortunes, with enhanced connections between this area and Britain. There is evidence in the Irish and Welsh annals of migration of people from southern Ireland to western Wales at some point in late antiquity, and a convincing case has been made to relate this to the *Attacotti* of the Roman sources. The derivation of the name is almost certainly from the Irish generic term for tributary peoples, *aithechthúatha*. The

Attacotti appear only briefly in the Roman histories as raiders in the 360s, but several units of *Atecotti* served in the Continental field armies in the later fourth century. This differentiates them from the *Picti* and *Scotti* who were not recruited for military service and suggests that elements of *Attacotti* had been formally allowed to settle inside the empire as federates. The Irish literary sources specify the expulsion of the *Déisi Muman* and the *Uí Liatháin* to Dyfed, and the distribution of late antique inscriptions using the Ogam script (evidently invented by a native Irish person with a knowledge of Latin) in southern Wales, provides important confirmation of this partial folk-migration. Ogam inscriptions are also common in southern Ireland, with smaller concentrations in northern Ireland, Cornwall and Scotland. It is an important reminder that what is often presented in Roman sources as raiding activity may have involved more complex patterns of migration and diaspora.

One of the most interesting consequences of Roman rule in Britain was the impact on the peoples of Free *Britannia*. There are signs that kingship and elite authority was strengthened in both Scotland and Ireland. Disparate and potentially warring factions were brought together into fewer, larger regional groupings. In response to Roman invasions of Scotland, the numerous peoples of Ptolemy were replaced in the later sources by *Caledonii* and *Maeatae* and they in turn by *Picti*. Although the heyday of the Pictish kingdom was to come after the departure of Rome, it is apparent that its ethnogenesis lay in the late Roman period as a response to Rome. From a position of self-defence against initial Roman invasions, by late Roman times the people of Scotland were increasingly taking the initiative in military action against Roman territory, conducting raids well inside the empire's frontiers. While Ireland was never subjected to Roman military adventures, there is little doubt that Rome's proximity and her desire to dominate even unconquered peoples through diplomatic pressure will have had an influence on the further development of Irish societies. Again, there are indications of the formation of larger territorial states as we progress through the Roman period, and of Irish military activity and migration extending well beyond *Hibernia* by late Roman times. One of the paradoxes of the collapse of Roman government in Britain is that the fringe territories were left far stronger and more vital than the old civil heartlands of lowland Britain.

15

Rural Culture and Identity

The rural population comprised in excess of 80 per cent of the estimated total of 2 million and was thus by far the largest and most diverse of the three main communities. The most visible group archaeologically was the elite, who at times constructed consciously Roman-style buildings and made a social display out of the consumption of devolved metropolitan culture. We must remember that they were a very small minority of the rural population at large (perhaps only 2 per cent). Archaeologically they are by far the most distinctive and, although the composition of this group was far from uniform, they shared some identity markers in common and also linked with elite behaviour and culture in the towns.

The rural elite included many of the wealthiest people in the province. As in other parts of the Roman world, the urban aristocracy were by and large supported by rural landholdings, and if fortunes were made in trade, manufacturing or some other profession, the common pattern was to invest in the most stable form of capital, a landed estate. The conquest of Britain created a land market of a type that had not existed previously, and opened up ownership of land to new patterns. On one of the few extant documents relating to landholding in Britain (dating to 118), the names of three landholders are given: Caesennius Vitalis, T. Valerius Silvinus and L. Iulius Bellicus – all three Roman citizens and at this date potentially immigrants, though the last-named has a British/Gallic cognomen. Certain parts of the landscape may have been opened up preferentially to non-British purchasers, and sale of land at cash prices may have favoured foreign investors over native Britons.

The British aristocracies and princely families in south-east England were affected both negatively and positively by the changes. On the one hand, old monopolies and rights were liable to be swept away, but in some cases the generosity of the victor to those who accepted Roman suzerainty could consolidate landholding in the interests of the existing elite. The classic success story relates to the family of Togidubnus in Sussex, where, in addition to the exceptional palace at Fishbourne, there are a number of other early and elaborate villas that can be plausibly related to the native elite. It is pretty clear that a substantial number of the rural elite in many parts of Britain were the descendants of British families who continued to farm ancestral lands. A significant change from the second century and later was that the rural aristocracy also fulfilled the role of urban elite, with second residences in towns.

The social position of Britons was not unchallenged and there may have been a considerable impact from outside investment, settlement of people from overseas and 'new money' augmenting the rural elite. A new province was a source of land for investment, with sale or lease of lands by the state being an important way to offset the initial high costs of incorporation of territory to the empire. The presence in Britain of immigrants from the Continent is evident in a number of areas of life. We have noted the numbers of people from northern Gaul among the epigraphic attestations in both towns and garrison settlements. Some at least of those probably invested in land and estates in the province. The army was another potential source of investors, with the retirement bonuses and savings specifically intended to allow veterans to purchase land and social position. In the early years of the province, of course, some may have chosen to return to their homelands on discharge, but the creation of veteran colonies for legionaries at Colchester, Gloucester and Lincoln established a firm base for settlement in the province. The existence of estates in the countryside around Lincoln is demonstrated by a rare tombstone reference from Branston to a rural estate: *in his praedis*. The distribution of discharge diplomas in the south may indicate areas where land was available for purchase or where groups of soldiers had already been settled. Walcot near Bath and Sydenham in west Kent are both in areas that may have been detached from *civitas* control and where lands may have been available for purchase. There are a few additional hints provided by finds of distinctly military artefacts at villa sites, perhaps most famously in the case of the Rudge Cup, the soldier's souvenir dish from Hadrian's Wall found at a villa in Wiltshire. A bronze cup with lettering of uncertain significance from the Yorkshire villa at Beadlam could be a similar marker of a retired soldier. The villa at Dalton Parlours in West Yorkshire overlies an Iron Age settlement site, but the excavators concluded that this was not a case of gradual evolution, but rather a supplanting of a native family by someone with close links to the legion at York (indicated by finds of military equipment, tile stamps of *legio* VI and of York tile fabrics). Some Britons serving in the Roman army will have in turn retired to the land. But farmers with military connections, whatever their ethnic background, will have had different cultural reference points that will have marked them out from their rural neighbours. They also had purchasing power. The one clear reference to the price of land (40 *denarii* for a 2-ha/5-acre wood in Kent) suggests that it was comparatively cheap. Although prices no doubt varied according to quality, a decent estate could probably have been purchased with a legionary's discharge bonus of 3,000 *denarii*.

The state and the imperial household will both have benefited from land confiscations following conquest and revolts, as well as from bequests from the provincial elite. The emperor was ultimately one of the largest landowners in most provinces, and these lands were administered through the procurator's office and its late Roman equivalent, both based in London. Another group of potential investors in rural development comprised members of the highest social classes in Rome, who took advantage of cheap land prices to establish estates. In the early fifth century we know that one of these absentee landowners, a women called Melania, chose to dispose of her multi-million property portfolio spread across Italy, Sicily, Spain, Africa and Britain.

Estates on public land, or owned by emperors and other absentee landlords, might be run by bailiffs or minor officials of state, by chief tenants, or through networks of tenurial arrangements. Their function was to cream off surpluses from the British occupiers of such lands. In the absence of much epigraphic testimony, it is difficult to detect these sorts of large estates on the ground, as in archaeological terms they may have resembled other private farms. The villa at Combe Down close to Bath is a notable example, as without a single lead seal referring to the province of *Britannia Superior* and an inscription recording the building work of an imperial freedman and assistant procurator, the interpretation of the site as a potential imperial estate would be highly contentious. A further example of an imperial estate can be postulated at Ickham in east Kent, where two groups of fourth-century imperial lead seals have been recovered. Other possible archaeological markers of major estates include atypical rural villages such as attested at Kingscote,

Gatcombe or Stonea Grange, where the scale of the sites, coupled with their architectural distinction, sets them apart from the regional rural backdrop.

The extent to which imperial officials had use of rural villas is uncertain. Given the short-term nature of their appointments, it is unlikely that they had the incentive to build and decorate villas for themselves, unless they intended to establish a long-term residence in the province. The likelihood of the state investing in lavish villas for high officials was low. Governors and senior officials may have had regular invitations to spend time at the rural retreats of prominent civilians and could have exploited their position to enjoy country living at someone else's expense. However, some minor officials had duties that were based on rural districts, as in the case of procurators of imperial property and of mines and quarries. Some at least of these people may have been based in comfortable but utilitarian residences that are architecturally classifiable as villas. Isolated examples of villa architecture in Cornwall or upland Wales or northern Britain may fall into this category.

Another group of potential villa owners would be wealthy refugees from the Continent, for instance in regions affected by major incursions across the Rhine frontier in the third century. The interpretation has been overplayed in the past in relation to the wave of spectacular late Roman villas in Britain, but the possibility that some at least of the late Roman investment came from newly arrived sources of capital should not be entirely dismissed. There are also a number of references to the exile of prominent individuals from elsewhere in the empire to Britain (for example, Ammianus Marcellinus refers to banishments in 361, before 369 and 370, and the suppression of the Priscillianists in the 380s provided another group). The Scillies was one possible destination, and would have been a particularly isolated and uncomfortable one for a person of high social standing. But other individuals may have fared better and purchase or lease of a suitable rural residence in southern Britain, where the governors could keep an eye on them, is a distinct possibility.

In late Roman times, following an empire-wide pattern, the Christian Church will have become a major landowner through endowments and testamentary gifts. The possibility that villas were taken on by senior clerics or even that some might have been converted into religious communities should be borne in mind, though proof is lacking.

A simple consideration of the information presented in the previous chapters shows that the regional patterns of rural development differed markedly across Britain, even in areas where villas flourished. The corollary of course is that elite fortunes likewise varied, as did the behaviour and lifestyle of high-status individuals. It also stands to reason that some individuals will have been more precocious than others in showing off their possession and understanding of high-status Roman culture. These may have included legionary veterans, merchants and craftsmen from Gaul, or members of Togidubnus' family and other high-status Britons seeking fast-track success under Roman rule. The palace at Fishbourne is an exceptional early manifestation of elite status games in the countryside, but most other villas and mosaics of early date represent special cases. In general, the take-up in Britain of the package of identity elements of a Roman elite class was both slow and uneven. The idea of a 'villa elite' as a broad category in south-east Britain is potentially anachronistic before the third century and is inapplicable for large parts of the south-west, west and north of Britain throughout the Roman period.

Not all the rural elite resided in villas, especially in the early centuries of Roman rule. We need to consider, for instance, how the indigenous peoples of the Fens, Cornwall, Wales and Scotland expressed their cultural superiority and difference from others in society and to what extent these practices were transformed by the reality of Roman suzerainty.

THE FASHIONING OF
ELITE BEHAVIOUR

Stone inscriptions were rare in the countryside, with milestones along roads being the most common occurrence. Britain is not unique in this respect and one of the primary reasons is that literate display was less suited to rural districts than to garrison communities or towns, where a greater density of literate individuals was to be found. The classic Roman milestone of northern and western Britain was a cylindrical column standing up to 2 m tall, whereas in southern Britain many examples were on smaller quadrangular blocks (some only c.30 cm cubes), with the content of inscriptions generally limited to imperial titulature. The majority of examples have been located close to known Roman roads, but there are some anomalous examples, including a series of finds from known villa sites situated several kilometres from the nearest road, and a cluster in Cornwall. It is possible that some at least of these rectangular pillars could have marked other significant landmarks, such as the boundary of imperial estates, or in the case of the Cornish pillars, for example, the limits of mining zones. A 'milestone' from the line of Ermine Street to the south of Water Newton seems to record public property (*publicum*), while another boundary stone from Thrapston in the Nene Valley marked '*PP*' could again indicate the terminus of public property. There must have been numerous boundary markers in the countryside, though the majority of them were probably of wood.

Another important class of rural inscription was the religious dedication. Many came from rural shrines, but others were found at or close by known villa sites (Chedworth, Daglingworth, West Coker, Shakenoak). The nature of the religious dedications varies. There are few inscribed altars, more numerous relief carvings of the deity accompanied by a brief text, a few engraved statuettes, rather more votive plaques shaped like feathers, considerable numbers of curse tablets and of individual bronze letters that could be bought as votives. Dedications to the imperial cult are highly unusual and in the case of two examples from near Bath seem to relate to imperial estates. The Combe Down text sought the welfare of the emperor on behalf of the assistant procurator Naevius, while at Somerdale, close to a major villa at Keynsham, a statue base to the *numen* of the deified emperors and Silvanus was erected by Gaius Indutius Felix, '*con vic ga*', perhaps a chief tenant (*conductor*) in control of an imperial estate village (*vicus*) whose name began with *Ga*.

Apart from the two large deposits of curse tablets found at Bath and Uley, isolated finds at a range of other sites, primarily rural temples, indicate that they are representative of a more general religious practice in southern Britain (Table 11, p. 312). Initial expectations that most of the curses will have been the work of specialist scribes operating at the temples have been confounded by the lack of duplication of hands at either Uley and Bath. It looks as though an important ingredient in the power of the curse was the personal engraving of them using model texts as a basis, even though the resulting documents often reveal defective knowledge of Latin and poor handwriting. This suggests that the business needed to be secret between the dedicant and the divinity to be efficacious – a point further emphasized by the practice of rolling or folding the lead sheets to prevent human eyes from reading them. The date range of the curses is established by changes in handwriting, with some at least as early as the late first or early second century and a few in the New Roman Cursive of the fourth century. The overall quality of literacy demonstrated by the rural curse tablets is about the same as that at Bath, suggesting no significant difference between the constituencies of worshippers in the small town and at the rural shrine. Some cross-over between the two groups may be suspected, as in the case of Docilianus, who lost a cloak at Bath and may be the same person with remarkably similar handwriting who calls himself Docilinus at Uley, when seeking vengeance against three named individuals whom he suspects of causing harm to one of his farm animals. How representative is Uley of the use of curses at rural temples? Although examples have also been found at Lydney, Brean Down, Pagan's Hill, Old Harlow, Weeting with Broomhill/Brandon, a number of features point to the area around Uley having been rather specially organized, perhaps as part of an imperial or other large-scale estate. The site may thus not have been typical, and at least one of the other rural temples yielding curse tablets lies closely adjacent to another suspected imperial estate (Pagan's Hill by Keynsham).

Tombstones (or engraved sarcophagi) are extremely rare on rural sites. There are three examples from Yorkshire, where the influence of the military community may be strongly suspected. Most of the other examples come from villas in southern Britain (Pitney, Wansford, Tarrant Hinton, Wool, Mansfield Woodhouse), or from the vicinity of small towns (Cricklade, Sea Mills, Bath, Charterhouse), with just a single example from a rural temple site (Wood Eaton). There are no examples that can be associated unequivocally with a non-villa rural settlement. A site at Barking in East London is of uncertain type, but also yielded tile stamps of the procurator based in London and may have been a villa similar to Saunderton in Bucks (from which came comparable stamped tiles). Three tombstones from Gloucestershire were all in fact found within a kilometre or two of the large nucleated site of Kingscote, itself a noted centre for religious inscriptions, relief carving and other decorative stonework. The special nature of Kingscote is emphasized by the identity of one of the people commemorated, Mettus a Getan (Dacian), who had evidently made a will, as an heir is mentioned.

Another significant hot spot of rural epigraphy lies just a few kilometres to the north-west at the temple of Uley. The unusual character of this part of Gloucestershire is emphasized by the fact that within an area of c.600 sq km we find one of the highest densities anywhere in Britain of rural epigraphy, religious iconography, sculptural works and decorative stonework, altars and tombstones. Certainty of interpretation is impossible, of course, but this part of the countryside was plainly out of the ordinary in its use of epigraphy.

Inscriptions incorporated in the schemes of interior decoration of rural buildings provide additional pointers to the literary pretensions of some villa owners. Mosaic inscriptions are exceedingly rare in Britain, with examples from the villas at Bignor, Colerne, Frampton, Hinton St Mary, Littleton, Lullingstone, Rudston, Thruxton, Winterton and Woodchester. There are fragmentary inscriptions on wall-paintings from villas at Alresford, Godmanchester, Greetwell, Lullingstone, Otford and Rockbourne, and graffiti scratched in plaster from Bancroft, East Malling, Fishbourne, Piddington, Rudston, Scampton, Tarrant Hinton. Although the examples are quite widespread, there are some hints that the distribution is skewed towards the more palatial villas (Bignor, Fishbourne, Woodchester) or to villas in proximity to the provincial capitals/*coloniae* (Alresford, East Malling, Greetwell, Lullingstone, Otford, Scampton, Winterton), or the military community (Rudston?), or areas of notably dense concentrations of villas with mosaics (Frampton, Hinton St Mary, Littleton, Rockbourne, Tarrant Hinton, Thruxton). Two of the mosaic inscriptions incorporate literary sounding phrases (Frampton, Lullingstone), one is a religious exhortation (Woodchester), but most are simply names of things depicted or perhaps the name of the artist (Winterton, Rudston, Colerne, Bignor). The Thruxton mosaic is unusual, both because it comes from a very modest aisled house and because it names 'Quintus Natalius Natalinus et Bodeni'. The first part gives the *tria nomina* of a provincial Roman citizen and the final name may be his *signum* or an alternative British name, Bodenus. He is presumed to be the owner of the villa in the fourth century. The mosaic-floored room was a late addition to a typical aisled house and may have been associated with an adjacent enclosure around an earlier grave and sacred pit. The unusual architectural context of the mosaic and perhaps the intent of this moderately well-to-do landowner seem a far cry from the more elaborate and larger villas of the Cotswolds.

A survey of evidence for writing implements has revealed numerous discoveries on rural sites. Unsurprisingly, the major concentrations are on villas (251 styli from seventy-three sites), though most sites yielded 1–2 styli at most, with only four sites totalling more than 10 styli (the largest total was 70 styli from the Hambledon villa in Buckinghamshire). Quite a bit of evidence also comes from non-villa settlements (94 styli from fifty sites). The data also suggest regional differences, though these could be a product of the scale of rural excavations in different counties, since the pattern is distorted by a few exceptional assemblages as at Hambledon, or the nucleated settlement at Tiddington in Warwickshire (30 styli). Nonetheless, a number of interesting blanks in the distribution can be noted (Cornwall, Devon, Leicestershire, Nottinghamshire, Derbyshire, Shropshire), corresponding to areas with comparatively few villas.

Although the peasantry may have been largely illiterate, some at least functioned within a literate system of landholding and many sites may have had economic interconnections (perhaps as components of larger estates) that are now inaccessible to us. A few exceptional survivals hint at what is lost: the writing tablet from London referring to the sale of a small wood in Kent is paralleled by a legalistic (but sadly fragmentary) tablet from the villa of Chew Stoke, perhaps guaranteeing vacant possession of a property being purchased. Fragments of further tablets have also been discovered at Claydon Pike and at a second-century rural site at Bicester, hinting at the once wide distribution of such documentation. In the most developed parts of the landscape, it is clear that land was measured, owned or leased, taxed and traded according to written documents.

The two areas highlighted already as ones in which significant imperial or other major estates may have existed (Avon/Somerset and Gloucestershire) have yielded over 22.5 per cent of all rural finds of styli in Britain, again emphasizing the potentially unusual character of these landscapes and the social outlook of the rural elite there.

Another indicator of literacy in the rural community is represented by graffiti on personal possessions, generally intended to mark ownership. As we have noted in earlier chapters, the practice was particularly common among the military community and is well attested also in towns. Of 151 sites recorded with graffiti on samian vessels, 73 were military sites (including 31 sites producing over five items), 26 were towns (14 with more than five items), 13 villas (only one with more than five items) and 39 other rural sites (none with more than five items). Some of the 'minor' rural sites were actually temples or what might be ranked as small towns in some classifications, but others were certainly relatively modest farms.

Personal names reveal much about the social mix in rural Britain, though the evidence is limited by the differing propensity of groups of people to record their names, and the homogenization of name forms through the spread of Roman citizenship. Stone inscriptions and religious dedications on metal votive plaques provide a first reference group, though we may presume that the bulk of this material relates to people of relatively elevated status in society, or those who saw themselves as such. Graffiti on personal possessions are often abbreviated, which makes reconstruction of the full set of names difficult. They do include some indisputably British or Gallic names among the more obvious Latin ones. Tile stamps from the Gloucester and Lincoln areas abbreviate the three names of Roman citizens (T. P. F. and L. V. L.), while stamps on pottery (especially mortaria) offer up 250 additional names (or abbreviations) of people whose workshops were often located in the countryside. The majority of named potters either had a single Latin name (over 60 examples) or a British/Gallic name (well over 100). Relatively few potters registered the *tria nomina*, but some were evidently citizens or foreigners, migrating in the wake of the army in the early post-conquest years. One man active in Kent in the first century was Q. Valerius Veranius, a citizen potter previously active in north-eastern Gaul. There were doubtless other entrepreneurs like him in the early stages of the occupation of Britain and the more successful of them may have invested in landed property.

Treasures such as the Hoxne hoard represent the topmost level in Romano-British society. Various items in the Hoxne treasure were engraved with personal names, including a lady Iuliana on a bracelet. A man named Aurelius Ursicinus features on ten spoons, along with a variety of other individuals with Latin or Greek names, Silvicola, Datianus, Peregrinus, Euherius (or Eutherius?), Patanta and Faustinus. The fortune represented by the hoard places this family in the top echelon of provincial society and their ultimate origins may well have been on the Continent, where the name Ursicinus was shared by a number of prominent individuals.

Some other individuals were clearly Roman citizens, as in the case of

Q. Neratius Proxsimus at Nettleham and Aurelia Concessa at Branston, both close to the colony at Lincoln. Many other names are straightforward Latin ones (though that does not preclude British origins): women called Secunda, Tertia, Fausta, Maxima, Simplicia, Veneria, or men called Censorinus, Firminus, Amatus, Licinius, Florentius and so forth. Others are equally 'Celtic' and thus probably of British or Gallic origin. Colasunius Bruccius and Colasunius Caratius who were jointly responsible for a statuette of Mars found near Lincoln fall into this category and there is a comparative wealth of other north-western European names: Bellicia, Mina, Mocuxsoma, Sulicena among women, and Bellicus, Satavacus, Tammonius, Vassinus, Vatiaucus, Vernicio among the men. It is important to remember that these need not all have been native Britons: Iventius (for Iuventius?) Sabinus attested at West Coker villa looks to have a fabricated citizen name, but his dedication to Mars Rigisamus suggests a Gallic origin as Rigisamus is attested only at *Avaricum* (Bourges).

The curse tablets from Uley and other rural sanctuaries potentially related to a wider social class, albeit still limited to the literate strata of society. Analysis of the names from Bath and Uley reveals a small majority of British/Gallic names over Latin ones (95 : 83 overall). Latin names occur as single *cognomina* (Saturninus/Saturninia), rather than the pairing of *nomen* and *cognomen*, which would normally indicate a Roman citizen. British names include Senovara (Bath) and Senovarus (Uley), while some names were evidently concocted on a British base – thus Docca, Docilis, Docilina, Docilianus at Bath and Docilius at Uley – all hinting at overlap between the 'congregations' at the two shrines. Another find from the sacred spring at Bath was a pewter plate engraved with a list of names and patronymics in the traditional British manner, as 'Marinianus Belcati . . . Bellaus Bellini' ('Marinianus son of Belcatus, . . . Bellaus son of Bellinus').

Some parts of the country are virtually devoid of recorded names. A rare example from Cornwall is Aelius Modestus, scratched on a pewter plate deposited in a well in the mining district. The likelihood in this case is that it records an incomer, perhaps a contractor or procuratorial official linked to tin extraction, or a military administrator.

Mosaics represented in Roman Britain the luxury art form *par excellence* and nearly 2,000 examples are now known, with the bulk of the numbers divided between villas and the major towns. Already utilized in the palace at Fishbourne, mosaics became a more widespread feature of rural villas and elite town houses during the second century. There are comparatively few securely dated third-century mosaics, but the early fourth century saw a massive resurgence and the majority of dated mosaics are assigned to this period. The spread of mosaics was to some extent conditional on the existence of workshops of trained craftsmen, and much analysis has focused on identifying regional schools, believed to have been based in major towns such as Cirencester.

Many of the early mosaics had geometric designs, some of considerable complexity, and in all periods such pavements remained numerically predominant. Figures are more common among the later material, often featuring mythological scenes. Two main schools of thought exist about the social significance of these images: the material is a random assemblage of standard Roman artistic motifs, without any specific personal or allegorical significance – the mosaics essentially represent what was available in the mosaicists' pattern books; or the selection of subject matter was something that rich patrons took great interest in and the deeper symbolic meanings of the scenes were all-important. In either interpretation there can be no doubt that mosaic floors represented a significant investment in a cultural artefact that was essentially a vehicle for presenting a person's claims of Roman identity and education.

The predominant themes in figured mosaics in Britain are all easily paralleled in the corpus of mosaic art from other provinces, though due to the poor preservation and/or inelegant artistic representation the precise iconographic identification sometimes remains disputed. Nonetheless, the overall pattern of British mosaic art does suggest some insular preferences, as perhaps in repeated allusions to the sea. The four seasons (Bignor, Chedworth, Lullingstone, and nine other sites), Orpheus charming the beasts (Barton Farm, Withington, Woodchester, Winterton, *inter alia*), Bacchus (Chedworth, Stonesfield, Pitney, Thruxton) are particularly well represented, but there are unambiguous representations of other classical myths, such as Bellerophon and the Chimaera (Croughton, Frampton, Hinton St Mary, Lullingstone), Europa and the bull (Keynsham, Lullingstone), Venus (Low Ham, Rudston), scenes from Virgil's *Aeneid* (Frampton, Low Ham), Jupiter and Ganymede (Bignor) and scenes from the life of Achilles (Keynsham, Horkstow?). British examples of other conventional subjects for mosaics include chariot or circus scenes (Colerne, Horkstow, Rudston), gladiators (Bignor, Brading), and wild animal hunts in the arena (Rudston). Animal hunts in general were popular images in elite art, representing one of the favoured leisure pursuits of the wealthy (Malton, Winterton). Representations of other gods and mythical beings are also attested: Mercury (Rudston), Neptune (Frampton, Withington, Rudston), Medusa (Bignor, Dalton Parlours), Theseus and the labyrinth (Oldcoates), pairs of mythological lovers (Pitney). Nymphs, cupids, peacocks, craters (the cantharus), dolphins, tritons and other marine beasts are common elements.

What is undeniable is that the repertoire is strictly limited to established classical themes, even if the details were occasionally bungled or misinterpreted by those responsible for laying the mosaic. The absence of scenes of rural life marks a contrast with some other provinces. All of this suggests strongly that a prime motivation for the laying of figural pavements was to show off real or claimed knowledge of classical culture. Knowledge was power in this society and mosaic art was used to the full to convey a sense of learning and status. The Low Ham and Frampton mosaics depicting scenes in the life of Aeneas can reasonably be seen to embody a claim to knowledge of Virgil's classic work. It has even been proposed that the inspiration of the mosaic panels was the commissioner's own manuscript of the text illustrated with miniature paintings, rather than pattern books owned by the mosaicist. Similarly, the mosaic inscription accompanying the scene of Europa and the bull at Lullingstone has been judged to evoke both the opening of the *Aeneid* and the poetic style of Ovid. The rarity of specific allusions in Roman Britain to classical literature makes these examples all the more striking. A fragmentary painted inscription from a fresco in a corridor at the villa of Otford in Kent almost certainly contains another reference to the *Aeneid*.

Evidence of a different kind is provided by some enigmatic coins of the usurper Carausius that surely contain abbreviated references to two successive lines of Virgil's Fourth *Eclogue*: *RSR* standing for *Redeunt Saturnia Regna* ('The Golden Age returns') and *INPCDA* for *Iam Nova Progenies Caelo Demittitur Alto* ('Now a new progeny is let down from heaven above'). There are further Virgilian allusions on the coins, all of which presupposes the existence of provincials schooled in Virgil or at least able to appreciate the cultural game-playing that Carausius was engaged in.

On such limited evidence it is impossible to assess fully the possible contents of personal libraries in Britain, but the mosaic evidence overall illustrates knowledge and understanding of classical mythology and genre among the provincial elite. The problem is the impossibility of getting inside the heads of those who commissioned and admired the works. That has not stopped scholars making the attempt, with varying degrees of success. The imagery of Orpheus, for instance, has been interpreted as being iconic of late Roman neo-Platonic philosophy. It is argued that Orpheus acquired a more profound philosophical and religious importance in late Roman paganism and thus in elite culture. Another suggestion is that he came to encapsulate British ideas about woodland gods. On the other hand, Orpheus had been a popular image in mosaic art from earlier centuries, perhaps not least because of the challenge of depicting the exotic menagerie of beasts that gathered around Orpheus when he played his lyre. The Orphic pavements in Britain were located within the most important reception rooms in the houses and villas where they were found. The most impressive example is the great pavement from Woodchester, situated in the principal dining-room in the centre of the main residential range. The fame of this mosaic will have spread in the West Country and some at least of the other Orpheus pavements may have been laid in emulation of it. All of these suggestions have some degree of plausibility about them. It is also quite possible that different factors may have motivated different people to adopt the image. The religious use of mosaic-floored rooms has sometimes been argued on the basis of the complex blending of imagery. An unusual Orpheus pavement from a tri-apsed hall at the Littlecote villa in Wiltshire has provoked the most discussion. Here Orpheus lacks his traditional menagerie, but is accompanied by four female figures (the seasons or goddesses), either on the backs of or standing alongside a range of different animals. The most detailed interpretation of the possible complex allegorical allusions is ingenious but ultimately unprovable and other evidence does not support the use of the room as a chapel of a neo-Platonic sect. The closest parallel for its architectural form is in late antique reception and dining-rooms.

The imagery of the vast majority of fourth-century mosaics is wholly pagan. Yet two Christian elements in mosaics from Frampton and Hinton St Mary in Dorset give pause for thought. Both incorporate the chi-rho symbol in mosaics that are otherwise loaded with traditional pagan elements (Bellerophon, hunting scenes, Bacchus, Neptune, Venus, Cupid, mythological couples and heroic tales, nereids, dolphins, hippocamps). Had the portions with the chi-rho symbols been damaged, we would have no difficulty fitting these pavements into the corpus of other pagan mosaics from Britain. Despite various attempts to explain the specific selections from pagan iconography in Christian terms (whether orthodox or Gnostic), it remains equally plausible that the late Roman aristocrats who commissioned these pavements saw no problem in juxtaposing the new Christian symbolism alongside the traditional visual language of the educated elite. The Christian identity was thus overlain on the established concept of *paideia*, by which the Roman elite across the empire sought to express social distance between themselves and those less well educated in the classical tradition. The same sort of mix of old and new traditions was matched at Lullingstone in Kent, where a subterranean room was converted into a Christian chapel – indicated by overtly Christian wall-paintings, while the main reception room retained its earlier mosaic floor depicting Bellerophon and the Chimaera, the seasons and Europa and Jupiter/bull.

The ability to recognize literary allusions or mythical figures represented in art forms, to recollect the details of the stories, to quote appropriate phrases from Virgil or another well-known author – these were attributes that defined someone of the top rank in society. It is reasonable to infer from the architecture and decor of certain villas that at least some individuals in Britain aspired to this exclusive status.

There is a lack of explicitly British content in mosaic iconography, though a few possible exceptions to this can be noted, such as the head of 'Neptune' from St Albans adorned with a pair of antlers and hinting at conflation with a British horned god. The Rudston Venus is frequently cited as an example of bad art, an inept British craftsperson botching the naked female form to hilarious effect. An alternative view is that the representation was deliberately abstracted in order to give prominence to 'Celtic' features and a preferred pear-shaped female form. There is no doubt that the art is naive, but the predominant cultural references here were Roman. In addition to Venus, the floor features a merman (triton), the head of Mercury (perhaps originally opposed by a now lost Bacchus), four hunters (*bestiarii* or *venatores*) and four animals fought in the arena. Two are specifically named: 'the bull called Man-killer' and 'the lion called Fiery'. Some of the other mosaics at Rudston reveal higher standards of representation, so it is possible that in this case the abstraction of the Venus pavement was related primarily to the non-availability of more skilled artists locally when it was laid down, perhaps at the end of the third century. A generation later, when the other pavements were laid down, the local standards of mosaic art were notably higher.

Much mosaic art from Britain was of comparably late date. There is no evidence to show a similar widely diffused familiarity with classical culture in, say, the second century. In fact the initial image bank appears to have been relatively restricted and, in the countryside at least, most early pavements were geometric. Many of the villas that were adorned with splendid mosaics in the fourth century did not even exist in the second. The cultural character of the late Roman countryside was remarkable, of course, but it represented a major change and expansion of elite behaviour at a comparatively late date. It is also clear that there was a significant gulf between the larger villas and their iconographically complex sets of images on the one hand, and the more tokenistic insertion of a single mosaic into a small farm on the other. While the culture was to some extent shared among the rural elite, not everyone bought into the knowledge at the same level or will have empathized with Roman elite culture to the same degree.

Other important decorative arts included wall-painting, which was widely incorporated in town and country houses. The models were developed from Mediterranean prototypes and the similarities in colour schemes, motifs and figural elements are striking. Inevitably, the material is much more fragmentary than mosaic art, but studies suggest that plastered and painted walls were overall far commoner than mosaic floors. Walls were often over-painted with imaginary architectural vistas – equivalent to the Pompeian second and fourth styles – and examples of these have been recognized in Britain. Many walls were treated as large panels of colour, with centrally placed miniature scenes, though some of the later Roman paintings involved large figures at near life-size covering the entire wall area above dado level (as at Kingscote). Where the subjects of figural scenes can be identified they conform to the repertoire of mosaic art in evoking standard themes in Roman mythology and society, including, evidently, scenes from Virgil at Otford in Kent and, perhaps, Venus and Mars at Kingscote or Narcissus and a Satyr from Tarrant Hinton. Marine scenes have been noted from a number of villa bath-suites, such as Fishbourne, Sparsholt, Lullingstone and Winterton.

Marble floor and wall veneers (*opus sectile*) are considerably rarer than mosaics and have been recorded in general only at exceptional sites, such as Bignor or the Fishbourne palace – whose marble workshop may also have supplied materials to nearby villas at Angmering and Buriton. Marble statuary appears to have been exceptionally rare in Britain, with Woodchester standing out for the number and quality of pieces recovered. Marble busts have been found at Lullingstone and Fishbourne, Broadbridge and Bosham, and marble statuettes have been found at a few other villas (Dryhill, Spoonley Wood, Bancroft) and at the rural temples at Maiden Castle and Uley.

Non-marble statuary and relief sculpture in the countryside was primarily a feature of the villas and the principal temples. Finds of religious sculpture from villas have led to theories that certain villas might have served as temples, with accommodation and baths for pilgrims. However, the overlap here is indicative of the close patronage links between villa owners and some rural temples and the incorporation of private shrines into villas.

The regional distribution of stone-carving on rural sites is drastically unequal in Britain, with a significant correlation with areas where there are abundant wealthy villas with mosaics. The Gloucestershire Cotswolds and the area around Bath are notably rich in this respect. In addition to anthropomorphic sculpture, much of it religious in nature, excavations at major sites in these areas have also yielded decorative architectural elements and items of stone furniture, such as chip-carved stone sideboards.

There are many crude carvings of heads in the round from different areas of Britain and Ireland. Some have come from known Roman villas, small towns or other settlements, but others lack a secure Roman provenance. These are often described as 'Celtic heads', though they lack coherence stylistically as a group. Although these have been included in the published volumes of sculpture from Roman Britain, their actual attribution is much debated and they may well cover a much longer time-span. Those that are of Roman date arguably represent a quite distinct branch of representational art from the elite products considered thus far. At any rate they are a reminder about how little understood are works of art that fall outside the normal classical repertoire of subjects.

Silver plate is another category of elite decorative art and Britain has produced some impressive collections, though interestingly with a strong concentration in East Anglia, a region not noted for the quality of its excavated villas. The two most extraordinary hoards recovered from rural contexts are the Mildenhall treasure and the Hoxne find. This latter hoard comprised almost 15,000 coins (569 gold and all but a tiny percentage of the rest silver), 29 items of gold jewellery, 78 silver spoons and 20 ladles, and 11 items of tableware (small bowls, vases and pepperpots). The Hoxne discovery is significant also because it lay close to the supposed location of a place recorded in the *Antonine Itinerary* as *Villa Faustini*, evidently a major estate adjacent to the Roman road. It is clear that the chest in which this hoard was deposited was not large enough to have held large plates and bowls, which were presumably part of a second (lost) cache.

Roman silver vessels had exercised an early fascination for the British elite, appearing in late Iron Age contexts, as in the case of two silver cups in a burial at Welwyn. Feasting and the display of luxury accoutrements was a feature held in common by Iron Age and Roman societies. The real mark of someone of elite status was the quality and quantity of his or her silver tableware. Some silverware was marked with its owner's name, a few pieces had ostentatious statements about their weight or capacity added. Britain was not just a consumer of exotic silverware manufactured elsewhere; there are strong indications of local manufacture. Production of pewter vessels, as a cheaper equivalent and some at least intended for votive deposition, is also attested by moulds from St Just in Cornwall, Camerton, Landsdown, Westbury and Nettleton (all close to Bath), Gloucester and Witcombe, Silchester and an outlier at Langton (Yorkshire). The design and decoration of pewter dishes plainly emulated silverware and, despite the comparatively rare survivals, indicate the widespread adoption of this material among the 'villa elite'. Standards could slip, however, as in the case of a neatly decorated pewter plate from Welney in Norfolk, where the standard invocation 'VTERE FELIX' or 'good luck to the user' appears to have been rendered as 'VERE FELEI'.

Where silver vessels were decorated with figures, we see the usual emphasis on classical mythology and pagan iconography. The Great Dish from the Mildenhall treasure has at its centre a head of Neptune, surrounded by hippocamps, nymphs and other sea beasts. The outer border is a Bacchic dance. Other vessels in the Mildenhall service featured the eclectic mixture of Bacchus, Alexander the Great, his mother and assorted wild beasts. But there are also three spoons with chi-rho symbols, indicating a potential Christian owner. Again, as with the mosaic evidence, the combination of Christian and pagan motifs is perhaps more problematic for us than it was for the late fourth-century aristocrats in a remote province. A scene of a boar hunt on a *lanx* from Risley Park (Derbyshire) again has pagan overtones but was donated by a Bishop Exuperius to the church of *Bogium* (location unknown).

Taken together, the luxury arts demonstrate that a significant group of the rural elite in Britain presented an identity that rested on a series of Roman cultural norms in other parts of the empire. Central to this conception was the rural villa and here we might draw a key distinction between a purely functional farmhouse with stone walls and a tile roof, and a building that incorporated additional features designed to reflect status and a Roman outlook (painted walls, mosaic or tessellated floors, baths, underfloor heating). Literacy was an assumed component of this cultural package and there is something of a correlation between the more grandiose villas and physical evidence of literate behaviour. This elite identity differed in significant respects from the military identity and though it overlapped with urban elite culture, there too we can trace divergence.

The conspicuous display of capital wealth in the form of architectural embellishment or interior decoration was strongest in areas of the countryside where social hierarchies were enshrined in Roman concepts of land tenure. Ownership of land, control of labour and tenants, and estate management were all buttressed by the use of an elite culture that reflected social proximity to Rome. Although some villa owners must have served in the army, the messages of power and social prestige we see in the rural archaeological record suggest that veterans eschewed many aspects of the military identity if they retired to the countryside. Power in the rural context was based primarily on legal title, cultural knowledge and education, rather than force. When veterans (whether aliens or Britons) joined the rural community they appear to have made efforts to fit in with those around them, even where that meant setting aside some aspects of their military identity. On the other hand, the frequent occurrence of items of Roman military equipment and of supposedly military-type brooches on rural sites could suggest that elements of dual military/rural identity traits could subsist side by side.

NON-ELITE RURAL CULTURE

There are many unresolved questions concerning the lifestyles of the rural population at large. In areas of villa estates, many of these people must have had relationships of dependency with the landowning elite and all were ultimately answerable to the tax demands of the state. The longevity of the roundhouse in the 'villa landscape' and the low penetration of Roman pottery styles and manufactured goods at many sites are striking testimony to a sort of resistant conservatism among the rural majority. Hopefully, future research will enable us to gain more insights on the rural lower orders and their experience of imperial rule.

In contrast to those who owned land or aspired to the social behaviour of the landowning class, the majority of the rural populace lived very different lives. Their utilization of new material culture was much more limited. Past studies of material culture have tended rather too easily to assume that the presence of 'Roman' artefacts can be equated with a desire to emulate Roman behaviour and fashions. Serving a meal in a samian vessel was not a great cultural advance if it was traditional food, prepared in a time-honoured way, which would previously have been eaten from special tableware (as had started to be adopted by some late Iron Age groups). The discovery of a Roman mixing bowl (mortarium) is potentially more interesting because it represents a different way of preparing food, as well as a new style of ceramic vessel. Patterns of consumption were subject to market forces as well as individual volition and some part of the uptake of new manufactured artefacts may have been due to nothing more than the greater availability of such products. For this reason, the nature of cultural change in rural districts is particularly interesting, as the range of manufactured goods was probably rather narrower here than in the towns or the garrison settlements. In addition we need to consider the use to which new material culture was put. The precise circumstances and context of use are thus important issues in the interpretation of mundane artefacts. Studies should also seek to identify types of artefact or behaviour that related more to a British or non-Roman identity.

Two major advances in the study of artefactual assemblages in Britain have been made in recent years. The first involves the close scrutiny of site assemblages and comparison between sites of similar types or distinct character. It is becoming clear that broad differences do exist between the military, urban and rural communities. Although part of the differences may relate to the varied supply and market arrangements, in part at least these represent the emergence of radically divergent notions of identity, with each group aiming both to reinforce its own version of being Roman and also to differentiate itself from others. Work on Roman ceramics suggests that rural assemblages were different from urban ones in terms of the relative proportions of functionally diverse vessels (for instance jars and tablewares) or by ceramic types. Non-villa settlements have low thresholds of occurrence of amphoras, decorated samian, mortaria, and so on, in comparison to villas, and villas in turn lag behind urban sites and military bases. Similar patterning has been revealed in overview studies of glass and animal bone.

The second approach is to examine the contextual data for the distribution of specific artefact classes across Britain in terms of broad categories of sites: military, major towns, other towns, villas, other rural settlements, and so on. A pioneer analysis of coins from 140 British sites, spread across the range of types, revealed broad differences in coin-use profiles between towns and rural sites and between east and west Britain. One interesting point to emerge is that the suburbs of major towns have coin profiles that are more similar to the countryside as a whole than to the pattern within the walled areas of these centres.

An analysis of the distribution of oil lamps has shown an overwhelming predominance in military contexts and at the two major centres of early Roman government, Colchester and London. Rural sites (including villas) represent a tiny fraction of the distribution. Olive oil was available in the civil zone in the first century (when most lamps were imported), but evidently it was not much used for lighting by native Britons. On the other hand, analysis of a range of small metal toilet implements, often produced in sets of 'tweezers, probes and nail cleaners', reveals a very different pattern. These items were introduced into Britain from the Roman empire in the late Iron Age and remained popular personal grooming items throughout the Roman period, though they became much more rare on the Continent. As such, they represent an insular cultural trait. They are rare at military sites and major towns (doubly so when one considers the volume of excavation at those categories of site), but are abundant at small towns, villas and other rural sites (cumulatively 66 per cent of all examples). Villas and rural sites together represent 38 per cent of all sites on which they have been located, with small towns another 32 per cent. These were status indicators in the late Iron Age, but appear to have achieved a broader distribution in the Roman period, plausibly representing the long-term maintenance of indigenous traditions about personal grooming.

The rest of this chapter will concentrate on three particularly important areas where alternative rural identities manifested themselves: diet, funerary practice and religion.

Consumption and diet

Food is a basic requirement of life, but it also reflects social beliefs within society. The differences implicit in the truism 'we are what we eat' should be demonstrable in archaeological terms. Basic variability in foodways ought to link with notions of identity. In many societies, diet is a conservative area of experience, linked to established subsistence economies and to a tendency for cooking traditions within rural households to be passed down from generation to generation. Major departures from traditional foodways thus require explanation. The elite in any society may occupy a distinctive niche in that they often employ cooks from outside their close agnate group, and these servants or slaves bring not only independent ideas to bear but are also less bound by tradition. In a colonial contact situation, there is a high potential for experimentation with food, both to denote status and to define new forms of social behaviour. Conversely, passive resistance to social change can also find an outlet in the maintenance of traditional foodways as a means of reinforcing a sense of identity.

In Britain under Roman rule there were certainly major innovations in diet and in the way that food was prepared and served. The army and the urban and rural elites were the people at the forefront of new practices and a distinctive material culture of food consumption. Imported commodities such as wine, olive oil and fish sauce are proxies for broader experimentation with radically changed styles of cuisine and taste. The late Iron Age aristocracies of the eastern and southern kingdoms had already experimented extensively in this area. Underneath the palatial villa of Fishbourne there was a high-status late Iron Age site, from which an assemblage of pottery and food remains closely correlates with Roman styles of feasting. This process was taken further under

Roman rule at some high-status sites as part of the elite demonstration of knowledge and understanding of Continental Roman culture. As we shall see, the process was neither uniform nor comprehensive. The occasional use of olive oil is something rather different from a permanent adoption of oil as the edible fat of choice.

Unsurprisingly, military sites and the major towns record the widest range of markers of changed dietary habits: higher ratios of cattle and pig bones and lower numbers of sheep and goats, the presence of numerous domestic fowl, a rise in consumption of fish and shellfish even with distance from major rivers and the sea, the occurrence of wine, oil and fish-sauce amphoras, botanical remains of 'luxury' and imported foodstuffs, and large numbers of specialized vessel forms in pottery and metal for the preparation, cooking and serving of food. Rural sites show less dramatic change in diet, though there appears to be both social and regional differentiation in the data. For instance, from non-villa sites, rural pottery assemblages tended to be dominated by jars used in cookery, with relatively smaller numbers of specialized vessels for food preparation and serving. Mortaria, flagons and amphoras – vessels that specifically link to foreign notions of food preparation and tastes – were notably rare, as were samian or other fineware serving dishes. Drinking vessels were generally larger-size beakers (suitable for beer) rather than the smaller cups normally used for wine. Animal-bone assemblages from rural settlements were dominated by sheep/goat, partly because these were the less sought-after animals in urban and military markets and thus more likely to be consumed in the country, partly because of an early development of wool production. Broadly speaking, there is a divide in British archaeology between the more 'Roman' sites where cattle and pigs predominate and those, primarily rural and 'native' in orientation, where sheep were the mainstay. Nonetheless, some rural sites show evidence of a shift towards beef production or pig-rearing in the Roman period and there is specific evidence from metrical analysis of cattle and sheep bones of increases in the size of stock, suggesting both introduction of new stock from the Continent and improved husbandry techniques. Regional differences were quite marked; for instance, cattle bones predominate in assemblages in the upper Thames Valley.

The role of meat in everyday diet has been much debated and it is generally agreed that in both Roman and British Iron Age societies meat was an occasional food of special status for most people. An association of meat with feasting and with religious sacrifice appears to have been a feature of both societies. Sheep were the preferred sacrificial animal at a number of British temple sites, such as Uley, Harlow and Great Chesterford, with a particular preference for young lambs. This suggests a seasonal cycle to cult activity at these religious sites. Otherwise, meat consumption was closely related to social status, and the financial where-withal to eat it more frequently was advertised by social customs of inviting others to witness and participate.

In parts of Britain, the material culture of many rural settlements is best characterized as impoverished, with few ostensibly Roman artefacts present. Cornwall and west Devon, Shropshire, Wales, the northern Midlands and northern Britain all fall into this broad category and the exceptional sites immediately excite curiosity. Perhaps it is better to see this as innate conservatism rather than resistance, but it may also reflect the reaction of people in areas of Britain that were offered less chance of wealth accumulation or social advancement than others.

By and large, higher-status rural sites, primarily villas but also includ-ing large villages such as Dragonby in Lincolnshire, do tend to show more experimentation with cultivated foodstuffs, animal products, cer-amics (large numbers of vessels from a wider range of forms and func-tional types). The differences between elite and non-elite foodways in Britain evidently widened in the Roman period. In the case of villas we can add in the architectural evidence of ornately decorated dining-rooms, serving as a suitable stage for the rich to play with their food. On the other hand, numbers of amphoras are low on all rural sites and this might suggest that despite a certain flirtation with wine and oil, perhaps for specific social functions, day-to-day cuisine remained fixed on the traditional mainstays of British diet, beer and butter. Neverthe-less, even on lower-status sites, there are some indications of changes and experimentation of diet across the centuries of the Roman presence in Britain; as more evidence is accumulated it should be possible to delineate this picture more precisely.

Funerary rituals and commemoration

Funerary practices provide important evidence for the behaviour of the non-elite elements in rural society, though as ever the high-status burials tend to dominate discussion. It is apparent that the period of Roman rule brought about extraordinary changes in the treatment of the body in death, but this was neither a rapid nor a straightforward process. In the late Iron Age there were already great regional differences in funerary practices, complicated by the widespread practice of excarnation (exposure of the body), human sacrifice and head cults. Human body parts turn up with some regularity in unusual contexts on Iron Age sites; sometimes associated with foundation deposits for houses, and in boundary features. They are not uncommon finds in Romano-British contexts either, though on sites with Iron Age antecedents the tendency is to assume that they were residual. Human sacrifice is perhaps most famously marked by the Lindow Man bog body from Cheshire, probably dating to the late first century and the time of Roman annexation of the region. Head cults (the curation of the skulls taken as trophies) are attested by the Roman literary sources and the archaeological data for some of the Iron Age peoples of Gaul. Archaeological finds of skulls from settlement sites in Britain suggest that the practice was also probably significant in some regions of the islands. Tell-tale signs are knife marks indicating de-fleshing of the skull and evidence for the polishing of the exposed parietal bone. A cluster of finds has been made in association with late Iron Age and Roman-period rural settlements in the southern Fenland, while a de-fleshed skull was located in a Roman context at the Folly Lane cemetery by St Albans, and a large number of skulls have been recovered from the Walbrook in London. All of this suggests that the influence of regional British practices with regard to death and the body may have had a long afterlife in the Roman period.

Elite burials dominate the funerary record, whether because of rare epigraphic commemoration or because of the quality of finds. A recent discovery of a pair of exceptional cremations from Harpenden near St Albans yielded a total of over 150 separate items, including 13 bronze vessels, 14 samian vessels, 9 of glass, 2 silver brooches and fragments of ivory. The date of the assemblage appears to be the early second century and the graves lay close to a probable early villa on the site of an earlier Iron Age settlement. The presence of some local pottery and a bronze strainer of Iron Age type may hint at a local origin of those buried here, but the overall assemblage reflects not only an adoption of a wide range of Roman elite culture, but, more importantly, access to it. On the other hand, the average numbers of grave goods in cremations from this part of Britain at this date is less than two, so we are dealing with exceptional individuals, whatever their precise origin.

In general, the areas of south-east Britain that had adopted the practice of furnished cremation burials in the late Iron Age continued to do so under Roman rule, with a gradual expansion in the range of artefacts deposited, to include more characteristically Roman grave goods such as coins and lamps. The difficulty is to differentiate between native Britons and incomers, as at all times native Britons probably dominate the archaeological record and at the local level practices may quickly have converged. Richly furnished cremation burials were a distinctive feature of the south-eastern counties but were rare beyond this zone in parts of Britain where inhumation or other methods of disposal of the dead had predominated in the Iron Age. The exceptions are primarily military sites. Within the south-east zone, regional differences stand out. For instance, larger numbers of vessels are commonly found in burials south of the Thames than in those north of it. This is another indicator that the Harpenden couple could have been immigrants.

Status was conveyed in various ways, with grave furnishings and funeral ritual being supplemented by choice of container, use of surface markers and treatment of the body. Elaborate above-ground structures in the south-east of England include large barrows, but mausolea and other built stone structures are also occasionally attested. Villas and military sites show a higher proportion of elite burials than towns, and contribute more to the overall total. For example, the Bartlow Hills cluster of seven barrows (Essex) probably related to a nearby villa. Villas associated with mausolea include Lullingstone and Bancroft.

The shift from cremation to inhumation was generally slower in rural areas than urban ones. However, by the end of the third century, most of southern Britain favoured the inhumation rite, with limited grave furniture and sometimes with coffins. In the later Roman period the influence of the major towns as cultural trendsetters is more evident, and a number of other innovations introduced from other parts of the empire, such as plaster packing in some elite burials, were primarily focused on the towns.

Nonetheless, there are aspects of the rural burial rite that appear to have remained distinctive and non-Roman. Burials were still commonly placed within boundary features and stray body parts at rural sites suggest that excarnation continued to be practised to a degree. Decapitation of the dead, with the head sometimes placed between the legs of the deceased in the grave, is occasionally encountered in urban cemeteries, but it is much more prevalent in rural contexts, especially in a broad band running from Dorset to the Wash. There are notable concentrations of decapitated burials in Dorset, Somerset, the upper Thames Valley, the Cotswolds, the Nene Valley, Essex and Cambridgeshire, and striking absences in east Kent, Norfolk, Sussex, Lincolnshire, the northern West Midlands. The significance of these burials is much debated and it is clear that more than one procedure was followed. A small minority appear to have been beheaded alive; in other cases the decapitation was performed *post mortem*; in yet others the skull appears to have been separated from the body after primary decomposition. Men, women and even infants are all represented. Punishment of criminals or deviants is inadequate as an overall explanation, though it is conceivable that the individuals were perceived in some sense as outsiders or on the margins of society. There may be links to pre-Roman practices related to head cults. At any rate, it is difficult to account for the regular appearance of this bizarre rite in terms of normative Roman burial practices. Although attested at several villa sites, it is associated with a wider range of rural settlements. Prone (face-down) burials also occur more commonly at rural sites. Both prone burials and decapitations when encountered in the managed urban cemeteries tend to be located on the fringes, suggesting that those interred in these ways were to some extent seen as outcasts or undesirables.

Infants were commonly buried in a different way from older children and adults and this is particularly clear-cut at rural sites. They were often interred below the floors of buildings, or incorporated in foundation deposits below the walls. Rather than interpret such discoveries as evidence of infanticide, some scholars argue that infant mortality was very much bound up with notions of fertility. The frequent association of infant burials with agricultural buildings suggests that some inherent link was being made between the death of a child and the productive potential of the land. In a similar way, the fact that a high proportion of decapitated burials involved women may also be linked to ideas about fertility and death. At any rate, such unusual customs were particularly prevalent in rural areas, suggesting a significant degree of cultural conservatism and non-Roman behaviour.

Religion

The practice of religion in the countryside differed in important respects from that of the military community and the urban centres, though there was of course a degree of overlap. We need to take account of the movement of the elite between town house and rural estate and of soldiers from fort to farm or simply visiting rural shrines. Our evidence for rural religion is almost entirely limited to the villa/civil zone of the province (Fig. 17). The religious practice of a large part of rural Britain, from Cornwall, through Wales and northern Britain, evidently remained unmonumentalized, non-epigraphic and aniconic.

The overwhelming majority of rural shrines were of Romano-Celtic type, though a few had a more basilical layout, as at Lydney Park. Some temples were sited close to roads or within village-type settlements (Nettleton, Heybridge, Westhawk Farm), but the positioning of others in significant topographic or cultural landmarks is also evident – as in the shrines established in the hillforts of Maiden Castle, Chanctonbury or South Cadbury, or offshore (Hayling Island). A number of the best-embellished rural temples, especially those producing epigraphic material, were located close to major villas or suspected imperial or other major estates: in the case of Uley one can cite Kingscote, Wood-chester and Frocester within a few miles and Pagan's Hill lay close by Keynsham. Many of the more isolated rural temples were set within sacred enclosures and surrounded by subsidiary buildings. The fourth-century temple to Mars Nodens at Lydney Park was erected within an abandoned promontory fort and the complex included accommodation and baths as well as the main shrine. Some at least of these sites had pre-Roman origins – notably Uley, Hayling Island, Wanborough.

The best-documented sites reveal evidence of animal sacrifices and of votive depositions of a wide range of personal items, including coins, items of jewellery and adornment, toilet implements, votive plaques/ leaves, letters, vessels and spoons, pottery and statuettes. Weapons were notably less common than in Iron Age ritual deposits, though model weapons and tools appear to have been substituted in some cases. Priestly regalia (some of distinctly non-Roman type), including ritual head-dresses and sceptres, have been found at Hockwold (Norfolk), Cavenham (Suffolk), Willingham Fen (Cambridgeshire) and Wan-borough (Surrey). The Wanborough head-dresses comprised chains

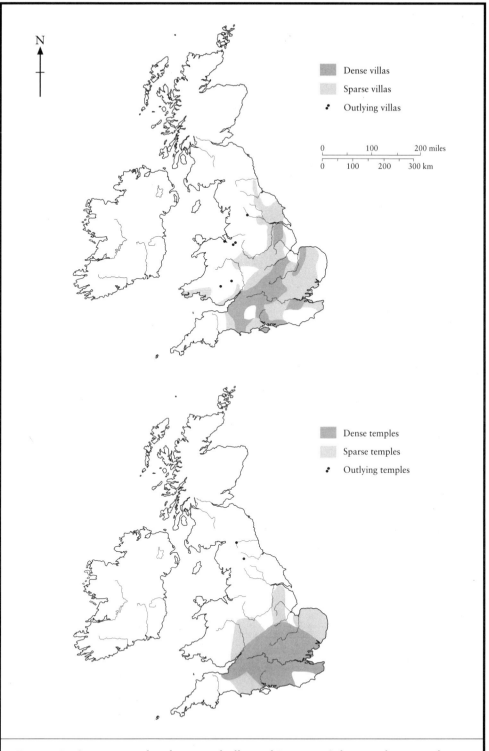

Figure 17. Comparitive distributions of villas and Romano-Celtic temples. Note the mosaic quality of the maps, illustrating not only major differences between south-east and western/northern Britain, but also variation within the so-called civil zone

supporting a wheel symbol on the top of the head. This motif is common in Iron Age and Roman religious contexts in Gaul and possibly to be associated with the Gallic equivalent of Jupiter. Some of the other examples are diadems incorporating silver plaques and small human masks. The sceptres often seem to have been topped with human or divine heads, or symbols of birds.

Although the old druidical order was effectively eliminated by Rome, there was a formal priesthood at many temple sites at later dates. The Lydney temple was ornamented with a fourth-century mosaic, paid for by offerings to the god and overseen by Titus Flavius Senilis, perhaps superintendent of the cult (*praefectus religionum*), and Victorinus, an interpreter of dreams. The secondary rank of Victorinus is emphasized both by his relegation to the second line of the dedication and by his single name as against the *tria nomina* of the superintendent. There is also an inscription from Bath relating to a dedication inspired by a vision.

Inscribed stone altars are notably rare at rural shrines, especially if we exclude the atypical Cotswolds/Bath region (Uley, Nettleton, Chedworth villa). Although inscribed votive metal plaques or leaves/feathers are known from several sanctuaries (Thistleton, West Coker villa, Lydney), stone inscriptions are generally rare. Alongside the engraved leaves and feather votive plaques, there were many plain ones, suggesting that a significant percentage of the clientele who could afford the offering lacked the skills to add a written message. The vast majority of 'votive' finds from temples are personal items of jewellery or coins, lacking any specific written communication with the god. At Bath and Uley the engraved curse tablets were accompanied by some unengraved examples, or ones where the text is an illiterate scrawl. Although the curse tablets in general reveal a previously unsuspected level of rural literacy, this suggests that literate skills were not essential in rural religious practice.

The Uley material is explicit in identifying Mercury as the main element of cult there, though Mars was also invoked. Harlow has yielded a fragment of an altar to the imperial *numen*, but the reference to the imperial cult was sometimes added to other dedications and the main focus at Harlow is thought to have been Mercury, named on a curse tablet. Another curse tablet from close to the Hockwold temple in Norfolk was addressed to Neptune, as was another from the Hamble estuary in Hampshire. Mars features in a *defixio* from the Marlborough

Downs and Minerva appears to be the goddess venerated by a gold votive leaf from Stonea Grange. In all these cases it is unclear if a British local cult lay behind the classical name.

Another possible indication of a lower engagement with literate religious practices concerns finds of single votive metal letters. These generally have nail-holes for affixing to vertical panels and have been found at a number of religious sanctuaries in southern Britain. Based on the comparatively wide range of letter-forms found at Lydney (A, C, D, E, F, L, M, N, O, P, R, S, T, V), it is sometimes assumed that dedicants bought individual characters to compose their own texts. But the fact that most sites where the material has been found have produced multiple examples of at most two or three letters, makes it more probable that individual letters had specific idiogrammatical significance. As such they could constitute a minimal sort of 'literate' religious transaction. It may be significant that they are virtually unattested at military sites or major towns.

Relief carvings and statuettes of the gods are more common, and classical deities are often recognizable by their attributes (Mercury with caduceus, goat/ram and cockerel for instance). The most common images in southern Britain are of Jupiter, Mars, Minerva, Mercury, Apollo, Hercules and Venus. On the other hand, most often the items are uninscribed, leaving open the question of whether the Roman god was worshipped in traditional form, syncretized with a British/Gallic cult, or if a local divinity had been accorded a classical representational form, but was being worshipped by its British name. Practice could have varied according to the outlook of different patrons at a shrine.

Individual rural temples sometimes featured more than one cult. At Uley, for instance, where Mercury was indisputably the main focus, there were also representations of Jupiter, Bacchus, Sol and Cupid; at Woodeaton, where Mars may have been the main cult, we find Venus, Hercules, Minerva and Cupid; at Nettleton, Apollo was accompanied by Diana, Silvanus and Mercury. Of course, the use of the classical names here is speculative and the imagery may equally be standing in for a range of British divinities. Two buried caches of votive plaques from Stony Stratford and Barkway included dedications to Jupiter, Vulcanus and Mars, and Mars and Neptune respectively (though the material could have derived from more than one temple in each case). Care must be taken not to confuse the most classically orthodox or

'Roman' representations of a god as indicative of practice in Britain as a whole. As one example, there is an impressive group of altars and other stone sculptures of Mars in classical panoply from a number of sites in Gloucestershire (Bisley Common, Custom's Scrubs Bisley, King's Stanley, Nailsworth). The atypicality of these reliefs is suggested by the fact that almost all were found within a few Roman miles of the great villa of Woodchester.

The clearest example of a British deity taking on Roman form, but not the Roman name is provided by a find from near Baldock, where twelve out of a hoard of nineteen votive plaques and a silver statuette clearly portray Minerva, but in all six instances where she is named it is as a hitherto unknown British goddess, Senuna. Sulis Minerva at Bath also occurs in her singular British form in many dedications. Other cults worshipped without reference to Roman names include Arnemetia at Buxton, possibly Veteris at Thistleton Dyer (otherwise only known in the military north), Viridius at Ancaster, Abandinus at Godmanchester and Dea Regina at Lemington.

Cases of syncretism are comparatively rare in the countryside. There is an altar to Apollo Cunomaglus dedicated by Corotica from the octagonal temple at Nettleton Scrub, along with a bronze plaque that names Apollo alone and relief carvings of Diana, Mercury and Rosmerta. A Roman citizen, presumably from the colony, erected an arch to Mars Rigonemetes in a rural sanctuary near Lincoln. Other paired dedications with Mars include Mars Rigisamus (West Coker), Mars Lenus (Chedworth), Mars Nodens (Lydney), Mars Olludius (Bisley), Mars Corotiacus (Martlesham), Mars Alator and Mars Toutatis (Barkway) – several of these second-named deities were Gallic cults. Although the social standing of the dedicants is uncertain, some at least appear to have been high-status individuals and not all were British – some may have been of Gallic immigrant stock. A set of silver spoons from Thetford, inscribed to Faunus in association with a variety of other names, is more difficult to interpret. Is it evidence of syncretism of Faunus with various British gods or did the British names refer to devotees of the cult?

A major gap in the epigraphy and iconography of rural shrines concerns the comparative lack of evidence for eastern cults and mystery religions. Aside from a possible statuette of Atys from Hockwold and an amulet from Woodeaton with links to the Isis cult, the bulk of the evidence relates to Christianity, which, once formally recognized in the fourth century, had a very different profile from other eastern cults. The range of deities from the classical pantheon or related to Roman state religion is also narrower in the countryside than in the towns.

The overall rarity of dedications to classical deities alone or to syncretized gods in southern Britain compared to the military zone is a strong indication that they represented a specific form of religious action by a small group, rather than the commonly assumed evidence of a broad social adoption of the *interpretatio Romana*. The dearth of altars and other dedications specifically mentioning the fulfilment of vows also marks a departure from the military practice and the exceptions can in part at least be attributed to the uppermost strata in rural society whose religious identity most closely followed Roman norms. On the other hand, the widespread adoption of curse tablets indicates that literacy was not the prime obstacle to the wider take-up of elements of Roman practice.

In line with the material from Bath, the rural curses are fundamentally focused on cases of theft (Table 11, p. 312). At Uley, we have reports to Mercury of thefts of draught animals, linen cloth, a gold ring and some fetters, a bridle, a piece of plate and four rings, linen, a cloak and two silver coins, and, in the most lengthy list of woes, the loss of two wheels, four cows and other goods from a house. Other rural curses record loss of money (Farley Heath, Pagan's Hill, Ratcliffe-on-Soar); farm equipment (Brean Down); personal items including jewellery (Lydney Park); writing implements (unprovenanced in Gloucestershire); an iron pan (Brandon near Hockwold); a mule, other items from a house and two bags; and gaiters, gloves, an axe and a knife (two examples from Ratcliffe-on-Soar). Some of the texts curse particular suspects (Vasicillus and his wife at Pagan's Hill, Tacita at Clothall near Bancroft, Senicianus at Lydney, Vitalinus and his son Natalinus at Uley). But many curses had to be enacted on anonymous criminals and the god's attention was specifically directed to the different possibilities: variants on the phrase 'whether man or woman, whether slave or free' occur commonly. In the longest list of possibilities from Uley we find 'whether boy or girl, whether male slave or female, whether man or woman, whether soldier or civilian'. Another curse from Weeting with Broomhill close to the Hockwold temple in Norfolk, asks for vengeance against a thief 'whether slave or free . . . whether civilian or soldier'. Although it is in the nature of the curse formulae to be inclusive of many different options, it is also probable that the selection is focused on plausible scenarios. The anticipated presence of both slaves and soldiers in rural districts and the fact that these are seen as separate from ordinary men and women is of interest, though it need not imply that either group was numerous. The iron fetters mentioned in one of the Uley tablets is another hint at a slave component in rural society.

Although the scale of many of the thefts was relatively small, suggesting that the dedicants included people of only moderate means, at least two instances involved quite substantial sums of money. The losses of 3,000 *denarii* at Pagan's Hill and 4,000 *denarii* at Farley Heath represent the equivalent of ten years' (or more) pay for a second-century legionary for example, and match or exceed the 3,000-*denarii* discharge bonus of a soldier. These larger sums were probably hoarded within houses and several of the other losses appear to relate to burglary of farmhouses and other rural buildings.

The religious practices among civilian communities were based on a complex process of selection and assimilation of different elements, rather than a straightforward correlation of British religious expression against standard Roman practices. There are close parallels with some of the developments in northern Gaul, and the influence of immigrants from this region in terms of importing cults (the Matres, Rosmerta, Epona, Granus, Lenus) and of temple architecture needs to be given serious consideration. However, there are likely to have been even more important influences from indigenous pre-Roman religious practices, difficult though these are to reconstruct from surviving evidence. One important late Iron Age development appears to be the cult of the individual, and the creation of some temples as hero cults for prominent princes has been canvassed on the basis of the Folly Lane sequence of chiefly burial succeeded by Romano-Celtic temple. Another good candidate appears to be the Hayling Island temple, which could have developed from the burial site of the Atrebatic king Commios.

A distinctive type of Romano-British brooch has also been associated with cult activity. This is the so-called horse and rider type, broadly third century in date, with enamelled decorative images of a figure on horseback. Its distribution is almost exclusively outside the military zone and major towns, with the vast majority of known examples from small towns and rural sites and, where context is clear, ritual deposits predominate. There is a particular clustering in East Anglia and a secondary south-western grouping (Dorset, Wiltshire, Somerset). Relief sculptures and statuettes of the warrior rider deity are also known (again with a non-military distribution) and the type is clearly a local cult distinct from the classical tradition of Mars, though one relief names the rider as Mars Corotiacus. This rural rider god may have gone by a variety of names in different regions.

In several respects, there is overlap between the British, Gallic and Germanic cults worshipped by the military and rural communities. For example, there are numerous British examples of horned gods, perhaps similar to the Continental Cernunos. Mother goddesses, often in groups of three, are well represented both on Hadrian's Wall and in the West Country. Another grouping of three figures, and with a similar distribution, are the Genii Cucullati, generally swathed in long hooded cloaks against the British weather (and looking for all the world like patron deities of fell-walkers).

Christianity is almost as elusive in the country as it is in the towns, given how pervasive it ought to have been by the later fourth century. There is a notable concentration of Christian votive deposits around the site of Icklingham (Suffolk), where a church and baptistery are also known. Both the density of Christian finds and the nature of the ritual deposits here are unusual and hint at underlying highly regional religious practices. Notwithstanding Christian mosaics at Hinton St Mary and Frampton, the house 'church' in the cellar at the Lullingstone villa and Christian symbols or inscriptions on portable items, other evidence is underwhelming. Indeed, as noted already, the 'Christian' mosaics and silverware were in large measure iconographically pagan. This represents a far from complete 'triumph of Christianity'. In certain parts of the West Country, there appears to have been a fourth-century boom at rural sanctuaries. This could in part have been a counterbalance to the decline of pagan cults in an urban context, where continuity of cult may have been harder to achieve in the face of increasingly tough imperial directives. The coin lists from many temples in the Cotswolds show that they remained active centres for offerings until the end of the fourth century and there was another such cluster in the Thames valley. In this instance, as in so many others, rural society appears to have diverged from the pattern of military and urban communities.

PART FIVE

Comparative Perspectives and Concluding Thoughts

16

Different Economies, Discrepant Identities

This history of Britain in the Roman empire has replaced the simplistic paradigm of Romanization with the idea of 'discrepant experiences' of empire. In the process, I hope to have communicated both the complexity of the evidence and the potential for us to draw out different perspectives on its political and cultural history. The balance sheet of how Britain fared as an imperial possession can now be redrawn, starting with an overview of its economic trajectory.

THE ECONOMY

The economy of Britain was profoundly affected by the desire of the Roman state to extract resources from the province and this was a constant of Roman imperialism. Conquest was regularly expected to yield a bounty to the expanding Roman empire, initially in the form of spoils of war that might substantially underwrite the cost of campaigns and subsequent triumphal celebrations, and then through the exploitation of a region's tangible resources: land, minerals, people. In return there was no doubt an implicit expectation that the empire would deliver certain services to its subjects. Politics was an important contributory factor in the timing of conquests, but there was also an underlying concern with what such territories were worth. When Strabo discussed the British archipelago in the time of Augustus he repeated what was surely an official line in stating that it was considered that the costs of direct rule would not yield a greater return than that already brought by tax and customs dues on trade. Strabo's list of British exports to the Continent in the early first century included grain, cattle, gold, silver, iron, slaves and hides. Almost a century after the Claudian invasion, the historian Appian observed that the British province was still not paying its way: '[The Romans] have occupied the better and greater part of it but they do not care for the rest. For even the part they do occupy is not very profitable to them.' This comment suggests there was some official measure of profitability, however crude, against which the provincial territories were measured. Were there any special features that contributed to the imbalance between costs and gains and what was the impact of this financial background on provincial government in Britain? The list of goods exported from Britain in late Roman times is quite similar to Strabo's (grain, textile goods, woollen goods, pottery, metals, slaves), but there are signs of economic progress. A late third-century panegyric to Constantius, celebrated his recovery of Britain after the usurpation of Carausius and Allectus in the following terms:

And, in truth . . . for the commonwealth it was no modest loss – of a land so fertile in cereals of all kinds, that rejoices in so great a number of pastures, so abundant in veins of metal, so productive of tax-revenues, so well provided with harbours, of so vast a circumference.

As this quote indicates, the most important elements of the British economy from a Roman perspective derived from the discrete activities of farming and mineral extraction. Farming was the mainstay of the ancient economy overall, given that the majority of people lived in the countryside. Metals were fundamental to the empire's coin supply, armaments and equipment, and had myriad uses in daily life. Studies of the Greenland icecap have revealed that the Roman period marks the largest pre-industrial peak in hemispheric copper and lead pollution, testimony to the scale of Roman smelting activity. Textile-making and clothing production will have been another important economic area, but is the least tangible archaeologically. In fact, none of our main economic elements yields the sort of archaeological evidence that allows easy quantification. In discussing productivity, imports and exports, we are obliged by the poor survival of the bulk of the material evidence to focus on a few more durable products such as pottery and coins. Here we must guard against making false assumptions about economic vitality based on abundance of finds. Although the presence of small change is a significant indicator of monetization, the periods of highest coin numbers, whether as site finds or hoards, are notoriously influenced by other factors, such as the extremely low value of many late third-century coins, or the political reasons for heightened levels of non-recovery of hoarded wealth.

One of the problems with evaluating Appian's comment is that what is commonly identified as the 'economy' of Roman Britain is in fact a composite of several different spheres of economic activity that over-lapped with one another, but which were in important respects distinct one from the other. Even in Roman times, when much fuller records were available, it must have been difficult to disentangle all the strands to determine total receipts and total costs of the province. In what follows, three different scenarios are proposed: the imperial economy, the provincial economy and the extra-provincial economy.

The imperial economy

A large amount of economic activity in Britain under Roman rule took place in the context of the empire's arrangements for extracting resources and for paying and provisioning her forces and officials. This can be broken down into a number of areas of activity.

The major costs of the imperial economy in Britain concerned the army (pay, bonuses, discharge bounties, materials, equipment and sup-plies), the provincial government infrastructure and transport costs, capital investment and running costs involving public lands and imperial properties, diplomatic subsidies to client tribes and kings. These are impossible to quantify with any degree of accuracy, but were un-doubtedly significant sums. The total salary and discharge bounty costs of the imperial army are estimated to have been in the order of 150 million *denarii* annually in the second century and if Britain nom-inally was responsible for 15 per cent of that, the bill was in excess of 22.5 million *denarii*. To that we need to add the considerable salaries of the key senatorial and equestrian officials. A consular governor of Roman Britain may have been paid as much as 200,000 *denarii* per annum (based on a reference to a governor of Africa in the early third century receiving 250,000 *denarii*). What we can say is that in all prob-ability the cost of the British territories amounted to some tens of millions of *denarii* each year in the early empire; it is by no means certain that the British province could yield that sort of revenue initially. This represents a huge sum to exact from a region that at the time of the conquest had no cities and, outside south-east England, relatively underdeveloped trading economies. The cul-de-sac status of the British province was an additional complication, since trade did not naturally flow through the territory towards other Roman provinces.

The Roman state and imperial household had a variety of means by which they could endeavour to recoup the investment in the province. The exploitation of people was done primarily through taxation and tribute demands, labour requirements and liturgies, enslavement, military recruitment. Private possessions, notably in the form of portable wealth, were a prime target of the army of conquest, but individual fortunes were periodically confiscated or received by the emperor in the form of legacies. Landed property was mobilized by state appropriation and redistribution, gains from legacies, disposals and land sales and rentals, imperial estates and state lands. Rural production more generally was tapped through rents, dues, requisitioning, price-fixing, measures for the provision of transport animals, and of course taxation (including in-kind levies). The exploitation of natural resources was another major area of state control and Tacitus explicitly referred to them as the 'spoils of victory'. Although primarily directed at mines and precious metals, monopolies were also extended to salt and decorative stone. There is some evidence to suggest that investment in and maintenance of the exploitation of natural resources was less intensive in the late Roman empire, as in the Spanish mining districts, with state revenues increasingly dependent on higher rates of taxation.

The state was also in a position to profit from the existence of markets, harbours and trade, through customs at provincial boundaries (*portoria*), market surcharges, and so on. Finally, the system of military supply had a profound effect on the evolution of trade more generally because of the way it operated (through contracts) and the nature and extent of transport (long-distance and under state subsidy). Some of these economic effects of empire were short-term, such as the initial plundering of conquered territories, but others evolved over much longer time-spans.

Fundamentally, though, the high costs of garrisoning Britain imposed an obligation on the provincial government to maximize as far as possible the benefits and to minimize the additional costs to the state. What that meant in practice was a concerted attempt to mobilize the economic potential of Britain in the interests of Rome, rather than an enlightened policy aimed at its broader economic development. The stark contrast between the lands of western and northern Britain when compared with the south-east strongly suggests that landholding arrangements and means of extracting surplus were different in the two areas, with the former being squeezed more heavily (in proportion to available surpluses) in order to reduce the costs of military supply. Similarly, it appears probable that major mineral deposits and other natural resources were exploited either directly by the state, or indirectly through contractors or by native Britons under some sort of licence or production agreements in which the state took a substantial share. There is no evidence that individual *civitates* reaped substantial benefits from the exploitation of natural resources in their commonly assumed territories, and districts containing such resources could have been separately designated as imperial or state land. There is strong evidence for initial direct exploitation of such resources under military supervision, and, by the second century, increasingly through the agency of contractors, probably answerable to procuratorial staff attached to mining districts. Although explicit evidence from Britain is limited, such transfers of the mechanisms of state wealth acquisition to private hands were typical of the Roman empire.

The taking of censuses and the collation of detailed records of land and property holdings were common to all parts of the empire. Despite the paucity of surviving documentation for what must have been an astonishing undertaking, we know that it formed the basis of provincial taxation, land allocation and both military and civil government. We can speculate on the existence of a Roman equivalent of the Norman Domesday Book. Certainly, Roman decisions about taxation, and ultimately the profitability of the province, were based on the cumulative records of successive phases of survey and information gathering as territory was incorporated. Epigraphic testimony of a census of the people of Annandale in southern Scotland carried out by the army at the end of the first century provides a glimpse of a process that we can assume took place in stages right across Britain.

Taxation in the early Roman empire was based on land and capitation (*tributum soli* and *tributum capitis*), though there was also a range of adventitious taxes on, for instance, slave sales, the emancipation of slaves and (for Roman citizens) inheritance. Practice and collection arrangements varied both inter- and intra-provincially and exemptions and immunities were much sought after by individuals and communities.

Although often levied in cash terms, it is clear that payment of tax was sometimes made in kind – a situation that may have been common in Britain, at least in the early years. Tax collection at various times involved tax-farmers, who gathered in the revenues under state contracts, local urban authorities and imperial fiscal officials – procurators, quaestors and imperial freedmen and slaves. We do not know how successful the state was at making tax collection in Britain the responsibility of the provincial urban elite; at all times one suspects there may have been a need for bolstering arrangements with tax-farmers and petty officials, especially with regard to the military regions and natural resources. In any imperial system, the efficiency of the tax system is counterbalanced by the relative success of subject peoples in evading assessment and full compliance. By the standards of pre-industrial societies, the Roman empire was relatively efficient at levying tax and in the areas of Britain that appear most resistant to Roman authority, the presence of the garrison gave strong support to the efforts of the tax collector. In areas of heavy assessment relative to productive capacity, a potential side-effect of the ongoing contest between tax collectors and tax evaders was the discouragement of displays of wealth and conspicuous consumption in native society. This is particularly clear in much of Cornwall, Wales, north-west England and Lowland Scotland.

. The imperial economy thus represented fundamental changes in the mobilization of resources in Britain, directed by the state, but also involving numerous private individuals motivated by the financial opportunities created by Roman colonialism. Following the 'regime change' of 43, the consolidation of the Roman province engendered resistance and financial speculation in equal measure.

The provincial economy

The parallel evolution of the provincial economy, based around markets, free trade and patterns of consumption, is hard to disassociate entirely from the operation of the imperial economy. It also profoundly affected pre-existing economic structures. The traditional economy of much of Britain pre-conquest was relatively underdeveloped, largely based on subsistence production and embedded in social relations, linked to extended family groupings or incipient elites. The market was comparatively poorly evolved outside the south-east, where trade with the near

Continent influenced it. Markets were a creation of the imperial economy, but their functioning across society made them key components of the provincial economy. Over time, the use of coinage to pay for commodities will have increased, though barter probably remained an important ingredient of many markets, especially in rural areas. It is arguable that the provincial economy grew significantly over time and answered not only to the top-down needs of the state, but also to the bottom-up desires of consumers and the ideas and innovations of manufacturers and traders. If measured in simple terms across the period 50–350, there is plenty of evidence for the evolution of urban markets and the integration of rural territories with them, of an increase in coin use, of expanded manufacturing activity and increased consumption of a wide range of goods across a broad spectrum of sites (military, urban and rural). On the other hand, it is also true that most of this vanished within a very short period after 400. Whatever else may have survived of 'Roman' life in Britain in the fifth century, the provincial economy can be said to have collapsed abruptly along with the imperial economy. This suggests that the provincial economy remained to a large extent dependent on its Siamese twin, the imperial one.

The supply and use of coinage was initially much more a part of the imperial economy, being needed to pay and service the troops and officials. Documents from *Vindolanda* show that military supply transactions commonly depended on cash, even if some were paper transfers. Within the rest of the province, the emergence of a cash economy was less rapid. The supply of money, especially small change that would facilitate everyday cash purchases, remained inadequate and erratic until the second century. In the mid-first century copies of official issues constituted a large proportion of the small denomination coinage in circulation in Britain, probably being produced specially for the military community. During the crisis years of the third century, supplies of official coinage were evidently disrupted and large numbers of low-value forgeries were put into circulation. This demonstrates the limited ability and interest of the state in providing abundant low-value specie to monetize the provincial economy at large.

The evolution of markets, notably at urban centres but also potentially at rural locations, was another key area where the state retained the prerogative to regulate arrangements – as is true of most major states. Markets had to be officially sanctioned and the privileges were generally

granted sparingly, with due regard to geographical spread and period-
icity (many ancient markets were fixed on periodic cycles within a region
or tied to particular religious festivals that brought additional consumers
to a town or rural sanctuary). Detailed documentary evidence for the
organization of markets in Britain is lacking, but it is clear that all the
major towns will have had designated market functions. Indeed three
towns were called *Venta* (of the *Belgae*, *Iceni* and *Silures*) and two more
are compounded with *-magus* after British words for 'market'. Many of
the larger small towns must also have had recognized market functions
and some sites may have specifically evolved in consequence of the
creation of a periodic market. The site of *Bannaventa* (Whilton Lodge)
is an obvious example.

In the absence of inscriptions attesting the location of official markets,
one clue to the potential pattern of markets is provided by the distribution of finds of oculists' (*collyrium*) stamps. These comprise multi-
sided stone dies for impressing into medicinal preparations for the
treatment of eye ailments. The inscriptions convey information on the
name of the preparation and of the man responsible for preparing
the medication. There are thirty known *collyrium* stamps from Britain
and they show a broad distribution up and down the main road network,
with about half the major towns having produced an example and most
of the rest coming from potential market centres among the small towns
(Bath, Cambridge, Kenchester, Staines). Given the even distribution of
these across Britain and the association of the stamps with the preparation of the salves as much as with their marketing, it is a reasonable
supposition that the bulk of these finds represent the settlement of
pharmacist doctors at convenient regional market centres.

The production of manufactured or processed goods was closely
linked to the evolution of markets. Whereas in pre-Roman times the
elite in society might have largely controlled the distribution of prestige
goods, a clear development of the Roman period was the expansion of
manufacturing activity tied to markets. Again, we encounter the problem
of how to differentiate army-related production from other manufacturing and in some cases they appear to be inseparable. The annual needs
of clothing for the army, for instance, have been estimated as a set of
tunic, cloak and blanket every two years, or 27,500 sets per year at peak
requirements, necessitating something in the order of 550,000 days'
labour and the wool from over 200,000 sheep. Servicing military needs

of key commodities absorbed significant amounts of time and resources for specialist producers and household weaving operations alike.

The growth of rural production in southern Britain is also indicative of a market-based economy. Studies of Iron Age farming technology and crop regimes have shown that agriculture and husbandry were both well advanced pre-conquest, with a series of major revolutions having occurred by the late first century BC. The key innovations of the Roman period were in terms of scale and specialization. Larger storage buildings, mechanical mills, corn-drying ovens all reflect market-oriented production, in part linked to villa-estate economies. There is evidence of improved ploughs for use on heavier soils, of advances in animal husbandry leading to overall improvement in the size of livestock, and some new introductions such as the grape vine, vegetables and orchard crops. The corn-drying ovens appear to have been at least dual purpose, but a major function appears to have been the malting of barley for the brewing of beer. The previous absence of such features on rural sites and their more common occurrence at upper-echelon Roman-period settlements suggest that they were not necessary for purely domestic production of beer. The construction of corn-dryers on many rural sites could thus be taken as proxy evidence for the manufacture of beer for wider markets. The late Roman peak in villas and other evidence for increased rural wealth are highly suggestive of a measure of growth in the provincial farming economy.

Some parts of the provinces of Britain appear to have always remained marginal to the provincial economy. The economic development of large parts of northern Britain was mostly arrested (garrison settlements like Catterick and the *civitas* of the *Carvetii* in the Eden Valley notwithstanding). The extraction of raw materials or the manufacture of goods for the northern frontier seems to link many secondary centres to the army, rather than to civil markets.

The extra-provincial economy

Inter-provincial trade was a feature of all Roman provinces, and set tariffs and customs dues on goods traded across provincial borders governed this. Certain classes of goods, for instance those carried under army supply contracts, were specifically excluded from the standard dues (*portoria*) payable near the provincial boundaries. Trade with the

Continent can be readily documented, both by distributions of artefacts but also by inscriptions. Sanctuaries near the mouth of the Rhine have yielded a dossier of inscriptions of merchants (*negotiatores*), with specific reference to traders in pottery and garments. It remains difficult to estimate the overall significance of cross-Channel trade because of the archaeological invisibility of commodities such as agricultural produce, textiles, garments, slaves and metals. Although metals ought to survive better than organic materials, it is rare to find ingots of pure metal and many metal artefacts were recycled in the past rather than thrown away with other household refuse.

The large volume of imported goods in Britain in the mid- to late first century is in part at least a reflection of the scale of state expenditure on the army and in pursuit of conquest. It is not indicative of the wealth of Britain or the health of the indigenous economy at that time. Even when not underwritten by state supply contracts, merchants and artisans were preferentially drawn to areas where army pay, state subsidies and so on could be accessed. This was notably the case at London and must explain its early commercial boom. The consumer base of veterans at Colchester, Lincoln and Gloucester also differentiated early economic development there from other towns. On the other hand, the flow of imports to the main settlements associated with the kingdom of Togidubnus and the evidence of foreign craftsmen at Chichester and Fishbourne reflected his access to resources (land revenues, subsidies from the emperors, pre-existing fortune) that were denied to most Britons in the aftermath of conquest.

From the late first century onwards imports into Britain actually decreased, and this is attributable to two factors. The completion of the conquest phase allowed a more stable garrison deployment to emerge. This favoured the development of supply sources closer at hand to the major bases. Secondly, in the long term, import substitution was vital if the costs of provisioning the army were to be brought lower. The success of import substitution can be judged by the fact that by the third and fourth centuries, manufactured goods from the Continent were rare in the British provinces. In large measure this represents their replacement by British manufactures, though it is conceivable that in part it was also the result of changes in official policy regarding military supply in order to reduce costs. For instance, from the early third century onwards imports of Spanish olive oil virtually ceased. The transition was abrupt and would appear to have been a deliberate policy decision. No doubt helped by the fact that the British garrison may have contained few troops of Mediterranean origin by this date, the decision to substitute other sources of fat for oil in the military diet could have yielded a substantial saving.

Reduction in the size of the military garrison in Britain, whether through temporary transfers or permanent withdrawals, was another obvious way for the state to try to trim costs. In consequence, export capacity in the provincial economy increased over time, as late Roman references to grain shipments to the Rhine indicate. Similarly, the rise of the provincial villa economy in the third and fourth centuries could be taken as a corollary of the reduction of the military burden and the improved performance of the provincial economy.

From the early third century, the subdivision of Britain into two provinces created internal *portoria* boundaries, in addition to those related to the Channel ports. Subsequent further divisions created at least four provinces within the British Diocese and this will have increased the regulatory importance of small towns along the main roads close to where the provincial boundaries were drawn.

The inter-provincial trade thus far discussed could be classed as part either of the imperial or the provincial economy. However, a distinguishing feature of *Britannia* is that it bordered on the limits of empire and the operation of economic relations with peoples dwelling beyond merits separate consideration. The extra-provincial economy is thus defined as the net material outcome of contacts with neighbouring societies. In the British context this included primarily the inhabitants of Scotland and Ireland, plus various island dwellers. There was also some potential for contact with the peoples of the North Sea coast beyond the Rhine. In the past the tendency has been to see these exchanges as very much controlled by the Roman state, whether passing out subsidies, presents or trade goods. The analysis of Roman goods in Ireland and Scotland suggests that the situation was more complex and that the indigenous societies were much more active agents in these contacts and that material culture from the Roman world was employed in regionally diverse ways within these societies.

There are indications that the extra-provincial economy involved a negative balance of trade and payments for the empire. Whereas in the east, this was because of the high-value trade goods coming along the

Silk Route, or up the Red Sea, in the northern provinces the maintenance of peace became increasingly expensive. There are references to cash payments to the *Maeatae* and *Caledonii* under Septimius Severus, and recently discovered hoards of silver *denarii* near the Moray Firth appear to be the physical manifestations of the practice. Similarly, the spectacular hoard of late Roman silverware from Traprain Law, much of it broken down into hack silver, or a superb gold crossbow brooch, again from the Moray region, are as likely to represent expensive gifts as they are plundered treasure. It is one of the ironies of Britain in the Roman world that under the different economic rules that governed extra-empire relations, these regions should have yielded some of the most exquisite Roman artefacts. The indigenous economies may have been relatively simple in Ireland and Scotland, but their chieftains were exposed to some of the most glittering prizes of Roman elite identity.

Contact with the Roman world also had negative impacts on these societies. The taking of slaves was not just a side-effect of Roman campaigns into Scotland, but was probably a continuous element of trade between the empire and her neighbours, with selling on of captives from inter-tribal wars that were themselves a symptom of the opportunity of the imperial presence. Similar impacts have been noted in West African societies in response to European slave stations on the coast. Recruitment of people from beyond the frontier into the Roman army is a definite possibility – one thinks of Lossio Veda the Caledonian attested at Colchester, or the origins of the *areani*. These people, who acted as scouts for the northern garrison and who evidently betrayed the province in the Barbarian Conspiracy, may have been recruited beyond the frontier. An enigmatic Irishman, Cunorix son of Maqqos-Colini, attested at Wroxeter, is another example of immigration to the empire.

One final aspect of the extra-provincial economy concerns the extent to which capital raised in Britain – through rents or extractive industry, trade or manufacturing – was taken off-shore. This is impossible to quantify, but the state, absentee landlords, foreign merchants, discharged soldiers who settled elsewhere, and investment partners in contracting companies could have removed substantial sums in specie, agricultural produce and metals.

DIFFERENT ECONOMIES AND DIFFERENT COMMUNITIES

Much of the rest of this chapter concerns the intersection between the different economies outlined above and the three main communities that this book has identified. The military community was primarily connected with the imperial economy, though the spending power of the soldiers both attracted economic activity to follow the army and could stimulate production in the provincial economy. The urban community had to operate within a structure that was drawn up initially to address the needs of the imperial economy. The first decades of Roman rule were undoubtedly difficult economically for the majority of Britons, but there were some civilians on hand to take advantage of any opportunities that presented. The provincial economy was ultimately built around the markets politically inscribed in the urban centres and fostered by their status as centres of consumption. The rural community was radically affected by the imperial economy, translating ownership, dues and obligations of land and production into economic structures that must first and foremost have provided an income for the state, and only secondly to local elites. In parts of the north and west, long-term socio-economic evolution of the societies seems to have been stifled by the over-riding needs of Rome. In broad terms, the areas closest to the army or where the major mineral wealth of the province lay do not seem to have been allowed the same potential for independent economic growth. This is not to idealize pre-Roman societies, which were often elite-dominated, slave-using and exploitative too, but it seems fair to suggest for some areas of the British province(s) that the burden of exploitation on the poorer stratum became heavier under Rome.

The economic vitality of the Romano-British towns remains difficult to judge from the accumulated and uneven evidence of periods of boom and bust. On the one hand, the record of civic munificence, public building and domestic housing seems to imply a low achievement by the standards of the rest of the empire. Craft production and commerce are easy to detect in the towns, though difficult to quantify in meaningful ways and seemingly indicative of a much lower level of long-distance trade than is commonly attested in the core Mediterranean provinces.

On the other hand, some scholars have postulated significant periods of economic growth from the rising counts of potsherds or the introduction of minor luxuries such as mosaics and tessellated floors, or painted plaster. It is equally clear that at certain periods some towns experienced crises, as at London and St Albans, where economic revival was very slow after second-century fires. In addition there was a gradual migration of manufacturing activity away from the major towns and into the small towns, such that in the early fourth century, when major towns were adorned with larger numbers of well-appointed houses, there seems to have been less of an urban productive base.

There are obvious pitfalls in trying to measure the success of the province's economy in terms of the flow of imports coming into harbour cities such as London. By the end of the second century, there were far smaller quantities (and percentages) of imported amphoras and fine-wares among the archaeological assemblages being formed in London. Yet this need not be entirely a sign of economic weakness. It could be argued that this was in part the result of successful import substitution by British products, thus contributing to a higher degree of economic independence in the province.

Equally important as the study of manufactured artefacts is the record of the evidence for food production and consumption represented by plant remains and animal bones. Typical 'signatures' have been proposed for bone assemblages from types of site and, as more such data accumulates to reinforce the model, this may prove a useful diagnostic for assessing the urban/non-urban status of some of the problematic small towns. Urban assemblages of animal bones are characterized by a high proportion of cattle bones and, by weight, beef was by far the most commonly consumed meat. This marks a major change from social and economic practices in the late Iron Age, when sheep predominated in many regions. In a household economy, the slaughter of a sheep or pig could generate meat for a feast, with surplus material that could be conserved. Large animals like cattle are better suited to urban markets, where the large quantities of meat and offal can be shared between numerous consumers. There is evidence of specialist butchery practices being evolved to process carcasses, including tanning and exploitation of horn, hoof and bone. How often and how much meat was eaten by the average town-dweller is uncertain. But the urban evidence shows that meat was readily available on a daily basis to those who could afford it, not simply on days of religious sacrifices. Specialized butchers operated in most major towns. This reflects the development of the provincial economy and is proxy evidence for centralized markets of other foodstuffs.

The invisible economy: products of the land

'Invisible' commodities were undoubtedly of far greater economic importance than cheap consumer durables like pottery, though quantification will always be difficult. Late Roman sources described Julian constructing a fleet of 600 ships and reinstituting exports of grain from Britain to supply the army and other sites on the Rhine frontier. This certainly suggests the availability of a very large surplus in Britain at this time, though how typical the size of fleet was in 360 and how long sustained this traffic in cereals was in the fourth century it is impossible to say. It is equally unclear how much of this grain was state-owned, being raised through taxation, and how much was being traded on the open market.

The rural economy yielded surpluses in a wide array of primary products (meat, grain, vegetables, herbs and medicinal compounds, pulses, timber) and secondary products (milk and dairy, tallow, hides, wool, beer), as well as manufactured goods utilizing rural products, such as textiles and clothes, shoes and leather goods, wooden vessels, tools and furniture. In all these economic areas there are hints of change and specialization, for example in the form of botanical evidence of new or luxury foods, or references in the primary sources to British hooded cloaks exported to the Continent. The evidence of increased rural wealth in the early fourth century implies greater success in mobilizing the traditional products of Britain within the provincial economy, perhaps at a time when the demands of the imperial economy bore less directly on the province with reductions in garrison size. It also suggests progressive building-up of capacity.

Rural productivity remained at the heart of both the imperial and provincial economies and the exploitation of land and labour by the state and the civilian elite went hand in hand. Within the provincial boundaries no one was immune from the exaction of tax and, where land tenure depended on higher ownership, rents. As in many other periods of history, peasants saw their surpluses creamed off. The growth of urban markets, accompanied by the existence of seasonal markets at major rural sanctuaries, encouraged greater economic integration, ensuring the supply of a range of necessities. Markets also fostered a higher degree of specialization in rural production, whether focused on livestock, or on cereals or on products like beer. The provincial economy like much else in Britain was sluggish in its early development, but by the third and fourth centuries was offering better opportunities for wider participation, as reflected in increased rates of conversion of traditional British farmsteads into stone-built farms and the spread of manufactured goods in rural communities.

Mines and metallurgy

Mineral resources are one of the most valued assets of colonial territories and the Roman state was especially alert to the possibilities. The chief mineral deposits in Britain comprised: silver-rich lead ores in the Mendip Hills, the Peak District and the Pennines, and various locations in Wales; copper from Parys Mountain in Anglesey and Llanymynech in Wales; tin (and other ores) from Cornwall; notable iron ore sources in the Weald, the Forest of Dean and the East Midlands; and a gold deposit in southern Wales at Dolaucothi. The Roman emperors from the time of Tiberius had tended to add new discoveries of precious metals to the imperial property portfolio, but there was equally scope for retaining lands with such resources as public property. Both solutions allowed the state to keep a controlling interest in the exploitation of the resource and to be the prime beneficiary therefrom. The British mineral fields were certainly less spectacular than those already developed in Spain, or indeed those to be brought into Roman control in *Dacia* in the early second century. However, they were significant in comparison to many other provinces and potentially crucial in Britain with its large military garrison and a potential problem with its balance of payments.

Most of these mineral fields lay beyond the territory overrun in 43 and were certainly one of the motors for further expansion to north and west. The rapidity with which extractive activity followed Rome gaining control of the Mendips (by the late 40s) and Wales (mid-70s) is a clear indication of the linkage between continuing conquest and the mobilization of key resources. Direct state exploitation, involving military personnel and possibly local and forced labour, appears to have been resorted to in the initial phases of exploitation. A Roman fort at

Charterhouse almost abuts the first lead rakes (surface trench mines) at the site, while there was a control fort at Pumpsaint close to the gold mine of Dolaucothi. Evidence from other provinces reveals considerable regional diversity in the precise administrative arrangements in mining districts, and given the different start-up dates and the diverse underlying geological conditions we should not expect a 'one-size-suits-all' treatment of the British deposits. The precious metals – gold and the richest silver-bearing lead ores – were the priority for exploitation under military supervision, especially early on. As the army moved forward, or the most easily accessible deposits were worked out, there was a tendency for mining districts either to be placed under the control of procurators, or to be leased to individual contractors or 'companies' based on groups of investors (*socii*).

Stamps on metal ingots from Britain reveal the different modes of operation. Lead ingots (pigs) were very heavy (average *c.*74 kg) and generally cast in moulds to produce a characteristic truncated and elongated pyramidical shape. Inscriptions were either cast retrograde in the mould or cold struck into the metal once cooled. Lead pigs from the Mendips were often marked with a series of control marks: imperial titulature; an indication of date; who was responsible for the production; and identifying them as products from the British mines (perhaps indicating that some of the metal was intended for shipment to the Continent, although only four British pigs have been found there). Many of the inscriptions specify that they came from the lead silver works (*ex arg.*) and some of the lead appears from analysis to have already had the silver extracted. The earliest Mendip pigs indicate the involvement of *legio II Augusta*, whereas by the Flavian period the mining district had a name *Veb* . . . and private companies were involved (*Socii Novaec* . . .). C. Nipius Ascanius who is attested working at Charterhouse under Nero, also appears on a pig from North Wales under Vespasian. It is possible that he was either a lessee or a mining procurator. Similarly, Ti. Claudius Triferus (or Triferna), known on Mendips' ingots, may be identifiable with *Ti. Cl. Tr.* on lead pigs from the Peak District field. In this case the name suggests the possibility that he may have been an imperial freedman, and thus a candidate for a supervisory role rather than a mine lessee. Even in cases when pigs were counter-stamped with the marks of *socii*, the implication of the imperial titles is that the metal was imperial property. The Derbyshire Peak production centred on the *metallum Lutudarense* (perhaps at Carsington), implying direct imperial exploitation in the early stages, when once again we find named individuals in charge. Probably of later date are ingots recording lessees, the *Socii Lutudarenses*. Some pigs from North Wales and some from Yorkshire mention the local peoples – *Deceangli* and *Brigantes* – but the ownership of the lead in both cases was clearly imperial, so the 'tribal' reference here is evidently to identify the lead source more closely.

Copper ingots from the major mine on Anglesey were bun-shaped and much lighter (*c.*13–20 kg) and, in the rare instances of preserved stamps, yield little more than an abbreviated name. In most instances, whether this was a mine controller or a mine lessee is uncertain, but one example refers to *sociorum Romae* or 'partners resident in Rome', again showing that at some stage at least these mines were leased under contract. Tin ingots from Cornwall are rare and only a single stamped example is known, marked as the property of a pair of reigning emperors. The only known ingots of pewter, an alloy of tin and lead, have all come from the Thames at London and appear to originate from a single workshop, being stamped as products of '*Syagrius*' and with Christian messages. Stamped silver ingots are mainly of fourth-century date, when they were issued in lieu of coin as payment to officials and troops. The surviving examples relate to a series of production centres (*officinae*) named after the person in charge: Civilis, Curmissus, Honorinus, Isas, Leo, Patricius, Ulpianus. Only one, of unusual form, specifies a location for the workshop, in Trier, and the rest may well have been produced with British silver.

Imperial titulature was no longer included on lead ingots after the late second century, perhaps indicating a shift in the administrative process, rather than a complete change in the production system. The empire presumably continued to take its cut on the production of the contractors active in the mining districts, but the requirement to mark that quota clearly seems to have been relaxed. Similar trends are evident in other mining districts of the Roman world. It is also possible that a greater proportion of lead was finding its way to civilian markets by this date, as the distribution of items such as lead sarcophagi, brine pans and baptismal fonts suggests. A late Roman cargo of 271 lead ingots (22 tonnes), wrecked on the coast of Brittany at Ploumanac'h, included a number evidently destined for the *civitates* of the *Iceni* and *Brigantes*. The concentration of evidence of pewter production around Bath is a further indication of the continuation of British lead-mining in concert with increased activity in the Cornish tin-fields.

Cornwall is the most enigmatic of Britain's mineral-rich areas, as evidence of large-scale Roman-period mining activity is lacking. This has often been attributed to the predominance of the Spanish tin sources in the early imperial period. Only from the third century, so the theory goes, was British tin required to fill the gap left by declining Spanish production. There are only a couple of Cornish sites with early imperial finds suggesting precocious production. Yet even in late Roman times, the evidence of tin-mining in Cornwall rests on a handful of ingots, a few Roman artefacts associated with known mining features and the evidence of the rise in British pewter production at this time. This relative lack of evidence could in part be due to the intensity of medieval and later mining activity obliterating or obscuring the Roman traces. The fact that later techniques of tin-streaming and ore-crushing were similar to Roman ones is a further hindrance to identifying the Roman traces in the landscape without excavation. There is surely much more to learn about Roman Cornwall. We should not exclude the presence of Roman officials or a key control site, as suggested already for the 'villa' of Magor at the heart of the Camborne mining district, or the pewter cup dedicated to Mars by Aelius Modestus found in a well at Bossence near St Ives. A man with this name was a military prefect on Hadrian's Wall, and, if the same person, he may have held a subsequent procuratorial position in Cornwall.

Iron production in Roman Britain was widespread, though three areas have produced more substantial evidence of mining and smelting. The Weald was probably the most significant of these in the early period (first–third centuries) and there is evidence of links with the British fleet at several of the major production sites, notably Beauport Park. The Forest of Dean and the East Midlands iron-fields were longer lived than the Weald, with production continuing into the fourth century. In all three areas smelting activity has been recorded at a broad spectrum of sites, from small-scale settlements to villages and more specialized operations accompanied by vast slag heaps. Three sites in the Weald have slag heaps in excess of 15,000 cubic metres (Beauport Park, Oaklands Park and Footlands), but many of the approximately eighty known smaller production sites may have been under effective state control, if the land was in imperial ownership and rents and taxes were taken in iron. Production appears to have peaked in the second century and to have declined during the third century, with only a few sites remaining active into the fourth century. Part of the reason may have been over-exploitation of the woodland cover on the Weald.

The Forest of Dean sites are numerous, but poorly explored, though again there appears to have been a mixture of numerous small-scale smelting sites operating alongside a smaller number of major centres. The chronological sequence appears to have been similar to the Weald, with some signs of reduced production in the later third century, though a number of villa sites seem to have provided a focus for continuing late Roman production here. In the East Midlands, there was a large number of generally small production sites and few of larger scale, though Laxton is the best example of a site with specialized iron-smelting function, having five major smelting furnaces and slag heaps of consider-able size (0.4 ha area). This was perhaps the centre of either a state production facility or a private contractor working under contract to the state. Another major production site lay at Clipsham, where a slag heap covering 1.2 ha has been recorded.

The exploitation of other natural resources under state control is also to be anticipated. For instance, the quarrying of Purbeck 'marble' from southern Dorset was unlikely to have been solely a private initiative. The specialist skills required favour a foreign contractor, taking on an option offered by the state. Early exploitation and long-range movement of fine-grained building stone, such as Bath stone, are also most easily explicable in terms of the provincial government either opening quarries or offering leases to contractors in attendance. The imperial freedman based at the Combe Down villa just outside Bath was possibly in charge of stone quarries there. Salt production was seen as a key resource in the Roman empire and was certainly viewed as something to monopolize or control (a position the Romans shared in common with other imperial powers of more recent times). Roman forts were established at the main brine springs and rock salt deposits (Droitwich, Northwich, Nantwich), indicating one line of initial control. Without surrendering property rights, the emperors may subsequently have leased exploitation of these deposits. Coastal salt workings were not banned, but some of the key wetland areas may have been retained as state property, with the inhabi-tants obliged to pay tax or rent in kind, regulated through the institution of the census and perhaps overseen by imperial officials.

Roman exploitation of the extensive British coalfields is also well attested, with over 200 sites having yielded evidence of the use of coal as a fuel. Many military sites in the north were supplied from the Durham coalfield, while specimens traceable to the Yorkshire, Nottinghamshire, Derbyshire, Forest of Dean, South Wales and Somerset fields are well represented in their localities. It is unclear to what extent the output came under state control – and some at least of the production found its way to towns and rural sites – but the regular use of coal at military sites indicates at the very least Roman appreciation of the economic value of coal.

Military supply

Feeding, clothing and supplying other needs of the armies of the Roman world were major undertakings. This was achieved by a combination of taxation/tribute collection, direct purchase and compulsory requisitioning (for which compensation was sometimes offered). Local sources of supply within the province were obviously to be preferred, but the initial circumstances of imperial conquest often worked against this. Despite the evidence of a developing economy in many parts of south-eastern Britain before the conquest, the size of the invading force and destabilization of local production necessitated high reliance on long-range supply in the first decades of the Roman province. Even basic foodstuffs such as grain were shipped from the Continent in support of the army (as demonstrated by botanical material from London, Alchester, Caerleon and South Shields, to name a few examples of widely differing date). Seaborne supply dictated the choice of many of the key early military bases on the coast or navigable tidal rivers. London emerged as the nodal point in overland communications precisely because the Thames allowed shipping to penetrate to a central location within the territories initially occupied, whereas Colchester lay at its eastern edge. Army supply contracts will have focused on foodstuffs, but many other manufactured goods could be obtained from the same locations that supplied food. Britain developed as an off-shoot of a prior pattern of military supply routes that ran up through Gaul from the Mediterranean in support of the armies on the Rhine. The key routes followed the Rhône river up to Lyon and then forked towards the upper Rhine in Switzerland, or towards the lower Rhine via the valleys of the

Saône and Mosel. State payments or subsidization of transport costs, relief from customs dues at provincial borders and similar inducements facilitated the movement of goods by sea, river and road.

Most of the surviving evidence for the working of military contracts comes from Egypt, but can be presumed to be typical of practice elsewhere. These were standard civil contracts (*locatio-conductio*) under Roman law, backed up by additional incentives to merchants to undertake them, such as provision of or payment for transport of goods included in the contract and exemption of such goods from taxes and dues. Some units evidently had supply specialists operating at long distances from the home base. 'Hunt's Pridianum', a military document relating to a unit based on the Danube in the early second century, shows that some personnel had been sent as far afield as Gaul in pursuit of specific supplies.

The organization of supply features prominently in the *Vindolanda* tablets. There are documents attesting to the organization of wagons for moving stone for a building project, the delivery of cartloads of grain by Britons, and accounts of grain allocations within the garrison. Someone called Octavius was author of one of the longest and most informative letters, sent to a man named Candidus. It is not certain whether the two men were soldiers or civilian traders, but the discovery of the letter in the fort probably favours the view that they were soldiers with special duties relating to the supply of the fort. Octavius requested money from Candidus to pay for grain he had purchased and was having threshed. At the same time he was also involved in cash deals involving sinew and animal hides. Octavius appears to have been operating some distance from his home fort – probably near Catterick – and was participating in a complex series of cash transactions on behalf of his unit. Several other tablets mention soldiers dispatched on special missions – carrying messages or engaged in supply activity – and in such cases they appear to have been required to provide accounts for travelling expenses.

In addition to military contract fixers, the system also depended on civilian entrepreneurs and traders who linked up with them. In Gaul and Germany, there is a huge concentration of inscriptions set up by merchants and freedmen (often involved in trade) along the military supply routes and in the Rhine frontier zone, though they are attested virtually nowhere else in Gaul.

The existence of military contracts underwrote trade and movement of other goods, and not only for the military markets. References in Roman legal sources imply that the reliefs and subsidies relating to goods being moved as military contracts were frequently abused. Mixed cargoes of goods partly under contract and partly excluded effectively shared the subsidy on transport costs. So merchants presumably tried to move more goods than actually contracted for in the same transport, illegally claiming the same exemptions to increase profit margins. There were many other loopholes for traders to exploit – packing items so that numbers were difficult to assess, claiming additional volume was needed to offset natural wastage and breakages en route. Painted inscriptions, stamps and brands, metal labels and tags, and shipping lists and papers could be used to help identify and quantify cargoes on the move. But in general, the state must have focused on dealing with the grossest abuses and have tolerated a measure of profit-taking by the traders. As a result, the operation of the imperial economy and the provincial economy are much more difficult to disentangle, since the supply of towns no doubt developed partly on the back of military supply.

Pottery: patterns of consumption

Pottery is disproportionately preserved in the archaeological record and is thus our most abundant evidence of economic activity. It is generally acknowledged that pottery was not a luxury commodity in the ancient world. Indeed, high-quality manufactured pottery appears to have been remarkably cheap and widely available to people at different levels of society. A distinct feature of the Roman empire was the scale of mass production of a range of wheel-made forms and the transport and distribution of vessels over great distances. The great terra sigillata (samian) production centres of southern Gaul, for instance, had huge kilns capable of holding over 10,000 pots in a single firing. The largest site at La Graufesenque is estimated to have produced millions of vessels for export across the western empire, including Britain. Nonetheless, there is a strong probability that what made such long-range trade in cheap ceramics possible was not the intrinsic value of the pottery itself but the side-by-side trade in other more valuable commodities and other hidden subsidies to the costs of transportation. It is also the case that the vast majority of pottery was *not* traded over long distances and the evidence of potters from north Gaul moving into Britain in the mid-first century suggests that greater proximity to consumers and new markets was an important consideration. Early potteries are attested at Colchester and between London and St Albans, notably at Brockley Hill. Even the major fineware production centres were not immune to change and La Graufesenque and other south Gaulish sites declined in favour of new manufactories in central and eastern Gaul. The extent to which pottery distributions can be read as proxy evidence for trade in foodstuffs is controversial, but it is plausible that changes in ceramic supply were bound up in more far-reaching changes in military supply to the province at the turn of the first/second centuries and later from the reign of Hadrian. As imports of mass-produced cheap pottery declined to negligible levels, so we might infer the growth in provincial agricultural production to the level when Britain in fact became a net exporter of grain to the Rhineland. The long-term trade links with the Continent reflected in terms of pottery supply patterns were with the Rhineland and northern Gaul.

Liquid commodities such as wine, olive oil and fish sauces were normally carried in amphoras, ceramic vessels of large capacity – typically 25 litres for wine and up to 70 litres for oil. Most of the wine amphoras imported to Britain were from southern Gaul, though already by the second century grape cultivation was well established in the Rhineland and wine from there seems generally to have been transported in barrels – making Rhenish wine imports to Britain impossible to quantify. The evidence of such perishable containers is mostly lost, though numerous barrel parts have been found at *Vindolanda*, many with branded information on contents and ownership, and barrels are occasionally recovered in waterlogged conditions at other sites where old casks had been used to line wells. Olive oil largely disappeared as an imported item in Britain with the cessation of imports of the Spanish Dressel 20 amphora in the early third century. Similarly, fish-sauce amphoras of later Roman types are rare. Whereas wine and fish-sauce supply could have switched to areas utilizing barrels (including Britain itself), this cannot apply to olive oil. The trend over time favoured closer sources of supply, self-sufficiency or doing without classic Mediterranean commodities.

The patterns of samian ware supply to military sites, major urban centres and small towns and other rural sites differed. The military community was a major consumer of imported tableware and its needs were probably filled largely through contracts. Samian is proportionally much more common as a percentage of total pottery in military assemblages and there is quite a high ratio of decorated to plain vessels, generally rising above the provincial average of 1 : 4. Major towns came closest to the military profile, with small towns and rural sites, including temples, having much lower thresholds of occurrence and lower ratios of decorated to plain forms. Samian assemblages from rural sites also tend to be small in numerical terms and vessels were often curated (and repaired) for considerable periods. The evidence from sanctuaries shows that samian was not adopted as a favoured votive offering, though other types of pottery were sometimes donated. There are significant regional variations in the inclusion of samian in early Roman burials; for instance, it is rare at St Albans, where Gallo-Belgic vessels were preferentially included, but more common in Kent. The attractiveness of glossy red pottery did not thus carry all before it in cultural terms and the contexts of use suggest that different groups in society were making distinct choices, not all economically based.

Regional patterns of pottery manufacture exploited the relative abundance of suitable clays and woodland, and most parts of south-eastern Britain feature in a gazetteer of kilns. Pottery production of Roman date differed in important respects from pre-conquest patterns. A higher proportion of pottery was wheel-made and fired in specialized kilns, as opposed to surface clamps. Coarse wares were characteristically reduced in firing to greyish fabrics, in comparison with the more irregularly fired fabrics of much Iron Age pottery. The exploitation of finer clays and innovations in preparation (levigation) allowed production of higher-quality vessels and of distinctive whitish/creamy fabrics for mortaria, the characteristic Roman mixing bowls. The repertoire of pottery types also expanded, especially in terms of serving and eating/drinking vessels, accompanied by innovations in surface treatment and use of slips for decoration. Some potters stamped their products, and construction of improved kilns allowed better control of firing conditions and more consistent results. By and large, domestic production of pottery was supplanted by manufactories, run by specialist potters who produced for markets. Similar comments could be applied for many other areas of craft production. The economic structures of the Roman empire encouraged the rise of the specialist artisan and the production of goods in workshops close to markets.

Though numerically the rural population was far larger, the two most accessible markets for manufactured goods were the military and the urban communities. Urban and military markets were more highly monetized and brought together the largest concentrations of consumers. In the first century military pottery supplies were serviced by three mechanisms: long-range imports from Gaul, orders from newly established potteries in southern Britain such as Brockley Hill, or auto-production by military potters at sites such as Brampton, Wilderspool or Holt. Stamps on mortaria can help us track the movement of some potters in the wake of the army's advance. C. Attius Marinus, for example, produced pots at Radlett and Brockley Hill in Hertfordshire, before moving north-west along Watling Street to Mancetter. In the long term, many civilian potters preferred to stay closer to civil markets that they could service alongside military contracts. Major centres of pottery production were thus generally located close to major Roman roads and urban centres, though more commonly favouring small towns than the major towns. Major towns, of course, were located for reasons other than proximity to the best clay sources, and such sites had large competing needs for the available fuel supplies. Colchester and Lincoln are both partial exceptions, but the predominant pottery industries were at places such as Water Newton or Mancetter. Some potteries were clearly sited closer to the major troop concentrations and one may infer that the availability of military contracts was a substantial factor in their *raison d'être*: examples include Doncaster, Littlechester (Derby), various sites either side of the Humber, Crambeck near Malton, and York. River and sea communications were factors in the success of potters in the Severn Valley, the Oxford area, the Poole Harbour region, the Thames estuary and perhaps the Nene Valley. Potteries at Alice Holt (Farnham), in the New Forest and at Mancetter were all more reliant on initial overland shipment of their products.

By the second century, most pottery was consumed within 25–50 km of its place of manufacture, but there were a number of notable exceptions to this rule, with a significant military focus of the non-local distribution. For instance, the products of kilns in the lower Severn Valley area have a bi-partite distribution, divided between their immediate locality and a dispersed secondary series of clusters around military sites up the west coast (Chester, the western end of Hadrian's Wall and western approaches and forts on the Antonine Wall). Similarly, the products of the Wilderspool kilns are predominantly recorded at military sites in north-western Britain, with the pattern suggesting some initial river and sea transportation. The eastern part of the northern frontier reveals a similar early reliance on the products of Colchester and a few other potteries close to the North Sea shipping routes. The fact that the major late Roman pottery manufactories in the Nene Valley, Oxfordshire, the New Forest and Alice Holt had a much more limited impact on northern military markets reflects both the growth of the provincial economy in the south and the changing nature of military purchasing arrangements.

The most extraordinary example of extra-regional distribution concerns a type of utilitarian pottery known as Black Burnished Ware. This was initially produced in the Poole Harbour region of Dorset, continuing an Iron Age tradition of hand-built and clamp-fired pottery. Imitations were in time produced in south-west Dorset, along the Thames estuary and at Rossington near Doncaster, but the south-east Dorset industry (SEDBB 1) remained the dominant enterprise. There are many highly peculiar aspects to the distribution of this long-lived pottery production (first to fourth centuries). It is found in small quantities throughout the British province(s) and occurs in very high percentages across a considerable swathe of south-west Britain and at sites up the west coast. It is present at most of the ports on the French Channel coast and is strongly represented at military sites in the north of Britain and in Wales. Its distribution range and the implicit volume of production set this industry apart from all other British pottery manufacture. The strongly conservative potting and firing techniques also run counter to the more general trends towards wheel-thrown pots and kiln-fired technique of most Roman pottery. Presumably the pots were cheap, robust and functional to have had such widespread and enduring success. But it is also apparent from the quantities of vessels from military sites and from the high numbers along the supply routes to the military zone that the distribution pattern is skewed by the need to service a primary institutional customer. Analysis of site finds has revealed that, as well as export by sea from Poole Harbour, a considerable amount of pottery appears to have been carried overland to the Severn estuary via Dorchester and Ilchester, with a previously unsuspected harbour site at Crandon Bridge now identified as the terminus from which it was shipped to other sites on both sides of the Bristol Channel, North Wales and north-western Britain. Based on the average occurrence of

SEDBB 1 as a proportion of all pottery at 121 sites in south-western Britain (c.31 per cent) and order of magnitude calculations of population levels, sizes of households and household needs in terms of pottery vessels, it has been calculated that annual production in the Poole Harbour area could have exceeded 1.28–1.66 million vessels. Packed in simple crates, the overland parts of the distribution could have involved 10,000–30,000 donkey loads each year. Ethnographic studies of traditional pottery industries suggest that on this basis something like 600 full-time potters would have been needed in this one area.

There are many uncertainties in these sorts of calculations, but it is indicative that at its peak the Romano-British pottery industry overall was probably producing several million vessels annually and providing employment for perhaps a few thousand individuals. The most astonishing aspect of the sub-Roman transition in the early fifth century is that this sort of manufacturing and consumer capacity collapsed so rapidly and so completely.

The second half of the fourth century seems to mark the onset of a more difficult economic climate, to judge from the evidence of change in towns and manufacturing industries. If the period 350–400 looks like one of moderately declining activity, the following fifty years represent economic catastrophe. One of the big questions about the ending of Roman rule in Britain concerns the sudden *caesura* of the economic structures that had characterized the earlier more successful phases. The final chapter will consider this issue in relation to our knowledge of the political circumstances of the secession. A few key changes of the late Roman economy may have contributed significantly to the sudden disintegration.

At all periods the provincial economy was peculiarly vulnerable to the performance and demands of the imperial economy. In the mid- to later third century, the political complications of the Gallic empire and the breakaway Carausian state can only have impeded the operation of the imperial economy by separating the British provinces from the insulating financial support of the empire as a whole. These may well have been times of increased financial exactions, and the relative lack of third-century mosaics may be an indicator of reduced wealth accumulation in the provincial economy in consequence. On the other hand, one of the factors that may have favoured the expansion of the provincial economy from the early fourth century was the reduction in the size of the provincial garrison. Even with a rising level of taxation in kind to supply the army, it is plausible that the costs of running the British provinces had been substantially reduced overall and that for the first time their revenues exceeded this. There may have been some easing of the overall financial burdens imposed on Britain and also more of the provincial surpluses available for trade towards the Continent. This would appear consistent with the evidence for greater wealth generation in the provincial sector at large. The respite was of comparatively short duration.

The concentration of the field army units in core provinces such as Gaul, Italy and *Illyricum*, along with the sequence of barbarian invasions, rebellions and civil wars, had created new priorities for raising revenues and supplies within the western prefectures. Although emperors tried to control the process of increases in taxation, praetorian prefects often felt obliged to make extraordinary levies because of shortfalls in the tax receipts, as Florentius evidently did in Gaul in 357. The usurpations of Magnentius and of Magnus Maximus no doubt exacerbated the situation of the British provinces; first, through extraordinary fiscal demands imposed on them by the pretenders and, secondly, once recovered by the empire, when punitive measures followed. An imperial agent, Paulus, was sent to Britain in late 353 'to fetch certain military men who had dared to join Magnentius', but he soon exceeded his brief and implicated many civilians in support for the pretender, targeting 'the fortunes of many people, spreading destruction and ruin in many forms', including imprisonment. The efforts at intercession by the *Vicarius* ended with his own arrest and suicide. In a sequel to these events, Libanius informs us that when Julian was Caesar in Gaul in the late 350s he 'sent accountants [to Britain] to supervise the expenditure that was nominally military but in practice was a source of income for the generals'. The financial abuses being investigated were those that had allowed usurpers like Magnentius to gain support in Britain, but any exercise that involved 'sending in the accountants' was liable to have wider ramifications and this one is specifically linked to the resumption of large-scale grain exports to the Rhine army in 360. Some (perhaps most) of this grain will have been raised as tax in kind.

The spate of pretenders proclaimed in late fourth-century Britain was perhaps symptomatic of profound discontent at higher taxation coupled with decreased security as a result of seaborne raids. The Roman state demanded more while giving less in return. When the last of these British usurpers vanished across the Channel in pursuit of his imperial destiny, there was a final British revolt. This time no usurper was put forward, but the entire Diocese seceded from the empire, bringing to an end the obligation to feed the imperial economy. It is an attractive possibility that increasing imperial exactions in the later fourth century were central to both the evident decline in economic activity and to the final rebellion of the province against Constantine III. It may also help to explain the finality of that step, with the abrupt cessation of the imperial economy also bringing down the provincial economy.

CULTURAL IDENTITIES: SOME CONCLUDING THOUGHTS

Cultural identity has been a major theme throughout this book. It will be apparent by now that there was no uniform 'Roman identity' for the provincial populations in Britain (or elsewhere) to measure up to. It is equally clear that the inhabitants of Britain did not share a common set of values and understanding of what it took to 'Become Roman', let alone that they were of one mind on the desirability of 'Being Roman'. Indeed many groups seem to have used culture not as a means of demonstrating the universality of Roman society, but rather as a measure of expressing their own distinctiveness and segregation from other groups in society. This is especially clear for the community of soldiers. One of the implications of this study is that there was an almost infinite number of possible versions of what 'Being Roman' meant. For convenience, this book has differentiated between aggregate group identities: the military, urban and rural communities, while also demonstrating some of the regional, chronological and social variance within each of these broad groups. These communities reflect not only geographical differences, but also states of mind, allowing for some degree of crossover of individuals into the physical space of a different community.

The existence of distinct community identities is perhaps best exemplified in differences in religious practice. Conventional Roman religion was governed by a calendar of festivals and a pantheon of recognized divinities, who had had well-developed representational (anthropomorphic) forms and attributes. Religious practice was often based on literate actions and was highly formulaic, even contractual, in the way it represented human interaction with divine powers. Previous studies have tended to identify uniformity across Britain, rather than seeking evidence of diversity of practice. It is clear that there were significant changes between pre- and post-conquest practice, notably the increased emphasis on anthropomorphic representations of deities, the importance of the written word as a medium for human messages to the divine, different components of ritual deposits, and so on. The analyses in earlier chapters have shown that very diverse practices of religion emerged in different parts of Britain, reflecting major discrepancies between the Roman army, urban communities and rural dwellers in the civil and military zones (Table 14). The army were the most enthusiastic fishers in the polytheistic pool, but also the most conventional in terms of practice. In south-eastern Britain, stone inscriptions and altars are exceedingly rare, but curse tablets occur in association with a particular temple type. Conversely, curse tablets and Romano-Celtic temples are practically unattested in the military zone. Urban communities in the province reflected a more hybrid approach to religion, evident in temple architecture that includes examples of conventional classical temples alongside numerous Romano-Celtic shrines, and at sites such as London

Table 14. Religious identity in Britain defined by differences in practice.

	TEMPLE TYPE	ALTARS	VOWS	VOTIVE FEATHERS/ LEAVES	VOTIVE LETTERS	CURSE TABLETS	VOTIVE DEPOSITS IN WATER	BRITISH CULTS	SYNCRETIZED CULTS	CLASSICAL CULTS
Military areas	Classical	Many	Many	Some	Rare	Rare	Some	Some	Many	Many
Urban centres incl. small towns	Classical/ Romano-Celtic	Some	Some	Many	Some	Many	Some	Some	Some	Some
Rural communities ('civil zone')	Romano-Celtic	Rare	Rare	Some	Many	Many	Many	Some	Some	Rare
Rural sites ('military zone')	None?	None	None	None	None	None	Some	Some	None	Rare

and Bath where we find both standard Roman religious inscriptions and curse tablets. Religious practices in much of the west and north of Britain remained non-representational and archaeologically elusive. The table summarizes these broad differences and these are interpreted as religious manifestations of discrepant identity.

Another major theme of this book has been the importance of regionalism in defining difference and identity. Many regional groupings can be traced to late Iron Age societies, but the negotiation between Rome and these groupings was also a vital part of what defined the maintenance or emphasis of regional traits under imperial rule. The trajectory of a people's or a kingdom's economic and social development was potentially contingent on the circumstances attending their surrender. Co-operation or resistance in the first generation of close Roman supervision could affect the steepness of that line positively or negatively. The countryside became a series of landscapes of imperialism, comprising a patchwork of different forms of landownership. Towns, small towns and road stations, roads and milestones, boundary markers, changes to field systems, new forms of rural structure (villas, temples, mausolea, villages), were physical manifestations of profound change, even if traditional habitations and field systems were long-lived in many districts. Military bases and their attendant garrison settlements were focal points in the road networks of the north and west.

There was no single model for the settlement and economic evolution of provincial landscapes, and the negotiation of power between Rome and subject peoples could produce very different results, as maps of Romano-Celtic temple and villa distributions indicate (Fig. 17, p. 481). Only a small part of the provincial territory (and equivalent to less than a quarter of the area of the British Isles) strongly adopted these two key markers of a Roman rural identity.

The Roman and native dialogue produced both punitive and generous land settlements for provincial people and the results can be crudely characterized as 'landscapes of resistance' and 'landscapes of opportunity'. In reality, of course, these are extreme ends of a continuous spectrum of possible scenarios and some peoples who initially suffered penalties may over time have been granted improved land allocation, while others initially treated mildly may have lost land and privileges through misbehaviour or arbitrary appropriation.

In south-east Britain, the following areas can be characterized as 'opportunistic': Cirencester and the Cotswolds, Chichester and Sussex, the Chiltern hills, north-western Kent. Resistant landscapes included those of Essex, Suffolk and Norfolk, the Fenland, the Weald, Salisbury Plain, the Wroxeter area and Cheshire. The 'resistant landscapes' closely correspond to the areas most profoundly affected by the Boudican revolt or the initial invasion of 43 or both, or to areas of natural resources over which the state chose to maintain exploitation rights. Overall, even in areas of villa development, the pace of rural development appears to have been quite slow, and if we limit our perspective to the first or early second centuries alone, there is very little evidence of 'opportunity'. The very richest areas in fourth-century Britain stand out as being unusual, and in some cases at least – as in parts of the Gloucestershire Cotswolds or the Bath area – the impact of imperial or other large estates is suspected to have played a part.

Most of the west and north appears highly 'resistant', though this may have had as much to do with Roman priorities as with the political or economic aspirations of rural communities. The option of releasing territory to civil government was closely controlled by the state and the lands that were passed from military or state control to British communities appear to have been geographically limited. The *Brigantes* shared the prime lands in the Vale of York with a legionary fortress and *colonia*; the *Silures* retained control of only part of the coastal strip in south Wales; the *Dumnonii* of Exeter were focused in east Devon, the *Carvetii* were narrowly based in the Eden Valley. The majority of lands in the military zone remained state controlled, with people allowed the use of lands subject to tribute and taxation payments.

Although we lack full detail of the way the non-civil territories of Britain were administered, it seems clear that military units frequently played an important role in local governance of regions (*regiones*). Britain's mineral wealth was not generally handed back to British com-munities for them to profit from. Whether through direct control by the military and procurators or through sub-contracts, the state sought to exploit these resources for its own profit. Areas such as the Peak District, Cornwall, the mining districts of south, central and northern Wales all reveal relatively unchanging patterns of native settlement against a backdrop of enhanced mineral exploitation in the Roman period. The profits of this activity are simply not visible in the British landscapes.

By definition, the extra-provincial areas were extremely resistant landscapes. However, even here we can see considerable variation in terms of settlement and societal evolution and in the use of Roman material culture. The areas most accessible to Rome's military arm in the Scottish Lowlands, both south and north-east of the Forth–Clyde isthmus, were clearly differentiated in this respect from other parts of Free *Britannia*. The dramatic evidence of successive waves of Roman marching camps imposed across this landscape reflects not only the ability of the Roman empire to inflict damage on extra-provincial communities, but direct attempts at conquest. Even if Roman armies were not sent into Atlantic Scotland and Ireland, the 'ambition' of Rome will have been clearly understood. Roman treaties and diplomacy accompanied mercantile contact with Ireland and played a part in shaping Irish politics.

Many accounts of Roman Britain have emphasized the threat posed to the provincial society by the unconquered 'barbarians' lying beyond. If we turn the argument around, however, it is also apparent that Rome posed a real and lasting threat to those British peoples. The initial Roman invasion of Scotland was an act of unprovoked aggression against relatively peaceable native societies. Rumours of possible Roman intervention in Ireland will not have been taken lightly across the Irish Sea. In the end, resistance in Scotland and Ireland created its own opportunities, with the rise of increasingly strong polities. Refugees from mainland Britain will have been absorbed into Irish society – there are a number of suggestive finds as we have seen – and possibly into Scotland also. More importantly, we can identify a higher level of ethnogenesis occurring in both Ireland and Scotland, culminating in the emergence of large kingdoms by late Roman times, capable of sending armies, raiding parties and settlers over considerable distances against the Roman provinces. At the same time that these larger confederated groupings arose, we can perceive a change in Rome's economic relations with these extra-provincial peoples. From a position of strength, wherein Rome could exact tribute and take slaves from peoples within easy reach of her borders, by the later Roman period the balance of power had clearly shifted, with Rome now frequently paying subsidies to secure the peace.

My vision of the operation of the Roman empire is a good deal less rosy than that of many modern commentators. Colonialism is an exploitative system of government and for over 350 years much of

Britain was under direct external rule. This was not a cosy dress-rehearsal for Britain's much later imperial age, even if the nineteenth-century British colonial servants drew readily on their knowledge of the Roman world to shape their own. Comparative study of colonial systems would suggest that their primary motivation is never the greatest good for the greatest number of provincial subjects. Although colonial regimes have often laid stress on their improving or civilizing qualities and the benefits of good administration and justice, this always comes at a price. The non-consensual aspect of imperial rule involves more than loss of auto-nomy, it also means loss of control of resources. The scale of exploitation of colonial resources and manpower varies greatly across time and space, but there is no doubt that the financial needs of the Roman empire were large and that this bore heavily on some provincials.

Opinion on the balance-sheet of Roman rule in Britain is sometimes polarized between those who extol the empire and the social and cultural benefits it brought and those who want to denigrate it. In my view, though, we must take due account of both the positive and negative aspects and impacts of empire. Although there has been a tendency in recent years to emphasize the importance of native agency, that is, the positive choices taken by Britons in shaping provincial development, this must be done with full awareness of the political context in which such preferences were expressed. The power dynamics of imperial rule are dramatically unequal and the globalizing influence of the colonizer should not be underestimated. The discrepant identities discussed in this book reflect a broad range of responses to Rome, from close integration to resistance, without privileging any one over the others. There were undoubtedly many individuals, from a variety of social and economic backgrounds, who closely espoused what they defined as Roman values and culture. More emphasis has been given here than in some recent studies to the activities of 'resident aliens' in the cultural transformations of the province. In particular there seems to have been a significant contribution by immigrants of northern Gallic and Rhineland extraction in the military community and among mercantile and skilled artisans. All these people profited from the opportunities presented by colonial rule and it is no surprise to see them adopting variants of conventional Roman identity as a means of social positioning in relation to the provincial administration that was often their paymaster. Indigenous Britons, notably of the upper order of society, made similar investment in the ideology and culture of the empire, but often not in precise emulation of the army, the bureaucrats or the foreigners. The engagement with normative elite behaviour and material culture was in some ways strongly conformist – especially in the top tier of villa-society by the fourth century – but in other respects one is struck by insular peculiarities. The low level of use of civil epigraphy and personal representation (including funerary commemoration) and the general lack of civic benefaction (euergetism) are striking instances amongst others of divergent behaviours. In general, the ways that Roman identity was manifested in terms of behaviour and material culture differed widely across society, space and time. It is equally apparent that at all times the majority of the British population lived their lives and defined their identity in ways that were consciously less Roman or more ambiguously constructed.

Resistance is harder to demonstrate archaeologically than conformity. However, we know that the Roman occupation engendered prolonged armed resistance in the first century and the Boudican revolt was a salutary lesson in the consequences of excessive zeal and brutality in dealing with newly subjected people. The loss of life that resulted cannot have helped reconcile the bulk of the population to the supposed justice and benefits of imperial rule. Roman possession of the British province was predicated on military force and violence and the participation of soldiers in the administration of civil zones will have continually reinforced the sense of living under occupation. The average subject of Roman authority in the first century could not have foreseen the potential benefits that might accrue below the level of the social elite, in the form of fully developed urban centres and the mature provincial economy. Their experience was the day-to-day reality of foreign domination, taxation and the petty injustices of a colonial system where the balance of power favoured soldiers, officials and Roman citizens over lesser provincials.

This is not to imply that all Britons were by definition anti-Roman or that all incomers (soldiers, merchants) shared the values of Italian upper-class Romans. People's aspirations and dreams will no doubt have varied with their status in society and regarding their position in relation to the power networks of the state. There will have been change over time, especially as incomers intermarried with indigenous Britons and more of the provincial garrison was recruited within Britain. What we must recognize, however, is that the existence of the Roman empire evoked a range of reactions from its subjects, including resistance or non-conformity alongside compliance and participation. The extent to which individuals found a comfortable accommodation with the culture of the imperial power increased over time as the socio-political structures became normalized to some degree. Some Romano-Britons may well have played a double game, at times presenting a cultured Roman face, at others a differently expressed British culture or identity. However, while people became accustomed to Rome, their subjugated status did not really change. It is irrelevant whether typical late Iron Age societies were more or less exploitative; Rome will have been judged by her subject peoples on her record. Increasingly in late Roman times the perception of many people in Britain will have focused on the taxation and predation of an off-shore power that was more interested in extracting revenue from them than in delivering security from enemies or justice from those who oppressed them.

One of the most extraordinary aspects of the Roman period in Britain is the scale and extent of physical and cultural changes that it brought about. It is arguable that, even without the invasion, parts of the island would have been profoundly changed by the globalizing impact of Roman culture and society. Indeed, the first indications of this process are manifest in the late Iron Age kingdoms of the south-east. Nonetheless, the architectural and material achievements of 350 years of direct rule are impressive, as visitors to any of the major towns, villas, forts or museums will be aware. The British Museum's collection of Romano-British memorabilia and treasure is particularly notable. Huge changes were registered in urbanization, architecture, construction techniques and materials, water-supply mechanisms and sanitation, luxury arts and a wider array of artistic products and manufactured artefacts, communications, transport, farming productivity, landscape markers, the market economy, coin use, mineral extraction and metal production, religion, funerary practices, dress, diet and cooking/dining habits, social practices such as bathing, literacy, education, census and record-keeping. It is clear in any overview that Britain shared many characteristics with other Roman provinces – and these have been the focus of much previous study under the Romanization paradigm.

Ultimately, there were profound differences that set the British experience apart from other areas under Roman rule. The story of Britain in the Roman empire does not describe a unilinear and ever-upwards path; rather it is a much more complex set of interwoven histories, both regionally and socially contingent, and with unexpected gradients up and down. The initial sluggish pace of development in town and country could be read as one sign of a lack of enthusiasm for Roman rule, the comparative stagnation of longer-term urban and villa development in the north and west as indicative of Roman domination and control there as much as native ineptitude. Similarly the sudden fall-off of Roman cultural traits in sub-Roman Britain is only hard to comprehend if we believe that virtually all Britons had wholeheartedly embraced Roman rule and Roman culture in the first place.

The insular position of Britain beyond the limits of the Continental empire contributed to this difference and its end-of-the-line location further weakened its integration. The size of the military garrison and its long-term maintenance in the island affected not only the character of a 'military' zone, but also profoundly influenced the governance of the 'civil' zone. The economic consequences of the high cost of the army can be read in the apparent efforts by the imperial government to extract all possible revenues from the province and thus to minimize the level of cross-subsidization from other parts of the empire. Put simply, Britain was squeezed harder than many other provinces. As we have seen, the moment of greatest visible growth and wealth generation in the provincial economy occurred in the early fourth century, when it appears that the size of the British garrison had been substantially reduced. The later fourth-century decline may equally reflect the re-imposition of higher demands as the western empire started to disintegrate militarily and revenues from the Gallic and German provinces fell.

17

'No Longer Subject to
Roman Laws'

The ending of Roman Britain is a subject of few facts and many theories. In archaeological terms, as noted in earlier sections, there is a major change detectable between 350 and 450. After 402 most of the conventional dating apparatus ceases to be helpful due to the shortage of imported coinage from the Continent and the collapse of manufacturing activity, leading to a lack of new artefactual styles. Even if items in circulation continued to be used for some time into the fifth century, this still marks a real cut-off point in material culture. No matter that some level of social continuity can be traced at a few towns and villas, the end date of Britain as part of the empire in 409 looks like a threshold to another sort of world.

Jerome memorably described Britain as 'fertile in usurpers'; certainly, the election of pretenders to the purple by the army played an important part in the final severance of the Diocese from the empire. Following major barbarian invasions across the Rhine, the ability of Honorius, the ruling emperor in the west, to respond to the needs of the British Diocese was clearly limited. Under threat of renewed seaborne attacks, some elements of the army in Britain followed the disreputable tradition of electing usurpers. In 406 or 407, they proclaimed Marcus emperor, but finding him not to their liking, soon murdered him and elected another. The second usurper, Gratian, lasted only four months before being treated likewise, and a third candidate was put forward. Constantine III had a talismanic name (evidently a key consideration in his being proclaimed in place of Gratian), but he seems to have rapidly left Britain with the field army units and to have won over to his cause the remnants of the army in Germany and Gaul. We know very little about the first two of these usurpers, but, given that the army was active in proclaiming them, it is most probable that they were all military men or Roman officials – the sort of people who might unite the armies of the western provinces. Constantine was soon embroiled in warfare both with barbarian invaders of the Gallic provinces and with Sarus, a general sent against him by Stilicho on behalf of Honorius. Despite initial setbacks, Constantine secured his control over much of Gaul and won over the Spanish provinces through an embassy made by his son Constans. In 409, Honorius was obliged to recognize Constantine as a co-ruler, not least because of the attack of Alaric and the Visigoths on Italy. The truce was short-lived and at the first opportunity in 410 Honorius sent another army, commanded by Count Constantius, against Constantine in southern Gaul. Constantine was captured and killed at Arles in 411.

In the meantime, Britain appears to have come under renewed Saxon attacks and, in the absence of support from Constantine, the Diocese revolted against him in 409. Zosimus, the key source for this, states that the inhabitants of Britain 'were obliged to throw off Roman rule and live independently, no longer subject to Roman laws. The Britons therefore took up arms and . . . freed their cities from the barbarians threatening them.' When Honorius regained control of the Gallic provinces in 411 he does not seem to have attempted to reunite Britain with the empire. Although Zosimus speaks of him sending letters to the 'British towns' in 410, 'bidding them to take precautions on their own behalf', this 'rescript' is now generally believed to relate to towns in *Bruttium* (southern Italy). The terminal date of my study is thus 409, marking the rebellion of the province against Constantine, and the idea of later letters passing between the British towns and Honorius is rejected. Given the chaotic state of the western empire at this date, with major barbarian incursions penetrating to Rome itself, Honorius was initially in no position to reunite Britain with the empire. When order was restored in Gaul, the empire might have been expected to try to reclaim its lost Diocese, yet no attempt appears to have been made to do so. This is perhaps an indication that Britain was perceived to have changed in the interim in a major and problematic way.

The economic consequences of the chaotic conditions on the near Continent and the British secession were spectacular. The lack both of imported coins after the earliest issues of Constantine III and of local imitations is a clear indication that the financial and taxation system of the Diocese had ceased to operate. Existing coins in circulation sufficed for a while, though increasingly clipped at the edges. That in itself indicates a breakdown of financial controls, and any long-term mainten-ance of the Roman tax system after 409 would surely have required fresh minting. Imperial expenditure also ceased and urban authorities were in no position to pick up the bill for soldiers or services. Already in decline before 409, the manufacture of pottery and a wide range of other goods cannot be shown to have continued for long into the fifth century, and trade in goods with the Continent appears to have halted abruptly. These are perhaps symptoms, rather than causes, of a more general collapse in the market economy and transport system of the Diocese. Even in the late Roman period, government contracts had underwritten some level of manufacturing, transport and market activity and mass production of artefacts by specialized artisans relied on cash customers and distribution networks.

Had a semblance of provincial government been maintained after 409, collapse might have been slower and less profound. The implication is that what followed the rebellion of 409 was anarchic and involved the breakdown of key institutions in society: provincial administra-tion, taxation, imperial rents and dues, the monetary economy, official purchases and orders, inter-regional trade, perhaps even the calendar of markets. This was the crucial difference between this and earlier secessionist phases in the third and fourth centuries, when Britain had continued to be run as though still a Roman territory. Constantine's governors were expelled, but not locally replaced by an effective shadow administration. Since urban government by the fifth century was an unwelcome and obligatory chore for the wealthy, the removal of upper tiers of provincial and Diocesan government may have created a cascade effect at the level of the *civitates*.

The military community had been weakened by the withdrawal of the best troops to support Constantine's bid for power; disaffection for his regime among the frontier and lower-grade troops that remained was stimulated by their isolation in the face of fresh seaborne raids, but perhaps also by issues relating to their future pay. In consequence, the power and influence of the army within Britain had never been weaker. The urban community clearly felt themselves under threat and ill-protected by the state. Urban lifestyles had been in decline for half a century, as a result of continuing heavy burdens imposed by the state. The rural communities were especially vulnerable to attacks and had particular reason to resent the provincial tax-collectors. There seems little doubt, therefore, that there were immediate reasons for dissatis-faction with the empire, building on the unpopularity that over 360 years of colonial rule had engendered in some parts of society. The three communities thus all had cause for repudiating the provincial administration at this time (or in the case of the military community of remaining passive as it was overthrown). If secession followed some sort of popular revolt, rather than a military coup, there is a good chance that crucial records in the provincial archives were destroyed, making subsequent reinstitution of colonial government structures all the harder. At any rate, the provincial and Diocesan system of government seems to have been replaced by something more regionally fragmented, based on the power of local rulers or *tyranni*.

The nature of the sub-Roman government is shadowy indeed. Gildas mentions some sort of British council still appealing for help to Aetius, the Roman commander in Gaul, towards the mid-fifth century, though other references suggest the increasing local dominance of tyrants and warlords. Credited in the best-known tradition with inviting the Saxons Hengist and Horsa into Britain as his allies, Vortigern may be an apocry-phal figure, but clearly he represented a type of local *tyrannus*. The sub-Roman polities or kingdoms may have evoked Roman terminology (as with the kingdom of *Dumnonia* in the south-west), but they do not seem to have correlated with the late Roman provinces. On balance, a greater fragmentation of power in Britain after 409 seems most probable, with towns serving as the focus of regional kingdoms dominated by individual rulers, and collective action of the neighbouring regions per-haps only very spasmodically achieved in moments of crisis. There are hints that some factions within Britain may have favoured reunion with the remnants of the empire, and at least one British war leader, Riothamus, crossed to the Continent in about 469 with a band of troops under terms of an alliance. But it is evident that not all were keen on being subjects of Rome again and there was no possibility of unified action.

Popular revolt against taxation has been suggested as a factor in the ending of provincial government and the certainty of the reintroduction of taxation had Britain been reincorporated was a strong disincentive to the process being initiated from the British side. When the Byzantine state recaptured Africa from the Vandals in the sixth century, the most serious military opposition came not from the Vandals, but from the

African peasantry, engendered by the re-imposition of the taxation system. Although some of the early medieval British sources imply a return of the Romans after 409, the key argument against this is the cessation of coin imports after about 407. Some late Roman tax was taken in kind, but without coins there was no provincial administration.

It now seems clear that there was no real continuity of urban community between Roman Britain and Saxon England. But when precisely did town life change out of recognition from the Roman model, since there is every difference between town life and life in towns? The evidence is contradictory: one substantial house and barn may have continued in occupation at St Albans into the fifth century, though the chronology of this is now being questioned; Saxon *Grubenhäuser* (sunken-floored buildings) appeared amid the ruins of Canterbury and Colchester; a chiefly residence was erected within the shell of the Baths Basilica at Wroxeter; a small church existed in the forum piazza at Lincoln. There are many other scraps of information hinting at continuing activity within the walled area of some towns, but lacking the coherence of the earlier phases. External structures, such as the amphitheatres at Cirencester and Chester, perhaps became fortified refuges. Craft production of many common goods appears to have ceased, though finds from sites such as the baths basilica at Wroxeter suggest careful curation and continued use of many 'Roman' artefacts well into the fifth century. Pottery repaired by rivets from a number of sites emphasizes the crucial difficulty of replacing such goods. The major towns and their public amenities had been showing signs of decline well before 409. The extreme change from early imperial standards was not entirely out of step with more widespread late antique urban developments, even in northern Italy. However, the British pattern seems to have diverged further and faster. The walled town of London appears to have been totally abandoned quite early in the fifth century, with Saxon *Lundenwic* later established 2 km west along the Thames. Always an important factor, the insularity of Britain was crucial in this sub-Roman period.

The final phases at military sites are equally difficult to follow, though at Birdoswald on Hadrian's Wall a sub-Roman chieftain appears to have erected a substantial hall over one of the fort's ruined granaries. Some activity continued within the *principia* of the fortress at York in the fifth and sixth centuries, though this looks more rural than military in orientation. More commonly, forts simply seem to have been abandoned and the key fortifications in the fifth century may have been the walled towns at the heart of the main farming regions. In the absence of any coherent naval force, effective defence against seaborne raiders depended on the ability to retreat within fortifications, and offensive operations will have focused on the ability to pursue small bands of raiders on horseback. To this extent, the British cities may initially have been relatively well placed to weather the effects of Pictish, Irish and Saxon raids. But the situation was to change profoundly with the Germanic settlements.

The latest phases of rural settlements are notoriously difficult to date and many sites have revealed traces of what excavators are prone to call 'squatter occupation'. The generic picture of widespread abandonment and of occasional small groups camping in the ruins of once grand villas must be treated with a certain caution. Most 'squatter occupation' could equally be interpreted as final adaptations to rural buildings, rather than reoccupation of essentially ruined or derelict places. Sites such as the small villa at Redlands Farm (Northamptonshire) appear to have been partially demolished in order to maintain a sector of the building as a dwelling. Occupation at a number of other villas clearly did extend into the fifth century, as at Piddington, Frocester and Whitley Grange near Wroxeter. St Patrick's family owned a small farm or *villula* in western Britain and this was still a going concern when he escaped from enslavement in Ireland, probably in the later fifth century. However, the largest and richest houses in areas close to the coast and navigable rivers, or in eastern England will have become targets for all manner of rural dangers, from brigandage to peasant revolt to external raiders. In the most unsettled areas and periods, the alternatives may have been leave or die. A number of hillforts were reoccupied at this date, perhaps as a safer alternative to the undefended villa residence (Crickley Hill in the Cotswold villa zone or South Cadbury).

Although the archaeological evidence is scanty, various historical materials point to a continuing intellectual vigour well into the fifth century. The continuance of the Christian Church was crucial to this. A major heresy in the fifth-century Church was sparked by the work of a British-born cleric called Pelagius. Pelagius spent most of his career outside Britain, and developed the doctrine that was condemned as heretical at Rome. Agricola, son of a Pelagian bishop Severianus, introduced his heresy to the British Church. Following the condemnation of his theological position as heresy in 418 and its suppression on the Continent, the continued adherence to Pelagianism of an important body within the British Church was a point of concern. There followed two visits to Britain by a prominent bishop, Germanus of Auxerre. The first of these took place in 429, the second perhaps in the mid-430s. Germanus is reputed to have won theological debates with the Pelagian clergy, secured the exile of heretics, healed the daughter of a tribune, visited (and extracted relics) from the tomb of St Alban and inspired British troops to victory over Picts and Saxons. Sorting fact from fiction is difficult, but it is clear that the Church remained an important institution in early fifth-century Britain and retained periodic contact with the Continent. On the other hand, the heresy issue and the exceptional nature of the visits of Germanus in themselves suggest that Christianity in Britain was already following an insular path.

The mission of Germanus to Britain was also mirrored in this sub-Roman period by the conversion of pagan Ireland and important monastic foundations in south-western Scotland. Redemptive Christianity evidently thrived in these troubled and traumatic times. The strongest evidence for a continuing Christian tradition in the late fifth and the sixth century thus all comes from western Britain, which appears to be the region where Gildas lived and researched his historical account, and from which area St Patrick was seized by Irish pirates. It is also the area where we find numerous Latin inscriptions (so-called class-1 inscriptions), many revealing still Latinized nomenclature and some referring to people of status by Latin terms – such as doctor, priest, magistrate. Given the paucity of fourth-century texts, the revival of civilian Latin epigraphy is striking and surely indicates a society undergoing a crisis of identity. There is an interesting overlap between these late Latin texts and the so-called Ogham inscriptions in an Irish language, which also occur widely in western Britain, often combined in bilingual texts. One plausible explanation is that they indicate the integration of Irish immigrants, mercenaries or military leaders into the increasingly beleaguered British society of Romano-Christian type.

This links to the other great change of the fifth century, namely the transformation of raiders into settlers and the long-term impact that this had on Britain. The scale of Germanic migration to Britain remains much debated and its ultimate origins are ambiguous. Gildas writes of a specific moment, the *Adventus Saxonum*, but archaeology hints at a more drawn-out process. One of the puzzles concerns how a relatively small set of Germanic groups could overwhelm the numerically far superior British. A factor here may have been the loss of control over Germanic mercenaries by one or more of the post-Roman British potentates. The use of Germanic mercenaries against other groups of Germans or barbarians is amply paralleled in the late Roman world, as is the granting of lands to some of these groups within provincial territories. It is by no means unlikely, therefore, that this was a line of approach given serious consideration by the British communities after 409, if it had not started earlier. The sources contain various versions of a tradition in which Saxon allies/mercenaries turned against their British employers and started to seize additional territory, backed up by reinforcement from the Germanic peoples of the North Sea coastlands. Gildas and other sources characterize this as a Saxon rebellion, after a period of co-operation.

A much-debated question is when the change occurred. Careful analysis of the available literary sources suggests that the nature of the 'Saxon' presence changed in about 440, though archaeological finds indicate that there was already an increasing number of specifically Germanic artefacts in cemeteries in eastern England from about 425. What we may be dealing with here is a gradual tilting of the scales as the balance of power shifted from the British communities to the Germanic groups. The Gallic Chronicle highlights 440–41 as a moment of some special triumph for the *Saxones* in Britain and in either 441–42 or 445–46 there appears to have been an explicit recognition that the island (or some significant part of it) had passed into Saxon jurisdiction. Probably writing early in the sixth century, Gildas is our best, but by no means reliable, guide to what happened next. The second half of the fifth century was marked by Germanic advance and British withdrawal, despite the celebrated resistance of Ambrosius Aurelianus at some point. Ambrosius Aurelianus is another of the mythic, though vaguely plausible, figures of sub-Roman Britain, second only to Arthur perhaps. His names suggest that he came from an aristocratic family; Gildas hints that his family may have been linked to the 'purple' at some stage (perhaps through kinship to a usurper), but more likely this simply indicates that he came from the highest provincial pedigree. It is reasonable to accept the existence of a war leader bearing these names and that he led resistance to the Germans at a time of crisis and for a time stemmed the tide. Whether the tales that link him with Vortigern have any basis in fact is much more debatable.

By the end of the fifth century, Britain was divided between a northern Pictish kingdom, an 'eastern' zone (with its western limits running through Hampshire, eastern Gloucestershire, Leicestershire, Lincolnshire and Yorkshire) characterized by Germanic cremation and inhumation cemeteries, and a series of western zones (Dorset, Somerset, Devon, Cornwall, Wales, north-western England) where a Christian and Latinate British culture survived in part, though also affected by Irish migrations into parts of Wales and Scotland. The Germanic groups had thus seized control of the productive heartlands of the Roman provinces. The future lay in their hands and those native Britons who lived under their authority evidently soon shared the cultural agenda they set. We should not envisage the complete replacement of one uniform ethnic group by another. On both the British and Germanic sides there were broad regional and ethnic subdivisions. But the cultural identity of early medieval England was to be predominantly Germanic, with markers typical of late antique Christian groups limited to the far west. Late antique imports from the Mediterranean world and Gaul are predominantly clustered along the western seaboard of Britain, emphasizing the fact that it was the western British who remained in partial contact with the old Roman world. The lack of trade between the Continent and the Germanic areas suggests a dramatic repudiation of Roman culture by the incomers in eastern Britain and the acceptance of this new un-Roman identity by the eastern Britons under 'Saxon' suzerainty.

The Germanic migrations and the transformation of sub-Roman Britain into Anglo-Saxon England are properly the subject of the next book in this series. Looked at from the Roman side of the chronological divide, there are some probable contributory factors to the relatively rapid and far-reaching collapse of Roman power in Britain. Firstly, the nature of Roman civilization itself was fundamentally different by the early fifth century from its form in the first century. As we have seen throughout this book, 'Being Roman' was a status game and was most thoroughly engaged in by those nearer the top of society. The literate stratum was at all times a relatively small proportion of the population (perhaps 10 per cent at best). Too large a number of people in Britain had an underdeveloped intellectual engagement with Roman civilization, and the effective cessation of markets and manufactures undermined their access to and use of material culture.

The archaeological evidence from the later fourth century suggests that the British elite class was already dwindling in numbers. If the fifth century was a century of woes – raiding, wars, plagues, anarchy, peasant revolts – as the sources suggest, this can only have eroded their numbers still further. Once a significant Germanic presence was established in eastern England by the mid- to later fifth century, the British elite, owning substantial land and wealth, was exceptionally vulnerable to attack. The distribution of the *c.*100 late Roman coin hoards found in Britain is revealing of massive failure of the elite groups in eastern England to retrieve their stored wealth. Set against the near absence of such hoards in western Britain, the evidence is particularly striking. The largest hoard, from Hoxne in Suffolk, comprised nearly 15,000 coins, with the latest issues being just two *siliquae* of Constantine III, dated 407–08. The heavy clipping of many of the other silver coins in the hoard suggests that the date of deposition could have been as much as several decades later.

When the upper social order was cut away or forced out of eastern England this led to the effective decapitation of an already demoralized society, while the initial Germanic repudiation of towns, villas and Christianity also undermined the sort of elite society established under Roman rule. In these regions, by the later fifth century there was no broad and strong foundation of *Romanitas* left. The emigration of some Britons to the Continent in the fifth century is attested in the sources, with particular concentrations ending up in Brittany, Gaul and northern Spain. Some of the outward trappings of Christian and Roman tradition were also maintained in sub-Roman Britain, especially in the western kingdoms. Paradoxically, these also marked something of a return to the sort of societies that had characterized pre-Roman Britain. The focus on chiefdoms and petty kingdoms and the reuse of hillforts and promontory forts are reminiscent, though the low level of cross-channel trade, the decline in pottery and craft production and the disappearance of coins all represent regression beyond the stage of social and economic evolution reached in the late Iron Age.

Some specialists in Dark Age archaeology insist that there were profound continuities with the Roman past and that Britain in the fifth century was similar to other late antique societies in the west. However, it remains hard to contest the view that the Roman occupation of Britain was ultimately very unpopular, having exacted a high price for too long. The ending of that rule saw the rapid emergence of very different sorts of society in consequence. Perhaps the ultimate irony of the sub-Roman period is that the regions that maintained for longest a semblance of Roman and Christian traditions were precisely those that had demonstrated the lowest levels of economic and social integration under Roman rule. The kingdoms of the Picts in Scotland, *Dumnonia* in Devon and Cornwall, *Dyfed* in south-west Wales, *Gwynedd* in north-west Wales and their equivalents in other parts of Wales and northern Britain were the final refuges of both a degenerated Roman identity and of the Iron Age Britons who had most strenuously resisted Rome.

Bibliographical Essay

The bibliography on Britain in the Roman empire is vast and I do not have space to refer to all the works I have consulted in researching this book. In trying to produce a useful resource for all levels of readers and researchers, there is a necessary emphasis on the work of the last twenty years, rather than earlier generations of scholarship. The progress in the subject since publication of P. Salway, *Roman Britain* (Oxford, 1981) will be particularly clear by comparison of our respective bibliographical essays. For convenience, I have structured the bibliographical essay in a similar way to the internal organization of chapters. I have also included many works that take a very different interpretative line from my own. Authors' initials and places of publication are omitted and titles sometimes abbreviated on second and subsequent citations of a work within a chapter.

GENERAL HISTORIES, RESOURCES AND ABBREVIATIONS

The best of the numerous general accounts with a strong narrative line is P. Salway, *Roman Britain* (Oxford, 1981), also available in repackaged and updated form as *The Oxford Illustrated History of Roman Britain* (Oxford, 1993); note also S. S. Frere, *Britannia: a history of Roman Britain* (3rd edn, London, 1987) and M. Todd, *Roman Britain (55 BC–AD 400)* (2nd edn, Oxford, 1997). An alternative, more thematic, approach was taken by I. Richmond in his classic short study, *Roman Britain* (Harmondsworth, 1955); the revised edition (edited by M. Todd, 1995) has extended the shelf-life to over fifty years. Two other historiographical milestones that I have particularly enjoyed revisiting are R. G. Collingwood and J. N. L. Myres, *Roman Britain and the English Settlements* (Oxford, 1937) and A. L. F. Rivet, *Town and Country in Roman Britain* (2nd edn, London, 1964).

M. Millett, *The Romanization of Britain. An essay in archaeological interpretation* (Cambridge, 1990) has been enormously influential, not least in advocating a much more archaeologically focused approach. J. Creighton, *Britannia. The Creation of a Roman Province* (London, 2006) offers a fresh perspective on the early phases. Other strong representatives of a thematic archaeological approach include M. Millett, *Roman Britain* (London, 1995); T. W. Potter, *Roman Britain* (London, 1997); T. W. Potter and C. Johns, *Roman Britain* (London, 1992); and P. Salway (ed.), *Short Oxford History of the British Isles. The Roman era* (Oxford, 2002). B. Jones and D. Mattingly, *An Atlas of Roman Britain* (reprint, Oxford, 2002) has broader coverage of topics than its title implies. R. J. A. Wilson, *A Guide to the Roman Remains in Britain* (4th edn, London, 2002) is the standard guidebook; there is also a useful gazetteer in P. Clayton, *Companion to Roman Britain* (Oxford, 1980). Of works treating the Roman interlude as part of a larger vision of British history, see D. Miles, *The Tribes of Britain* (London, 2005); F. Pryor, *Britain BC* (London, 2002) and *Britain AD* (London, 2004); and C. A. Snyder, *The Britons* (Oxford, 2003).

For bibliographical research, work to 1959 is listed in W. Bonser, *A Romano-British Bibliography* (Oxford, 1964). *Archaeological Bulletin for the British Isles / Archaeological Bibliography* (1949–87) covered the years 1940–80, and was subsequently replaced by *British Archaeological Abstracts* (1987–91) and *British Archaeological Bibliography* (1992–). Guidance on more recent work and resources is to be found in A. C. King, *British and Irish Archaeology. A bibliographical guide* (Manchester/New York, 1994) and C. Lavell, *Handbook for British and Irish Archaeology. Sources and resources* (Edinburgh, 1997). Annual summaries of excavations and discoveries of Roman-period sites in Britain can be found in *Journal of Roman Studies* (1921–69) and in *Britannia* (1970–).

The inscriptions of Roman Britain are exceptionally well published:

RIB I = R. G. Collingwood and R. P. Wright, *The Roman Inscriptions of Britain. Vol. I: Inscriptions on Stone* (Oxford, 1964, revised edition (with addenda and corrigenda by R. S. O. Tomlin), Stroud, 1995).

RIB II.1 = S. S. Frere, M. Roxan and R. S. O. Tomlin, *The Roman Inscriptions of Britain. Vol. II: Instrumentum Domesticum. Fasc. 1. The military diplomata; metal ingots; tesserae; dies; labels; and lead sealings* (Stroud, 1990); *RIB* II.2 = S. S. Frere and R. S. O. Tomlin, *Fasc. 2. Weights; gold vessel; silver vessels; bronze vessels; lead vessels; pewter vessels; shale vessels; glass vessels; spoons* (Stroud, 1991); *RIB* II.3 = S. S. Frere and R. S. O. Tomlin, *Fasc. 3. Brooches, rings, gems, bracelets, helmets, shields, weapons, iron tools, baldric fittings, votives in gold, silver and bronze, lead pipes, roundels, sheets and other lead objects, stone roundels, pottery and bone roundels, other objects of bone* (Stroud, 1991); *RIB* II.4 = S. S. Frere and R. S. O. Tomlin, *Fasc. 4. Wooden barrels, stilus-tablets, objects of wood, leather, oculists' stamps, wallplaster, mosaics, handmills, stone tablets, stone balls, stone pebbles, small stone votives, miscellaneous objects of stone, jet, clay figurines, clay objects, antefixes, tile-stamps of legion II Augusta, of legion VI Victrix, of legion IX Hispana, of legion XX Valeria Victrix, tile-stamps of the auxiliaries* (Stroud, 1992); *RIB* II.5 = S. S. Frere and R. S. O. Tomlin, *Fasc. 5. Tile-stamps of the Classis Britannica; imperial, procuratorial and civic tile-stamps; stamps of private tilers; inscriptions on relief-patterned tiles and graffiti on tiles* (Stroud, 1993); *RIB* II.6 = S. S. Frere and R. S. O. Tomlin, *Fasc. 6. Dipinti and graffiti on amphorae, dipinti and graffiti on mortaria, inscriptions in white barbotine, dipinti on coarse pottery, samian barbotine or moulded inscriptions* (Stroud, 1994); *RIB* II.7 = S. S. Frere, and R. S. O. Tomlin, *Fasc. 7. Graffiti on samian ware (terra sigillata)* (Stroud, 1995); *RIB* II.8 = S. S. Frere and R. S. O. Tomlin, *Fasc. 8. Graffiti on coarse pottery cut before and after firing; stamp on coarse pottery. Addenda and corrigenda to fascicules 1–8* (Stroud, 1995).

RIB III = *The Roman Inscriptions of Britain. Vol. III: Inscriptions on Stone* (forthcoming) (this latter will replace annual listings of new discoveries in *Journal of Roman Studies* (1955–69) and *Britannia* (since 1970).

Note also R. Goodburn and H. W. Waugh, *The Roman Inscriptions of Britain. I. Inscriptions on stone. Epigraphic indexes* (Gloucester, 1983); S. S. Frere, *The Roman Inscriptions of Britain. II. Instrumentum Domesticum. Combined epigraphic indexes* (Stroud, 1995).

Another important series concerns the publication of sculptural and decorative stonework: *CSIR* 1.1 = E. J. Phillips, *Corpus Signorum Imperii Romani. Great Britain. Vol. 1. Fasc. 1. Corbridge, Hadrian's Wall east of the North Tyne* (London, 1977); *CSIR* 1.2 = B. W. Cunliffe and M. G. Fulford, *Corpus Signorum Imperii Romani. Great Britain. Vol. 1. Fasc. 2. Bath and the rest of Wessex* (London, 1982); *CSIR* 1.3 = S. R. Tufi, *Corpus Signorum Imperii Romani. Great Britain. Vol. 1. Fasc. 3. Yorkshire* (London, 1982); *CSIR* 1.4 = L. J. F. Keppie and B. J. Arnold, *Corpus Signorum Imperii Romani. Great Britain. Vol. 1. Fasc. 4. Scotland* (London, 1984); *CSIR* 1.5 = R. Brewer, *Corpus Signorum Imperii Romani. Great Britain. Vol. 1. Fasc. 5. Wales* (London, 1986); *CSIR* 1.6 = J. C. Coulston and E. J. Phillips, *Corpus Signorum Imperii Romani. Great Britain. Vol. 1. Fasc. 6. Hadrian's Wall west of the North Tyne, and Carlisle* (London, 1988); *CSIR* 1.7 = M. Henig, *Corpus Signorum Imperii Romani. Great Britain. Vol. 1. Fasc. 7. Roman sculpture from the Cotswolds* (London, 1993); *CSIR* 1.8 = J. Huskinson, *Corpus Signorum Imperii Romani. Great*

Britain. Vol. 1. Fasc. 8. Roman sculpture from eastern England (London, 1994); *CSIR 1.9* = M. Henig, *Corpus Signorum Imperii Romani. Great Britain. Vol. 1. Fasc. 9. Roman sculpture from the West Midlands* (London, 2004). For Roman London, not yet covered by *CSIR*, see M. Henig, 'Art in Roman London', in I. Haynes et al., *London Under Ground* (Oxford, 2000); C. Hill et al., *The Roman Riverside Wall and Monumental Arch in London* (London, 1980).

One of the most important developments of the 1990s was the initiation of a postgraduate conference in Roman archaeology, reinvigorating debate through new theoretical approaches: *TRAC 1* = E. Scott (ed.), *Theoretical Roman Archaeology: First Conference Proceedings* (Avebury, 1993); *TRAC 2* = P. Rush (ed.), *Theoretical Roman Archaeology: Second Conference Proceedings* (Aldershot, 1995); *TRAC 3* = A. Leslie (ed.), *Theoretical Roman Archaeology and Architecture. The Third Conference Proceedings* (Glasgow, 1999); *TRAC 4* = S. Cottam, D. Dungworth, S. Scott and J. Taylor (eds), *TRAC 94. Proceedings of the Fourth Annual Theoretical Roman Archaeology Conference, Durham 1994* (Oxford, 1995); *TRAC 5* = not published (though some papers featured in R. Laurence and J. Berry, *Cultural Identity in the Roman Empire* (London, 1998)); *TRAC 6* = K. Meadows, C. Lemke and J. Heron (eds), *TRAC 96. Proceedings of the Sixth Annual Theoretical Roman Archaeology Conference, Sheffield* (Oxford, 1997); *TRAC 7* = C. Forcey, J. Hawthorne and R. Witcher (eds), *TRAC 97: Proceedings of the Seventh Annual Theoretical Roman Archaeology Conference, Nottingham* (Oxford, 1998); *TRAC 8* = P. Baker, C. Forcey, S. Jundi and R. Witcher (eds), *TRAC 98: Proceedings of the Eighth Annual Theoretical Roman Archaeology Conference, Leicester* (Oxford, 1999); *TRAC 9* = G. Fincham, G. Harrison, R. Holland and L. Revell (eds), *TRAC 99: Proceedings of the Ninth Annual Theoretical Roman Archaeology Conference, Durham* (Oxford, 2000); *TRAC 10* = G. Davies, A. Gardner and K. Lockyear (eds), *TRAC 2000: Proceedings of the Tenth Annual Theoretical Roman Archaeology Conference, London* (Oxford, 2001); *TRAC 11* = M. Carruthers, C. van Driel-Murray, A. Gardner, J. Lucas, L. Revell and E. Swift (eds), *TRAC 2001: Proceedings of the Eleventh Annual Theoretical Roman Archaeology Conference, Glasgow* (Oxford, 2002); *TRAC 12* = G. Carr, E. Swift and J. Weekes (eds), *TRAC 2002: Proceedings of the Twelfth Annual Theoretical Roman Archaeology Conference, Canterbury* (Oxford, 2003); *TRAC 13* = B. Croxford, H. Eckardt, J. Meade and J. Weekes (eds), *TRAC 2003: Proceedings of the Thirteenth Annual Theoretical Roman Archaeology Conference, Leicester* (Oxford, 2004); *TRAC 14* = J. Bruhn, B. Croxford and D. Grigoropolous (eds), *TRAC 2004: Proceedings of the Fourteenth Annual Theoretical Roman Archaeology Conference, Durham* (Oxford, 2005).

There are increasingly good websites on the subject, but these are not considered stable enough for citation in a work of this kind.

Some of the more commonplace abbreviations used below are: *AJA* = *American Journal of Archaeology*; *ANRW* = *Aufstieg und Niedergang der Römischen Welt. Geschichte und Kultur Roms in Spiegel der neueren Forschung*; *Ant. J.* = *Antiquaries Journal*; *Arch. J.* = *Archaeological Journal*; *JRA* = *Journal of Roman Archaeology*; *JRS* = *Journal of Roman Studies*; *OJA* = *Oxford Journal of Archaeology*; *PPS* = *Proceedings of the Prehistoric Society*; *PSAS* = *Proceedings of the Society of Antiquaries Scotland*; RCAHMS, RCAHMW = Royal Commission on Ancient Historic Monuments (Scotland and Wales); RCHME = Royal Commission on Historical Monuments (England).

I   THE SPECTRE OF EMPIRE

The first quote is from W. C. Sellar and R. J. Yeatman, *1066 and All That: a memorable history of England, comprising all the parts you can remember, including 103 good things, 5 bad kings and 2 genuine dates* (London, 1930), far superior to the more recent spoof history, T. Deary, *Rotten Romans* (London, 1994). The second quote is from F. Haverfield, *The Romanization of Roman Britain* (Oxford, 1915).

In addition to the general works already noted, other books on the subject (some of which treat it as largely unproblematic) include, J. Alcock, *Life in Roman Britain* (London, 1997); G. de la Bédoyère, *Companion to Roman Britain* (Stroud, 1999); A. R. Birley, *Life in Roman Britain* (London, 1964); K. Branigan, *Roman Britain, Life in an Imperial Province* (London, 1980); S. Hill and S. Ireland, *Roman Britain* (London, 1996); T. McAleavy, *Life in Roman Britain* (London, 1999); H. H. Scullard, *Roman Britain – Outpost of the Empire* (London, 1979); D. Shotter, *Roman Britain* (London, 1998); J. S. Wacher, *Roman Britain* (London, 1978).

R. Reece, *My Roman Britain* (Cirencester, 1988) was a profoundly unconventional, irreverent and influential antidote to the canonical approaches. R. Hingley was one of the first younger scholars to take up the challenge, 'Past, present and future – the study of Roman Britain', *Scottish Archaeological Review* 8 (1991); 'Attitudes to Roman imperialism', in *TRAC* 1 (1993). On the historiography of Britain and the Roman empire, R. Hingley, *Roman Officers and English Gentlemen. The imperial origins of Roman archaeology* (London, 2000); on the rediscovery of Boudica and her modern reception, R. Hingley and C. Unwin, *Boudica. Iron Age warrior queen* (Hambledon and London, 2005). For the contribution of F. Haverfield, see *The Romanization of Roman Britain* (1915); *The Roman Occupation of Britain* (rev. edn with G. Macdonald, Oxford, 1924); also P. Freeman in D. J. Mattingly (ed.), *Dialogues in Roman Imperialism. Power, discourse and discrepant experience in the Roman empire* (Portsmouth, RI, 1997); G. Woolf, 'Romans as civilizers. The ideological pre-conditions of Romanization', in J. Metzler et al., *Integration in the Early Roman West* (Luxembourg, 1995). Generally positive judgements of the Roman empire underscore works such as P. Wilkinson, *What the Romans Did for Us* (London, 2000).

On globalization and Roman imperialism: R. Hingley, *Globalising Roman Culture. Unity, diversity and empire* (London, 2005); note also R. Witcher, 'Globalisation and Roman imperialism. Perspectives on identities in Roman Italy', in E. Herring and K. Lomas (eds), *The Emergence of State Identities in Italy in the First Millennium BC* (London, 2000); G. Woolf, 'World systems analysis and the Roman empire', *Journal of Roman Archaeology* 3 (1990). Classic studies in post-colonialism include, E. W. Said, *Orientalism* (Harmondsworth, 1978) and *Culture and Imperialism* (London, 1992). For post-colonial approaches in Roman archaeology, see J. Webster and N. Cooper (eds), *Roman Imperialism: post-colonial perspectives* (Leicester, 1996); Mattingly (ed.), *Dialogues in Roman Imperialism* (1997); J. Webster, 'Creolising Roman Britain', *AJA* 105.2 (2001).

Note also the Theoretical Roman Archaeology Conference (*TRAC*) volumes cited above; J. C. Barrett, 'Theorising Roman archaeology', *TRAC* 6 (1997); S. L. Dyson, 'From new to New Age archaeology, archaeological theory and classical archaeology: a 1990s perspective', *AJA* 97.2 (1993); S. James, 'Roman archaeology: crisis and revolution', *Antiquity* 295 (2003); G. Woolf, 'The present state and future scope of Roman archaeology: a comment', *AJA* 108 (2004).

Comparative work on empires I have found useful includes, S. Alcock et al., *Empires* (Cambridge, 2001); M. Hardt and A. Negri, *Empire* (London, 2000); D. Lieven, *Empire: the Russian empire and its rivals* (2000). On the Roman empire, see P. A. Brunt, *Roman Imperial Themes* (Oxford, 1990); C. B. Champion, *Roman Imperialism. Readings and sources* (Oxford, 2004); J. S. Wacher, *The Roman Empire* (London, 1987) and *The Roman World* (2 vols, London, 1987); C. Wells, *The Roman Empire* (London, 1992); G. Woolf (ed.), *The Cambridge Illustrated History of the Roman World* (Cambridge, 2004); *The Cambridge Ancient History*, especially volumes X–XIII. Useful sources for individuals, explanations of terms and institutes are G. Shipley, J. Vanderspoel, D. Mattingly, L. Foxhall, *The Cambridge Guide to Classical Civilization* (Cambridge, 2006); S. Hornblower and A. Spawforth, *The Oxford Classical Dictionary* (3rd edn, Oxford, 1996). On the inclusivity of the Roman empire's power structures, see A. Birley, *The African Emperor. Septimius Severus* (London, 1988). On cultural interactions between empire, enemies and subjects, J. C. Barrett et al. (eds), *Barbarians and Romans in North-West Europe* (Oxford, 1989); B. C. Burnham and H. B. Johnson (eds), *Invasion and Response: the case of Roman Britain*

(Oxford, 1979); T. F. C. Blagg and A. C. King (eds), *Military and Civilian in Roman Britain. Cultural relationships in a frontier province* (Oxford, 1984).

Dramatic reflections on empire: T. Stoppard, *Indian Ink* (London, 1995); H. Brenton, *Plays: 2. The Romans in Britain, and Others* (London, 1989).

Comparative studies in colonialism include important works by C. Gosden, *Archaeology and Colonialism. Cultural contact from 5000 BC to the present* (Cambridge, 2004); M. Given, *The Archaeology of the Colonized* (London, 2004); H. Hurst and S. Owen (eds), *Ancient Colonizations. Analogy, similarity and difference* (London, 2005); C. L. Lyons and J. K. Papadopoulos, *The Archaeology of Colonialism* (Los Angeles, 2002). G. Fincham, 'Writing colonial conflict, acknowledging colonial weakness', *TRAC* 10 (2001), makes the important point that the behaviour of colonial powers is often driven by their self-perception of their weakness and vulnerability in occupied territory.

The key modern work on Romanization is M. Millett, *The Romanization of Britain* (1990). The debate is summarized from a number of viewpoints in articles by P. Freeman and J. Barratt, in D. J. Mattingly (ed.), *Dialogues in Roman Imperialism* (Portsmouth, RI, 1997); W. S. Hanson, 'Dealing with barbarians: the Romanization of Britain', *Building on the Past. Papers celebrating 150 years of the Royal Archaeological Institute* (London, 1994); S. James, 'Romanization and the peoples of Britain', in S. Keay and N. Terrenato (eds), *Italy and the West. Comparative issues in Romanization* (Oxford, 2001); D. J. Mattingly, 'Vulgar and weak Romanization, or time for a paradigm shift?', *JRA* 15 (2002); J. Metzler et al. (eds), *Integration in the Early Roman West. The role of culture and ideology* (Luxembourg, 1995); M. Wood and F. Queiroga (eds), *Current Research on the Romanization of the Western Provinces* (Oxford, 1992); G. Woolf, 'The unity and diversity of Romanization', *JRA* 5 (1992); *Becoming Roman: the origins of provincial civilization in Gaul* (Cambridge, 1998). There is also an interesting cluster of Romanization papers in *TRAC* 6 (1997) and 7 (1998). *Archaeological Dialogues* 9.1 (2002) featured papers by G. Woolf and J. Slofstra on social change in Gaul, with substantial focus on the Romanization debate.

For a strong defence of imperial intentionality, C. R. Whittaker, 'Imperialism and culture: the Roman initiative', in Mattingly (ed.), *Dialogues* (1997). The late twentieth-century consensus on cultural change in Britain is also reflected in K. Branigan, 'The new Roman Britain – a view from the West Country', *Trans. Bristol and Gloucester Arch. Soc.* 112 (1994); B. C. Burnham, 'Celts and Romans. Towards a Romano-Celtic society', in M. Green (ed.), *The Celtic World* (London, 1995); J. Huskinson, 'Culture and social relations in the Roman Province', in P. Salway (ed), *Short Oxford History of the British Isles. The Roman era* (Oxford, 2002); T. F. C. Blagg and M. Millett, *The Early Roman Empire in the West* (Oxford, 1990).

Important comparative studies from northern Gaul, the Rhineland and the German frontier: R. Brandt and J. Slofstra (eds), *Roman and Native in the Low Countries: spheres of interaction* (Oxford, 1983); M. Carroll, *Romans, Celts and Germans. The German provinces of Rome* (Stroud, 2001); J. D. Creighton and R. J. A. Wilson, *Roman Germany: studies in cultural interaction* (Portsmouth, RI, 1999); T. Derks, *Gods, Temples and Ritual Practices: the transformation of religious ideas and values in Roman Gaul* (Amsterdam, 1998); J. F. Drinkwater, *Roman Gaul: the three provinces, 58 BC–AD 260* (London, 1983); A. King, *Roman Gaul and Germany* (London, 1990); N. Roymans (ed.), *From the Sword to the Plough: three studies on the earliest Romanisation of Northern Gaul* (Amsterdam, 1996); E. M. Wightman, *Gallia Belgica* (London, 1985); W. Willems, *Romans and Batavians* (Amsterdam, 1986); Woolf, *Becoming Roman* (1998).

Alternative approaches to cultural change and identity in the Roman empire can be found in D. J. Mattingly, 'Being Roman: expressing identity in a provincial setting', *JRA* 17 (2004); A. Gardner, 'Social identity and the duality of structure in late Roman-period Britain', *Journal of Social Archaeology* 2.3 (2002); R. Hingley, *Globalizing Roman Culture* (London, 2005); S. Jones, *The Archaeology of Ethnicity. Constructing identities in the past and present* (London, 1997); P. Wells, *The Barbarians Speak. How the conquered peoples shaped Roman Europe* (Princeton, 1999) and *Beyond Celts, Germans and Scythians: archaeology and identity in Iron Age Europe* (London, 2001).

The quote on economic worth is from M. P. Charlesworth, *The Lost Province or the Worth of Britain* (Cardiff, 1949).

On resistance as a theme, see, *inter alia*, J. F. Drinkwater and H. Vertet, 'Opportunity or opposition in Roman Gaul', in Wood and Queiroga, *Current Research on the Romanization of the Western Provinces* (1992); R. Hingley, 'Resistance and domination: social change in Roman Britain', in Mattingly (ed.), *Dialogues* (1997).

2 SOURCES OF INFORMATION AND RULES OF EVIDENCE

The sources

The standard review of Roman sources dealing with the geography of Britain is A. L. F. Rivet and C. Smith, *The Place-Names of Roman Britain* (London, 1979); see also B. Jones and D. Mattingly, *An Atlas of Roman Britain* (reprint, Oxford, 2002). Useful selections of historical sources include S. Ireland, *Roman Britain: a sourcebook* (2nd edn, London, 1996); J. C. Mann and R. G. Penman, *Literary Sources for Roman Britain* (LACTOR 11, London, 1985). Sources dealing specifically with Ireland are collected in P. Freeman, *Ireland and the Classical World* (Austin, 2001). Good discussions of sources are to be found in P. Salway, *Roman Britain* (Oxford, 1981), with a useful listing of standard texts of all the main classical sources in his extensive bibliography; see also W. S. Hanson, *Agricola and the Conquest of the North* (London, 1987). On problems with the way these sources present the 'Barbarian Other', see, *inter alia*, B. W. Cunliffe, *Greeks, Romans and Barbarians* (London, 1988); J. Webster, 'The just war: Graeco-Roman texts as colonial discourse', in *TRAC 4* (Oxford, 1995); 'Ethnographic barbarity: colonial discourse and Celtic warrior societies', in J. Webster and N. Cooper (eds), *Roman Imperialism: post-colonial perspectives* (Leicester, 1996); 'There be dragons! The continuing influence of Roman attitudes to northern Britain', in B. Bevan, *Northern Exposure* (Leicester, 1999); G. Woolf, 'Beyond Romans and natives', *World Archaeology* 28.3 (1997). On the druids, see now M. Green, *Exploring the World of the Druids* (London, 1997); S. Piggott, *The Druids* (London, 1975); A. Ross, *Druids. Preachers of immortality* (Stroud, 1999); J. Webster, 'At the end of the world: druidic and other revitalization movements in post-conquest Gaul and Britain', *Britannia* 30 (1999).

The Penguin Classics series has good translations of the works of Livy, Caesar, Tacitus, Suetonius, Ammianus Marcellinus, the *Historia Augusta* (Lives of the Later Caesars). Ptolemy is most readily accessible in E. L. Stevenson, *Claudius Ptolemy. The Geography* (New York, 1932). For discussion of sub-Roman sources, K. Dark, *Britain and the End of the Roman Empire* (Stroud, 2000).

On the literary constructions of the image of Britain in the sources, K. Clarke, 'An island nation: re-reading Tacitus' Agricola', *JRS* 91 (2001); P. C. N. Stewart, 'Inventing Britain: the creation and adaptation of an image', *Britannia* 26 (1995).

Standard epigraphic corpora (*RIB* I, etc.) are detailed above; for useful editions of selected texts, B. Dobson and V. Maxfield (eds), *Inscriptions from Roman Britain* (LACTOR 4, London, 1995); S. Ireland, *Roman Britain: a sourcebook* (1996). Spatial analysis of the distribution of inscriptions in Britain by M. Biró, 'The inscriptions of Roman Britain', *Acta Archaeologica Academiae Scientiarum Hungaricae* 27 (1975) remains insightful. On the use of epigraphy, see L. Keppie, *Understanding Roman Inscriptions* (London, 1991).

For the publication of the *Vindolanda* tablets, A. K. Bowman and J. D. Thomas, *Vindolanda: the Latin writing tablets* (London, 1983), is now supplanted by A. K. Bowman and J. D. Thomas, *The Vindolanda Writing Tablets (Tabulae Vindolandenses II)* (London, 1994) and *The Vindolanda Writing Tablets (Tabulae Vindolandenses III)* (London, 2003). There is also an excellent website.

The curse tablets from Bath are published by R. S. O. Tomlin, in B. W. Cunliffe (ed.), *The*

Temple of Sulis Minerva at Bath, Vol. 2: The Finds from the Sacred Spring (Oxford, 1988); preliminary discussion of the Uley finds by Tomlin can be found in *Britannia* reports on new texts and in A. Woodward and P. Leach, *The Uley Shrines: excavation of a ritual complex on West Hill, Uley, Gloucestershire: 1977–9* (London, 1993).

What sort of picture has been constructed?

On literacy in the Roman empire and in Britain, A. K. Bowman and G. Woolf (eds), *Literacy and Power in the Ancient World* (Cambridge, 1994); A. E. Cooley (ed.), *Becoming Roman, Writing Latin? Literacy and epigraphy in the Roman West* (Portsmouth, RI, 2002); J. H. Humphrey (ed.), *Literacy in the Roman World* (Ann Arbor, 1991); W. S. Harris, *Ancient Literacy* (Cambridge, MA, 1989). Note also, J. N. Adams, 'British Latin: the text, interpretation and language of the Bath curse tablets', *Britannia* 23 (1992) and 'The language of the Vindolanda writing tablets: an interim report', *JRS* 85 (1995); E. P. Hamp, 'Social gradience in British spoken Latin', *Britannia* 6 (1975); J. C. Mann, 'Spoken Latin in Britain as evidenced in the inscriptions', *Britannia* 2 (1971).

On British toponyms, see Rivet and Smith, *Place-Names* (1979); A. L. F. Rivet, 'Celtic names and Roman places', *Britannia* 11 (1980); S. Esmonde Cleary, 'Britannia Superior and Britannia Inferior', in R. J. A. Talbert (ed.), *Barrington Atlas of the Greek and Roman World* (Princeton, 2000); Ordnance Survey, *Map of Roman Britain* (4th edn, Southampton, 1978); Tabula Imperii Romani, *Condate–Glevum–Londinium–Lutetia* (London, 1983); Tabula Imperii Romani, *Britannia Septentrionalis* (London, 1987).

Prosopographical evidence is definitively presented by A. Birley, *The Fasti of Roman Britain* (Oxford, 1981); *The Roman Government of Britain* (Oxford, 2005), which is essentially a major revision of the *Fasti*; see also his *The People of Roman Britain* (London, 1979). The epigraphic indexes of *RIB*, the *Vindolanda* tablets and the Bath curse tablets will help the interested reader track most of the individuals referred to in this book.

On the frameworks of government, D. Braund, *The Administration of the Roman Empire 241 B.C.–A.D. 193* (Exeter, 1988); W. Eck, in *Cambridge Ancient History* XI (2000); B. Levick, *The Government of the Roman Empire. A sourcebook* (London, 1985); M. Goodman, *The Roman World 44 BC–AD 180* (London, 1997); D. S. Potter, *The Roman Empire at Bay AD 180–395* (London, 2004); G. H. Stevenson, *Roman Provincial Administration till the Age of the Antonines* (Oxford, 1949).

Archaeology

Works reflecting the development of the discipline and current agendas include R. G. Collingwood and I. A. Richmond, *The Archaeology of Roman Britain* (London, 1969); M. Todd (ed.), *Research on Roman Britain: 1960–89* (London, 1989); R. F. J. Jones (ed.), *Roman Britain: recent trends* (Sheffield, 1991); S. James and M. Millett, *Britons and Romans: advancing an archaeological agenda* (York, 2001); P. Salway (ed.), *Short Oxford History of the British Isles. The Roman era* (Oxford, 2002); M. Todd (ed.), *A Companion to Roman Britain* (Oxford, 2004).

For aerial photography, see S. S. Frere and J. K. S. St Joseph, *Roman Britain from the Air* (Cambridge, 1983); G. S. Maxwell and D. R. Wilson, 'Air reconnaissance in Roman Britain 1977–84', *Britannia* 18 (1987); J. K. S. St Joseph, 'Air reconnaissance in Britain 1969–72', *JRS* 63 (1973); 'Air reconnaissance in Roman Britain, 1973–76', *JRS* 67 (1977).

Studies of the Roman army in Britain are covered below in Chapters 4–8. Published proceedings of Roman Frontier Studies conferences contain many papers relating to Britain; see, *inter alia*, W. S. Hanson and L. Keppie (eds), *Roman Frontier Studies 1979* (Oxford, 1980); M. Planck (ed.), *Studien zur Militärgrenzen Roms III, 13 Internationaler Limes Kongress Aalen 1983* (Stuttgart, 1986); H. Vetters and M. Kandler (eds), *Der Römische Limes in Österreich. Akten der 14 Internationalen Limeskongresses 1986, Carnuntum* (Vienna, 1990); V. A. Maxfield and B. Dobson, *Roman Frontier Studies 1989* (Exeter, 1991);

W. Groenman-van Waateringe et al. (eds), *Roman Frontier Studies 1995* (Oxford, 1997); P. Freeman et al. (eds), *Limes XVIII: Proceedings of the XVIIIth International Congress of Roman Frontier Studies held in Amman, Jordan* (Oxford, 2002); S. Visy, *Proceedings of the XIXth International Limeskongress* (Pecs, 2005).

Roman roads, I. Margary, *Roman Roads in Britain* (London, 1967). Water supplies, A. Burgers, *The Water Supplies and Related Structures of Roman Britain* (Oxford, 2001). Architecture and architectural sculpture, T. F. C. Blagg, 'Schools of stonemasons in Roman Britain', in J. Munby and M. Henig (eds), *Roman Life and Art in Britain* (Oxford, 1977); 'Art and architecture', in Todd (ed.), *Research on Roman Britain* (1989); *Roman Architectural Ornament in Britain* (Oxford, 2002); P. Johnson and I. Haynes, *Architecture in Roman Britain* (London, 1996). Sculpture is largely published in the CSIR series of volumes (see above).

General studies of Roman art, J. M. C. Toynbee, *Art in Britain under the Romans* (London, 1965); *Art in Roman Britain* (London, 1962); M. Henig, *The Art of Roman Britain* (London, 1995); Munby and Henig (eds), *Roman Life and Art in Britain* (1977). Less authoritative is J. Laing, *Art and Society in Roman Britain* (Gloucester, 1997). For more theoretically informed approaches, see now S. Scott and J. Webster (eds), *Roman Imperialism and Provincial Art* (Cambridge, 2003). For mosaics, see D. Neal, *Roman Mosaics in Britain* (London, 1983); D. Neal and S. Cosh, *Roman Mosaics of Britain. Vol. 1: Northern Britain* (London, 2002). Wall-painting, N. Davey and R. Ling, *Romano-British Wall Painting* (London, 1981); R. Ling, *Romano-British Wall Painting* (Princes Risborough, 1985); 'Wall-painting since Wheeler', in S. Greep (ed.), *Roman Towns. The Wheeler inheritance* (York, 1993); B. Philp, *The Roman House with Bacchic Murals at Dover* (Dover, 1989).

Jewellery: C. Johns, *The Jewellery of Roman Britain. Celtic and classical traditions* (London, 1996); C. Johns and T. Potter, *The Thetford Treasure* (London, 1983); Ear-rings: L. Allason-Jones, *The Ear-rings in Roman Britain* (Oxford, 1989); Beads: M. Guido, *The Glass Beads of the Prehistoric and Roman Periods in Britain and Ireland* (London, 1978); Brooches: J. Bayley and S. Butcher, *Roman Brooches in Britain: a technological and typological study based on the Richborough collection* (London, 2004); R. Hattatt, *A Visual Catalogue of Richard Hattatt's Ancient Brooches* (Oxford, 2000); gemstones: M. Henig, *A Corpus of Roman Engraved Gemstones from British Sites* (2 vols, Oxford, 1974); C. Johns, *The Snettisham Roman Jeweller's Hoard* (London, 1997). A general introduction to a wide range of artefacts is G. de la Bédoyère, *The Finds of Roman Britain* (London, 1989).

Coins and coin hoards: R. Reece, *Coinage in Roman Britain* (London, 1987); *Roman Coins from 140 sites in Britain* (London, 1991); 'British sites and their coins', *Antiquity* 67 (1993); 'Site finds in Roman Britain', *Britannia* 26 (1995); *The Coinage of Roman Britain* (Stroud, 2002); A. S. Robertson, *An Inventory of Romano-British Coin Hoards* (London, 2000).

Burial archaeology: R. F. J. Jones, 'Burial customs of Rome and the provinces', in J. S. Wacher, *The Roman World*, 2 vols (London, 1987); J. Pearce et al. (eds), *Burial in the Roman World* (Oxford, 2001); R. Philpott, *Burial Practices in Roman Britain: a survey of grave treatment and furnishing AD 43–410* (Oxford, 1991); R. Reece (ed.), *Burial in the Roman World* (London, 1977).

The percentage figures on different excavations are taken from R. Hingley, *Roman Officers and English Gentlemen* (London, 2000).

3 'NOTHING FOR US TO FEAR OR REJOICE AT.' BRITAIN, BRITONS AND THE ROMAN EMPIRE

For ancient sources on pre-Roman Britain, see A. L. F. Rivet and C. Smith, *The Place-Names of Roman Britain* (London, 1979). On the problems with the term 'Celts', see S. James, *The Atlantic Celts: ancient people or modern invention?* (London, 1999); J. Collis, *The Celts.*

Origins, myths and inventions (Stroud, 2003). On the European Iron Age context, J. Collis, *The European Iron Age* (London, 1984); B. W. Cunliffe (ed.), *Oxford Prehistory of Europe* (Oxford, 1994); M. Green (ed.), *The Celtic World* (London, 1995). For the outdated 'Belgic' migration models, see, for example, C. Hawkes, 'The British Iron Age', in S. S. Frere (ed.), *Problems of the Iron Age in Southern Britain* (London, 1961). The Ordnance Survey *Map of Southern Britain in the Iron Age* (Chessington, 1962) is old, but still useful.

The British Iron Age

The most detailed synthesis remains B. W. Cunliffe, *Iron Age Communities in Britain* (London, 1st edn, 1974; 2nd edn, 1979; 3rd edn, 1991; 4th edn, 2005); see also his *Iron Age Britain* (London, 1995). On the 'Wessex model', see, *inter alia*, G. Bersu, 'Excavations at Little Woodbury, Wiltshire', *PPS* 6 (1940); B. W. Cunliffe, *Danebury: an Iron Age hillfort in Hampshire. Vol. 6: A Hillfort Community in Perspective* (York, 1995); B. W. Cunliffe and D. Miles (eds), *Aspects of the Iron Age in Central Southern Britain* (Oxford, 1984); A. P. Fitzpatrick and E. Morris (eds), *The Iron Age in Wessex: recent work* (Salisbury, 1994); D. W. Harding, *The Iron Age in Lowland Britain* (London, 1974).

Criticisms of the Wessex model and works emphasizing regional diversity include T. Champion and J. Collis (eds), *The Iron Age in Britain and Ireland. Recent trends* (Sheffield, 1996); A. Gwilt and C. C. Haselgrove (eds), *Reconstructing Iron Age Societies* (Oxford, 1997); J. D. Hill, 'Re-thinking the Iron Age', *Scottish Archaeological Review* 6 (1989); J. D. Hill and C. Cumberpatch (eds), *Different Iron Ages: Studies in the archaeology of Iron Age Europe* (Oxford, 1995). See also the research agenda set out by C. C. Haselgrove et al., *Understanding the British Iron Age: an agenda for action* (Salisbury, 2001).

Recent succinct syntheses: J. Collis, 'The Iron Age', in B. Vyner (ed.), *Building on the Past: papers celebrating 150 years of the Royal Archaeological Institute* (London, 1995); C. C. Haselgrove, 'The Iron Age', in J. Hunter and I. Ralston (eds), *The Archaeology of Britain* (London, 1999); J. D. Hill, 'The Iron Age in Britain and Ireland: an overview', *Journal of World Prehistory* 9.1 (1995).

On iron metalwork and craft production, see B. W. Cunliffe, *The Celtic World* (London, 1997); S. James and V. Rigby, *Britain and the Celtic Iron Age* (London, 1997); I. M. Stead, *Celtic Art in Britain before the Roman Conquest* (London, 1985).

For East Yorkshire 'chariots', see I. M. Stead, *Iron Age Cemeteries in East Yorkshire* (London, 1991); and the Ferrybridge chariot, A. Boyle, 'Riding into history', *British Archaeology* (May 2004).

Caesar's British adventure

Caesar's campaigns and their background are well discussed in D. Braund, *Ruling Roman Britain* (London, 1996). G. Grainge, *The Roman Invasions of Britain* (Stroud, 2005) reviews the maritime dimension of various campaigns from Caesar to the later Roman period.

Britain between the (Roman) wars

On Iron Age coinage see notably, J. Creighton, *Coins and Power in Late Iron Age Britain* (Cambridge, 2000), which has much influenced my writing of this section; B. W. Cunliffe (ed.), *Coinage and Society in Britain and Gaul: some current problems* (London, 1981); C. C. Haselgrove, *Iron Age Coinage in South-east England: the archaeological context* (Oxford, 1987); R. Hobbs, *British Iron Age Coins in the British Museum* (London, 1996); M. Mays (ed.), *Celtic Coinage: Britain and beyond* (Oxford, 1992); R. D. Van Arsdell, *Celtic Coinage of Britain* (London, 1989).

Client kingdoms are explored at length by Creighton, *Coins and Power*; and more fancifully by M. Henig, *The Heirs of King Verica* (Stroud, 2002). On the Roman practice, see D. Braund, *Rome and the Friendly King* (London, 1984); *Ruling Roman Britain* (1996).

Trade with the Continent, see B. W. Cunliffe, 'Relations between Britain and Gaul in the first century BC and early first century AD', in S. Macready and F. H. Thompson (eds), *Cross-Channel Trade between Gaul and Britain in the Pre-Roman Iron Age* (London, 1984).

Cultural change pre-43, C. C. Haselgrove, 'Romanisation before the conquest: Gaulish precedents and British consequences', in T. F. C. Blagg and A. C. King (eds), *Military and Civilian in Roman Britain* (Oxford, 1984); 'The Romanisation of Belgic Gaul: archaeological perspectives', in T. F. C. Blagg and M. Millett, *The Early Roman Empire in the West* (Oxford, 1990).

The 'Peoples of Roman Britain' consists of an incomplete series of volumes on the archaeology of the main *civitates* identified by Rome. Although the territorial limits and the back-projection of these entities on to the late Iron Age are more problematic than the books generally acknowledge, the volumes are useful regional studies for both Iron Age and Roman periods: K. Branigan, *The Catuvellauni* (Gloucester, 1987); B. W. Cunliffe, *The Regni* (London, 1973); A. Detsicas, *The Cantiaci* (Gloucester, 1983); R. Dunnett, *The Trinovantes* (London, 1975); B. Hartley and L. Fitts, *The Brigantes* (Gloucester, 1988); N. Higham and B. Jones, *The Carvetii* (Gloucester, 1985); H. Ramm, *The Parisi* (London, 1978); M. Todd, *The Coritani* (revised edn, Gloucester, 1991); G. Webster, *The Cornovii* (revised edn, Gloucester, 1991).

Among key excavations, B. W. Cunliffe, *Danebury: an Iron Age hillfort in Hampshire* (6 vols, York, 1984–95); *The Danebury Environs Programme: the prehistory of a Wessex landscape* (Oxford, 2000–2003); *Hengistbury Head, Dorset* (Oxford, 1987); A. P. Fitzpatrick, *Archaeological Excavations on the Route of the A27 Westhampnett Bypass, West Sussex. Vol. 2: The Cemeteries* (Salisbury, 1997); J. Foster, *The Lexden Tumulus. A reappraisal of an Iron Age burial from Colchester, Essex* (Oxford, 1986); M. Fulford and J. Timby, *Late Iron Age and Roman Silchester: excavations of the site of the forum basilica, 1977, 1980–86* (London, 2000); C. C. Haselgrove and M. Millett, 'Verulamion reconsidered', in Gwilt and Haselgrove, *Reconstructing Iron Age Societies* (1997); C. F. C. Hawkes and P. Crummy, *Camulodunum 2* (Colchester, 1996); J. Manley and D. Rudkin, *Facing the Palace. Excavations in front of the Roman palace at Fishbourne* (Lewes, 2005); R. Niblett, *The Excavation of a Ceremonial Site at Folly Lane, Verulamium* (London, 1999); K. Parfitt, *Iron Age Burials from Mill Hill, Deal* (London, 1995); N. Sharples, *Maiden Castle: excavation and field survey 1985–86* (London, 1991); Stead, *Iron Age Cemeteries in East Yorkshire* (1991); 'The Snettisham treasure: excavations in 1990', *Antiquity* 65 (1991); I. M. Stead and V. Rigby, *Baldock: the excavation of a Roman and pre-Roman settlement* (London, 1986); I. M. Stead and V. Rigby, *Verulamium. The King Harry Lane site* (London, 1989); I. M. Stead et al., *Lindow Man. The body in the bog* (London, 1986); G. J. Wainwright, *Gussage All Saints: an Iron Age settlement in Dorset* (London, 1979). Cunliffe, *Iron Age Communities* (2005) contains an appendix listing bibliographical references for principal Iron Age sites.

Structured ritual deposition is well introduced in J. D. Hill, *Ritual and Rubbish in the Iron Age of Wessex* (Oxford, 1995); for its possible relevance to Roman period hoards, see the debate between M. Millett and C. Johns, in *TRAC* 4 (1995).

Beyond the client kingdoms

The picture has been transformed since early pioneering studies, such as S. S. Frere (ed.), *The Iron Age in Lowland Britain* (London, 1978); A. L. F. Rivet (ed.), *The Iron Age in Northern Britain* (Edinburgh, 1966); C. Thomas, *The Iron Age in the Irish Sea Province* (London, 1972). Cunliffe's regional survey in *Iron Age Communities* remains a key starting point; while C. C. Haselgrove, 'Iron Age societies in central Britain: retrospect and prospect', and other papers in B. Bevan, *Northern Exposure: interpretative devolution and the Iron Age in Britain* (Leicester 1999), bring out the profound differences between the south-eastern kingdoms and the peripheral peoples of central, north and west Britain. Other regional reviews include, P. Clay, *The Prehistory of the East Midlands Claylands* (Leicester, 2002);

J. Davies and T. Williamson (eds), *Land of the Iceni: the Iron Age in northern East Anglia* (Norwich, 1999); D. W. Harding, *The Iron Age in Northern Britain* (London, 2004); R. Hingley, 'Society in Scotland from 700 BC to AD 200', *PSAS* 122 (1992); F. Lynch et al., *Prehistoric Wales* (Stroud, 2000); B. Raftery (ed.), *Sites and Sights of the Iron Age* (Oxford, 1996). See further, references for Chapters 13–14.

On Dobunnic coinage and territory, R. D. van Arsdell, *The Coinage of the Dobunni. Money supply and coin circulation in Dobunnic territory* (Oxford, 1994). On the east Leicestershire hoard, see V. Priest et al., 'Iron Age gold from Leicestershire', *Current Archaeology* 188 (2003).

4   THE IRON FIST: CONQUEST (43–83) AND AFTERMATH

For general accounts of the Roman army, see Y. Le Bohec, *The Imperial Roman Army* (London, 1994); A. Goldsworthy, *Roman Warfare* (London, 2000); for sources, B. Campbell, *The Roman Army 31 BC–AD 337. A sourcebook* (London, 1994). The history of the conquest is well discussed by S. S. Frere, *Britannia: A history of Roman Britain* (3rd edn, London, 1987) and P. Salway, *Roman Britain* (Oxford, 1981); with graphic illustrations in B. Jones and D. Mattingly, *Atlas of Roman Britain* (reprint, Oxford, 2002). See also D. Braund, *Ruling Roman Britain* (London, 1996) for a very source-led account. Marching camps are illustrated in S. S. Frere and J. K. S. St Joseph, *Roman Britain from the Air* (Cambridge, 1983); H. Welfare and V. G. Swann, *Roman Camps in England. The field archaeology* (London, 1995). For other important evidence of the conduct of the army on campaign, see F. Lepper and S. S. Frere, *Trajan's Column* (Gloucester, 1988). P. Wells, *The Battle that Stopped Rome* (New York, 2003) provides a vivid insight into the clash of the Roman and northern European military traditions, in the context of the famous defeat of Varus in the Teutoberg forest.

The return of the Romans

On the events of 43, favouring landing in Kent see S. S. Frere and M. Fulford, 'The Roman invasion of AD 43', *Britannia* 32 (2001); for Hampshire, D. G. Bird, 'The Claudian invasion reconsidered', *OJA* 19.1 (2000); J. F. Manley, *The Roman Invasion of Britain: a reassessment* (Stroud, 2002); E. Sauer, 'The Roman invasion of Britain (AD 43) in imperial perspective: a response to Frere and Fulford', *OJA* 21.4 (2002). On the Claudian conquest phase more generally, M. Todd, 'The Claudian conquest and its consequences', in M. Todd (ed.), *A Companion to Roman Britain* (Oxford, 2004); for older views see J. Wacher, *The Coming of Rome* (London, 1979); G. Webster, *The Roman Invasion of Britain* (London, 1980).

Continued resistance and rebellions 47–69

C. J. Arnold and J. L. Davies, *Roman and Early Medieval Wales* (Stroud, 2000); W. Manning, 'The conquest of Wales', in Todd, *Companion* (2004); G. Webster, *Rome Against Caratacus. The Roman Campaigns in Britain AD 48–58* (London, 1981).

On Boudica, R. Hingley and C. Unwin, *Boudica. Iron Age Warrior Queen* (London, 2005); note also, G. de la Bédoyère, *Defying Rome. The rebels of Roman Britain* (Stroud, 2003); G. Webster, *Boudica: the British revolt against Rome AD 60* (London, 1978).

Civil war and the Flavian advance

Arnold and Davies, *Roman and Early Medieval Wales* (2002); A. R. Birley, 'Britain 71–105: advance and retrenchment', in L. de Ligt et al. (eds), *Roman Rule and Civic Life: local and regional perspectives* (Amsterdam, 2004); D. J. Breeze, *Roman Scotland* (London, 1996); W. S. Hanson, *Agricola and the Conquest of the North* (London, 1987); G. Maxwell, *A Battle Lost: Romans and Caledonians at Mons Graupius* (Edinburgh, 1990); 'The Roman penetration of the north in the late first century AD', in Todd, *Companion* (2004), on marching camp evidence.

The aftermath of conquest

S. S. Frere, 'M. Maenius Agrippa, the expeditio Britannica and Maryport', *Britannia* 31 (2000); N. Hodgson, 'Were there two Antonine occupations of Scotland?', *Britannia* 26 (1995); A. R. Birley, *The African Emperor. Septimius Severus* (London, 1988).

D. B. Campbell, 'The Roman siege at Burnswark', *Britannia* 34 (2003) argues against the view that these were practice siege works.

5   *BRITANNIA PERDOMITA*: THE GARRISONING OF THE PROVINCES

See also bibliography for Chapter 6. On general issues of troop deployment, see M. Bishop, 'Praesidium: social, military and logistical aspects of the Roman army's provincial distribution during the early Principate', in A. Goldsworthy and I. Haynes, *The Roman Army as a Community* (Portsmonth, RI, 1999). A critical view of the strengths and weaknesses of current knowledge of the Roman army is provided by S. James, 'Writing the legions: the development and future of Roman military studies in Britain', *Arch. J.* 159 (2002).

The changing nature of military dispositions

Overall summaries, W. S. Hanson, 'Roman Britain. The military dimension', in J. Hunter and I. Ralston (eds), *The Archaeology of Britain* (London, 1999); B. Jones and D. Mattingly, *An Atlas of Roman Britain* (reprint, Oxford, 2002).

General studies of Roman forts and fortresses in Britain, P. Bidwell, *Roman Forts in Britain* (London, 1997); A. Johnson, *Roman Forts* (London, 1983). On the legions in Britain, see R. Brewer (ed.), *Roman Fortresses and their Legions* (London, 2000).

The regional summaries below highlight useful overviews and key excavations/sites.

South-east and south-west Britain

P. Crummy, *City of Victory: the story of Colchester – Britain's first Roman town* (Colchester, 1997); S. S. Frere and J. K. S. St Joseph, *Roman Britain from the Air* (Cambridge, 1983); B. J. Philp, *Roman Forts of the Classis Britannica at Dover* (Dover, 1981). V. A. Maxfield, 'The Roman military occupation of south-west England: further light and fresh problems', in W. S. Hanson and L. Keppie (eds), *Roman Frontier Studies 1979* (Oxford, 1980); 'Pre-Flavian forts and their garrisons', *Britannia* 17 (1986); 'The Roman army', in R. Kain and W. Ravenhill, *Historical Atlas of South-west England* (Exeter, 1999); E. Sauer, 'Alchester, a Claudian vexillation fortress near the western boundary of the Catuvellauni: new light on the Roman invasion of Britain', *Arch. J.* 157 (2000); M. Todd, 'Oppida and the Roman army: a review of recent evidence', *OJA* 4.2 (1985); *The Coritani* (1991); cf. M. Jones, *Roman Lincoln* (Stroud, 2002).

The Marches and Wales

H. R. Hurst, *Kingsholm* (Gloucester, 1985). D. J. P. Mason, *Roman Chester: City of the Eagles* (Stroud, 2001). C. J. Arnold and J. L. Davies, *Roman and Early Medieval Wales* (Stroud, 2002); B. C. Burnham and J. L. Davies, *Conquest, Coexistence and Change* (Lampeter, 1990); J. L. Davies, 'Soldiers, peasants and markets in Wales and the Marches', in T. F. C. Blagg and A. C. King (eds), *Military and Civilian in Roman Britain* (Oxford, 1984); 'Military deployment in Wales and the Marches from Pius to Theodosius', in V. A. Maxfield and B. Dobson, *Roman Frontier Studies 1989* (Exeter, 1991); 'Soldier and civilian in Wales', in M. Todd (ed.), *Companion to Roman Britain* (Oxford, 2004); V. E. Nash-Williams, *The Roman Frontier in Wales* (2nd edn, with M. Jarrett (ed.), Cardiff, 1969).

Specific sites: G. Boon, *The Legionary Fortress at Caerleon-Isca* (Caerphilly, 1987); J. Casey et al., *Excavations at Segontium (Caernarfon) Roman Fort* (London, 1993); W. Manning, *Report on the Excavations at Usk* (Cardiff, 1981/1989); A. G. Marvell and H. S. Owen-John, *Leucarum: excavations at the Roman auxiliary fort at Loughor, W. Glamorgan, 1982–4 and 1987–8* (London, 1997); D. Zienkiewicz, *The Legionary Fortress Baths* (Cardiff, 1986).

Northern England and Scotland

D. J. Breeze, 'Agricola the builder', *Scottish Archaeological Forum* 12 (1980); *The Northern Frontiers of Roman Britain* (London, 1982); 'The frontier in Britain, 1979–1983', in M. Planck (ed.), *Studien zur Militargrenzen Roms III* (Stuttgart, 1986); *Roman Scotland* (London, 1996); W. S. Hanson, *Agricola and the Conquest of the North* (London, 1987); 'Scotland and the northern frontier: second to fourth centuries AD', in Todd, *Companion* (2004); N. Hodgson, 'Were there two Antonine occupations of Scotland?', *Britannia* 26 (1995); R. Newman, *The Archaeology of Lancashire. Present state and future priorities* (Lancaster, 1996).

Specific sites: P. Bidwell, *The Roman Fort at Vindolanda* (London, 1985); P. Bidwell and S. Speak, *Excavations at South Shields Roman Fort* (Newcastle, 1994); R. Birley, *Vindolanda Research Reports I, The Early Wooden Forts* (Hexham, 1994); M. Bishop and J. Dore, *Corbridge. Excavations of the Roman Fort and Town* (London, 1989); K. Buxton and C. Howard-Davis, *Brementenacum. Excavations at Roman Ribchester 1980, 1989–1990* (Lancaster, 2000); S. S. Frere and J. Wilkes, *Strageath. Excavations within the Roman fort* (London, 1989); L. F. Pitts and J. K. St Joseph, *Inchtuthil: the Roman legionary fortress excavations 1952–65* (Gloucester, 1985).

Building requirements: E. Shirley, *Building a Roman Legionary Fortress* (Stroud, 2001).

The Roman linear frontiers: Hadrian's Wall and the Antonine Wall

General works on Roman frontiers include, H. Elton, *Frontiers of the Roman Empire* (London, 1996); E. N. Luttwak, *The Grand Strategy of the Roman Empire* (Baltimore, 1976); J. Wacher (ed.), *The Roman World* (London, 1987) (good summaries of Roman frontiers around the empire); C. R. Whittaker, *The Frontiers of the Roman Empire. A social and economic study* (Baltimore, 1994).

For Hadrian's Wall: P. Bidwell (ed.), *Hadrian's Wall 1989–1999* (Carlisle, 1999); D. J. Breeze and B. Dobson, *Hadrian's Wall* (4th edn, London, 2000); J. Crow, 'The northern frontier of Britain from Trajan to Antoninus Pius: Roman builders and native Britons', in Todd, *Companion* (2004); G. de la Bédoyère, *Hadrian's Wall* (Stroud, 1998); C. M. Daniels, *Handbook to the Roman Wall* (13th edn, Newcastle, 1978); S. Johnson, *Hadrian's Wall* (London, 1989); G. D. B. Jones and D. Woolliscroft, *Hadrian's Wall from the Air* (Stroud, 2001); D. J. A. Taylor, *The Forts on Hadrian's Wall. A comparative analysis of the form and construction of some buildings* (Oxford, 2000); R. J. A. Wilson and I. Caruana (eds), *Romans on the Solway* (Kendal, 2004); R. Woodside and J. Crow, *Hadrian's Wall: a historic landscape* (London, 1999). Construction: P. R. Hill, *The Construction of Hadrian's Wall*

(Oxford, 2004); R. Kendal, 'Transport logistics associated with the building of Hadrian's Wall', *Britannia* 27 (1996).

For the Antonine Wall: W. S. Hanson and G. S. Maxwell, *Rome's North West Frontier: the Antonine Wall* (Edinburgh, 1983); L. J. F. Keppie, 'The Antonine Wall 1960–1980', *Britannia* 13 (1982); A. S. Robertson, *The Antonine Wall* (3rd edn, Glasgow, 1979).

Inside Roman forts

Complementary accounts of the *Vindolanda* discoveries are to be found in A. R. Birley, *Garrison Life at Vindolanda. A band of brothers* (Stroud, 2003); A. K. Bowman, *Life and Letters on the Roman Frontier. Vindolanda and its people* (2nd edn, London, 2003). On the internal layout, see, Frere and St Joseph, *Roman Britain from the Air* (1983); M. Hassall, 'The internal planning of Roman auxiliary forts', in B. R. Hartley and J. S. Wacher (eds), *Rome and her Northern Provinces* (Gloucester, 1983); N. Hodgson and P. Bidwell, 'Auxiliary barracks in a new light: recent discoveries on Hadrian's Wall', *Britannia* 35 (2004). On defences, M. J. Jones, *Roman Fort Defences to AD 117* (Oxford, 1975); J. Lander, *Roman Stone Fortifications. Variation and change from the first century AD to the fourth* (Oxford, 1984).

On the Carlisle tablets, see R. S. O. Tomlin, 'Roman manuscripts from Carlisle: the ink writing tablets', *Britannia* 29 (1998); 'The missing lances, or making the machine work', in Goldsworthy and Haynes, *The Roman Army as a Community* (1999).

6   THE COMMUNITY OF SOLDIERS

General studies of the Roman army in Britain include, G. de la Bédoyère, *Eagles over Britannia. The Roman army in Britain* (Stroud, 2001); P. A. Holder, *The Roman Army in Britain* (London, 1982); M. G. Jarrett, 'Non-legionary troops in Roman Britain: part one, the units', *Britannia* 25 (1994). On the British legions see, R. J. Brewer (ed.), *Roman Fortresses and their Legions* (Cardiff, 2000); L. Keppie, in Y. Le Bohec, *Les légions de Rome sous le Haut-Empire* (2 vols, Lyon, 2000). On the auxiliaries, G. L. Cheeseman, *The Auxilia of the Roman Imperial Army* (Oxford, 1914); K. R. Dixon and P. Southern, *The Roman Cavalry from the First to the Third Century AD (London, 1992); P. A. Holder, Studies in the Auxilia of the Roman Army from Augustus to Trajan* (Oxford, 1980); J. Spaul, *Ala. The auxiliary cavalry units of the pre-Diocletianic imperial Roman army* (Aldershot, 1994); *Cohors. The evidence for and a short history of the auxiliary infantry units of the imperial Roman army* (Oxford, 2000). On recruitment, B. Dobson and J. C. Mann, 'The Roman army in Britain and Britons in the Roman army', *Britannia* 4 (1973).

On the idea of the community of soldiers, see notably, A. Goldsworthy and I. Haynes, *The Roman Army as a Community* (Portsmouth, RI, 1999); S. James, 'The community of soldiers: a major identity and centre of power in the Roman empire', in *TRAC* 8 (Oxford, 1999). Compare also, T. F. C. Blagg and A. C. King (eds), *Military and Civilian in Roman Britain. Cultural relationships in a frontier province* (Oxford, 1984); V. A. Maxfield, *Soldier and Civilian: life beyond the ramparts. The Eighth Annual Caerleon Lecture* (Cardiff, 1995). On conditions of military service, see R. W. Davies, *Service in the Roman Army* (Edinburgh, 1985); G. R. Watson, *The Roman Soldier* (London, 1969). On the political roles, B. Rankov, 'The governor's men: the officium consularis in provincial administration', in Goldsworthy and Haynes, *The Roman Army as a Community* (1999).

Civilians and the military community

On '*vici*'/garrison communities, see C. S. Somner, *The Military Vici in Roman Britain* (Oxford, 1984); 'The Roman army in SW Germany as an instrument of colonisation: the relationship of forts to military and civilian vici', in Goldsworthy and Haynes, *The Roman*

Army as a Community (1999); J. L. Davies, 'Military vici: recent research and its significance', in B. C. Burnham and J. L. Davies, *Conquest, Coexistence and Change* (Lampeter, 1990). For specific examples, see J. A. Biggins and D. J. A. Taylor, 'Survey of the Roman fort and settlement at Birdoswald', *Britannia* 30 (1999) and *Britannia* 35 (2004). At the upper end, the settlements resemble towns, M. Bishop and J. Dore, *Corbridge. Excavations of the Roman fort and town* (London, 1989); P. Wilson, *Cataractonium. Roman Catterick and its hinterland. Excavations and research 1958–1997, Parts 1 and 2* (York, 2002).

On the civil community in northern Britain at large, see P. Salway, *The Frontier People of Roman Britain* (Cambridge, 1965); B. Hartley and L. Fitts, *The Brigantes* (Gloucester, 1988); N. Higham and B. Jones, *The Carvetii* (Gloucester, 1985). For the definitive publication of the *Vindolanda* tablets, see references cited under Chapter 2.

The best general accounts of the military community at *Vindolanda* are, A. R. Birley, *Garrison Life at Vindolanda. A band of brothers* (Stroud, 2003); A. K. Bowman, *Life and Letters on the Roman Frontier. Vindolanda and its people* (London, 2003). The *Anavionenses* census is discussed in detail by A. R. Birley, 'The Anavionenses', in N. Higham (ed.), *Archaeology of the Roman Empire. A tribute to the life and works of Professor Barri Jones* (Oxford, 2001).

On women on the northern frontier, see L. Allason-Jones, *Women in Roman Britain* (London, 1989); 'Women and the Roman army in Britain', in Goldsworthy and Haynes, *The Roman Army as a Community* (1999). On women inside barracks, C. van Driel-Murray, 'Gender in question', in *TRAC* 2 (Aldershot, 1995).

The sexual servicing of garrisons under other imperial regimes is considered by R. Hyam, *Empire and Sexuality. The British experience* (Manchester, 1990).

Members of the community of soldiers

This section made extensive use of *RIB* I and II, with particular support from A. R. Birley, *The People of Roman Britain* (1979), *The Fasti of Roman Britain* (Oxford, 1981) and *The Roman Government of Britain* (Oxford, 2005). Note also, H. Devijver, *The Equestrian Officers of the Roman Army* (Stuttgart, 1992).

North Africans in the British garrison, V. Swann, 'The twentieth legion and the history of the Antonine Wall reconsidered', *PSAS* 129 (1999).

On discharge diplomas relating to the *auxilia*, *RIB* II.1 (with further references); patterns of veteran settlement, J. C. Mann, 'The settlement of veterans discharged from auxiliary units stationed in Britain', *Britannia* 33 (2002); M. Roxan, 'Settlement of veterans of the auxilia – a preliminary study', in W. Groenman-van Waateringe et al. (eds), *Roman Frontier Studies 1995* (Oxford, 1997).

7   THE FASHIONING OF THE MILITARY IDENTITY

Key readings include, I. Haynes, 'Introduction: the Roman army as a community', in A. Goldsworthy and I. Haynes, *The Roman Army as a Community* (Portsmouth, RI, 1999); A. Gardner, 'Military identities in Roman Britain', *OJA* 18.4 (1999); S. James, 'Soldiers and civilians: identity and interaction in Roman Britain', in S. James and M. Millett, *Britons and Romans* (York, 2001). On the material culture of the army, L. Allason-Jones, 'Material culture and identity', in James and Millett, *Britons and Romans* (2001); I. Haynes, 'Military service and cultural identity in the auxilia', in Goldsworthy and Haynes, *The Roman Army as a Community* (1999).

Language and literacy: the epigraphic habit

Vindolanda material, see sources referenced above (pp. 546–7), plus J. N. Adams, 'The language of the Vindolanda writing tablets: an interim report', *JRS* 85 (1995). Finds from *Vindolanda*, see E. Birley et al., *Vindolanda Research Reports. Vol. II: Reports on the Auxiliaries, the Writing Tablets, Inscriptions, Brands and Graffiti* (Hexham, 1993); C. van Driel-Murray et al., *Vindolanda Research Reports. Vol. III: Reports on Leather, Textiles, Environmental Evidence and Dendrochronology* (Hexham, 1993). Note also, J. C. Mann, 'Epigraphic consciousness', *JRS* 75 (1985); J. Evans, 'Graffiti: evidence of literacy and pottery use in Roman Britain', *Arch. J.* 144 (1987); M. Hassall, 'Epigraphy and the Roman army in Britain', in T. F. C. Blagg and A. C. King (eds), *Military and Civilian in Roman Britain* (Oxford, 1984); M. E. Raybould, *A Study of Inscribed Material from Roman Britain* (Oxford, 1999). On commemorative tombstones, see A. C. Anderson, *Roman Military Tombstones* (Princes Risborough, 1984); V. Hope, 'Words and pictures: the interpretation of Romano-British tombstones', *Britannia* 28 (1997).

Cultural and social traits

There is much military sculpture in the British *CSIR* volumes (see pp. 542–3 above); also L. Keppie, *Roman Inscribed and Sculpted Stones in the Hunterian Museum University of Glasgow* (London, 1998); on patronage, see M. Henig, 'Artistic patronage and the Roman military community', in Goldsworthy and Haynes, *The Roman Army as a Community* (1999). Military dress is well discussed from a variety of angles in M. Bishop and J. C. Coulston, *Roman Military Equipment from the Punic Wars to the Fall of Rome* (2nd edn, Oxford, 2005); A. Croom, *Roman Clothing and Fashion* (Stroud, 2002); S. James, *Excavations at Dura-Europus, Final Report VII, the Arms and Armour and other Military Equipment* (London, 2004); J. P. Wild, 'Textiles and dress', in M. Todd (ed.), *A Companion to Roman Britain* (Oxford, 2004).

On jewellery and personal ornament, see A. Croom, 'Personal ornament', in Todd, *Companion* (2004); M. Henig, *A Corpus of Roman Engraved Gemstones* (Oxford, 1974); C. Johns, *The Jewellery of Roman Britain* (London, 1996). For initial publication of the Ilam *trulla*, see *Britannia* 35 (2004). For lighting equipment from military sites, see H. Eckardt, *Illuminating Roman Britain* (Montagnac, 2002).

The outstanding analyses of material cultural assemblages at forts/garrison settlements are H. E. M. Cool and C. Philo, *Roman Castleford. Vol. 1: The Small Finds* (Wakefield, 1998); H. E. M. Cool et al., *Finds from the Fortress. The Archaeology of York 10* (York, 1995); H. E. M. Cool in P. Wilson, *Cataractonium. Roman Catterick and its hinterland. Excavations and research 1958–1997, Part 2* (York, 2002). Also asking interesting questions about the interpretation of material culture at a military site, S. Clarke, 'Abandonment, rubbish disposal and special deposits at Newstead', in *TRAC 6* (1997); 'In search of a different Roman period: the finds assemblage at the Newstead military complex', in *TRAC 9* (2000); A. Gardner, 'Identities in the late Roman army: material and textual perspectives', *TRAC* 10 (2001).

Religion

There is a tendency to conflate the diverse religious practices of military and civil communities in Britain, typified by G. de la Bédoyère, *Gods with Thunderbolts. Religion in Roman Britain* (Stroud, 2002); M. Henig, *Religion in Roman Britain* (London, 1984); 'Roman religion and culture in Britain', in Todd, *Companion* (2004). Similarly, work attempting to reconstruct native British religion via military evidence is flawed; M. Green, *The Gods of the Celts* (Gloucester, 1986); M. Aldhouse-Green, 'Gallo-British deities and their shrines', in Todd, *Companion* (2004). See now, D. Mattingly, 'Being Roman. Expressing identity in a provincial setting', *JRA* 17 (2004).

For focused epigraphic studies of military practice and cults followed, see M. Aldhouse-Green and M. Raybould, 'Deities with Gallo-British names recorded in inscriptions from Roman Britain', *Studia Celtica* 33 (1999); E. Birley, 'The deities of Roman Britain', in *ANRW* II.18, *Religion, Principat* (1986); G. L. Irby-Massie, *Military Religion in Roman Britain* (Brill, 1999); A. Zoll, 'A view through inscriptions: the epigraphic evidence for religion at Hadrian's Wall', in J. Metzler et al., *Integration in the Early Roman West* (Luxembourg, 1995); 'Patterns of worship in Roman Britain: double named deities in context', in *TRAC* 4 (1995).

On the colonial context of *interpretatio*, compelling arguments have been advanced by J. Webster, 'Translation and subjection: interpretatio and the Celtic gods', in J. D. Hill and C. Cumberpatch (eds), *Different Iron Ages* (Oxford, 1995); 'Interpretatio: Roman word power and the Celtic gods', *Britannia* 26 (1995); 'A negotiated syncretism: readings on the development of Romano-Celtic religion', in D. Mattingly (ed.), *Dialogues in Roman Imperialism* (Portsmouth, RI, 1997). Cf. G. Webster, 'What the Britons required from the gods as seen through the pairing of Roman and Celtic deities and the character of votive offerings', in M. Henig and A. King, *Pagan Gods and Shrines of the Roman Empire* (Oxford, 1986).

For votive assemblages and religious artefacts, see L. Allason-Jones and B. McKay, *Coventina's Well* (Gloucester, 1985); M. Green, *Small Cult Objects from the Military Areas in Roman Britain* (Oxford, 1978).

Diet and consumption

Feeding the army: A. R. Birley, *Garrison Life at Vindolanda* (Stroud, 2003); R. W. Davies, 'The Roman military diet', *Britannia* 2 (1971); B. A. Knights et al., 'Evidence concerning the Roman military diet at Bearsden, Scotland in the 2nd century AD', *Journal of Archaeological Science* 10 (1983); J. Pearce, 'Food as substance and symbol in the Roman army: a case study from Vindolanda', in P. Freeman et al. (eds), *Limes XVIII* (Oxford, 2002). Archaeozoological studies, A. Grant, 'Domestic animals and their uses', in Todd, *Companion* (2004); A. King, 'Animal bones and the dietary identity of military and civilian groups in Roman Britain, Germany and Gaul', in Blagg and King, *Military and Civilian in Roman Britain* (1984); 'Animals and the Roman army: the evidence of animal bones', in Goldsworthy and Haynes, *The Roman Army as a Community* (1999); 'The Romanization of diet in the western empire: comparative archaeozoological studies', in S. Keay and N. Terrenato (eds), *Italy and the West* (Oxford, 2001); S. Stallibrass, 'Cattle, culture, status and soldiers in northern England', *TRAC* 9 (2000).

Deviations from the archetypal military identity

These are superbly illustrated in H. E. M. Cool, *The Roman Cemetery at Brougham* (London, 2004).

8 *DE EXCIDIO BRITANNIAE*: DECLINE AND FALL?

Among general surveys of the late Roman empire, see the excellent account by D. S. Potter, *The Roman Empire at Bay AD 180–395* (London, 2004). A. H. M. Jones, *The Later Roman Empire 284–602* (2 vols, Oxford, 1964) remains indispensable, despite its lack of attention to the archaeological record. The best of the general accounts of late Roman Britain are S. Esmonde Cleary, *The Ending of Roman Britain* (London, 1989); and S. Johnson, *Later Roman Britain* (St Albans, 1978).

Third-century crisis: A. C. King and M. Henig (eds), *The Roman West in the Third Century: contributions from archaeology and history* (Oxford, 1981); C. Witschel, 'Re-evaluating the

Roman west in the 3rd c. A.D.', *JRA* 17 (2004). On the Tetrarchy, S. Williams, *Diocletian and the Roman Recovery* (London, 1985). On Ammianus and the fourth century, J. Matthews, *The Roman Empire of Ammianus* (London, 1989). On Germanization, see P. Wells, *The Barbarians Speak* (Princeton, 1999). On the breakaway state of Carausius and Allectus, P. J. Casey, *Carausius and Allectus. The British usurpers* (London, 1994); H. P. G. Williams, *Carausius: a consideration of the historical, archaeological and numismatic aspects of his reign* (Oxford, 2003).

Changes to military structure in the late empire

P. J. Casey, *The Legions in the Later Roman Empire* (Cardiff, 1991); P. A. Holder, *The Roman Army in Britain* (London, 1982); S. James, 'Britain and the late Roman army', in T. F. C. Blagg and A. C. King (eds), *Military and Civilian in Roman Britain* (Oxford, 1984); P. Southern, 'The army in late Roman Britain', in M. Todd, *A Companion to Roman Britain*, (Oxford, 2004); P. Southern and K. Dixon, *The Late Roman Army* (London, 1996). Note also relevant sections of B. Campbell, *The Roman Army 31 BC–AD 337* (London, 1994). For the *Notitia*, see M. Hassall, 'Britain in the Notitia', in R. Goodburn and P. Bartholomew (eds), *Aspects of the Notitia Dignitatum* (Oxford, 1976); N. Hodgson, 'The Notitia Dignitatum and the later Roman garrison of Britain', in V. A. Maxfield and B. Dobson, *Roman Frontier Studies 1989* (Exeter, 1991).

Changes to Roman fortifications: S. Johnson, *Late Roman Fortifications* (London, 1983); J. Lander, *Roman Stone Fortifications. Variation and change from the first century AD to the fourth* (Oxford, 1984); D. A. Welsby, *The Roman Military Defence of the British Province in its Later Phases* (Oxford, 1982). The Saxon Shore defences are well covered by S. Johnson, *The Roman Forts of the Saxon Shore* (London, 1979); D. E. Johnston (ed.), *The Saxon Shore* (London, 1977); V. A. Maxfield, *The Saxon Shore* (Exeter, 1989). A. Pearson, *The Roman Shore Forts. Coastal defences of southern Britain* (Stroud, 2002), asks new questions about the materials, logistics and programme of construction.

Wales: P. J. Casey, 'Coin evidence and the end of Roman Wales', *Arch. J.* 146 (1989); J. L. Davies, 'Military deployment in Wales and the Marches from Pius to Theodosius', in Maxfield and Dobson, *Roman Frontier Studies 1989* (1991). Northern frontier: D. J. Breeze, *The Northern Frontiers of Roman Britain* (London, 1982); D. J. Breeze and B. Dobson, *Hadrian's Wall* (4th edn, London, 2000); W. S. Hanson, 'Scotland and the northern frontier: second to fourth centuries AD', in Todd, *Companion* (2004). Chalet barracks are dispensed with by N. Hodgson and P. Bidwell, 'Auxiliary barracks in a new light: recent discoveries on Hadrian's Wall', *Britannia* 35 (2004).

Changes to the military community and military identity

Arms and armour: M. Bishop and J. C. Coulston, *Roman Military Equipment* (2nd edn, Oxford, 2005); S. James, *Excavations at Dura-Europos, Final Report VII. The Arms and Armour and other Military Equipment* (London, 2004).

Other so-called military metalwork is well reviewed in its European context by E. Swift, *The End of the Western Roman Empire: an archaeological investigation* (Stroud, 2000); *Regionality in Dress Accessories in the Late Roman West* (Montagnac, 2000).

Birdoswald: T. Wilmott, *Birdoswald: excavations of a Roman fort on Hadrian's Wall and its successor settlements: 1987–92* (London, 1998).

Kipling's poem is from C. R. Fletcher and R. Kipling, *A School History of England* (Oxford, 1911).

9 *FORMA URBIS*: THE DEVELOPMENT OF TOWNS

Proto-urbanism and urbanization in the Roman empire, B. W. Cunliffe and T. Rowley (eds), *Oppida: the beginnings of urbanization in barbarian Europe* (Oxford, 1976); F. Grew and B. Hobley (eds), *Roman Urban Topography in Britain and the Western Empire* (London, 1985); W. S. Hanson, 'Administration, urbanisation and acculturation in the Roman west', in D. Braund (ed.), *The Administration of the Roman Empire 241 BC–AD 193* (Exeter, 1988); J. C. Mann, *Britain and the Roman Empire* (Aldershot, 1996).

Study of Roman urbanization in Britain rests on the magisterial account of J. Wacher, *The Towns of Roman Britain* (2nd edn, London, 1995). Other useful overviews or general surveys include, R. G. Collingwood and I. A. Richmond, *The Archaeology of Roman Britain* (London, 1969); G. de la Bédoyère, *The Towns of Roman Britain* (London, 1992); A. S. Esmonde Cleary, 'Roman Britain. Civil and rural society', in J. Hunter and I. Ralston (eds), *The Archaeology of Britain* (London, 1999); S. Greep (ed.), *Roman Towns: the Wheeler inheritance. A review of 50 years' research* (York, 1993); M. J. Jones, 'Cities and urban life', in M. Todd, *A Companion to Roman Britain* (Oxford, 2004); R. F. J. Jones, 'The urbanisation of Roman Britain', in R. F. J. Jones (ed.), *Roman Britain: recent trends* (Sheffield, 1991); P. Ottaway, *Archaeology in British Towns from the Emperor Claudius to the Black Death* (London, 1992); A. L. F. Rivet, *Town and Country in Roman Britain* (2nd edn, London, 1964); J. S. Wacher (ed.), *The Civitas Capitals of Roman Britain* (Leicester, 1966); P. Wilson (ed.), *The Archaeology of Roman Towns. Studies in honour of John S. Wacher* (Oxford, 2003).

New agendas are reflected in B. C. Burnham et al., 'Themes for urban research c.100 BC to AD 200' and M. Millett, 'Approaches to urban societies', both in S. James and M. Millett, *Britons and Romans* (York, 2001). J. Creighton's *Britannia. The Creation of a Roman Province* (London, 2006) provides a fascinating rethink of the early stages of urbanization.

Roads and the *cursus publicus*: E. W. Black, *Cursus Publicus. The infrastructure of government in Roman Britain* (Oxford, 1995); R. Chevallier, *Roman Roads* (London, 1976); H. Davies, *Roman Roads in Britain* (Stroud, 2002); B. Jones and D. Mattingly, *An Atlas of Roman Britain* (reprint, Oxford, 2002); I. Margary, *Roman Roads in Britain* (London, 1967).

The function of Roman towns

L. de Ligt et al. (eds), *Roman Rule and Civic Life: local and regional perspectives* (Amsterdam, 2004); E. Fentress (ed.), *Romanization and the City: creation, dynamics and failures* (Portsmouth, RI, 2000).

Origins and early development

Compare the views of P. Salway, 'Geography and the growth of towns, with special reference to Britain', in Grew and Hobley (eds), *Roman Urban Topography* (1985) – arguing for deliberate foundations, with M. Millett, *The Romanization of Britain* (Cambridge, 1990) – stressing native agency; see also A. S. Esmonde Cleary, 'The origins of towns in Roman Britain. The contributions of Romans and Britons', in A. Rodriguez Colmenero, *Los Orígenes de la Ciudad en el Noroeste Hispánico* (San Marcos, 1998); P. Crummy, 'The origins of some major Romano-British towns', *Britannia* 13 (1982); H. Hurst (ed.), *The Coloniae of Roman Britain: New studies and a review* (Portsmouth, RI, 1999); M. Todd, 'The early cities', in M. Todd (ed.), *Research on Roman Britain: 1960–89* (London, 1989); G. Webster (ed.), *Fortress into City: the consolidation of Roman Britain* (London, 1988).

Architecture: T. Blagg, 'Art and architecture', in Todd, *Research on Roman Britain* (1989);

'Buildings', in Jones, *Roman Britain: recent trends* (1991); G. de la Bédoyère, *The Buildings of Roman Britain* (London, 1991); P. J. Drury, *Structural Reconstruction* (Oxford, 1982); P. Johnson and I. Haynes, *Architecture in Roman Britain* (London, 1996); M. J. Jones, 'Lincoln and the British fora in context', in Hurst (ed.), *The Coloniae of Roman Britain* (1999); D. Perring, *The Roman House in Britain* (London, 2002).

Water supply: A. Burgers, *The Water Supplies and Related Structures of Roman Britain* (Oxford, 2001); A. T. Hodge, *Roman Aqueducts and Water Supply* (Leeds, 1992). For peripheral development, A. S. Esmonde Cleary, *Extra-Mural Areas of Romano-British Towns* (Oxford, 1987).

Regional studies: The 'Peoples of Roman Britain' volumes serve some areas of the country. Note also, A. McWhirr, *Roman Gloucestershire* (Gloucester, 1981); P. Wilson, 'The Roman towns of Yorkshire 30 years on', in Wilson (ed.), *Archaeology of Roman Towns* (2003). For specific sites, in addition to sections in Wacher's *Towns of Roman Britain* (1995), see also:

London: J. Bird et al. (eds), *Interpreting Roman London* (Oxford, 1996); I. Haynes et al. (eds), *London under Ground. The archaeology of a city* (Oxford, 2000); C. Maloney, *The Upper Walbrook Valley in the Roman Period* (London, 1990); D. Perring, *Roman London* (London, 1991); D. Perring and S. Roskams, *Early Development of Roman London West of the Walbrook* (London, 1991); J. Shepherd, *The Temple of Mithras London* (London, 1998); B. Watson (ed.), *Roman London: recent archaeological work* (Portsmouth, RI, 1998); T. Wilmott, *Excavations in the Middle Walbrook Valley* (London, 1991); T. Williams, *Public Buildings in the South-West Quarter of Roman London* (London, 1993); 'Water and the Roman city: life in Roman London', in Wilson, *The Archaeology of Roman Towns* (2003).

Colchester: P. Crummy, *Excavations at Lion Walk, Balkerne Lane and Middlesborough, Colchester* (Colchester, 1984); *Excavations at Culver Street and Miscellaneous Sites 1971–85* (Colchester, 1992); *City of Victory: the story of Colchester – Britain's first Roman town* (Colchester, 1997); 'Making towns out of fortresses and the first urban fortifications in Britain', in Hurst (ed.), *The Coloniae of Roman Britain* (1999); N. Crummy et al., *Excavations of Roman and Later Cemeteries, Churches and Monastic Sites in Colchester* (Colchester, 1993); C. F. C. Hawkes and P. Crummy, *Camulodunum 2* (Colchester, 1996); R. Niblett, *Sheepen: an early Roman industrial site at Colchester* (London, 1985). Note also the pioneering and influential, N. Crummy, *The Roman Small Finds from Excavations in Colchester 1971–79* (Colchester, 1983).

Lincoln: M. J. Jones, 'Roman Lincoln: changing perspectives', in Hurst (ed.), *The Coloniae of Roman Britain* (1999); *Roman Lincoln. Conquest, colony and capital* (Stroud, 2002); K. Steane et al., *The Archaeology of Wigford and the Brayford Pool* (Oxford, 2001); D. Stocker (ed.), *The City by the Pool* (Oxford, 2003).

Gloucester: H. R. Hurst, various chapters, and J. Timby, 'Pottery supply to Gloucester colonia', in Hurst (ed.), *The Coloniae of Roman Britain* (1999).

York: P. Ottaway, *Roman York* (London, 1993); 'York, the study of a late Roman colonia', and S. Roskams, 'The hinterlands of Roman York', both in Hurst (ed.), *The Coloniae of Roman Britain* (1999). Note also, A. Hall and H. Kenward, *Environmental Evidence from the Colonia* (York, 1990); K. Dobney et al., 'It's all garbage . . . a review of bioarchaeology in the four English colonia towns', in Hurst (ed.), *The Coloniae of Roman Britain* (1999).

St Albans: S. S. Frere, *Verulamium I–III* (London/Oxford, 1972, 1983, 1984); R. Niblett, *Verulamium. The Roman city of St Albans* (Stroud, 2001).

Silchester: G. C. Boon, *Silchester: The Roman town of Calleva* (London, 1974); A. Clarke and M. G. Fulford, 'The excavation of insula IX, Silchester: the first five years of the Town Life Project 1997–2001', *Britannia* 33 (2002); M. G. Fulford, *Silchester: excavations on the defences 1974–80* (London, 1984); *The Silchester Amphitheatre Excavations 1979–85* (London, 1989); 'Julio-Claudian and early Flavian Calleva', in Wilson (ed.), *The Archaeology* *of Roman Towns* (2003); M. G. Fulford and J. Timby, *Late Iron Age and Roman Silchester: excavations of the site of the forum basilica, 1977, 1980–86* (London, 2000).

Leicester: A Connor and R. Buckley, *Roman and Medieval Occupation in Causeway Lane, Leicester* (Leicester, 1999); N. J. Cooper and R. Buckley, 'New light on Roman Leicester', in Wilson (ed.), *The Archaeology of Roman Towns* (2003).

Cirencester: N. Holbrook (ed.), *Cirencester. The town defences, public buildings and shops* (Cirencester, 1998); A. McWhirr, *Roman Houses in Cirencester* (Cirencester, 1983); 'Cirencester – Corinium Dobunnorum', in Greep (ed.), *Roman Towns* (1993).

Wroxeter: P. Barker et al., *The Baths Basilica Wroxeter. Excavations 1966–90* (London, 2000); P. Ellis (ed.), *The Forum Baths and Marcellum at Wroxeter. Excavations by Graham Webster 1955–85* (London, 2000); R. White and P. Barker, *Wroxeter. Life and death of a Roman city* (Stroud, 1998); R. White and V. Gaffney, 'Resolving the paradox: the work of the Wroxeter Hinterland Project', in Wilson (ed.), *The Archaeology of Roman Towns* (2003).

Canterbury: K. Blockley et al., *Excavation in the Marlowe Car Park and Surrounding Areas* (2 vols, Canterbury, 1995).

Other major towns: H. James, *Roman Carmarthen, Excavations 1978–1993* (London, 2004); C. S. Dobinson, *Aldborough Roman Town, North Yorkshire* (London, 1995); with M. Bishop, *Finds from Roman Aldborough* (Oxford, 1996).

Different urbanisms: the 'small towns'

A. E. Brown (ed.), *Roman Small Towns in Eastern England and Beyond* (Oxford, 1995); B. C. Burnham, 'The origins of Romano-British small towns', *OJA* 5.2 (1986); B. C. Burnham and J. S. Wacher, *The Small Towns of Roman Britain* (London, 1990); Millett, *The Romanization of Britain* (1990); W. Rodwell and T. Rowley (eds), *The Small Towns of Roman Britain* (Oxford, 1975); R. F. Smith, *Roadside Settlements in Lowland Roman Britain* (Oxford, 1987); M. Todd, 'The small towns of Roman Britain', *Britannia* 1 (1970). On *vici* and administrative functions, see now M. Tarpin, *Vici et pagi dans l'occident romain* (Rome, 2002).

Specific sites: A. S. Anderson et al., *The Romano-British 'Small Town' at Wanborough, Wiltshire* (London, 2001); M. Atkinson and S. J. Preston, 'The late Iron Age and Roman settlement at Elms Farm, Heybridge, Essex, excavations 1993–5: an interim report', *Britannia* 29 (1998); T. J. Blagg et al., *Excavations at a Large Romano-British Settlement at Hacheston, Suffolk 1973–74* (Ipswich, 2004); P. Booth et al., *Excavations in the Extramural Settlement of Roman Alchester, Oxfordshire 1991* (Oxford, 2002); A. Cracknell and C. Mahany, *Roman Alcester, Southern Extramural Area, Parts 1–2* (York, 1994); G. Fincham, *Durobrivae: a Roman town between Fen and upland* (Stroud, 2004); A. R. Hands, *The Romano-British Roadside Settlement at Wilcote, Oxfordshire I–III* (Oxford, 1993/2004); P. Leach and C. J. Evans, *Excavation of a Romano-British Roadside Settlement in Somerset, Fosse Lane, Shepton Mallet 1990* (London, 2001); M. Millett and T. Wilmott, 'Rethinking Richborough', in Wilson (ed), *The Archaeology of Roman Towns* (2003); J. H. Williams, 'New light on Roman Kent', *JRA* 16 (2003) (on Westhawk Farm).

10 TOWNSPEOPLE: DEMOGRAPHY, CULTURE AND IDENTITY

Studies of townspeople in general: A. Birley, *The People of Roman Britain* (London, 1979). For social aspects of the study of Romano-British towns, see B. C. Burnham et al., 'Themes for urban research c.100 BC to AD 200', in S. James and M. Millett, *Britons and Romans*

(York, 2001); R. F. J. Jones, 'Cultural change in Roman Britain', in R. F. J. Jones (ed.), *Roman Britain: recent trends* (Sheffield, 1991); M. Millett, 'Approaches to urban societies', in James and Millett, *Britons and Romans* (2001).

On military personnel in towns: M. C. Bishop, 'Soldiers and military equipment in the towns of Roman Britain', in V. A. Maxfield and B. Dobson, *Roman Frontier Studies 1989* (Exeter, 1991); B. Yule and B. Rankov, 'Legionary soldiers in 3rd-century Southwark', in B. Watson (ed.), *Roman London: recent archaeological work* (Portsmouth, RI, 1998).

Slaves in Britain: R. S. O. Tomlin, ' "The girl in question": a new text from Roman London', *Britannia* 34 (2003). *Peregrini*, veterans and other immigrants, see S. S. Frere and M. G. Fulford, 'The collegium peregrinorum at Silchester', *Britannia* 33 (2002); articles by M. Fulford and M. Millett, in H. Hurst (ed.), *The Coloniae of Roman Britain* (Portsmouth, RI, 1999); J. C. Mann, *Legionary Recruitment and Veteran Settlement During the Principate* (London, 1983).

The epigraphic habit

Distribution of inscriptions in Gaul, G. Woolf, *Becoming Roman* (Cambridge, 1998); in Britain, B. Jones and D. Mattingly, *An Atlas of Roman Britain* (reprint, Oxford, 2002): M. E. Raybould, *A Study of Inscribed Material from Roman Britain* (Oxford, 1999). See also M. Biró, 'The inscriptions of Roman Britain', *Acta Archaeologica Academiae Scientiarum Hungaricae* 27 (1975). Patterns of dedication of buildings compared, T. F. C. Blagg, 'Architectural munificence in Britain: the evidence of inscriptions', *Britannia* 21 (1990). On tombstones, V. Hope, 'Words and pictures: the interpretation of Romano-British tombstones', *Britannia* 28 (1997).

Urban religious practices, M. Henig, 'Roman religion and Roman culture in Britain', in M. Todd, *A Companion to Roman Britain* (Oxford, 2004); M. Henig and A. King, *Pagan Gods and Shrines of the Roman Empire* (Oxford, 1986). One of the more detailed case-studies is I. Haynes, 'Religion in Roman London', in I. Haynes et al., *London Under Ground* (Oxford, 2000).

Classical temples: see B. W. Cunliffe and P. Davenport, *The Temple of Sulis Minerva at Bath* (Oxford, 1985); P. J. Drury, 'The temple of Claudius at Colchester reconsidered', *Britannia* 15 (1984). Romano-Celtic temples, P. J. Drury, 'Non-classical religious buildings in Iron Age and Roman Britain', and P. D. Horne and A. King, 'Romano-Celtic temples in Continental Europe: a gazetteer of those with known plans', both in W. Rodwell (ed.), *Temples, Churches and Religion: recent research in Roman Britain* (Oxford, 1980); M. T. Lewis, *Temples in Roman Britain* (Cambridge, 1966); A. Woodward, *Shrines and Sacrifices* (London, 1992). On evidence for structured use of space and depositional patterns, see A. Smith, *The Differential Use of Constructed Sacred Space in Southern Britain from the Late Iron Age to the 4th Century AD* (Oxford, 2001).

Eastern cults: E. and J. Harris, *The Oriental Cults in Roman Britain* (Leiden, 1965); J. Shepherd, *The Temple of Mithras London* (London, 1998). Imperial cult: D. Fishwick, 'The provincial centre at Colchester: towards an historical context', *Britannia* 28 (1997), with reference to his important earlier studies.

Curse tablets: R. S. O. Tomlin, 'Tabellae Sulis: Roman inscribed tablets of tin and lead from the sacred springs at Bath', in B. W. Cunliffe (ed.), *The Temple of Sulis Minerva at Bath*, Vol. 2: *The Finds from the Sacred Spring* (Oxford, 1988); 'Writing to the gods in Britain', in A. E. Cooley (ed.), *Becoming Roman, Writing Latin?* (Portsmouth, RI, 2002). Ritual deposition in watery contexts: R. Bradley, *The Passage of Arms: an archaeological analysis of prehistoric hoards and votive deposits* (Oxford, 1998); G. Wait, *Ritual and Religion in Iron Age Britain* (Oxford, 1985); but note that ritual deposition in the Walbrook is not accepted by T. Wilmott, *Excavations in the Middle Walbrook Valley* (London, 1991).

Material matters

Patterns of urban consumption distinct from military and rural ones, H. E. M. Cool and M. Baxter, 'Peeling the onion: an approach to comparing vessel glass assemblages', *JRA* 12 (1999). On dress, J. P. Wild, 'The clothing of Britannia, Gallia Belgica and Germania Inferior', in *ANRW* II.12.3 Principat (1985); 'Textiles and dress' in Todd, *Companion* (2004).

Interior decoration (mosaics and wall-paintings): I. Ferris, 'Collage and spectacle. Urban art in Roman Britain', in P. Wilson (ed.), *The Archaeology of Roman Towns* (Oxford, 2003); P. Johnson, 'Town mosaics and urban officinae', and R. Ling, 'Wall-painting since Wheeler', both in S. Greep (ed.), *Roman Towns: the Wheeler inheritance* (York, 1993); R. Ling, 'Mosaics in Roman Britain: discoveries and research since 1945', *Britannia* 28 (1997); D. Neal and S. Cosh, *Roman Mosaics of Britain. Vol. 1, Northern Britain.* (London, 2002).

Diet, see bibliography for Chapter 15 below. On the economic hinterlands of towns, see D. Perring (ed.), *Town and Country in England. Frameworks for archaeological research* (York, 2002); S. Roskams, 'The hinterlands of Roman York', in Hurst (ed.), *The Coloniae of Roman Britain* (1999). Amphoras in British towns, A. Connor and R. Buckley, *Roman and Medieval Occupation in Causeway Lane, Leicester* (Leicester, 1999). Palaeopathology, C. Roberts and M. Cox, 'The human population: health and disease', in Todd, *Companion* (2004); *Health and Disease in Britain: prehistory to the present day* (Stroud, 2003). On urban cemeteries, see Chapter 11, below.

11 THE URBAN FAILURE?

Traditional progressive model, S. Frere, *Britannia* (London, 1987); the argument of early decline is exemplified by R. Reece, 'Town and country: the end of Roman Britain', *World Archaeology* 12.1 (1980); 'The end of Roman Britain revisited', *Scottish Archaeological Review* 2.2 (1983). For a modified view of later fourth-century decline, A. S. Esmonde Cleary, *The Ending of Roman Britain* (London, 1989); N. Faulkner, *The Decline and Fall of Roman Britain* (Stroud, 2000), who models decline through analysis of statistical data. Cf. G. de la Bédoyère, *The Golden Age of Roman Britain* (Stroud, 1999). On the late Roman town in Britain and beyond, T. R. Slater (ed.), *Towns in Decline AD 100–1600* (Aldershot, 2000).

Rising significance of small towns, see A. E. Brown (ed.), *Roman Small Towns in Eastern England and Beyond* (Oxford, 1995); B. C. Burnham and J. S. Wacher, *The Small Towns of Roman Britain* (London, 1990); M. Millett, *The Romanization of Britain* (Cambridge, 1990).

Town defences

J. Crickmore, *Romano-British Urban Defences* (Oxford, 1984); A. S. Esmonde Cleary, 'Civil defences in the west under the high empire', in P. Wilson (ed.), *The Archaeology of Roman Towns* (Oxford, 2003); S. S. Frere, 'British urban defences in earthwork', *Britannia* 15 (1984); B. R. Hartley, 'The enclosure of Romano-British towns in the second century AD', in B. R. Hartley and J. S. Wacher (eds), *Rome and her Northern Provinces* (Gloucester, 1983); J. Maloney and B. Hobley (eds), *Roman Urban Defences in the West* (London, 1985); J. S. Wacher, 'The dating of town walls in Roman Britain', in J. Bird (ed.), *Form and Fabric: studies in Rome's material past* (Oxford, 1998).

Some specific reports: C. Colyer et al., *The Defences of the Lower City. Excavations at the Park and West Parade 1970–72 and a discussion of other sites and excavations up to 1994* (York, 1999); S. S. Frere et al., *Excavations on the Roman and Medieval Defences at Canterbury* (Canterbury, 1982); M. G. Fulford, *Silchester: excavations on the defences 1974–80* (London, 1984); N. Holbrook (ed.), *Cirencester. The town defences, public buildings and shops* (Cirencester, 1998); H. R. Hurst, *Gloucester: the Roman and later defences* (Gloucester, 1986); papers on Colchester, Chichester and Caerwent, in Wilson, *Archaeology of Roman Towns* (2003).

Change and reorientation

On plagues, see J. Wacher, *The Towns of Roman Britain* (2nd edn, London, 1995).

On the late Roman provincial and civil administration, see A. Birley, *The Roman Government of Britain* (Oxford, 2005). Discussions of late Roman urban housing include de la Bédoyère, *The Golden Age of Roman Britain* (1999); C. Walthew, 'The town house and the villa house in Roman Britain', *Britannia* 6 (1975); cf. A. McWhirr, *Roman Houses in Cirencester* (Cirencester, 1982), for rural-type structures in an urban context.

On occupation of domestic structures, Faulkner, *Decline and Fall of Roman Britain* (2000). The implications of rubbish pits and wells in London are discussed by P. Marsden and B. West, 'Population change in Roman London', *Britannia* 23 (1992). On the fourth-century commercial activity at Silchester, see A. Clarke and M. G. Fulford, 'The excavation of insula IX, Silchester: the first five years of the Town Life Project 1997–2001', *Britannia* 33 (2002). The debate about continuity into the fifth century at St Albans centres on S. S. Frere, *Verulamium II* (London, 1982); but see now, D. Neal, 'Building 2, insula XXVII from Verulamium. A reinterpretation of the evidence', in Wilson, *Archaeology of Roman Towns* (2003), casting doubt on the fifth-century sequence.

Dark earth, B. Watson, 'Dark earth and urban decline in late Roman London', in B. Watson (ed.), *Roman London: recent archaeological work* (Portsmouth, RI, 1998); B. Yule, 'The dark earth and late Roman London', *Antiquity* 64 (1990). Changing water supply at London, T. Williams, 'Water and the Roman city: life in Roman London', in Wilson, *Archaeology of Roman Towns* (2003).

Locational and structural aspects of urban cemeteries, A. S. Esmonde Cleary, *Extra-Mural Areas of Romano-British Towns* (Oxford, 1987); 'Putting the dead in their place: burial location in Roman Britain', in J. Pearce et al. (eds), *Burial in the Roman World* (Oxford, 2001); R. F. J. Jones, 'Burial customs of Rome and the provinces', in J. S. Wacher, *The Roman World* (2 vols, London, 1987); I. Morris, *Death-ritual and Social Structure in Classical Antiquity* (Cambridge, 1992).

On burial practices in Britain and in their wider context, Pearce et al. (eds), *Burial in the Roman World* (2001); R. Philpott, *Burial Practices in Roman Britain: a survey of grave treatment and furnishing AD 43–410* (Oxford, 1991). On the gender imbalance, C. Davison, 'Gender imbalances in Romano-British cemetery populations: a re-evaluation of the evidence', in Pearce et al., *Burial in the Roman World* (2001).

Specific excavations: B. Barber and D. Bowler, *The Eastern Cemetery of Roman London. Excavations 1983–1990* (London, 2000); B. Barber and J. Hall, 'Digging up the people of Roman London', in I. Haynes et al., *London Under Ground* (Oxford, 2000); G. Clarke, *The Roman Cemetery at Lankhills* (Oxford, 1979); D. Farwell and T. Molleson, *Excavations at Poundbury 1966–80. Vol. 2: The Cemeteries* (Dorchester, 1993); R. Niblett, *The Excavation of a Ceremonial Site at Folly Lane, Verulamium* (London, 1999); A. McWhirr et al., *Romano-British Cemeteries at Cirencester* (Cirencester, 1982); L. P. Wenham, *The Romano-British Cemetery at Trentholme Drive, York* (London, 1968).

On late Roman belts and personal ornaments, E. Swift, *The End of the Western Roman Empire: an archaeological investigation* (Stroud, 2000); *Regionality in Dress Accessories in the Late Roman West* (Montagnac, 2000).

Christianity and funerary context, C. J. S. Green, 'The significance of plaster burials for the recognition of Christian cemeteries', in R. Reece (ed.), *Burial in the Roman World* (London, 1977); cf. L. Cooper, 'A Roman cemetery in Newarke Street, Leicester', *Transactions of the Leicestershire Archaeological and Historical Society* 70 (1996); D. Watts, *Christians and Pagans in Roman Britain* (London, 1991). Churches and other evidence of Christianity, W. Rodwell (ed.), *Temples, Churches and Religion: recent research in Roman*

Britain (Oxford, 1980); C. Thomas, *Christianity in Roman Britain to AD 400* (London, 1981); D. Watts, *Religion in Late Roman Britain. Force of change* (London, 1998); on the possible London basilica, D. Sankey, in Watson (ed.), *Roman London* (1998). Water Newton treasure, K. S. Painter, *The Water Newton Early Christian Silver* (London, 1977).

12 THE VILLA AND THE ROUNDHOUSE

B. Campbell, *The Writings of the Roman Land Surveyors* (London, 2000); O. A. W. Dilke, *The Roman Land Surveyors* (Newton Abbot, 1971). For comparable examples of Rome's ability to bring about major change in rural structures, I. Haynes and W. Hanson (eds), *Roman Dacia. The making of a provincial society* (Portsmouth, RI, 2004).

General overviews of landscapes of Roman Britain, M. Corney, 'Characterising the land-scape of Roman Britain', in D. Hooke (ed.), *Landscape, the Richest Historical Record* (Amesbury, 2000); K. and P. Dark, *The Landscape of Roman Britain* (Gloucester, 1997); A. S. Esmonde Cleary, 'The countryside of Britain in the 4th and 5th centuries – an archaeology', in P. Ouzoulias et al. (eds), *Les campagnes de la Gaule à la fin de l'antiquité* (Antibes, 2001); R. Hingley, 'The Romano-British countryside – the significance of rural settlement forms', in R. F. J. Jones (ed.), *Roman Britain: recent trends* (Sheffield, 1991); R. Hingley and D. Miles, 'The human impact on the landscape: agriculture, settlement, industry, infrastructure', in P. Salway (ed.), *Short Oxford History of the British Isles. The Roman era* (Oxford, 2002); papers by R. Hingley and A. King in M. Todd (ed.), *A Companion to Roman Britain* (Oxford, 2004); B. Jones and D. Mattingly, *An Atlas of Roman Britain* (reprint, Oxford, 2002); D. Miles (ed.), *The Romano-British Countryside* (2 vols. Oxford, 1982); D. Miles, 'The Romano-British Countryside', in M. Todd (ed.), *Research on Roman Britain: 1960–89* (London, 1989); J. Taylor, 'Rural Society in Roman Britain', in S. James and M. Millett, *Britons and Romans* (York, 2001).

Links between town and country in the Roman world, M. Fulford, 'Town and country in Roman Britain – a parasitical relationship?', in Miles, *Romano-British Countryside* (1982); cf. J. Rich and A. Wallace-Hadrill (eds), *City and Country in the Ancient World* (London, 1991); A. L. F. Rivet, *Town and Country in Roman Britain* (2nd edn, London, 1964); I. Hodder and M. Millett, 'Romano-British villas and towns: a systematic analysis', *World Archaeology* 12 (1980).

On the contribution of aerial photography, see R. H. Bewley, *Lincolnshire's Archaeology from the Air* (Lincoln, 1998); S. S. Frere and J. K. St Joseph, *Roman Britain from the Air* (Cambridge, 1983); D. Riley, *Early Landscapes from the Air* (Sheffield, 1980); R. Whimster, *The Emerging Past: air photography and the buried landscape* (London, 1989); D. R. Wilson, 'Romano-British villas from the air', *Britannia* 5 (1974). The effects of new discoveries on knowledge of the most susceptible landscapes for air-photography, M. G. Fulford and E. Nichols (eds), *Developing Landscapes of Lowland Britain. The archaeology of the British gravels: a review* (London, 1992).

Mapping of 'Roman' countryside, Ordnance Survey *Map of Roman Britain* (Southampton, 1st edn, 1924, 2nd edn, 1928, 3rd edn, 1956, 4th edn, 1976, rev. 4th edn, 1994, 5th edn, 2001). See also works cited in relation to place-names in Chapter 2.

Various models of the geographical structure of Britain are to be found in N. Davies, *The Isles. A History* (Oxford, 1999); C. Fox, *The Personality of Britain* (Cardiff, 1943); W. G. Hoskins, *The Making of the English Landscape* (London, 1955); B. Roberts and S. Wrathmell, *Region and Place. A study of English rural settlement* (London, 2002).

Land sales, see now R. S. O. Tomlin, 'A five acre wood in Kent', in J. Bird et al. (eds), *Interpreting Roman London* (Oxford, 1996).

Pre-Roman and Roman landscapes

See works cited in Chapter 3; also I. Armit, *Celtic Scotland* (London, 1997); J. Taylor, 'Space and place: some thoughts on Iron Age and Romano-British landscapes', in A. Gwilt and C. C. Haselgrove (eds), *Reconstructing Iron Age Societies* (Oxford, 1997). On environment and ecology, P. Dark, *The Environment of Britain in the First Millennium AD* (London, 2000); M. van der Veen, *Crop Husbandry Regimes: an archaeobotanical study of farming in northern England 1000 BC–AD 500* (Sheffield, 1992), for impressive evidence of pre-Roman agricultural development; cf. M. K. Jones, 'Crop production in Roman Britain', in Miles, *Romano-British Countryside* (1982).

Note that many early studies on landscapes of ancient Britain emphasized regionalism, C. Thomas, *Rural Settlement in Roman Britain* (London, 1966). The major study of the Roman agrarian economy in Britain remains S. Applebaum, 'Roman Britain', in H. P. R. Finberg (ed.), *The Agrarian History of England and Wales*, I. ii (Cambridge, 1972); see also K. Branigan and D. Miles, *The Economies of Romano-British Villas* (Sheffield, 1988).

Villa-dominated accounts include G. de la Bédoyère, *Roman Villas and the Countryside* (London, 1993); R. G. Collingwood and I. A. Richmond, *The Archaeology of Roman Britain* (London, 1969). Compare the pioneering work of R. Hingley, *Rural Settlement in Roman Britain* (London, 1989). On Roman introductions to British farming, M. van der Veen and T. P. O. O'Connor, 'The expansion of agricultural production in late Iron Age and Roman Britain', in J. Bayley (ed.), *Science in Archaeology: an agenda for the future* (London, 1998). On population, M. Millett, *Romanization of Britain* (1990) provides a good overview of previous estimates.

The villa in Britain

Key studies of the Romano-British villa (and wider villa context) include, J. Percival, *The Roman Villa: an historical introduction* (London, 1976); A. L. F. Rivet (ed.), *The Roman Villa in Britain* (London, 1969); M. Todd (ed.), *Studies in the Romano-British Villa* (Leicester, 1978); M. Todd, 'Villa and fundus', in Branigan and Miles, *Economies of Romano-British Villas* (1988). A number of papers in P. Johnson and I. Haynes, *Architecture in Roman Britain* (London, 1996) deal with architectural aspects of villas. An individual and challenging study that emphasizes social relations as a factor in villa-planning is J. T. Smith, *The Roman Villa* (London, 1998); see also 'Villas as a key to social structure', in Todd, *Studies in the Romano-British Villa* (1978). Other discussions of villas as estates, M. Gregson, 'The villa as private property', in Branigan and Miles, *Economies of Romano-British Villas* (1988); H. J. M. Green, 'A villa estate at Godmanchester', in Todd, *Studies in the Romano-British Villa* (1978).

Non-villa settlement in the countryside

Hingley, *Rural Settlement* (1989) is fundamental. On roundhouses see also R. M. and D. E. Friendship-Taylor, *From Roundhouse to Villa* (Hackleton, 1997); A. Oswald, 'A doorway on the past: practical and mystic concerns in the orientation of roundhouse doorways', in Gwilt and Haselgrove, *Reconstructing Iron Age Societies* (1997). Other rectangular buildings, P. Morris, *Agricultural Buildings in Roman Britain* (Oxford, 1979); J. Hadham, 'Aisled buildings in Roman Britain', in Todd, *Studies in the Romano-British Villa* (1978). Note also Iron Age rectangular structures, T. Moore, 'Rectangular houses in the British Iron Age? Squaring the circle', in J. Humphrey (ed.), *Re-searching the Iron Age* (Leicester, 2003). Typical of the Iron Age to Roman transition on rural settlements are the Midlands sites discussed in R. J. Zeepvat, *Three Iron Age and Romano-British Rural Settlements on English Gravels* (Oxford, 2000). On cave-dwelling in Roman Britain, note K. Branigan and M. Deane, *Romano-British Cavemen* (Oxford, 1992). For village settlements, R. Hanley, *Villages in Roman Britain* (Princes Risborough, 2000).

13 PROVINCIAL LANDSCAPES

Regional research frameworks are in the course of development for much of Britain, providing important syntheses of rural settlement studies – though most existed only as web resources during the course of my research for this chapter.

South-east Britain

The eastern counties

Cambridgeshire, Essex and Suffolk. General works: D. M. Browne, *Roman Cambridgeshire* (Cambridge, 1977); P. J. Drury and W. Rodwell, 'Settlement in the Iron Age and Roman periods', in D. G. Buckley (ed.), *Archaeology in Essex to AD 1500* (London, 1980); R. Dunnett, *The Trinovantes* (London, 1975); C. Going, 'The Roman countryside', in O. Bedwin (ed.), *The Archaeology of Essex* (Chelmsford, 1996); J. Kemble, *Prehistoric and Roman Essex* (Stroud, 2001); W. R. Powell, *The Victoria History of the Counties of England. A history of the county of Essex*. Vol. 3: *Roman Essex* (London, 1963); I. E. Moore, *The Archaeology of Roman Suffolk* (Ipswich, 1988); T. M. Williamson, 'The Roman countryside: settlement and agriculture in NW Essex', *Britannia* 15 (1984).

Specific sites, G. A. Cater, *Excavation at the Orsett 'Cock' Enclosure, Essex, 1976* (Chelmsford, 1998); C. P. Clarker, *Excavation to the South of Chignall Roman Villa, Essex* (Chelmsford, 1998); W. J. and K. A. Rodwell, *Rivenhall: investigations of a villa, church and village 1950–77* (2 vols, York, 1986/1993).

Hertfordshire, Bedfordshire, Buckinghamshire and Northamptonshire. General works: K. Branigan, *Town and Country. The Archaeology of Verulamium and the Roman Chilterns* (Bourne End, 1973); *The Catuvellauni* (Gloucester, 1987); S. Bryant and R. Niblett, 'The late Iron Age in Hertfordshire and the north Chilterns', in A. Gwilt and C. C. Haselgrove (eds), *Reconstructing Iron Age Societies* (Oxford, 1997); R. A. Croft and D. C. Mynard, *The Changing Landscape of Milton Keynes* (Aylesbury, 1993); M. Dawson (ed.), *Prehistoric, Roman and Post-Roman Landscapes of the Great Ouse Valley* (York, 2000): M. Dawson, *Archaeology in the Bedford Region* (Oxford, 2004); J. R. Hunn, *Reconstruction, and Measurement of Landscape Change* (Oxford, 1994); R. Niblett, *Roman Hertfordshire* (Wimbourne, 1995); *Verulamium. The Roman city of St Albans* (Stroud, 2001); A. Simco, *Survey of Bedfordshire. The Roman period* (Bedford, 1984).

Specific sites: K. Branigan, *Latimer. Belgic, Roman, Dark Age and Early Modern Farm* (Bristol, 1971); D. S. Neal, *The Roman Villa at Gadebridge Park, Hemel Hempstead 1963–68* (London, 1974); D. S. Neal et al., *Excavation of the Iron Age, Roman and Medieval Settlement at Gorhambury, St Albans* (London, 1990); R. J. Williams et al., *Wavedon Gate. A late Iron Age and Roman settlement in Milton Keynes* (Aylesbury, 1996); R. J. Williams and R. J. Zeepvat, *Bancroft. Late Bronze Age and Iron Age settlements, Roman temple-mausoleum and Roman villa* (Aylesbury, 1994); R. J. Zeepvat et al., *Caldecotte, Milton Keynes. Excavations and fieldwork 1966–91* (Aylesbury, 1994).

East Anglia. J. Davies and T. Williamson (eds), *Land of the Iceni: the Iron Age in northern East Anglia* (Norwich, 1999); T. Gregory, 'Romano-British settlement in west Norfolk and on the Norfolk Fen edge', in D. Miles (ed.), *The Romano-British Countryside*, (2 vols, Oxford, 1982); D. Gurney (ed.), *Settlement, Religion and Industry on the Fen Edge: three Romano-British settlements in Norfolk* (Norwich, 1986); 'Small towns and villages of Roman Norfolk', in A. E. Brown (ed.), *Roman Small Towns in Eastern England and Beyond* (Oxford, 1995).

The Fenland: G. Fincham, *Landscapes of Imperialism. Roman and native interaction in the East Anglian Fenland* (Oxford, 2002); D. Hall and J. Coles, *Fenland Survey: an essay in landscape and perspective* (London, 1994); P. P. Hayes and T. W. Lane, *The Fenland Project*

Number 5: Lincolnshire survey, the south-west Fens (Sleaford, 1992); C. W. Phillips, *The Fenland in Roman Times* (London, 1970); T. Potter, 'Recent work on the Roman Fens and the question of imperial estates', *JRA* 2 (1989).

Specific sites: K. Jackson and T. Potter, *Excavations at Stonea, Cambridgeshire 1980–85* (London, 1996); D. Mackreth, *Monument 97, Orton Longueville, Cambridgeshire: a late pre-Roman Iron Age and early Roman farmstead* (Manchester, 2001).

Comparative British wetlands: J. R. L. Allen and M. G. Fulford, 'Romano-British settlement and industry in the wetlands of the Severn estuary', *Ant. J.* 62 (1987); S. Rippon, *The Gwent Levels. The evolution of a wetland landscape* (York, 1996); *Severn Estuary: landscape evolution and wetland reclamation* (London, 1997); 'The Romano-British exploitation of coastal wetlands: survey and excavation on the north Somerset Levels, 1993–1997', *Britannia* 31 (2000).

The south-eastern counties

General overview: E. W. Black, *The Roman Villas of South-East England* (Oxford, 1987); P. Drewett et al., *The South East to AD 1000* (London, 1988).

Kent. General works: C. Andrews, 'Romanisation: a Kentish perspective', *Archaeologia Cantiana* 121 (2001); T. Blagg, 'Roman Kent', in P. Leach (ed.), *The Archaeology in Kent to AD 1500* (London, 1982); A. Detsicas, *The Cantiaci* (Gloucester, 1983); J. H. Williams, 'New Light on Roman Kent', *JRA* 16 (2003).

Specific sites: G. W. Meates, *The Roman Villa at Lullingstone* (2 vols, Maidstone, 1979/1987). London area, D. G. Bird, 'The London region in the Roman period', in J. Bird et al. (eds), *Interpreting Roman London* (Oxford, 1996); D. Perring and T. Brigham, 'Londinium and its hinterland: the Roman period', in *The Archaeology of Greater London* (London, 2000).

The central southern counties

Sussex. General works: B. W. Cunliffe, *The Regni* (London, 1973); D. R. Rudling, 'Rural settlement in late iron age and Roman Sussex', in Miles, *Romano-British Countryside* (1982); 'The development of Roman villas in Sussex', *Sussex Archaeological Collections* 136 (1998).

Specific sites: B. W. Cunliffe, *Excavations at Fishbourne 1961–1969* (2 vols, Leeds, 1971); *Fishbourne Roman Palace* (Stroud, 1998); S. Frere, 'The Bignor Villa', *Britannia* 13 (1982).

Surrey/Berkshire. D. G. Bird, 'The Romano-British period in Surrey', in J. and D. G. Bird, *The Archaeology of Surrey to 1540* (Guildford, 1987); D. G. Bird, *Roman Surrey* (Stroud, 2004); M. Corney, 'Field survey of the extra-mural region', in M. Fulford (ed.), *Silchester Defences 1974–1980* (London, 1984).

Hampshire/Wiltshire. B. W. Cunliffe, *Wessex to AD 1000* (London, 1993); P. Ellis (ed.), *Roman Wiltshire and After* (Devizes, 2001); A. P. Fitzpatrick and E. L. Morris, *The Iron Age in Wessex: recent work* (Salisbury, 1994); D. Johnston, 'Villas of Hampshire and the Isle of Wight', in M. Todd (ed.), *Studies in the Romano-British Villa* (Leicester, 1978); D. McOrmish et al., *The Field Archaeology of the Salisbury Plain Training Area* (Swindon, 2002); R. Palmer, *Danebury. An Iron Age hillfort in Hampshire. An aerial photographic interpretation of its environs* (London, 1984); D. Tomalin, *Roman Wight. A guide catalogue* (Newport, 1987).

Specific sites: B. W. Cunliffe, 'Roman Danebury', *Current Archaeology* 188 (2003); A. King, 'The south-east façade of Meonstoke aisled building', in P. Johnson and I. Haynes (eds), *Architecture in Roman Britain* (London, 1996).

The East Midlands

General works: R. H. Bewley, *Lincolnshire's Archaeology from the Air* (Lincoln, 1998); D. Hall, 'Survey work in eastern England', in S. Macready and F. H. Thompson (eds), *Field Survey in Britain and Abroad* (London, 1985); M. Parker-Pearson and R. T. Schadla-Hall, *Looking at the Land. Archaeological landscapes in Eastern England. Recent work and future directions* (Leicester, 1994); RCHME, *Northamptonshire: an Archaeological Atlas* (London, 1980); M. Todd, *The Coritani* (rev. edn, Gloucester, 1991); J. B. Whitwell, *Roman Lincoln-shire* (Lincoln, 1970).

Nene Valley: C. Taylor, 'Roman settlements in the Nene Valley: the impact of recent archaeology', in P. Fowler (ed.), *Recent Work in Rural Archaeology* (Bradford on Avon, 1975); J. P. Wild, 'Villas in the lower Nene Valley', in Todd, *Studies in the Romano-British Villa* (1978).

Specific sites: N. Cooper, *The Archaeology of Rutland Water: Excavations in the Gwash Valley, Rutland* (London, 2000); D. A. Jackson and T. Ambrose, 'Excavations at Wakerley, Northants 1972–5', *Britannia* 9 (1978); G. Keevil and P. Booth, 'Settlement, sequence and structure: Romano-British stone-built roundhouses at Redlands Farm, Stanwick and Alchester', in R. M. and D. E. Friendship-Taylor (eds), *From Roundhouse to Villa* (Hackleton, 1997); D. F. Mackreth, *Orton Hall Farm: a Roman and early Anglo-Saxon farmstead* (Manchester, 1996); J. May, *Dragonby: report on excavations at an Iron Age and Romano-British settlement in north Lincolnshire* (2 vols, Oxford, 1996); D. S. Neal, 'The Stanwick villa, Northants: an interim report', *Britannia* 20 (1989); I. Stead, *Excavations at Winterton Roman Villa* (London, 1976); S. Upex, 'The Roman villa at Cotterstock, Northamptonshire', *Britannia* 32 (2001).

The West Midlands and west England

West Midlands, Warwickshire and Oxfordshire. General works: P. Booth, 'Warwickshire in the Roman period: a review of recent work', *Transactions Birmingham and Warwickshire Archaeological Society* 100 (1996); D. Benson and D. Miles, *The Upper Thames Valley. An archaeological survey of the river gravels* (Oxford, 1974); M. Fulford, 'Iron Age to Roman: a period of radical change on the gravels', in M. Fulford and E. Nichols (eds), *Developing Landscapes of Lowland Britain. The archaeology of the British gravels: a review* (London, 1992); M. Henig and P. Booth, *Roman Oxfordshire* (Stroud, 2000); T. Gates, *The Middle Thames Valley* (Reading, 1975); D. Miles, 'Confusion in the countryside: some comments on the upper Thames region', in Miles, *The Romano-British Countryside* (1982); M. Tingle, *The Vale of the White Horse Survey* (Oxford, 1991).

Specific sites: T. G. Allen, *An Iron Age and Romano-British Enclosed Settlement at Watkins Farm, Northmoor, Oxon* (Oxford, 1990); T. G. Allen et al., *Excavations at Roughground Farm, Lechlade, Gloucestershire: a prehistoric and Roman landscape* (Oxford, 1993); V. Gaffney and M. Tingle, *The Maddle Farm Project* (Oxford, 1989); G. Lambrick and M. Robinson, *Iron Age and Roman Riverside Settlements at Farmoor, Oxfordshire* (Oxford, 1979); D. Miles (ed.), *Archaeology at Barton Court Farm, Abingdon, Oxon* (Oxford, 1984); D. Wilson, 'The North Leigh Roman villa: its plan reviewed', *Britannia* 35 (2004).

Western Cotswolds, Gloucestershire and Avon. General works: R. Leech, *The Upper Thames Valley in Gloucestershire and Wiltshire* (Bristol, 1977); K. Branigan and P. J. Fowler, *The Roman West Country* (London, 1976); T. Darvill and G. Gerrard, *Cirencester: town and landscape* (Cirencester, 1994); A. McWhirr, *Roman Gloucestershire* (Gloucester, 1981); RCHME, *Iron Age and Romano-British Monuments in the Gloucestershire Cotswolds* (London, 1976).

Specific sites: K. Branigan, *Gatcombe. The excavation and study of a Romano-British villa estate, 1967–1976* (Oxford, 1977); N. Holbrook, 'Turkdean Roman villa, Gloucestershire: archaeological investigations 1997–1998', *Britannia* 35 (2004); P. Leach et al., *Great Witcombe Roman Villa, Gloucestershire* (Oxford, 1998); E. Price, *Frocester. A Romano-British settlement, its antecedents and successors. Vol. 1: The Sites; Vol. 2: Finds* (Stonehouse, 2000); J. Timby, *Excavations at Kingscote and Wycomb, Gloucestershire* (Cirencester, 1998); S. Trow and S. James, 'Ditches villa, North Cerney. An example of locational conservatism in the early Roman Cotswolds', in K. Branigan and D. Miles, *The Economies of Romano-British Villas* (Sheffield, 1988).

The South-western counties

General works: K. Branigan, *The Roman Villa in South-west England* (Bradford-on-Avon, 1976); H. C. Bowen and P. J. Fowler, 'Romano-British settlements in Dorset and Wiltshire', in C. Thomas, *Rural Settlement in Roman Britain* (London, 1966); P. Ellis (ed.), *Roman Wiltshire and After* (Devizes, 2001); D. McOrmish, et al., *The Field Archaeology of the Salisbury Plain Training Area* (Swindon, 2002); P. Leach, *Roman Somerset* (Wimbourne, 2002); D. Putnam, *Roman Dorset* (Wimbourne, 1984).

Specific sites: R. Leech, *Excavations at Catsgore 1970–73. A Romano-British village* (Bristol, 1982).

West and north Britain

R. Kain and W. Ravenhill, *Historical Atlas of South-west England* (Exeter, 1999); S. Pearce, *The Kingdom of Dumnonia* (Padstow, 1978); M. Todd, *The South West to AD 1000* (London, 1987).

Eastern Devon

General works: A. P. Fitzpatrick et al., *Prehistoric and Roman Sites in East Devon: the A30 Honiton to Exeter Improvement DBFO Scheme 1996–9* (2 vols, Salisbury, 1999); F. Griffith, *Devon's Past. An aerial view* (Exeter, 1988); H. Riley and R. Eilson-North, *The Field Archaeology of Exmoor* (Swindon, 2001); C. Thomas, 'The character and origin of Roman Dumnonia', in Thomas, *Rural Settlement* (1966); M. Todd, *Roman Devon* (Exeter, 2001).

Specific sites: R. Silvester, 'Excavations at Honeyditches villa, Seaton, in 1978', *Proceedings of Devon Arch. Soc.* 39 (1981).

Cornwall and western Devon

General works: N. Johnson and P. Rose, 'Defended settlement in Cornwall – an illustrated discussion', in Miles, *The Romano-British Countryside* (1982); H. Quinnell, 'Cornwall during the Iron Age and the Roman Period', *Cornish Archaeology* 25 (1986); C. Thomas, *Exploration of a Drowned Landscape. Archaeology and history of the Isles of Scilly* (London, 1985).

Specific sites: N. Appleton-Fox, 'Excavations at a Romano-British round, Reawkla, Gwinear, Cornwall', *Cornish Archaeology* 31 (1992); P. M. Christie, 'The excavation of an Iron Age souterrain and settlement at Carn Euny, Sancreed, Cornwall', *PPS* 44 (1978); H. Quinnell, *Excavations at Trethurgy Round, St Austell: insights into Roman and post-Roman Cornwall* (Cornwall County Council, 2004).

The Marches

General works: R. White and P. Barker, *Wroxeter. Life and Death of a Roman City* (Stroud, 1998); G. Webster, *The Cornovii* (rev. edn, Gloucester, 1991); cf. K. J. Matthews, 'Immaterial culture: invisible peasants and consumer subcultures in north-west Britain', in *TRAC 6* (1997); S. Stanford, *The Archaeology of the Welsh Marches* (London, 1991); R. Whimster, *The Emerging Past* (London, 1989).

Wales

General works: C. J. Arnold and J. L. Davies, *Roman and Early Medieval Wales* (Stroud, 2000); B. C. Burnham and J. L. Davies, *Conquest, Coexistence and Change* (Lampeter, 1990); J. Davies, *A History of Wales* (Harmondsworth, 1990); J. L. Davies, 'The early Celts in Wales', in M. Green (ed.), *The Celtic World* (London, 1995); A. H. A. Hogg, 'Invasion and response: the problem in Wales', in B. C. Burnham and H. B. Johnson (eds), *Invasion and Response* (Oxford, 1979); F. Lynch et al., *Prehistoric Wales* (Stroud, 2000); W. Manning, *A Pocket Guide. Roman Wales* (Cardiff, 2001).

Regional peoples: M. G. Jarrett and J. C. Mann, 'The tribes of Wales', *Welsh History Review* 4 (1969).

South-west Wales. H. James and G. Williams, 'Rural settlement in Dyfed', in Miles, *The Romano-British Countryside* (1982); G. Williams, 'Recent work on rural settlement in south-west Wales', in Burnham and Davies, *Conquest, Coexistence and Change* (1990).

Specific sites: G. Wainwright, 'The excavation of the fortified settlement at Walesland Rath, Pembrokeshire', *Britannia* 2 (1971); *The Coygan Camp* (Cardiff, 1967).

Environment: A. Caseldine, *Environmental Archaeology in Wales* (Lampeter, 1990).

South-east Wales. S. Rippon, *Gwent Levels: the evolution of a wetland landscape* (York, 1996).

Specific sites: A. Hogg, 'The Llantwit Major villa: a reconsideration of the evidence', *Britannia* 5 (1974); M. Jarrett and S. Wrathmell, *Whitton. An Iron Age and Roman farmstead in south Glamorgan* (Cardiff, 1981); D. M. Robinson (ed.), *Biglis, Caldicot and Llandough. Three late Iron Age and Romano-British sites in south-east Wales* (Oxford, 1988).

North-east Wales. K. Blockley, 'The Romano-British period', in J. Manley et al., *The Archaeology of Clwyd* (Mold, 1991).

Specific sites: K. Blockley, *Prestatyn 1984–5. An Iron Age farmstead and Romano-British industrial settlement in north Wales* (Oxford, 1989); T. O'Leary, *Pentre Farm, Flint* (Oxford, 1989).

North-west Wales. P. J. Fasham et al., *The Graeanog Ridge. The evolution of a farming landscape and its settlements in north-west Wales* (Aberystwyth, 1998); R. S. Kelly, 'Recent research on the hut group settlements of north-west Wales', in Burnham and Davies, *Conquest, Coexistence and Change* (1990); RCAHMW, *An Inventory of the Ancient Monuments in Caernarvonshire* (vols I/III, London, 1956/1964).

Specific sites: D. Longley et al., 'Excavations on two farms of the Romano-British period at Bryn Eryr and Bush Farm, Gwynedd', *Britannia* 29 (1998).

Northern England

General works: J. Chapman and H. Mytum, *Settlement in North Britain 1000 BC–AD 1000* (Oxford, 1983); P. Clack, 'The northern frontier: farmers in the military zone', in Miles, *Romano-British Countryside* (1982); P. Clack and C. C. Haselgrove, *Rural Settlement in the Roman North* (Durham, 1982); D. W. Harding, *The Iron Age in Northern Britain* (London, 2004); J. Harding (ed.), *Northern Pasts: Interpretations of the later prehistory of northern England and southern Scotland* (Oxford, 2000); N. Higham, *The Northern Counties to AD 1000* (London and New York, 1986); R. Miket and C. Burgess (eds), *Between and Beyond the Walls: Essays on the prehistory and history of North Britain in honour of G. Jobey* (Edinburgh, 1984); C. Tolan-Smith, *Landscape Archaeology in Tynedale* (Newcastle, 1997); P. Wilson et al. (eds), *Settlement and Society in the Roman North* (Bradford, 1984).

Regional peoples: B. Hartley and L. Fitts, *The Brigantes* (Gloucester, 1988); C. C. Haselgrove, 'The Iron Age', in R. Newman, *The Archaeology of Lancashire: present state and future priorities* (1996); 'Iron Age societies in central Britain: retrospect and prospect', in B. Bevan, *Northern Exposure* (Leicester, 1999); N. Higham and B. Jones, *The Carvetii* (Gloucester, 1985); H. Ramm, *The Parisi* (London, 1978).

Studies of particular sub-regions: J. Barnatt and K. Smith, *The Peak District* (London, 1997); R. Bewley, *Prehistoric and Romano-British Settlement in the Solway Plain, Cumbria* (Oxford, 1994); K. Branigan, 'Villas in the north', in K. Branigan (ed.), *Rome and the Brigantes. The impact of Rome on northern England* (Sheffield, 1980); M. Faull and S. Moorhouse, *West Yorkshire: an archaeological survey to AD 1500* (Wakefield, 1981); T. Gates, *The Hadrian's Wall Landscape from Chesters to Greenhead: an air photographic survey* (Hexham, 1999); P. Halkon and M. Millett, *Rural Settlement and Industry: Studies in the Iron Age and Roman archaeology of lowland East Yorkshire* (Leeds, 1999); N. Higham and G. D. B. Jones, 'Frontiers, forts and farmers: the Cumbrian aerial survey 1974–75', *Arch. J.* 132 (1976); G. A. Makepeace, 'Romano-British rural settlements in the Peak District and north-east Staffordshire', *Derbyshire Arch. J.* 118 (1998); M. Neville (ed.), *Living on the Edge of Empire: models, methodology and marginality* (Manchester, 1999); Newman, *The Archaeology of Lancashire* (1996); J. Price and P. Wilson, *Recent Research in Roman Yorkshire* (Oxford, 1988); D. Riley, *Early Landscapes from the Air* (Sheffield, 1980); D. Shotter, *Romans and Britons in North-west England* (Lancaster, 2004); C. Stoertz, *Ancient Landscapes of the Yorkshire Wolds* (London, 1997).

Specific sites: D. H. Heslop, *The Excavation of an Iron Age Settlement at Thorpe Thewles* (London, 1988); D. Neal, *Excavations on the Roman Villa at Beadlam, Yorkshire* (Leeds, 1996); I. Stead, *Rudston Roman Villa* (Leeds, 1980); S. Wrathmell and A. Nicholson, *Dalton Parlours: Iron Age settlement and Roman villa* (Wakefield, 1990); M. van der Veen, *Crop Husbandry Regimes: an archaeobotanical study of farming in northern England 1000 BC–AD 500* (Sheffield, 1992).

Scotland

General studies: I. Armit, 'Cultural landscapes and identities: a case study in the Scottish Iron Age', in Gwilt and Haselgrove, *Reconstructing Iron Age Societies* (1997); 'The abandonment of souterrains', *PSAS* 129 (1999); J. C. Barrett et al. (eds), *Barbarians and Romans in North-West Europe* (Oxford, 1989); D. Breeze, *Roman Scotland* (London, 1996); W. S. Hanson, 'The Roman presence: brief interludes', in K. J. Edwards and I. B. M. Ralston (eds), *Scotland: environment and archaeology 8000 BC–AD 1000* (Edinburgh, 1997); R. Hingley, 'Society in Scotland from 700 BC to AD 200', *PSAS* 122 (1992); Harding, *The Iron Age in Northern Britain* (2004); I. Ralston, 'Recent work on the Iron Age settlement record in Scotland', in T. Champion and J. R. Collis, *The Iron Age in Britain and Ireland: recent trends* (Sheffield, 1996); G. Wittington and K. J. Edwards, 'Ubi solitudinem faciunt pacem appellant: the Romans in Scotland, a palaeo-environmental contribution', *Britannia* 24 (1993).

Regional peoples: R. Hingley, *Settlement and Sacrifice. The later prehistoric people of Scotland* (Edinburgh, 1998). On the distribution of Roman artefacts, F. Hunter, 'Roman and native in Scotland: new approaches', *JRA* 14 (2001).

Studies of specific sub-regions: D. W. Harding, *Later Prehistoric Settlement in South-west Scotland* (Edinburgh, 1982); G. S. Maxwell, 'Settlement in southern Pictland: a new overview', in A. Small (ed.), *The Picts: a new look at an old problem* (Dundee, 1987); RCAHMS, *North-east Perth: an archaeological landscape* (London, 1990); *South-east Perth: an archaeological landscape* (London, 1994); *Eastern Dumfriesshire: an archaeological landscape* (London, 1997); J. S. Rideout et al., *Hillforts of Southern Scotland* (Edinburgh, 1992).

Lowland brochs: L. McInnes, 'Brochs and the Roman occupation of Lowland Scotland', *PSAS* 114 (1994); E. Mackie, 'The Leckie broch, Stirlingshire: an interim report', *Glasgow Arch. J.* 9 (1982); L. Main, 'Excavations of a timber round-house and broch at Fairy Knowe, Buchlyvie, Stirlingshire, 1975–8', *PSAS* 128 (1998).

For figures on the potential impact of Rome in Wales and Scotland, see D. Breeze, 'The impact of the Roman army on the native peoples of northern Britain', in H. Vetters and M. Kandler, *Der Römische Limes in Österreich. Akten der 14 Internationalen Limeskongresses 1986, Carnuntum* (Vienna, 1990); J. L. Davies, 'Native producers and Roman consumers: the mechanisms of military supply in Wales from Claudius to Theodosius', in W. Groenman-van Waateringe et al. (eds), *Roman Frontier Studies 1995* (Oxford, 1997).

14   FREE *BRITANNIA*: BEYOND THE FRONTIERS

Northern and western Scotland

General works: D. Breeze, 'The edge of the world: the imperial frontier and beyond', in P. Salway (ed.), *Short Oxford History of the British Isles. The Roman era* (2002); K. J. Edwards and I. B. M. Ralston (eds), *Scotland: environment and archaeology, 8000 BC–AD*

1000 (Edinburgh, 1997); R. Hingley, 'Society in Scotland from 700 BC to AD 200', *PSAS* 122 (1992); L. Keppie, 'Beyond the northern frontier: Romans and natives in Scotland', in M. Todd (ed.), *Research on Roman Britain: 1960–89* (London, 1989).

Regional peoples: W. A. Cummins, *The Age of the Picts* (Gloucester, 1995); S. M. Foster, *Picts, Gaels and Scots. Early historic Scotland* (London, 1996); E. MacKie, 'The early Celts in Scotland', in M. Green, *The Celtic World* (London, 1995).

On brochs and other settlement types: I. Armit, 'Broch building in northern Scotland: the context of innovation', *World Archaeology* 21 (1989); *Towers in the North. The brochs of Scotland* (Stroud, 2003); N. Dixon, *The Crannogs of Scotland* (Stroud, 2004); E. MacKie, *The Roundhouses, Brochs and Wheelhouses of Atlantic Scotland c.700 BC–AD 500* (Oxford, 2002); N. Sharples and M. Parker-Pearson, 'Why were brochs built?', in A. Gwilt and C. C. Haselgrove (eds), *Reconstructing Iron Age Societies* (Oxford, 1997).

Regional studies: I. Armit, *The Archaeology of Skye and the Western Isles* (Edinburgh, 1995); A. Fenton, *The Northern Isles: Orkney and Shetland* (Edinburgh, 1978).

Ireland

General works: G. Cooney and E. Grogan, *Irish Prehistory. A social perspective* (Bray, 1994); P. Freeman, *Ireland and the Classical World* (Austin, 2001); J. P. Mallory and T. E. McNeill, *The Archaeology of Ulster from Colonization to Plantation* (Belfast, 1991); B. Raftery, *La Tène in Ireland: problems of origin and chronology* (Marburg, 1984); *Pagan Celtic Ireland. The enigma of the Irish Iron Age* (London, 1994); 'Ireland: a world without Romans', in Green, *The Celtic World* (1995); 'Iron Age studies in Ireland: some recent developments', in T. Champion and J. R. Collis, *The Iron Age in Britain and Ireland: recent trends* (Sheffield, 1996); M. Stout, *The Irish Ringfort* (Dublin, 1997).

Specific sites: B. Raftery, 'Drumanagh and Roman Ireland', *Archaeology Ireland* 35 (10.1) (1996). On the *Attacotti*, see the convincing arguments of P. Rance, 'Attacotti, Deisi and Magnus Maximus: the case for Irish federates in late Roman Britain', *Britannia* 32 (2001).

Roman and imported finds in Ireland: J. D. Bateson, 'Roman material from Ireland: a re-examination', *Proc. Royal Irish Acad.* 73C (1973); R. Warner, 'Some observations on the context and importation of exotic material in Ireland from the first century BC to the second century AD', *Proc. Royal Irish Acad.* 76C (1976).

15 RURAL CULTURE AND IDENTITY

The land document referred to is published by R. S. O. Tomlin, 'A five-acre wood in Kent', in J. Bird et al. (eds), *Interpreting Roman London* (Oxford, 1996). On the overlap between military and rural identity, E. W. Black, 'Villa owners: Romano-British gentlemen and officers', *Britannia* 25 (1994); N. Roymans, 'Romanization and the transformation of a martial-elite ideology in a frontier province', in J. Metzler et al., *Integration in the Roman West* (Luxembourg, 1995). On Melania, see E. A. Clark, *The Life of Melania the Younger* (New York, 1984).

Various categories of portable artefacts referred to in the chapter can be found in the fascicules of *RIB* II. Details about people can mostly be found in A. Birley's, *The People of Roman Britain* (London, 1979); L. Allason-Jones, *Women in Roman Britain* (London, 1989).

The fashioning of elite behaviour

On the general articulation of 'villa' culture, see, *inter alia*, G. de la Bédoyère, *Roman Villas and the Countryside* (London, 1993); *The Golden Age of Roman Britain* (Stroud, 1999); P. Dark, *The Landscape of Roman Britain* (Gloucester, 1997). Cf. M. Millett, *Roman Britain* (London, 1995).

Stone inscriptions: *RIB* I; M. E. Raybould, *A Study of Inscribed Material from Roman*

Britain (Oxford, 1999). Thruxton villa, see M. Henig and G. Soffe, 'The Thruxton Roman villa and its mosaic pavement', *Journal of the British Archaeological Association* 146 (1993); B. Cunliffe, 'Roman Danebury', *Current Archaeology* 188 (2003). Writing implements: W. S. Hanson and R. Conolly, 'Language and literacy in Roman Britain: some archaeological considerations', in A. E. Cooley (ed.), *Becoming Roman, Writing Latin?* (Portsmouth, RI, 2002). Graffiti on personal possessions: see *RIB* II; also J. Evans, 'Evidence of literacy and pottery use in Roman Britain', *Arch. J.* 144 (1987). Hoxne hoard: R. Bland and C. Johns, *The Hoxne Treasure* (London, 1993). Names at Bath and Uley: R. S. O. Tomlin, 'Writing to the gods in Britain', in Cooley, *Becoming Roman, Writing Latin?* (2002).

Art and culture: M. Henig (ed.), *A Handbook of Roman Art* (Oxford, 1983); *The Art of Roman Britain* (London, 1995); R. and L. Ling, *Making Classical Art: process and practice* (Stroud, 2000); J. M. C. Toynbee, *Art in Roman Britain* (London, 1962); *Art in Britain under the Romans* (London, 1965). For mosaics, in addition to works cited in Chapter 2, see A. Rainey, *Mosaics in Roman Britain* (Newton Abbot, 1973); D. J. Smith, 'The mosaic pavements', in A. L. F. Rivert (ed.), *The Roman Villa in Britain* (London, 1969).

Iconography of mosaics and knowledge of Classics: S. Scott, 'The power of images in the late Roman house', in R. Laurence and A. Wallace-Hadrill (eds), *Domestic Space in the Roman World: Pompeii and beyond* (Ann Arbor, 1997); *Art and Society in Fourth-Century Britain. Villa mosaics in context* (Oxford, 2000); cf. A. A. Barrett, 'The literary classics in Roman Britain', *Britannia* 9 (1978).

On Orpheus in art: S. Scott, 'Symbols of power and nature: the Orpheus mosaics of fourth-century Britain and their architectural contexts', in *TRAC* 2 (1995); P. Witts, 'Mosaics and room function: the evidence from some fourth-century Romano-British villas', *Britannia* 31 (2000). Christian and Gnostic elements in mosaics: D. Perring, 'Gnosticism in fourth-century Britain: the Frampton mosaics reconsidered', *Britannia* 34 (2003). Coins of Carausius and Virgil's Fourth *Eclogue*: G. de la Bédoyère, *The Golden Age of Roman Britain* (London, 1999).

Question of British content in provincial art, see the opposing views of C. Johns, 'Art, Romanisation and competence', M. Henig, 'Art and aesthetics: a personal view', and J. Webster, 'Art as resistance and negotiation', in S. Scott and J. Webster (eds), *Roman Imperialism and Provincial Art* (Cambridge, 2003).

Wall-painting: N. Davey and R. Ling, *Romano-British Wall Painting* (London, 1981). Marble statuary: see *CSIR* volumes for the sparse and fragmentary traces. On so-called Celtic heads, cf. A. Ross, *Pagan Celtic Britain* (London, 1967); and the increasingly cautious comments of the *CSIR* volume editors. Silver plate: J. P. C. Kent and K. S. Painter, *Wealth of the Roman World AD 300–700* (London, 1977); K. S. Painter, *The Mildenhall Treasure* (London, 1977).

Villa architecture see Chapter 12. For the argument that villa elaboration may reflect individual identity more than an unvaried group identity based on conspicuous consumption, see C. Martins, 'Becoming consumers: looking beyond wealth as an explanation for villa variability', in *TRAC* 12 (2003).

Non-elite rural culture

C. Evans, 'Britons and Romans at Chatteris: investigations at Langwood Farm', *Britannia* 34 (2003); C. Gosden and G. Lock, 'Becoming Roman on the Berkshire Downs: the evidence from Alfred's Castle', *Britannia* 34 (2003); R. Hingley, *Rural Settlement in Roman Britain* (London, 1989); R. Hingley and D. Miles, 'The human impact on the landscape: agriculture, settlement, industry, infrastructure', in P. Salway (ed.), *Short Oxford History of the British Isles. The Roman era* (Oxford, 2002). On the social use of state in domestic buildings, see papers by R. Hingley and S. Scott in R. Samson (ed.), *The Social Archaeology of Houses* (Edinburgh, 1990).

Comparison of site assemblages of pottery and other finds: see publications by H. E. M. Cool in Chapter 7; H. E. M. Cool and M. J. Baxter, 'Exploring Romano-British finds assemblages', *OJA* 21.4 (2002); D. Longley et al., 'Excavations on two farms of the Romano-British period at Bryn Eryr and Bush Farm, Gwynedd', *Britannia* 29 (1998).

Contextual data on individual finds classes: H. E. M. Cool, 'Roman metal hairpins from southern Britain', *Arch. J.* 147 (1990); 'Some notes on spoons and mortaria', in *TRAC* 13 (2004); H. E. M. Cool and M. Baxter, 'Peeling the onion: an approach to comparing vessel glass assemblages', *JRA* 12 (1999); N. Crummy and H. Eckardt, 'Regional identities and technologies of the self: nail-cleaners in Roman Britain', *Arch. J.* 160 (2003); H. Eckardt, 'Material matters: the social distribution of Roman artefacts', *JRA* 18 (2005) – an important and insightful paper; S. Jundi and J. D. Hill, 'Brooches and identity in first-century AD Britain: more than meets the eye?', *TRAC* 7 (1998); S. Puttock, *Ritual Significance of Personal Ornament in Roman Britain* (Oxford, 2002). Note also various papers in R. Hingley and S. Willis (eds), *Roman Finds: context and theory* (Oxford, 2005).

Consumption and diet

On diet: J. Hamshaw-Thomas, 'When in Britain do as the Britons: dietary identity in early Roman Britain', in P. Rowly-Conwy (ed.), *Animal Bones, Human Societies* (Oxford, 2000); K. Meadows, 'You are what you eat: diet, identity and Romanization', *TRAC* 4 (1995); 'The appetites of households in early Roman Britain', in P. Allison (ed.), *The Archaeology of Household Activities* (London, 1999); G. Hawkes, 'Wolves' nipples and otters' noses? Rural foodways in Roman Britain', in *TRAC* 11 (2002). For other studies on animal bones, see bibliography for Chapters 7 and 10.

Pottery assemblages: papers by P. Rush and S. Willis in *TRAC* 6 (1997); P. Booth, 'Inter-site comparisons between pottery assemblages in Roman Warwickshire. Ceramics as indicators of site status', *Journal of Roman Pottery Studies* 4 (1991); J. Evans, 'Material approaches to different Romano-British site types', in S. James and M. Millett (eds), *Britons and Romans* (York, 2001).

Funerary rituals and commemoration

Lindow man and human sacrifice: M. Aldhouse-Green, *Dying for the Gods: human sacrifice in ancient Europe* (Stroud, 2001). Note also, R. Whimster, *Burial Practices in Iron Age Britain* (Oxford, 1981).

Harpenden cremations: preliminary publication in N. Faulkner, *Hidden Treasure. Digging up Britain's past* (London, 2003). Decapitation: R. Philpott, *Burial Practices in Roman Britain* (Oxford, 1991); A. Taylor, *Burial Practice in Early England* (Stroud, 2001). Infant burials:, E. Scott, *The Archaeology of Infancy and Infant Death* (Oxford, 1999). Note also, S. L. Keegan, *Inhumation Rites in Late Roman Britain: the treatment of the engendered body* (Oxford, 2002).

Religion

Location of temples and shrines: B. Jones and D. Mattingly, *An Atlas of Roman Britain* (reprint, Oxford, 2002); A. Smith, *The Differential Use of Constructed Sacred Space in Southern Britain from the Late Iron Age to the 4th Century AD* (Oxford, 2001). Type of temples, see Chapter 10.

Relatively unquestioning of the degree to which rural communities diverged from mainstream Romano-British religion are, G. de la Bédoyère, *Gods with Thunderbolts. Religion in Roman Britain* (Stroud, 2002); M. Henig, *Religion in Roman Britain* (London, 1984); G. Webster, *The British Celts and their Gods under Rome* (London, 1986).

Newer approaches: M. Millett, 'Rethinking religion in Romanization', in J. Metzler et al., *Integration and the Early Roman West* (Luxembourg, 1995); J. Webster, 'Necessary comparisons: a post-colonial approach to religious syncretism in the Roman provinces', *World Archaeology* 28.3 (1997). Understanding of pre-Roman religion: M. J. Green, *The Gods of Roman Britain* (Princes Risborough, 1983); *The Gods of the Celts* (Gloucester, 1986); *Symbol and Image in Celtic Religious Art* (London, 1989); 'The gods and the supernatural', in M. Green (ed.), *The Celtic World* (London, 1995); A. King, 'The emergence of Romano-Celtic religion', in T. F. C. Blagg and M. Millett, *The Early Roman Empire in the West* (Oxford, 1990). Ritual deposits and practices: A. Woodward, *Shrines and Sacrifices* (London, 1992). Religious material from southern Britain, M. J. Green, *The Religions of Civilian Roman Britain* (Oxford, 1976).

Some key excavations: I. M. Ferris et al., *The Excavation of a Romano-British Shrine at Orton's Pasture, Rocester, Staffordshire* (Oxford, 2000); N. E. France and B. M. Gobel, *The Romano-British Temple at Harlow* (Gloucester, 1985); T. Gregory, *Excavations in Thetford 1980–82, Fison Way* (Dereham, 1991); R. Leech, 'The excavation of a Romano-Celtic temple and a later cemetery on Lamyatt Beacon, Somerset', *Britannia* 17 (1986); M. J. O'Connell and J. Bird, 'The Roman temple at Wanborough, excavation 1985–86', *Surrey Archaeological Collections* 82 (1994); W. J. Wedlake, *The Excavation of the Shrine of Apollo at Nettleton, Wiltshire, 1956–1971* (London, 1982); A. Woodward and P. Leach, *The Uley Shrines* (London, 1993).

For Senuna, see N. Faulkner, *Hidden Treasure. Digging up Britain's Past* (London, 2003). On syncretism in the countryside, J. Webster, 'Interpretatio: Roman word power and the Celtic gods', *Britannia* 26 (1995); 'A negotiated syncretism: readings on the development of Romano-Celtic religion', in D. Mattingly (ed.), *Dialogues in Roman Imperialism* (Portsmouth, RI, 1997); cf. G. Webster, 'What the Britons required from the gods as seen through the pairing of Roman and Celtic deities and the character of votive offerings', in M. Henig and A. King, *Pagan Gods and Shrines of the Roman Empire* (Oxford, 1986); A. Zoll, 'Patterns of worship in Roman Britain: double named deities in context', in *TRAC* 4 (1995).

Curse tablets: see bibliography for Chapter 10, but especially Tomlin, in Cooley, *Becoming Roman, Writing Latin?* (2002).

Hero cults: R. Niblett, *The Excavation of a Ceremonial Site of Folly Lane, Verulamium* (London, 1999); cf. C. Forcey, 'Whatever happened to the heroes? Ancestral cults and the enigma of Romano-Celtic temples', in *TRAC* 7 (1998). Horse and rider brooches: H. Eckardt, 'Material matters: the social distribution of Roman artefacts', *JRA* 18 (2005).

Christianity: C. F. Mawer and C. Frances, *Evidence for Christianity in Roman Britain* (Oxford, 1995); D. Petts, *Christianity in Roman Britain* (Stroud, 2003); S. M. Pearce (ed.), *The Early Church in Western Britain and Ireland* (Oxford, 1982); see also references in Chapter 10.

On villa society, see also bibliography for Chapter 12.

16 DIFFERENT ECONOMIES, DISCREPANT IDENTITIES

The economy

Greenland icecap evidence of Roman period pollution, discussed by A. I. Wilson, 'Machines, power and the ancient economy', *JRS* 92 (2002). General studies of economy of Britain under Rome: M. G. Fulford, 'The economy of Roman Britain', in M. Todd (ed.), *Research on Roman Britain: 1960–89* (London, 1989); 'Britain and the Roman empire: the evidence for regional and long distance trade', in R. F. J. Jones (ed.), *Roman Britain: recent trends* (Sheffield, 1991); 'Economic structures', in M. Todd (ed.), *A Companion to Roman Britain* (Oxford, 2004). On embedded economies, see I. Hodder, 'Pre-Roman and Romano-British tribal economies', in B. C. Burnham and H. B. Johnson (eds), *Invasion and Response* (Oxford, 1979). Cross-channel trade from pre-Roman to Roman times is covered in S. Macready and F. H. Thompson (eds), *Cross-Channel Trade between Gaul and Britain in the pre-Roman Iron Age* (London, 1984); J. du Plat Taylor and H. Cleere (eds), *Roman Shipping and Trade: Britain and the Rhine provinces* (London, 1978).

The imperial economy

On the costs of the army and state bureaucracy, see R. P. Duncan-Jones, *Money and Government in the Roman Empire* (Cambridge, 1994). General studies of the Roman economy, see K. Greene, *The Archaeology of the Roman Economy* (London, 1986); D. J. Mattingly, 'The imperial economy', in D. S. Potter (ed.), *Companion to the Roman Empire* (Oxford, 2006). Roman censuses: W. Eck, 'Provincial administration and finance', in *Cambridge Ancient History* XI (2000). Taxation, see R. P. Duncan Jones, *Structure and Scale in the Roman Economy* (Cambridge, 1990). Economic demands of the army: W. S. Hanson, 'The Roman presence: brief interludes', in K. J. Edwards and I. B. M. Ralston (eds), *Scotland: environment and archaeology 8000 BC–AD 1000* (Edinburgh, 1997). Dependence: M. G. Fulford, 'Demonstrating Britannia's economic dependence in the first and second centuries', in T. F. C. Blagg and A. C. King (eds), *Military and Civilian* (Oxford, 1984).

The provincial economy

Money supply: P. J. Casey, *Understanding Ancient Coins* (London, 1986); 'The monetization of a third world economy: money supply in Britain in the first century AD', in M. Wood and F. Queiroga (eds), *Current Research on the Romanization of the Western Provinces* (Oxford, 1992); R. Reece, 'Site finds in Roman Britain', *Britannia* 26 (1995); *The Coinage of Roman Britain* (Stroud, 2002). On wider context: M. G. Fulford, 'Economic hotspots and provincial backwaters: modelling the late Roman economy', in C. E. King and D. G. Wigg (eds), *Coin Finds and Coin Use in the Roman World* (Berlin, 1996).

Markets: L. de Ligt, *Fairs and Markets in the Roman Empire: economic and social aspects of periodic trade in a pre-industrial society* (Amsterdam, 1993). Oculists' stamps: R. Jackson, 'A new collyrium stamp from Staines and some thoughts on eye medicine in Roman London', in J. Bird et al. (eds), *Interpreting Roman London* (Oxford, 1996).

Manufacturing expansion: H. Cleere, 'Industry in the Romano-British countryside', in D. Miles (ed.), *The Romano-British Countryside* (2 vols, Oxford, 1982); A. McWhirr, *Roman Crafts and Industries* (Princes Risborough, 1982).

Extra-provincial economy

Inter-provincial trade: K. Greene, 'Roman trade between Britain and the Rhine provinces: the evidence of pottery to c.AD 250', in Taylor and Cleere, *Roman Shipping and Trade* (1978); M. G. Fulford, 'Pottery and Britain's foreign trade in the later Roman period', in D. P. S. Peacock, *Pottery and Early Commerce: characterisation and trade in Roman and later ceramics* (London, 1977). On harbours: H. Cleere, 'Roman harbours in Britain south of Hadrian's Wall', in Taylor and Cleere, *Roman Shipping and Trade* (1978); G. Milne, *The Port of Roman London* (London, 1985). For Roman ships and boats, N. Nayling and S. McGrail, *The Barland's Farm Romano-Celtic Boat* (York, 2004); P. Marsden, *Ships of the Port of London, First to Eleventh Century* (London, 1994); A. J. Parker, *Ancient Shipwrecks of the Mediterranean and the Roman Provinces* (Oxford, 1992). Sanctuaries near the Rhine mouth, see M. Hassall, 'Britain and the Rhine provinces: epigraphic evidence for Roman trade', in Taylor and Cleere, *Roman Shipping and Trade* (1978). Imports of wine from the Continent are discussed by D. P. S. Peacock, 'The Rhine and the problem of Gaulish wine in Roman Britain' in Taylor and Cleere, *Roman Shipping and Trade* (1978). Luxury foods: C. Bakels and S. Jacomet, 'Access to luxury foods in central Europe during the Roman period: the archaeobotanical evidence', *World Archaeology* 34.3 (2003).

Trade (and tribute levying) with Free *Britannia*: W. S. Hanson, 'Across the frontier: addressing the ambiguities', in W. Groenman-van Waateringe et al. (eds), *Roman Frontier Studies 1995* (Oxford, 1997). L. Jorgensen et al., *The Spoils of Victory. The north in the shadow of the Roman empire* (Copenhagen, 2003) is a superbly illustrated account of extra-provincial contacts in northern Europe.

Different economies and different communities

The invisible economy: products of the land

K. Branigan and D. Miles, *The Economies of Romano-British Villas* (Sheffield, 1988); A. Grant, 'Animals in Roman Britain', in Todd, *Research on Roman Britain* (1989); 'Domestic animals and their uses', in Todd, *Companion* (2004); M. K. Jones, 'Crop production in Roman Britain', in Miles, *Romano-British Countryside* (1982); A. King, 'Animal bones and dietary identity of military and civilian groups in Roman Britain, Germany and Gaul', in Blagg and King, *Military and Civilian* (1984); 'Diet in the Roman world: a regional comparison of the mammal bones', *JRA* 12 (1999); M. Maltby, 'Iron Age, Romano-British and Anglo-Saxon husbandry – a review of the faunal evidence', in M. Jones and G. Dimbleby (eds), *The Environment of Man: the Iron Age to the Saxon period* (Oxford, 1981); 'Animal bones and the Romano-British economy', in C. Grigson and J. Clutton-Brock (eds), *Animals and Archaeology*. Vol. V: *Husbandry in Europe* (Oxford, 1984). Textiles and leather: J. P. Wild, 'Cross-Channel trade and the textile industry', in Taylor and Cleere (eds), *Roman Shipping and Trade* (1978); 'The textile industries of Roman Britain', *Britannia* 33 (2002).

Mines and metallurgy

General accounts of Roman mining in Britain: O. Davies, *Roman Mines in Europe* (Oxford, 1935); G. D. B. Jones and P. R. Lewis, 'Ancient mining and the environment', in P. Raatz (ed.), *Rescue Archaeology* (London, 1974); B. Jones and D. Mattingly, *An Atlas of Roman Britain* (reprint, Oxford, 2002). On Dolaucothi: B. C. and H. Burnham, *Dolaucothi-Pumsaint: survey and excavation, 1987–1999* (Oxford, 2004); P. R. Lewis and G. D. B. Jones, 'The Dolaucothi gold mines, I: The surface evidence', *Arch. J.* 89 (1969). Ingots from mining sites: see *RIB* II.1. Iron production: H. Cleere, 'The Roman iron industry in the Weald and its connection with the Classis Britannica', *Archaeological Journal* 131 (1985); H. Cleere and D. Crossley, *The Iron Industry of the Weald* (Leicester, 1986); I. Schrüfer-Kolb, *Roman Iron Production in Britain. Technological and socio-economic landscape development along the Jurassic Ridge* (Oxford, 2004); D. Sim and I. Ridge, *Iron for the Eagles. The iron industry of Roman Britain* (Stroud, 2002).

Purbeck marble: D. Hinton (ed.), *Purbeck Papers* (Oxford, 2002). For salt production: M. Nevell and A. P. Fielding, *Brine in Britannia. Recent archaeological work on the Roman salt industry in Cheshire* (Manchester, 2005); J. D. Hurst, *A Multiperiod Salt Production Site at Droitwich* (York, 1997); T. Lane and E. L. Morris, *A Millennium of Salt-Making. Prehistoric and Romano-British salt production in the Fenland* (Lincoln, 2001); S. Woodiwiss (ed.), *Iron Age and Roman Salt Production and the Medieval Town of Droitwich* (London, 1992). The use and sources of coal are surveyed by M. Dearne and K. Branigan, 'The use of coal in Roman Britain', *Ant. J.* 75 (1995); A. Smith, 'Provenance of coals from Romano-British sites in England and Wales', *Britannia* 28 (1997).

Military supply

P. P. M. Erdkamp (ed.), *The Roman Army and the Economy* (Amsterdam, 2002); C. R. Whittaker, *The Frontiers of the Roman Empire. A social and economic study* (Baltimore, 1994).

Pottery: patterns of consumption

Of general studies on Roman Britain, the fundamental work is P. Tyers, *The Pottery of Roman Britain* (London, 1996); see also M. Fulford and K. Huddleston, *The Current State of Romano-British Pottery Studies* (London, 1991); K. Greene, *Roman Pottery* (London, 1992); V. G. Swan, *Pottery in Roman Britain* (4th edn, Princes Risborough, 1988); P. V. Webster, *Roman Samian Pottery in Britain* (York, 1996); S. Willis, 'Samian pottery in Britain; exploiting its distribution and archaeological potential', *Arch. J.* 155 (1998). There are many relevant papers in A. C. and A. S. Anderson (eds), *Roman Pottery Research in Britain and*

North-West Europe: papers presented to Graham Webster (Oxford, 1981); J. Bird (ed.), *Form and Fabric: studies in Rome's material past in honour of B. R. Hartley* (Oxford, 1998); A. Detsicas (ed.), *Current Research on Romano-British Coarse Pottery* (London, 1973); J. N. Dore and K. Greene, *Roman Pottery Studies in Britain and Beyond* (Oxford, 1977); note also the *Journal of Roman Pottery Studies* (since 1984). On production technology, see the outstanding survey of V. G. Swan, *The Pottery Kilns of Roman Britain* (London, 1984). On the scale of pottery production: D. P. S. Peacock, *Pottery in the Roman World* (London, 1982); J. Gillam and K. Greene, 'Roman pottery and the economy', in Anderson and Anderson (eds), *Roman Pottery Research in Britain and North-West Europe* (1981).

On the meaning of pottery distributions: I. Hodder, 'Some marketing models for Romano-British pottery', *Britannia* 5 (1974); S. Willis, 'The Romanization of pottery assemblages in the east and north-east of England during the first century AD', *Britannia* 27 (1996); 'Samian, beyond dating', in *TRAC* 6 (1997); N. Cooper, 'Searching for the blank generation: consumer choice in Roman and post-Roman Britain', in J. Webster and N. Cooper (eds), *Roman Imperialism: post-colonial perspectives* (Leicester, 1996), argues for economic over social factors in artefact distributions. Amphoras: P. P. A. Funari, *Dressel 20 Inscriptions from Britain and the Consumption of Spanish Olive Oil* (Oxford, 1996); *Journal of Roman Pottery Studies* 10 (amphoras in Britain and the western empire) (2003); D. P. S. Peacock and D. F. Williams, *Amphorae and the Roman Economy: an introductory guide* (London, 1986). Impact of military supply on pottery distributions: Jones and Mattingly, *An Atlas of Roman Britain* (2002).

Regional pottery production (major wares): J. R. L. Allen and M. G. Fulford, 'Distribution of South-East Dorset Black Burnished Category 1 pottery in south-west Britain', *Britannia* 27 (1996); M. G. Fulford, *New Forest Roman Pottery* (Oxford, 1975); M. D. Howe et al., *Roman Pottery from the Nene Valley: a guide* (Peterborough, 1980); M. Lyne and R. S. Jeffreys, *The Alice Holt/Farnham Road Pottery Industry* (London, 1979); R. J. Pollard, *The Roman Pottery of Kent* (Maidstone, 1988); P. R. Wilson (ed.), *The Crambeck Roman Pottery Industry* (Leeds, 1989); C. J. Young, *Oxfordshire Roman Pottery* (Oxford, 1977).

Cultural identities: some concluding thoughts

See notably the bibliographies for Chapters 7, 10 and 15.

17 'NO LONGER SUBJECT TO ROMAN LAWS'

L. Webster and M. Brown (eds), *The Transformation of the Roman World 400–900* (Cambridge, 1997). For the archaeological context of late Antiquity: J. K. Knight, *The End of Antiquity: Archaeology, society and religion AD 235–700* (Stroud, 1999); E. A. Thompson, *Romans and Barbarians. The decline of the western empire* (Madison, 1982). R. Reece, *The Later Roman Empire: an archaeology* (Stroud, 1999) emphasizes that Britain was if anything more insular and isolated from the mainstream than it had been in the early Roman period.

For a variety of readings of events of the late fourth and early fifth centuries: J. F. Drinkwater, 'The usurpers Constantine III (407–411) and Jovinus (411–413)', *Britannia* 29 (1998); M. E. Jones, *The End of Roman Britain* (London, 1996); J. P. C. Kent, 'The end of Roman Britain: the literary and numismatic evidence', in J. Casey, *The Ending of Roman Britain* (Oxford, 1979); M. Kulikowski, 'Barbarians in Gaul, usurpers in Britain', *Britannia* 31 (2000); E. A. Thompson, 'Britain AD 406–410', *Britannia* 8 (1977); *St Germanus of Auxerre and the End of Roman Britain* (Woodbridge, 1984); I. Wood, 'The fall of the western empire and the end of Roman Britain', *Britannia* 18 (1987); 'The final phase', in M. Todd, *A Companion to Roman Britain* (Oxford, 2004). More archaeologically based accounts: C. Arnold, *Roman Britain to Saxon England* (London, 1984); P. J. Casey (ed.), *The End of Roman Britain* (Oxford, 1979); N. Higham, *Rome, Britain and the Anglo-Saxons* (London, 1992); E. James, *Britain in the First Millennium* (London, 2001).

On the debate as to whether the sub-Roman period marked a complete break with the past or was a continuation of late Antiquity: R. Collins and J. Gerrard (eds), *Debating Late Antiquity in Britain AD 300–700* (Oxford, 2004); arguing for substantial continuity (on thin evidence) is K. Dark, *Civitas to Kingdom: British political continuity 300–800* (Leicester, 1994); *Britain and the End of the Roman Empire* (Stroud, 2000). Contemporary Gaul: J. Drinkwater and H. Elton (eds), *Fifth-century Gaul: a crisis of identity?* (Cambridge, 1992). On the problems of late Roman and sub-Roman sources: D. N. Dumville, 'Sub-Roman Britain: history and legend', *History* 62 (1977); Dark, *Britain and the End of the Roman Empire* (2000). For the idea of a peasant revolt contributing to secession, N. Faulkner, *The Decline and Fall of Roman Britain* (Stroud, 2000). Convincing arguments against the validity of the rescript of 410 (and much other sensible commentary on the late sources besides), A. Birley, *The Roman Government of Britain* (Oxford, 2005).

Archaeological evidence for early fifth-century towns, D. A. Brooks, 'A review of the evidence for continuity in British towns in the fifth and sixth centuries', *OJA* 5.1 (1986); S. Loseby, 'Power and towns in late Roman and early Anglo-Saxon England', in G. Ripoli and J. M. Gurt, *Sedes Regiae* (Barcelona, 2000); R. Reece, 'The end of the city in Roman Britain', in J. Rich (ed.), *The City in Late Antiquity* (London, 1996). The end of coin imports and coin use: see P. Guest, *The Late Roman Gold and Silver Coins from the Hoxne Treasure* (London, 2005).

On regional responses to the collapse of Roman authority, C. J. Arnold and J. L. Davies, *Roman and Early Medieval Wales* (Stroud, 2000); C. Thomas, *Christian Celts: Messages and Images* (Stroud, 1998); T. Wilmott and P. Wilson (eds), *The Late Roman Transition in the North* (Oxford, 2000).

Index

Page-numbers in italics refer to maps and tables

Abandinus 484
Abergavenny 144, 412
Abingdon 390
accountants, sent to Britain by Julian 519
Achilles 464
Acton Scott *380*, 408–9
actress 301
Addedomarus 73
Adel 420
administration, breakdown of 531–3; civil
  260–61, 273, 275–6, 281, 291, 295,
  335, 339, 360–61, 525; military 93–4,
  186, 273, 291; third-century reforms
  227, 236; see also provincial government
Adminius 72, 75, 300; flight to Rome 94
Adventus Saxonicum, the 536
aedile, see magistrates
Aelius Brocchus, auxiliary officer 183–4
Aelius Modestus 463, 509
Aeneas, see Virgil
Aeresius Saenus, C. 209
Aesurilinus 300
Aetius 532
ager assignati 354; *a. publicus* 353, 354,
  359, 385, 407; *a. stipendiarius* 361;
  agri arcifini 359–60; see also land,
  status of
agency 15, 525
aggression 89–90; and 'terror' 91
Agricola, biography by Tacitus 26–7, 98
Agricola, Cn. Iulius, governor 5, 8, 91, 98;

and Ireland 441; and Scotland 88, 150;
  and urban development 277–8; career in
  Britain 116–19, 132, 145, 177–8,
  431–2
agriculture 58; changes under Rome
  366–9; crops 365, 366; pre-Roman
  expansion of 363–6; scale 366
agrimensores, see land surveyors
air-photography 356–7, 361, 368, 392–3,
  394, 402, 433
aisled hall, see villas
Akeman Street, Roman road 143
ala Augusta 121; *a. I Thracum* 190; *a.
  Indiana* 190; *a. Petriana* 181; *a.
  Sebosiana* 163, 184–5
alae, see auxilliaries
Alaisiagae 217, 223
Alamanni, Germanic people in Britain 241,
  250
Alaric 530
Albion (Britain) 29, 31, 437, 442
Alchester 110, *137*, 141–2, 329, 395;
  dendrochronology date 142; fortress
  142, 265; imported grain 221; small
  town at 142, 265, 395
Aldborough 149, 257, 258, 268, 276;
  Brigantian centre 262, 328, 419–20;
  mosaics and wall-paintings 320–21
Alderney 244
Aldwincle 193
Alfenus Senecio, L. governor 123

581

Alice Holt, pottery manufacturing 389, 516–17

Allectus, usurper 9, 176, 230–33, 231

Almondbury 419

altars 121, 169, 210, 302, 484, 521; and military religion 206, 215–17, 306–7; dedicated by civilians 306–7; rarity in rural zone 458, 482, 485, 521

Ambleside 193

Ambrosius Aurelianus 536–7

Amiens Patera 213–14

Ammaedara 360

Ammianus Marcellinus 27, 231, 232, 234–5, 456

amphitheatres 152, 268, 269, 282–3, 337–8

amphoras 221–2, 322–3, 360, 473, 475–6, 504, 514

Anavionenses, people of Annandale and Nithsdale 49, 148, 150, 174, 423, 495

Ancaster 484

Anencletus 300

Anglesey (*Mona*) 29; as granary of North Wales 145; conquest by Rome 97, 105, 112, 116; settlement on 416–17

Anglo-Saxon England 537

Angmering 381, 387–8, 469

Angus 429–39

Anicius Maximus, P. 186

animal bone 504–5; from Iron Age contexts 56; from military sites 220–21, 473, 475; from rural settlement 221, 363, 473, 475–6; from urban sites 221, 322–3, 473, 475

animals, domesticated species in Britain 475

Annandale 150, 425

annexation of territory 91

Annianus 313

Antenociticus 217–18

Antistius Adventus, Q., governor 179

Antonine Itinerary 32, 256–9, 257–8, 265, 470

Antonine Wall 8, 31, 120, 148, 152, 155, 159–60, 187–8; construction sequence 121–2, 159–60; design of 159; distance slabs from 209–10; epigraphic evidence 159; gates, fortlets and forts 159; military way 159

Antoninus Pius, emperor 8, 27; and advance into Scotland 121

Antonius Lucretianus, *beneficiarius consularis* 302

Apollo 403–4; altar to 216; A. Cunomaglus 484; on Iron Age coinage 68–9

Appian, view of Britain's unprofitability 492–3

aqueducts 268, 269, 279, 284, 341, 358

Aquilinus, imperial freedman 300, 302, 304

archaeology 19; evidence from 5, 44–6; urban a. 263–5

arches 302; Richborough 280

archipelago, British 29, 32

architecture, and change 362, 400; and continuity of tradition 392, 400; and elites 367; and identity 373, 377, 383; and technology 376; in Fens 385; in Sussex 387; Roman, 366, 370, 527; vernacular in Britain 367–9, 394

areani (frontier scouts) 231, 234, 235, 236, 502

aristocrats, aristocracy, see elites

Arminia 312

Arminius, German leader 71

Armoricans, people of Brittany 403

arms and armour 212, 248; in early Principate 206–8; late Roman changes 248–9

arms workshops, state run (*fabricae*) 249

army 88, 239; and law 204–5, 315; and literacy 199–204, 222, 247–8; and women 195–7; brutality to civilians 108, 173, 205; cost of 493; discipline 164, 205, 207, 251; early Roman organization 130–65; ethnic diversity and regional diversity 130–32, 166–9, 187–8, 190, 197, 199–201, 203,

215–16, 222–4, 228–9, 248–50; field army units, (comitatenses) 239, 240, 529; frontier troops (limitanei, ripenses) 228, 239, 531; hierarchy 217; identity and culture 199, 205–14, 250–52; interaction with civilians 166, 170–76, 185, 191, 198, 206–7, 412; careers 176–83, 204; late Roman organization 166, 182–5, 227–8, 238–47, 248, 250–52; Latin as lingua franca 166, 167, 199–202; levies and conscription 92–3, 153–4, 166; officers 180–85, 208, 216–17, 250; on campaign 88–9; pay and conditions 166, 184–5, 227; record-keeping in 130, 162–5, 200–202; recruitment of Britons 92–3, 128, 169, 186–7, 361; religious practice/ceremony 204, 214–18, 219, 220; role in civil government 128–30, 167, 171, 177, 186–9, 359; relationship with imperial government 125, 212; see also garrison, soldiers

Arnemetia 484

Arras culture 61

artefacts, Roman 430, 440; varied composition of assemblages 472–3

Arthur 237, 536

Asclepiodotus 233

Ashford Carbonell, 380, 408–9

Ashill 272

Ashstead 389

assize tours/courts, see justice

Atlantic Scotland 431–7, 439

Atrebates, people of Berkshire and Surrey 49, 95, 97, 99, 137, 262, 265, 381; civitas centre and settlement 389

Atrebates, people of northern Gaul 68–70

Atrectus, brewer 164

atrocities, in Roman sources 89, 91, 412

Attacotti, people of Ireland 37, 232, 235, 240–41, 437, 451–2

Attius Marinus, C. 516

Atys 484

Auchendavy 155, 195, 197, 216

Augustus, emperor 8, 72; dealings with Britain 70–72; Res Gestae 28

Aulus Plautius, governor 95, 97, 134

Aurelia Aia 196

Aurelia Concessa 463

Aurelia Eubia 196

Aurelia Lupula 197

Aurelia Quartilla 196

Aurelia Romana 196

Aurelia Sabina 196

Aurelian, emperor 233, 266

Aurelius Lunaris, M., merchant 298

Aurelius Marcus 196

Aurelius Modestus, M. 219

Aurelius Nepos, M. 186, 208

Aurelius Pusinnus 194

Aurelius Saturninus 313

Aurelius Senecio 318

Aurelius Ursicinus 462

Aurelius Verus, C. 298

Aurelius Victor, M. 189, 231

Auteini, people of Ireland 49, 443

autobiography 27

auxiliaries, 88; alae, 131, 228; and law 204; and North African pottery 223; armour of 207; Batavian units 131–2; brewing 222; careers 189–90; clothing 208–9; cohortes, cohortes equitatae 131; deployment of 131–2; in garrison 92–3, 130–31; numeri 92, 239; origins and nomenclature 189–90; pay and status 189–90, 192–3; quingenaria and milliaria units 131; recruitment 168–9, 192, 222; size of units in fourth century 238, 239, 246; tombstones 208; Tungrian Units 132, 168

Aves Ditch 81

Avienus 25

Avon Valley 398–9

Aylesford-Swarling culture 61–2

Ayrshire 422–6

Bacchus 348, 464, 471, 483

Baienus Blassianus, Q. 182–3

bailiffs 455

Bagendon *59*, 397

Baldock *55*, 76–7; and goddess Senuna 484

Balline, hoard *440*, 450–51

Ballinrees, hoard *440*, 450–51

Balmuildy *155*

Bancroft *381*, 478

banishment to Britain 456

banquet, scenes on tombstones 209

baptismal fonts 349

Bar Hill *155*

Barathes, Syrian *173*, 196

Barbarian Conspiracy 9, 232, 235–7, 502

barbarians, 'Barbarian Other' 9, 34, *120*, 524, 529–30; in sculpture 208, 210–11; 248, 428

Barbaricum 22, 24, 36

barbarism, model of progressive 34–6

Barkway 483

barley 220, 224, 365

Barnsley Park 396, 398

barracks, and cavalry 246; 'chalet' type 245–6; in 'villa'? 401; presence of women in 242, 245

barrels 221, 514

barrows 476

Bartlow Hills 478

Barton Court Farm 395

Barwick in Elmet 419

basilicas 336–7, 348; see also fora

bastion towers, see towers

Batavians 131–2; and brewing 222; compared with Gurkas 169; see also auxiliaries

Bath 186, 211, 214, 258, 259, 264, 289–90, 329, 396; baths at 283, *303*; *collyrium* stamp 498; curse tablets 310–15, *312*, *313*, 458–9, 482; inscriptions from 307–8, 399, 482; personal nomenclature in curse tablets 463; sacred spring 289; small town 287; stone quarries 510; temple 62, 186, 281

baths 259, 527; at forts 171; at temples 480; in towns 268, 269, 283–4, 338, 341; in villas 383, 471

Battersea shield 62

Baudihillia 223

Beadlam 214, *381*, 420, 454

beakers, and beer drinking 323, 475

beans 220, 221, 365

Bearsden *155*, 221

Beauport Park 509

Beda, see Alaisiagae

Bede 37

Bedfordshire 136, 383

beef 476

beer 475–6; as typical British beverage 323; drunk by garrison 164, 220–22; production of 220–22, 499

Belatucadrus 198

Belgae, people of southern Britain 49, 99, 262, 265, *380*, 389–90, 399, 498

'Belgic migration' 53–4

Bellaus Bellini 463

Bellerophon 464, 467

belt fittings 212, 249–51; Germanic 336; 395

Beltingham, inscription 219

beneficiarii 129, *173*, 188–9; inscriptions of 219, 296, 302, *302*, 303, 307

Benwell 217–18

Berikos, see Verica

Berkshire 139, 389

Betaghstown 449

Biccus *314*

Bicester 461

Bignor 374, *381*, 388, 469

Bilbury Rings 99

billeting of troops 129

Binchester 189

biography, ancient 26–8

Birdlip 396

Birdoswald *155*, 211, 215, 533; inscription from 245

Birnie, coin hoards from *430*, 438

Birrens 169; altar from 216, 257

bishops and bishoprics 348–9

Bisley Common 484

Black Burnished ware 212–13, 400, 517–18; see also pottery

Black Pig's Dyke *440*, 448

Boadicea, see Boudica

boar, wild 185, 210

board game 78

Bodmin Moor 140, *364*

Bogium, see Risley Park

Bolerion promontorium 28

Bollihope Common, boar hunt 184–5

books 201

bone, see animal

Bosham 469

Bossence 509

botanical remains, in military contexts 221; see also vegetation history

Boudica of *Iceni* 4

Boudican revolt 8, 75, 97, 110–13, 138, 331, 384, 526; accounts of 106–8; causes of 107–10, 261, 271, 293, 354; casualties in 93, 110–13

Boulogne 129, 133, 243

boundary markers 360–61, 365–6, 458, 477–8, 522

Bourton on the Water 398

Bowling Green Farm 394

Bowness *155*

Box *380*, 399

Boxmoor 383

Boyne Valley *440*

Bradford on Avon 379, *396*

Brading 463

Bradwell 242

Brampton 329, 516

Brancaster 242

branding iron 203

Brandon (Norfolk) *313*, 485

Brandon Camp, see Leintwardine

Branston, rural estate 454

Brantingham 420

Bratton Seymour 400

Braughing *55*, 76, *313*

Bray Head *440*, 449

braziers, North African type 188

bread 204, 220

bread wheat 365

Brean Down 48, *313*, *396*

Brecon Gaer 144

Breckland, Norfolk 364

Bretannoi 25

brewing, see beer

Bridgeness 210

bridges 149, 366

Briga, fort mentioned in *Vindolanda* tablets 183

Brigantes, major people of Northern England 8, 49, 82–3, 90, 97, 98, *137*, 148, 262, 381, 508, 523; annexation of kingdom 115–17; *civitas* centre 149; client kingdom 100; garrisoning of 146, 149; intimidation of 141; revolt? 121–2; resistance 102, 104, *120*; settlement 418–20; 442

Brigantes, *people of Ireland* 49, 443

Brigantian kingdom 98, 229

Brisley Farm 61

Britain, *passim*, contact with Rome in Iron Age 48; insularity of 528; names in sources 31; visits of emperors to 176–7

Britanni, *Brittones* 38, 92, *120*

Britannia 22, 29, 31–2, 229, 231; and first sub-division of province 126, 177; and second sub-division of province 227–8, 334–5; B. *Inferior*, third-century province 126, 177, 179, 180, 229; B. *Prima*, fourth-century province 227–8, 229, 334–5; B. *Secunda*, fourth-century province 227–8, 229, 334–5; B. *Superior*, third-century province 126, 177, 179, 229, 455; *diocese* 229, 519–20, 529–32; garrison 128–65; image of B. subdued on coinage 122; isolation of 20, 24, 126, 176, 234, 334, 362

Britannicus Maximus 234

Britanny 403, 538

Brithonic Celtic (P-Celtic) 52, 431, 436, 443

British Museum, Iron Age finds in 59–60; Roman finds in 527

Britons, described in ancient sources 33–7, 51; see also sources

Brittunculi, 'little Brits' 36, 165

Broadbridge 489

brochs 357, 423, 426, 430, 433–4

Brockley Hill 514, 516

Brompton *135*

brooches 209, 212, 406; crossbow type 249–51, 500; decline in use 209; Germanic types 336; horse and rider type 486–7; typology and distribution 213, 319–20, 471

brothels 175, 195

Brougham *148, 155*, 214; cemetery 224; personal names attested at 198

Brough-on-Humber 243–4, 256, 257, 258, 268, 276, 302, 328; possible *civitas* centre and settlement 420

Brough on Noe 135

Broxmouth 423, 430

Bryn Eryr *380*, 417

Bu Njem 215

bucket pendants 224

Buckinghamshire 136

building technology 376

Buittle 438

Bulmore 396, 412, 414–15

bureaucracy 129, 374; increased in fourth century 335

Burgh Castle 242

Burghhead *430*, 436, 439

burglary, attested in curse tablets 311, 485–6

burial clubs 194

burial rites, and status 345; Christian 343, 347; late Iron Age 77–80; orientation 347; see also funerary rites

burials 205, 343–7; British elite 100, 109; cremations 224; decapitated 478–9; demographic patterns 323–4; German influence/belts in 346–7; infant 246, 323, 347, 479; inhumations 344–5; palaeopathological data 323–4; warrior 61; see also cemeteries, grave goods, funerary rites

Buriton 469

Burnswark 121, 419, *430*

Burrow in Lonsdale 194

Bury Barton 402

Bury Close 394

Bury Hill 58

butchers 504

Butser Hill, experimental farm 365

butter 220, 476

Butu *313*

Buxton 264, 484

byres 363

Cadbury Castle 99

Caecilius Donatianus 215

Caer Gybi 243

Caer Leb 417

Caer Mead, see Llantwit Major

Caerhun 243

Caereni, people of western Scotland 49, 429–31

Caerleon, legionary fortress *137*, 144, 186, 211, 258, *258*, 262, 264, 396, 411; garrison settlement 192; ink writing tablets from 200, 204; sculpture from 205–6; grain imports 221; garrison 244

Caernarfon *137*, 145–6, 206, 243–4, 257, 258–9, 264, 418

Caersws *137*, 146, 418

Caerwent 243, 258, 259, 262, 268, 276, 328; basilica 336; *civitas* centre 205, 412, 414–15; graffiti 321; houses in 284–5; mosaics 320; statue dedication from 318; wells 341

Caesar, Iulius 8; account of Britons 34, 50; assasination 70; first campaign 64–5; second campaign 65–7; literary works 24, 28, 34; political background to campaigns 64–6

Caesennius Vitalis 453

Caistor-by-Norwich, *civitas* centre *55*, 139, 257, 258, 262, 268, 276, 279, 311, *313*, 328, 337, 384; auxilliary discharge diploma 193

Caithness 439

Caldicot 414

Caledonia 35; forest 30, 429

Caledonii, people of northern Scotland 35, 49, *120*, *148*, *231*; and Roman campaigns in Scotland 122–4, 132; relations with Rome 429–32, 435–6, 452, 502

calendar 531; and military life 204; and religion 215, 521

Calgacus, British chief 117, 119, 431

Caligula (Gaius), emperor *8*; planned invasion 72; accession 94, 117

Calleva, see Silchester

Callow Hill 394

Calpurnia Trifosa 300

Calpurnius Concessinius Q., cavalry prefect 121

Calpurnius Agricola, S., governor 179

Calpurnius Receptus, C., priest 300

Camborne 404

Cambridge 498

Cambridgeshire 384–5

Camelon *148*, 150, 152, *155*, 159

Camerton 470

camp prefects 185

campaigns in Britain 8, 9, 97, 98, 177, 231–2; evidence of 88, 121; of Agricola 117–19, 132, 435, 438; of Claudius 94–100; of Iulius Caesar 64–7; of Hadrian 119–20; of Scapula 102–6; of Septimius Severus 123–4, 152, 435; of Constantine 234; of Stilicho? 238; of Vespasian 114–19, 139

Campania Dubitata 197

Camphouse 438

Camulodunon, see Colchester

canabae, see garrison settlements

Candida Barita 305

candlesticks 214

cannibalism 34, 37, 428

Canterbury, *civitas* centre *55*, 257, 262, 268, 276, 279, 328, 386–7, 533; burial 205, 347; dark earth 340–41; early development 271; territory 386

Cantiaci, people of Kent 49, *137*, 262, 287, 307, *381*; territory and settlement 386–7

Cantissena 312

Cantium, kings of 50; *promontorium* 28, 29

capital, imperial 226

capitolia, rarity in Britain 281

Capricorn 210

captives, in sculpture 210

Caracalla, emperor 9, 27, 176; campaigns in Scotland 123–4, 152; extension of Roman citizenship, 192, 291; murder of brother Geta 124; withdrawal from Scotland 152–3

Caratacus, British prince 73, 75, 81, 94, 97; as war leader 96, 100–105, 145

Carausius, usurper 9, *231*, 176; career of 230–33; coins refering to Virgil's *Eclogue* 465; uses barbarians in army 241

Cardiff *137*, 144, 243, 245, 412

Carlisle *148*, *155*, 257, 258, 262, 264, 268, 328; and occupation of Scotland 150; fort at 115, 157, 243; ink writing tablets from 163, 200; inscription 121; Murrell Hill lady 209; possible *civitas* centre 261; rebuild of fort in 83–4 (winter) 118; regional centurion at 186–7

Carmarthen *137*, 276, 328, 411; fort 145; *civitas* centre 243, 258, 258, 262–3, 268

Carn Brea *380*, 404

Carn Euny 405

Carnonacae, people of western Scotland 49, 429–31

Carpow 124, *148*, 152–3, 188

Carr Dyke *383*, 385

Carrawburgh *155*, 157; religious dedications 215–16; sculpture from 206

Carriden *155*, 159; *vicus* inscription from 172

Carrock Fell 419

Carsington 393, 508

Cartimandua, queen of *Brigantes* 97, 98, 229; and relations with Rome 83, 90, 102, 104; and Brigantian revolt 114–15

Carvetii, people of Eden Valley 49, *148*, *174*, 260, 262, *380*, *418*, 499, 523

Carvoran *155*, 206, 215

Carvossa *380*, 406

Cassiterides, islands of 30

Cassius Dio 26, 97, 120, 122, 134, 293; description of Britons 35; on Boudican revolt 106–8, 110; on eastern kingdom 81; on invasion 96, 100

Cassivellaunos, British king 65–6

Castell Collen 144

Castell Henllys *380*, 411

Castledykes *148*, 426

Castleford *148*, 264, 420; and *regio Lagitiensis* 187

Castor (by Water Newton) 385

casualties (human impact) 6, 67, 93, 111–13, 118, 120; see also civilians

Cataurus, Ti. Claudius, see Claudius Cataurus

Catterick *148*, 257, 258, 264, 329, 512; *beneficiarius consularis* attested at 189; garrison settlement 172, 286, 420, 499

cattle, and military diet 220–21; and urban diet 322, 475, 504; in Iron Age 365; in Ireland 448; as export to continent 491

Catuvellauni, people of southern Britain 49, 68, 81, 97, 98, 100, 111, *137*, 137–8, 223, 262, 335, *381*, *382*–3

Cauci, people of Ireland 49, 443

cavalry 63, 87–8, 161, 181, 190, 210, 228, 248; armour and imagery 207; tombstones 189, 208; see also *ala*, auxiliaries

Cavenham 480

Cave's Inn 263

Cawthorn 136

Celtic, heads 206, 469; language 52, 429–31, 436, 443

'Celts' 51–2, 83–4

cemeteries 251; Brougham 224; Germanic 537; Iron Age 60–62, 77–80; military 224; rural 357; urban 223–4, 243–7;

war 99; see also burials, funerary practice

Cenacus 314

Cenimagi 65; see also *Iceni*

census 43, 174, 360–61, 495, 527

centuriation, regular division of land 359–60; lack of British evidence 359–60

centurio regionarius, see regional centurion

centurions 185–7, 189, 205, 208; duties 186; ethnic origins of 186; in towns 300; the first centurion (*primus pilus*) 186

ceramics, see pottery

Cerialis, see Flavius Cerialis, Petillius Cerialis

cereals 220–22; and storage 55–6; pre-Roman 364–5; see also grain

Cernunos 487

chain mail, see armour

Chalton (Hants) 390

chamfrons 203, 207

Channel, English 24–5, 30, 65, 129, 258

Chapel House Farm 421

chariots 34–5, 48; c. burials 48; c.- and horse-gear 48, 58, 60; c. racing 282–3; c. warfare 63; Ferrybridge c. 48; in art 464

Charlton (Kent) 387

Charterhouse on Mendip 264, 396; mining 135, 290, 317, 506–7

Chatteris *381*, 384–5

Chedworth 374, 396, 397–8

Chelmsford 259, 329

Chertsey shield 62

Cheshire 523

Chester *137*, *148*, 172, 257, 258, 262, 264, *380*, 533; and coastal defence 243; *beneficiarius* at 189; legionary fortress 146, 204, 211, 415; garrison settlement 192, 415; reduction of garrison 244–5; tombstone from 208

Chesters *155*, 189, 193, 197

Chesterton *313*

Chew Stoke, writing tablet 461

Chichester 109, *137*, 142, 257, 258, 262,

267–8, 269, 276–7, 302, 321, 328, 381, 523; *civitas* centre 59, 76, 387; Iron Age origins 96–7; military site at 100, 139, 266

chiefdoms 50, 56

Chignall St James 379–82, *381*

children, and dress 209; and military community 170, 183, 197, 204, 209, 224; and mortality 323–4, 344–5

Chilterns 382, 523

Chimaera 464

chi-rho symbol 349, 466–7, 471

Chisenbury Warren 390

Christianity 9, 228, 248, 485, 487, 535–9; and Christian iconography 466–7, 471, 487; at Lullingstone villa 387, 467; impact on towns 325–6, 348; imperial attitudes to 325; influence on burial practice 345–7; sparcity of British evidence 326, 348–9

christians 325

Church, the, as landowner 456; in sub-Roman Britain 534–5

church councils 348–9

churches 348–9, 485

Chysauster 405

Cicereius Felix, P. *313*

Cicero, M. Tullius 47, 64, 67

Cintusmus 299

circus, 283; at Colchester 268–9, 282; theme in mosaic art 464

Cirencester, *civitas* centre 137, 190, 229, *258*, 262, 269, 302, 328, 523; and early military occupation 142; and *Antonine Itinerary* 259; cemetery 343; defences 331; Jupiter column 334–5; mosaics 320, 321, 464; *municipium*? 263; provincial capital? 228; public buildings 282–3, 533; seal from 317; imperial sculpture/tombstone 208, 318; rural buildings 340; urban development 276–7

citizens and citizenship, Roman 130, 189–90, 192, 204, 261, 274, 299–300, 303, 337, 453, 460, 462, 526; and children of soldiers 204; edict of Caracalla 192, 291

civil government, and local administration 337; army role in 129–30, 188–9; governors 129, 227–8; late Roman changes 227–8, 334; see also imperial household, procurators, soldiers, taxation

civil war 8, 9, 125, 231, 232; after Nero 113; impact of 249; and army 123–4, 248–9; and Agricola 177–8; and Third-Century Crisis 225–6; and urban defences 327

civil zone 129–30, 202, 528

civilians, and collateral damage 91–2; and civic status 330–33; and military community 108, 170–76, 191, 199, 206–7, 251–2; and officials 259; assault by soldiers 205; bias in law 204; clothing 208–9, 319–20; diet 220–21; in garrison settlements 193, 202; reprisals against 235; sculpture 206, 318–19; trade 221

Civilis *312*

civitas centres 260–63, 272–3, 276–86, 317, 320, 384; and defences 332; and manufacturing 321–2; and public benefaction 303; and small towns 286; and villa settlement 382; failed examples 265–6; mosaics and wall paintings 320–21; recognition by Rome 263; territories and economic resources assigned to 281, 354–7, 359, 495; workshops 337

civitates, see peoples

Classicianus, see Iulius C.

Classis Britannia, see fleets

Claudia Martina 300

Claudia Severa, birthday invitation to Sulpicia Lepidina 183, 201–2

Claudian, poet 238

Claudius, emperor *8*, 176; arch of (Rome) 96; death and impact on Britain 104; invasion of Britain 75, 84, 94–100;

Claudius, emperor – *cont.*
  temple at Colchester 107, 110, 271,
  281
Claudius Cataurus, Ti. 300
Claudius Hieronymianus, legionary legate
  302, 304
Claudius Ligur . . . , citizen *303*
Claudius Paulinus, Ti., legate of *legio II*
  Augusta 179–81, 318; governor of
  Britannia Inferior 179–81; letter to
  Sennius Sollemnis 179–81
Claudius Tirintius, Ti. 190
Claudius Triferus, Ti. 507
Claydon Pike *381, 395, 396,* 461
clearance of woodland, see deforestation
client kingdoms 8, 67–72, 97, 98, 138,
  229; and Roman interference 75, 90–91,
  94–5, 100; annexation of 101, 138–9,
  258, 387; archaeological evidence for
  75–80, 137–8; hostages from 71; land
  allocations to 361; of Togidubnus
  265–9, 277; post-conquest clients
  99–101; relationship with other clients
  81–4; succession in 72, 75, 91
client rulers 267
cliff castles, see promontory forts
Clifford 144
climate 37
Clipsham 510
Clodius Albinus, D. governor and usurper
  9, 123, 125, 126, 176, 233, 237, 327
Clothall *313,* 485
clothing and textiles 336, 492, 498–9; and
  military supply 498–9; cloaks 208–9,
  249, 318–19, 505; female 209, 318–19;
  Gallic coat 208, 319; in military
  sculpture 208–10; trousers 208; toga
  210, 319; see also dress, shoes,
  underpants, *Vindolanda* tablets
clubs (*collegia*), see guilds
Clwyd 145–6, 415–17
Clydesdale 425–6
Clyro *137,* 144
coal and coalfields 511
coastal defences 242–3; down Solway

coast 157; in Gaul 242; western Britain
  243; north-eastern Britain 243–4; in
  Channel 243–4; see also Saxon Shore
cob walling 394
Cocceia Irene 196
Cocceius Firmus, M. 195, 216
Cocidius 218
coffins 478; lead-lined 344; gypsum-packed
  344, 478
Cogidubnus, see Togidubnus
cohors I Hispanorum 183; *c. I Tungrorum*
  162–3; *c. II Asturum* 183; *c. II*
  Britannorum 92; *c. II Tungrorum* 169,
  216; *c. IV Lingonum* 181; *c. Usiporum*
  132; *c. VI Thracum* 142, 190; *c. III*
  Batavorum 162–3; *c. VIIII Batavorum*
  162–3, 181; *c. I Vardulorum* 162–3
cohortes 238; see also auxiliaries
coins, Iron Age 59, 68–9, 70–74; and
  Cunobelin 74; changes post-Caesar 69,
  80; classical imagery on 68–9, 72–4;
  distribution of 56, 373; hoards 141;
  imports 69; in ritual deposits 62–3;
  Latin legends on 38, 69, 71, 73–4; of
  Iceni 81; of *Corieltavi* 81–2, 141; of
  Dobunni 82; of *Durotriges* 82;
  portraiture 74; serial imagery on 69, 80;
  mint mark on 73; used for dynastic
  legitimation 70–71, 73–4
coins, Roman 226, 497, 527, 531, 538;
  and coin supply 492, 497; as evidence
  for military deployment 232, 244; as
  votive offerings 480; end of imports
  from Roman empire 529–30; forgeries
  497; in Scotland 438; in Ireland 449;
  issued by usurpers 232; late Roman
  clipped 530–31, 538; late Roman
  distribution 338, 473; subdued *Britannia*
  image 122; see also hoards, monetization
Colasunius Bruccius/Caratius 463
Colchester 42, *55,* 97, 109, 137, 142, 229,
  257, 258, 262, 268, 276–7, 328, 511,
  533; Balkerne Gate 331; capture of
  95–6; circus at 271–2, 282; *colonia* 108,
  137, 192–3, 260–61, 265, 282, 292,

354; Gosbecks and Iron Age settlement
59, 75, 271; inscriptions from 181, 186,
190, 208; Iron Age burials 77; legionary
fortress established 126, 271; mosaics
from 320–21; native Britons attached to
colonia 110, 260–61, 271–2, 379;
pottery 212–13, 514, 516–17; sacked by
Boudica 106, 271, 333; Sheepen area 75;
temple of Claudius at 107, 110, 271,
281; veteran settlement 187, 271–2
collaboration with Rome 525–6
collateral damage 91–2
collegia see guilds
colonialism 4, 109, 375–6, 524–5; and
religion 215; archaeology of 13–14;
impacts of 63, 91–2; modern 525
colonies (*coloniae*) in Britain 108, 137,
142, 222, 260–61, 266, 271–2, 301,
390; administrative responsibilities of
355; and centuriation 360; defences 332;
auxilliary veterans at 193; honorary
c. 261; re-use of fortress buildings 272;
tombstones from 305, 318–19
Colsterworth 393
Combe Down, imperial estate *380*, *396*,
399, *455*, *458*, *510*
comes Britanniarum (Count of Britain)
238–9, *239*
comites, see counts
commentarii, record keepers 129
Commios (Commius), Gallic then British
king 66, 69–70
Commodus, emperor *8*, 122, 125, *125*;
statue of 211
communications 527; civil 274; *cursus
publicus* 259, military 142; see also
roads
communities 18, 218, 333, 355, 461, 502,
520–22, 531; and economy 503–20;
military 291–2, 306, 525; rural 356,
453–87; urban 267, 292–324
community of soldiers 18, 241, 247; and
ethnicity 223, 250; and literacy
199–204, 247–8; and native women
220–22; diet 220–22; dress 206–9,

248–9; distinct from civilians 206–7,
250–52; hierarchical nature of 206;
material culture of 205–14, 222, 230,
247–9; membership of 166–8, 202, 213;
religion 214–20; representations of
206–11; ritual and ceremony 204
concubines 175, 190
Condrausius 187
confederation 66, 418–20, 423, 431–2
conquest, Roman 7, *8*, 72, 97, 98;
progressive impact of 367
conscription 168, 249; of native peoples
169, 176
Constans, emperor *9*, 76; winter visit to
Britain 25, 231, 234–5
Constantine I (the Great), emperor *9*, 176,
227, 231, 234, 237; and Christianity
228; bust of 211; campaigns in Britain?
234; declared emperor at York 234,
241
Constantine II *9*
Constantine III, usurper 176, 232, 520,
529–31, 538; depletion of British
garrison 237–8
Constantius I (Chlorus), emperor 176, 231;
campaigns in Britain 230, 233–4; dies at
York 233; *panegyric* to 223, 492
Constantius II, emperor *9*, 234–5
construction 527; see also towns
consumption, of foodstuffs 220–22,
321–3, 504–5; of Roman material
culture 212, 321–3; 453, 472–6, 496,
502
continuity, in towns 325, 533, 538
Conwy Mountain, hillfort 416
cooking 474
cooking stands, North African 188
copper, mining in Britain 145, 409, 417
copper-alloy artefacts 201, 207, 211, 213
coppicing 365
Corbridge, fort and garrison settlement
121–2, *148*, *155*, 157, 163, 174, 188,
215, 257, 264, 269, 329; and occupation
of Scotland 150, 152; small town 172,
261, 289

cord rig, cultivation 425
Cordius Candidus 302
core–periphery model 56–7
Coria (Corbridge), referred to in
    Vindolanda tablets 183
Corieltavi, people of East Midlands 49, 97,
    137, 262, 381; coinage and hoard 81–2,
    140–42; conquest of 98, 101; garrison
    140–42; settlement 390
Coriondi, people of Ireland 49, 443
Corionotatae, people of Northumberland?
    121
Cornavii, people of northern Scotland 49,
    429–31
corn-drying ovens 363, 410, 415, 499
Cornelius Peregrinus 181
corniticularii, governor's staff 129
Cornovia, see Cornwall
Cornovii, people of Cornwall? 49, 137,
    140, 262, 380, 407
Cornovii, people of Shropshire 42–3, 49,
    137, 223, 262, 380, 408
Cornwall 140, 402–8, 456, 463, 523, 539;
    administered separately from Devon
    under Rome? 140, 402–8; mineral
    resources 30, 403, 406–7, 506, 508–9;
    settlement 403–5
Corotica 484
corvées, forced labour 335
Cossutius Saturninus, C. 187
Cote 394
Cotswolds 141, 393, 396
council, of Three Gallic Provinces 181;
    provincial c. 299
councils, Church 9, 348–9; of Arles 348
Count of Saxon Shore 239, 239, 242–3
counts (comites) 232, 235–6, 239–40,
    242–3
courts, assizes 337; in towns 337
courtyard houses, Cornish settlement type
    259
Coventina 215–16
Covesea Cave 439
Cow Roast 76
Cowbridge 412

Coygan Camp 380, 411
craft production 290, 533
craftsmen 295; and epigraphic habit 109;
    immigrant 500, 525
Craig Phadraig 436
Crambeck, pottery 516
Cramond 148, 152, 155, 426
Crandon Bridge 396, 516
Crannogs 430, 433
Crediton 380, 401
cremation, see burials
Creones, people of western Scotland 49,
    429–31
Crickley Hill 534
crime 164; see also justice, army, civil
    government
Croes Carn Einion 413
Cromwell 381, 392
crops, introductions in Roman period
    366
Cruchain, Connaght in Ulster Cycle 440,
    444, 446
Cúchúlainn 443
cultivation 340–41, 363–6, 421, 433; see
    also agriculture, husbandry
cults, head 477, 479; hero 486
Cumbria 146–9, 421–2
cuneus Frisiorum 223
Cunobelin (Cunobelinus), British king 8,
    72, 81, 109–10; coinage 74; succession
    94
Cunorix, son of Maqqos-Colini 502
cupids 483
curatores 163
curia Textoverdorum, people of Hadrian's
    Wall area 218
curial class, numbers in Britain 293;
    paucity of inscriptions set up by 318–19
currency bars, see ingots
curse tablets (defixiones) 40, 310–15,
    312–14, 521; curses and binding spells
    310; distribution in Britain 310–14, 521;
    emphasis on theft curses 40, 310, 485;
    from Bath 311, 312–13, 314–15,
    458–9, 463, 521–2; from London 311,

313, 314, 521–2; from rural districts
313, 458–9, 463; from Uley 458–9, 463,
482, 485–6; illiterate versions 482;
nomenclature on 311–14; ritual nature
of deposition 311, 315
cursus publicus 32, 259, 333, 358
customs dues (*portoria*) 158, 491, 494,
501; exemptions from 499–500, 512
Cwymbrywn *380*, 410

Dacia, annexation of 355; 'extermination'
of Dacian people 355–6; mineral
resources of 506
Dal Riata 431–2, 437, 444
Dalswinton *148*, 150
Dalton Parlours *381*, 420, 454–5
Damastown *440*, 449
Dan y Coed 411
Dan y Graig 413
Danebury 54–6, *55*, 58
Dane's Cast *440*, 448
Dannicus 190, 208
Darenth 387
Darini, people of Ireland 49, 442
Dark Ages and Dark Age archaeology 538
'dark earth' 340–41
Dartmoor 140, 364
dates, chronology xvi, *8, 9*
Dea Regina 484
debts 191
Decantae, people of northern Scotland 49,
429
decapitations, see inhumations
Deceangli, people of north-east Wales 49,
97, 102, 116, *137*, 262, *380*, 508;
garrison 145, settlement 415–16
Decianus Catus, procurator 106–7
Decimus Caerellius Victor, prefect *219*
decline 225, 325
decurions, urban magistrates 189, 299
dedications *219, 302, 303*; at Brougham
198; by women 197, 216, 317; collective
217–18; in army and garrison
settlements 194, 202; of public buildings
301; of religious buildings 315; to

foreign gods 188; using paired names
216–17
dediticii, see submitted peoples
deer, roe 220–21
defences, Iron Age 54, 56, 58–9, 66, 76–7,
83; defended farmsteads 56, 58; see also
hillforts, *oppida*, rural settlement
defences, urban 326–33, *328, 329*;
addition of walls 330–31; and insecurity
331; as symbols of civic status 331–2;
dating 326–7
defixiones, see curse tablets
deforestation 363–6, 423, 429
deities 206, 211, 214–18, 219, 220; British
215–18, 308–9, 484, 486–7, 521;
classical 215–16, 308, 482–4, 520–21;
Eastern 309–10, 484–5; Gallic 217,
484, 486; Germanic 223; paired
214–17; recorded at *Vindolanda* 218,
219–20
Delfinus 197
delimitation, outline survey of land 359
Demetae, people of south-west Wales 49,
116, *137*, 262, *380*; garrison 144–5;
settlement 410–12
Demetrius, explorer of northern seas 25
demography, male:female imbalance in
urban society 323–4, 344–5
dendrochronology 154
deposition, ritual 53, 62, 310; structured
62
Derbyshire 507–8
Dere Street, Roman road 147–8
deterrence 91, 158
development, regional 379–427
Devil's Dyke 76
Devon 135, 523, 539; garrison 139–40;
settlement 401–8
Dewlish 400
Diana 216, 308, 483–4
Didius Gallus, A., governor 104
dies 203–4
diet 527; at *Vindolanda* 220–22; in army
213, 220–22, 474; in towns 221, 322–3,
474; rural 221, 474–6

Din Lligwy 417
dining rooms 466, 476
Dinorben 380, 415
Dio, see Cassius Dio
Diocese, see Britannia
Diocletian, emperor 9, 227, 249; reforms
    of 374
Diodorus Siculus 28
Dionysius Fortunatus 197
diplomacy 68, 75, 89–90, 524
diplomas, auxiliary, distribution of
    discharge certificates 172, 192–3,
    454
disarmament 97, 101, 110
discharge, from army 204, 214; diplomas
    172–3, 193
discipline, military 164
discrepant experience 17, 222, 491; d.
    identity 18, 522, 525; diversity of
    experience 15
distance slabs 209–10
Ditches, The 374, 396, 397
Ditchley 394
Diviciacus 53–4
Dobunni, people of West Country 49, 97,
    137, 262, 380, 381; and territory 81,
    398–9; and urban development 265;
    coinage 82; conquest and garrison 98,
    101, 141–2; settlement 395–7
Docilianus 312, 459
Docilius, decurion 163
Docimedes 313
documents, and Roman administration
    361; see also sources
dogs 184, 365
Dolaucothi 380, 411
Domitia Attiola 313
Domitian, emperor 8; and Agricola 178;
    withdrawal from Scotland 118, 151
Domitianus, emperor 226
Doncaster 420, 516
Dorchester (Dorset), civitas centre 142,
    258, 259, 262, 269, 276, 399, 517;
    graffiti 321; mosaics 320; Poundbury
    cemetery 328, 343, 347

Dorchester (Oxon) 55, 302, 329, 393;
    beneficiarius 189; oppidum 81
Dorset 139, 399–400
Dorsey, The 440, 448
Dover 129, 138, 242, 257, 264, 302
Draco 214
Draethen 414
Dragonby 55, 381, 393, 476
Drayton 381, 392
dreams and visions 482
dress 527; female 209, 319–20; military
    167, 206–8, 248–9, 336, 498–9; see
    also clothing
Droitwich 135–6, 290, 510
druids (druides) 50–51, 97, 310, 482; and
    resistance 105–6
Drumanagh 439, 440, 441–2, 447–9
Dryburn Bridge 423, 430
Dubnovellaunos 73
Duccius Rufinus, L. 208
duces 228
Dulcitius, dux Britanniarium 236
Dumbarton Rock 436
Dumfries and Galloway 422–6
Dumnonia, sub-Roman kingdom 532, 539
Dumnonii, people of Clyde valley 49, 148,
    150, 423, 426
Dumnonii, people of East Devon 49, 97,
    137, 139–40, 262, 380, 523; territory
    and settlement 401–8
Dun Ailinne 440, 445–6, 449
Duncote Farm 409
duns 357, 423, 426, 430, 433–4
Dunston's Clump 421
Durobrivae, see Water Newton
Durocornovium 140
Durotriges, people of Somerset and Dorset
    49, 97, 137, 262, 380; coinage 82;
    submission 98; garrison deployment 139;
    status in late Roman period 335;
    settlement 399–400
dux Britanniarum 232, 236, 238, 239
Dyfed 144–5, 410–12
Dyfed, sub-Roman kingdom 539
Dyke Hills cemetery, Dorchester 344, 346

dykes 58–9, 76, 385
dynastic marriage 81

East Midlands, iron production 509–10;
    rural settlement 364, *381*, 390, *391*
Eastbourne *381*, 387–8
Easter Happrew 426
eastern kingdom 49, 55, 68, 97, 137, 474;
    coinage of 68–71, 73–4; conquest 95–8;
    expansion of 80–81; garrison 138–9;
    principal *oppida* 75–6
Eblani, people of Ireland 49, 442–3
Eccles *313*, 386–7
Ecimius Bellicianus Vitalis, L. 187
economic development 499, 504, 518–9
economies 491–520, 528; and
    monetization 492, 497, 516; collapse of
    Roman 497, 518–20, 530–31;
    embedded 496; extra-provincial
    499–502; Imperial 493–6, 503; market
    527, 531; provincial 496–9, 503; rural
    505–6
Edict of Milan 9
Edinburgh 424, *430*, 438
Egnatius Tyranus T. *313*
Eildon Hill North 424–5, *430*, 438
elephants, in Britain with Claudius 96
elites 10, 93, 453–60, 465–7, 470–71; and
    burials 345; and estates 356; and
    housing 339; and public buildings 338;
    and villas 367, 376, 386; in eastern
    counties 379–82, 384; in post-conquest
    period 100, 109, 175, 183, 281, 303,
    306; in Scotland 433, 438, 502; late
    Roman wealth 325
Ely *380*
Emain Macha (Narvan), royal centre in
    Ireland 444–5
emigration, of Britons to Britanny and
    Spain 538
emmer wheat 365
emperors 7, 176; and landholding 362,
    538; origins 227
empire 13; British 251; impact on
    scholarship 3–5; nostalgia for 5

Empire, Roman 6–7, 22–3, 524–8;
    balance sheet of 525; decline and
    political change 225–38; economic
    impact 19, 493–6; human cost 6;
    imagery of 212; division of 227; impact
    on Britain 6, 12, 19; rise of Christianity
    228; unpopularity 532; 'without limits'
    89, 94
enamel and enammeling 213–14
enclosed farmstead/settlement 56, 58, 374,
    383; see also rural settlement, defences,
    Iron Age
Enderby 393
Engleton 408–9
entertainers 301
environmental data 363–6
Epaticcus 73, 81
Epidii, people of western Scotland 49,
    429–31
Epidium promontorium (Kintyre) 431
epigraphic habit 38, 202–4, 296–318; and
    burial 345; late Roman decline of
    247–9, 335
epigraphy 38–41, 43, 222, 241, 335, 526,
    535; see also inscriptions
Epona 216–17, 486
Epperstone 392
equestrians 10, 180–85, 227; careers in
    military (*tres militiae*) 181–2, 186; from
    British towns 299, 301; number of posts
    in Britain 180; origins of equestrian
    officers in Britain 181–2; property
    qualification 182
Eratosthenes 28
Ermin Street, Roman road near Gloucester
    143
Ermine Street, Roman road 141, 458
Erpeditani, people of Ireland 49, 443
Essendon 76
Essex 379, 382, 523
estates, imperial 353, 354, 359, 371–2,
    384–6, 455–6, 459, 493, 523; in Africa
    371–2
estates, private 359, 453–5, 472, 499; and
    elite 356

ethnicity, and Germans 222–4, 248, 250; and identity 223

ethnogensis 452

ethnography, ancient 34–6; 418

euergetism, see public benefaction

Europa, and the bull 464–5, 467

Eusebius 231

Eutropius 231, 232, 428

events, historical 8–9

evidence, rules of 21–46

Ewell 389

Excingus 223

Exeter 137, 140, 258, 259, 262, 269, 272, 276, 328, 336–7, 347, 401, 523

Exmoor 140, 364

expansionism 90, 126, 158, 178, 353; and Roman power 97

exports from Britain 505–6, 514; grain for Rhine provinces 501, 505; in Iron Age 491; in Roman period 492

Exsuperius 312

Exuperius, bishop 349, 471

eye doctors, see oculists

Fairy Knowe 430, 439

Fal Estuary, Roman harbour? 406

familia Caesaris, see imperial household

family 204, 209, 245

famine 112

Farley Heath 313, 485–6

farming, and invisible economy 505–6; changes in scale under Rome 366, 499, 527; economic importance of 492; in Iron Age 361, 363–6, 499; structures 363; within towns 340

Farmington 398

farmsteads 382; isolated 383; defended 56; see also rural settlement

Farnham 389

Faunus 484

Favonius Facilis, M. 186–7, 208

feasting 306, 470, 474–6

federates 230; settled in Britain 240–41

Feigh Mountain 440, 449

Fen Causeway, Roman road across Fens 139

Fenland 477, 523; administration of 385; and saltmaking 384; Iron Age/Roman settlement 384–5; lack of villas 385

Ferrybridge 48–50

fertility, notions of 479

festivals 204, 290, 337, 520

Ffrith 380, 415–16

fibulae, see brooches

field survey 356, 368, 383

fields 262, 283, 389–90, 522; Iron Age field systems 360–61, 364–5

Fife 429–39, 435

Fifehead Neville 400

fifth-century crisis 325

Filey 244

Fimmilena, see Alaisiagae

finger rings 212–13, 317

fires, urban 233–4

fiscus, imperial treasury 166

fish and fish sauce 220, 322, 474–5, 514

Fishbourne 76; late Iron Age activity at 474; military activity at 100, 139, 266; 'palace' 373–4, 381, 387–8, 454, 469

Flavia Augustina 209

Flavia Caesariensis, fourth-century province 227–8, 229, 334–5

Flavian dynasty 177–8; and urban development 266; and conquest of Britain 113–19; military deployments 135–54

Flavius Cerialis, prefect at Vindolanda 162, 164, 177; career 181–3

Flavius Jovinus 250

Flavius Quietus, S. 186

Flavius Sanctus 250

Flavius Senilis, T., religious prefect? 482

Flavius Stilicho 230

Flavius Verecundus 187

Flavius Virilis, T. 185

fleet, the British (classis Britannica) 129, 138, 156, 182–3, 230, 240–41, 386; later f. 233, 241–3

Flint 415

Florentius, praetorian prefect 519

Floridius Natalis, T. 186

Flower Hill 440, 449

Folkestone, villa 381, 386

Folly Lane 77, 270–71, 477, 486

food, see diet

Footlands 509

fora at major towns 263, 279, 281, 336–7; at Gloucester 366; at London 275, 280–81, 336–7; at Silchester 270, 281; at St. Albans 277; changes in late Roman period 336–7; function 281

force, exemplary 89–90, 99

Forden Gaer 146, 244, 418

foreigners 108–9, 261, 526; and urban community 293–4, 298; inscriptions 300–306; settlement in Britain 386–7

forest, Caledonian 429; myth of primeval cover 38; F. of Dean 396, 509–10

Forth–Clyde isthmus 123, 150–52, 154, 155, 159, 430; Agricolan forts 117; and Antonine Wall 121

fortlets 152, 156, 159

fortresses 143–6, 150, 533–4; and civil communities 168; animal bone assemblages 220–21; distribution 133, 134; for vexillations 133, 134, 142–3, 147, 152–3; internal layout and construction 160–61; legionary 133, 142–4, 146, 161, 204, 244, 250; re-use for urban foundations 390; sculpture from 205–6, 211; see also garrison pattern

forts, 132–65, 133, 177, 239, 241, 424, 426, 534; and absence of 431; animal bone assemblages 220–21; annexes 171; barracks 160, 245–6; commanding officer's house 184, 246; construction and layout 160–61; defences 160, 242; distribution 132–65; for auxilliary units 148, 172, 205; fourth-century 242, 244–6; garrison communities 168, 170–76, 246; 'glen blockers' 151; headquarters building 215; lamps from 211; numbers of 153–4; f. of Saxon shore 239; on Antonine Wall 159–60;

on Hadrian's Wall 156–8; parade grounds 207; religious buildings 217–18; sculpture from 206; size of 160; slaves in 194; variable occupation at Vindolanda 162; women in 242, 246; see also garrison pattern

Fortunata, slave 'girl in question' 294–5

forum/basilica complexes, see fora

Fosse Way, Roman road 134, 143, 401

Fotheringhay, village and villa 383

four seasons, representations of 464

Frampton 380, 465–7, 487

Franci, people of Germany 226, 231, 241

Fraomarius 250

Free Britannia 119, 150, 428–52, 523–4

freedmen 187, 294, 301; and religious practice 309; as merchants 298; as seviri Augustales 298; in imperial service 295, 300, 302, 303–4, 399, 455

freedwomen 294, 300

Freestone Hill 440, 449

friendly kings, see client rulers

Friagabis 223

Frilford 287

Frisia, pottery from 223

Frisii, people of Holland 132

Frocester Court 380, 396, 397–8, 480, 534

frontiers, Roman 119, 154; see also Hadrian's Wall, Antonine Wall

Frontinus, S. Iulius, governor 116, 145, 178

Fronto 120, 120

Frumentius 216

Fullerton 381, 390

Fullofaudes 235–6, 250

funerary inscriptions, and commemoration 526; and military community 207–8, 210; rarity in rural and urban communities 202, 210, 526; and women 196–7, 299–300, 318; see also inscriptions

funerary rites 527; and identity 223–4; cremation 477–8; excarnation 477–8; inhumation 478–9; in Iron Age 477; in rural districts 476–9; see also burial

furnaces 336–7

Gabbroic wares 403

Gabrantovices, people of northern Britain 418

Gadebridge 383

Gaelic 443

Gaius, see Caligula

Galba, emperor 113–14

Galerius 9, 228, 234

Galian, Leinster in Ulster cycle 444

Gallia Belgica, province of northern Gaul 8, 22, 303, 307; cultural similarities with *Britannia* 486; *G. Lugdunensis* 22

Gallic Chronicle 536

Gallic coat 208–9

Gallic Empire 8, 9, 226–33, 231

Gallienus 226

Gangani, people of Ireland 49, 443

Ganymede 464

Garn Boduan 380, 416

garrison settlements 170–76, 260, 264, 499, 522; administration of 171–2; and identity 291–2; and native Britons 198; auxilliary veterans at 193; by forts (*vici*) 170; by legionary bases (*canabae*) 192, 216, 222; culture of 171; epigraphic evidence for 170–71; fourth-century decline 246; impact on settlement 420, 422, 426; inhabitants of 192–8, 205; in Wales 415; *mansiones* in 259; relationship with forts 171–6; religious dedications from 194–5, 217–18

garrisons, military 128, 522; and empire 128, 166–7; and government 177; and mining 411; Claudio-Neronian 134; coastal defence 135; economic impact of 153, 161–2; Flavian 135–6, 150; Trajanic-Hadrianic 135; in northern Britain 135, 146–9; in Scotland 149–53, 434–5; in south-east 136–42; in south-west 136–42; in Wales 142–6, 239–40, 412; late Roman reductions 501, 528; on Hadrian's Wall 157–8; on Antonine Wall 159–60; relationship with civil community 166–7, 251–2; Severan

152–3; size in Africa 131; size in Britain 130–31, 153–4, 166, 222, 237–8, 528; third-century changes 238–47; see also army, auxilliaries, legions,

Gask Ridge, watchtowers and road on 148, 151

Gatcombe 380, 396, 399, 456

gates 326, 331

Gaul 530–31; contact with 109

Gayton Thorpe 378

gemstones, imagery on 212

Genii Cucullati 487

genius loci 219; *g.* of the land of Britain 216; *g.* of the *praetorium* 218, 219

Genounian territory 122

geography, ancient 28–37

Germania 22, 169

Germanic peoples 223–4, 350; raids across Rhine and Danube 226; recruits in army 248, 250; resettlement within empire 228, 240–41, 250; settlement in Britain 543–8

Germanization 223–4, 228, 536

Germanus of Auxerre 535

Germany 154

Geta, emperor 9, 123–4; murder of 124; visit to Britain 176

Gildas 37, 225, 232, 532, 535–6

gladiators 282–3; as theme in mosaic art 464–5; at Leicester 301; female? 301

Glamorgan 412–15

glass 473; at military sites 211; beads in burial 224; engraved 317; in Cornwall 406; mould blown 316–17

Glenlochar 148, 150, 152

globalization 17, 525, 527

Gloucester, fortress 137, 142, 208; *colonia* 192, 260, 272, 279, 397; and *Antonine Itinerary* 258, 258; and urban development 262, 268, 276, 279, 396; decline 340–41; forum 366; imperial statue from 318; mosaics 320, provincial capital? 228; seal from 317; temple 281

Gloucestershire 396, 397

Gnostic, interpretation of mosaics 467

goats 220, 322 see also ovicaprids

Godmanchester 259, 289, 329, 348, 484

Gododdin, 424, 432

gods, horned 487, see also deities

Goidelic Celtic (Q-Celtic) 52, 431, 443

gold 403–4, 491–2, 506–7; mine at
    Dolaucothi 411; workshop at Malton
    171

Goldborough 244

Goldcliffe, 'drainage' inscription 414

Golden *440*, 449

Goldherring 405

Gordian I, emperor 176

Gorhambury 76, *381*, 382–3

Gosbecks, see Colchester

Goths 9

government, provincial 128–30, 493–6,
    531–2; and *beneficiarii* 129, 188–9,
    303; civil 255–61, 334–5; local 260–61,
    280, 532

governor's staff 129, 188–9, 275, 303;
    numbers 129; *stratores* 129, 303; use of
    soldiers on 129, 188–9, 526

governors 129, 173, 493; careers 177–80;
    changes in third century 227; early
    Roman (*legati*) 177–80; ethnic origins
    179, 250; late Roman (*vicarii* and
    praesides) 227–8, 250; numbers known
    334–5, 337; public benefactions of 303;
    role and average term 177–8, 255–6

graffiti 38, 188, 395; on walls 321; see also
    inscriptions, words on things

grain 491–2, 501, 505, 511; see also
    cereals

Grampian region 429

granaries 55, 363–4

Grandford 139, 385

grape vine 366, 384

Grateley South 390

Gratian, emperor 9, 232

Gratian, usurper 176, 232, 237, 250, 529

grave goods 249, 345–6, 477–8; at
    Brougham 224; at Winchester 346; shoes
    346

Gravelly Guy 394–5

Great Bulmore 244

Great Casterton 329, 392

Great Chesterford *137*, 239, 476

Great Dunham 193

Great Witcombe 396, 397

Greaves Ash 421

Greta Bridge 189, 193, 196

Grim's Ditch 55, 81; *oppidum* and villas
    393–4

growth, economic 499, 504, 528

Grubenhäuser (sunken floored buildings)
    533

guilds (*collegia*) 194, 298, 303; craft 109,
    267, 298, 302; military 169, 217;
    religious 216; see also clubs

Gurness 434

Gussage All Saints 58

Gwent 412–15

Gwynedd, sub-Roman kingdom 539

gynaeceum, state weaving works 335

gypsum 345, 347

HA see *Historia Augusta*

Hadrian, emperor 8, 27, 119–20, 158,
    173; visit and expedition to Britain *120*,
    156, 176,

Hadrian's Wall 8, 31, *120*, 135, 148, 149,
    154–60, *155*, 182, 188, 258; Antonine
    abandonment 121, 159; construction
    119, 154–7, 162; design of 156, 174;
    final phases 533; forts on 157–9; forts
    damaged in 180s? 122; fourth-century
    garrisoning 233, 238, 241, 245, 251,
    355; function of 156–8; gates, towers
    and milecastles 156–9; later Antonine
    recommissioning 121, 159; pollen cores
    near 364; pottery production 213;
    second-century garrisoning 157–8;
    'separated Romans and barbarians'?
    158, 174; sequence 156; Severan
    renovation 152; souvenir metal vessels
    from 213–14; stone and turf sections
    156; the Vallum 157–9; whitewashed?
    156; workforce 156–7, 335

Halcombe *380*

Hallstatt culture 52–3, 451

Halstock 378, 400

Ham Hill 139

Hamble Estuary, curse tablet *313*, 482

Hambledon 461

hamlets, see villages

Hampshire 389–90

handwriting, at *Vindolanda* 201–2; styles 314–15

harbours, see ports

hare 221

harness gear 207; see also chariots

Harlow 476, 482

Harpenden, richly furnished cremation burials 477–8

Harpham *381*, 420

Haterius, Nepos, T., attested in *Vindolanda* tablets 174; census of *Anavionenses* 174

Haverfield, Francis 4–5

Hayes Farm 402

Hayling Island *55*, 62, 480, 486

headquarters building, see forts

health 323

hearths 246, 336–7

Hebrides 29

heirs 204, 459

Hembury 140

Hengist and Horsa 532

Hengistbury Head *55*, 56

Hercules 211, 216, 483; H. Saegon 309

Herefordshire 143

heresy 534

hero cults, see cults

Herodian 27, 36, *120*, *125*

Heronbridge *380*, 415

Hertfordshire 136, 382–3

Heybridge *264*, *381*, 480

hides, animal 491

High Cross 143

High Ham 400

High Rochester 257

Highland line 429, 431–6

hillforts 54–6, 143, 410, 416–19, 430, 440, 447; and Roman conquest 99, 139;

in Scotland 432; reoccupied in late antiquity 534, 538

Hinton St Mary *380*, 400, 466–7, 487

Historia Augusta 27, *120*, *125*, 231

history, Roman, key dates 8–9

hoards 406, 492–3, 502; Carn Brea 404; fourth-century hoards 326; Hoxne 462, 470, 538; Ipswich 59; in Ireland 450–51; in Scotland 438; Iron Age 59–60; Mildenhall 470; non-recovery of 493, 538; Snettisham 59, 212; south-east Leicestershire 140; Traprain Law 357; Water Newton 349

Hockwold 384, 480, 482, 484; curse tablet 485–6

Hod Hill *55*, 99, 139

Holcombe 401

Holme House *381*, 420–21

Holt 172, 187–8, 415, 516

Holyhead 243

honey 220

Honeyditches (Seaton) 401

Honorius, western emperor 9, 230, 529–30; rescript to British towns? 530

Horkstow 464

horses, in Iron Age 59, 365; in burials 224; and Roman cavalry 207

hostages (*obsides*) 71, 75

Houghton Down 390

houses, aisled-halls 339; courtyard 285, 339–40; in towns 281, 284–6, 339; strip buildings 285, 287, 295, 320; winged corridor 285, 339; see also towns, villas

Housesteads *155*, 169, 172, 189, 197; Germans at 223; women at 246

housing, domestic 281, 284–7, 326, 338–40

Howe 434

Hoxne treasure 470; coins from 470; personal names on items 462

Humberside 141, 392

Huntcliffe 244

hunting 221; as elite activity 184–5, 465; evidence of *Vindolanda* tablets 184;

as arena entertainment 282–3, 465,
467–8
hunting nets 184
Hunt's Pridianum 512
Hurly Hawkin 430, 439
husbandry, animal 475, 499; crop 499
hypocaust heating 410

Iavolenus Priscus, L., *iuridicus* 275
Iceni, people of East Anglia 49, 91, 97,
137, 138, 262, 381, 498, 508;
annexation and revolt of 106–8, 384;
client kingdom 100–101; coinage of 81
Ickham 386, 455
Icklingham, Christian finds 348, 487;
church 485
Icknield Way 138–9
iconography, funerary 207–9, 318–19
identity 18–19, 292, 520–28; and
architecture 373; and dress 206–9, 213,
249; and ethnicity 223, 230; and
funerary practices 345–7; and material
culture 205–14, 247–9, 321–3, 472;
and origins 189–90, 296–8; and religion
210, 347–50, 520–21; and rural
communities 358, 377, 386, 453–87,
520–21; and status 223; and the military
199–214, 222–4, 230, 247–52, 520–22;
and the urban community 292, 321–2,
326–33, 339, 520–21; and British Iron
Age traditions 17, 59, 83–4, 472;
'Roman' 199, 520, 525, 539; see also
discrepant identity
Ilam, metal vessel from 213–14
Ilchester 264, 269, 287, 289, 329, 344,
517; possible *civitas* centre 261; villas
near 399–400
Ilchester Mead, villa 396, 400
Ilkley 148
imagery, power of 207–10, 212
Imilcho 300
immigrants 318–19, 324, 374, 454, 500,
525; see also foreigners
imperial cult 219; and provincial council
299; at military sites 310; dedications to

imperial *numen* 307, 310; in countryside
458, 482; in towns, 298, 310; temple at
Colchester 310
imperial estates, see estates
imperial household, slaves and freedmen in
provincial administration 294–5, 303–4,
458, 496, 510
imperialism 522, 524–8; legacy of
nineteenth- and twentieth-century
attitudes 4–5, 7, 11, 14–15, 17, 128,
525; non-consensual nature 525; Roman
315
imports to Britain 61, 75–81, 214, 221–2,
322–3, 511–12; import subsitution 500,
504; late antique 537
Inchtuthil 148, 151, 436, 430; construction
of fortress 161
India, British 92
industrial settlements 290–91
Indutius Felix, C. 458
infant burials see burials
infant mortality 344; and infanticide 479
infantry 63, 87–8, 208, 228, 248
Ingelborough 419
ingots 500; copper 417, 449, 508; iron 57;
lead 139, 409, 416, 507; pewter 508;
silver 450, 508; stamped 139, 416, 450,
507–8; tin 405, 508
inheritance 204
inhumations, decapitated 478–9; in coffins
344; in shrouds 344, 346; in organized
urban cemeteries 343–7; prone 479; see
also burials, funerary practice
Innocentia 349
inscriptions 39, 43, 179, 180, 184–5, 189,
197, 209–10, 302–3, 399; distribution
in Gaul 296; distribution pattern in
Britain 39, 202, 217, 318, 336; fourth
century 222, 244, 247–8; from
Hadrian's Wall 156, 223, 245; from
countryside 454, 457–60, 482; from
towns 267, 296–306, 325, 334; graffiti
188, 203, 321; on stone 202–3, 335;
religious 215–18, 219–20, 302–3, 349;
recording military victories 121; sub-

inscriptions – *cont.*
Roman class I type 535; words on possessions (*instrumentum domesticum*) 38–40, 203–4, 207, 213–14, 296, 316–18, 461–2, 513

intaglio rings, see finger rings

interior decoration 183–4, 211, 320–21, 339; see also mosaics, wall-paintings

interpretatio Romana, see syncretism

invasion 8, 24, 94–100, 97; of Caesar 47; of Claudius 75, 84, 95–100

Inveresk 426

Inverness 118

I.O.M., see Jupiter Optimus Maximus

Iovinus, *magister equitum* 236

Iraq 91–2

Irchester 329, 383

Ireland (*Hibernia*) 29, 32, 49, 439–52, 440, 524; and Irish Sea 441–2; claims of Roman invasion of 439–41; conversion to Christianity 535; economy 448, 501; in Ptolemy's *Geography* 442–3; La Tène culture in 448; linear earthworks 440, 448; literary sources 428, 442–4; material culture of 448; migrations to western Scotland? 537; migrations to western Wales? 451, 535, 537; peoples of 442–5; raids 534; Roman material in 439–41, 440, 448–52; royal sites 440, 443, 445–7, 449; settlement types 440, 446–8

iron 213; major ore deposits 136, 140, 386–7, 392, 491, 506, 509–10; smithing 405, 407

Iron Age, burial 60–62; client kingdoms 68–83; hoards 59–60; in Britain 5, 8, 48, 83–4, 266; in Europe 52–3; leadership/kingship 60, 74; religion 62–4; settlement, society and economy 12, 50, 54–5, 57–64, 83–4, 361–6; warfare 63–4

iron fist, exemplary use of force 87–90, 99; punitive action 106

Isis 484

Isle of Man 29

Isle of Wight 29, 98

Islip 394

itineraries and road maps 32–3, 256–9, 257–8, 265

Iulia Brica 305

Iulia Fortunata 305

Iulia Velva 305

Iuliana 462

Iuliona 196

Iulius Agricola, see Agricola

Iulius Bellicus, L. 453

Iulius Caesar, see Caesar

Iulius Classicianus, C., procurator 112; tombstone in London 265

Iulius Frontinus, see Frontinus

Iulius Maximus 197

Iulius Quadratus, M. 186

Iulius Severus, S., governor 121, 179

Iulius Verecundus 163

Iulius Verus, Cn., governor 159, 179

Iulius Vitalis 187

Iuventius Sabinus 463

Iuthungi, Germanic people 226

Iverni, people of Ireland 49, 443

Jarrow monument 119

Jerome 37, 529

jet 441–2

jewellery 209, 211–13, 480

Josephus 10, 100

Juba II 100

Julian, emperor 9, 235, 519

Jupiter 216, 308, 482–3; J. columns 302, 334–5; J. Dolichenus 217; J. Optimus Maximus 215, 218, 219

justice 164, 256, 281, 337; administration of 129; summary 93

Juvenal 205; poetic allusion to Ireland 441

Kelvedon *313, 381*

Kenchester 264, 329, 498

Kennell Hall Knowe 421

Kent 386–8, 523; Iron Age coinage from 80; kings of 66; sale of woodland in 361; Keynsham *380*, 401; villa and possible imperial estate 396, 399, 458, 480 kilns 513, 516–17

Kimmeridge shale 400

King Harry Lane cemetery 61, 78–80

kingdoms 97; of Scotland 432; of Ireland 444–9

kings and kingship 8, 97, 428, 524; surrender to Claudius 96; see also client kings, client kingdoms

Kingscote 264, 380, 396, 397–8, 445, 480; tombstones from 459; wallpaintings 468

Kingsholm 110, 137, 142

Kinvaston 137, 143

Kipling, Rudyard 251

Kirk Sink 380, 419

Kirkbride 155, 183

Kirkby Thore 193

Knock Hill 421

Knockadigeen 440, 447

Knocknashee 440, 447

Knowth 449

La Graufesenque 513–14

La Tène culture 52–3, 440, 448, 451

labels, lead 317–18

Laeti 240–41

Laigan (Galian), Leinster in Ulster Cycle 444

Lake District 136

Lake Farm 137

Lambay Island 440, 441–2

lamps 211, 478; distribution of 214, 473

Lancashire 146–7, 418–19

Lancaster 148, 189, 243

Lanchester 189

land, allocation of 191–2, 353–5, 359, 362, 369, 412–15; clearance 361; confiscation 272, 353, 379, 384, 455; economic mobilization of 494; ownership 354, 358, 453, 471; public or state 172, 353–4, 359, 455–6, 494; reclamation 414; rents 494, 505; sales 354, 361, 453; status of 359, 373; surveyors (agrimensores) 353, 359–60; see also ager

land survey 359

landholding, patterns of 108, 355, 358–60, 371–2, 382, 427

landowners, and conscription 249; women 455

landscapes, and change 362–3, 366–9, 383, 407; categories of 367–8; Iron Age 363–6; of imperialism 355, 358, 366, 428; of opportunity and resistance 369, 385, 522–4; Roman provincial 379–427, 522, 527

language, British 52; 'Celtic' 52, 429–31, 433; Greek 296; Latin 199–202, 296, 311, 450, 458; Neo-Punic 188

Lankhills, Winchester 343, 346

late antiquity 538–9

Latin 173, 212; as lingua franca 166; as spoken in the army (sermo militaris) 167, 181, 199–202; late antique inscriptions 535; names 187–8, 189–90, 199–200, 203, 217; place-names 42–3; spoken by Britons 71

Launceston 140

law 315, 336; and military community 204–5; British customary 261; martial 93; Roman 205, 261, 337, 347, 512

Laxton 510

Lea Cross 408–9

lead 139, 145, 398, 409, 415, 506–8; in Cornwall 403; labels and seals 317–18; tanks 349, 508

Lease Rigg 136

Leckie 430, 439

legacies 204; as source of imperial landholding in Britain 494

legal experts (iuridici) 275

legal systems 37

legio I Minervia 179; II Adiutrix 90, 115, 131, 179, 188; II Augusta 96, 110, 114–15, 130, 139, 152–3, 179, 185–6, 210, 239, 244, 401, 507; III Augusta 185; III Parthica 185; VI Ferrata 179; VI Victrix 126, 131, 153, 180, 185–6, 188, 223, 238, 244; VII Gemina 119; VIII Augusta 119, 131; IX Hispana 90, 98, 110, 115, 131, 180, 188; X Fretensis

legio I Minervia – cont.
185; *XIV Gemina* 90, 98, 110, 113–15, 130, 188; *XX Valeria Victrix* 98, 110, 115, 130–31, 142, 173, 185–6, 210, 223, 244, 416; *XXII Primigenia* 119

legionaries 187–9

legionary, centurions 185–7; legates (numbers and tenure) 180, 184, 189, 210, 302, 303; tribunes 180

legions 22, 130–31, 144, 156, 159, 239; late Roman reductions 239; numbers and size of 131–2; outposting 188; vexillations of 134; withdrawals from Britain 188; see also army, garrison, *legio*

Leicester 55, 137, 141–2, 257, 258, 262, 269, 276, 279, 297, 301, 328, 391; amphoras from 323; *civitas* centre 390; damage to basilica 336; date of street grid 279; mosaics 320–21; Newarke Street cemetery 343; seals from 318

Leicestershire 62, 77, 317

Leighton *137*, 143

Leintwardine 143, 264, *313*

levies, military 6, 221

Lexden tumulus 62, 77–80

libraries 466

lighting 214

Lilliesheaf 438

limitanei 228, 239

Lincoln 55, *137*, 228, 229, 257, 258, 262, 268, 276, 302, 318, 320, 328, 391; bishopric 348; Brayford Pool 141; church (St Paul in the Bail) 347–8, 533; colony 141, 192, 260, 272, 279, 390; dark earth 340–41; forum 272, 281, 348; legionary fortress 141, 390; pottery production 516; provincial capital? 335; temple 281; veterans at 193

Lincolnshire 392–3

Lindow Man 62, 477

Linley *380*, 409

literacy 38–41, 43, 130, 471, 521, 527, 537; allusions to Virgil 201, 464–5, 467–8; and army 38, 130, 199–204,

215, 222, 247–8; and curse tablets 482, 485–6; and intaglio rings 212; and religious practice 202, 215, 218, 308, 310–15, *313–14*; and rural society 482–3; and stone inscriptions 202, 215; and urban society 308, 315–18; at *Vindolanda* 40, 183; of women 183, 201–2; writing implements as evidence of 461–2

literature, Roman 38, 201, 464–5, 467–8; Welsh 237

Littlechester, Derbyshire pottery 516

Littlecote 466

liturgies 494

Livy 6, 26

Llandeilo 144

Llandough 413

Llangollen 145

Llantwit Major (Cae'r Mead) 205, *380*, 413

Llanymynech 99, 145, *380*, 409, 417

Llyn Cerrig Bach, hoard 55, 62

Llys Brychan *350*, 410

loans, to British elite 107–10

local government, as function of towns 335–7; late Roman 339

Lockington *381*, 392

Lockleys 370

Lollia Bodicca 185, 187

Lollius Urbicus, Q., governor 121, 179

London 32, *137*, 192, 207, 211, 221, 229, 236, 256, 257, 258, 262, 268, 276–7, 302, 328; amphitheatre at 265; as capital of British diocese 276; as centre of government 265, 275; as port and trading centre 500, 504, 511; bishopric 348; cemeteries 344–5; *colonia* status? 261, 275; commercial centre 273–5; Cripplegate fort at 265, 275; crossing point of Thames 273; curse tablets *313*; dedications at *302*, *304*, 348; demography 323–4; fires 333–4; forum/basilica complex 275, 280–81, 336–7, 348; foreign merchants at 109; 'governor's palace' 275; harbour facilities 284; housing 284–5; in Saxon times 533; military presence 138, 188–9, 273–5; mint at 335; mithraeum 348; mosaics and wallpaintings 320; provincial capital 228, 274, 280, 335; regional treasury at 335; sacked by Boudica 323; seals from 318; size of 263, 275; slaves attested at 294–5; urban development at 265, 274–5, 321; Walbrook stream 315–17, 341–3; wells and rubbish pits 338, 341–3; writing tablets from 200, 275

Longinus Sdapeze 190
Longthorpe 110, 137, 138
Lossio Veda, Caledonian 297, 309, 502
Lothian 422–6
Loudon Hill 152
Loughor 144, 243
Lovernisca 312
Low Ham 465
Lucinius 234
Lucius Verus, emperor 8
Lucullus, son of Amminius 300, 307
Lufton 400–401
Lugi, people of northern Scotland 49, 429–31
Lullingstone 381, 387, 465, 467, 469, 478, 487
Lupicinus, magister equitum sent to Britain 235, 240
Lurio 197
luxury foodstuffs 184, 475, 505
Lydney 313, 396, 480, 482–5; curse tablet 485
Lympne 242, 257, 264

Machen 396
Maeatae, people of north-eastern Scotland 35, 120, 122–4, 148, 153, 432, 435–6, 452, 502
Maenius Agrippa 183
Maesderwen 380, 413
Maesius Auspicatus, P. 304
magister equitum, m. peditum 228
magistrates 260, 299, 337, 361; aedile 260

Magnentius, usurper 9, 231, 235, 237, 519
Magnus Maximus, usurper 9, 176, 232, 237, 240, 519
Magor 380, 406–7
magus, British term for market 498
Maiden Castle 55, 139, 480; siege at 99
makers' marks, see inscriptions
malnutrition 323
Malpas 193
Malton 136, 148, 171, 193, 264, 420
Mam Tor 419
Manapii, people of Ireland 49, 443
Mancetter 137, 143
Manchester 5, 148, 516
Mandela, Nelson, at Jongintaba's 'villa' 375–6
Mandubracius 64, 68, 70
Mansfield Woodhouse 381, 392
mansiones 177, 259, 289
Mantinia Maerica 305
manufacturing 321, 333–4, 338, 498–500, 504, 515–18, 527; and markets 338, 515; fifth-century collapse of 529, 531, 533, 538
maps 28; Roman (formae) 360; modern 356–8
marble 307, 387, 397, 469; arch at Richborough 280; floor and wall veneers 469; see also Purbeck 'marble', statues
Marches, the Welsh 142–3, 408–9
marching camps 424; as evidence of campaign routes 88, 115, 117, 123–4, 145, 151, 435; Stracathro type 117
Marcommanic wars 169
Marcus, usurper 176, 232, 529
Marcus Aurelius, emperor 8
marine scenes, in art 464–5, 468–70
Marinianus Belcati 463
Marinus of Tyre 31
market buildings (macella) 268–9
markets 289, 338, 494, 527; and place-name evidence 498; as regional centres 506; cessation of 538; evolution 496–9; land m. 453; slave m. 294; supervision of 129, 331, 358

Marlborough Downs, curse tablet *313*, 482

Mars 210, 216, 218, *219*, 308, *313*, 315, 463, 467–8, 482; M. Alator 484; M. Belatucadrus 216; M. Camulus 217, 307; M. Cocidius 214, 216; M. Corotiacus 484, 487; M. Lenus 309, 484; M. Medocius 309; M. Nodens *313*, 484; M. Ocelus 309; M. Olludius 484; M. Rigisamus 463, 484; M. Rigonometes 309, 484; M. Thincsus 217, 223; M. Toutatis 217, 484

martial ethos 212

Martiannius Pulcher, M., governor *302*, 304

Maryport 148, *155*, 157, 183, 215, 243

massacres 105

material culture 363; aceramic 408, 415, 422; and identity 52–3, 205–14, 293, 472–4, 526; and evidence of literacy 199–205; and contact with Ireland 439–41, 448–52, 524; and contact with Scotland 426, 428–9, 437, 524; and resistant conservatism 472; changes in fifth century 529; in western and northern Britain 476

Matres, see mother goddesses

Mauretanian kingdom 94, 100

mausolea 210, 478

Maxentius 231, 234

Maxima Caesariensis, fourth-century province 227–8, 229, 334–5

Maximian, emperor 9, 227, 230, 231, 232–4

measurement xvi, 359

meat and meat consumption 220–22, 322–3, 475–6; salt m. 221, 386; urban processing of 322

medical implements 78

Mediterranean Sea 24

Medusa 465

Mela (Pomponius Mela) 28, 30, 448

Melania 455

Menai Straits 145

Mendip hills 396; mineral resources 506–7

Meole Brace 408

Meols 380, 415

Meonstoke 377

mercenaries, Germanic 536; Irish 535

merchants 108–9, 173, 202, 303; and military supply 512–13; as landowners 456; attested in Britain 297–8, 525–6; commemorated by inscriptions 305–6; named at sanctuaries of Domburg and Colijnsplaat 297, 500

Mercury *219*, 308, *313*, *314*, 315, 465, 467, 482–5; M. Andescocivoucos 308–9

messengers 129

metals 492, 500, 527

metalware 184, 211, 213

metalworking 384; in ex-public buildings 336–7

Mettus 459

Metunus *313*, 315

Middlewich 135–6, 172, 380, 409; auxiliary discharge diploma from 173, 193

Mide (Brega), Meath in Ulster Cycle 444

migrations, 'Belgic' 53–4; Germanic 230; Irish 411, 451–2; Saxon 535–8

Milan 224

Mildenhall 329; figural scenes on treasure 470–71

milestones 335, 457–8, 522; from Cornwall 458

Milford Haven 145

military community, see community of soldiers

military disaster (*clades*) 106

military records, see army

military treasury (*aerarium militare*) 166

military zone 528

Milking Gap 158

Mill Hill 61

mills, rotary grain 499; see also querns

mineral resources 64, 115, 145, 363, 398–9, 494–5, 506–7, 523, 527; as motor of expansion 101, 134–6; location of 136; exploitation of 139, 362, 407, 414–16, 418; forts linked with 135, 418; in *Dacia* 506; in Spain 415;

Minerva 216, 308–9, 483–4; see also Sulis Minerva

mines 361, 494, 506–11; and mining districts 317, 523; Cornwall 406–7, 508–9; Mendips 506–7; north Wales 415–17, 506–8; organization of 409, 411, 415–17, 506–7; Peak District 506–8; south Wales 412, 414, 506–7

mining 290; economic importance of 492, 494; involvement of troops in 130, 415–16; involvement of procurators 507; involvement of socii 507–8; in Cornwall 406–7, 508; in Spain 415, 509

mints 63, 73

mithraea 304, 309, 348

Mithras 217, 309–10

monetization 492, 497, 516

money-lending 108–9, 191

Monmouth 144, 412

Mons Graupius, battle of 98, 117–18, 135, 151; casualties at 93

Montanus, imperial slave 294

Moray 429–39; M. Firth 429–30, 435–6; Roman finds from 502

moritix, see merchants

mortaria, mixing bowls 472–3, 475, 515–16

mosaicists, regional schools of 398, 464

mosaics, and Christian allusions 466–7, 487; and patrons 464; classical themes and cultural character 320–21, 465, 471; date 466, 468; fourth-century boom 320, 326, 464; from temples 482; in towns 285, 320–21, 339–40, 463–4; in villas and rural sites 393, 399–400, 457, 460, 463–8; inscriptions on 321, 460; pattern books 464; predominant themes 464–8; rarity at garrison settlements 211, 320; rarity in third century 518; second-century 464

mother goddesses (Matres) 219, 309, 486–7

Mount Batten 403, 406

Mounth, The, division between Maeatae and Caledonii 436

Mousa 434

Mull of Kintyre (Epidium Promontorium) 431

Mumha, Munster in Ulster Cycle 444

municipia 260–63, 279, 355

murder, of soldiers at Canterbury 205

Murrell Hill lady 209

mutationes 259, 289

mutiny 89, 114, 124–5, 125, 132; and deserters 164

Mynnydd Bychan 414

mythological scenes 464, 466–8, 470

Naevius, assistant procurator 458

Nagnatae, people of Ireland 49, 443

nails, from Roman forts 161

names, see nomenclature

Nanstallon 137, 140

Nantwich 510

Narcissus, mythical character 468

Natalinus 314

Natalius Natalinus, Q. 460

natural disasters, see fire, plague

natural resources 362, 427, 491, 525; modes of exploitation by Rome 362; see also mineral resources

Navan 440, 444–5

navy, see fleet

Neath 144, 243

Nectaridus, Count of Saxon Shore? 235, 250

Nehallenia, goddess 297, 500

Nemeto Statio, see Bury Barton

Nemetona 309

Nemmonius Verecundus 305

Nene Valley 383–4; pottery 516–17

Neo-Platonic philosophy 466

Neo-Punic inscription 188

Neptune 219, 308, 313, 315, 465, 470, 482–3; as horned god? 467

Neratius Proxsimus, Q. 302, 463

Nero, emperor 107–9; suicide of 113; attitude towards Claudius and Britain 104

Nerva, emperor 8

Nettleham 302

Nettleton 396, 483–4

New Forest, pottery 516–17

Newcastle-on-Tyne 155, 156

Newgrange 440, 449

Newstead 148, 150, 152, 207, 259, 425–6

Newton Kyme 420

Newton on Trent 137

Nipius Ascanius, C. 507

nomenclature, of peoples and tribes 418,
    432; and military community 167, 174,
    181, 187, 190, 196–8, 217, 224; and
    rural community 460, 462–3; and urban
    community 305; British/'Celtic' 197,
    224, 305, 462–3; Gallic 197, 463;
    Germanic 197, 217, 224; Greek 197,
    462; late antique west British 535;
    Roman 217, 224, 300, 462–3

Norfolk 138–9, 384–6, 523

North Cerney, see Ditches, The

North Leigh 381, 393

North Tawton 140

North Wanborough 377

North Yorks Moors 136

Northamptonshire 383–4

Northmoor 394

Northumberland 421

Northwich 135–6, 172, 380, 409, 510

Notitia Dignitatum 33, 130, 238–47,
    334–5; late Roman military dispositions
    239

Novantae, people of Scotland 49, 148,
    423, 425

Novantico, soldier from Leicester 297

Novicius, freedman 187

numeri, see auxiliaries

numerus Hnaudifridi 223

Numidia 100, 131

nymphs 215, 465

Oaklands Park 509

Ocean (Oceanus) 22, 24–5, 67

Ocelus Vellaunos 309

Ocrinum promontory 403

Octavius, author of Vindolanda letter 512

oculists, collyrium stamps 498

officium consularis, see governor's staff

Ogham script 452, 535

Okehampton 137, 140

Old Carlisle, vicani inscription from 172,
    193

Old Durham 420

Old Harlow 313

Old Kirkpatrick 159

Old Oswestry 417

Old Penrith 193

olive oil 220, 322, 473–6, 514; and
    lamps 214; cessation of imports
    500–501; imports from Spain 220,
    323, 514

olives 220

oppida 58–9, 142, 266–8, 270–71, 332,
    374, 393, 397, 419, 447

opportunities, of Roman rule 369, 525

oppression, of civilians in provinces 10,
    107–8, 204–5

optiones, junior army officers 163

orchard crops, introduced in Roman period
    362, 364

Ordnance Survey, Map of Roman Britain
    356–7, 370

Ordovices, people of north-west Wales 49,
    97–8, 102, 105, 116, 137, 145, 262,
    416–17

Orkas promontorium 30, 380

Orkney islands (Orcades) 29; king of 428;
    Roman finds from 428, 439; brochs on
    434

ornament, and style 213–14

Orosius 232

Orpheus 464; and Neo-Platonism 466

Osmanthorpe 137

Ostorius Scapula, governor 97, 101, 266,
    412; campaigns in Wales 102–6; death
    104

Otford 465, 468

'Other', the 36

Otho, emperor 113–14

Otterton Point 401

Ouse valley 383

ovicaprids (sheep and goats) 220–21, 322, 475–6, 504
Ovid 465
Oxfordshire 394–5; pottery production 516–17
Oystermouth 413

pacification measures 98–106
Pagan's Hill, temple 396, 459, 480; curse tablets 313, 459, 485–6
paganism, late fourth-century revival of 9, 335, 348, 487; outlawed in towns 228, 348; strength in countryside 487
pagi, see rural districts
paideia (knowledge of classical culture) 467
Panegyric, see Constantius
parade grounds 207
Parisi, people of East Yorkshire 49, 82–3, 137, 148, 260, 262, 381, 418, 420; garrisoning of 146–7
Park Brow 389
Park Street 381, 383
Parys Mountain 417
pastoralism 36
patronage 182
Paullinus, see Suetonius Paullinus
Paulus, imperial agent 235, 519
Pausanius 120, 122
pax romana 99
Peddars Way, Roman road 139
Pegasus 210
Pelagius and Pelagian heresy 534–5
Pen y Coed 411
Pennines 258, 418–22, 506
peoples of Britain 47–64, 47, 97–8, 120; and farming 50; and land ownership 353–4, 358–9, 362; impact of Roman army on 91–4, 107, 132–54, 169, 175–6, 335; in classical sources 33–6, 51, 149; insular character 62, 375–6; of Ireland 439–45; of Scotland 422–6, 429–32
Perennis, praetorian prefect 125
persecution 228, 325

personal names, see nomenclature
Perthshire 429–39
Pertinax, P. Helvius, governor and emperor, 124–5, 125, 176; career 182
Petillius Cerialis, Q, governor 98, 110, 115, 132, 168, 180, 201; career 178
petitions, to emperors 204, 255, 330; to governors 204; to the gods 306, 314
Petronius Fortunatus 185
Petronius Turpilianus, governor 113
Petronius Urbicus, Q., prefect 219
Pevensey 241–2
pewter vessels, inscribed 470; moulds and production centres 470, 508–9; ingots from Thames 508
Philus 318
Pictavia, Pictland 436, 539
Picti, late Roman people of northern Britain 231–2, 235, 237–8, 241, 432, 435–7, 444, 452, 534–5
Pictish, art 436; heartlands 434; kingdom 537, 539; language 52, 436; settlement 435–6
Piddington 534
Piercebridge 172, 420
pigs 220, 322, 365, 475, 504
pirates 535
Pitney 464
place-names xvi, 28, 31–3; British 42–3; Irish 443, 445; Latin 42–3
plague 334, 538
Plas Coch 380, 415
Platorius Nepos, governor 156
Plautius, see Aulus Plautius
Pliny the Elder 28–30, 184
ploughshares 363, 499
Ploumanac'h wreck 508
Plutarch 25
Plymouth 264, 402–3; Roman occupation at 405–6; Iron Age occupation, see Mount Batten
Poenius Postumus, camp prefect of legio II Augusta 110
poetry 215

policing 154, 158, 331
pollen cores, evidence of environment
363–6
pollution 492
Polybius 10
Polyclitus, imperial freedman 112
polygamy 34–5
polytheism 216, 218
Pomeroy Wood 402
Pompeius Homullus, Cn. 185
Pompeius Optatus 195
Pomponius Valens, C. 187, 296
Poole Harbour 264, 400; pottery
production 516–18
poppy, opium 221
population, in towns 323–4, 334; of
Britain 293, 356, 368; rural 356–7, 405,
453
Porthmeor 405
Portchester 242
ports 138, 256, 257–8, 280, 284, 358,
386, 415, 492, 494, 504; in Cornwall
406
Poseidonius 28
post stations, see cursus publicus
post-colonialism 5, 11–12, 17
Postumus, emperor 231
potters 462; migration to Britain 299
pottery 472, 492, 513–18, 538; aceramic
cultures 408; African styles in Britain
187–8, 223; Alice Holt 389; and
military supply 212, 516–17; Black
Burnished ware 400, 517–18; differences
between military, rural and urban
assemblages 212, 290, 338, 408, 473,
475; domestic production supplanted by
manufactories 514–16; Gallo-Belgic
wares 515; location of main British
production sites 290–91, 516; Frisian
223; Gabbroic wares 403; Iron Age
regional styles 517; range of products
515; scale of production 513, 517–18;
stamps 203; see also amphora, mortaria,
samian, terra sigillata
poultry 220, 322, 365, 475

Poundbury, Dorchester 243, 347
power 97, 169, 325; and land 358; and
religious practice 105–6, 215–16;
devolution of p. 7; juridical 256;
relationships of p. 16, 56, 81, 93, 103,
185, 196, 199, 205, 207–8, 226, 252,
281, 525; symbols of p. 156, 158,
210–11
power-sharing 10, 227, 525–6
Powys 145–6, 416–18
Prae Wood 66
praepositus, of region 186
praesides (late Roman governors) 335
praetorian guard, in Britain 123
praetorium (commanding officer's house)
259; at Vindolanda 183–4
Prasutagus, king of Iceni 90, 106, 109
prata legionis 409
prefects, praetorian 227–8, 229; tribal
187, 277
Prestatyn 137, 380, 415–16
pretenders, and the British provinces 125,
176; see also usurpers
priests, at Bath 299
priestly regalia 480–81
primus pilus, see centurions
princeps, see emperors
Priscillianists 456
Priscus, son of Toutius 299
Probus, emperor 231, 240–41
Procopius 36,
procurator, financial official 129, 256, 275,
295, 459, 496; mining procurators? 507,
523
promontory forts 404, 410–11
prosopography 42–3
prostitutes 175, 195
Protacius, C. 303
provinces (of Britain) 9, 227–8; division
into four p. 227–8, 229, 334–5, 501;
division into two p. 126, 177, 229, 501;
locations and capitals of British p. 228,
229, 334–5; possible fifth p. 228; see
also Britannia Superior, Britannia
Inferior, Maxima Caesariensis, Britannia

Prima, Britannia Secunda, Flavia Caesariensis, Valentia
provincial council 299–300, 304, 310
provincial government 255–61, 275–6, 360–61; and towns 334–5; third-century changes to 227–8; fourth-century changes 335–6
provincial governors, see governors
Ptolemy (Claudius Ptolemaeus) 28, 30; and Ireland 441–5, 452; *Geography* 49, 140, 418, 429, 435; problems with assignation of sites to British *civitates* 31, 398, 403, 423–5
Publianus 349
public benefaction (euergetism) 280, 301–4, *302–3*, 526
public buildings, disrepair 336–8; provision of in towns 280–81, 336–8; see also towns
Pudens (?) son of Pudentinus 267, 298, *302*, 304
Pulborough *381*, 387–8
Pumpsaint 507
punishment, and *Iceni* 384; military 205
Purbeck 'marble' 267, 300, 307, 400, 510

Quarry Farm 421
quays 284
queens, see Cartimandua
querns (rotary) 363, 404, 433, 440, 451
Quintus Veranius, governor 97, 178

Radlett 516
Raetia 169
raids 226, 302; on Britain 230, 232; seaborne 230, 235, 331, 388, 437, 529–32, 534–5
Rangeworthy 396
rape 107
Ratcliffe on Soar *313*, 485
Rathgall 440, 449
raths 410, 447–8
Ravenglass 193, 243, 257, 258
Ravenna Cosmography 33

rebellion 535–6; see also Boudican revolt, revolts
record, archaeological 44–6
recruitment, military 88, 130, 168–9, 186, 192, 494, 502; by regions of empire 131–2, 187–8; of Britons 187, 222, 251; of federates 230, 248–50; see also army
Reculver 242
Redlands Farm 534
refugees 105–6, 141, 441–2, 524; and villa ownership 456
Regia, royal centre in Ireland 443, 445
Regina, freedwoman 196, 209, 223, 296–7
regional centurion (*centurio regionarius*) 186–7, 303, *303*
regions and regionalism 477, 522–4; divergent rural histories of 15–17, 522–4
Regni, people of Sussex 49, 99, 262, 265, *381*, 387
religion 527; and the military community 166–7, 194, 204, 212, 214–20, *219–20*; and rural communities 217–18, 458–9, 480–87, 521; British 105–6, 108, 198, 215, 308–9, 484, 521; Christianity 228, 337, 345–6, 348–9; Eastern cults 212, 215, 309–10, 484–5; Germanic 217; Imperial cult 166, 215, 218, 298, 458; in towns 306–16; the Roman pantheon 212, 215, 482–3, 520, *521*; see also Christianity, paganism, syncretism
religious practice *219*, 358, 520–22; and festivals 204; and literacy 521; and status 216–17; dedications by civilians 307–8; dedications by soldiers 167, 188, 194, 215; dedications by women 197–216; in military community 166, 204, 210, 214–20, 222, 521; in rural community 384, 480–87, 521; in urban community 306–16, 335, 347–9, 458–9, 521; Iron Age 306; lustration 215; name-pairing (syncretism) 214–17, 484–5; sacrifice 210, 215, 308, 476, 480; votive offerings 215, 308, 480; see also curse tablets, ritual

resistance 4, 12, 65–6, 90–92, 101–21, 399, 496, 522–7, 539; cultural 472, 474, 476; Caratacus as r. leader 101–3; Roman responses to r. 103–4; r. to colonization 107–8; see also landscapes of r.

resources, see mineral resources, natural resources, salt

revitalization movements 105

revolts 98, 120, 167, 231–2, 384; Batavian 132, 168; Boudican 8, 75, 97, 106–13, 138, 271, 354, 384; Brigantian 8, 97, 114–16; Gallic 8; Jewish 21

Rhineland 303, 307, 500

Rhuddgaer 417

Rhuddlan 415

Rhyn Park 137, 145

Ribchester 148, 186, 197, 207, 243

Richborough 236, 242, 244, 257, 264, 280

ring-forts (Wales) 410–11

rings, see finger rings

Riothamus 532

ripenses 228, 239

Risca 414

Risingham 196–7

Risley Park 349, 471

ritual 204, 306; watery deposition and 62–3

Rivenhall 379, 381

river Aire 421; r. Annan 150, 425–6; r. Avon 395, 398–9; r. Clyde 29, 150, 155, 159, 426; r. Darent 386–7; r. Dee 415; r. Eden 149, 418, 422; r. Exe 29, 140, 401, 407; r. Fal 403, 406; r. Forth 155, 159, 423; r. Humber 141, 244, 392, 419; r. Irthing 156; r. Lune 422; r. Medway 386–7; r. Mersey 147, 422; r. Mersey reach of sea-going ships 172; r. Nene 29; r. North Tyne 425; r. Ouse (Yorks) 29, 419–20; r. Ribble 172, 422; r. Severn 29, 142–3, 146, 244, 259, 408, 517; r. Soar 141; r. Stour 271; r. Tamar 140, 403, 406; r. Taw 140, 403; r. Tay 150–51, 429, 432, 435–7; r. Tees 29, 244, 420–21; r. Thames 29, 95, 138,

142, 273–4, 394–5, 511; r. Trent 141, 392, 491; r. Tweed 150, 424–5; r. Tyne 29, 149, 155, 156, 244, 418; Tyne bridge 149; r. Ure 419; r. Usk 144, 412–14; r. Witham 141; r. Wye 144, 412

rivers and navigation 511

road stations 522, see also cursus publicus

roads 32–3, 141–3, 146–8, 150, 152, 243, 358, 393, 401, 458, 522; and Antonine Itinerary 256–9, 257–8; and military 138, 154, 157, 159; and towns 256, 265, 268–71, 341; as engineered routes 136, 366; as property boundaries 359, 361; country 378, 384; in Scotland 127; trans-Pennine 147, 258

Robogdii, people of Ireland 49, 442

Rochester 287, 329

Rockbourne 378, 400

Roman army, see army, Roman

'Roman Britain', contrasted with 'Britain in the Roman Empire' 26, 357

Romanization 199; defective paradigm xii, 14–17, 491, 527

Rome, history of 8–9

Roscius Coelius 114

Rosewarne 406–7

Rosmerta 484, 486

Rossington 137, 148

roundels, in bone and pottery 317

roundhouse 55, 357, 365, 367, 375–6, 382–3, 404; and compounds 382, 387; and other circular buildings 376; as British architectural norm 367, 375; co-existence with villas 367, 375–6, 383, 472; in Scotland 434; in towns 279, 285–6, 288–9; size and materials 375–7

rounds (of Cornwall) 357, 404

rubbish disposal 337–8, 340–43

Rudge Cup 213–14, 454

Rudston 61, 381, 420; Venus mosaic 467–8

Rufus Sita 190, 208

rural districts (pagi) 286, 355, 359, 361; administrative status 358–9

rural settlement, and enclosures

(compounds) 362, 374, 377–8, 382–3, 387, 397; and field systems 383; and military connections 158, 355, 412, 422, 426, 454–5, 471; and squatter occupation 534; and social hierarchy 379–82, 385; central southern counties 380–81, 389–90; density, numbers and population 356, 368, 390, 424; East Midlands 364, 381, 390, 391; eastern counties 364, 379–86, 381; Ireland 440; non-villa settlement 367–9, 375–8, 382, 389, 390, 392, 394, 402; northern counties 364, 418–22; nucleated 362, 378–9, 382, 384, 401–2; pattern 358, 364, 368–9, 386, 395, 399, 412, 414, 419, 424, 432–3; regional heterogeneity 358–64; Scotland 364, 422–6, 429–39, 430; south-western counties 364, 380, 396, 399–408; south-eastern counties 364, 381, 385–9; unenclosed 432; villas and 'Roman' 356–7, 368–75, 396; Wales and Marches 364, 380, 408–18; West Midlands 364, 380

Ruthin 415

sacred enclosures (temenoi) 307
sacred grove (nemeton) 62–3, 105, 112, 306
sacrifice 210, 215, 480; human 62, 112, 477; animal offerings 322, 476
Saham Toney 55, 138–9, 384
St Alban 535
St Albans 55, 109, 137, 142, 257, 258–9, 262, 263, 270, 276–8, 320–21, 328; and Boudican revolt 278, 333; and Folly Lane enclosure 78–9, 137–8, 270–71; baths and water supply 283, 341; cemeteries at 78–80, 302; dark earth 340–41; defences 331; early Roman layout 278; fires 333–4; forum 277; housing 284; Insula XXVII house 340; Iron Age activity at 59, 75–80, 270; late Roman occupation 333, 337, 339–43, 533; mosaics and wall-painting 320–21, 467; municipium status and Flavian

expansion 261, 278; theatre and other public buildings at 278, 282; theatre reused as rubbish dump 337, 343; villa settlements near 382
St Patrick 37, 534–5
Salisbury Plain 523; settlement on 396
Salmanes 197
Salmonsbury 393
salt 143, 213, 220–21, 290, 384, 400; as imperial monopoly 363, 496, 510; mines and brine springs 510; winning 363, 510
Salvius Liberalis, C., iuridicus 275
samian ware 203, 211, 513; graffiti on 461–2; patterns of supply 514–15; on rural sites 472, 475, 515
Samnite Wars 6
sandals 191
sarcophagus 344, 508
Sarmatians, cavalry sent to Britain 122, 169
Saturnina 314
Saxon Shore, military command 239, 388; forts of 135, 241–3
Saxones, Germanic peoples 9, 231–2, 235, 238, 241, 388, 530, 532–7
Scampton 381, 392
Scapula, see Ostorius Scapula
Scarborough 244
Scilly Isles (Sillina) 29, 407–8, 456
Scotland 8–9, 29, 98, 120, 149–53, 426, 434–5, 437–9, 524; debate about Antonine phases of occupation 151–2; economic relations with Britannia 501; native settlement 422–6, 429–36, 430
Scotti, people of northern Ireland and western Scotland 231–2, 235, 237–8, 241, 432, 452; linked with Dal Riata 437, 444–5
sculptor 210–11
sculpture 205, 211–12, 248, 325; and identity 205–6, 208–10, 318–19; on anthropomorphic s. 206, 217–18, 458, 469, 483; military tombstones 208, 224; quality of 210–11, 469; relief s. 206,

sculpture – *cont.*
209, 211; religious 308; see also Celtic heads, statues
scythes 363
Sea Mills 142
seals, lead 317–18, 455
Seaton *380*
secession *125*, 231; of Britain (in 409) 530–33
seeds, carbonized 363
Selgovae, people of Tweed valley 49, *148*, 150, 423–4
Selsey Bill 76
senators 10; career paths and service in provinces 182
Seneca, loans to Britons 107, 293
Sennius Sollemnis, letter from British governor 179–81
Senuna, goddess worshipped at Baldock 484
Septimius, Lucius governor *302*; dedication of Cirencester Jupiter column 335
Septimius Severus, emperor 9, 10, 88, *125*, 176, 233; campaigns in Britain 123–4; death at York 124; planned reoccupation of Scotland 123–4, 152; victory in civil war 126
Serapis, temple of 304
Setantii, people of northern Britain 418
settlement, see rural settlement
settlers 420
Severius Emeritus, C. 186, *303*
Severn Valley, pottery 516
Severus, *comes domesticorum* 236
seviri Augustales, see freedmen
sewers and sewage 221, 284, 341
sex, and the Roman army 174–6, 195–6
Sextus Valerius 208
Shakenoak 394
Shapwick 396
Sharpstones Hill 408
sheep 220, 322, 365; see also ovicaprids
Sheepen, see Colchester
shellfish 322, 475
Shetland islands, 29, 30, 434

shoes 209, in burials 346
shrines 52, 62, 186, 215, 217–18, *302*, see also temples
Shropshire 408–9
sickles 404
Siculus Flaccus, *agrimensor* 353–4, 360–61
sideboards, in chip-carved stone 469
sieges 121
signal stations 244, 248; see also Gask Ridge
Silchester *55*, *137*, *142*, 257–8, 256–9, 262, 263, 269, 276–7, 328; amphitheatre 270; and rural settlement 389; baths 270; church 348; defences 332; Iron Age origins 59, 76–7, 268–9; early development 267–70; faunal assemblage 322; forum 270, 281, 336; guild of foreigners 298, 307; housing 284–5; insula IX excavations 269–70, 339–40; military finds at 100, *139*, 270; mosaics and wall-paintings 320–21; seals from 318; street grid 270; temples 270; wells 341
Silures, people of south-east Wales 35, 49, 97–8, 498; Roman conquest of 102, 104–5, 116, 134, *137*, 143–4, 180; and *civitas* centre 260, 262; rural settlement *380*, 411–15
Silvanus 219, 308, 483; S. Callirius 308
silver 450, 491, 506–8; from rural sites 470–71; in Iron Age contexts 470; mineral deposits 398, 415; silverware 211, 326, 349, 470–71; spoons 470–71, 484
Similis 307–9
singulares (governor's bodyguard) 129
skulls, human, deposited in Walbrook 477; defleshed 477, 479
slavery 6; operation of in Britain 108–9, 294–5, 494, 502
slaves 47, 171, 183, 294–5, 300, 491; and identity 295; cost of 295; domestic 295; female 195–6; from Ireland 451; literacy and 183; of imperial household 275,

294–5; owned by other slaves 294–5; owned by soldiers 170–71, 187, 194, 300–301; rural and mining slaves 295, 485–6; savings of 295; sexual demands on 195–6

Sleaford 55

small towns 58, 264, 286–9, 302–3, 522; and economy 321, 334; and garrison settlements 286; and manufacturing 504; and provincial borders 501; and sanctuaries 289–90; and villas 289; baths in 283; cemeteries 344; definition and legal status 286; morphology 287–8; roundhouses in 285–6, 288–9; tombstones from 459; with defences 289, 327–33; with entertainment buildings 283

Smertae, people of northern Scotland 49, 429–31

Snettisham 55; torcs 59–60; Roman 'jeweller's hoard' 212

Snowdonia 145–6, 416–17

society, Iron Age 63, 503, 522, 527, 538; provincial 503; Roman 525–6; Sub-Roman 531–9

socii (investors), see mining

socks 190, 209

Sol 483

soldiers, and families 194–6, 204, 245–7; and literacy 199–204, 215, 222, 247–8, and religious pratice 215–18, 219–20, 248, 250; and veteran settlement 355; careers 204, community of 166, 176–98; discipline 205, 251; ethnic origins of 222; in civil government 129, 189; interactions with civilians 199, 205–7, 251–2; involved with supply 512; marriage ban on 170, 175; material culture and dress 205–14, 248–9; murder of 205; pay and conditions 227, 248, 250–52; not cultural ambassadors 166, 199; referred to in curse tablets 485–6; see also army, community, governor's staff, veterans

Solent, The 95, 233

Solinus *312*, 442

Solway Firth 29, *155*, *156*

Somerdale 458

Somerset 399–400

Somerset Levels 364

soothsayer 299

sources 21–43, 97–8, 120, 125, 231–2; annalistic 26; archaeological 5, 19, 21, 220–22; bias in 36, 233, 412; Christian 37; epigraphic 38–41, 418; geographical 28–37; Greek 21, 28, 30; legal 37; on Britain 7, 10–11, 19, 94; on peoples of Britain 48–64, 101, 103, 149

souterrains 426, *430*, 432, 448

South Cadbury 139, 480, 534

South Shields *155*, 160, 173, 196, 209, 223, 244; barrack excavations 161, 246–7; imported grain at 221

southern kingdom 55, 68, 95, 97, *137*, 267–9, 474; *oppida* of 76–7; organization post-conquest 99–100, 139–40; see also Commios, Togidubnus, Verica

Southwark 264, 275, 341

Southwell *381*, 392

Southwick 387–8

spa sites 289–90

Spain, mineral resources 506

Sparsholt 469

Spaxton 400

Spettisbury 99

spices 220

Spinan's Hill 440, 447

Spitalfields 344

Spoonley Wood 397

springs 215

'squatters' 337, 534

Staffordshire 143, 213–14

Staines 498

Stainmore Pass 115

stamps, on ingots 507–8; on pottery 203–4, 462, 516; on tile 386

standard bearer 207–8, 210

Stane Street, Roman road 388–9

Stanegate, 'frontier' 154, 157; Roman road 154, 159
Stanford in the Vale 394
Stannigton 193
Stanway 62, 77–8
Stanwick, *oppidum* of *Brigantes* 55, 59, 83, 115, *381*, 419; elite enclosure at The Tofts 419
Stanwick (Northants), villa 383
Stanwix, fort *155*
state, Roman, see government, imperial
Statius Priscus, M. 181
statues and statuary, copper-alloy 206, 211, 406; imperial and equestrian 318, 272; lack of individual honorific 318; marble 211, 469; non-marble 211, 469; of Claudius Paullinus at Caerwent 318
status, and religious practice 212, 216–18; and the military 206, 221, 223, 248–9; civilians 331–2
stereotypes 34, 428
Stilicho 232, 240, 250, 530
stock-raising 365, 395, 411
Stoke Gabriel 402
Stonea Grange 384–5, *381*, 456, 483
Stonesfield 294
Stony Stratford 483
Stonyford 449
Strabo 19, 28, 30, 47; on worth of Britain 491; description of Britons 34–5, 428
Stracathro 151, *148*
Strathmore 88, *120*
stratores (grooms) 129, *302*
street grids, see towns
stripbuildings, see houses
style, artistic 205–14; convergence of Roman and British 210, 213
subjugation 97, 216
submitted peoples 97, 98–9, 167; conditions imposed on 353–4, 358, 369
Sub-Roman Britain 528
suburbs 473; see also towns
Suddern Farm 58
Suessiones, people of northern Gaul 53
Suetonius Paullinus, C., governor, and Boudican revolt 106–8, 110; invasion of Anglesey 105; military record of 178; support for Otho in civil war 179
Suetonius Tranquillus, C., biographer 27, 97; offered post in Britain 183; on Cunobelin 74; on Nero 104; Vespasian's campaigns 98
Suffolk 384–6
Suleviae 307, 309
Sulinus, son of Brucetus 307
Sulinus, son of Maturus 307
Sulis Minerva 309, 311, *312–13*, 315, 484
Sulpicia Lepidina, wife of Flavius Cerialis 162, 183, 201
supply, military 152–3, 158, 162, 212, 220–22, 369, 415, 494–5, 499–500, 511–14, 516; and contracts 512
surplus production 365
Surrey 389
surveyors, Roman 28, 94
Sussex 387–9
Sutton Walls 99
swords 63, 207
Syagrius 508
Sydenham 193
syncretism 215–17, 308, 484–5, 521; prevalence among military community 309; see also religion

tablets, see writing tablets
Tabula Peutingeriana 32–3
Tacita *313*
Tacitus, C. Cornelius, historian 26–8, 35, 41, 91, 93–100, 97, 98, 125; on Roman abuses of power 108; on Agricola 117; on Britons 35, 416; on Brigantes 104, 115–16, 418; on Boudican revolt 106–11; on peoples of Scotland 431–2; on Ireland 444; on events in reign of Nero 114, 117; on Ostorius Scapula 101–4, 142; on London 265, 274; 'spoils of victory' 494
Taexali, people of north-eastern Scotland 49, *148*, 151, 429, 435, 437

Tammonii, prominent family at Silchester 305

Tara, Hill of 440, 445–7, 449

Tarbock, tile production at 173

Tarrant Hinton 468

Tasciovanus 73

tax and taxation 94, 221, 360–61, 472, 491, 494–6, 505, 511, 526–7, 531–3; assessment and collection of 360–61, 496, 531–2; capitation 361, 495; higher rates in late Roman period 519; inheritance, land and sales t. 495

technology, building 376; farming 366–7

Tectoverdi, people of northern Britain 418

Templeborough 193, 223

temples 522; and curse tablets 458; and tombstones 459; and religious sculpture 469; in towns 268–9, 302–3, 337–8, 348; of divine Claudius at Colchester 271, 281; Romano-Celtic type 271, 282, 306–7, 348, 480, 481, 521; classical type 215, 279, 281–2, 521

termini, see boundary markers

territory (territoria), legionary (prata) 409; of civitates and other towns 281, 286, 358

terror 91

Tetrarchs and Tetrarchy 223–4, 227

textiles 184, 211, 318, see also clothing

theatres 268–9, 282–3, 337–8

theft 311; attested in curse tablets 310–15, 312–14, 485–6

Theodosius, Count, commander 232; campaign in Britain 228, 235–7, 330; and restoration work 237

Theodosius, emperor 9, 176, 228, 230, 237

theory, and Roman archaeology xii

Theseus 465

Thetford 55, 62, 138–9, 384; spoons dedicated to Faunus 484

'Third-Century Crisis' 225–7, 231

Thistleton 381, 392, 484

Thornford 400

Thorpe Thewles 364

Thorwell Farm 414

Thruxton 396, 460

Thule 30

Tiberinus Celerianus, Londoner 298, 304

Tiberius, emperor 8; and mineral resources 506

Tiddington 461

tile, flue 388; production 173, 290; roofs 410; stamps 270, 275, 386, 401, 416, 454, 459, 462

time, and military life 204

tin 30, 403, 405, 506, 508–9

Tincomarus 71, 73

Titus, emperor 8, 117, 176, 180

Titus Caninus, prefect 219

togas 210; lack of British representations 319

Togidubnus, Ti. Claudius (Cogidubnus), British client king 90, 109, 139, 229, 276, 300, 387–8, 454, 500; and Fishbourne 373–4; and urban development 265–8; origin and identity 99–100

Togodumnus, British prince 75, 81, 94

toilet implements, as votive oferings 480; common in rural society 473–4

tombstones 119, 186–7, 300, 304–6, 325; distribution 194, 305, 459; iconography 210, military 194, 198, 202, 204, 206–8, 216, 224, 305; numbers 194, 305; rarity in southern Britain 209–10, 305, 318–19, 459

Topsham 402

torcs 59–60, 441–2, 450–51

Torrs, hoard 62

Torwoodlee 248, 430

towers, military 244, 328–9, 330–31, 384–5; see also signal stations

towns 255–91, 262, 264, 268–9, 328–9 358, 366, 522; administrative function 255, 260–63, 291, 331, 334–5, 337, 354–5, 358–9; and urban community 267, 292–324, 344–5; Antonine Itinerary 256–9, 257–8, and public benefaction 303–3; baths in 272, 279, 283–4, 338; cemeteries 279, 343–7;

towns – *cont.*
    churches in 348–9; coin-loss patterns
and 332, 473; construction in stone 278,
280, 284, 339; construction in timber
284; consumption of meat and other
foodstuffs 322–3; councils 260, 280,
293; dearth of religious inscriptions 318;
decline of 333–50; decline of paganism
in 325–6; defences 243, 279, 326–33,
534; distribution and numbers of, 261,
262, 263, 264; donation of public
buildings 280, 338; economic function
275–6, 331, 503–5; entertainment
buildings 279, 282–3; fate in sub-
Roman Britain 530–33; features of
279–80; Flavian consolidation 276–9; in
client kingdom of Togidubnus 265–8;
forum/basilica complexes 263, 268–9,
279, 281, 336–7; functions of 260;
health and nutrition in 323–4, 334;
housing 281, 284–5, 326, 338–40;
Julio-Claudian initiatives 276–7, 279;
lack of tombstones 318–19; *mansiones*
in 259; mosaics and wall-paintings 285,
310–21; population in 323–4, 334;
premature decline of 292, 338, 349–50,
528; origins 266–77, 279, 332; retarded
pace of development of 280, 349–50,
373–4, 528; reuse of abandoned
fortresses 271–3; risk of fires in 333–4,
504; road grids 263, 276, 279, 332;
roundhouses and other rural building
types at 279, 285–6, 340; rubbish
disposal 337–8, 341–3; shops and
workshops 285; size of 263; small towns
263, 283, 286–7, 344; temples in 267,
270–71, 279, 281–2; typology of
260–63; water supply 279, 284, 342
tracks 362
trade 318, 492–4; contact with Continent
25, 30, 56, 68, 72, 221–2, 499–501,
531; decline in sub-Roman period 538
traders, at garrison settlements 173; beaten
at *Vindolanda* 173, 202; dealing in
pottery and garments 500

Trajan, emperor 8
transport costs, subsidization by state
    512
Traprain Law 357, 423–4, *430*, 438, 500
Tre'r Ceiri *380*, 416
treaties 67, 72, 151, 524
Trebellius Maximus, governor 113–14,
    124, *125*
Trelissey *380*, 410
Trethurgy *380*, 404–5
Tretia Maria *313*
tria nomina, see nomenclature, Roman
tribal prefects (*praefecti genti*) 187, 277
'tribes' 59, 83–4; and tribal groupings 56,
    63
tribunes 189; senatorial (*tribuni laticlavii*)
    180; equestrian (*tribuni angusticlavii*)
    180–85
tribute 23, 174, 354, 360–61, 494, 511,
    524; see also tax
Trier 193, 227
Trinovantes, people of Essex 49, 65–6, 68,
    97, *137*, 262, 381; conquest by Rome
    98, 100; role in Boudican revolt 106–8;
    associated with *colonia* at Colchester
    108–9, *137*, 271–2; rural settlements of
    379–82
triumphs 6, 93
Tuathal Techtmar, Irish chieftain 441
Tulsk (Roscommon) 446
Tungrians 132, 168
Turkdean 374, *396*, 397–8
Tyne-Solway isthmus 150–51, 154, *155*,
    160
tyrants (*tyranni*) 532

Ulaidh, Ulster in Ulster Cycle 444
Uley 55, 322, *396*, 397–8; curse tablets
    314, 458–9, 482, 485–6; personal
    nomenclature in curse tablets *314*, 463;
    sacrifices at 476; temple 62, 460, 480,
    482–3
Ulpius Ianuarius, M. 302
Ulpius Marcellus, governor *120*, 122
Ulpius Quintus, M. 297

Ulster 443–5

Ulster Cycle, The 443–5, 448, 451; peoples
mentioned in 444–5

underpants and socks 190–91, 208–9

urban community, see community

urbanism 19, 255, 277, 292, 325–5

urbanization 272, 527; Roman policy
260–61, 273

Ursa 197

Usdiae, people of Ireland 49, 443

Usipi, Germanic people 132

Usk 137, 144, 412

usurpers 9, 125, 226, 231–2, 519–20,
529–30, 536; proclaimed in Britain 529;
and effects on Britain 226, 235; Britain
'fertile in' 235, 240, 529

Vacomagi, people of eastern Scotland 49,
148, 151, 429, 433, 435, 437

Vale of Pickering 149, 420

Vale of York 149, 419–20

Valens, emperor 9, 240

Valentia, fourth-century province 228,
236, 334–5

Valentinian I, emperor 9, 236, 240

Valentinian II, emperor 9

Valentinus 236

Valerian 226

Valerius Genialis, S. 190

Valerius Iustus, C. 196

Valerius Silvanus, T. 453

Valerius Veranius, Q. 462

Vallum, see Hadrian's Wall

Valurius, S. 208

Vandals 240–41

Varius Severus, M. 302

vectigal, see tribute

vegetation history 364–6

Vegetius, scout ships in Britain 242

Vegetus, slave 294

Veldedeius (Veldeius), groom 203

Vellabori, people of Ireland 49, 43

vengeance 112

Venicones, people of Fife and Tayside 49,
148, 151–2, 429, 433, 435, 437

Vennicnii, people of Ireland 49, 443

Venta, term for market 335, 498

Venus 467–8, 484

Venutius, consort of Cartimandua 98, 104,
114

Veranius, Q., governor 104–5

Vercingetorix 4, 66

Verecunda Rufilia 223, 297

Verecundinus 312

Verecundius Diogenes, M., merchant 297,
305

Verica, British client king 8, 73, 95, 100,

Verlamion, see St Albans

Verona List 334

Vespasian, emperor 8, 113, 176, 178;
death 117; initiates forward policy
114–19; role in Claudian conquest 96,
98–9

veteran colonies, see coloniae

veterans 191–3, 205, 214, 457, 500; and
land grants/purchases 353, 454;
inscriptions of 193, 301, 305; settled at
coloniae 260–61; settled round military
bases 420,

Veteres (Vitiri, Hveteri) 217–18, 219–20,
484

Vettius Benignus 300

Vettius Bolanus, governor 98, 114

vexillation fortresses 141; in East Midlands
141; in West Midlands 143;

Vibia Pacata 187

vicars (vicarii) 227, 335

Victorinus, interpreter of dreams? 250,
482

Victory 123, 216

vicus, vici 170–71, 302, 355; as term for
small town 171, 286; in military context
172; see also, garrison settlements

Viducius Placidus, L. 298, 304; dedication
of arch and shrine at York 302

Vilbia 312

Villa Faustini 384, 470

villages 522; and brochs 434; and hamlets
357, 378; and small towns 288–9, 378,
387; and villas 378, 382–3

villas 369–75, 379, 382–3, 477, 481, 522, 526; absence of 385–6, 389–90, 400; and aisled houses 371, 377, 382, 384–5, 390, 460; and baths 371, 375, 377, 382, 387, 468–9; and economy 501; and British vernacular traditions 392–3; and marble 387, 397; and mosaics 371–4, 377, 387–8, 392, 397, 410, 463–8; and sculpture 469; and material culture 472–3; and roundhouses 367, 374, 376, 382, 394; and rural settlement patterns 379–422; and social architecture of extended clans 377–8; and the elite 368–9, 372–4, 376, 379–82, 457, 471–2; and imperial servants 456; and wall-paintings 410; as common stereotype of Roman countryside 356; as estates 382, 389–90, 392, 397, 400; definitions, typology and features of 369–73; distribution and numbers of 368, 370–71, 379–427; early group in Sussex 373–4, 454; late florescence of 374, 499; palatial examples 370, 373, 386–8, 393, 397–8, 410, 413, 469; religious practice at 458, 469; significance of 372; slow uptake of 367, 373–4, 376, 393, 399; tombstones from 459; winged corridor type 371, 379–82, 387

Vindolanda 119, 148, 155, 157, 165, 170, 174, 189; barracks 246; barrels from 221, 514; beer brewing 222; discharge diploma 193; inscribed and stamped possessions 203; religious dedications from 218, 219–20

Vindolanda tablets 8, 36, 40, 130, 132, 153, 162–5, 186–7, 189, 200–204; addresses 200; administration of justice 164; dealing with supply 163, 191, 220, 497, 512; diet 184, 191, 220–22; feasting and festivals 204; handwriting styles 201–2; household inventories 183–4; hunting 184–5, 221; inspections (renuntia) 163; references to warfare, natives and other civilians 164–5,

171–3; leave requests (commeatus) 163; letters of recommendation 164; meeting with governor 177; names of soldiers in 174, 190, 198; names of women in 183, 190, 201; personal letters 164, 183; purchases by soldiers in 190, 220; references to clothing 183, 190–91; references to textiles 184; routine activities 163, 200; strength report 163; types of document 162

vineyard 384

violence, colonial 12, 91–2

Virgil, 201, 467–8; Aeneid as subject of mosaics and wall paintings 464–5; Eclogue on coins of Carausius 465

Virgo Caelestis 215

Viridius 484

Virius Lupus, governor 123

Visigoths 530

Vitalinus 314

Vitellius, emperor 113–14, 125

Viventia 349

Viventius, bishop 349

Volcanus 218, 219

Voluntii, people of Ireland 49, 442, 444

Volusenus 70

Volusia Faustina 305, 318

Vortigern 532, 537

Votadini, people of Lothian 49, 148, 150, 423, 424

votives, 480, 482–3, 521; leaf or feather shaped 308, 349, 458, 480, 483, 521; letters 308, 459, 483, 521; plaques 308, 349, 482; vows 200, 215, 308

Vulcanus 483

Waddan Hill 139

Wakerley 383, 393

Walbrook, mithraeum 217; springline 341; rubbish or 'ritual' deposits in 342–3, 477

Walcot 193

Waldgirmes 273

Wales 29, 97–8, 240, 539; absent from

Notitia 239–40, 245; effectiveness of Roman military garrison 145–6; late military activity 153–4, 243–5; migration of Irish 451; mineral resources 506; settlement 409–18; villas 456

Walesland Rath 380, 410

Wall 137, 143, 259

Wall-paintings 410, 468–9, 471; and Christian allusions 467; classical themes 320–21, 468; in towns 285, 320–21, 339; painted inscriptions and graffiti 460

Wallsend 155, 156, 161, 245–6

Walsingham 384

Walton Castle 242

Walton Heath 382

Walton le Dale 172

Wanborough 314, 396; priestly regalia 480, 482

warehouses 284

warfare 8, 105–7, 117, 119–27, 120, 231; and sieges 99, 121; guerrilla w. 91; impact on civilians 105–6; impact on imperial stability 225; in late Roman period 230, 248–9; Iron Age 63–4; Roman 87–94

warrior bands (*comitatus*) 60

Warwickshire 395

Wash, The 29, 391

Wasperton 395

watchtowers, see signal towers, towers

Water Newton 263, 264, 269, 289–90, 329, 349, 386, 458; possibly *civitas* centre 261; pottery production 516

water supply and disposal 279, 284, 341, 527; see also aqueducts, sewers, towns, wells

Waterloo helmet 62, 207

Watkins Farm 394

Watling Street, Roman road 143, 258, 333

Weald, the 386–7, 523; ironworking on 509–10

wealth 385, 471, 505

weapons, votive offerings 480; see also arms

weather, described by ancient sources 37

weaving works, state (*gynaeceum*) 335

weeds 363, 365

weights 317

Welland Valley 383

Welney 470

Welwyn 76, 470

Wemberham 400

Werwell 390

West Coker 463

West Hill Uley, see Uley

West Midlands 393–9

Western Isles (Hebrides) 29

Westhampnett 61

Westhawk Farm 264, 381, 387, 480

Westland 400

Weston-under-Penyard 144

wetlands 384–6, 396, 400, 414

Wetwang Slack 61

wharves 342

wheat 221, 365; distributions at *Vindolanda* 220; see also cereals

Wheathampstead 55, 58, 66

Wheeldale Moor 136

wheel-houses 430, 434

Wheeting with Broomhill 314, 485–6

Whilton Lodge 498

Whitby 136, 244

Whitchurch 135–6, 172, 257, 258, 380, 409

Whithorn 438

Whitley Castle 135

Whitley Grange 380, 408–9, 534

Whitton 380, 413

Wicklewood 384

Wilderspool 172, 516

Willingham Fen 480

Willington 393

wills, testamentary 204

Wiltshire 389–90

Winchester 55, 142, 189, 257–8, 259, 262, 269, 276–7, 328; as a centre of southern kingdom 76; as *civitas* centre 267, 302, 389–90; dark earth 340–41; hoard 70; Lankhills cemetery 343, 346

wine 220, 322–3, 474–6; from Gaul 221,
514; from Italy 74, 84; from Rhineland
514; produced in Britain? 384
Winterton 319, 381, 469
Withington 465
woad 34
Woden Law 430
Wollaston 381, 383–4
women 455; and literacy 201–2; and
military community 170, 173–6, 183–4,
187, 194–7, 204, 209, 223–4, 242, 246;
and religious dedications 216–17; and
urban community 318–20, 323–4;
British 185, 187; unbalanced urban
demography 344–5; see also
freedwomen
Woodchester 370, 374, 390, 396, 397,
469, 480, 484; great pavement 466
Woodeaton 483–4
woodland, management 363, 365; tablet
concerning sale of 286–7, 361, 454,
461
Woodside 411
wool 208–9; combs 363; production 475,
498
workshops 320–21, see also towns
Wrekin, the 99, 143
writing implements 461

writing tablets 40, 162–5, 275, 286, 361;
stylus/wax and ink/leaf 40, 200; use in
military record-keeping 43, 200, 208;
use in civil record keeping 361; used on
rural estates 461
Wroxeter 257–8, 262, 269, 302, 329, 380,
502, 523; baths basilica site 338, 533;
civitas centre 143, 258, 272, 276, 278,
336, 408–9; church? 348; defences 331;
discharge diploma from 193;
Hinterlands Survey 408; military phase
137, 142–3, 146, 189–90

Yarchester 380, 409
Year of the Four Emperors 113
York, bishopric 348; burials 344, 347;
military occupation at 146, 192–3, 211,
228, 229, 238, 244–5, 256, 257, 258,
262, 268; merchants at 297–8, 302;
material culture from 318, 320; people
from 305; provincial capital 335;
regional impact 420; sewers 341; sub-
Roman period 533–4; urban centre at
261, 328, 523
Yorkshire 61, 146–9, 418–20

Zosimus 37; and ending of Roman Britain
231–2, 530